Mahabharata

NORTHWESTERN WORLD CLASSICS

*Northwestern World Classics brings readers
the world's greatest literature. The series features
essential new editions of well-known works,
lesser-known books that merit reconsideration,
and lost classics of fiction, drama, and poetry.
Insightful commentary and compelling new translations
help readers discover the joy of outstanding writing
from all regions of the world.*

Mahabharata

Adapted and edited by David R. Slavitt

Introduction by Henry L. Carrigan Jr.

Northwestern University Press ✦ *Evanston, Illinois*

This book has been published with the generous support of Nina Robinson Vitow.

Northwestern University Press
www.nupress.northwestern.edu

This translation is adapted from Kisari Mohan Ganguli, *The Mahabharata of Krishna-Dwaipayana Vyasa Translated into English Prose* (Calcutta: Bharata Press, 1883–1896). "Agni," chapter 16 of the present translation, appeared in *Per Contra: An International Journal of the Arts, Literature, and Ideas*, no. 35 (2015).

Printed in the United States of America

10 9 8 7 6 5 4 3 2 1

Library of Congress Cataloging-in-Publication Data

Slavitt, David R., 1935– author.
   Mahabharata / adapted and edited by David R. Slavitt ; foreword by Henry L.
   Carrigan Jr.
      pages cm — (Northwestern world classics)
      ISBN 978-0-8101-3059-3 (pbk. : alk. paper) — ISBN 978-0-8101-3060-9 (e-book)
      1. Mahabharata—Adaptations. 2. Hindu mythology—Poetry. 3. Hindu gods—Poetry.
   4. Epic poetry, Sanskrit—Adaptations. I. Carrigan, Henry L., 1954– writer of preface.
   II. Title. III. Series: Northwestern world classics.
      BL1138.25.S59 2015
      294.5923—dc23

                                                                                  2014050149

The War

The general pattern and sweep of the *Mahabharata* remind us in some ways of *Der Ring des Nibelungen* and its representation of the Twilight of the Gods. In the Sanskrit epic, the quarrel and then the war between the Kaurava and the Pandava branches of the Bharata family begin in an age (*yuga*) of communication and intercourse between gods and men, an age that ends at the great battle at Kurukshetra, during which more than 1.6 million men are said to have been killed. Compared to the *Mahabarata*, however, the *Ring* is a mere sketch. Moreover, the *Mahabharata*, at some nine thousand printed pages in its first complete English translation, is about eight times longer than the two Homeric epics combined (see Kisari Mohan Ganguli, *The Mahabharata of Krishna-Dwaipayana Vyasa Translated into English Prose, published in Calcutta between 1883 and 1896 by Bharata Press*). That the Tibetan *Gesar* epic is even longer is cold comfort.

For this adaptation, the principle on which I based my decisions about what to include and what to omit was fidelity to the story. I see the poem as describing a great arc, from the conception and birth of Bhishma to that hero's death, his body pierced by so many arrows on all sides that he cannot fall down. I followed some other lines of narrative, at least for a while, but it was Bhishma's career that I kept in mind, and to which I continually returned. Perhaps it would be fairer to say that my preferences played only a minor role: I left it to the poem itself to declare its shape and size.

So this is, and isn't, the *Mahabharata*. The core of the poem, however, is here—the relatively straightforward story of a quarrel and its dire consequences not only for the dynasty and India but also for mankind.

The poem is in some ways the Hindu equivalent of the Old Testament (with occasional striking similarities, such as a baby abandoned and set adrift in a basket on a river). The legend about the *Mahabharata* is that it came to Vyasa (a *rishi*, or divinely inspired poet) through Brahma's grace and that, as the rishi Vyasa recited it, Ganesha (the god with the elephant head) served as his amanuensis and took it down. (It is said that at a certain moment, when Ganesha's stylus wore out, he broke off one of his tusks and used that to continue writing.) What is more probable is that the work was not composed all at once.

Earlier versions, dating as far back as 1500 BCE, concentrate on how the Pandavas and the Kauravas met to do battle for eighteen days on the field of Kurukshetra. The poem's title is thus the *maha* (big, great, noble) story of the Bharata family. There are breaks in the action, some of them quite substantial; and, over the centuries, there have been expansions and interpolations. The entirety of the *Bhagavad Gita* (Song of the Blessed One) is one such section.

In the sixth book of the *Mahabharata*, the Gita is a lengthy discussion between Krishna and Arjuna about how to live by negotiating the three paths of knowledge, action, and devotion. I have omitted it partly because it was almost certainly a later addition and partly because there are a number of versions of this popular section of the poem, but mostly because I find it preachy and tiresome. Mahatma Ghandi liked it well enough to make a translation of it while serving time in a British prison in Poona. I assume that some readers will be disappointed or even angry that I left it out, but I have limited tolerance for high-mindedness. My Western preference is for any religious feeling on my part to arise from narratives of character in action, and there is the gods' plenty of that in these startling stories.

I should probably explain that my adaptation of this work is not a translation directly from the Sanskrit (which I am not competent to undertake) but rather a recasting of Ganguli's version, cited earlier. There are two major reasons for my having taken this approach. The first and foremost is that Ganguli's prose translation leaves altogether too much to the reader's literary imagination. A poem wants to be in "poetry," which is to say in a form that presents itself to the reader as entailing some minimal degree of linguistic activity beyond the basics of exposition and description. I could not imagine trying to reproduce the swing of the Sanskrit *sloka* couplets, as Romesh C. Dutt did in his version (*The Ramayana and the Mahabharata Condensed into English Verse*, published in London in 1899). What I settled for was the least intrusive presentation I could contrive of lines broken more or less according to the requirements of breathing or syntax, which sometimes coincide. I wanted to suggest the feel of chanting, and to produce a text that doesn't just plod along but dances, at least a bit. The second reason for my having recast the Ganguli rendition is that its language is antique, with *thou* and *hadst* and other such affectations, which were probably supposed to give the text a certain loftiness but are now only distracting and silly. The sense of Ganguli's prose translation is generally accessible, but its mannerisms are dismaying, particularly in such a long work. Therefore, I saw Ganguli's version as an opportunity to work with what were, in effect, notes for a poem and turn them into a text that would not ask so much from a sympathetic reader. Nevertheless, I did let a small number of these mannerisms stand because they give a slight but appropriately exotic flavor to the language of gods and of men and women distant from our own time and culture.

My overall purpose in undertaking this adaptation was to make something that pleased me and might conceivably engage a contemporary sensibility. But I hope that the poem speaks eloquently for itself. It is engaging, thrilling, funny, charming, and finally awesome, with a range in timbre from the impish naïveté of fairy tales to the solemnity of our greatest epics. There are movies, television series, and even comic books based on the poem, and they all work well because there is so much action, with so many extravagantly bloody scenes. (I am informed that in India, during telecasts of the series, some families burned incense as they stared, transfixed, at the tube.) Few "great works of literature" offer so lively a sequence of wonders.

My hope when I began my work was to convey both the rip-roaring and the pious aspects of this tale, which still deserves to be read, enjoyed, and admired. If

I have done that for Anglophone readers of our time, I shall consider myself to have accomplished a very great service.

David R. Slavitt
Cambridge, Massachusetts
February 2015

Henry L. Carrigan Jr.

"There is a very mysterious, extraordinary, rich, and totally unknown epic, *The Mahabharata.* One of its great virtues is almost nobody coming to it [in the West] knows what's going to happen next. Imagine you were going to see *Hamlet* not knowing what's going to happen next."[1]

On Halloween night 1987, hundreds of New Yorkers sat through an all-night performance of Peter Brook's production of the *Mahabharata.* As the audience witnessed the multilayered stories of this sprawling epic being acted out, the differences between Hindu and Western philosophy and myth dawned on many there. In the West, actors and individuals often choose their mythic character in a dramatization of enduring Western epics such as the *Odyssey* or the Hebrew Bible; actors choose to play Odysseus or Samson or Esther, momentarily embracing the role but seldom allowing the character's role to embrace them. In Indian epics such as the *Mahabharata,* however, one's role in life is inseparable from the role one finds oneself has been playing all along in life (king, lover, mother, friend of Krishna). That is, the separation between myth and reality that so heavily marks Western culture is noticeably absent in Hindu culture and philosophy. Watching a performance like Brooks's could move someone to discover what role in life she had been playing all along without knowing it.

Entering into the world of the *Mahabharata,* in this newly abridged retelling and editing by the respected poet and translator David Slavitt, thus requires for most readers in the West a willingness to experience a collection of stories that has never really been fixed in any canonical way and that focuses on remembering—the events and characters are inextricably bound to other events, characters, and stories in the Hindu tradition—rather than simply just hearing or reading. In the West, the power of orality that originally marked the foundational myths of Greece and Rome, as well as of Israel and Jerusalem, relatively quickly became fixed and static in written form so that myth gave way to doctrine or philosophical treatise. Hero stories thus became little more than inspiring tales that illustrate certain virtues—courage, prudence, wisdom—and heroes became one-dimensional characters that stand for a single idea. In India, the myths of its two greatest epics, the *Ramayana* and the *Mahabharata,* remain fluid, dynamic, and unfixed in a single canon of texts. In a culture rich with epics and the characters who populate them, Hindus continue to retell the stories of the *Mahabharata* both because individuals remember them from their earliest hearing and because their heroes and gods continue to live and breathe as a part of the fabric of their lives. The *Mahabharata* is thus unlike Western epics because it is not fixed in time and space in a single written authoritative form—everyone who retells it makes it his or her own; all who read it enter into a communal experience of living out various social roles and discovering the impact of those roles on self and other.

Indian literature contains two kinds of classic literature: the *Rig Veda*, which contains many of the central religious concepts of Hinduism, especially as some of those principles are illustrated in the Vedic collections of texts known as the *Upanishads*, and the *Mahabharata* (or the tale of the Bharata dynasty), the great epic of the Kurukshetra War. The *Rig Veda* is a collection of hymns that contains myths of the creation of the world, as well as ancient prayers to be recited at various rituals. The hymns praise gods such as Indra, exalted for having slain his enemy, Vrtra; Agni, the sacrificial fire; and Soma, the sacred potion or seed and the plant from which the potion is made. The *Rig Veda* was likely preserved orally over 3,000 years, likely between 1700 BCE and 1100 BCE.

The *Mahabharata* is one of two great epic poems (the other is the *Ramayana*), and it is composed of more than 100,000 verses, or three million words (ten times as long as the *Rig Veda* and fifteen times the combined length of the Hebrew Bible and the New Testament). The composition, provenance, and dates of composition of the epic remain fluid, for it was preserved both in oral and in written form, so that there is no single *Mahabharata*. There is a story to be discovered and told, over and over again, even as there exist hundreds of different manuscript versions. The *Mahabharata* even contains a signal of its own remarkable fluidity in the story at the end of the epic where the Jain sage Hemachandra reworks its meaning for his own religious tradition. As the scholar David Shulman put it, "the *Mahabharata* is co-terminous with the world—not a modest claim, perhaps, but one that does help clarify the aims of this text. There is no escape built into it from its relentless, bleak vision. It presents itself not as a work of art but as reality itself. No boundary marks off this text from the rest of the world."[2] Although the origins of the Kurukshetra War can be traced to around 1200 BCE, the Bharata battle—the epic's central battle—likely occurred around 950 BCE, and though each of these dates is approximate, the kernel of the *Mahabharata* can be traced to the tenth century BCE, while the process of composition continued well into the fifth century BCE.

Whereas the *Rig Veda* was considered divine and typified by being heard, the *Mahabharata* was man-made, typified by its being remembered and transmitted orally, its fluid character characterized by the shape-shifting contours of storytelling.

In at least one of the stories of the *Mahabharata*'s origins, Vyasa summons the elephant-headed god Ganesha (patron of intellectuals and merchants) to be his scribe. Ganesha agrees to perform this task but only on the condition that Vyasa would not lag behind and keep Ganesha waiting for the next line; Vyasa stipulated that Ganesha could not write down anything he could not understand. When Ganesha seemed to be getting ahead of Vyasa, the latter would throw in a "knot" that would cause Ganesha to pause for a moment; many scholars attribute the many conceptual and linguistic stumbling blocks in the manuscript traditions to this story.

Like many ancient epics, the *Mahabharata* is a tale of family conflict, family rivalry, jealousy, pride, ambition, honor, defeat, and love, all played out against the backdrop of the founding of a culture. At its core is the bitter struggle and ongoing conflict between two rival families for control and possession of the Bharata kingdom and its capital, Hāstinapura, the "city of the elephant," on the Ganges River in north central India. The five sons of the dead king Pandu—called the five Pandavas—engage in protracted war with the one hundred sons of the blind king Dhritarashtra. The Pandavas are children of the gods: Dharma (law, morality) is the father of Yudhishthira; Vayu (the god of the wind) is the father of Bhima; the king of the gods, Indra, is the father of Arjuna; and, the Ashvins are the father of the twins, Nakula and Sahadeva.

With a simple roll in a game of dice, Yudhishthira loses the kingdom to his cousins. The cousins ship the Pandavas, and their wives, the Draupadi, into exile for twelve years. Once they have their cousins in exile, the Dhartarashtra party behaves cruelly toward them. After enduring harsh treatment, the Pandavas are aided by Krishna, the incarnation of the god Vishnu, who arrives to rescue Law, Good Deeds, Right, Virtue, and Justice from the Dhartarashtras, who are depicted as evil and defiling dharma. A cataclysmic battle ensues between the rival families, wiping out each side almost entirely. Although Krishna is invoked to help the Pandavas, the poem often portrays him as desiring the war in order to purge from the world those who stand in the way of right practice and right action.

Through its tale—and its many smaller subplots and plot twists—of family rivalry and the bitter war that concludes it—the *Mahabharata* deals with questions of duty, right, virtue, love, spiritual freedom, war, death, sacrifice, and justice. David Slavitt's illuminating modern retelling sheds new light on the meaning of the epic for us today.

Notes

1. Peter Brook, quoted in Wendy Doniger O'Flaherty, *Other People's Myths* (New York: Macmillan, 1988), 140.

2. David Shulman, quoted in Doniger O'Flaherty, *Other People's Myths*, 59.

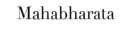Mahabharata

Prologue

Om!

Having bowed down to Narayana and Nara,
                                      the most exalted male being,
and also to the goddess Saraswati,
                                      we must utter the word for Victory:

Jaya!

✦

Ugrasrava, the son of Lomaharshana, surnamed Sauti,
well versed in the Puranas, one day approached the munis,
those great sages of rigid vows, sitting at their ease.
Those ascetics, wishing to hear his wonderful narrations,
greeted him with due respect. Sauti saluted those munis with joined palms
and inquired about the progress of their asceticism. When they were again
    seated,
and the son of Lomaharshana had taken the seat assigned to him,
one of the munis asked him: "Where do you come from, O lotus-eyed Sauti,
and where have you been spending your time?"
Sauti gave a full and proper answer in words consonant with their way of life:
"Having heard the diverse sacred and wonderful stories
which were composed in his *Mahabharata* by Vyasa
and recited in full by Vaisampayana at the snake sacrifice
of the high-souled royal sage Janamejaya,
and having wandered about, visiting many sacred waters and holy shrines,
I journeyed to that country called Samantapanchaka,
venerated by the Dwijas, the twice born,
where formerly was fought the battle
between the children of Kuru and Pandu,
                              and all the chiefs of the land ranged on either side.
From there, eager to see you, I came here. You reverend sages,
who have concluded the silent meditations, have fed the holy fire,
and are sitting in tranquillity, should I recount the sacred stories, collected in
    the Puranas,
containing precepts of religious duty and of worldly profit
and the acts of illustrious saints and sovereigns of mankind?"
The rishi replied: "The Puranas, first promulgated by the great rishi Vyasa,

diversified both in diction and division, possessing subtle meanings logically
    combined,
and gleaned from the Vedas, are a sacred work.
                            Composed in elegant language,
they include the subjects of other books. They comprehend the sense of the
    four Vedas.
We are desirous of hearing that history called the *Bharata*,
the holy composition of the wonderful Vyasa,
just as it was cheerfully recited under the direction of Vyasa himself
                         at the snake sacrifice of Raja Janamejaya."
Sauti then said: "Having bowed down to the primordial being Isana,
to whom multitudes make offerings, and who is adored by the multitude;
who is the true incorruptible one, Brahma, perceptible, imperceptible, eternal;
who is both a non-existing and an existing non-existing being;
who is the universe and also distinct from the existing and non-existing universe;
who is the creator of high and low, the ancient, exalted, inexhaustible one;
who is Vishnu, the beneficent and benevolence itself,
worthy of all preference, pure and immaculate; who is Hari, the ruler of the
    faculties,
the guide of all things movable and immovable;
I will declare the sacred thoughts of the illustrious sage Vyasa.
Some charanas, or bards, have already published this history, some are now
    teaching it,
and others, in like manner, will hereafter promulgate it upon the earth.
It is a great source of knowledge,
established throughout the three regions of the world.
It is possessed by the twice born in both detailed and compendious forms.
It is the delight of the learned for its elegant expressions,
its conversations human and divine, and its variety of poetical measures."

✦

Sauti then recited: "*In this world, when it was destitute of brightness and light,*
and enveloped all around in total darkness,
there came into being, as the primal cause of creation, a mighty egg,
the one inexhaustible seed of all created beings.
It is called Mahadivya and was formed at the beginning of the yuga, the age,
in which we are told was the true light Brahma, the eternal one,
the wonderful and inconceivable being present alike in all places,
the invisible and subtle cause, whose nature partakes of entity and non-entity.
From this egg came out the lord Pitamaha Brahma,
the one and only Prajapati, with Suraguru and Sthanu.
Then appeared the twenty-one Prajapatis: Manu, Vasishtha, and Parameshthi;
ten Prachetas; Daksha; and the seven sons of Daksha.
Then appeared the man of inconceivable nature whom all the rishis know
and also the Viswe-devas, the Adityas, the Vasus, and the twin Aswins,
the Yakshas, the Sadhyas, the Pisachas, the Guhyakas, and the Pitris.

After these were produced the wise and most holy Brahmarshis
and the numerous Rajarshis distinguished by every noble quality;
so also the water, the heavens, the earth, the air, the sky,
the points of the heavens, the years, the seasons, the months,
the fortnights, with day and night in due succession.
And thus were produced all things which are known to mankind.
What is seen in the universe, whether animate or inanimate, of created things
will at the end of the world, and after the expiration of the yuga,
be again confounded. And, at the commencement of other yugas,
all things will be renovated and, like the various fruits of the earth,
succeed each other in the due order of their seasons.
Thus continues perpetually to revolve in the world,
without beginning and without end,
this wheel which causes the destruction of all things. "

✦

Sauti continued: "When that learned Brahmarshi of strict vows, the noble Vyasa,
had finished composing this greatest of narrations,
he began to consider how he might teach it to his disciples.
The possessor of the six attributes, Brahma, the world's preceptor,
knowing of his anxiety, came to him in person to gratify the saint and benefit the
people.
When Vyasa saw him, he was surprised and, standing with joined palms,
bowed low and ordered a seat to be brought.
Vyasa walked around him who is called Hiranyagarbha on that distinguished seat
and then stood before it. Commanded by Brahma, he sat down near the seat,
smiling in joy. Then Vyasa addressed the god, saying:
'O divine Brahma, I have composed a poem that is greatly respected.
In this poem, I explain the mystery of the Veda,
and other subjects: the various rituals of the Upanishads with the Angas;
the compilation of the Puranas, and history composed by me
and named after the three divisions of time—past, present, and future;
the determination of the nature of decay, fear, disease, existence, and
non-existence;
a description of creeds and of the various modes of life;
rules for the four castes, and the import of all the Puranas;
an account of asceticism and of the duties of a religious student;
the dimensions of the sun and moon, the planets, the constellations, and the
stars,
together with the duration of the four ages; the Rig, Sama, and Yajur Vedas,
and also the *Adhyatma*; sciences and the treatment of diseases;
charity and Pasupatadharma; birth celestial and human, for particular purposes;
also a description of places of pilgrimage and other holy places,
of rivers, mountains, forests, the ocean, and of heavenly cities and aeons;
the art of war; the different kinds of nations and languages;
the nature of the manners of the people; and the all-pervading spirit.

All these have been represented.

But, after all, no writer of this work is to be found on earth.'

Brahma said: 'I hold you in high esteem for your knowledge of divine mysteries,

you who are foremost among the whole body of celebrated munis,

distinguished for the sanctity of their lives.

I know you have revealed the divine word, even from its first utterance,

in the language of truth. You have called your present work a "*poem*,"

wherefore it shall be a poem. There shall be no poets whose works may equal

the descriptions of this poem. Let Ganesha be thought of, O muni,

for the purpose of writing it down.' "

Sauti continued his recitation: "Brahma, having spoken thus to Vyasa,

retired to his own abode. Vyasa then called Ganesha to mind.

And Ganesha, obviator of obstacles, and ready to fulfill the desires of his
    votaries,

was no sooner thought of than he appeared at the place where Vyasa was seated.

When Ganesha had been saluted and was seated,

Vyasa said: 'O guide of the Ganas! be the writer of the *Bharata*,

which I have formed in my imagination and am about to repeat.'

Ganesha answered: 'I will be the writer of your work,

provided that my pen does not run dry.'

And Vyasa instructed that divinity: 'Wherever there is anything you do not
    comprehend,

cease writing.' Ganesha signified his assent by repeating the word *Om!*

He then took up his pen, and Vyasa began dictating this work as he had agreed."

✦

Sauti continued: "From the mystery of their meaning, no one is able, to this day,

to penetrate those closely knit, difficult *couplets*.

Even the omniscient Ganesha took a moment to consider

while Vyasa continued to compose other verses in great abundance.

The wisdom of this work, like eyedrops, has cleared the eyes of an inquisitive
    world

that were blinded by the darkness of ignorance. As the sun dispels the darkness,

so does the *Bharata*, with its discourses on religion, profit, pleasure, and final
    release,

dispel the ignorance of men.

As the full moon by its mild light expands the buds of the water lily,

so have the Puranas, by exposing the light of what is heard or revealed through
    direct experience,

expanded the human intellect.

By the lamp of history, which destroys the darkness of ignorance,

the whole mansion of nature is properly and completely illuminated."

Beginnings

Ganga

The Ganges, the holy river.
Ganga, she is called, or *Ma-Ganga, Mother Ganga.*
Daughter of the Himalayas and Menaka, the most beautiful of the Apsaras.
She flows from the toes of Vishnu. She purifies the ashes
of the sixty thousand sons of King Sagara.

✦

One day the celestials had assembled to worship Brahma.
Among the royal sages there was King Mahabhisha.
Ganga, the queen of rivers, also came to pray.
Her garments, white as moonbeams, were displaced by the wind.
Her body was exposed. The celestials bent their heads or looked away.
But Mahabhisha stared openly at the queen of rivers.
For this he was cursed by Brahma: "Wretch, you have forgotten yourself.
For staring at Ganga, you shall be reborn on earth
and suffer the agonies of human beings. But again and again
you shall attain to these regions. She, too, shall be born in the world of men
and shall do you injuries. But when your wrath shall be provoked,
then shall you be freed from my curse."
King Mahabhisha, in his sadness, thought of the least bad human life he might
    lead.
Considering all the monarchs and ascetics on earth,
he declared that he wished to be born as son to Pratipa,
son of Bhimasena, light of the Kuru race, and unrivaled on earth.
But still his face was deeply woeful. And Ganga, the queen of rivers,
seeing King Mahabhisha's dejection, went away, thinking of him wistfully.
On her way, she saw the eight Vasus, dwellers in heaven,
pursuing the same path. And the queen of rivers asked them:
"Why do you look so dejected? You are gods in heaven. Is anything wrong?"
The Vasus answered, saying: "O queen of rivers,
we have been cursed for a minor fault, having provoked the anger of the
    Brahma.
Vasishtha, foremost among seven excellent rishis,
had been engaged in twilight prayers, but seated as he was, we could not see him.

In ignorance, we crossed between him and the sun.
He cursed us, saying: 'Be you born among men!'
It is beyond our power to frustrate an utterance of Brahma.
Therefore, O river, become a human female
and make us, the Vasus, your children. We are unwilling to enter the womb
of any human female." The queen of rivers told them: "Be it so"
and asked them: "On earth, who is that foremost among men whom you would
    choose to be your father?"
The Vasus replied: "On earth, Pratipa shall have a son, Shantanu,
who will be a king of universal fame."
And Ganga then said: "Gods, my wish is exactly what you sinless ones have
    expressed.
I shall do good to that Shantanu."
The Vasus then said: "And then you must throw your children into the water,
so that we may be rescued soon
without having to live on earth for any length of time."
Ganga then said: "I shall do what you desire.
But in order that Shantanu's intercourse with me may not be entirely fruitless,
allow one son at least to live."
                The Vasus agreed.
"We shall each contribute an eighth part of our respective energies.
With the sum of these, you shall have one son
                according to your wishes and his.
But this son shall not beget any children on earth.
This son of yours, for all his great energy, shall be childless."

✦

This Pratipa of whom the Vasus had made mention
spent many years in ascetic penances at the source of the river Ganga.
The lovely Ganga, assuming the form of a beautiful female,
arose one day from the waters of the river and approached the monarch.
The royal sage was engaged in his austere exercises
when the celestial maiden, endowed with ravishing beauty,
came to him and sat upon his right thigh
that was, for manly strength, a veritable sala tree.
When the lovely maiden had sat upon his lap in this way, the monarch said
    to her:
"O beautiful girl, what do you desire? What shall I do?"
The maiden answered: "I desire you, O king. I wish you to be my husband!
O foremost among Kurus, make me your wife!
To refuse a woman who comes to you of her own accord is never approved by
    the wise."
Pratipa answered: "O fairest maiden, even when moved by lust,
I never go to others' wives or to women not of my order. I have taken an oath."
The maiden replied: "I am not ugly. I am in every way worthy of your favor.
I am a celestial maiden, and I desire you for my husband.

Do not refuse me, O king." To this Pratipa answered: "Dear maiden,
still I must abstain from what you would have me do.
If I break my vow, sin will overwhelm and kill me.
You have embraced me, sitting on my right thigh.
But this is the seat for daughters and daughters-in-law.
The left lap is for the wife, but you did not choose that.
O fairest of women, I therefore cannot enjoy you as an object of desire.
But be my daughter-in-law. I accept you for my son!"
The damsel then said: "O virtuous one, let it be as you have said.
Let me be united with your son.
Because of my great respect for you, I shall be a wife of the celebrated Bharata
    race.
You, who descend from Bharata, are the refuge of all the monarchs on earth!
I am incapable of numbering the virtues of the Bharatas
even if I had a hundred years in which to do so.
But, O lord of all, let it be understood now that when I become your
    daughter-in-law,
your son shall not be able to judge of the propriety of any of my actions.
Living thus with your son, I shall do good to him and increase his happiness.
And he shall finally attain to heaven in consequence of the sons I shall bear him,
                    and of his virtues and excellent conduct."
The celestial damsel then disappeared.
And Pratipa, too, departed to wait for the birth of his son
and the fulfillment of her promise.

✦

After much time, when Pratipa was old, a son was born to him and his wife,
and the child was called Shantanu, meaning "*Control*,"
because he was born after his father had controlled his passions for so long
and had carried out so many ascetic penances. Shantanu became the best of
    Kurus,
understanding that this region of indestructible bliss
can be acquired by deeds alone.
When Shantanu grew up into a youth, Pratipa addressed him:
"Some time ago, O Shantanu, a celestial damsel came to me for your good.
If you meet that fair-complexioned one, and if she solicits you for children,
accept her as your wife. And do not judge of the propriety or impropriety of her
    actions,
and do not ask who she is, or from whom or whence she comes,
but accept her as your wife. This is my command!"
Having thus commanded his son Shantanu, Pratipa installed him on his throne
and retired into the woods.
            King Shantanu then ruled with great intelligence and dignity.
He loved hunting and passed much of his time in the woods,
where this most excellent monarch slew many deer and buffalo.
One day, as he wandered along the bank of the Ganges,

he saw a lovely maiden of blazing beauty as dazzling as the goddess Sri.
Of faultless pearly teeth, and decked with celestial ornaments,
she was attired in garments of a texture as fine as the filaments of the lotus.
Seeing her, the monarch was astonished—his raptures made his skin tingle.
With an unwavering gaze, his eyes drank in her charms,
but still he failed to quench his thirst.
Seeing the monarch of blazing splendor moving about in great agitation,
the damsel was herself moved and felt a great attraction to him.
She gazed and gazed and longed to gaze on him forever.
The monarch then addressed her in soft words:
"O slender-waisted one, whether you be a goddess or the daughter of a Danava,
or of the race of the Gandharvas or the Apsaras,
or of the Yakshas or the Nagas, or of human origin,
O woman of celestial beauty, I ask you to be my wife!"
The maiden, hearing the soft and sweet words of the smiling monarch,
and remembering her promise to the Vasus, answered the king;
faultless of feature, the damsel sent a thrill of pleasure into his heart
with every word she uttered: "O king, I shall become your wife
and obey your commands. But you must not interfere with me in anything I do,
whether it be agreeable or disagreeable,
nor shall you ever speak to me in an unkindly way.
As long as you are gentle and kind, I promise to live with you.
But I shall leave you the moment that you interfere with me
or speak a harsh word to me." The king answered: "So be it."
And thereupon the damsel, obtaining that excellent monarch,
that foremost exemplar of the Bharata race, as her husband, was highly pleased.
And King Shantanu also, obtaining her as his wife,
enjoyed to the full the pleasure of her company.
Adhering to his promise, he refrained from asking her anything.
Shantanu became exceedingly gratified with her conduct,
beauty, magnanimity, and attention to his comforts.
And Ganga, the goddess of the three realms—celestial, terrestrial, and
    subterranean—
having assumed a human form of superior complexion,
and endowed with celestial beauty, lived happily as the wife of Shantanu,
having as the fruit of her virtuous acts obtained as her husband
that tiger among kings equal unto Indra himself in splendor.
She gratified the king by her attractiveness and affection,
by her wiles and love, by her music and dance, and was herself gratified.
The monarch was so enraptured with his beautiful wife
that months, seasons, and years rolled on without his being conscious of them.
And the king, while thus enjoying himself with his wife,
had eight children born to him who in beauty were like the very celestials
    themselves.
But those children, one after another, as soon as they were born,
Ganga threw into the river, saying: "This is for your good."
And the children sank, to rise no more.

The king could not have been pleased with such conduct.
But he never spoke a word about it, lest his wife leave him.
But when the eighth child was born,
and his wife, as before, was about to throw it smilingly into the river,
the king with a most sorrowful countenance, and wanting to save it from
    destruction,
addressed her and said: "Do not kill him! Who are you?
From whom do you come? Why do you kill your own children?
Murderess of our sons, the weight of your sins is great!"
His wife replied: "You want children? Now you have a child.
I shall not destroy this one.
But according to our agreement, my stay with you is at an end.
I am Ganga, the daughter of mountains. I am worshipped by the great sages.
I have lived with you so long to accomplish the purposes of the celestials.
The eight illustrious Vasus, endowed with great energy,
were condemned by Vasishtha's curse to assume human forms.
On earth, besides you, there was none else to deserve the honor of begetting
    them.
Nor was there any woman on earth except one like me,
a celestial of human form, to become their mother.
I assumed human form to bring them forth.
You, too, having become the father of the eight Vasus,
have acquired many regions of perennial bliss.
It was also agreed between myself and the Vasus
that I should free them from their human forms as soon as they were born.
I have thus freed them from their curse.
                    Blessings upon you. I now leave you, O king!
But rear this child of rigid vows. That I should live with you as long as I have
was the promise I gave to the Vasus. Let the child be called Gangadatta."
Shantanu asked: "What was the fault of the Vasus, and whose curse
condemned them to be born among men?
What also has this child of ours, Gangadatta, done so that he has to live among
    men?
O daughter of mountains, tell me all."
The celestial Ganga replied to her husband:
"O best of Bharata's race, he who was obtained as a son by Varuna was called
    Vasishtha,
who afterward came to be known as Apava.
He had his asylum on the breast of Meru, king of mountains.
The spot was sacred, abounding with birds and beasts,
and at all times of the year there bloomed flowers of every season.
Apava, that foremost among virtuous men, the son of Varuna,
practiced his ascetic penances in those woods blessed with sweet roots and water.
Daksha had a daughter known by the name of Surabhi,
who, for the benefit of the world, brought forth,
by her connection with Kasyapa, a daughter—Nandini—in the form of a cow,
foremost among cows, the cow of plenty, capable of granting every desire.

The virtuous son of Varuna obtained Nandini for his Homa rites.
And Nandini, dwelling in that hermitage that was adored by munis,
roamed fearlessly in those sacred and delightful woods.
One day there came into those woods adored by the gods and celestial rishis
the Vasus, with Prithu at their head. Wandering there with their wives,
they enjoyed themselves in those delightful precincts.
And strolling there, the slender-waisted wife of one of the Vasus
saw in those woods Nandini, the cow of plenty, with her wealth of
     accomplishments,
large eyes, full udders, fine tail, beautiful hooves, and every other auspicious
     sign,
and yielding much milk.
She showed the animal to her husband, Dyaus, who also admired her fine
     qualities.
He said to his wife: 'O black-eyed girl of fair thighs,
this excellent cow belongs to the rishi who owns this delightful refuge.
O slender-waisted one, any mortal who drinks the sweet milk of this cow
remains youthful for ten thousand years.'
Hearing this, the wife addressed her lord of blazing splendor, saying:
'There is on earth a friend of mine, Jitavati by name,
possessed of great beauty and youth.
She is the daughter of that god among men, the royal sage Usinara,
endowed with intelligence and devoted to truth.
I desire to have this cow and her calf, O illustrious one, for that friend of mine.
Therefore, bring me that cow so that my friend on earth, drinking of her milk,
may become free from disease and decrepitude.
O illustrious and blameless one, there is nothing I should like better.'
Hearing these words of his wife, and moved by the desire of humoring her,
Dyaus stole the cow, aided by his brothers Prithu and the others.
Indeed, Dyaus, commanded by his lotus-eyed wife, did her bidding,
forgetting for the moment the ascetic merits of the rishi who owned the cow.
He did not think at the time that he was going to fall into the sin of stealing
     the cow.
When Apava, son of Varuna, returned to his holdings in the evening
with fruits he had collected, he did not see the cow or her calf.
He searched for them in the woods but failed to find them,
and he understood by his ascetic vision that she had been stolen by the Vasus.
His wrath was at once aroused, and he cursed the Vasus, saying:
'Because they have stolen my cow of sweet milk and handsome tail,
therefore, shall they be born on earth!' "

Ganga continued: "O bull of Bharata's race, the illustrious rishi Apava thus
     cursed the Vasus in his anger
and, having cursed them, the illustrious one set his heart once more
                              on ascetic meditation.
The Vasus came to know of Apava's curse and speedily came to his house.

Addressing the rishi, they endeavored to pacify him, but they failed to obtain
pardon.
Apava said: 'You Vasus have been cursed by me.
But you shall be freed from my curse within a year of your birth among men.
But Dyaus, for whose deed you have all been cursed,
shall for his sinful act be required to dwell on earth a length of time,
for I shall not make futile the words I have uttered in wrath.
Dyaus, though dwelling on earth, shall not beget children.
He shall be virtuous, however, and conversant with the scriptures.
He shall be an obedient son to his father,
but he shall have to abstain from the pleasure of female companionship.'
Thus addressing the Vasus, the great rishi went away. The Vasus then
together came to me. And they begged of me that as soon as they would be
born,
I should throw them into the water.
And I did so to free them from their earthly lives.
                         From the rishi's curse,
this one only—Dyaus—is to live for some time on earth."
Having said this, the goddess disappeared, taking with her the child.
That child of Shantanu was named both Gangeya and Devavrata
and afterward came to be known as Bhishma.
And he surpassed his father in all accomplishments.
Shantanu, after the disappearance of his wife, returned to Hastinapura, his
capital,
                         with a sorrowful heart.

Satyavati

A river called Suktimati flowed by King Vasu's capital.
This river was once attacked by a life-endowed mountain called Kolahala
that had been maddened by lust.
                        Vasu, beholding the foul attempt,
struck the mountain with his foot, a kick so hard as to enable the river
to free herself of the mountain's unwelcome embraces.
Still, the mountain had begotten on the river twins,
which the river, grateful to Vasu for his having rescued her,
gave to Vasu.
                        The son he made the generalissimo of his forces.
The daughter, who was called Girika, he married.

One day, Girika, after her menstrual course and purifying bath,
presented herself to Vasu, her lord.
                        But that very day the Pitris of Vasu
had come to that best of monarchs and foremost among wise men
to ask him to slay a deer for their Sraddha rites, which honor the dead.
The king, reluctant to disobey his household gods,
                        went hunting,
but at every moment he was thinking only of Girika,
who was so beautiful as to rival the goddess Sri.

It was springtime, and the woods were as delightful
as the gardens of the king of the Gandharvas. There were asokas, champakas,
chutas, and atimuktas in abundance, and there were punnagas and karnikaras
and vakulas and divya patalas and patalas and narikelas, chandanas and arjunas
and other such sacred trees, resplendent with fragrant flowers and sweet fruits.
The whole forest was roused by the sweet notes of the blackbird
and echoed with the hum of maddened bees.
The king felt great desire, but Girika was not with him.
He roamed this way and that, and he saw a beautiful asoka
decked with dense foliage, its branches covered with flowers.
The king sat at his ease in the tree's shade. Excited further by the fragrance of
    the season,
the charming odors of the flowers all around, and the delicious breeze,

the king could not keep his from mind thoughts of his beautiful wife.
Noticing a strong hawk that was resting near him, the king addressed him,
    saying:
"Good bird, carry my seed to my wife, Girika, and give it to her."
The hawk took it from the king and flew swiftly through the air,
but on his way he was seen by another of his species.
Supposing that the first was carrying meat from a recent kill,
the second flew at him, and the two fought each other
high in the sky with their sharp beaks and talons. As they fought, the seed fell
into the Yamuna, in the waters of which dwelled Adrika, an Apsara of the higher
    rank,
who had been transformed by a Brahmana's curse into a fish.
Vasu's seed fell from the claws of the hawk and into the water,
and Adrika swallowed it at once.
In the tenth month after the fish Adrika swallowed the seed, she was caught by
    fishermen.
From her stomach emerged a male and a female child of human form.
The fishermen rushed to King Uparichara to report the strange thing that had
    happened.
They said: "O king, these two beings of human shape emerged from a fish's
    body!"
The male child was taken by King Uparichara, and afterward he became the
    virtuous, truthful monarch Matsya.
After the twins' birth, the Apsara, freed from her curse,
left her fish form and resumed her celestial shape. The Apsara then rose up
to walk the path of the siddhas, rishis, and charanas.
The king gave the fishermen the girl, saying: "Let this one be your daughter."

She was given the name of Satyavati and had great beauty and every virtue,
but because she lived with fishermen and fish, she had a distinctly fishy smell.
To serve her foster fathers, she plied a boat on the waters of the Yamuna.
One day while she was out on the water, the great rishi Parasara saw Satyavati.
So great was her beauty that even an anchorite would have desired her.
As soon as he saw her, the rishi burned to have her.
That bull among munis addressed the girl of celestial beauty and tapering
    thighs:
"Accept my embraces, O lovely one!" Satyavati replied: "O, but see the rishis
standing on either bank of the river. If they are looking on, how can I grant your
    wish?"
The ascetic created a fog to envelop them in darkness.
The maiden, seeing the fog summoned up by the great rishi, was amazed.
Helpless and blushing, she said: "O holy one, I am a maiden. If I accept your
    embraces,
my virginity will be sullied. How shall I then, O rishi, be able to return home?
Indeed, for my shame, I should not be able to bear life.
Illustrious one, do what should be done." That rishi, gratified with all she had
    said,

answered: "You shall remain a virgin, even if you grant my wish.
And, O lovely girl of fair smiles, I shall grant you your fondest wish,
whatever it may be." The maiden asked that her body might lose its odor of fish
and have instead a sweet smell. The illustrious rishi granted that wish of her
heart.
She thereupon accepted the embraces of the rishi and was then known
among men
as Gandhavati the Sweet-Scented. Men could catch her scent
from the distance of a *yojana*, eight miles. And for this reason she was also
known
as Yojanagandha, one who scatters her scent for a *yojana* in every direction.
The illustrious Parasara, after this, went to his own domain,
while Satyavati, happy that her wish had been granted,
and having become sweet-scented, and with her virginity still unsullied,
conceived from Parasara's embraces, and she brought forth that very day,
on an island in the Yamuna, the son sired upon her by Parasara.
The child, with the permission of his mother, set his mind on asceticism.
And he went away, saying: "Whenever you think of me and call upon me,
whatever the occasion, I shall appear before you."

✦

Thus was Vyasa born of Satyavati by Parasara.
Because he was born on an island, he was called Dwaipayana, meaning
"*Island-Born.*"
And the learned Dwaipayana, seeing that virtue
is destined in each *yuga* to become lame in one leg—virtue having four legs in
all—
and that the period of life and the strength of men followed the *yugas*,
and moved by the desire of obtaining the favor of Brahman and the Brahmanas,
arranged the Vedas. And for this he came to be called Vyasa, meaning "*Divider*"
or "*Arranger.*"
The boon-giving great one then taught to Sumanta, to Jaimini,
to Paila, to his son Suka, and to Vaisampayana the Vedas and the *Mahabharata*.
And the compilation of the *Bharata* was published by him.

✦

Shantanu reigned in Hastinapura for thirty-six years, and his subjects lived in
peace,
inspired by dharma and charity. He was a virtuous king,
his words and the truth going hand in hand.
One day he went out into the woods to hunt for deer.
He was chasing an animal that one of his arrows had wounded,
when he noticed that the waters of the Ganga in a certain spot were running
shallow.
He asked himself how this could be. As he stared at the river, he saw

a handsome young man pushing the surface of the river downward with divine
    weapons.
This was his son, whom he did not recognize, having seen him only briefly at his
    birth.
But the boy recognized his father and, dazzling him with his divine powers,
    disappeared.
After a moment, Shantanu addressed the river: "Ganga, show me my son."
And Ganga brought him forth, leading the richly dressed youth by her right
    hand.
This was Gangadatta of great energy and fame and immeasurable splendor,
sprung from the component parts of the eight Vasus and born
of the womb of Ganga through King Shantanu. "I looked after him well," said
    Ganga.
"He knows the Vedas. He is skilled in all the weapons. And he is able in
    statecraft."
Shantanu took him to Hastinapura, his capital city,
                            and he made his son Gangadatta his heir.

✦

Four years later, Shantanu was again in the woods
by the banks of the Yamuna. It had been a long day, and the king was tired.
He sent a servant back to Hastinapura with his horse and weapons,
saying he himself would go instead by boat and rest during the journey.
Other servants hailed a boatman, who agreed to take a passenger to the city,
but the boatman recognized Shantanu, his king.
Honored to have so distinguished a passenger, the boatman invited the king
to take refreshment at his cottage nearby. Shantanu accepted,
and the boatman made the king as comfortable as he could,
offering him the best pillow and serving him fruit and milk.
He had his daughter serve the king. Shantanu noticed her perfume,
a fragrance finer than that of any flower, and felt the sharp nip of desire.
For a fisherman's daughter? Even so.
Shantanu asked the boatman for the girl's hand in marriage.
The father was happy to agree and said he would be glad to give her to the king,
but only if the king would promise . . .
                            "Promise what?"
"That her son and none other shall be your heir."
Shantanu shook his head and had the boatman take him to Hastinapura.
For many days he brooded. He wanted the girl, but he could not turn his back
on his son Gangadatta. Not many days later, Gangadatta noticed his father's
    sadness.
"Prosperity attends you. All kings pay you tribute. Why do you grieve?" he asked.
Shantanu sighed deeply. "You are my only son," he said. "You are worth a
    hundred sons.
But life is uncertain. And you know the saying—that he who has but one son has
    no son.

It is not that I wish to remarry. I trust that you will live long and add luster to our
  dynasty.
I know, too, that I shall attain heaven for having fathered you.
But you are a great warrior, always ready for battle. And if I should lose you,
if you should die, what will become of our line?"
Gangadatta was an intelligent and perceptive young man.
He made further inquiries and learned from one of the king's counselors
about the fisherman's daughter and the harsh condition the father had
  demanded.
He went forthwith to the fisherman's cottage and said to him:
"Hear my vow, O fisherman. Never has there been and never shall there be
  again one like it.
I make my vow that your daughter's son shall be our king."
The fisherman considered this. "I know you are a righteous man," he said.
"I believe you will keep your vow. I do not doubt your word.
But how do I know that your children will also keep your word and honor your
  promise?
I speak as a father concerned for his daughter's welfare."
Gangadatta replied: "Then hear me again, O fisherman. I have already
  surrendered my claim to the throne.
Now I give you my further vow—that I shall never marry nor lie with a woman.
You need not fear on account of any child of mine.
I shall attain heaven, even though I have no sons."
The fisherman was delighted. "I give my daughter to the king," he said.
At that moment, from heaven, the Apsaras and the gods and sages sent down
on Gangadatta's head a rain of flowers as together they proclaimed:
"He shall be known henceforth as Bhishma, the maker of the awesome vow."
Bhishma beckoned to the fisherman's daughter. "Come, mother," he said,
"ascend into my chariot. Together we shall go to the palace."
When Shantanu heard of Bhishma's vow,
he was deeply moved. "I shall give you a gift," he said.
"So long as you wish to live, death shall not touch you.
You will die only when you wish to die."

Vyasa

King Shantanu established his beautiful bride in his household.
Soon after was born of Satyavati a heroic son of Shantanu, named Chitrangada,
after the powerful king of the Gandharvas.
He was endowed with great energy and became an eminent man.
King Shantanu also begot upon Satyavati another son, named Vichitravirya,
who was a mighty bowman and became king after his father.
Before Vichitravirya reached his majority,
Shantanu realized the inevitable depredation of time and ascended to heaven.
Bhishma, placing himself under the command of Satyavati,
installed Chitrangada on the throne of the Kurus. Chitrangada soon vanquished
    all other monarchs
and considered no man his equal.
His namesake, seeing that Chitrangada could vanquish men,
challenged him to an encounter.
Between that Gandharva king and the king of the Kurus, both powerful,
there was a fierce combat on the field of Kurukshetra, by the banks of the
    Saraswati,
which lasted three full years. In that long and terrible shower of weapons
and outpouring of blood, the Gandharva king, who had greater powers of
    deception,
slew the Kuru prince. Having slain the younger Chitrangada,
the elder Chitrangada, the Gandharva king, ascended to heaven.
Bhishma, his half brother having been slain,
performed his obsequies and installed Vichitravirya, still in his minority,
on the throne of the Kurus. Vichitravirya placed himself under the command
of Bhishma as he ruled the ancestral kingdom. He adored Bhishma,
who was wise and conversant with all the rules of religion and law.
Bhishma was his protector and made sure that he was obedient to the dictates of
    duty.
And Bhishma, while ruling the kingdom with Vichitravirya on the throne,
placed himself under the command of Satyavati, his father's widow.
When Vichitravirya attained his majority, Bhishma told him he must marry.
It was at this time that Bhishma heard of the three daughters of the king of Kasi,
all equal in beauty to the Apsaras themselves.

All three were to be married on the same day, and to select their husbands
    themselves.
Bhishma went to the city of Varanasi in a single chariot
and saw there innumerable monarchs who had come from all directions.
He also saw those three maidens who would select their own husbands.
When the time came for each of the kings to be mentioned by name,
Bhishma chose those three maidens on behalf of Vichitravirya
and, taking them upon his chariot, addressed the kings.
"O monarchs," he said, in a voice deep as the clouds' thunder,
"the wise have directed that when an accomplished person has been invited,
a maiden may be bestowed on him, decked with ornaments
and provided with many valuable presents. Others may bestow their daughters
by accepting a couple of cows. Yet others give their daughters by taking a
    fixed sum,
and there are also some who take maidens away by force.
Some wed with the consent of the maidens, some by drugging them into
    consent,
and some by going to the maidens' parents and obtaining their sanction.
Others again obtain wives as presents for assisting at sacrifices.
Of these, the learned always applaud the eighth form of marriage.
Kings, however, speak highly of the *swyamvara*, the fifth form,
and wed accordingly. The sages have said that a wife is dearly to be prized
who is taken away by force after the slaughter of opponents
from within the midst of a concourse of princes and kings invited to a self-choice
    ceremony.
Therefore, you monarchs, I bear away these maidens by force.
Strive to the best of your might to vanquish me or be vanquished.
Monarchs, I stand here resolved to fight!"
Having said this to the assembled rulers and to the king of Kasi,
the Kuru prince, with the three maidens in his chariot, sped away.
The challenged monarchs all stood up, slapping their arms and biting their
    lower lips.
Loud was the din they produced as, in a great hurry,
they cast off their ornaments and put on their armor.
The motion of their ornaments and armor resembled the flashing of meteors in
    the sky.
With brows furrowed and eyes red with rage, the kings moved in impatience,
armor and ornaments dazzling or waving with each agitated step.
The charioteers brought handsome cars with fine horses in harness.
Equipped with all kinds of weapons, the monarchs raced in their chariots
and pursued the retreating chief of the Kurus. Then occurred the terrible
    encounter
between those innumerable monarchs on the one side and Bhishma alone on
    the other.
The monarchs fired ten thousand arrows at the same time.
Bhishma, however, responded to those numerous arrows
with a shower of his own, as innumerable as the down on the body.

The kings surrounded him and rained down arrows, like clouds showering a
  mountainside.
With his own shafts, Bhishma countered that deadly downpour,
piercing each of the monarchs with three more arrows.
They in turn hit Bhishma, each with five shafts,
but Bhishma resisted those by his strength and prowess
and struck each opposing king with two more arrows.
The combat was so fierce with the heavy downpour of missiles
that it looked like the ancient encounter between the celestials and the Asuras,
and men of courage who took no part in it were struck by fear
even to witness the scene. With his arrows, Bhishma cut off bows and flagstaffs,
coats of mail, and human heads by the hundreds and thousands.
Such was his prowess and lightness of hand,
and such the skill with which he protected himself,
that the contending car warriors, although they were his enemies, applauded
  him loudly.
Then Bhishma, that foremost among wielders of weapons, having vanquished all
  those monarchs,
pursued his way toward the capital of the Bharatas, taking the maidens with him.

✦

It was then that the car warrior King Salya of Madra, pursuing Bhishma, the son
  of Shantanu,
challenged him to an encounter. Eager to obtain the maidens for himself,
Salya came upon Bhishma like the leader of a herd of elephants rushing upon
  another
and tearing him with his tusks at the sight of a female in heat.
Thus Salya of mighty arms, moved by fury, addressed Bhishma, saying: "Wait!
  Wait!"
Bhishma, tiger among men and destroyer of hostile armies, flamed up like a
  blazing fire.
Bow in hand, and forehead furrowed, he stayed on his car
in accordance with Kshatriya usage, waiting for the enemy.
All the rulers stood there to watch the encounter between Bhishma and Salya.
Like roaring bulls at the sight of a cow in rut, the two menaced each other.
Salya covered Bhishma with hundreds and thousands of swift-winged arrows.
And the kings, seeing Salya's innumerable shafts, uttered loud shouts of
  admiration.
But Bhishma, subjugator of hostile towns, hearing those shouts of the Kshatriyas,
grew enraged and said: "Wait! Wait!" In a fury, he commanded his charioteer:
"Lead my car to Salya so that I may slay him instantly, as Garuda slays a serpent."
Then the Kuru chief fixed the Varuna weapon on his bowstring
and with it wounded the four steeds of King Salya.
Then the Kuru chief, warding off with his weapons those of his foe,
killed Salya's charioteer. Wielding the Aindra weapon,
Bhishma killed the noble steeds of his adversary.

He then vanquished that best of monarchs but left him with his life.
Salya, after his defeat, returned to his kingdom and continued to rule it
  virtuously.
And the other kings also, who had come to witness the self-choice ceremony,
                    returned to their own kingdoms.

✦

After this victory, Bhishma set out with the maidens
for Hastinapura, where the virtuous Vichitravirya
ruled with the wisdom and justice of his father, Shantanu.
Passing through many forests, rivers, hills, and woods,
Bhishma, son of the great Ganga, brought the daughters of the king of Kasi to
  the Kurus
as tenderly if they were his daughters-in-law, or younger sisters, or daughters.
Eager to benefit his half brother, he offered those accomplished maidens
to Vichitravirya and began preparations for his half brother's wedding.
But when everything about the wedding had been arranged
in consultation with Satyavati, the eldest daughter of the king of Kasi said:
"In my heart, I had chosen the king of Saubha as my husband,
and he in his heart had accepted me as his wife. This was also approved by my
  father.
At the self-choice ceremony, I would have chosen him as my lord.
You are conversant with all the dictates of virtue.
                    Knowing all this, do as you think best."
Thus addressed in the presence of the Brahmanas,
Bhishma reflected as to what should be done.
He consulted the Brahmanas, who had mastered the Vedas,
and decided to permit Amba, the eldest daughter of the king of Kasi, to do as
  she liked.
But the other two daughters, Ambika and Ambalika, he bestowed with the
  proper rites on his half brother.
Vichitravirya was virtuous and abstemious but proud of youth and beauty,
and he soon became lustful after his marriage. Both Ambika and Ambalika
  were tall
and of the complexion of molten gold. Their heads were covered with black
  curly hair
and their fingernails were long and red. Their hips were fat and round,
and their breasts full and deep. Endowed with every auspicious mark,
the desirable young ladies considered themselves to be wedded to a husband
in every way worthy of themselves. They loved and respected Vichitravirya,
and he, having the prowess of the celestials and the beauty of the twin Aswins,
could steal the heart of any beautiful woman.
Vichitravirya passed seven years in the company of his wives.
But while yet in the prime of youth, King Vichitravirya contracted tuberculosis.
Friends and relatives tried to find a cure. But in spite of all efforts, the Kuru king
  died,

setting like the evening sun. Bhishma was grief-stricken.
In consultation with Satyavati, he directed that the rites of obsequy be
    performed
by learned priests and eminent members of the Kuru clan.

✦

Satyavati was in deepest grief at the loss of her son.
After the funeral rites, she consoled her weeping daughters-in-law
as best she could. And, turning her eyes to religion
and to the paternal and maternal ancestors of the Kurus, she addressed
    Bhishma:
"The funeral cake, the achievements, and the perpetuation of the line
of the virtuous and celebrated Shantanu of Kuru's race now depend on you.
As the attainment of heaven is inseparable from good deeds,
as long life is inseparable from truth and faith, so is virtue inseparable from you.
O virtuous one, you are well acquainted with the dictates of virtue.
You know very well that you are equal to Sukra and Angiras
in steadfastness and knowledge of the customs of families in difficult
    circumstances.
I rely upon you, therefore, as I raise a most delicate matter.
O bull among men, my son and your brother has gone childless to heaven
while still a youth. These wives of his, the amiable daughters of the ruler of Kasi,
possessing beauty and youth, are desirous of children.
At my command, therefore, sire offspring on them for the perpetuation of our
    line.
It behooves you to guard virtue against ruin.
Install yourself on the throne, and rule the kingdom of the Bharatas. Take a
    wife.
                    Do not plunge your ancestors into hell."
Addressed in this fashion by his mother and by friends and relatives, Bhishma
    replied:
"O mother, what you say is certainly sanctioned by virtue.
But you know my vow in the matter of begetting children.
You also know all that happened when your father gave his consent for your
    marriage
to my father. O Satyavati, I repeat the pledge I once gave:
I would renounce the three worlds, the empire of heaven, and anything greater
    than that,
but I can never renounce truth. The earth may renounce its scent;
water, its wetness; light, its power to show forms; air, its attribute of touch;
the sun, his glory; fire, its heat; the moon, his cooling rays;
space, its capacity of transmitting sound; the slayer of Vritra, his prowess;
and the god of justice, his impartiality. But I cannot renounce truth."
To this Satyavati answered: "I know what your vow was on my account.
But in this emergency, you bear the burden of the duty one owes one's
    ancestors.

O punisher of foes, act in such a way that the line may not be broken,
and that our friends and relatives may not grieve."
The weeping Satyavati spoke such words prompted by grief
at the loss of her son. Bhishma said: "O queen, do not turn your eyes away from
  virtue.
Do not destroy us. A breach of truth by a Kshatriya is never applauded
in our treatises on religion. I shall soon tell you what the established Kshatriya
  usage is
to prevent Shantanu's line from becoming extinct on earth.
Hearing me, reflect on what should be done, in consultation with learned priests
and those acquainted with what is allowable in times of emergency and distress,
while not forgetting what the ordinary course of social conduct should be.
In ancient days, Rama, the son of Jamadagni, angered by the death of his father,
slew with his battle-ax the king of the Haihayas. And Rama,
by cutting off the thousand arms of Arjuna, the Haihaya king,
achieved a feat most difficult in the world.
Not content with this, he set out on his chariot for the conquest of the world.
Taking up his bow, he cast around his mighty weapons to exterminate the
  Kshatriyas.
And with his swift arrows he annihilated the Kshatriya tribe one and twenty
  times.
When the earth was thus deprived of Kshatriyas by the great rishi,
the Kshatriya ladies all over the land had offspring raised by Brahmanas
skilled in the Vedas. It has been said in the Vedas
that the sons so raised belong to whoever has married the mother.
So the Kshatriya ladies went to the Brahmanas, not lustfully but from motives of
  virtue.
Indeed, it was thus that the Kshatriya race was revived.
In this connection, there is another old history that I will tell you.
There was in the old days a wise rishi of the name of Utathya.
He had a wife named Mamata, whom he dearly loved.
One day Utathya's younger brother Vrihaspati, a priest of the celestials
endowed with great energy, approached Mamata.
The latter, however, told her husband's younger brother that she had conceived
and that, therefore, he should not seek for the consummation of his desires.
She continued: 'O illustrious Vrihaspati, the child I have conceived
has studied the Vedas in his mother's womb. His opinion is that your seed will be
  wasted.
How can this womb of mine afford room for two children at a time?
It is wrong, therefore, for you to approach me at such a time.'
Thus addressed, Vrihaspati, though possessed of great wisdom,
still could not suppress his desire, and he attempted to lie with her.
The child in the womb then addressed him: 'O father, cease your attempt.
There is no space in here for two. The room is small, and I occupied it first.
Do not assault me.' But Vrihaspati, without listening to that child in the womb,
continued to embrace Mamata, who possessed the most beautiful eyes.
He penetrated her and ejaculated, but the child in her womb

blocked his seed with the soles of his feet, forcing it out so that it fell to the
    ground.
Seeing this, Vrihaspati became indignant, reproached Utathya's child,
and cursed him, saying: 'Because you have spoken to me as you have,
at a time of pleasure sought by all creatures, perpetual darkness shall overtake
    you.'
And from this curse, Utathya's child was born blind
and came to be called Dirghatamas, meaning *"Enveloped in Perpetual Darkness."*
The wise Dirghatamas, although born blind, possessed a knowledge of the
    Vedas.
By virtue of his learning, he succeeded in obtaining as his wife
a young and handsome Brahmana maiden named Pradweshi.
For the continuation of Utathya's race, the illustrious Dirghatamas
sired upon her several children, Gautama being the eldest.
These children, however, were all given to covetousness and folly.
Dirghatamas, possessing complete mastery over the Vedas,
learned from Surabhi's son the practices of their order
and fearlessly conformed himself to those practices.
The other munis believed that he was transgressing the limits of propriety
and became indignant, seeing sin where there was none.
They said: 'This man no longer deserves a place among us.
Therefore shall we all cast this sinful wretch out.'
                    His wife, too, became indignant with him.
The husband asked his wife: 'Why is it that you, too, have been dissatisfied
    with me?'
His wife answered: 'The husband is called the *bhartri* because he supports the
    wife.
He is called *pati* because he protects her. But you are neither to me!
You have great ascetic merit, but you have been blind from birth,
so it is I who have supported you and your children. I shall not do so in future.'
Hearing these words, the rishi became indignant and said to her and her
    children,
'Take me to the Kshatriyas, and you shall then be rich.'
His wife replied: 'I desire no wealth procured by you,
for that can never bring me happiness. O best of Brahmanas, do as you like.
I shall not maintain you as before.' At these words of his wife, Dirghatamas said,
'I lay down from this day as a rule that every woman shall adhere to one husband
    for life.
Be the husband dead or alive, it shall not be lawful for a woman
to have connection with another. And she who may have such connection
shall be regarded as a fallen woman. A woman without a husband
shall always be liable to be sinful. And even if she be wealthy,
she shall not be able to enjoy that wealth. Calumny shall always dog her.'
Hearing these words of her husband, Pradweshi became angry
and commanded her sons, saying: 'Throw him into the waters of Ganga!'
The wicked Gautama and his brothers exclaimed: 'Why should we support this
    old man?'

They tied Dirghatamas to a raft, committed him to the mercy of the stream,
and returned home without compunction. The blind old man, drifting along
    the stream,
passed through the territories of many kings until one day a king named Vali,
conversant with every duty, went to the Ganges to perform his ablutions.
And as the monarch was thus engaged, the rishi's raft approached him.
The king rescued the old man. The virtuous Vali, ever devoted to truth,
then learned whom he had saved, and he chose him for siring offspring.
The rishi expressed his willingness. Thereupon King Vali sent his wife,
    Sudeshna,
to Dirghatamas. But the queen, knowing that the man was blind and old,
did not go to him but sent her nurse instead. And upon that Sudra woman
the virtuous rishi, his passions under full control, sired eleven children,
of whom Kakshivat was the eldest. King Vali one day asked Dirghatamas,
'Are these children mine?' Dirghatamas replied: 'No, they are mine.
Kakshivat and others have been sired by me upon a Sudra woman.
Your unfortunate queen, Sudeshna, seeing that I was blind and old,
insulted me by not coming herself but sending her nurse instead.'
The king then pacified that best of rishis and sent Queen Sudeshna to him.
Dirghatamas, merely by touching her person, said to her,
'You shall have five children—Anga, Vanga, Kalinga, Pundra, and Suhma—
who shall be like the sun himself in glory.
And after their names as many countries shall be known on earth.'
It is after their names that their dominions have come to be called
Anga, Vanga, Kalinga, Pundra. and Suhma.
It was thus that the line of Vali was perpetuated by a great rishi.
And it was thus that many mighty bowmen and great car warriors, wedded to
    virtue,
sprang in the Kshatriya race from the seed of Brahmanas.
Hearing this, O mother, do as you think best, as regards the matter at hand."
Bhishma continued: "Listen as I indicate the means by which the Bharata line
may be perpetuated. Let an accomplished Brahmana be invited
by an offer of wealth, and let him sire offspring upon the wives of Vichitravirya."
Satyavati, smiling softly, and in a voice broken by bashfulness,
then addressed Bhishma, saying: "What you say is true. From my confidence
    in you,
I shall now indicate how we may perpetuate our line, if you approve,
conversant as you are with the practices permitted in seasons of distress, for of
    our race
you are virtue and you are truth, and you are our sole refuge.
Hearing what I say, therefore, tell me what you think may be proper.
My father was a virtuous man who kept a ferryboat.
One day, in the prime of my youth, I went to ply his boat,
and it happened that the great and wise rishi Parasara came to my boat
to cross the Yamuna. As I was rowing him across the river, he became excited
and addressed me in soft words. The fear of my father was uppermost in my
    mind.

But there were men on the shore who could see us,
and their presence was another reason for my refusal.
But my fear of the rishi's curse prevailed, and having obtained from him a great
    boon,
I could not refuse his solicitations. The rishi, by his energy,
brought me under his complete control, and having first enveloped the two of us
                            in a thick fog, he gratified his desire.
Before this happened, there had been a revolting fishy odor in my body,
but the rishi dispelled it and gave me my present fragrance.
The rishi also told me that even after bringing forth his child
on an island of the river, I would still be a virgin.
The child of Parasara so born of me in my maidenhood
has become a great rishi endowed with great ascetic powers
and known by the name of Dwaipayana.
But having by his ascetic power divided the Vedas into four parts,
he has come to be called on earth by the name of Vyasa
and, for his dark color, by the name of Krishna, meaning *The Dark*." Truthful in
    speech, free from passion,
a mighty ascetic who has burned away all his sins,
he went away with his father immediately after his birth.
Appointed by me and by you also, that rishi of incomparable splendor
will certainly beget good children upon the wives of your brother.
He told me when he went away: 'Mother, think of me when you are in difficulty.'
I will now call upon him, if you think it right, and I am sure that great ascetic
                            will plow Vichitravirya's fields."
Bhishma joined his palms and said: "That man is truly intelligent
who fixes his eyes on virtue, profit, and pleasure, and who, after reflecting with
    patience,
acts so that virtue may lead to future virtue, profit to future profit,
and pleasure to future pleasure. What you have said, therefore,
being beneficial to us and consistent with virtue,
is certainly the best course and has my full approval."
When Bhishma had said this, Satyavati focused her mind on the muni
    Dwaipayana,
who was then engaged in interpreting the Vedas. Realizing that his mother was
    calling,
he came instantly. Satyavati greeted her son and embraced him, bathing him in
    her tears
and sobbing at the sight of her son after so long a time.
Her first son, the great Vyasa, moved by her grief, washed her with cool water
and bowed to her. "I have come, O mother, to comply with your wishes," he said.
"Command me without delay. I shall accomplish your desire."
                    The family priest of the Bharatas
then worshipped the great rishi, who accepted the offerings, uttering the usual
    mantras.
Pleased by the worship, he took his seat. Satyavati addressed him and said:
"O learned one, sons derive their birth both from the father and the mother.

They are, therefore, the common property of both parents.
There cannot be the least doubt that the mother has as much power over them
as the father. As you are indeed my eldest son, according to the ordinance,
so is Vichitravirya my youngest son. And as Bhishma is Vichitravirya's brother
on the father's side, so are you his brother on the mother's side.
This Bhishma, the son of Shantanu, devoted to truth, does not,
for the sake of his vow, entertain the desire of begetting children
or of ruling the kingdom. Therefore, from affection for your brother
    Vichitravirya,
and for the perpetuation of our dynasty, for the sake of this Bhishma's request
and my command, for kindness to all creatures, for the protection of the people,
and from the liberality of your heart, I ask you to do what I say.
Your younger brother has left two widows, the equals of the daughters of the
    celestials,
endowed with youth and great beauty.
For the sake of virtue and religion, they have become desirous of offspring.
You are the fittest person to be appointed. Beget upon them, therefore,
children worthy of our race, for the continuance of our line."
Hearing this, Vyasa said: "O Satyavati, you know what virtue is,
both in respect to this life and the other. Your desires are based on virtue.
At your bidding, therefore, making virtue my motive, I shall do what you desire.
Indeed, this practice is conformable to the true and eternal religion,
and I shall give to my brother children that shall be like Mitra and Varuna.
Let the ladies then duly observe for one full year the vow I indicate.
They shall then be purified. No women shall ever approach me
                            without having observed this rigid vow."
Satyavati then said: "O sinless one, it shall be as you say.
But take such steps that the ladies may conceive immediately.
In a kingdom where there is no king, the people perish from want of protection.
Sacrifices and other holy acts are suspended. The clouds send no showers,
and the gods disappear. How can a kingdom be protected that has no king?
See that the ladies conceive. Bhishma will watch over the children
as long as they are in their mothers' wombs."
Vyasa replied: "If I am to give my brother children so unseasonably,
then let the ladies bear my ugliness. That in itself shall be the most austere of
    penances.
If the princess of Kosala can bear my strong odor, my ugly and grim visage,
my attire and body, then she shall conceive an excellent child."
Vyasa then said to Satyavati: "Let the princess of Kosala,
clad in clean attire and decked with ornaments, wait for me in her bedchamber."
                            Saying this, he disappeared.
Satyavati then went to her daughter-in-law and spoke to her privately:
"O princess of Kosala, listen to what I say. It is consistent with virtue.
The dynasty of the Bharatas has become extinct.
Beholding my affliction and the extinction of his paternal line,
the wise Bhishma has made a suggestion, which, for its achievement, depends
    on you.

Accomplish it, O daughter, and restore the lost line of the Bharatas.

O woman of fair hips, bring forth a child equal in splendor to the chief of the celestials.

He shall bear the burden of this our hereditary kingdom."

Satyavati having with great difficulty procured the assent

of her daughter-in-law to her proposal, which was not inconsistent with virtue,

then fed Brahmanas and rishis and numberless guests who arrived on the occasion.

Soon after the monthly season of the princess of Kosala was over,

Satyavati, purifying her daughter-in-law with a bath, led her into the sleeping apartment.

Seating her upon a luxurious bed, she addressed her: "O princess,

your husband has an elder half brother who shall this day enter your womb

to give you a child. Wait for him without dropping off to sleep."

The princess lay on her bed, thinking of Bhishma and the other elders of the Kuru race.

Then Vyasa entered her chamber while the lamp was burning.

The princess, seeing his dark visage, his matted locks of copper hue,

his blazing eyes, and his grim beard, closed her eyes in fear.

Vyasa, to accomplish his mother's wishes, lay with her anyway.

But the princess, stricken with fear, never once opened her eyes to look at him.

And when Vyasa left her, he was met by his mother, who asked:

"Shall the princess have an accomplished son?"

He replied: "The son she will bring forth will be equal in might

to ten thousand elephants. He will be an illustrious royal sage of great learning,

intelligence, and energy. This noble-souled one shall have in his time a century of sons.

But from the fault of his mother he shall be blind.

And he shall be called Dhritarashtra, meaning '*The Blind One.*'"

To these words, Satyavati responded: "How can one who is blind

become a monarch worthy of the Kurus? How can a blind man

become the protector of his relatives and family, and the glory of his father's race?

You must give the Kurus another king."

                              "So be it," Vyasa said, and he went away.

The first princess of Kosala in due time brought forth a blind son.

Soon after that, Satyavati again summoned Vyasa,

having secured the assent of her second daughter-in-law, Abalika.

In accordance with his promise, Vyasa approached the second wife of his brother.

And Ambalika, beholding him, became pale with fear.

Seeing her so afflicted and pale with fear, Vyasa addressed her:

"Because you have blanched at the sight of my grim face,

your child shall be pale in complexion.

And the name your child shall bear will be Pandu, meaning '*The Pale.*'"

                              Saying this, Vyasa left her chamber.

As he left her, he was met by his mother, who asked him about the child he had begotten.

Vyasa told her that the child would be of pale complexion and called Pandu.
Satyavati again begged another child of her son,
and Vyasa replied: "So be it."
Ambalika, when her time came, brought forth a son of pale complexion.
Blazing with beauty, the child was endowed with all auspicious marks.
It was this child who afterward became the father of the Pandavas, those mighty
   archers.
Some time after, when the elder of Vichitravirya's widows
again had her monthly season, she was solicited by Satyavati
to approach Vyasa once again. Possessed of beauty like the daughter of a
   celestial,
and remembering the grim visage and strong odor of Vyasa,
the princess refused to do her mother-in-law's bidding.
But she sent to Vyasa one of her own maids, one with the beauty of an Apsara
and decked with her own ornaments. When Vyasa arrived, the maid rose up
and saluted him. She waited on him and took her seat near him when asked.
Vyasa was well pleased with her, and when he rose to go away,
he said: "Dear girl, you shall be a slave no longer. Your child also
shall be fortunate and virtuous, and foremost among all intelligent men on
   earth!"
And the son thus begotten upon her by Krishna-Dwaipayana
was afterward known by the name of Vidura.
He was thus the brother of Dhritarashtra and the illustrious Pandu.
And Vidura, free from desire and passion, was conversant with the rules of
   government.
He was the god of justice born on earth,
under the curse of the Brahmana Mandavya.
And Krishna-Dwaipayana, when he met his mother as before,
informed her regarding how he had been deceived by the elder princess
and how he had begotten a son upon a Sudra woman.
Having spoken thus unto his mother, he disappeared from her sight.
Thus were born those celestial children, the propagators of the Kuru race.

✦

But what did the god of justice do to be cursed?
And who was Mandavya, the Brahmana ascetic
from whose curse the god had to be born in the Sudra caste?
Mandavya, conversant with all duties, was devoted to religion, truth, and
   asceticism.
He used to sit at the entrance of his house, at the foot of a tree,
with his arms upraised in observance of the vow of silence.
He sat there for years, until one day there came into his domain
a band of robbers laden with their loot. They were being pursued
by a body of guardians of the peace. The thieves, on entering that domain,
hid their booty there and in fear concealed themselves before the guards
   appeared.

But just as they did so, the pursuing constables arrived.

Seeing Mandavya sitting under the tree, they questioned him:

"O best of Brahmanas, which way have the thieves gone?

Point, so that we may follow them without loss of time."

The ascetic said not a word in reply. The officers of the king, on searching the
property,

soon discovered the thieves concealed there, together with their plunder.

Their suspicion then fell upon Mandavya, and they seized him along with the
thieves.

They brought him before the king, who sentenced him to be executed

with his supposed associates. The constables carried out the sentence,

impaling the celebrated rishi. Having done so, they went to the king

with the booty they had recovered. But the virtuous rishi, though impaled

and kept without food, remained in that state for a long time without dying.

And the rishi, by his ascetic power, not only preserved his life

but summoned other rishis to the scene. They came in the night

in the forms of birds and, seeing him engaged in ascetic meditation

although fixed on that stake, were plunged into grief.

Telling that best of Brahmanas who they were, they asked:

"O Brahmana, what was the sin for which you have thus been made to suffer

the tortures of impalement?"

To this, that tiger among munis answered the rishis of ascetic achievement:

"Whom shall I blame for this? In fact, none but myself!"

After this, the constables, seeing him still alive, informed the king,

who consulted his advisers and then came to Mandavya, who was impaled on the
stake.

The king said: "O best of rishis, I have offended against you in ignorance.

I beseech your pardon. Do not be angry with me."

Mandavya was pacified. And the king, seeing that Mandavya was free from wrath,

raised him up and endeavored to extract the stake from his body.

But he could not do this. So he cut it off just outside the body.

Mandavya, with most of the stake still within him, walked about

and in that condition practiced the most austere penances

and conquered numberless regions unattainable by others.

And because part of the stake was within him, he came to be known in the three
worlds

by the name of Ani-Mandavya, meaning "*Mandavya with the Stake in Him.*"

One day that Brahamana, acquainted with the highest truth of religion,

went to the abode of the god of justice.

The god was seated on his throne, and the rishi reproached him, saying:

"What, pray, is the sinful act I have committed, even unconsciously,

for which I am being punished? Behold the power of my asceticism, and tell me!"

The god of justice replied: "O rishi of ascetic achievement,

you once pierced a little insect on a blade of grass.

You now bear the consequence of that act.

Just as a gift, however small, multiplies in respect of its religious merits,

so does a sinful act multiply in respect of the woe it brings in its train."

On hearing this, Ani-Mandavya asked: "When did I commit this act?"
The god of justice told him that he had committed it when he was a child.
The rishi then pointed out: "That shall not be a sin which is done
by a child up to the twelfth year of age. The scriptures do not recognize it as
      sinful.
The punishment you have inflicted on me for such a venial offense
is disproportionate in its severity.
The killing of a Brahmana involves a sin that is heavier
than the killing of any other living being.
You shall, therefore, O god of justice, have to be born among men,
even of a woman of the Sudra order. And from this day I establish
that an act shall not be sinful when committed by one below the age of fourteen.
But when committed by one above that age, it shall be regarded as sin."
Cursed for this fault by that illustrious rishi,
the god of justice had his birth as Vidura of the Sudra order.
And Vidura was well versed in the doctrines of morality and also in politics
and worldly profit. And he was entirely free from covetousness and wrath.
Possessed of great foresight and undisturbed tranquillity of mind,
Vidura was always devoted to the welfare of the Kurus.

4

Pandu

The Kurus grew in prosperity. The earth yielded abundant harvests,
and the crops were of good quality. The clouds poured rain in season,
and the trees were full of fruits and flowers.
The oxen were happy, and the birds and animals rejoiced.
The cities and towns were filled with merchants, artisans, traders,
and artists of every description, and the people were brave, learned, honest, and
    cheerful.
There were neither robbers nor anyone who was sinful.
It seemed that a golden age had come upon every part of the kingdom.
The capital of the Kurus was a second Amaravati, full of palaces and mansions
and possessing great gates and arches. In delight, men sported on lakes and
    rivers,
in fine groves and pleasing woodlands.
The southern Kurus, in their virtuous rivalry with their northern kinsmen,
walked in the company of siddhas, rishis, and charanas.
In the prosperity fostered by the Kurus there were no misers or widows.
The wells and lakes were always full, the groves abounded with trees,
and the houses of the Brahmanas were prosperous and wealthy.
Ruled by the virtuous Bhishma, the kingdom was adorned
with hundreds of sacrificial stakes. And the wheel of virtue
having been set in motion by Bhishma, the country became so contented
that subjects of other kingdoms, quitting their homes,
came to dwell there and increase its population.
Seeing the youthful acts of their illustrious princes, the citizens were filled with
    hope.
In the house of the Kuru chiefs, as also in those of the principal citizens,
give and *eat* were the words most frequently heard.
Dhritarashtra, Pandu, and Vidura, of great intelligence,
were from their birth raised by Bhishma as if they had been his own sons.
And the children, having passed through the usual rites of their order,
devoted themselves to vows and study.
They grew into fine young men skilled in the Vedas and all sports.
They became well skilled in the practice of the bow,
in horsemanship, in encounters with mace, sword, and shield,
in the management of elephants in battle, and in the science of morality.

Well read in history and the various branches of learning,
and acquainted with the truths of the Vedas, they acquired knowledge
that was both versatile and deep.
Pandu surpassed all men in archery, while Dhritarashtra surpassed all in
    personal strength,
and in the three worlds there was no one equal to Vidura
in devotion to virtue and knowledge of the dictates of morality.
With the restoration of the extinct line of Shantanu,
people in all countries said that among mothers of heroes,
the daughters of the king of Kasi were the first;
that among countries, Kurujangala was the first;
that among virtuous men, Vidura was the first;
and that among cities, Hastinapura was the first.
Because Dhritarashtra was blind, and Vidura had been born of a Sudra woman,
Pandu became king. One day Bhishma addressed Vidura, saying:
"Our celebrated race, resplendent with every virtue and accomplishment,
has sovereignty over all other monarchs on earth.
Its glory has been maintained by many virtuous and illustrious monarchs of old.
Vyasa, Satyavati, and I have raised you three in order that our line may not be
    extinct.
You and I must take such steps that the dynasty may expand as does the sea.
I have heard that there are three maidens worthy of being allied to our race.
One is the daughter of Surasena of the Yadavas, the second is the daughter of
    Suvala,
and the third is the princess of Madra. All these maidens are of course of blue
    blood,
possessed of great beauty, and eminently fit for an alliance with our family.
                              We should choose them for the continuing of our race."
Vidura replied: "You are our father and our mother, too.
You are our spiritual instructor. Therefore, do what is best for us in your eyes."
Soon afterward, Bhishma heard from the Brahmanas
that Gandhari, the daughter of Suvala, had prayed to Shiva
and had obtained from the deity the boon that she should have a hundred sons.
Bhishma thereupon sent messengers to King Suvala of Gandhara.
Suvala hesitated at first, on account of the blindness of the bridegroom.
But, taking into consideration the Kurus' fame and behavior,
he gave his virtuous daughter to Dhritarashtra.
The chaste Gandhari, hearing that Dhritarashtra was blind
and that her parents had consented to marry her to him,
out of love and respect for her future husband blindfolded her own eyes.
Sakuni, Suvala's son, brought his beautiful sister to the Kurus
and formally gave her away to Dhritarashtra.
Gandhari was received with great respect, and the nuptials were celebrated
with much pomp under Bhishma's direction.
Sakuni, after having bestowed his sister along with her many valuable robes,
and after having received Bhishma's adorations, returned to his own city.
And the beautiful Gandhari gratified all the Kurus with her respectful behavior.

Devoted to her husband, Gandhari pleased the family with her good conduct.
She was so chaste, moreover, that she never referred even with words
to men other than her husband and his elders.

✦

Among the Yadavas was a chief named Sura, who had a daughter called Kunti,
    also called Pritha,
unrivaled for beauty. Sura gave his firstborn daughter
to his childless cousin and friend, the illustrious Kuntibhoja.
And in the house of her adoptive father, Kunti looked after the duties of
    hospitality
to Brahmanas and other guests. Once she particularly pleased
Durvasa, the awesome Brahmana of rigid vows.
This sage, anticipating by his spiritual power the future distress
that would befall Pandu for the unrighteous act of slaying a deer
while it was copulating with its mate,
imparted to her a formula of invocation for summoning any of the celestials.
The rishi said: "Those celestials whom you shall summon by this mantra
                         shall approach you and give you children."
Thus addressed by the Brahmana, the amiable Kunti became curious
and in her maidenhood summoned Arka, the god of the sun.
As soon as she pronounced the mantra, that effulgent deity appeared.
The maiden was overcome with surprise.
But Arka, near at hand, said: "Here I am, O black-eyed girl!
Tell me what I am to do for you." Kunti said: "O slayer of foes,
a certain Brahmana gave me this formula of invocation as a boon,
and I have summoned you only to test its efficacy.
For this offense, I bow to you and beg forgiveness.
A woman, whatever be her offense, always deserves pardon."
Arka replied: "I know that Durvasa has granted you this boon.
But cast off your fears, and grant me your embraces.
My approach cannot be futile but must bear fruit.
You have summoned me, and if it be for nothing,
it shall certainly be recorded as your transgression."
The god of the sun said many things to her to allay her fears,
but the maiden, out of modesty and fear of her relatives,
did not consent to grant his request. Arka addressed her again:
"O princess, for my sake, it shall not be sinful for you to grant my wish."
Thus the illuminator of the universe persuaded her.
And of this connection there was immediately born a son
known throughout the world as Karna.
Dressed in natural armor, and with his face adorned by earrings,
the heroic Karna was first among wielders of weapons,
blessed with good fortune, and endowed with the beauty of a celestial child.
After the birth of this child, Arka restored her maidenhood to Kunti
and ascended to heaven. The princess, beholding her son with sorrow,

reflected on what was best for her to do.

From fear of her relatives, she decided to conceal the evidence of her folly,
$\qquad$ and she cast her child into the water.

At some distance downstream, the shepherdess Radha, wife of Adhiratha,
took up the child, and she and Adhiratha brought him up as their own son.
Radha and her husband gave him the name Vasusena, meaning *"Born to Wealth,"*
because he was born with natural armor and earrings.

He would worship the sun until his back was heated by its rays,
and during these hours of adoration there was nothing on earth
Vasusena would not give to the Brahmanas.

Indra, chief of the celestials, wanting to benefit his own son, Arjuna,
assumed the form of a Brahmana and approached Vasusena
to beg of him his natural armor. Vasusena took off his natural armor,
joined his palms in reverence, and gave it to Indra,
who was well pleased with Vasusena's liberality
and therefore gave him a fine dart, saying: "That one and only one
among the celestials, the Asuras, men, the Gandharvas,
the Nagas, and the Rakshasas whom you wish to conquer
$\qquad$ shall be certainly slain with this dart."

The son of Surya had been known before by the name of Vasusena.
But after he cut off his natural armor, he came to be called Karna,
meaning *"Peeler of His Own Covering."*

✦

Kunti was endowed with beauty and every accomplishment,
devoted to virtue, and possessed of every good quality.
But, young and beautiful though she was, no king had asked for her hand.
Her father, Kuntibhoja, therefore invited the princes and kings of other
$\qquad$ countries
and desired his daughter to select a husband from among the guests.
Kunti, entering the amphitheater, beheld Pandu, foremost among the Bharatas.
Proud as a lion, broad-chested, bull-eyed, endowed with great strength,
and outshining all other monarchs, he looked like another Indra.
Beholding Pandu in that assembly, Kunti became agitated.
Advancing with modesty and quivering with emotion,
she placed the nuptial garland about Pandu's neck.
The other monarchs then returned to their respective kingdoms
on elephants, on horses, and in chariots, as they had come.
The bride's father caused the nuptial rites to be performed.
The Kuru king and the daughter of Kuntibhoja
formed a couple like Maghavat and Paulomi, the king and queen of the
$\qquad$ celestials.
King Kuntibhoja presented his son-in-law with much wealth
and sent him back to his capital. Accompanied by a large force bearing various
$\qquad$ banners,
and eulogized by Brahmanas and by great rishis pronouncing benedictions,

Pandu reached his capital, arrived at his palace, and installed his queen in it.
Some time later, Bhishma decided that Pandu should have a second wife.
Accompanied by four kinds of armed troops, and also by aged counselors,
Brahmanas, and great rishis, Bhishma went to the capital of Salya, the king of
    Madra.
Hearing that Bhishma had arrived, the king of Madra went out to receive him
and invited him to his palace. There, the king offered Bhishma a white carpet
    for a seat
and water with which to wash his feet.
When he was at his ease, the king asked him the reason for his visit.
Bhishma said: "I have come for the hand of a maiden.
I have heard that you have a sister named Madri,
celebrated for beauty and endowed with every virtue. I would choose her for
    Pandu.
You are in every respect worthy of an alliance with us,
                    as we also are worthy of one with you."
The ruler of Madra replied: "To my mind, there is no one
other than one of your family with whom I can enter into an alliance."
Bhishma gave Salya much gold, both coined and uncoined,
and precious stones of various colors by the thousands, and elephants,
and horses and cars, and much cloth and many gems, pearls, and corals.
Salya accepted these gifts and then gave away his sister,
decked in ornaments, to that bull of the Kuru race.
The wise Bhishma, son of Ganga, delighted by the success of his mission,
took Madri with him and returned to the Kuru capital.

On an auspicious day, and at a moment chosen by the wise,
King Pandu married Madri, and he established his beautiful bride
in handsome quarters. That best of monarchs then gave himself up to
    enjoyment
in the company of his two wives, as most he liked and to the limit of his desires.
After thirty days, the Kuru king started off from his capital to conquer the world.
He saluted and bowed to Bhishma and the other Kuru elders,
bade goodbye to Dhritarashtra, and set out on his campaign
with a large force of elephants, horses, and chariots,
cheered by the blessings and auspicious rites
performed by the citizens with their prayers for his success.
That tiger among men first subjugated the robber tribes of Asarna.
He next turned his army against Dhirga, the ruler of the kingdom of Maghadha,
who was proud of his strength and had offended many monarchs.
Pandu attacked Dhirga's capital, slew him there, and took everything in his
    treasury
and also vehicles and draft animals without number.
He then marched into Mithila and subjugated the Videhas.
Then he led his army against Kasi, Sumbha, and Pundra
and by the strength of his arms spread the fame of the Kurus.
Like a mighty fire whose far-reaching flames were represented by his arrows

and the splendor of his weapons, he consumed all the kings with whom he came
  in contact.
These, along with their forces, were made the vassals of the Kurus.
And all the kings of the world regarded Pandu as the single hero on earth,
even as the celestials regard Indra in heaven.
With joined palms, the kings of the earth bowed to Pandu
and waited on him with presents of various kinds of gems,
precious pearls and corals, and much gold and silver
as well as first-class cows and handsome horses,
and fine cars and elephants, and asses and camels and buffalo, goats and sheep,
and blankets and beautiful hides and furs.
The king of Hastinapura accepted those offerings and returned to his capital,
to the great delight of his subjects, all of whom said:
"O, the fame of the achievements of Shantanu, that tiger among kings,
and of the wise Bharata has been revived in our day by Pandu.
Those who once robbed the Kurus of both territory and wealth,
                    Pandu has subjugated and made to pay tribute."
With Bhishma at their head, all the citizens went out to receive the victorious
  king.
They had not gone far when they saw his attendants, laden with much wealth.
The train of various conveyances and of elephants, horses, cars,
cows, camels, and other animals was so long that they could not see its end.
Pandu came before Bhishma, worshipped at his feet,
and saluted the citizens as each deserved. Bhishma embraced Pandu as his son.
He wept in joy as Pandu, with a flourish of trumpets and kettledrums, entered
  his capital.
At the command of Dhritarashtra, Pandu offered the wealth he had acquired
to Bhishma, their grandmother Satyavati, and their mothers.
And he sent a portion of his wealth to Vidura also.
The virtuous Pandu gave his other relatives similar presents.
Satyavati, Bhishma, and the Kosala princes were all given gifts
from that which Pandu had acquired on his campaign.
Ambalika in particular, embracing her son of incomparable prowess,
was as glad as the queen of heaven embracing Jayanta.
With the wealth Pandu had acquired, Dhritarashtra performed five great
  sacrifices
equal to a hundred great horse sacrifices,
at all of which there were lavish offerings to the Brahmanas.
Thereupon Pandu, who had achieved victory over sloth and lethargy,
retired into the woods, accompanied by his two wives, Kunti and Madri.
Leaving behind his splendid palace with its luxurious beds,
he became a permanent inhabitant of the woods and devoted his time to
  hunting deer.
From his abode in a hilly region overgrown with huge sala trees
on the southern slope of the Himavat mountains, he roamed in perfect
  freedom.
Pandu and his wives wandered in those woods like Airavata

accompanied by two she-elephants. People who dwelled in those woods
saw the heroic Bharata prince, armed with sword and bow and arrow,
clad in his beautiful armor, and skilled in all weapons,
and they considered him a god wandering among them.
At the command of Dhritarashtra, people supplied Pandu
with every object of pleasure and enjoyment.
Meanwhile, Bhishma, son of the oceangoing Ganga,
heard that King Devaka had a young and beautiful daughter born of a Sudra wife.
Bringing her from her father's abode, Bhishma married her to Vidura.
And Vidura begot upon her many children like himself in their
     accomplishments.
Dhritarashtra begot upon Gandhari a hundred sons,
and upon a Vaisya wife another besides those hundred.
Pandu had by his two wives, Kunti and Madri, five sons,
great charioteers begotten by the celestials for the perpetuation of the Kuru line.
But how did Gandhari bring forth those hundred sons, and in how many years?
And what was the life span allotted to each?
How did Dhritarashtra also beget another son on a Vaisya wife?
How did Dhritarashtra behave toward his obedient and virtuous wife, Gandhari?
And how were the five sons of Pandu, those mighty charioteers, begotten
even though Pandu labored under the curse of the great rishi he had slain?
One day Gandhari entertained the great Vyasa,
who had come to her abode exhausted and hungry.
Pleased with Gandhari's hospitality, the rishi granted her wish
that she should have a century of sons, each equal to her lord
in strength and accomplishments. Some time later, Gandhari conceived
and bore the burden in her womb for two long years without being delivered.
She was greatly distressed by this. And it was then that she heard that Kunti
had brought forth a son whose splendor was like that of the morning sun.
Impatient of the length of her pregnancy, which had been so prolonged
and deprived of reason by her grief, she struck her womb violently,
without the knowledge of her husband.
And out of her womb after two years' growth came a hard mass of flesh like an
     iron ball.
She was about to throw it away, but Vyasa came to her and, seeing that ball of
     flesh,
asked her: "What have you done?"
Gandhari said: "Having heard that Kunti has brought forth a splendid son,
I struck at my womb. You granted me my wish that I should have a hundred sons,
but here is only this ball of flesh!" Vyasa then said: "My words can never be futile.
I have never spoken an untruth even in jest. Let a hundred pots full of clarified
     butter
be brought, and let them be placed in some concealed spot.
Meanwhile, let cool water be sprinkled over this ball of flesh."
The ball of flesh, sprinkled with water, divided into a hundred and one parts,
each about the size of a thumb. These were then put into those pots of clarified
     butter

and were watched with care. The illustrious Vyasa then said to the daughter of
  Suvala
that she should open the covers of the pots after two years.
He then went to the Himavat mountains to devote himself to asceticism and
  meditation.
In time, King Duryodhana was born from among those pieces of the ball of flesh
that had been put into those pots. News of Duryodhana's birth was brought
to Bhishma and Vidura. The day that the haughty Duryodhana was born
was also the birthday of Bhima of mighty arms and great prowess.
As soon as Duryodhana was born, he began to cry and bray like an ass.
Hearing that sound, the asses, vultures, jackals, and crows uttered their
  respective cries.
Violent winds began to blow, and there were fires in all directions.
In great fear, King Dhritarashtra summoned Bhishma and Vidura
and all the Kurus and numberless Brahmanas and addressed them:
"The oldest of the princes, Yudhishthira, is the perpetuator of our line.
By virtue of his birth, he has acquired the kingdom.
We have nothing to say to this. But shall this my son born after him become
  king?
Tell me what is lawful and right under these circumstances."
As soon as these words were spoken, jackals and other carnivorous animals
began to howl ominously. Taking note of those frightful omens,
the assembled Brahmanas and the wise Vidura replied: "O king,
with these frightful omens at the birth of your eldest son, it is clear that
  Duryodhana shall be
the exterminator of our race. The prosperity of all depends on abandoning him.
To keep him would be a calamity. If you abandon him, there still remain
your nine and ninety sons. Do good to the world and to your line
by casting off this one child. It has been said that an individual should be cast off
for the sake of the family, that a family should be cast off for the sake of a village,
that a village may be abandoned for the sake of the whole country,
and that the earth itself may be abandoned for the sake of the soul."
This is what Vidura and the Brahmanas said,
but King Dhritarashtra did not have the heart to follow their advice.
Then, within a month, were born a full hundred sons to Dhritarashtra
and a daughter also in excess of this hundred.
During the time when Gandhari was in an advanced state of pregnancy,
there was a maidservant of the Vaisya class who used to attend on Dhritarashtra.
During that year, Dhritarashtra begot upon her a son endowed with great
  intelligence,
who was afterward named Yuyutsu. And because he was begotten by a Kshatriya
upon a Vaisya woman, he came to be called Karna.
Thus were born unto the wise Dhritarashtra a hundred sons, all heroes
and mighty chariot fighters, and a daughter, Duhsala, over and above the
  hundred,
and another son, Yuyutsu, of great energy and strength, begotten upon a Vaisya
  woman.

But if the ball of flesh was distributed by the great rishi only into a hundred parts,
and if Gandhari did not conceive on any other occasion, how, then, was Duhsala
  born?
When the illustrious rishi sprinkled water over that ball of flesh,
it began to divide into parts. As it was dividing,
the nurse began to take up the parts and put them into those pots of clarified
  butter.
While this was going on, Gandhari, realizing the affection one feels for a daughter,
said to herself: *There is no doubt that I shall have a hundred sons.*
The muni having said so, it cannot be otherwise.
But I should be very happy if a daughter were born to me
over and above these hundred sons, and junior to them all.
My husband then may attain to those worlds
that the possession of a daughter's sons confers.
It is also true that the affection women feel for their sons-in-law is great.
If, therefore, I obtain a daughter over and above my hundred sons,
then, surrounded by sons and a daughter's sons, I would feel supremely blessed.
If ever I have practiced ascetic austerities, if ever I have given anything in charity,
if ever I have performed the Homa through the Brahmanas,
if ever I have gratified my superiors by respectful attentions,
then, as the reward for those acts, let a daughter be born to me—
all this while Vyasa, that illustrious and best of rishis, was dividing the ball of
  flesh.
Counting a full hundred of the parts, he said to the daughter of Suvala:
"Here are your hundred sons. I did not speak anything to you that was false.
Here, however, is one part in excess of the hundred,
intended for giving you a daughter's son.
This part shall develop into an amiable and fortunate daughter, as you have
  desired."
Then Vyasa brought another pot full of butter and put the hundred and first
  part into it.

✦

The names of Dhritarashtra's sons, according to the order of their birth, were
Duryodhana, Yuyutsu, Duhsasana, Duhsaha,
Jalasandha, Sama, Saha, Vinda and Anuvinda,
Durdharsha, Suvahu, Dushpradharshana, Durmarshana and Durmukha,
Dushkarna and Karna, Vivinsati and Vikarna, Sala, Satwa,
Sulochana, Chitra and Upachitra, Chitraksha,
Charuchitra, Sarasana, Durmada and Durvigaha,
Vivitsu, Vikatanana, Urnanabha and Sunabha, then Nandaka and Upanandaka,
Chitravana, Chitravarman, Suvarman, Durvimochana,
Ayovahu, Mahavahu, Chitranga, Chitrakundala, Bhimavega,
Bhimavala, Balaki, Balavardhana, Ugrayudha,

Bhima, Karna, Kanakaya, Dridhayudha, Dridhavarman,
Dridhakshatra, Somakitri, Anudara, Dridhasandha, Jarasandha,
Satyasandha, Sada, Suvak, Ugrasravas, Ugrasena, Senani, Dushparajaya,
Aparajita, Kundasayin, Visalaksha, Duradhara, Dridhahasta, Suhasta,
Vatavega and Suvarchas, Adityaketu, Vahvashin, Nagadatta,
Agrayayin, Kavachin, Krathana, Kunda, Kundadhara, Dhanurdhara,
the heroes Ugra and Bhimaratha, Viravahu, Alolupa, Abhaya and
    Raudrakarman,
and Dridharatha, Anadhrishya, Kundabhedin, Viravi,
Dhirghalochana Pramatha, and Pramathi and the powerful Dhirgharoma,
Dirghavahu, Mahavahu, Vyudhoru, Kanakadhvaja, Kundasi and Virajas.
Besides these hundred sons, there was a daughter, named Duhsala.
All the sons were heroes, skilled in warfare and learned in the Vedas.
Worthy wives were in time selected for all by Dhritarashtra.
And King Dhritarashtra also bestowed Duhsala upon Jayadratha, the king of
    Sindhu.

✦

One day Pandu was roaming the woods, and he saw a large deer, the leader of a
    herd,
servicing his mate. The monarch pierced them both with five of his sharp, swift
    arrows.
Yet it was no deer Pandu had hit but a rishi's son of great merit,
enjoying his mate in the form of a deer. Pierced by Pandu's arrows
while engaged in the act of intercourse, the deer fell to the ground,
uttering cries of a man, and wept bitterly.
Then he said to Pandu: "O king, even men who are slaves to lust and wrath,
and devoid of reason, and ever sinful, avoid committing so cruel an act as this.
Individual judgment does not prevail against the ordinance,
but the ordinance prevails against individual judgment.
You were born, O Bharata, to a race that has ever been virtuous.
How is it, therefore, that you suffer yourself to be overpowered by passion and
    wrath
                      and to lose your reason?"
Pandu replied: "O deer, kings slay animals of your species
exactly as they slay foes. You should not reprove me thus from ignorance.
Animals of your species are slain by open or covert means.
The rishi Agastya, engaged in the performance of a grand sacrifice,
chased deer and dedicated every deer in the forest to the gods in general.
You have been slain according to the usage sanctioned by such precedent.
For his sacrifices, Agastya performed the Homa with fat of the deer.
                    Why, then, do you reprove me?"
The deer replied: "O king, men do not let fly their arrows at their enemies
when the latter are unprepared. There is a time for doing that—
after the declaration of hostilities. Slaughter at such a time is not censurable."
Pandu replied: "Men slay deer by various means,

whether the animals are careful or careless. Therefore, O deer, why do you
   reprove me?"
The deer said: "I did not blame you for having killed a deer,
or for the injury you have done me. But you should have waited
until the completion of my act of intercourse.
What man of wisdom and virtue is there who can kill a deer engaged in such
   an act?
The time of sexual intercourse is agreeable to every creature
and productive of good to all the world.
With my mate I was engaged in the gratification of my sexual desire.
But that effort of mine has been rendered futile.
O king of the Kurus, as you were born to the race of the Pauravas, noted for
   virtuous deeds,
such an act is scarcely worthy of you.
O Bharata, this act must be regarded as extremely cruel, execrable, infamous,
   and sinful,
and leading certainly to hell. You are acquainted with the pleasures of sexual
   intercourse.
You are acquainted also with the morality and the dictates of duty.
You are like a celestial, and it does not behoove you to perform an act that leads
   to hell.
Your duty is to chastise all who act cruelly or are engaged in sinful practices
and who have thrown to the winds religion, profit, and pleasure,
as explained in the scriptures. What have you done, O best of men,
in killing me, who gave you no offense? I am a muni, disguised as a deer,
who subsists on fruits and roots. I was living in the woods, at peace with all.
Yet you have killed me, O king, for which I will curse you.
As you have been cruel to a couple of opposite sex, surely shall death overtake you
as soon as you feel sexual desire. I am Kindama, a muni of ascetic merit,
and was engaged in intercourse with this deer because my feelings of modesty
did not permit me to indulge in such an act in human society.
As a deer I roved the deep woods in the company of other deer.
You have slain me without knowing that I am a Brahmana,
and the sin of having slain a Brahmana shall not, therefore, be yours.
But as you have killed me, disguised as a deer, at a like time my fate shall become
   yours.
When you, approaching your wife lustfully, unite with her,
as I had done with mine, in that very state you shall be obliged to go to the world
   of the spirits.
And that wife with whom you may be united in intercourse at the time of your
   death
shall follow you with affection and reverence to the domain of the king of the
   dead.
You brought me grief when I was happy. So shall it come to you when you are
   happy."
Saying this, the deer gave up the ghost, and Pandu was plunged into woe at the
   sight.

After the death of that deer, King Pandu and his wives wept bitterly.
Pandu said: "The wicked, even if born to virtuous families,
when deluded by their own passions are overwhelmed with misery at the fruit of
     their deeds.
I have heard that my father, though begotten by Shantanu of virtuous soul,
was cut down while still a youth because he had become a slave to his lust.
In the soil of that lustful king, the illustrious Krishna-Dwaipayana begot me.
Though I am the son of such a being, with my wicked heart wedded to vice,
I am yet leading a wandering life in the woods, hunting deer.
The gods have forsaken me! I shall seek salvation now.
The great impediments to salvation are the desire to beget children,
and other concerns of the world. I shall now adopt the Brahmacharya mode of
     life
and follow on the path of my father. I will bring my passions under complete
     control
by severe ascetic penances. Forsaking my wives and other relatives,
and shaving my head, I will wander the earth alone, begging for my subsistence
from each of these trees standing here. Forsaking every object
of affection and aversion, and covering my body with dust,
I shall make the shelter of trees or deserted houses my home.
I shall never yield to the influence of sorrow or joy,
and I shall regard slander and flattery in the same light. I shall not seek
     benedictions.
I shall be at peace with all and shall accept no gifts.
I shall not mock anyone, nor shall I scowl at anyone,
but shall be ever cheerful and devoted to the good of all creatures.
I shall not harm any of the four orders of life—
oviparous and viviparous creatures, worms and vegetables—
but shall show an equality of behavior toward all, as if they were my own
     children.
Once a day shall I beg of five or ten families, at the most,
and if I do not succeed in obtaining alms, I shall then go without food.
I shall rather stint myself than beg more than once of the same person.
If I do not obtain anything after completing my round of seven or ten houses,
I shall not enlarge my round. Whether I obtain or fail to obtain alms,
I shall be equally unmoved, like a great ascetic.
One lopping off an arm of mine with a hatchet
and one smearing the other arm with sandalwood paste shall be regarded by me
     equally.
I shall not wish prosperity to the one or misery to the other.
I shall not be pleased with life or displeased with death.
I shall desire neither to live nor to die.
Washing my heart of all sins, I shall transcend those sacred rites
productive of happiness that men perform in auspicious moments, days, and
     months.
I shall abstain from all acts of religion and profit
and also from those that lead to the gratification of the senses.

Freed from all sins and snares of the world, I shall be like the wind, subject to
    no one.
Following the path of fearlessness, I shall at last lay down my life.
Destitute of the power of begetting children, and firmly adhering to the line of
    duty,
I shall not deviate from that plan so as to tread on the vile path
of the world, so full of misery. Whether respected or disrespected in the world,
that man who from covetousness casts on others a begging look behaves like a
    dog."
The king, having thus wept in sorrow, looked at his two wives,
Kunti and Madri, and said to them: "Let the princess of Kosala, my mother,
    Vidura,
the king with our friends, the venerable Satyavati,
Bhishma, the priests of our family, the illustrious soma-drinking Brahmanas,
and all elderly citizens whom we support be informed
that Pandu has retired to the woods to lead a life of asceticism."
Hearing these words of their lord, both Kunti and Madri said to him:
"O bull of Bharata's race, there are many other modes of life
you can adopt in which you can undergo the severest penances
along with us, your wedded wives, and in which, for the salvation of your body
and freedom from rebirth, you may obtain heaven.
We also, in the company of our lord and for his benefit,
controlling our passions and bidding adieu to all luxuries,
shall subject ourselves to the severest austerities.
O king, if you abandon us, we shall this very day depart from this world."
Pandu replied: "If this resolve of yours springs from virtue,
then with you both I shall follow on the imperishable path of my fathers.
Abandoning the luxuries of cities and towns, clad in barks of trees,
and living on fruits and roots, I shall wander the woods, practicing the severest
    penances.
Bathing morning and evening, I shall perform the Homa. I shall reduce my body
by eating very sparingly and shall wear rags and skins
and knotted locks on my head. Exposing myself to heat and cold,
and disregarding hunger and thirst, I shall live in solitude
and give myself up to contemplation. I shall eat what fruit I find, ripe or green.
To those household gods called the Pitris
and to the other gods I shall make offerings of speech, water, and the fruits of
    the wilderness.
I shall not see, far less harm, any of the denizens of the woods,
or any of my relatives, or any of the residents of cities and towns.
Until I lay this body down, I shall thus practice the severe ordinances
of the Vanaprastha scriptures, always searching for ordinances even more severe
    that they may contain."
The Kuru king, having spoken thus to his wives,
gave away to Brahmanas the big jewel in his diadem,
his necklace of precious gold, his bracelets, his large earrings,
his valuable robes, and all the ornaments of his wives.

Then, summoning his attendants, he said to them: "Return to Hastinapura,
and proclaim to all that Pandu and his wives have gone into the woods,
forgoing wealth, desire, happiness, and sexual appetite."
His followers and attendants set up a loud wail: "O! we are undone!"
Then, with hot tears trickling down their cheeks, they left the king
and returned to Hastinapura, carrying with them the wealth to be distributed in
    charity.
Dhritarashtra, hearing what had happened in the woods, wept for his brother.
Pandu and his two wives went to the mountains of Nagasata, eating fruits and
    roots.
Then Pandu went to Chaitraratha, and then across the Kalakuta,
and finally, crossing the Himavat, he arrived at Gandhamadana.
Protected by mahabhutas, siddhas, and great rishis, Pandu lived
sometimes on level ground and sometimes on mountain slopes.
He journeyed on to the lake of Indradyumna, crossed the mountains of
    Hansakuta,
and continued to the mountain of a hundred peaks, where he practiced ascetic
    austerities.
Within a short time he became the favorite of the whole body of the siddhas
and charanas residing there. And—devoted to the service of his spiritual masters,
free from vanity, with his mind under complete control
and his passions fully subdued—Pandu earned the right to enter heaven.
Some of the rishis would call him brother and some friend,
while others cherished him as their son. At last Pandu became
like a Brahmarshi, even though he was a Kshatriya by birth.

✦

On a day of the new moon, the great rishis of rigid vows
assembled and, desiring to behold Brahman,
were on the point of starting their expedition. Pandu asked: "Where are we
    going?"
The rishis answered: "In the abode of Brahman
there will be today a great gathering of celestials, rishis, and Pitris,
                            and today we shall go there."
Pandu was eager to visit heaven along with the great rishis.
With his two wives, he was on the point of following the rishis
in the northerly direction from the mountain of a hundred peaks,
but those ascetics said to him: "In our northward march, ascending the king of
    mountains,
we have seen on its breast many regions inaccessible to mortals;
retreats also of the gods and Gandharvas and Apsaras,
with palatial mansions by the hundreds resounding with sweet notes of celestial
    music;
the gardens of Kuvera, on even and uneven ground; mighty rivers; and deep
    caverns.
There are many regions on those heights that are covered with perpetual snow

and utterly destitute of vegetable and animal existence.
In some places, the downpour of rain is so heavy
that they are perfectly inaccessible and unfit for habitation.
Not to speak of other animals, even winged creatures cannot cross them.
The only thing that can go there is air; and the only beings, siddhas and great
    rishis.
How shall these princesses ascend those heights of the king of mountains?
Unaccustomed to pain, shall they not droop in affliction?
Therefore, do not come with us, O bull of Bharata's race!"
Pandu replied: "Fortunate ones, it is said that for the sonless
there is no admittance into heaven. I am sonless! In affliction I speak to you!
I am afflicted because I have not been able to discharge my debt to my
    ancestors.
With the dissolution of my body, my ancestors perish!
Men are born on this earth with four debts—
those due to deceased ancestors, to the gods, to the rishis, and to other men.
These must be discharged. No regions of bliss exist for those
who neglect to pay these debts in due time.
The gods are paid by sacrifices; the rishis, by study, meditation, and asceticism;
the ancestors, by the begetting of children and the offering of the funeral cake;
and other men, by the leading of a humane and inoffensive life.
I have justly discharged my obligations to the rishis, the gods, and other men.
But my ancestors are sure to perish with the dissolution of my body!
I am not yet freed from the debt I owe them.
I would ask you, should children be begotten on my wives
as I myself was begotten on the wife of my father by an eminent rishi?"
The rishis said: "O king, there are progeny in store for you,
sinless and blessed with good fortune, and like to the gods.
We see this with our prophetic eyes. Therefore, accomplish by your own acts
that which destiny points to. Men of intelligence, acting with prudence,
always obtain good fruits. The fruits you would obtain are distinctly visible."
Pandu remembered the loss of his procreative powers and the curse of the deer.
Calling Kunti to him, he told her: "Strive to raise offspring at this time of
    distress.
Those who are wise in the eternal religion declare that a son is the cause of
    virtuous fame
in the three worlds. It is said that sacrifices, charitable gifts, penances,
and vows observed most carefully do not confer religious merit on a sonless man.
I am certain that, as I am sonless, I shall never obtain the regions of true felicity.
Wretch that I was, and addicted to cruel deeds,
my power of procreation has been destroyed by the curse of the deer.
The religious institutes mention six kinds of sons that are heirs and kinsmen,
and six other kinds that are not heirs but kinsmen.
They are, first, the son begotten by oneself upon one's wedded wife;
second, the son begotten on one's wife by an accomplished person out of
    kindness;
third, the son begotten upon one's wife by a person for pecuniary consideration;

fourth, the son begotten upon the wife after the husband's death; fifth, the
maiden-born son;

sixth, the son born of an unchaste wife; seventh, the son given;

eighth, the son bought for a consideration; ninth, the son self-given;

tenth, the son received with a pregnant bride; eleventh, the brother's son;

and, twelfth, the son begotten upon a wife of lower caste.

On failure to have offspring of a higher class, the mother should try to have
offspring

of the next class. In times of distress, men solicit offspring

from accomplished younger brothers. The self-born Manu has said

that men failing to have legitimate offspring of their own

may have offspring begotten upon their wives by others,

for sons confer the highest religious merit.

Therefore, O Kunti, being destitute myself of the power of procreation,

I command you to raise good offspring through some person."

Kunti answered: "Do not to say this to me. I am your wedded wife, devoted to you.

O Bharata of mighty arms, you shall yourself beget children upon me,

and then I shall ascend to heaven with you. Receive me in your embrace,

to beget children. I shall not even in imagination accept any other man.

What man is there in this world superior to you?"

King Pandu replied: "Kunti, what you have said is sweet to hear.

But I shall now tell you of the practices of old indicated by illustrious rishis.

Formerly women were not immured within houses

and dependent on husbands and other relatives.

They used to go about freely, enjoying themselves as they liked.

They did not then adhere to their husbands faithfully,

and yet they were not regarded as sinful, for that was the usage of the times.

That usage is followed to this day by birds and beasts, without any signs of
jealousy.

That custom, sanctioned by precedent, is applauded by great rishis

and is still regarded with respect among the northern Kurus.

Indeed, that custom, so lenient to women, has the sanction of antiquity.

The present custom of confining women to one husband for life

has been established only recently. I shall tell you who established it, and why.

There was a great rishi, named Uddalaka, who had a son named Swetaketu,

who also was an ascetic of merit. The present virtuous custom was established

by that Swetaketu, out of anger. One day, in the presence of Swetaketu's father,

a Brahmana came and, catching Swetaketu's mother by the hand, told her: 'Let
us go.'

Seeing his mother seized by the hand and taken away apparently by force,

the son was moved by wrath. But Uddalaka told him: 'Do not be angry, O son!

This is the custom sanctioned by antiquity. The women of all orders in this world

are free. Men in this matter, as regards their respective orders, act as cattle.'

But the rishi's son, Swetaketu, disapproved of that custom

and established in the world the present custom as regards men and women.

Accordingly, it is considered sinful for women not to adhere to their husbands.

Women transgressing the limits assigned by the rishi have abortions.

And, men, too, violating a chaste wife who has from her maidenhood
observed the vow of purity, become guilty of the same sin.
The woman also who, being commanded by her husband to raise offspring,
refuses to do his bidding, becomes equally sinful.' "
Ever attentive to what was agreeable and beneficial to her lord, Kunti replied:
"In my girlhood, O lord, I was in my father's house, attending upon his guests.
I used to wait respectfully upon Brahmanas of rigid vows and great ascetic merit.
One day, my attentions particularly pleased that Brahmana whom people call
    Durvasa,
of fully controlled mind and possessing knowledge of all the mysteries of religion.
Pleased with my services, that Brahmana granted me a boon
in the form of a mantra for calling into my presence any one of the celestials I
    liked.
And the rishi, addressing me, said: 'Any one of the celestials upon whom you call
shall approach you and be obedient to your will, willingly or not.
And you shall have offspring through his grace.'
That Brahmana told me this when I lived in my father's house.
The words uttered by a Brahmana can never be false. The time has come
when they may yield fruit. Commanded by you, O royal sage,
I can by that mantra summon any of the celestials so that we may have good
    children.
Tell me which of the celestials I shall summon. I await your command."
Pandu replied: "Strive this very day to gratify our wishes.
Summon the god of justice, the most virtuous of the celestials.
The god of justice and virtue will never be able to pollute us with sin.
The world also will then think that what we do can never be unholy.
The son we shall obtain from him will be foremost among the Kurus in virtue.
Begotten by the god of justice and morality, he will never set his heart
upon anything sinful or unholy. Therefore, woman of sweet smiles,
attending to virtue, summon the god of justice with your mantra."
Then Kunti said: "So be it." And, bowing down to Pandu
and reverently circumambulating his person, she resolved to do his bidding.
It was when Gandhari was a full year into her pregnancy
that Kunti summoned the eternal god of justice to obtain offspring from him.
She offered sacrifices to the god and repeated the manta Durvasa had given her.
At the spot where Kunti was seated, the god arrived
in his car resplendent as the sun and asked: "O Kunti, what am I to give you?"
Smiling in her turn, Kunti replied: "You must give me offspring."
Then Kunti was united in intercourse with the god of justice in his spiritual form
and obtained from him a son devoted to the good of all creatures.
She brought forth his excellent child, who lived to acquire great fame,
at the eighth *muhurta*, called *abhijit*, at the hour of noon
of that very auspicious day of Kartika, the seventh month,
when the star Jyeshtha in conjunction with the moon was ascendant.
As soon as the child was born, an incorporeal voice from the sky said:
"This child shall be the best of men, foremost among those who are virtuous.
Endowed with great prowess and truthful in speech, he shall rule the earth.

And this first child of Pandu shall be known by the name of Yudhishthira.
He shall be a famous king, known throughout the three worlds."
Having obtained that virtuous son, Pandu again addressed his wife:
"The wise have declared that a Kshatriya must be endowed with physical
   strength,
or else he is no Kshatriya. Therefore, ask for an offspring of superior strength."
Thus commanded by her lord, Kunti invoked Vayu, the mighty god of wind.
And Vayu came to her, riding on a deer, and said: "What am I to give you?
   Tell me what is in your heart."
Smiling in modesty, she said: "Give me, O best of celestials,
a child with great strength and large limbs, capable of humbling the pride of all."
The god of wind thereupon begot upon her the child afterward known as Bhima
   of mighty arms and fierce prowess.
And upon the birth of the child Bhima, also called Vrikodara, who was endowed
   with extraordinary strength,
an incorporeal voice said: "This child shall be foremost among men in strength."
And he was indeed so strong that when he fell from the lap of his mother,
high up on the mountain's breast, the violence of the fall broke into fragments
the stone upon which he landed, without the infant's body being injured in the
   least.
He had fallen from his mother's lap because Kunti,
frightened by a tiger, had risen up suddenly, unconscious of the child asleep on
   her lap.
And as she had risen, the infant, falling upon the mountainside,
broke the rocky mass upon which he fell into a hundred fragments.
It so happened that the very day on which Vrikodara was born
was also the birthday of Duryodhana, who afterward became the ruler of the
   whole earth.
After the birth of Vrikodara, Pandu began to think about how to obtain a
   superior son
who would achieve worldwide fame. "Everything in the world
depends on destiny and exertion," he reasoned. "But destiny can never be
   successful
except by timely exertion. We have heard it said that Indra is the chief of the gods.
Indeed, he is endowed with immeasurable might and energy and prowess and
   glory.
Pleasing him with my asceticism, I shall obtain from him a son of great strength.
Indeed, the son he gives me must be superior to all
and capable of vanquishing in battle all men and all creatures other than men.
I shall therefore practice the severest austerities in heart, deed, and speech."
Taking counsel with the great rishis, Pandu commanded Kunti
to observe an auspicious vow for one full year
while he himself commenced to stand on one leg from morning to evening
and to practice other severe austerities
with his mind rapt in meditation for gratifying the lord of the celestials.
It was after a long time that Indra, gratified by such devotion,
approached Pandu and said: "I shall give you a son who will be celebrated

all over the three worlds and who will promote the welfare of Brahmanas,
cattle, and all honest men. The son I give you will smite the wicked
and delight friends and relatives. He will be a slayer of all foes."
Thus addressed by the king of the celestials, the king of the Kuru race said to
   Kunti:
"O fortunate one, your vow has become successful.
The lord of the celestials is willing to give you a son such as we desire,
of superhuman achievements and great fame.
He will be the oppressor of all enemies and possessed of great wisdom.
Endowed with a great soul, in splendor equal to the sun,
invincible in battles, and of great achievements, he will also be extremely
   handsome.
O woman of fair hips and sweet smiles, the lord of the celestials
has become gracious to you. Invoke him and bring forth a child
who will be the very home of all Kshatriya virtues."
The celebrated Kunti invoked the king of the gods,
who thereupon came to her and begot the son who was afterward called Arjuna.
And as soon as this child was born, an incorporeal voice, loud and deep,
and filling the whole vault of heaven, said to Kunti:
"This child, O Kunti, will be equal to Kartavirya in energy and to Shiva in prowess.
Invincible like Sakra, he will spread your fame far and wide.
As Vishnu, the youngest of Aditi's sons, enhanced her joy,
so shall this child enhance your joy. Subjugating the Madras, the Kurus, the
   Somakas,
and the people of Chedi, Kasi and Karusha, he will maintain the prosperity of
   the Kurus.
This mighty hero, vanquishing all the effeminate monarchs of the earth,
will with his brothers perform three great sacrifices.
In prowess, he will be even as Jamadagnya or Vishnu.
Foremost among men, he will achieve great fame.
He will gratify by his heroism Sankara, the Mahadeva, the god of gods,
and will receive from him the great weapon named Pashupatastra.
Your son will also slay, at Indra's command,
those Daityas called the Nivatakavachas, who are the enemies of the gods.
He will acquire all kinds of celestial weapons,
and this bull among men will retrieve the fortunes of his race."
Hearing those words uttered so loudly, the ascetics
dwelling on the mountain of a hundred peaks, and the celestials with Indra
sitting in their cars, became most glad.
Sounds of an invisible drum filled the entire welkin.
The whole region was covered with flowers showered down by invisible agents.
The various tribes of celestials assembled to offer adorations to the son of Pritha.
The Gandharvas and Apsaras came there also.
The various tribes of Apsaras, decked with celestial garlands and every ornament
and attired in fine robes, came there and danced in joy, chanting the praises of
   Arjuna.
All around, the great rishis began to utter propitiatory formulas.

And Tumvuru, that best of singers, began to sing in charming notes.
Bhimasena and Ugrasena, Urnayus and Anagha,
Gopati and Dhritarashtra and Suryavarchas the eighth,
Yugapa and Trinapa, Karshni, Nandi, and Chitraratha,
Suvarna of great fame, Viswavasu, Bhumanyu, Suchandra,
Sam and the tribes of Haha and Huhu, gifted with wonderful melody of voice—
these celestial Gandharvas all went there.
Many illustrious Apsaras also came to dance and sing.
Only great rishis crowned with ascetic success and no others
saw those celestials and other beings seated in their cars or waiting on mountain
    peaks.
Those best of munis, beholding that wonderful sight, were amazed,
and their love and affection for the children of Pandu were in consequence
    enhanced.

✦

Pandu, desiring even more children, again asked his wife to invoke some other
    god.
But Kunti said: "The wise do not sanction a fourth delivery even in a season of
    distress.
A woman having intercourse with four different men is called a *swairini*, wanton,
while she who has intercourse with five is a whore.
You are well acquainted with the scripture on this subject.
Why, then, do you ask me this, in seeming forgetfulness of the ordinance?"
After the birth of Kunti's sons, and also of the hundred sons of Dhritarashtra,
the daughter of the king of Madra addressed Pandu:
"O slayer of foes, I have no complaint, even though you have been unpropitious
    to me.
I have no complaint that, even though by birth I am superior to Kunti,
I am inferior to her in station. I do not grieve that Gandhari has a hundred sons.
But this is my great grief—that while Kunti and I are equal,
I should be childless while you should have offspring by her alone.
If the daughter of Kuntibhoja should so provide that I should have offspring,
she would be doing me a great favor also, and benefiting you.
She is my rival, and I feel a delicacy in soliciting any favor from her.
If you be kindly disposed to me, then ask her to grant my desire."
Pandu answered: "O Madri, I do revolve this matter often in my own mind,
but I have hitherto hesitated to tell you anything, not knowing how you would
    receive it.
Now that I know what your wishes are, I shall strive after that end.
I think that, if I ask her, Kunti will not refuse."
After this, Pandu addressed Kunti in private:
"Grant me more offspring for the expansion of my race and the benefit of the
    world.
Provide that I myself, my ancestors, and yours also
may always have the funeral cake offered to us.

Do what is beneficial to me, O blameless one, and rescue Madri as by a raft.
Grant her the means of obtaining offspring, and achieve for yourself
imperishable fame by making her a mother of children."
Kunti readily yielded and said to Madri: "Without loss of time, think of some celestial,
and you shall obtain from him a child like him."
Madri thought of the twin Aswins, who came to her with great speed
and begot upon her twin sons, named Nakula and Sahadeva,
unrivaled on earth for personal beauty. As soon as they were born,
an incorporeal voice said: "In energy and beauty these twins shall transcend
even the twin Aswins themselves."
After all the children were born, the rishis dwelling on the mountain of a hundred peaks,
uttering blessings on them, performed the first rites of birth and named them.
The eldest of Kunti's children was called Yudhishthira; the second, Bhimasena;
and the third, Arjuna. And of Madri's sons, the firstborn of the twins was called Nakula
and the next, Sahadeva.
King Pandu, beholding his children of celestial beauty and boundless energy,
of great strength and prowess and largeness of soul, rejoiced.
And the children became great favorites of the rishis
and also of their wives, dwelling on the mountain of a hundred peaks.
Sometime later, Pandu again made a request to Kunti on behalf of Madri.
But Kunti replied: "Having received the formula of invocation only once,
she has, O king, managed to obtain two sons. Have I not been thus deceived by her?
I fear, O king, that she will surpass me in the number of her children.
This is the way of all wicked women. Fool that I was,
I did not know that by invoking the twin gods I could obtain, at one birth, twin children.
I beseech you, O king, do not command me any further."
Thus were born to Pandu five sons, begotten by celestials
and endowed with great strength, who all lived to achieve great fame
and expand the Kuru race. Each bore every auspicious mark on his person.
Handsome like Soma, as proud as the lion, well skilled in the use of the bow,
and of leonine tread, breast, heart, eyes, neck, and prowess,
these foremost among men began to grow up.
Seeing them and their virtues growing with the years,
the great rishis dwelling on that snowcapped sacred mountain were filled with wonder.
And the five Pandavas and the hundred sons of Dhritarashtra
grew up, like a cluster of lotuses in a lake.
Pandu, meanwhile, felt the strength of his arms revive.
One day in the season of spring, which maddens every creature,
the king, accompanied by his wife Madri, wandered the woods,
where every tree had put forth new blossoms.
All around him were palasas and tilakas and mangoes and champakas

and parihadrakas and karnikaras, asokas and kesaras and atimuktas and
    kuruvakas,
with swarms of maddened bees humming about.
There were flowers of blossoming parijatas, with the blackbirds pouring forth
    their melodies
from under every twig that echoed with the sweet hum of the black bees.
And he saw as well other kinds of trees bent down with the weight of their
    flowers and fruits.
There were also many fine pools of water overgrown with fragrant lotuses.
Pandu felt the sweet bite of desire. Wandering like a celestial
with a light heart in the midst of such scenery, Pandu was alone with Madri,
who was in semitransparent attire. And beholding the youthful Madri thus
    attired,
the king felt his desire flame up like a forest fire.
Unable to suppress the desire thus kindled at the sight of his wife,
he was overpowered. The king then seized her against her will,
but Madri, trembling in fear, resisted him to the best of her might.
Consumed by desire, Pandu forgot all about his misfortune.
And, unrestrained by the fear of the rishi's curse, and impelled by fate,
the monarch forcibly sought the embraces of Madri,
as if he wished to put an end to his own life.
His reason, thus beguiled by the great destroyer himself, was lost along with his
    life.
The Kuru king Pandu, of virtuous soul, thus succumbed
to the inevitable influence of time while united in intercourse with his wife.
Madri, clasping the body of her senseless lord, began to weep.
And Kunti, with her sons and the twins of Madri, hearing those cries of grief,
came to where the king lay dead. In a piteous voice, Madri said:
"Come here alone, O Kunti. Let the children stay there."
Kunti bade the children stay, and she ran.
Seeing Pandu and Madri prostrate on the ground, she said, "O woe!
I have watched this hero with care. How did he forget the rishi's curse
and approach you with desire? You should have protected this foremost
    among men.
Why did you tempt him? He was always melancholy at the thought of the rishi's
    curse.
How did he come to be merry alone with you here?
Princess of Valhika, more fortunate than myself, you are to be envied,
for you have seen the face of our lord suffused with gladness and joy."
Madri replied: "Revered sister, I resisted the king, but he could not control
    himself.
It was as if he were making the rishi's curse come true."
Kunti then said: "I am the older of his wedded wives.
The chief religious merit must be mine.
Do not prevent me, therefore, from achieving what must be achieved.
I must follow our lord to the region of the dead.
Rise up, O Madri, and yield me his body. And rear these children."

Madri replied: "I clasp our lord yet, and I have not allowed him to depart.
Therefore, I shall follow him. My appetite has not been appeased.
You are my older sister. Let me have your permission.
This foremost among Bharata princes approached me, desiring intercourse.
His appetite was unsatisfied. Shall I not follow him to the region of Yama and
   gratify him?
If I survive you, it is certain I shall not be able to rear your children as if they
   were mine.
Will not sin touch me on that account? But you, O Kunti,
will be able to bring my sons up as if they were yours.
The king, in seeking me, has gone to the region of spirits.
My body, therefore, should be burned with his.
O sister, do not withhold your permission for what I desire."
Having said this, the daughter of the king of Madra,
wife of Pandu, ascended the pyre of her lord, that bull among men.

◆

In Hastinapura, King Dhritarashtra directed Vidura and Bhishma
to celebrate the funeral ceremonies of that lion among kings in royal style,
distributing cattle, cloths, gems, and diverse kinds of wealth.
"Let Kunti perform the last rites of Madri in such manner as may please her,"
Dhritarashtra said, "and let Madri's body be so carefully wrapped up
that neither the god of the sun nor the god of wind may behold it.
Do not lament for the sinless Pandu.
He was a worthy king and left behind five heroic sons, equal to the celestials."
Vidura and Bhishma said: "So be it." And they fixed upon a sacred spot for the
   rites.
The family priests went out of the city, carrying with them the sacred fire
fed with clarified butter by which it was rendered fragrant.
Then friends, relatives, and adherents decked the wrapped body of the monarch
with flowers of the season and sprinkled it with various perfumes.
They also decked the hearse itself with garlands and rich hangings.
Placing the covered body of the king with that of his queen
on that bier decked out so brightly, they carried it on their shoulders
with the white umbrella of state held over the hearse
and with waving yak tails and sounds of various musical instruments.
Hundreds of people distributed gems among the crowd.
Priests clad in white walked at the forefront of the procession,
pouring libations of clarified butter on the sacred fire
that blazed in an ornamental vessel.
And Brahmanas and Kshatriyas and Vaisyas and Sudras by the thousands
followed the deceased king, wailing loudly.
And Bhishma and Vidura and the Pandavas all wept aloud.
At last they came to a romantic wood on the banks of the Ganga.
There they set down the hearse on which lay the lionhearted king and his
   spouse.

They brought water in golden vessels, washed the king's body,
besmeared it with several kinds of fragrant paste, and dressed it in white.
The king seemed as if he were living, and only asleep on a costly bed.
When the ceremonies were finished, the Kauravas set fire to the bodies,
bringing lotuses, sandalwood paste, and other fragrant substances to the pyre.

Seeing the bodies aflame, Kausalya burst out: "O my son, my son!"
And she fell senseless to the ground.
The citizens wailed, and the birds of the air and the beasts of the field
were touched by the lamentations of Kunti.
And Bhishma, son of Shantanu, and wise Vidura and others grieved deeply
    there.
The Pandavas and their friends renounced their beds and slept on the ground.
Young and old, all the citizens went into mourning for twelve days,
in condolence for the weeping Pandavas.

5

Bhima

Seeing the grief of all the subjects, the venerable Vyasa said to his mother,
  Satyavati:
"Our days of happiness have gone by, and days of calamity have succeeded.
Sin increases day by day. The world has become old.
Because of wrong and oppression, the empire of the Kauravas cannot endure.
Go, then, into the forest, and devote yourself to contemplation through Yoga,
for society will be filled with deceit and wrong. Good work will cease.
Do not witness the annihilation of your race in your old age."
Acquiescing to his words, Satyavati entered the inner apartments
and said to her daughter-in-law: "O Ambika, because of the deeds of your
  grandsons,
I hear that this Bharata dynasty and its subjects will perish.
If you will permit, I shall go to the forest with Kausalya,
who is so grieved at the loss of her son."
The queen asked permission of Bhishma also
and then went to the forest with her two daughters-in-law.
She engaged in contemplation, and in good time, leaving her body, ascended to
  heaven.

✦

The sons of King Pandu grew up in princely style in the home of their father.
Whenever they were engaged in play with the sons of Dhritarashtra,
their superiority of strength was evident. In speed, in striking distant objects,
in consuming food, and in scattering dust, Bhimasena beat all the sons of
  Dhritarashtra.
The son of the wind god pulled them by the hair and made them fight with one
  another,
always laughing. And Vrikodara easily defeated those hundred and one children,
as if they were one rather than many. The second Pandava would seize them by
  the hair
and throw them down, dragging them along the ground.
Some had their knees broken, some their heads, and some their shoulders.
That youth, sometimes holding ten of them, plunged them under water
                              until they nearly drowned.

When the sons of Dhritarashtra climbed the boughs of a tree to pluck fruits,
Bhima used to shake that tree, striking it with his foot,
so that the fruits and the fruit pickers came down together.
Those princes were no match for Bhima in boxing, in speed, or in skill.
Bhima used to display his strength by tormenting them
in childishness, but not from malice.
Because of these displays of strength by Bhima,
Duryodhana, the eldest son of Dhritarashtra, conceived a hostility toward him.
The wicked and unrighteous Duryodhana, through ignorance and ambition,
prepared himself for an act of sin.
He considered that there was no one who could compare with Bhima in
prowess,
and that he would therefore have to destroy him by artifice.
Bhima dared a century of us to combat, he said to himself,
but when he is asleep in the garden, I can throw him into the Ganga.
Afterward, confining his eldest brother, Yudhishthira, and his younger brother, Arjuna,
I shall reign as sole king, without fear of molestation.
From then on, Duryodhana was always alert to any opportunity to injure Bhima.
At length, at a beautiful place called Pramanakoti,
on the banks of the Ganga, he built a palace decorated with hangings of rich
stuffs
and filled it with all kinds of pretty objects and fine foods.
Gay flags waved from the roof of this mansion.
When all was ready, Duryodhana, that wicked prince, said to the Pandavas:
"Let us all go to the banks of the Ganga, graced with trees and crowned with
flowers,
and swim, sail, and sport there in the water." Yudhishthira agreed to this,
and the sons of Dhritarashtra, taking the Pandavas with them,
mounted country-born elephants of great size and left the capital.
Arriving at the palace, the princes dismissed their attendants
and, admiring the beauty of the gardens and the groves,
entered like lions entering their mountain caves.
They saw that the architects had handsomely plastered the walls and the ceilings,
and that painters had decorated them lavishly.
Through the windows, they could see the splendid fountains.
Here and there were tanks of clear water in which lotuses blossomed.
The riverbanks were decked with various flowers, whose fragrance filled the air.
The Kauravas and the Pandavas sat down to enjoy the delicacies that were
served.
They laughed and played and exchanged morsels of food with one another.
Meanwhile, Duryodhana had mixed a poison with some of the food
so that he could make away with Bhima.
That wicked youth with nectar on his tongue and a razor in his heart
rose at length and, in a friendly manner, fed Bhima with that poisoned food.
Duryodhana smiled because he had accomplished his objective.
The sons of Dhritarashtra and Pandu sported together in the water.
Then they dressed themselves in white and decked themselves with ornaments.

Fatigued by their exertions, they went to rest in the pleasure house in the
    garden.
Bhima was more fatigued than anyone else, having been more strenuous in his
    exertions.
On rising from the water, he lay down on the ground,
                                weary and beginning to feel the poison.
The cool air spread the toxin through all his frame so that he lost consciousness
    at once.
Duryodhana bound him with cords of vines
and threw him into the water, where he sank down
until he reached the Naga kingdom on the riverbed.
Nagas by the thousands bit him with their fangs, containing virulent venom.
The serpents bit him all over his body except on his chest,
where the skin was so tough that their fangs could not penetrate it.
The snake poison neutralized the vegetable poison in the blood of the wind
    god's son.
Regaining consciousness, the son of Kunti burst his bonds
and pressed the snakes down under the riverbed.
A few fled for their lives and went to their king, Vasuki.
"O king of snakes," they said, "a man drowned under the water, bound in vines.
Probably he had drunk poison, for when he fell among us, he was insensible.
But when we began to bite him, he regained his senses, burst his fetters, and
    attacked us.
May it please Your Majesty to inquire who he is?"
Having been asked by the inferior Nagas, Vasuki went to Bhimasena.
One of the serpents, named Aryaka, was the grandfather of the father of Kunti.
The lord of the serpents saw his relative and embraced him.
Vasuki, learning all of this, was pleased with Bhima and asked Aryaka:
"How can we make him happy? Let him have money and gems in profusion."
Aryaka answered: "O king of serpents, if Your Majesty is pleased with him,
he has no need of wealth! But permit him to drink from the *rasakunda*, the
    nectar vessels,
and thus acquire immeasurable strength.
There is the strength of a thousand elephants in each vessel.
Let this prince drink as much as he can."
The king of serpents gave his consent, and the serpents began the rites.
Purifying himself carefully, Bhimasena faced the east and began to drink the
    nectar.
At one draft, he drained the contents of a whole vessel
and in this manner drank from eight successive jars, until he was full.
At length the serpents prepared a bed for him, on which he lay down to rest.

✦

Meanwhile, the Kauravas and the Pandavas, having had such a good time,
set off without Bhima from the river palace for Hastinapura,
some on horses, some on elephants, and some in cars and other conveyances.

On their way, they said to one another: "Perhaps Bhima has gone before us."
The wicked Duryodhana was delighted by Bhima's absence
and in great joy entered the city with his brothers.
Yudhishthira, unacquainted with wickedness, assumed others were as honest as he.
The eldest son of Pritha went to his mother and asked her if Bhima had come.
"Where could he have gone?" he said. "We looked for him everywhere
                            in the gardens and the woods,
but found no sign of him, and we decided that he had preceded us home.
We hurried here in great anxiety. Have you sent him anywhere? I am full of
    worry.
He had been asleep, and then he was gone. I fear that he is no more."
Kunti shrieked in alarm and said she had not seen Bhima. He had not come
    home.
"Go back in haste with your brothers," she said, "and search for him."
She summoned Vidura and said: "Bhimasena is missing!
The other brothers have all come back from the gardens, but Bhima has not
    appeared.
Duryodhana does not like him. The Kaurava is crooked
and malicious and low-minded and imprudent. He covets the throne.
I am afraid that in a fit of anger he may have slain my darling."
Vidura replied: "Say not so! Protect your other sons with care.
If the wicked Duryodhana be accused, he may slay your remaining sons.
The great sage has said that all your sons will be long-lived.
Bhima will surely return, therefore, to gladden your heart."
The wise Vidura then returned to his abode while Kunti continued in great
    anxiety.

✦

Meanwhile, Bhimasena awoke from his slumber on the eighth day,
feeling strength beyond measure because of the nectar he had drunk.
The Nagas consoled and encouraged him, saying:
"The strength-giving liquor will give you the might of ten thousand elephants!
No one now will be able to vanquish you in a fight. Bathe in this holy water,
and then return home. Your brothers are disconsolate on your account."
Bhima purified himself in those waters and, decked in white robes and flowery
    garlands,
ate of the *paramanna*, the pudding of rice and sugar, offered by the Nagas.
He received the adorations and blessings of the snakes,
saluted them in return, and rose from the nether region.
Bearing up the lotus-eyed Pandava from under the waters,
the Nagas put him back in the garden from which he had vanished.
Having reached the surface of the earth, Bhima ran with all speed to his mother.
He bowed down to her and his eldest brother
                        and smelled the heads of his younger brothers.
His mother and his brothers embraced him, exclaiming: "Oh! what joy we have
    today!"

Bhima told his brothers about Duryodhana's villainy
and the lucky and unlucky events that had befallen him in the world of the
    serpents.
Yudhishthira said: "Be silent about this. Speak of it to no one.
From now on, you must all protect one another. Be careful!"
Thus warned by Yudhishthira, they all became very vigilant.
And lest any of the sons of Kunti relax or grow negligent,
Vidura continually offered them his sage counsel.
Sometime later, Duryodhana again mixed a fresh and virulent poison into
    Bhima's food.
But Yuyutsu, Dhritarashtra's son by a Vaisya wife, in friendship for the Pandavas,
informed them of this. Nevertheless, Bhima swallowed it without hesitation
and digested it completely. And although it was deadly, the poison had no effect
    on him.
When the poison failed to have any effect,
Duryodhana, Karna, and Sakuni tried many other plans for killing the Pandavas.
Every one of these plans was known to the Pandavas,
                  but in accordance with Vidura's advice,
they suppressed their indignation and said nothing.

6

Drona

King Dhritarashtra realized that the Kuru princes were passing their time in
idleness.
He appointed Kripa as their tutor and sent them to him for instruction.
Born of a clump of heath, Kripa was well skilled in the Vedas,
and under his tutelage the Kuru princes studied the use of arms.
But how did Kripa spring from a clump of heath?
And where did he get his weapons?
The great sage Gautama had a son named Saradwat, born with arrows in his hand.
This son of Gautama exhibited great aptitude for the study of weapons,
but none for the other sciences. Saradwat acquired his weapons through those
austerities
by which Brahmanas acquire knowledge of the Vedas.
His father, Gautama, with his skill in weaponry and through his austerities,
had made the great Indra fear him. The chief of the gods
summoned a celestial damsel named Janapadi and sent her to Gautama, saying:
"Do your best to disturb the austerities of Gautama."
The Apsara tempted the ascetic.
As Gautama beheld her, alone in those woods and clad only in a single piece of
cloth,
her figure unrivaled on earth for beauty,
his eyes grew wide with delight, his bow and arrows slipped from his hand,
and his body shook all over with passion.
But with ascetic fortitude and strength of soul, the sage resisted the temptation.
Nevertheless, the suddenness of his mental agitation
caused an uncontrollable emission of his vital fluid.
Leaving his bow and arrows and deerskin behind, he fled from the Apsara.
His vital fluid, however, having fallen upon a clump of heath,
was divided into two parts, from which sprang twins.
It happened that a soldier attending King Shantanu
while the monarch was out hunting saw the twins.
He also saw the bow and arrows and deerskin on the ground.
He thought these infants might be the offspring of some Brahmana proficient in
arms.
He took up the children along with the bow and arrows and brought them to
the king,

who was moved with pity. "Let these become my children," the king said,
and he brought them to his palace. Then Shantanu performed the prescribed rites
and brought them up. He called them Kripa and Kripi
because he had adopted them out of *kripa*, pity.
Gautama continued his study of the science of arms,
and through his spiritual insight he learned that his son and his daughter
were in Shantanu's palace. He went to the palace and told the king about his
 lineage.
He then taught Kripa the science of arms, and various other kinds of knowledge.
In a short time, Kripa became an eminent master of arms.
And the hundred sons of Dhritarashtra, and the Pandavas,
along with the Yadavas and the Vrishnis,
and many other princes from various lands—all received lessons from him in
 that science.
Eager to give his grandsons a superior education,
Bhishma had been seeking for those Kuru princes a teacher with energy and
 skill.
He wanted none who was not possessed of great intelligence, none who was not
 illustrious
or a perfect master of the science of arms, and none who was not of godlike
 might.
The son of Ganga placed the Pandavas and the Kauravas
under the tuition of Bharadwaja's son, Drona, who was skilled in all the Vedas.
Drona of worldwide fame accepted the princes as his pupils
and taught them the science of arms in all its branches.
And the Kauravas as well as the Pandavas became proficient in a short time
     in the use of all kinds of arms.

✦

How was Drona born? And how did he acquire his arms?
And how and why did he come to the Kurus?
At the source of the Ganga there lived a great sage named Bharadwaja,
ceaselessly observing the most rigid vows.
One day, intending to celebrate the Agnihotra sacrifice,
he went along with many great rishis to the Ganga to perform his ablutions.
At the bank of the river he saw Ghritachi, an Apsara endowed with youth and
 beauty.
With a proud countenance and voluptuous languor,
the damsel emerged from the water after her ablutions were over.
And as she walked along the bank, her attire became disordered.
The sage was smitten with desire. His vital fluid erupted in the violence of his
 emotion.
The rishi caught it in a vessel called a *drona*.
Then Drona sprang from the fluid in that vessel, fluid preserved by the wise
 Bharadwaja.
And the child thus born studied all the Vedas and their branches.

✦

There was a king named Prishata, who was a great friend of Bharadwaja.
Prishata had a son named Drupada, who used to come every day
to the hermitage of Bharadwaja to play with Drona and study in his company.
When Prishata died, Drupada became the king of the northern Panchalas.
About this time, the illustrious Bharadwaja also ascended to heaven.
Drona continued to reside in his father's hermitage, devoting himself to
    austerities.
Well versed in the Vedas, and having burned out all his sins by asceticism,
the celebrated Drona, moved by the desire of offspring, married Kripi,
the daughter of Saradwat. This woman, always engaged in virtuous acts
and the most austere of penances, bore a son named Aswatthaman.
And as soon as Aswatthaman was born, he neighed like the celestial steed
    Ucchaihsravas.
An invisible being in the skies said: "The voice of this child
is like the neighing of a horse and has been audible all around.
The child shall, therefore, be known as Aswatthaman, meaning '*Horse-Voiced.*'"
Drona was exceedingly glad at having a son.
He continued to live in that hermitage
and devoted himself to the study of the science of arms.
It was also about this time that Drona heard that Jamadagnya, illustrious Brahmana
and foremost among wielders of weapons, wanted to give away all his wealth to
    Brahmanas.
Having heard of Rama's knowledge of arms and of his celestial weapons,
Drona set his heart on them, as also on the knowledge of morality that Rama
    possessed.
Drona set out for the Mahendra mountains, accompanied by disciples
who were all devoted to vows of ascetic austerities.
At Mahendra, the son of Bharadwaja beheld the son of Bhrigu.
Drona approached that scion of the Bhrigu race, gave his name,
and told him of his birth in the line of Angiras.
Touching the ground with his head, he worshipped at Rama's feet.
And seeing the illustrious son of Jamadagni intent upon retiring into the woods
after having given away all his wealth, Drona said:
"Know that I sprang from Bharadwaja, but not in any woman's womb!
I am a Brahmana of high birth, Drona by name,
come to you with the desire of obtaining your wealth."
Rama Jamadagnya replied: "You are welcome! Tell me what you desire."
Drona answered that foremost among smiters: "I am a candidate for your eternal
    wealth."
Rama told him: "My gold and other riches have been given away to Brahmanas.
I have left now only my body and my various valuable weapons.
I am prepared to give either my body or my weapons.
Which would you have? Say, and I will give it!"
Drona answered: "Give me the weapons and the art of hurling and recalling
    them."

"So be it," the son of Bhrigu said, and he gave all his weapons to Drona
along with the whole science of arms, with its rules and mysteries.
Accepting them, and thinking himself well rewarded,
Drona set out for the city of his friend Drupada and presented himself to that
    monarch.
"Know me as your friend," he said. But the lord of the Panchalas was displeased.
Intoxicated with the pride of wealth, the king scowled in anger and said:
"Your intelligence is not of a high order. You say that you are my friend!
Do you not know that great kings can never be friends
with such luckless and indigent persons as you?
It is true that there was once a friendship between us, but that was when we were
    equals.
Time, which destroys everything in its course, destroys friendship also.
In this world, friendship never endures forever in any heart.
Time wears it away, and anger ruins it. Do not claim a worn-out friendship.
Think of it no longer. Friendship can never exist between a poor man and a
    rich man,
between a man of letters and an unlettered mind, or between a hero and a
    coward.
Why do you desire an impossible thing? There may be friendship or hostility
between persons equal in wealth or might. But the rich and the poor
can neither be friends nor quarrel with each other.
One of impure birth can never be a friend to one of pure birth.
One who is not a chariot warrior can never be a friend to one who is.
And one who is not a king can never have a king for his friend.
Why, then, do you desire the continuance of our former friendship?'
Angered, Drona wished to check the insolence of the Panchala king.
He hastened toward the capital of the Kurus, named after the elephant.
At Hastinapura, he lived privately in the house of Kripa.
Drona's mighty son, Aswatthaman, at intervals when Kripa was not teaching him,
used to give the sons of Kunti lessons in the use of arms.
But as yet none knew of Aswatthaman's prowess.
One day the heroic princes all came out of Hastinapura
and began to play with a ball and roamed about in gladness of heart.
It happened that the ball they had been playing with fell into a dry well.
The princes strove to recover it, but their efforts proved futile.
They eyed one another bashfully and were ashamed of themselves.
Just at this time, they saw approaching a Brahmana of darkish hue, decrepit and
    lean,
and sanctified by the performance of the Agnihotra sacrifice.
He had finished his daily rites of worship. The princes surrounded him
    immediately.
Drona—for he was that Brahmana—smiled a little and said:
"Shame on your Kshatriya might, and shame also on your skill in arms!
You are of the race of Bharata! How is it that you cannot recover a ball from a well?
Promise me a dinner today, and I will with these blades of grass
bring up not only the ball you have lost but also this ring that I now throw down!"

Drona then took off his ring and threw it into the dry well.

Yudhishthira, the son of Kunti, addressed Drona, saying:

"O Brahmana, you ask for a trifle! With Kripa's permission, ask of us

what will last you for life!" With smiles, Drona replied to the Bharata princes:

"This handful of long grass I would invest, by my mantras, with the virtue of
weapons.

Behold, these blades possess virtues that other weapons do not have!

I will with one of these blades pierce the ball

and then pierce that blade with another, and that other with a third,

and thus by a chain I shall bring up the ball."

Drona did exactly what he had said. The princes were amazed,

and their eyes were wide with delight. They said: "O learned Brahmana,

bring up the ring also, without loss of time."

Drona took a bow and arrow, pierced the ring with the arrow,

and brought it up at once. Coolly, he gave it to the astonished princes.

They said: "We bow to you, O Brahmana! No one else possesses such skill.

We long to know who you are, and whose son. What can we do for you?"

Drona answered the princes: "Go to Bhishma, and describe to him my likeness

and skill. He will recognize me." The princes did so, and Bhishma at once
understood

that the Brahmana had to be Drona. He realized at once

that Drona would make an ideal teacher for the princes.

Bhishma went to Drona, welcomed him respectfully, and brought him to the
palace.

Adroitly, Bhishma asked Drona why he had come to Hastinapura,

and Drona told him everything that had happened:

"Long ago, I went to the great rishi Agnivesa to obtain from him his weapons

and to learn the science of arms. I lived with him for many years

in the guise of a Brahmacharin, with matted locks on my head.

At that time, and for the same reasons, the prince of Panchala,

the mighty Yajnasena, also lived in the same hermitage.

We lived together for a long time, and from our earliest years we studied
together.

He was my friend from boyhood, always saying and doing what was agreeable
to me.

He used to tell me: 'O Drona, I am the favorite child of my illustrious father.

When the king installs me as monarch of the Panchalas,

the kingdom shall be yours. This is my solemn promise.

My dominion, wealth, and happiness shall all depend on you.'

At last the time came for his departure, and he returned to his country.

I wished him well and remembered his words.

Some time later, in obedience to the injunctions of my father,

and prompted also by the desire of offspring, I married Kripi,

of short hair and great intelligence, who had observed many rigid vows.

She was always engaged in the Agnihotra and other sacrifices and austerities.

In time, she gave birth to a son, named Aswatthaman, of great prowess

and equal in splendor to the sun himself. I was as pleased to obtain Aswatthaman

as my father had been to obtain me. One day Aswatthaman
observed some rich men's sons drinking milk, and he began to cry.
At this I was so upset that I lost all knowledge of the points of the compass.
Instead of asking a man who had only a few cows to give me one,
which would leave him unable to perform his sacrifices
and make it impossible for him to sustain his virtue,
I thought it would be better to obtain a cow from one who had many,
and for that I wandered from country to country,
but I was unsuccessful and failed to obtain a milk cow.
After I had come home, some of my son's playmates gave him water
mixed with powdered rice, and the poor boy was fooled into thinking it was milk.
He danced in joy, crying out: 'Oh! I have taken milk! I have taken milk!'
Those playmates smiled at his simplicity and called out derisively:
'Look at poor Drona, who does not strive to earn wealth,
and whose son drinks water mixed with powdered rice and mistakes it for milk.'
I resolved that even if I should be cast off and censured by Brahmanas,
I still would not, from desire for wealth, be anybody's servant.
For our former friendship, O Bhishma, I went to the king of the Somakas,
with my dear child and wife. He had been installed on the throne of the
      Somakas,
and with high hopes I went to that dear friend of mine seated on the throne.
I said: 'O tiger among men, know me for your friend!'
But Drupada laughed in derision and cast me off as if I were some stranger.
He said: 'Your intelligence scarcely seems to be of a high order
inasmuch as you approach me suddenly and say you are my friend!
But time, which destroys everything in its course, destroys friendship also.
In this world, friendship never endures forever in any heart.
Friendship can only exist between people of equal rank
and does not last forever. Time ruins friendships, as anger destroys them.
Do not cling, then, to our worn-out friendship. Think of it no longer.
The friendship I had with you was for a special purpose.
One who is not a king can never have a king for his friend.
I do not remember ever having promised you my kingdom.
But I can give you food and shelter for one night.'
I left his presence quickly, vowing to do what I will certainly do soon enough.
Thus insulted by Drupada, O Bhishma, I have been filled with wrath
and have come to the Kurus to obtain intelligent and docile pupils.
I come to Hastinapura to gratify your wishes. Tell me what I am to do."
Bhishma said to him: "String your bow, O Brahmana,
and make the Kuru princes accomplished in arms.
Worshipped by the Kurus, enjoy every comfort in their abode.
You are the lord, O Brahmana, of the wealth of the Kurus and of their
      sovereignty!
From this day, the Kurus are yours. Think of what may be in your heart
as already accomplished. It is our great good fortune, O Brahmana, that you are
      here.
The favor you conferred upon me by your coming here is immeasurable."

✦

Drona, that first of men, took up his quarters in the abode of the Kurus.
Bhishma gave him a house that was tidy and neat and filled with every kind of
    wealth.
After Drona had rested a while, Bhishma took his grandsons, the Kaurava princes,
and gave them to Drona as pupils. He also gave him many valuable presents.
Having accepted them all as his pupils, Drona called them apart one day
and, making them touch his feet, said to them with a swelling heart:
"I have in my mind a particular purpose. Promise me
that when you have become skilled in arms, you will accomplish it."
The Kuru princes were silent. But Arjuna vowed to accomplish whatever it was.
Drona clasped Arjuna to his bosom and took the scent of his head, weeping in joy.
Drona taught the sons of Pandu the use of many weapons, both celestial and
    human.
And many other princes also flocked to him for instruction in arms,
as did Karna, the adopted son of Radha of the Suta caste, and became his pupils.
Out of jealousy, the *Suta* child Karna frequently defied Arjuna,
and with Duryodhana's support he used to insult the Pandavas.
Arjuna, however, from devotion to the science of arms, always stayed by Drona's
    side,
and in skill, strength of arms, and perseverance he surpassed all his fellow
    students.
Although the instruction the teacher gave was the same for all,
in lightness and skill Arjuna was foremost.
Drona was convinced that none of his pupils would ever equal that son of Indra.
Drona gave lessons to all the princes in the science of weapons,
and while he gave every one of his pupils a narrow-mouthed vessel
so that they would spend much time in filling those vessels,
he gave his own son Aswatthaman a broad-mouthed vessel,
which he could fill quickly, so that he might return sooner.
And in this extra time, Drona instructed his son in superior methods of using
    weapons.
Arjuna figured this out and began filling his narrow-mouthed vessel with water
by means of the Varuna weapon. Thus he could come to his preceptor
at the same time as his preceptor's son. Accordingly, Arjuna was in no way
    inferior
to Aswatthaman in excellence and skill. Arjuna's devotion to his preceptor was
    very great,
and he became Drona's favorite. Seeing his pupil's devotion to arms,
Drona summoned the cook and instructed him in secret:
"Never give Arjuna his food in the dark or tell him that I have told you this."
A few days later, however, when Arjuna was eating, a wind arose, and the lamp
    went out,
but Arjuna continued eating in the dark, his hand going to his mouth out of
    habit.
Realizing the force of habit, Arjuna began practicing with his bow at night.

Drona heard the twang of Arjuna's bowstring in the darkness, came to Arjuna,
  and said:
"I shall teach you so that there shall be no archer equal to you."
Thereafter, Drona began to teach Arjuna the art of fighting on horseback,
on the backs of elephants, on chariots, and on the ground.
Drona also instructed Arjuna in fighting with mace, sword, lance, spear, and dart
and in using many weapons and fighting with many men at the same time.

✦

Kings and princes, eager to learn the science of arms, flocked to Drona by the
  thousands,
and among those was a prince named Ekalavya,
the son of Hiranyadhanus, king of the Nishadas, the lowest of the mixed orders.
Drona, however, would not accept the prince as his pupil, because he was a
  Nishada
who might in time surpass his highborn pupils.
But the Nishada prince touched Drona's feet with bent head
and went into the forest, where he made a clay image of Drona.
He worshipped it respectfully, as if it were his real preceptor,
and practiced weaponry before it with rigid regularity.
Because of his exceptional reverence for his preceptor and his devotion to his
  purpose,
he became adept at fixing arrows on the bowstring, aiming, and letting go.
One day the Kuru and Pandava princes, with Drona's permission, set out to hunt.
A servant followed the party at leisure with the usual implements and a dog.
In the woods they wandered, looking for game. The dog wandered, too,
and came upon the Nishada prince, Ekalavya. He was of dark hue,
with his body smeared in filth. He was dressed in black and had matted locks on
  his head,
and so the dog began to bark. The Nishada prince, wanting to exhibit his
  lightness of hand,
sent seven arrows into the dog's mouth before the animal could shut it.
Pierced with these seven arrows, the dog returned to the Pandavas, who were
  amazed.
Ashamed of their own skill, they praised the lightness of hand and precision of aim
of the unknown archer. They searched the woods for the unknown bowman
and soon found him ceaselessly discharging arrows from his bow.
He was a total stranger to them, and they asked: "Who are you, and whose son
  are you?"
He replied: "I am the son of Hiranyadhanus, king of the Nishadas.
I am a pupil of Drona's, laboring for mastery of the art of arms."
The Pandavas then returned to the city to tell Drona
of the wonderful feat of archery they had witnessed in the woods.
Arjuna, thinking that this might be Ekalavya, went to Drona in private and said:
"You told me, clasping me to your bosom, that no pupil of yours should be equal
  to me.

Why, then, is this pupil, the mighty son of the Nishada king, superior to me?"
Drona reflected for a moment and decided what to do.
He took Arjuna with him and went into the woods to the Nishada prince.
He saw Ekalavya, with his body smeared with filth, with matted locks on his head,
and clad in rags. When Ekalavya saw Drona approaching, he went a few steps
    forward,
touched his feet, and prostrated himself on the ground.
The son of the Nishada king, worshipping Drona,
represented himself as his pupil and, clasping his hands in reverence,
stood before him awaiting his commands. Drona addressed him, saying:
"If you are really my pupil, give me my fee."
Ekalavya was much gratified and answered: "O illustrious teacher, command me,
for there is nothing that I would not give."
Drona answered: "I should like the thumb of your right hand."
Ekalavya, devoted to truth and feeling obliged to keep his promise,
with a cheerful face and an unafflicted heart cut off his thumb and gave it to
    Drona.
After this, when the Nishada prince shot with his remaining fingers,
he found that he had lost his former lightness of hand.
And Arjuna was happy, the fever of jealousy having left him.

✦

Two of Drona's pupils became very proficient in the use of the mace.
These were Druvodhana and Bhima, and they were always jealous of each other.
Aswatthaman surpassed everyone in the mysteries of the science of arms.
The twins, Nakula and Sahadeva, outshone everyone in handling the sword.
Yudhishthira outperformed everyone as a car warrior,
but Arjuna exceeded them all in every respect—
in intelligence, resourcefulness, strength, and perseverance.
Accomplished in all weapons, Arjuna became the best of the best of car warriors.
His fame spread all over the earth, to the shores of the sea.
And although the instruction was the same, the mighty Arjuna surpassed all the
    princes.
In weapons as well as in devotion to his preceptor, he was the best of them all.
Among all the princes, Arjuna alone became an atiratha,
a car warrior capable of fighting sixty thousand foes.
Dhritarashtra's wicked sons, seeing that Bhimasena was endowed with great
    strength,
and that Arjuna was accomplished in all arms, became jealous of them.
One day Drona decided to test the comparative excellence of all his pupils
and collected them together after their education had been completed.
Before doing this, he had ordered that an artificial bird be placed on top of a
    tree,
to serve as a target. When they were all together, Drona said to them:
"Take up your bows quickly, and stand here, aiming at that bird on the tree,
with arrows fixed on your bowstrings. Shoot when I give the order,

and cut off the bird's head. I shall give each of you a turn."
He first called Yudhishthira, saying: "Aim with your arrow, and shoot when I
    tell you."
Yudhishthira took up the bow and aimed at the bird.
But Drona addressed the Kuru prince, saying:
"You see that bird on top of the tree?" Yudhishthira answered: "I do."
Then Drona again asked him: "What do you see now, O prince?
Do you see the tree, myself, or your brothers?"
Yudhishthira answered: "I see the tree, you, my brothers, and the bird."
Drona repeated his question many times but was answered as often in the same
    words.
Vexed with Yudhishthira, Drona said: "Stand apart. It is not for you to strike the
    bird."
Then Drona repeated the experiment with Duryodhana
and the other sons of Dhritarashtra, one after another,
as also with his other pupils, Bhima and the rest,
including the princes who had come unto him from other lands.
But the answer in every case was the same as Yudhishthira's:
"I see the tree, you, our fellow pupils, and the bird."
They were all ordered, one after another, to stand apart.
Then Drona called on Arjuna and said: "It is by you that the target must be shot.
Therefore, turn your eyes to it. You must let fly the arrow as soon as I give the
    order.
Stand here with bow and arrow for an instant."
Arjuna aimed at the bird with his bow bent.
Drona then asked him as he had asked others:
"Do you see the bird there, the tree, and myself?"
Arjuna replied: "I see the bird only, not the tree or you."
Drona was well pleased with Arjuna and said to that mighty car warrior:
"If you see the vulture, then describe it to me."
Arjuna said: "I see only the head of the bird, not its body."
At these words, the hair on Drona's body stood on end from delight.
He then said to Arjuna: "Shoot." And the pupil let fly his arrow
and with his sharp shaft struck off the head of the vulture and brought it down.
No sooner was the deed done than Drona clasped Arjuna to his bosom,
confident that Drupada with his friends had already been vanquished.
Sometime later, Drona and his pupils went to the bank of the Ganga to bathe.
When Drona plunged into the stream, a strong alligator—sent, as it were, by
    death himself—
seized him by the thigh. And though he was himself quite capable,
Drona, seeming to be in trouble, asked his pupil to rescue him.
Instantly Arjuna struck the monster in the water with five sharp arrows
while the other pupils stood confounded. On this evidence of Arjuna's readiness,
Drona considered him his foremost pupil.
The monster, in the meantime, cut into pieces by Arjuna's arrows,
released Drona's thigh and gave up the ghost.
The son of Bharadwaja then addressed the mighty car warrior Arjuna and said:

"Accept this superior and irresistible weapon called Brahmasira
along with the methods of hurling and recalling it.
You must never use it against any human foe, however,
for if its foe is endowed with inferior energy, it might burn the whole universe.
It is said that this weapon has no peer in the three worlds.
Keep it, therefore, with great care, and listen to what I say.
If ever any foe who is not human contends against you,
you may then employ it against him and bring about his death in battle."
Pledging himself to do as he was bidden, with joined palms Arjuna received the
     weapon.
Drona then said: "No one else in this world will ever become a bowman superior
     to you.
You shall never be vanquished by any foe, and your achievements shall be great."

✦

When the sons of Dhritarashtra and Pandu showed themselves
to be accomplished in arms, Drona addressed the king
in the presence of Kripa, Somadatta, Valhika, Bhishma, Vyasa, and Vidura
and said: "Your children have completed their education.
With your permission, O king, let them now demonstrate their proficiency."
The gladdened king said: "O best of Brahmanas, you have accomplished a great
     deed.
Tell me where and when and how the trial may be held.
My blindness makes me envy those who are blessed with sight
and will behold my children's prowess in arms.
Vidura, do all that Drona says. There is nothing that can be more agreeable
     to me."
Vidura went out to do as he had been bidden.
Drona measured out a piece of land that was devoid of trees and thickets
and furnished with wells and springs. He selected a lunar day,
when the star ascendant was auspicious, and offered sacrifice to the gods
in the presence of the citizens assembled by proclamation to witness this.
Then the artificers of the king built a large and elegant stage,
according to the rules of the scriptures, and furnished it with all kinds of
     weapons.
They also built a second elegant hall for the lady spectators.
And the citizens constructed many platforms while the wealthier pitched tents
     all around.
When the day fixed for the tournament came, the king and his ministers,
with Bhishma and Kripa walking ahead,
came to that theater of almost celestial beauty, constructed of pure gold
and decked with strings of pearls and stones of lapis lazuli.
Gandhari and Kunti and the other ladies of the royal household,
in gorgeous attire and accompanied by their waiting women,
ascended the platforms, like celestial ladies ascending the Sumeru mountain.
The four orders, including the Brahmanas and the Kshatriyas,

eager to behold the princes' skill in arms, left the city and came running to the
    spot.
With the sounds of trumpets and drums and the noise of voices,
that vast concourse was an agitated ocean.
At last, accompanied by his son, Drona, dressed in white
with a white sacred thread, white locks, white beard, white garlands,
and white sandalwood paste rubbed over his body, entered the lists.
He was the moon accompanied by the planet Mars in an unclouded sky.
Bharadwaja worshipped and ordered Brahmanas to celebrate the auspicious
    rites.
When sweet-sounding musical instruments had sounded as a propitiatory
    ceremony,
several competitors entered, equipped with various arms.
Having girded their loins, those mighty warriors of Bharata's race appeared,
wearing finger protectors and carrying bows and quivers.
With Yudhishthira at their head, the princes came in order of age,
and they displayed their wonderful skill with their weapons.
Riding on horses that they managed dexterously,
the princes hit marks with arrows engraved with their respective names.
The spectators thought that they were beholding the city of the Gandharvas
and were filled with amazement. Some hundreds and thousands,
with eyes wide in wonder, exclaimed: "Well done! Well done!"
Having shown their skill and dexterity in the use of bows and arrows
and in the management of cars, the warriors took up their swords and bucklers
and entered the lists, plying their weapons.
Their agility, the symmetry of their bodies, their grace, their calm,
the firmness of their grasp, and their deftness in the use of sword and buckler
                    impressed and delighted the spectators.
Vrikodara and Suyodhana, delighted by the prospect of fighting,
entered the arena, mace in hand, like two single-peaked mountains.
They braced their loins, summoned all their energy, and roared,
like two infuriated elephants contending for a cow elephant.
They careered right and left, circling the lists,
as Vidura described to Dhritarashtra and to Kunti and Gandhari the feats of the
    princes.
When Durhodhana and Bhima entered the arena,
the spectators were divided into two parties.
Some cried: "Behold the heroic king of the Kurus!" And some cried: "Behold
    Bhima!"
There was a loud uproar. The intelligent Bharadwaja said to Drona's son,
    Aswatthaman:
"Restrain these warriors. Do not let the ire of the crowd be provoked by this
    combat."
Aswatthaman restrained the combatants with their maces uplifted.
And Drona himself entered the arena and commanded the musicians to stop.
With a voice as deep as that of the clouds he said:
"See how Arjuna is dearer to me than my own son."

And having performed the propitiatory rites, Arjuna appeared in the lists,
like an evening cloud reflecting the rays of the setting sun
and lit by the hues of the rainbow and flashes of lightning.
Conchs were blown, and other musical instruments sounded.
The spectators shouted: "This is the son of Kunti! This is the middle Pandava!
This is the son of the mighty Indra! This is the protector of the Kurus!
This is the one foremost among those versed in arms! This is the foremost
 cherisher of virtue!
This is the great repository of the knowledge of manners!"
As Kunti heard these shouts, her tears mixed with the milk of her breast
and wetted her bosom. Hearing that uproar, Dhritarashtra asked Vidura:
"What are they shouting? It is like a troubled ocean rising up to rend the
 heavens!"
Vidura replied: "O king, Arjuna has entered the lists. This uproar is for him."
Dhritarashtra said: "I have indeed been blessed, favored, and protected!"
When the spectators had quieted, Arjuna began to display his skill in weaponry.
With the Agneya weapon he created fire, and with the Varuna weapon he
 created water;
with the Vayavya weapon he created air; and with the Parjanya weapon, clouds;
and with the Bhauma weapon, land; and with the Parvatya weapon,
he brought mountains into being. With the Antardhana weapon,
all these were made to disappear. Now Arjuna appeared tall, and now short;
now he was seen on the yoke of his car, and now on the car itself;
and the next moment he was on the ground.
Like one shaft, he let fly five arrows at a time into the mouth of a moving iron
 boar.
And he discharged one and twenty into the hollow of a cow's horn
hung on a rope, swaying to and fro. In this manner, Arjuna showed his great skill
in the use of sword, bow, and mace. When the exhibition had nearly ended
and the sounds of instruments had faded, there came from the gate a sound
of the slapping of arms, like a roar of thunder.
The multitude wondered: "Are the mountains splitting? Is the earth rending
 asunder?
Or is the dome of heaven resounding with the roar of gathering clouds?"
The spectators turned their eyes toward the gate where Drona stood,
 surrounded
by the five brothers, like the moon and the five-starred constellation Hasta.
Duryodhana stood up in haste and was surrounded by his hundred haughty
 brothers,
with Aswatthaman among them. That prince, mace in hand,
appeared like Purandara in days of yore, encircled by the celestial host
on the occasion of the battle with the Danavas.
The spectators gaped as Karna, that hero with his natural mail
and face brightened with earrings, took up his bow, girded on his sword,
and entered the lists. He was the one who was born of Pritha in her maidenhood
and was an heir of the hot-beamed sun. His energy was like that of a lion or a bull,
or the leader of a herd of elephants. In splendor, he resembled the sun;

in loveliness, the moon; and in energy, fire.
He was tall like a golden palm tree and endowed with the vigor of youth.
He was capable of slaying a lion. He bowed indifferently to Drona and Kripa.
The entire assembly, as they gazed at him, asked: "Who is he?"
In a voice as deep as that of the clouds, he addressed his unknown brother,
　　Arjuna,
saying: "O Arjuna, I shall perform feats before this gazing multitude,
surpassing all you have performed! You shall be amazed."
The spectators all stood up at once. Duryodhana was filled with delight,
while Vibhatsu was abashed and angry. Then, with the permission of Drona,
Karna did all that Arjuna had done before.
Duryodhana and his brothers embraced Karna in joy and said:
"Welcome, O mighty-armed warrior! It is our good fortune that you have come.
Live as you please, and command us and the kingdom of the Kurus."
Karna replied: "I regard it as already accomplished. All I want is your friendship.
And my wish is for single combat with Arjuna."
Duryodhana said: "Enjoy the good things of life with me!
Be the benefactor of your friends, and place your feet on the heads of all my foes."
Arjuna felt disgraced and said to Karna: "The path of the unwelcome intruder
and of the uninvited talker shall be yours, O Karna, for you shall be slain by me."
Karna replied: "This arena is meant for all, not for you alone!
There are kings who are superior in energy, and the Kshatriya regard might alone.
What need of argument, which is the exercise of the weak?
Speak instead in arrows, until with arrows I strike off your head before your
　　master."
With Drona's permission, Arjuna advanced for the combat.
On the other side, Karna took up his bow and arrows and stood ready for the
　　fight.
The firmament was enveloped in clouds emitting flashes of lightning,
and the colored bow of Indra appeared, shedding its effulgent rays.
The clouds seemed to laugh because of the rows of white cranes then on the wing.
Indra thus watched the arena from affection for his son,
while the sun dispersed the clouds from over his own offspring.
Arjuna remained hidden under cover of the clouds,
while Karna remained visible in bright sunshine.
The son of Dhritarashtra stood by Karna,
and Bharadwaja and Kripa and Bhishma remained with Arjuna.
Those assembled were divided, as also were the female spectators.
Kunti swooned away, but, with the help of female attendants, Vidura revived her
by sprinkling her with sandalwood paste and water. Restored to consciousness,
Kunti saw her two sons clad in mail. She was terrified
but could do nothing to protect them. Both had strung bows in their hands.
Kripa addressed Karna, saying: "This Pandava, Kunti's youngest son,
who belongs to the Kaurava race—he will engage in combat with you.
But you, too, must tell us your lineage and the royal line of which you are the
　　ornament.
Arjuna will fight with you or not, as he thinks fit.

Sons of kings never fight with men of inglorious lineage."
Karna's countenance became like a pale lotus torn by pelting showers.
Duryodhana said: "O master, the scriptures have it that three classes of persons
can claim royalty—persons of the blood royal, heroes, and those who lead armies.
If Arjuna is unwilling to fight with one who is not a king,
I will install Karna as king of Anga."
At that very moment, on a golden seat with fried paddy and with flowers and
    water pots
and much gold, the mighty warrior Karna was installed as king
by Brahmanas versed in mantras. A royal umbrella was held over his head
                while yak tails waved around him.
When the cheers ceased, King Karna said to the Kaurava Duryodhana:
"Tiger among monarchs, what shall I give you that may compare
with your gift of a kingdom? O king, I will do all that you bid!"
Duryodhana answered: "I wish only for your friendship." And Karna replied: "Be
    it so."
                    They embraced in joy and happiness.
Then Adhiratha entered the lists
with his sheet hanging down loosely, trembling and supporting himself on a staff.
Karna put down his bow and, moved by filial regard, bowed down his head.
Then the charioteer covered his feet with the end of his sheet
and addressed Karna as his son. The charioteer embraced Karna
and bedewed his head, still damp from the coronation, with many tears.
Bhima realized that Karna was a charioteer's son and taunted him: "O son of a
    charioteer,
you do not deserve death at the hands of Arjuna. As befits your lineage, go get a
    whip.
You are no more worthy to rule the kingdom of Anga
than a dog is deserving of butter that has been placed before the sacrificial fire."
With quivering lips, Karna sighed. Duryodhana looked up at the god of day in
    the skies
and, like a mad elephant that emerges from a pool of lotuses,
rose in wrath from among his brothers. He said to Bhima:
"You should not speak such words. Might is the cardinal virtue of a Kshatriya,
and even a Kshatriya of inferior birth deserves to be fought with.
The lineage of heroes, like the source of a lordly river, is often unknown.
The fire that covers the whole world rises from the waters.
The thunder that slays the Danavas was made of the bone of a mortal named
    Dadhichi.
The illustrious god Guha, who combines in himself portions of all the other
    deities,
is of unknown lineage. Some call him the offspring of Agni; some, of Krittika;
some, of Rudra; and some, of Ganga.
We have heard that persons born in the Kshatriya order have become Brahmanas.
Viswamitra and others born Kshatriyas have obtained the eternal Brahma.
Drona was born in a water pot, and Kripa sprang up from a clump of heath.
And I know the births of you Pandava princes.

Can a she-deer bring forth a tiger like Karna, of the splendor of the sun,
and born with natural mail and earrings?
This prince among men deserves sovereignty not only over Anga but over the
    world
because of the might of his arm and my swearing to obey him in everything.
If there be anybody here to whom what I have done to Karna seems intolerable,
let him ascend his chariot and bend his bow."
A confused murmur arose among the spectators who approved of Duryodhana's
    speech.
But then the sun went down, and Duryodhana took Karna's hand
and led him from the arena's countless lamps.
                    The Pandavas also returned to their dwelling.
Some people thought Arjuna had won the day; some, Karna; and some,
    Duryodhana.
Kunti, recognizing her son in Karna by the various marks on his person,
and seeing him installed in the sovereignty of Anga, felt motherly affection and
    pride.
Duryodhana, having obtained Karna in this way as an ally, banished his fears
of Arjuna's proficiency in arms. And the heroic Karna gratified Duryodhana
by sweet speeches while Yudhishthira was sure that no warrior on earth was like
    Karna.

◆

The Pandavas and the son of Dhritarashtra had demonstrated such
    accomplishment
that Drona thought the time had come when he could demand his fee.
Assembling his pupils together one day, Drona told them what recompense he
    wanted:
"Seize Drupada, the king of Panchala, and bring him to me.
That shall be the most acceptable payment." Those warriors answered: "So be it."
And they mounted their chariots and marched out with him.
Smiting the Panchalas on their way, they laid siege to the capital of the great
    Drupada.
Duryodhana and Karna and the mighty Yuyutsu, and Duhsasana
and Vikarna and Jalasandha and Sulochana—these and many other Kshatriya
    princes
vied with one another to be foremost in the attack.
The princes in their fine chariots entered the hostile capital and passed along
    the streets.
The king of Panchala, seeing that mighty force and hearing its loud clamor,
emerged from his palace accompanied by his brothers.
Though King Yajnasena was well armed, the Kuru army assailed him
with a shower of arrows, uttering their war cry.
Yajnasena, however, was not easy to subdue in battle
and, approaching the Kurus upon his white chariot, rained his fierce arrows all
    around.

Before the battle started, Arjuna addressed Drona, that best of Brahmanas,
and said: "We shall exert ourselves after they have displayed their prowess.
The king of Panchala can never be taken on the field of battle by any of these."
Having said this, the son of Kunti, surrounded by his brothers, waited outside
the town.
Drupada saw the Kuru host, rushed forward, and showered arrows all around.
Such was his lightness of motion on the field of battle that,
although he was fighting unsupported on a single chariot,
the Kurus supposed that there were many Drupadas opposed to them.
The fierce arrows of that monarch fell fast on all sides
until conchs and trumpets and drums by the thousands
were sounded by the Panchalas from their houses, giving the alarm.
Then there arose from the Panchala host a roar as terrible as that of a lion,
while the twang of their bowstrings seemed to rend the very heavens.
Duryodhana and Vikarna, Suvahu and Dirghalochana and Duhsasana,
in fury, showered their arrows upon the enemy.
But the mighty bowman, Prishata's son, invincible in battle,
though pierced with many arrows, afflicted the hostile ranks with greater vigor.
Careering over the field of battle like a fiery wheel,
King Drupada smote Duryodhana and Vikarna and even the mighty Karna
and many other heroic princes and numberless warriors, slaking their thirst for
battle.
All the citizens showered the Kurus with various missiles, like clouds pouring
raindrops.
Young and old, they rushed to battle, assailing the Kurus.
The Kauravas, seeing how frightful the fighting had become,
then broke and fled toward the Pandavas. The Pandavas heard the wail of the
beaten host,
saluted Drona, and mounted their chariots.
Arjuna bade Yudhishthira not to engage in the fight
and then rushed forward, appointing Nakula and Sahadeva, those sons of Madri,
as the protectors of his chariot wheels. Bhimasena, mace in hand, ran ahead.
Arjuna and his brothers advanced toward the enemy,
filling the whole region with the rattle of chariot wheels.
Like a Makara entering the sea, the mighty Bhima, resembling a second Yama,
entered the Panchala ranks mace in hand and roaring like the ocean in a storm.
He first rushed toward the array of elephants,
while Arjuna attacked that force with the prowess of his arms.
Like the great destroyer himself, Bhima slew elephants with his mace.
Those animals, huge as mountains, struck by Bhima's mace,
had their heads broken into pieces. Covered with streams of blood, they fell to
the ground,
like cliffs loosened by thunder. The Pandavas thus littered the ground
with elephants and horses and cars by the thousands
as they killed many foot soldiers and car warriors.
As a herdsman in the woods drives before him with his staff countless cattle,

so did Vrikodara drive before him the chariots and elephants of the hostile force.
Meanwhile, Arjuna assailed the son of Prishata with a shower of arrows
and felled him from his elephant. Like the terrible fire that consumes all things
at the end of the *yuga*, Arjuna brought down horses and cars and elephants by
    the thousands.
The Panchalas and the Srinjayas, thus assailed by the Pandava,
met him with a perfect shower of weapons of various kinds.
They sent up a loud shout and fought desperately with Arjuna
in a battle that was furious and terrible to behold.
Hearing the enemy's shouts, the son of Indra was filled with wrath.
He assailed the hostile host with a thick shower of arrows
and rushed toward it furiously, afflicting it with renewed vigor.
Those who saw the illustrious Arjuna at that time
could not mark any interval between his fixing the arrows on the bowstring
and letting them go. Loud were the shouts that arose there,
mingled with cheers of approval. Then the king of the Panchalas,
accompanied by Satyajit, rushed at Arjuna, like the Asura Samvara
rushing at the chief of the celestials in olden days.
Arjuna covered the king of Panchala with a shower of arrows.
There was a frightful uproar among the Panchala host,
like the roar of a mighty lion springing at the leader of a herd of elephants.
And seeing Arjuna rushing at the king of Panchala, Satyajit rushed at him.
The two warriors, like Indra and the Asura Virochana's son Vali,
drew closer to each other and ground down each other's ranks.
With great force, Arjuna pierced Satyajit with ten keen shafts,
at which feat the spectators were amazed. But without losing any time,
Satyajit assailed Arjuna with a hundred shafts. Then Arjuna,
thus covered by that shower of arrows, with remarkable lightness of motion
rubbed his bowstring to increase the force and velocity of his shafts.
Cutting his antagonist's bow in half, Arjuna rushed at the king of the Panchalas,
but Satyajit took up a tougher bow and pierced with his arrows
Arjuna, his chariot, his charioteer, and his horses. Arjuna, thus assailed,
was eager to slay Satyajit at once, and he pierced with arrows his antagonist's
    horses,
his flags, his bow, his clenched fist, his charioteer, and the attendant at his back.
Satyajit, with his bows repeatedly broken and his horses slain,
                          desisted at last from the fight.
The king of the Panchalas, when his general was thus discomfited,
showered arrows upon the Pandava prince.
Arjuna fought furiously and cut his enemy's bow in two as well as his flagstaff.
He pierced his antagonist's horses and charioteer also with five arrows.
Then, throwing aside his bow, Arjuna took a scimitar from his quiver
and, with a loud shout, leaped from his own chariot to that of Drupada.
With perfect fearlessness, he seized him as Garuda seizes a huge snake
after agitating the waters of the ocean. At the sight of this, the Panchala troops
                          ran away in all directions.

Arjuna then sent forth a loud shout and returned from the Panchala ranks.

The princes saw him coming with his captive and began to lay waste Drupada's
    capital.

Arjuna said: "Drupada is a relative of the Kuru heroes. Therefore, O Bhima,
do not slay his soldiers. Let us only give our preceptor his fee."

The mighty Bhima, though still eager for battle, refrained from the act of
    slaughter.

The princes took Drupada, his friends, and his counselors and offered them to
    Drona.

There was Drupada—captured, humiliated, and deprived of wealth—
and Drona said: "I have laid waste your kingdom and capital.

But do not fear for your life, although it depends now on the will of your foe.

Do you now desire to revive your friendship with me?"

Drona smiled a little and again said: "Fear not for your life, brave king!

We Brahmanas are ever forgiving. And my affection and love for you

have grown with me since we sported together as children.

O king, I therefore ask for your friendship again.

And, as a favor, I give you half of the kingdom that was yours.

You told me before that none who was not a king could be a king's friend.

Therefore, I retain half your kingdom. You are the king of all the territory

lying on the southern side of the Bhagirathi, while I will be the king

of all the territory on the north of that river. If this pleases you, we can now be
    friends."

Drupada answered: "You are of noble soul and great prowess,

O Brahmana. I am therefore not surprised at what you do.

                        I am gratified, and I desire your eternal friendship."

Drona then released the king of Panchala and bestowed upon him half the
    kingdom.

Thenceforth a sorrowful Drupada resided in the city of Kampilya

on the banks of the Ganga, in the province of Makandi,

filled with many towns and cities. And Drupada also ruled

the southern Panchalas up to the bank of the Charmanwati River.

From that day, Drupada was convinced that he could not, by Kshatriya might
    alone,

defeat Drona, being very much his inferior in spiritual Brahma power.

He therefore began to wander the earth, to find out how to obtain a son

who would subjugate his Brahmana foe.

Drona, meanwhile, resided in Ahicchatra and ruled the territory of Ahicchatra

that Arjuna had obtained for him, full of towns and cities.

7

Kanika

A year later, Dhritarashtra, thinking of his people, installed Yudhishthira, son of
  Pandu,
as heir apparent to the kingdom because of his firmness, fortitude, patience,
benevolence, frankness, and honesty. Soon Yudhishthira, the son of Kunti,
overshadowed the deeds of his father with his good behavior, manners,
and application to business. Bhima took lessons from Sankarshana in the sword
  and mace
and on the chariot, and after his education was finished,
he became as strong as Dyumatsena himself. Arjuna was celebrated
for the firmness of his grasp of weapons, the lightness of his motion, the
  precision of his aim,
and his proficiency in use of the Kshura, Naracha, Vala, and Vipatha weapons,
and, indeed, of all weapons, straight or crooked, heavy or light.
Drona said there was no equal in the world to Arjuna in dexterity and ability.
One day, Drona addressed Arjuna before the assembled Kaurava princes:
"There was a disciple of Agastya in the science of arms called Agnivesa.
He was my preceptor; and I, his disciple. By ascetic merit, I obtained from him a
  weapon
called *Brahmasira*, which could never be futile and was capable
of consuming the whole earth. That weapon may now pass from disciple to
  disciple.
While imparting it to me, my preceptor said: 'Never hurl this weapon
at any human being, especially a weak one. You have obtained this celestial
  weapon.
No one else deserves it. But obey Agnivesa's command.'
And now, in the presence of your cousins and relatives, give me my preceptorial
  fee."
Arjuna pledged that he would give what the preceptor demanded,
and Drona said: "O sinless one, you must fight with me when I fight with you."
And that bull among the Kuru princes swore to Drona that he would
                          and, touching his feet, went away northward.
A loud shout arose that there was no bowman in the world like Arjuna.
Arjuna and the other Pandava princes became so powerful
that they slew in battle the great Sauvira and the king of the Yavanas,
whom Pandu had failed to bring under subjection.

Vipula, king of the Sauviras, who had always shown a disregard for the Kurus,
was made by the intelligent Arjuna to feel the edge of his power.
Arjuna also repressed by means of his arrows the pride of King Sumitra of
  Sauvira.
The third of the Pandava princes, assisted by Bhima on a single car,
subjugated all the kings of the east, backed by ten thousand cars.
In the same way, having conquered on a single car the whole of the south,
Dhananjaya sent a large booty to the kingdom of the Kurus.
As King Dhritarashtra beheld the great prowess and strength of those mighty
  bowmen,
his thoughts about the Pandavas were poisoned,
and from that day the monarch became so anxious that he could hardly sleep.
Summoning to his side Kanika, that foremost among ministers,
well versed in the science of politics, and an expert in counsels,
the king said: "The Pandavas are overshadowing the earth. I am jealous of them.
Should I have peace or war with them? Advise me, for I shall do as you think
  best."
Kanika answered him in these pointed words: "Listen to me, O sinless king,
and do not be angry with me after hearing what I say.
Kings should always be ready with uplifted maces to strike when necessary,
and they should always increase their power. Avoiding all faults themselves,
they should watch over the faults of their foes and take advantage of them.
If the king be always ready to strike, everybody will fear him.
The king, therefore, should always have the power to punish, in all that he does.
He should conduct himself so that his foe may not detect any weakness in him.
But by means of the weakness he detects in his foe, he should pursue him to
  destruction.
As the tortoise conceals its body, so should the king always conceal his means
  and ends
and always hide his own weakness from the sight of others.
Having begun a particular act, he should accomplish it thoroughly.
You know how a thorn, if not extracted wholly, produces a festering sore.
The slaughter of a foe who does you evil is always praiseworthy.
If the foe be one of great prowess, one should watch for the hour of his disaster
and then kill him without scruple. If the foe should happen to be a great
  warrior,
his hour of vulnerability should be watched, and he should then be induced to fly.
Sire, an enemy, however contemptible, should never be scorned.
A spark of fire is capable of consuming an extensive forest,
if only it can spread from one object to another.
Kings should sometimes feign blindness and deafness,
for if they cannot chastise, they should seem not to notice faults that call for
  chastisement.
On such occasions, let them regard their bows as made of straw.
But they should be always on the alert, like a herd of deer sleeping in the woods.
When your foe is in your power, destroy him by any means necessary.
Show him no mercy, even though he seek your protection.

A foe, or one who has once injured you, should be destroyed by the lavishing of
    money,
if that be necessary, for by killing him you may be at your ease.
The dead can never inspire fear. You must destroy your foes, root and branch.
Then you should destroy their allies and partisans, who cannot exist
if the principal be destroyed. If the root of the tree be torn up,
the branches and twigs cannot continue.
Carefully concealing your own means and ends, you should always watch your
    foes.
Maintaining the perpetual fire by sacrifices, by brown cloths, by matted locks,
and by hides of animals for your bedding, you should at first gain your foes'
    confidence,
and when you have gained it, you should spring upon them like a wolf.
It has been said that in the acquisition of wealth, the garb of holiness may be
    employed
as a hooked staff, to bend down a branch in order to pluck the fruits that are ripe.
This should be the method also in destroying foes, for you should proceed
on the principle of selection. Bear your foe upon your shoulders until the time
    comes
when you can throw him down, breaking him into pieces like an earthen pot
thrown with violence upon a stony surface.
The foe must never be let off, even though he address you most piteously.
Show no pity, but slay him at once. By the arts of conciliation
or the expenditure of money, or by the creation of disunion among his allies,
or by force—indeed, by every means in your power—destroy your foe."
Dhritarashtra said: "Tell me how a foe can be destroyed by the arts of
    conciliation
or the expenditure of money, or by the production of disunion or the
    employment of force."
Kanika replied: "Listen, O monarch, to the history of a jackal dwelling in the forest
in days of yore and fully acquainted with the science of politics.
There was a wise jackal, mindful of his own interests,
who lived in the company of four friends—a tiger, a mouse, a wolf, and a
    mongoose.
One day they saw in the woods a strong deer, the leader of a herd,
whom they could not seize because of his fleetness and strength.
They called a council for consultation. The jackal opened the proceedings and
    said:
'O tiger, you have made many an effort to seize this deer, but all in vain,
because this deer is young, fleet, and very smart.
Let the mouse go and eat into its feet when it lies asleep.
And when this is done, let the tiger approach and seize it.
Then, with great pleasure, we shall all feast on it.'
They all set to work very cautiously, as the jackal had directed.
And the mouse ate into the feet of the deer, and the tiger killed it.
With the body of the deer lying on the ground, the jackal said to his companions:
'Blessings upon you! Go and perform your ablutions.

In the meantime, I will look after the deer.'

They all went into a stream while the jackal waited there, meditating.

The tiger returned first, after having performed his ablutions.

He saw the jackal there, plunged in meditation.

The tiger said: 'Why are you so sorrowful? You are foremost among all intelligent
beings.

Let us enjoy ourselves today by feasting on this carcass.'

The jackal said: 'Hear, O tiger, what the mouse has said. He said:

"Fie on the strength of the king of the beasts!

I was the one who slew this deer. By my might will he today gratify his hunger."

When he has boasted in such language, I do not wish to touch this food.'

The tiger replied: 'If indeed the mouse hath said so, my sense is now awakened.

I shall, from now on, slay with the might of my own arms

creatures ranging the forest, and then feast on their flesh.'

Having said this, the tiger went away.

After the tiger had left the spot, the mouse came.

And the jackal addressed him: 'Blessings, O mouse, but hear what the mongoose
said.

He said: "The tiger touched the carcass of this deer with his claws,

and it is poisoned. I will not eat of it. On the other hand, if you, O jackal, permit it,
I will slay the mouse and feast on him."

Hearing this, the mouse became alarmed and ran to his hole.

After the mouse had gone, the wolf came there, having performed his ablutions.

And the jackal said to him: 'The king of the beasts has been angry with you.

Evil is certain to overtake you. He is expected here with his wife. Do as you
please.'

Thus the jackal got rid of the wolf also, for the wolf fled,

contracting his body into the smallest dimensions.

It was then that the mongoose came. And the jackal said to him: 'By the might
of my arm

I have defeated the others who have fled. Fight with me first,

and then eat of this flesh as you please.'

The mongoose replied: 'When indeed the tiger, the wolf, and the intelligent
mouse

have all been defeated by you, heroes though they are, you seem to be a greater
hero still.

I do not desire to fight with you.' Saying this, the mongoose also went away."

Kanika continued: "When they all had gone away, the jackal,

well pleased with the success of his policy, ate up all that venison by himself.

If kings act in this way, they can be happy. Thus should you treat the timid,

by exciting their fears; the courageous, by the arts of conciliation;

the covetous, by gifts of wealth; and equals and inferiors,

by an exhibition of prowess to bring them under your sway."

Kanika continued: "If your son, friend, brother, father, or even your spiritual
preceptor

should become your foe, you should, if you want to prosper, slay him without
scruple.

By curses and incantations, by gifts of wealth, by poison, or by deception,
the foe should be slain. He should never be disdained.
If both parties be equal and success uncertain,
then he who acts with diligence will grow in prosperity.
If the spiritual preceptor himself be vain, ignorant of what should be done
and what left undone, and vicious in his ways, even he should be chastised.
If you be angry, show yourself as if you are not so, speaking with a smile on your
lips.
Never reprove anyone with indications of anger. Speak soft words before you
smite,
and even while you are smiting! After the smiting is over, pity the victim,
and grieve for him. Even shed tears.
Comfort your foe by conciliation, by gifts of wealth, and by gentle behavior.
But you must smite him when he misbehaves.
You should also smile at the heinous offender who lives by the practice of virtue,
for the garb of virtue simply covers his offenses as black clouds cover the
mountains.
Burn the house of anyone you punish with death.
And never permit beggars or atheists or thieves to dwell in your kingdom.
By a sudden sally or pitched battle, by poison or by corruption of his allies,
by gifts of wealth, and by any other means in your power, you should destroy
your foe.
You may have to act with the greatest cruelty.
You should make your teeth sharp, to give a fatal bite.
And you should ever smite so effectually that your foe may not again raise his
head.
You should always fear even someone whom there is no cause to fear,
and fear even more someone for whom there is such cause.
For if the first should ever become powerful, he may destroy you for your
unpreparedness.
You should never trust the faithless, nor trust too much those who are faithful,
for if those in whom you confide prove to be your foes, you are certain to be
annihilated.
After testing their faithfulness, you should employ spies
in your own kingdom and in the kingdoms of others.
Your spies in foreign kingdoms should be accomplished deceivers
and persons in the garb of ascetics. Your spies should be placed in gardens,
places of amusement, temples, and holy places as well as in drinking halls and
streets.
You should also have them pay attention to the ministers, the chief priest,
the heir presumptive, the commander in chief, the gatekeepers of the court,
persons in the inner apartments, the jailor, the chief surveyor, the head of the
treasury,
the general administrator of orders, the chief of the town police,
the chief architect, the chief justice, the president of the council,
the commander of the fort, the chief of the arsenal,
the chief of the frontier guards, and the keeper of the forests.

And they should be in places of sacrifice, near wells, on mountains and in rivers,
in forests, and in all places where people congregate.
In speech, you should always be humble, but let your heart be ever sharp as a
    razor.
And when you are committing a very cruel and terrible act, speak with smiles on
    your lips.
If you want to prosper, you should adopt all arts—
humility, oath, conciliation, worshipping the feet of others by lowering your
    head,
and inspiring hope. A person conversant with the rules of policy
is like a tree decked with flowers but bearing no fruit;
or, if bearing fruit, these must be at a great height not easily attainable from the
    ground;
and if any of these fruits seem to be ripe, care must be taken to make them
    appear green.
Conducting himself in such a way, he shall never fade.
Virtue, wealth, and pleasure have both their evil and their good effects.
While benefiting from those effects that are good, he should avoid those that are
    evil.
Those who are virtuous are made unhappy for want of wealth and neglect of
    pleasure.
Those who pursue wealth are made unhappy for neglect of the other two.
And so those who pursue pleasure suffer for their inattention to virtue and
    wealth.
You should therefore pursue virtue, wealth, and pleasure
in such a way that you may avoid suffering. With humiliation and attention,
without jealousy, and with care to accomplish your purpose,
you should consult with the Brahmanas. When you have fallen, you should raise
    yourself
by any means, gentle or violent; and after you have raised yourself,
you should practice virtue. He who has never been afflicted with calamity
                    can never have prosperity.
This may be seen in the life of one who survives his calamities.
He who is afflicted with sorrow should be consoled
by the recitation of the history of persons of former times.
He who is afflicted with sorrow should be consoled with the hope of future
    prosperity.
He who has concluded a treaty with an enemy and reposes at his ease
is like a person who awakens after falling from the top of a tree he had slept in.
A king should keep to himself his counsels, without fear of calumny;
and, while watching everything with the eyes of his spies,
he should take care to conceal his own emotions before his enemies' spies.
Like a fisherman who becomes prosperous by catching and killing fish,
a king can never grow prosperous without tearing the vitals of his enemy
and without doing violent deeds. The might of your foe,
as represented by his armed force, should always be completely destroyed,
plowed up like weeds and mowed down and otherwise afflicted

with disease, starvation, and want of drink.
A person in want never approaches one in affluence motivated by love.
And when one's purpose has been accomplished,
one has no need to approach him to whom one had hitherto looked for aid.
Therefore, when you do anything, never do it completely,
but always leave something to be desired by others whose services you may need.
One who wants prosperity should diligently seek allies and means
and carefully conduct his wars. His exertions in these respects
should always be guided by prudence.
A prudent king should always act so that friends and foes never know his motives
before he acts. Let them know all when the act has been commenced or ended.
As long as danger does not come, act as if you are afraid.
But when danger overtakes you, grapple with it courageously.
He who trusts in a foe who has been subjugated by force
invites his own death, as does a crab by her act of conception.
Always reckon the future act as already arrived,
and devise measures for meeting it; or else, from panic and haste,
you may overlook an important point in coping with it when it occurs.
A person who wants prosperity should always act with prudence,
conforming his plans to time and place. He should also act with an eye to
    destiny
as capable of being regulated by mantras and sacrificial rites.
If a foe be insignificant, he should not be despised,
for he may grow like a palmyra tree extending its roots
or a spark of fire in the deep woods that bursts into an extensive conflagration.
As a little fire gradually fed with kindling soon becomes capable
of consuming even the greatest of forests, so the person who increases his power
by making alliances and friendships becomes capable of subjugating
                              even the most formidable of foes.
The hope you give your foe should be long deferred before it is fulfilled;
and when the time comes for its fulfillment, invent some pretext for deferring it
    further.
Let that pretext be founded upon some reason, and let that reason be made to
    appear
as founded on some other reason. A king should, in the matter of destroying his
    foes,
always resemble a razor in every way—as unpitying as the razor is sharp,
hiding his intent just as the razor is concealed in its leather case,
striking when the opportunity comes just as the razor is used on the proper
    occasion,
and sweeping off his foes, with all their allies and dependents,
just as the razor shaves the head or the chin without leaving a single hair.
O supporter of the Kurus, bearing yourself toward the Pandavas and others
as policy dictates, act in such a way that you may not have to grieve in future.
Well do I know that you are endowed with every blessing
and possessed of every mark of good fortune.
Therefore, O king, protect yourself from the sons of Pandu!

The sons of Pandu are stronger than your sons, who are their cousins.
Therefore, O chastiser of foes, I tell you plainly what you should do.
Listen to my advice, O king! You and your children
must exert yourselves to do what is necessary.
Act in such a way that there may not be any fear of you on the part of the
    Pandavas."
Having spoken thus, Kanika returned to his abode,
while King Dhritarashtra became pensive and melancholy.

8

Duryodhana

King Duryodhana, Duhsasana, and Kama formed an evil conspiracy
to burn Kunti and her five sons to death. But Vidura,
capable of reading the heart by external signs, ascertained their wicked intention
just by observing their faces. Vidura decided that Kunti and her sons should flee.
Providing a boat strong enough to withstand wind and wave, he said to Kunti:
"Dhritarashtra was born to destroy the fame and offspring of the Kuru race.
He is about to abandon all virtue. I have ready on the river a boat
by which you can escape from the net that death has spread around you and
   your children."
Kunti was deeply grieved and, with her sons, stepped into the boat and crossed
   the Ganges.
The Pandavas took with them the wealth given them at Varanavata by their
   enemies,
                        and they went deep into woods.

                              ✦

The wicked Duryodhana, seeing that Bhima could surpass everybody in strength,
and that Arjuna was the most accomplished in arms, became morose.
In public squares and in courtyards and other places,
the people talked of Yudhishthira, the eldest son of Pandu,
as being the best qualified for ruling the kingdom.
They said: "Dhritarashtra, having been born blind, had not obtained the
   kingdom before.
How can he become king now? And Bhishma, the son of Shantanu,
having relinquished sovereignty, would never accept it now.
We shall now, therefore, install on the throne, with proper ceremonies,
the eldest of the Pandavas. Worshipping Bhishma and Dhritarashtra,
he will maintain the former and the latter with his children in every kind of
   enjoyment."
Duryodhana, hearing these words of the partisans of Yudhishthira,
became distressed. The wicked prince could not put up with those speeches.
Mad with jealousy, he went to Dhritarashtra, saluted him with reverence,
and addressed the monarch: "O father, I have heard the citizens' words of ill
   omen.

Passing you by, and Bhishma, too, they desire the son of Pandu to be their king.
Bhishma will permit this, for he will not rule the kingdom.
It seems that the citizens are trying to inflict a great injury on us.
Pandu obtained the ancestral kingdom by virtue of his own accomplishments,
but you, from blindness, did not obtain the kingdom, although fully qualified to
    have it.
If Pandu's son now obtains the kingdom as his inheritance,
his son will obtain it after him, and that son's son also, and so on it will descend
in Pandu's line. In that case, we and our children will be excluded from the
    royal line
and shall be disregarded by all men. Therefore, O king, adopt such counsels
that we may not forever suffer distress and have to depend on others for food.
O king, if you had obtained sovereignty before, we would have succeeded to it,
    however much the people might be unfavorable to us."
King Dhritarashtra, hearing these words of his son,
and recollecting what Kanika had said to him, became sorrowful and began to
    waver.
Then Duryodhana and Karna and Sakuni and Duhsasana held a consultation.
Duryodhana said to Dhritarashtra: "Father, send the Pandavas to the town of
    Varanavata.
    We shall have no fear of them there."
Dhritarashtra reflected for a moment and replied: "Pandu always behaved
    dutifully
toward all his relatives, but particularly toward me.
He cared little for enjoyments of the world but gave everything to me, even the
    kingdom.
His son is as devoted to virtue as he and is possessed of every accomplishment.
He is the favorite of the people. He has many allies.
How can we exile him from his ancestral kingdom?
The counselors and soldiers and their sons and grandsons have all been
    maintained
by Pandu. Shall not the citizens slay us, with all our friends and relatives,
    on account of Yudhishthira?"
Duryodhana answered: "What you say is true.
But in view of the evil looming in your future, if we conciliate the people
with wealth and honors, they will side with us. The treasury and the ministers of
    state
are under our control. Therefore, it behooves you now to banish the Pandavas,
by some gentle means, to the town of Varanavata.
When sovereignty shall have vested in me, then Kunti and her children
    may come back from that place."
Dhritarashtra replied: "This is the thought I had, too. But because of its
    sinfulness,
I have never given expression to it. Neither Bhishma nor Drona nor Kripa
will ever allow the exile of the Pandavas. In their eyes, dear son, among the Kurus,
we and the Pandavas are equal. Those wise and virtuous persons
see no difference between us. But if we behave so toward the Pandavas,

shall we not deserve death at the hands of the Kurus?"

"Bhishma has no excess of affection for either side," Duryodhana answered,
"and will therefore be neutral in any dispute. The son of Drona, Aswatthaman,
is on my side. There is no doubt that where the son is, there the father will be.
Kripa, the son of Saradwat, must be on the same side as Drona and
Aswatthaman.
He will never abandon Drona and Aswatthaman, his sister's son.
Vidura is dependent on us for his livelihood, although he is secretly with the foe.
If he sides with the Pandavas, he alone can do us no injury.
Exile the Pandavas therefore to Varanavata, without fear,
and take such steps that they may go there this very day.
By this act, you can extinguish the grief that consumes me like a blazing fire,
robs me of sleep, and pierces my heart like a terrible dart."
Prince Duryodhana and his brothers began to win the people over to their side
by grants of wealth and honors. Meanwhile, some counselors
loyal to Dhritarashtra spoke up in court about the town of Varanavata,
describing it as a charming place. They said that the festival of Pasupati, or
Shiva,
had commenced in that town, that the concourse of people was great,
and that the procession was the most delightful on earth.
While they were speaking in this way, the Pandavas felt desire to go to there.
And when King Dhritarashtra saw how the Pandavas' curiosity had been
awakened,
he said: "These men often speak of Varanavata as the most delightful town in the
world.
If you desire to witness that festival, go there with your followers and friends,
and enjoy yourselves there like the celestials.
Give pearls and gems to the Brahmanas and the musicians assembled there.
Relax there for as long as you please, and enjoy yourselves as much as you like
before you return here to Hastinapura."
Yudhishthira understood the motives of Dhritarashtra
and, considering that he was weak and friendless, replied to the king: "So be it."
Then—addressing Bhishma, son of Shantanu, and the wise Vidura,
and Drona, Valhika, the Kauravas, Somadatta, Kripa, Aswatthaman, and
Bhurisravas,
and the other counselors, Brahmanas, and ascetics, and the priests and citizens—
he said, slowly and humbly: "With our friends and followers,
we go to the delightful town of Varanavata at the command of Dhritarashtra.
Give us your benedictions so that we may prosper and not be touched by sin."
Thus addressed by the eldest of Pandu's sons, the Kaurava chiefs
all pronounced blessings on them, saying: "Sons of Pandu,
let all the elements bless you along your way, and let not the slightest evil befall
you."
The Pandavas performed propitiatory rites, finished their preparations, and
set out.

✦

Duryodhana then summoned his counselor Purochana, took his right hand, and
    said:
"O Purochana, this rich world is now mine. But it is yours, too.
You ought, therefore, to protect it. Do then as I ask, keep my counsel,
and exterminate my foes. Dhritarashtra has sent the Pandavas to Varanavata,
where they will enjoy themselves during the festivities.
Do what you must to reach Varanavata today in a car drawn by swift mules,
and in the neighborhood of the arsenal have a quadrangular palace built there,
rich in materials and furniture. Guard the mansion well from prying eyes.
And use for erecting it hemp, resin, and whatever other inflammable materials
    you find.
Mix a little earth with clarified butter and oil and fat and a large quantity of lac,
and use that to make the plaster for lining the walls.
Scatter those things around the house in such a way that neither the Pandavas
nor anyone else, even with scrutiny, may see them or realize that the house is a
    firetrap.
And having built the mansion, arrange it that the Pandavas dwell in it
with Kunti and all their friends. Furnish it with seats and conveyances and beds
all of the best workmanship, suitable for the Pandavas,
so that Dhritarashtra may have no reason to complain.
Also manage it all so that none of Varanavata may know anything of this
until our purpose is accomplished. When the Pandavas are sleeping in the house
confidently and without fear, set fire to it, with the flames starting at the outer
    door.
The Pandavas will be burned to death, but the people will say it was an accident."
"So be it," Purochana said to the Kuru prince, and he went off to Varanavata
in a car drawn by fleet mules to obey Duryodhana and do as the prince had
    bidden him.

✦

Meanwhile, the Pandavas got into their cars, to which they yoked horses as fast as
    the wind.
When they were about to enter their cars, they touched the feet of Bhishma,
of King Dhritarashtra, of the illustrious Drona, of Kripa, of Vidura,
and of the other elders of the Kuru race. They saluted with reverence all the
    older men,
embraced their equals, received the farewells of the children,
and took leave of all the venerable ladies, walking around them respectfully,
and then they said goodbye to all the citizens. Vidura of great wisdom and the
    other Kurus
and the citizens also, in great sadness, followed those tigers among men to some
    distance.
Those among the citizens and the country people who followed the Pandavas
were afflicted beyond measure, seeing the sons of Pandu in such distress,
and said aloud: "King Dhritarashtra of wicked soul sees nothing.
The Kuru monarch is blind to virtue. Neither sinless Yudhishthira

nor Bhima, mightiest of men, nor Dhananjaya, the youngest son of Kunti,
will ever be guilty of waging a rebellion. If these remain quiet,
what shall the son of Madri do? How is it that Bhishma suffers the exile of the
 Pandavas
to that wretched place and permits this act of great injustice?
Vichitravirya, the son of Shantanu, and Pandu, the royal sage of Kuru's race,
both cherished us with fatherly care. But now that Pandu has ascended to heaven,
Dhritarashtra cannot tolerate these princes, who are Pandu's children.
We who do not sanction this exile shall all go where Yudhishthira goes,
                    leaving this excellent town and our own homes."
The virtuous Yudhishthira reflected for a few moments and then said to the
 citizens:
"The king is our father, worthy of regard, our spiritual guide and our superior.
To obey with unsuspicious hearts whatever he orders is our duty.
You are our friends. Walking around us and making us happy by your blessings,
return now to your houses. When the time comes for us to act,
you may accomplish all that is agreeable and beneficial to us."
Thus addressed, the citizens walked around the Pandavas,
gave them their blessings, and returned to their respective abodes.

✦

After the citizens had stopped following them,
Vidura, who wanted to warn the eldest of the Pandavas of the dangers,
addressed the learned Yudhishthira in the dialect of the Mlechchhas,
which was unintelligible to any in the party but the two of them.
He said: "One who can infer the schemes of his foes from the dictates of political
 science
should act in such a way as to avoid danger. He knows there are sharp weapons
capable of cutting the body that are not made of steel,
and he understands how to ward them off. Such a man can never be injured by
 foes.
The blind man does not see his way and has no knowledge of direction.
He who is without firmness will never acquire prosperity.
Remember this, and be on your guard. The man who faces a weapon
not made of steel but of fire can escape from the flames
by making his house like that of a jackal, with many escape routes.
By wandering, a man may acquire the knowledge of ways,
and by the stars he can ascertain his direction. He who keeps his five senses
 under control
                    can never be oppressed by his enemies."
Yudhishthira then replied to Vidura, saying: "I have understood you."

✦

The Pandavas set out on the eighth day of the month of Phalguna,
when the star Rohini was in the ascendant, and they arrived at Varanavata

and beheld the town and the people. By the thousands, the people of Varanavata
approached the sons of Kunti, blessed them, and surrounded them.
Yudhishthira looked resplendent, an Indra with the thunderbolt in his hands
in the midst of the celestials. Welcomed by the citizens, and greeting the citizens
     in return,
the Pandavas entered the populous town of Varanavata.
Those heroes first went to the dwellings of Brahmanas,
then to the abodes of the officials of the town,
and then to the houses of the Sutas and the Vaisyas and to those of even the
     Sudras.
The Pandavas followed Purochana to his palace, where he gave them food and
     drink
and beds and carpets, all of the first quality. Attired in costly robes,
the Pandavas lived there for ten nights, enjoying the deference of Purochana
and the people of Varanavata. After the tenth night, Purochana spoke to them
of the mansion he had built for them. He called it t*he Blessed House,*
although in reality it was the cursed house.
Yudhishthira inspected the house and said to Bhima that it was built
of inflammable materials. Smelling the fat mixed with clarified butter
and preparations of lac, he told Bhima: "With trusted artists
well skilled in the construction of houses, the enemy have procured hemp, resin,
heath, straw, and bamboos, all soaked in butter. This wicked Purochana,
following Duryodhana's orders, stays here with the object of burning me to death
when he sees that I trust him. But Vidura knew of this danger, and warned me."
Bhima replied: "If you know this house to be such a tinderbox,
it would then be well for us to return to where we had first taken up our quarters."
Yudhishthira disagreed: "No, we should continue to live here,
pretending not to be suspicious but all the while alert and with our eyes peeled.
And we must find some means of escape. If Purochana realizes
that we have fathomed his designs, he may act in haste and suddenly burn us to
     death.
Purochana cares little for obloquy or sin. The wretch stays here,
acting under Duryodhana's instructions.
If we are burned to death, will our grandfather Bhishma be angry?
Will he show his wrath and make the Kauravas angry with him?
If, from fear of being burned, we fly from here, then Duryodhana,
who is ambitious and wants sovereignty, will accomplish our deaths by other
     means—
spies or assassins. We have no rank or power, but Duryodhana has both;
we have no friends or allies, but Duryodhana has both;
we are without wealth, but Duryodhana has at his command a full treasury.
Will he not therefore destroy us, one way or another?
Let us, therefore, deceive this wretch Purochana and that other wretch
     Duryodhana
and pass our days in feigning. Let us lead a hunting life, wandering over the
     earth.
We shall then, if we have to escape our enemies, be familiar with all paths.

We shall also, this very day, cause a subterranean passage to be dug in our
    chamber,
in great secrecy. If we conceal what we do from all, fire shall never consume us.
We shall live here, doing everything for our safety,
but with such privacy that neither Purochana nor anyone else in Varanavata
                  knows what we are doing."

❖

A friend of Vidura's, well skilled in mining, came to the Pandavas in secret
and said: "Vidura has sent me to serve you.
Purochana will set fire to the door of your house on the fourteenth night
to burn you to death, with your mother. Vidura also told you something
in the Mlechchha tongue, to which you replied in same language.
         I tell you this to establish my credentials."
Yudhishthira replied: "I now know that you are a dear and trusted friend to
    Vidura,
true and devoted to him. There is nothing that he does not know.
As you are his friend, so are you ours.
Protect us as the learned Vidura has always protected us.
I know that this inflammable house has been contrived for me
by Purochana, at the command of Dhritarashtra's son.
That wretch who commands wealth and allies pursues us relentlessly.
Save us from the impending conflagration. If we are burned to death here,
Duryodhana's most cherished desire will be satisfied.
Here is that scoundrel's well-furnished arsenal.
This large mansion has been built next to it, without any way to escape.
But this unholy plan of Duryodhana was known to Vidura from the first,
and it was he who warned us. Save us from it, without Purochana's knowledge."
The miner said: "So be it." And he carefully began his work of excavation,
making a large subterranean passage. The mouth of that passage
was in the center of that house, on a level with the floor and closed up with
    planks,
hidden from Purochana. The Pandavas slept in their chambers,
with arms ready for use, while during the day they went hunting in the forests.
Thus they deceived Purochana by a show of trustfulness and contentment,
while in reality they were wary and discontented.
Nor did the citizens of Varanavata know anything about these plans of the
    Pandavas.
         In fact, no one knew except the miner, Vidura's friend.

❖

The Pandavas lived there cheerfully and without arousing suspicion,
and Purochana was exceedingly pleased.
Yudhishthira said to Bhima and Arjuna and to the twins, Nakula and Sahadeva:
"The blackguard has been well deceived, and I think it is time for our escape.

Let us set fire to the arsenal and burn Purochana to death
while the six of us flee, unobserved by anyone."
Then, on the occasion of an almsgiving, Kunti fed a large number of Brahmanas
and also a number of ladies who ate and drank and enjoyed themselves and then,
by Kunti's leave, returned to their respective homes.
There came to the feast—hoping to obtain food, and as though impelled by fate
in the course of her wanderings—a Nishada woman with her five sons.
She and her children, intoxicated with wine, could not stay awake.
More dead than alive, they lay down in that mansion to sleep.
Then a violent wind arose in the night, and Bhima set fire to the house
where Purochana was sleeping. Then he torched the mansion in several places
    all around.
And when the sons of Pandu were satisfied that the house was ablaze,
they and their mother entered the subterranean passage.
The heat and the roar of the fire became intense and awakened the townspeople.
Seeing the house in flames, the citizens said that Purochana of wicked soul
had, under Duryodhana's instruction, built this house
for the destruction of his employer's relatives.
"He has burned to death, as if he were their foe, the sinless heirs of Pandu!" they
    said.
"And the sinful Purochana, who has burned those best of men,
the innocent and unsuspicious princes, has himself been burned to death."

✦

The Pandavas, however, had fled through the tunnel, unnoticed.
With their mother, they could not proceed in haste,
but Bhimasena, with his awesome strength and swiftness,
took up all his brothers and his mother and carried them through the darkness,
with his mother on his shoulder, the twins on his sides,
and Yudhishthira and Arjuna on his arms. With the speed of the wind he
    traveled,
breaking the trees with his breast and pressing the earth deep with his feet.
Meanwhile, Vidura had sent a trusted man into those woods.
He found the Pandavas with their mother,
where they were measuring the depth of the Ganga.
Vidura's emissary showed the Pandavas a boat with sails and flags,
constructed by trusted shipwrights and capable of withstanding wind and wave.
As the miner had done, so did he demonstrate that he had truly been sent by
    Vidura
and was his trusted agent. He delivered Vidura's message:
"O son of Kunti, you shall surely defeat in battle Karna,
and Duryodhana with his brothers, and Sakuni."
He also pointed out the boat that was ready for them
and would glide pleasantly and bear them all safely from these regions.
He instructed them to board the boat and accompanied them himself.
He said: "Vidura has smelled your heads and embraced you mentally,

and he has said again that in commencing your journey, you should never be
    careless."
Vidura's emissary then took those bulls among men to the other side of the Ganga
and, seeing them all safe on the opposite bank, he uttered the word *jaya*,
wished them success, and then returned to the place from which he had come.

✦

When dawn broke, many of the townspeople came to see the house
in which the sons of Pandu had been living, and which was now burned down.
Duryodhana's counselor Purochana had died in the fire.
The people wailed aloud and observed that this had been done
for the wicked Duryodhana by Purochana for the destruction of the Pandavas.
They agreed that Duryodhana could not have managed this
without King Dhritarashtra's knowledge and assent.
There was little doubt then that even Bhishma, the son of Shantanu,
and Drona and Vidura and Kripa and other Kauravas had failed in their duty.
They resolved to send a message to King Dhritarashtra, to say:
"Your great desire has been achieved! You have burned the Pandavas to death!"
They sifted through the embers for some trace of the Pandavas,
and they saw the corpses of the innocent Nishada woman with her five sons.
While the people were going through the ruined house,
the miner Vidura had covered with ashes the hole he had dug,
in such a way that it remained unnoticed.
The citizens then sent word to Dhritarashtra that the Pandavas
and his counselor Purochana had been burned to death.
King Dhritarashtra, on hearing of the death of the Pandavas, wept in great sorrow.
He said: "King Pandu, my brother of great fame, died today
when those heroic sons of his and their mother burned to death.
Go quickly to Varanavata, and have the funeral rites performed for those heroes
and for the daughter of Kuntiraj! Let the bones of the dead be sanctified
with the usual ceremonies, and let all the beneficial and respectful acts be
    performed.
Let the friends and relatives of those who have been burned to death go there.
Let there be a dispensation of alms that ought, under the circumstances, to be
    done
                            by us for the Pandavas and for Kunti."
Having said this, Dhritarashtra, the son of Ambika, offered oblations of water
to the sons of Pandu. And all of the family, afflicted with great sorrow, wailed
    aloud:
"O Yudhishthira! O prince of the Kuru race!" Others cried: "O Bhima! O
    Phalguna!"
And yet others called out in their grief: "O twins! O Kunti!"
Thus did they sorrow for the Pandavas and make offerings of water to their
    spirits.
The citizens, too, wept for the Pandavas. Only Vidura did not grieve deeply,
                        because he knew the truth.

9

Hidimva

The Pandavas and their mother arrived at the banks of the Ganga,
which they crossed quickly because of the strength of the boatmen's arms,
the rapidity of the current, and a favorable wind. Leaving the river behind,
they proceeded south, finding their way by starlight. After great exertion,
they reached a dense forest. They were tired and thirsty; sleep was closing their
    eyes.
Yudhishthira addressed Bhima and asked: "What can be more painful than this?
We are now deep in the woods. We have no idea where we are or where we are
    going.
We cannot go on. We do not know if that wretch Purochana has been burned to
    death.
How shall we escape from these dangers? O Bhima, take us up as you did before.
              You alone among us are as strong and swift as the wind."
The mighty Bhimasena, taking up Kunti and his brothers, traveled with greatest
    speed,
and the whole forest with its trees and their branches trembled
as he crashed through them. The motion of his thighs raised a wind
as strong as those that blow during May and June. As Bhima made a path for
    himself,
he trod down the saplings and creepers and uprooted large trees that stood in
    his way,
like the leader of a herd of elephants, an old bull elephant, angry and full of
    strength,
during the season of rut, when the juices trickle down the three parts of his body.
The Pandavas disguised themselves on their way, for fear of the sons of
    Dhritarashtra.
Toward evening, Bhima reached a terrible forest where fruits and water were
    scarce,
and which resounded with the frightening cries of birds and beasts
that became more fierce as twilight deepened and darkness shrouded everything.
The Pandava princes were unable to proceed further.
They sat down in that forest without food and drink. Kunti said to her sons:
"I am the mother of the five Pandavas, and yet among them I burn with thirst!"
Bhima, hearing these words, his heart stirred by compassion,
resolved to keep going through that terrible forest.

At last he saw a beautiful banyan tree with wide-spreading branches.
Setting his brothers and his mother down beneath it, he said to them:
"Rest here while I go in search of water. I hear the cries of aquatic birds.
        I think there must be a large pool close by."
Bhima went off in the direction of the bird cries, and within four miles he came
  to a lake,
where he bathed and slaked his thirst. And for his mother and his brothers
he brought water by soaking his upper garments. Hastily retracing his way,
he returned to his mother and his brothers.
He was filled with sorrow at seeing them asleep on the bare ground
and began to sigh like a snake. Bhima exclaimed: "What a wretch I am
to behold my brothers asleep this way! Alas, they who at Varanavata
lay on the softest and costliest beds now stretch out on the cold ground!
Kuntiraja, decked with every auspicious mark, as resplendent as the filaments of
  the lotus
and as delicate and tender, and fit to sleep on the costliest couch, sleeps there
  on the dirt!
And these tigers among men, my brothers, also asleep on the ground!
The virtuous Yudhishthira, who deserves the sovereignty of the three worlds,
sleeps like an ordinary man, on hard ground!
Arjuna of the darkish hue of blue clouds, unequaled among men,
sleeps on the ground like any ordinary man! The twins,
who in beauty are like the twin Aswins among the celestials,
are asleep like common mortals on the poor earth!
The man who has no jealous or wicked relatives lives in happiness in this world,
like a single tree in a village. The tree that stands alone in its village
with its leaves and fruits, and in the absence of others of the same species,
  becomes sacred
and is worshipped and venerated by all. And those who have many relatives
who are all heroic and virtuous also live happily in the world, without sorrow of
  any kind.
They may be powerful and prosperous, but they gladden their friends and
  relatives
and live in dependence on one another, like tall trees growing in the same forest.
We, however, have been forced into exile by the wicked Dhritarashtra and his sons
and have escaped, with difficulty and by sheer good fortune, from a fiery death.
Having escaped from the fire, we now rest in the shade of this tree.
Having already suffered so much, where are we to go now?
You sons of Dhritarashtra, you wicked men, enjoy your success,
but know that it is temporary. The gods are certainly auspicious to you now.
But you are still alive only because Yudhishthira does not command me
to take your wretched lives. Otherwise this very day, full of righteous wrath,
I would send you, O Duryodhana, to the regions of Yama
with your children and your friends and your brothers!
But what can I do if the virtuous King Yudhishthira,
the eldest of the Pandavas, is not yet angry with you?"
Having said this, Bhima squeezed his palms and sighed deeply in his affliction.

Like an extinguished fire that blazes up suddenly,
Bhima once more looked at his brothers, sleeping on the ground like ordinary
    persons.
And he said to himself: *There must be some town not far off from this forest.*
They all are sleeping, so I will stay awake to protect them.
I will be able to slake their thirst after they arise refreshed from their rest.
And he sat there, keeping watch over his mother and his brothers.

✦

Not far from the place where the Pandavas were asleep, a flesh-eating Rakshasa
    named Hidimva
lived on the sala tree. He was a cruel cannibal, of visage that was grim
because of his sharp and long teeth. He was now hungry and longing for human
    flesh.
Long of leg, and with a large belly, he had hair and beard that were both red
    in hue,
as were his eyes. His shoulders were as broad as the trunk of a tree.
His ears were like arrows, and his features were frightful.
This monster saw the sons of Pandu sleeping in the woods and longed for
    human flesh.
Shaking his grizzly locks and scratching them with his fingers,
                    the large-mouthed cannibal stared at them.
Sniffing the delicious odor of man, he said to his sister, also named Hidimva:
"It is a long time since I have discovered such agreeable food!
My mouth waters at it. I shall sink my eight teeth today into the most delicious
    flesh.
Attacking their throats and opening their veins, I shall drink much human
    blood,
hot and fresh and frothy. Go and find out who they are. The strong scent of man
pleases my nostrils. Slaughter them all, and bring them to me. They are in my
    territory.
You need not fear them. Do as I bid you, for we shall soon dine together,
tearing their bodies apart at our leisure. And after we have feasted to our fill,
                    we shall dance together to lively music!"
At her brother's command, Hidimva, the female cannibal, went
to where the Pandavas were asleep with their mother, with Bhimasena sitting
    awake.
Bhimasena, unrivaled on earth for beauty, was like a vigorous sala tree,
and the Rakshasa woman immediately fell in love with him. She said to herself:
This person with skin the color of heated gold and with mighty arms,
with shoulders as broad as the lion's and eyes like lotus petals,
is worthy of being my husband. I shall not obey the cruel command of my brother.
A woman's love for her husband is stronger than her affection for her brother.
If I slay him, my brother's gratification as well as mine will be only momentary.
But if I let him live, my joy with him will last forever and ever.
The Rakshasa woman was capable of assuming any form at will,

and she assumed the appearance of an excellent human woman.
With slow steps, and with smiles and a modest gait, she approached Bhima and
    said:
"O bull among men, from where have you come, and who are you?
Who are these persons of celestial beauty sleeping here?
Who, sleeping so trustfully in these woods, as if she were lying in her own
    chamber,
is this lady of transcendent loveliness? Do you not know
that this forest is the abode of a wicked Rakshasa called Hidimva?
You beings of celestial beauty, I have been sent here by that Rakshasa, my
    brother,
to kill you for his food. But, beholding you as resplendent as a celestial,
I want instead to marry you, and I would have no one for my husband but you!
Knowing this, do what is proper. My heart and my body
have been pierced by the shafts of Kama. I desire you; make me yours.
I will rescue you from the Rakshasa, who eats human flesh.
Be my husband, and we shall live on the breasts of mountains
inaccessible to ordinary mortals. I can range through the air as I please.
You may enjoy great happiness with me in those faraway regions."
To these words, Bhima replied: "O Rakshasa woman,
who can abandon his sleeping mother and his elder and younger brothers?
What man would go to gratify his lust, leaving his mother and his brothers
                        as food for a Rakshasa ?"
The Rakshasa woman replied: "Awaken them, and I shall do what is agreeable
    to you.
I shall rescue you all from my cannibal brother." Bhima then said:
"I will not awaken my brothers and my mother, sleeping comfortably in the
    woods,
because of your wicked brother. Rakshasas cannot bear the prowess of my arms.
Neither men nor Gandharvas nor Yakshas can withstand my might.
You may stay or go as you like, or even send your cannibal brother. I don't care."
Hidimva thought that his sister had not returned quickly enough.
He alit from his tree and hurried to where the Pandavas were.
Alarmed, the Rakshasa woman said to Bhima: "The cannibal is coming, and he is
    angry.
I beg you to do with your brothers as I have told you to do.
I am endowed with the powers of a Rakshasa and am capable of going wherever
    I like.
Awaken your brothers and your mother. Then climb up on my hips,
and I will carry all of you through the skies." Bhima answered: "Do not be afraid.
No Rakshasa is capable of injuring any of them as long as I am here.
I will slay this cannibal before your very eyes.
The worst of Rakshasas is no worthy antagonist of mine,
nor can all the Rakshasas together withstand the strength of my arms,
each like the trunk of an elephant. See also these thighs of mine, like iron maces,
and see this broad and powerful chest. O beautiful one, you shall see my
    prowess,

like that of Indra. Do not underestimate me, fair one, because I am a man."
Hidimva replied: "I do not hold you in contempt. But I have seen the outcome
when Rakshasas contend with men." Then the wrathful flesh-eating Rakshasa
heard what Bhima had been saying, and he saw his sister disguised in human
    form—
her head decked with garlands of flowers, her face like the full moon,
and her eyebrows and nose and eyes and ringlets all of the handsomest
    description,
her nails and complexion of the most delicate hue—
and wearing every kind of ornament, and attired in fine transparent robes.
The cannibal suspected that she was desirous of sexual intercourse
and, angry with his sister, he dilated his eyes and said: "What senseless creature
wishes to throw obstacles in my path now, when I am hungry?
Have you so lost your mind, O Hidimva, that you do not fear my wrath?
Shame on you, unchaste woman! You are even now eager for carnal pleasure
and willing to do me an injury. You are ready to sacrifice the honor and good
    name
of all the Rakshasas, your ancestors! Those with whose aid you would do me this
    injury,
                              I will slay along with you."
Hidimva ran at her to kill her then and there, but Bhima, that eminent smiter,
seeing him rush at his sister, rebuked him: "Stop! Stop!"
Bhima smiled in derision, and said: "O Hidimva,
what need is there for you to awaken these persons sleeping so comfortably?
Approach me first, without loss of time. Smite me first. It is not right to kill a
    woman,
especially when she has been sinned against instead of sinning.
This girl is scarcely responsible for desiring intercourse with me.
She has been moved by the deity of desire, who pervades every living thing.
You wicked wretch and most infamous of Rakshasas,
your sister came here at your command. Seeing my person, she desires me.
In that, the timid girl does you no injury. It is the deity of desire who has offended.
Do not injure her for this offense. You shall not slay a woman when I am here.
Come with me, O cannibal, and fight with me singly, and I shall send you today
to the abode of Yama. Your head today will be pressed down by my might
and pounded to pieces, as though pressed by the tread of a mighty elephant.
When you are slain in the battle, herons, hawks, and jackals will tear your limbs
    in glee.
I shall make this forest destitute of Rakshasas—this forest that you have ruled for
    so long,
you devourer of human flesh! Your sister shall see you become like a huge
    elephant
dragged by a lion. Once I have killed you, men will range these woods without
    fear."
Hidimva said: "What need is there for this boasting?
Accomplish all this, and then you may boast and vaunt. You think you are strong,
but today you shall try that strength in your encounter with me.

Until then, I will not slay your brothers. Let them sleep comfortably. But I will
    slay you,
and then, after drinking your blood, I will slay these also, and then, last of all,
                this sister of mine, who has done me an injury."
Saying this, the cannibal extended his arms and ran in wrath toward Bhimasena.
Bhima of terrible prowess quickly seized the arms of the Rakshasa as though in
    sport
and dragged him a full thirty-two cubits, like a lion dragging a little animal.
The Rakshasa, feeling the weight of Bhima's strength, became very angry.
Clasping the Pandava, he sent forth a terrible yell.
The mighty Bhima then dragged the Rakshasa to a greater distance,
lest his yelling awaken his brothers. Clasping and dragging each other,
both Hidimva and Bhimasena struggled like two full-grown elephants mad with
    rage,
and they broke down trees and tore the creepers that grew around.
And at those sounds, the sleeping Pandavas woke up with their mother
and saw the female Hidimva sitting before them.
Beholding her extraordinary beauty, they were filled with wonder.
Kunti addressed her sweetly and gave her every assurance, saying:
"O splendid daughter of the celestials, whose are you, and who are you?
On what business have you come hither, and from whence?
If you are the deity of these woods or an Apsara, tell me all about yourself."
Hidimva replied: "This broad forest that you see is the abode of a Rakshasa
of the name of Hidimva. I am the sister of the chief of the Rakshasas.
I had been sent by my brother to kill you and your children.
But when I got here, I beheld your mighty son
and was brought under the control of your son by the deity of love,
who pervades the nature of all beings. I then chose that mighty son of yours
as my husband. I tried to convey you from here, but your son would not permit it.
Then the cannibal came to kill you and your children.
But he has been dragged away by your mighty son—my husband.
Look now at the two of them, man and Rakshasa, engaged in combat,
grinding each other and filling the whole region with their shouts."
Hearing those words, Yudhishthira rose up and Arjuna also and Nakula and
    Sahadeva,
and they beheld Bhima and the Rakshasa fighting,
each eager to overcome the other, and each dragging the other with great force.
The dust raised by their feet looked like the smoke of a forest fire.
Their bodies, covered with that dust, resembled two tall cliffs enveloped in mist.
Then Arjuna, seeing that Bhima was hard pressed in the fight with the Rakshasa,
    said:
"Fear not, Bhima! We had been asleep and did not know
that you were engaged with a terrible Rakshasa and beginning to tire.
Here am I to help you. Let me slay the Rakshasa, and let Nakula and Sahadeva
                protect our mother."
But Bhima answered: "Look on this encounter, O brother, as if you were a
    stranger.

Do not worry about the result. Having come within reach of my arms,
he shall not escape with his life."
Then Arjuna said: "What is the point, O Bhima, of keeping the Rakshasa alive so
    long?
We must not dawdle here. The east is reddening. The dawn approaches.
The Rakshasa becomes stronger at daybreak! Do not play with your victim,
but slay the Rakshasa soon. At dusk and at dawn, Rakshasas use their powers of
    deception.
Exert all your strength."
At this speech by Arjuna, Bhima blazed up with anger
and summoned the might that Vayu, his father, puts forth at the universal
    dissolution.
In rage, he raised the Rakshasa's body high in the air and whirled it a hundred
    times.
He then said to the cannibal: "O Rakshasa, your intelligence was given to you in
    vain,
and in vain have you grown and thrived on unsanctified flesh.
You deserve, therefore, an unholy death, and I shall reduce you to nothing.
I shall make this forest blessed today, like one without prickly plants.
You shall no longer slay human beings for food."
Arjuna at this point said: "O Bhima, if you think it is difficult to overcome this
    Rakshasa,
let me help you. If you can, slay him yourself now. Or let me slay him.
You are tired and have almost finished him. You deserve rest."
Hearing Arjuna's words, Bhima was fired with rage
and dashed the Rakshasa to the ground, slaying him as if he were an animal.
The dying Rakshasa sent forth a terrible yell that filled the whole forest
and was as deep as the sound of a wet drum.
Then the mighty Bhima, holding the Rakshasa's body with his hands, bent it
    double
and broke it in the middle. Beholding Hidimva slain, the Pandavas rejoiced.
Arjuna bowed to the illustrious Bhima and said to him:
"Revered brother, I think there is a town not far from this forest.
Let us go there quickly, so that Duryodhana may not trace us."
All those mighty car warriors, those tigers among men, said: "So be it."
And they proceeded with their mother, followed by Hidimva, the Rakshasa
    woman.

✦

Turning back to Hidimva, Bhima said to her:
"Rakshasas avenge themselves on their enemies by adopting deceptions
that cannot be penetrated. I do not trust you.
Therefore, go the way your brother has gone."
But Yudhishthira saw that Bhima was enraged and said: "However angry you
    may be,

do not slay a woman. The observance of virtue is a higher duty
than the protection of life. Hidimva came to slay us, but you have slain him.
This woman is the sister of that Rakshasa, but what can she do to us,
even if she has malign intentions?" Hidimva reverentially saluted Kunti
and her son Yudhishthira and said, with joined palms: "O revered lady,
you know the pangs women feel at the hands of the god of love. Blessed woman,
these pangs Bhimasena has caused are torturing me.
I have been waiting for the time when your son could assuage them.
That time is now come. I hoped I would be made happy.
Casting off my friends and relations and the customs of my race,
I have chosen this son of yours, this tiger among men, as my husband.
I tell you truly, dear lady, that if I am cast off by that hero or by you,
I will no longer be able to bear this life of mine.
Therefore, you must show me mercy and think of me as your obedient slave.
Unite me with your son, and let him be my husband.
He has the form of a celestial. Let me take him with me wherever I like.
Trust me, I will again bring him back to all of you.
And when you think of me, I will come to you immediately
and convey you wherever you may command. I will rescue you from all dangers
and carry you across inaccessible and uneven regions, bearing you on my back
whenever you desire to proceed with swiftness. Be gracious to me,
and make Bhima accept me. It has been said that in a season of distress
one should protect one's life by any means.
He who seeks to discharge that duty should not scruple about the means.
He who, in a season of distress, keeps his virtue is foremost among virtuous men.
It is virtue that protects life, and thus is virtue called the giver of life.
Hence the means by which virtue is secured is never censurable."
Yudhishthira agreed: "It is as you say, Hidimva. But you must act as you have said.
After he has washed himself and said his prayers and performed the propitiatory
    rites,
Bhima will pay his attentions to you until the sun sets. Sport with him as you like
during the day. But you must bring Bhimasena back here every evening."
Bhima assented to all that Yudhishthira had said, and he said to Hidimva:
"Listen to me, O Rakshasa woman! Truly do I make this engagement with you—
that I will stay with you until you obtain a son."
And Hidimva answered: "So be it." And she took Bhima upon her body
and sped through the countryside on mountain peaks of gorgeous vistas
and regions, sacred to the gods, that abounded with grazing herds
and echoed with the melodies of feathered flocks.
She assumed the most beautiful form, decked with every ornament,
and she sported with the Pandava and studied to make him happy in every way.
In inaccessible regions of forests, and on mountain breasts
overgrown with blossoming trees, on lakes resplendent with lotuses and lilies,
on the islands of rivers and on the rivers' pebbly banks, in woods with
    blossoming trees,
in Himalayan bowers and in various caves, on crystal pools smiling with lotuses,

on seashores shining with gold and pearls, in beautiful towns and fine gardens,

in woods sacred to the gods and on hillsides, in the regions of Guhyakas and
ascetics,

on the banks of the Manasarovara that abounded with the fruits and flowers of
every season,

Hidimva sported with Bhima and studied to make him happy until, in time, she
conceived

and brought forth a mighty son begotten upon her by the Pandava.

Rakshasa women bring forth the very day they conceive.

The child, of terrible eyes and large mouth and with pointy ears, was fearsome
to behold.

His lips were as brown as copper, and his teeth were sharp. He had a loud roar,

mighty arms, and great strength, and he became a mighty bowman.

Of long nose, broad chest, muscular calves, speedy motion, and great strength,

he had nothing human in his countenance, although he was born of man.

And he surpassed in strength and prowess all Pisachas and kindred tribes

as well as all Rakshasas. Although he was a little child, he grew and became a
youth

in the hour when he was born. The mighty hero soon acquired high proficiency

in the use of all weapons. The baldheaded child, soon after his birth,

bowed down to his mother and touched her feet and the feet also of his father.

His parents then gave him a name. His mother had remarked that his head

was bald as a *ghata*, a water pot, and so both his parents called him Ghatotkacha,

meaning "*Pot-Headed.*" And Ghatotkacha was exceedingly devoted to the Pandavas

and became a great favorite with them—indeed, almost one of them.

Hidimva knew that the period of her stay with Bhima had come to an end,

and she saluted the Pandavas and repeated her promise

that she would come to them whenever they called on her. Then she went away.

And Ghatotkacha also promised his father that he would come whenever he was
wanted,

saluted them, and went away northward. Indeed, it was the illustrious Indra who
created,

by lending a portion of himself, the mighty car warrior Ghatotkacha

as a fit antagonist of Karna because of the dart he had given Karna,

which would kill anyone it was used against.

10

Vaka

The heroic Pandavas then went from forest to forest, killing animals for food.
In the course of their wanderings, they saw the countries of the Matsyas,
the Trigartas, the Panchalas, and the Kichakas, and many beautiful woods and
   lakes.
They had matted locks and wore tree bark and animal skins.
They appeared to be a group of ascetics. Sometimes they traveled in haste,
carrying their mother on their backs, and sometimes they went in disguise.
They studied the Rig and the other Vedas and all the Vedangas
                       as well as the sciences of morals and politics.
In course of their wanderings, they met their grandfather Vyasa.
Saluting the illustrious Krishna-Dwaipayana, those chastisers of enemies
and their mother stood before him with joined palms. Vyasa then said to them:
"I knew beforehand of this affliction of yours, and of your exile by the son of
   Dhritarashtra.
And I have come to you to do you great good. Do not grieve for what has
   happened,
but know that all this is for your happiness. The sons of Dhritarashtra and you
are all equal to me. But men are always partial to those in misfortune or of
   tender years.
My affection for you is therefore greater now, and I desire to do you good.
Listen to me! Not far off is a delightful town where no danger can overtake you.
                       Live there in disguise and wait for my return."
Vyasa, the son of Satyavati, thus comforted the Pandavas, and he led them
into the town of Ekachakra. The master also comforted Kunti, saying: "Live, O
   daughter!
This son of yours, Yudhishthira, having by his justice conquered the entire earth,
will rule over all the other monarchs. There is no doubt
that with Bhima's and Arjuna's prowess he will conquer the whole world
with her belt of seas, and he will enjoy sovereignty over it all.
Your sons and those of Madri will enjoy themselves in their dominions.
These tigers among men will perform sacrifices, such as the Rajasuya
and the horse sacrifice, in which the presents to the Brahmanas are very large.
And your sons will rule their ancestral kingdom, maintaining their friends and
   relatives
                       in luxury and affluence and happiness."

With these words, Vyasa introduced them into the dwelling of a Brahmana.
And the island-born rishi, addressing the eldest of the Pandavas, said:
"Wait here for me! I will come back! Adapt yourselves to the country and the occasion,
and you will be happy." Then the Pandavas said to the rishi: "So be it."
And the illustrious rishi Vyasa returned to the region from which he had come.

✦

In Ekachakra, the sons of Kunti lived for a short time in the abode of that Brahmana.
Leading the life of mendicants, they became great favorites of the townsmen,
and at nightfall they placed before Kunti all they had gathered in their begging tours.
Kunti used to divide the sum among them, with each taking what was allotted to him.
And those heroes and their mother together took a half
while the mighty Bhima alone took the other half.
In this way, the illustrious Pandavas lived there for some time.
One day, while they were out on their begging tour and Bhima was at home
with his mother, Kunti heard a loud wail from within the apartments of the Brahmana.
Kunti could not bear to listen to these cries with indifference and said to Bhima:
"Our woes have been diminished, and we are living happily in the Brahmana's house,
respected by him and unknown to Dhritarashtra's son.
I think of the good I should do to this Brahmana, as guests should do for their hosts!
He is a man upon whom favors are not lost. He pays back to others
more than what he receives at their hands. Some affliction has overtaken him.
If we could be of any help to him, we should only be repaying his kindnesses."
Bhima replied: "I shall try to ascertain the nature of the Brahmana's distress.
And, however difficult the task the task may prove, I shall relieve it."
While mother and son were thus talking, they heard another wail of sorrow
from the Brahmana and his wife. Kunti quickly entered their inner apartments,
like a cow running toward her tethered calf. She saw the Brahmana, his wife,
and his son and daughter sitting with woeful faces and heard him say:
"Oh! how miserable is this earthly life, hollow as the reed and fruitless.
All is sorrow. There is no freedom from misery! Life is suffering and sickness;
it is a path of pain! The soul is one; but it pursues virtue, wealth, and pleasure.
And because these three are pursued at the same time,
there is frequently a disagreement that can be the source of much misery.
Some say that salvation is the highest object of our desire.
But I believe it can never be attained. The acquisition of wealth is hell:
the pursuit of wealth is attended with misery, and there is more misery
after one has acquired it, for one loves one's possessions, and if one loses them,
that is an occasion of woe. I do not see how I can escape from this danger

nor how I can flee with my wife to some region free from peril.

Remember, dear wife, that I wanted to move somewhere else where we would be
 happy,

but you did not listen to me. You said: 'I was born here, and I have grown old
 here;

this is the home of my ancestors.' Your father and mother ascended to heaven
 long ago.

Your relatives are also all dead. Why then did you prefer to live here?

The time has now come when you are to witness the death of a member of our
 family.

How sad is that spectacle for me! Or perhaps the time has come for my own
 death,

for I shall never be able to abandon cruelly one of my own as long as I myself am
 alive.

You are my helpmate, self-denying and as affectionate to me as a mother.

The gods have given you to me as a true friend.

You are of pure lineage and good disposition, the mother of my children,

devoted to me, and altogether innocent. I chose you and married you,

and I cannot abandon you now, even to save my life.

And how shall I bring myself to sacrifice my son, a child of tender years,

without the first down of manhood? How shall I sacrifice my daughter,

who has been placed in my hands by the Creator for me to bestow on a husband,

and through whom I hope to enjoy those regions attainable only

by those who have daughters' sons? Some people think that a father's affection

for a son is greater; others, that his affection for a daughter is greater.

Mine, however, is equal. How can I give up the innocent daughter

upon whom rest the regions of bliss obtainable by me in the afterlife?

But then, if I sacrifice myself, I should scarcely know any peace,

for those whom I leave behind would not be able to feed and house themselves.

Without me, my survivors will certainly perish. My distress is great,

and I know no means of escape. What course shall I take?

Perhaps, if we can live together no longer, we should all die together."

On hearing these words of the Brahmana, his wife answered:

"Do not grieve like an ordinary man. This is not the time for mourning.

You have learning, and you know that all men are sure to die.

None should grieve for what is inevitable. Wife, son, and daughter,

you sought all these for yourself. As you are wise, kill your sorrows.

I will go there myself. This, indeed, is the highest duty of a woman—

that by sacrificing her life she should seek the good of her husband.

Such an act of mine will make you happy and will bring me fame

in this world and the next. This is the highest virtue,

and by this you may acquire both righteousness and happiness.

The object for which one desires a wife has already been achieved.

I have borne you a daughter and a son and have been freed from the debt I had
 owed you.

You are well able to support and cherish the children, as I can never do.

You are my life, my wealth, and my lord.

Without you, how shall these children of tender years—how shall I myself—exist?
Widowed and masterless, with two children depending on me,
how shall I support them and myself, leading an honest life?
If your daughter is solicited in marriage by dishonorable persons,
vain and unworthy of contracting an alliance with your line, how shall I protect
  her?
As birds seek avidly for meat that has been thrown away on the ground,
so do men solicit a woman who has lost her husband.
Approached by wicked men, I may waver, and I may not be able to stay on the
  right path.
How shall I be able to keep this sole daughter of your house, this innocent girl,
in the decency in which her ancestors have always walked?
How shall I be able to impart to your son every desirable accomplishment,
to make him as virtuous as you are, in that season of want when I shall be a
  widow?
Unworthy persons will demand the hand of your daughter,
like Sudras desiring to hear the Vedas. And if I do not bestow upon them
this girl of your blood and qualities, they may even take her by force,
like crows carrying away sacrificial butter. And if your son becomes unlike you,
and your daughter is placed under the control of unworthy persons,
I shall be despised in the world by even dishonorable and evil persons,
and I will certainly die. These children, bereft of you and me, will also perish
like fish when the lake dries up. Therefore, I am the one who must be sacrificed.
Persons conversant with morals have said that for women who have borne
  children,
to predecease their husbands is an act of the highest merit.
I am ready to abandon this son and this daughter, and life itself, for you.
For a woman to do well for her lord is a higher duty than sacrifices,
asceticism, vows, and charities of every description.
The act I intend to perform is consonant with the highest virtue and is for your
  good
and that of your race. The wise have declared that children and relatives and wife
and all things held dear are cherished for the purpose of liberating oneself
from danger and distress. One must guard one's wealth for freeing oneself from
  danger,
and it is by his wealth that he should cherish and protect his wife.
But he must protect himself both by means of his wife and his wealth.
The learned have enunciated the truth that a wife, son, wealth, and house
are acquired to provide against accidents, foreseen or unforeseen.
The wise have also said that all one's relations weighed against oneself
would not be equal to oneself. Protect yourself therefore by abandoning me.
Give me leave to sacrifice myself, and cherish my children.
Those who are conversant with morals have said that women should never be
  slaughtered,
and the Rakshasas are not ignorant of the rules of morality.
It is certain that the Rakshasa will kill a man, but it is doubtful that he will kill a
  woman.

Therefore, place me before the Rakshasa. I have enjoyed much happiness
and have obtained much that is agreeable to me. I have had children who are
    dear to me.
I have also acquired great religious merit. For these reasons, I am not unhappy
    to die.
I have thought carefully and have come to this resolution.
O dear husband, also think that by abandoning me you may obtain another,
    younger wife.
By her you may again acquire religious merit. There is no sin in this.
For a man, polygamy is an act of merit, but for a woman to take a second husband
after the death of the first is sinful. Your sacrifice of yourself would be censurable.
Liberate, then, yourself and these your children, and abandon me."
The Brahmana embraced her, and they both wept in silence.
Hearing these words of her parents, and seeing them weep,
the daughter was filled with grief and said to them: "Why are you so afflicted,
and why do you weep so, as if you had none to look after you?
There is no doubt that you are bound in duty to abandon me eventually.
So abandon me now, and save everything at my expense.
Men desire to have children, thinking that children will save them
in this world as well as in the next. Cross your stream of difficulties,
making use of my poor self, as if I were a raft.
A child rescues his parents in this region and the next;
therefore is the child called by the learned Putra, meaning '*Rescuer.*'
The ancestors desire daughter's sons from me as a special means of salvation.
But without children, I will rescue them by protecting the life of my father.
My brother is of tender years and will perish if you die now.
If you die and my brother follows you, the funeral cake of the Pitris will be
    suspended,
and they will be injured. Left behind by my father and brother, and my mother
    also,
for she will not survive her husband and son,
I shall be plunged deeper and deeper into woe and will perish in great distress.
There can be no question that if you escape from this danger
with my mother and infant brother, then your race and the ancestral cake
will be perpetuated. The son is one's own self, the wife is one's friend,
but the daughter is a source of trouble. Save yourself, then,
by removing that source of trouble, and set me on the path of virtue.
As a girl, father, I shall be helpless without you and plunged into grief.
I am therefore resolved to rescue my father's race and earn the merit of that act.
               If you, O best of Brahmanas, go to the Rakshasa,
leaving me here, I shall be very much pained. Be kind to me, then, O best of men,
for our sake, for that of virtue, and also for that of your race, save yourself.
    Abandon me,
from whom you shall one day be forced to part. There need be no delay
in doing what is inevitable. What can be more painful than that we, when you
    have risen
to heaven, shall have to go about begging our food, like dogs, from strangers?

But if you are rescued with your relatives, I shall live happily
in the region of the celestials. If you bestow your daughter in this way,
and you then offer oblations to the gods and the celestials, they will be propitious."
Listening to these words of their daughter, the Brahmana and his wife
became even sadder than before, and the three of them wept together.
Their son then lisped these words in a sweet and fluty tone:
"Do not weep, O father, or you, mother, or you, my sister!"
The child approached each of them and, with a blade of grass he held between
    his fingers,
said: "I will slay the man-eating Rakshasa with this!"
Although all of them had been plunged into deep grief, joy now appeared on
    their faces.
Kunti decided that this might be the proper opportunity
and approached the group and said these words, which revived them,
even as nectar revives a person who is dead:
"Tell me the cause of your grief. I will remove it, if I can."
The Brahmana replied: "Your speech is worthy of you.
But no human being can remove this grief of ours.
Not far from this town there lives a Rakshasa named Vaka,
a cannibal who is the lord of this country and town.
He thrives on human flesh, and with his strength he rules this country.
We have no fear from the machinations of any enemy, or indeed from any living
    soul.
The cannibal's fee, however, is his food, which consists of a cartload of rice,
two buffalo, and the human being who delivers them to him.
One after another, the householders have to send him this food.
The duty comes to each family after an interval of many long years.
If any seek to avoid it, the Rakshasa slays them with their children and wives,
and he devours them all. There is, in this country, a city called Vetrakiya,
where the king of these territories lives. He is ignorant of the science of
    government,
and has little intelligence. He does not care how these territories may be
    rendered safe.
So we bear our burden, for we live within the dominion of that wretched and
    weak king,
in perpetual fear. Brahmanas can never be made to dwell permanently
    anywhere,
for they are dependent on no one, and they live like birds, ranging everywhere
    in freedom.
It has been said that one must secure a good king, then a wife, and then wealth.
But as regards the acquisition of these three, my actions have been
in the reverse direction, and I am suffering sorely.
It is now my turn to give the Rakshasa his food as I have described to you,
including the one human being. I have no wealth with which to buy a man.
I cannot consent to part with any one of my family, nor do I see any way of escape
from the Rakshasa. I am now sunk in an ocean of grief from which there is no
    escape.

I shall therefore go to that Rakshasa today, with all my family,
in order that the monster might devour us all at once."
Kunti said: "Do not grieve, O Brahmana.
I see a way by which to rescue you from that Rakshasa.
You have only one son, of very tender years, and one daughter, young and
    helpless,
and I do not like it that any of these, or your wife, or even you yourself should go
to the Rakshasa. I have five sons, O Brahmana.
Let one of them go, carrying on your behalf the tribute to that Rakshasa."
The Brahmana replied: "To save my own life, I shall never suffer this to be done.
I shall never sacrifice the life of a Brahmana or of a guest.
Even those of low origin and of sinful practices would refuse to do what you ask
    of me.
It is said that one should sacrifice oneself and one's offspring
for the benefit of a Brahmana. This is excellent advice, and I intend to follow it.
When I have to choose between the death of a Brahmana and my own,
I should prefer the latter. The killing of a Brahmana is the highest sin,
and there is no expiation for it. A reluctant sacrifice of oneself is better
than the reluctant sacrifice of a Brahmana. O dear lady, in sacrificing myself
I do not become guilty of suicide. No sin can attach to me if another takes
    my life.
But if I deliberately consent to the death of a Brahmana, that would be a
    sinful act,
from the consequence of which there would no escape.
The learned have said that the abandonment of one who has come to your
    house
or who sought your protection is like the killing of one who seeks death at your
    hands
and is both cruel and sinful. Those conversant with practices that are allowed
in seasons of distress have said that one should never perform an act that is cruel
and censurable. It is better for me to perish with my wife
                    than to sanction the death of a Brahmana."
Kunti said: "I agree with you, O Brahmana, that Brahmanas should always be
    protected.
But this Rakshasa will not be able to kill my son, who is endowed with great
    strength
and skilled in mantras. He will faithfully deliver the food to the Rakshasa
but will rescue himself. I have seen before many Rakshasas of huge bodies
engaged in combat with my heroic son and killed by him.
But do not tell anybody, for if it were known, persons eager to obtain this power
would trouble my sons, if only out of curiosity. The wise have said
that if my son imparts any knowledge to anyone without the assent of his
    preceptor,
my son himself will no longer be able to profit by that knowledge."
The Brahmana with his wife were exceedingly glad to hear this,
and they assented to Kunti's suggestion and welcomed her words, which were as
    nectar.

When Kunti and the Brahmana went to Bhima to ask him to accomplish this
    task,

Bhima replied: "So be it."

✦

After Bhima had promised to accomplish the task,
the Pandavas returned home with the alms they had received during the day.
From Bhima's countenance, Yudhishthira suspected the nature of the task
he had undertaken. Sitting by the side of his mother, Yudhishthira asked her in
    private:
"What is the task that Bhima seeks to accomplish? Does he do so at your
    command
or of his own accord?" Kunti replied: "It is at my command that Bhima will do
    this deed,
for the good of the Brahmana and for the liberation of this town."
Yudhishthira said: "What a rash act, O mother! It almost amounts to suicide!
The learned never applaud the abandonment of one's own child.
Why do you wish to sacrifice your child for the sake of another's?
You have acted against the course of human practices and the teachings of the
    Vedas.
We rely on Bhima's arms when we sleep in the night,
and he is our hope of recovering the kingdom of which we have been deprived
by the covetous son of Dhritarashtra. It is Bhima by whose prowess we were
    rescued
from the palace of lac and various other dangers. Bhima caused the death of
    Purochana,
and, relying on his might, we regard ourselves as having already slain
    Dhritarashtra's sons
and acquired the whole earth with all her wealth. Upon what considerations, O
    mother,
have you resolved upon abandoning him? Have you lost your reason?
Has your understanding been clouded by the calamities you have undergone?"
Kunti answered: "O Yudhishthira, you need not be anxious.
I have not come to this resolve because of any weakness of understanding.
Respected by him, and with our sorrows assuaged, we have been living
in the house of this Brahmana, unknown to the sons of Dhritarashtra.
For repayment of that Brahmana's kindness, I resolved to do this.
He is a man upon whom good offices are never lost. The measure of his requital
becomes greater than the measure of the services he receives.
Considering the prowess of Bhima in our escape from the house of lac
and from the destruction also of Hidimva, my confidence in him is great.
The might of Bhima's arms equals that of ten thousand elephants.
That was how he succeeded in carrying you all, each heavy as an elephant,
from Varanavata. No one on earth is equal to Bhima in might;
he may even overcome that foremost among warriors, the holder of the
    thunderbolt himself.

Soon after his birth, he fell from my lap onto the breast of the mountain.
By the weight of his body, the mass of stone on which he fell broke into pieces.
From this also I have come to know Bhima's might.
For this reason, I resolved to set him against the Brahmana's foe.
I have not done this from foolishness or ignorance or from any motive of gain.
I have deliberately resolved to do this virtuous deed.
By this act, O Yudhishthira, two objects will be accomplished:
one is to requite the services rendered by the Brahmana, and the other
is to acquire high religious merit. It is my conviction that the Kshatriya
who renders help to a Brahmana acquires regions of bliss hereafter.
So also a Kshatriya who saves the life of a Kshatriya
achieves great fame in this world as well as in the other.
A Kshatriya giving help to a Vaisya also on this earth acquires worldwide approval.
One of the kingly tribe should protect even the Sudra who comes to him for
    protection.
If he does so, in his next life he receives his birth in a royal line,
commanding prosperity and the respect of other kings.
My son, the illustrious Vyasa, who acquired wisdom by hard ascetic toil,
told me these things long ago. That is why I have resolved upon accomplishing
    this."
Yudhishthira replied: "What you have deliberately done, moved by compassion
for the afflicted Brahmana, is indeed excellent. Bhima will certainly come back
    alive
after having slain the cannibal. But tell the Brahmana not to do anything
whereby the dwellers in this town may know about it,
                and make him promise to comply with your request."
Then, when the night passed away, Bhimasena, the son of Pandu,
took the Rakshasa's food and set out for the place where the cannibal lived.
Approaching the forest where the Rakshasa dwelled, he began to eat the food he
    had carried
and called loudly to the Rakshasa by name. The Rakshasa, inflamed with anger,
approached the place where Bhima was sitting. Of huge body and great strength,
of red eyes, red beard, and red hair, he was terrible to behold as he advanced,
pressing the earth deep with his tread. The opening of his mouth was from ear
    to ear,
and his ears themselves were straight as arrows. Of grim visage,
he had a forehead furrowed into three lines. Beholding Bhima eating his food,
the Rakshasa advanced, biting his nether lip and expanding his eyes in wrath.
"Who is this fool," he asked, "eager to go to the abode of Yama,
who eats in my very sight the food intended for me?"
Bhima smiled in derision and disregarded the Rakshasa.
He continued eating with averted face. The cannibal uttered a frightful yell
and with both arms upraised ran at Bhima, intending to kill him there and then.
Still disregarding the Rakshasa and casting only a single glance at him,
Bhima continued to eat the Rakshasa's food.
Furious, the Rakshasa struck from behind with both his arms a heavy blow
on Bhima's back. Bhima did not even look up but continued to eat as before.

Then the mighty Rakshasa, even more furious, tore up a tree and ran at Bhima
to strike him again. Meanwhile, the mighty Bhima had leisurely eaten up all the
    food.
Washing himself, he stood at last, ready to fight.
He smiled in derision as, with his left hand, he caught the tree
the Rakshasa hurled at him. The Rakshasa tore up many more trees
and hurled them at Bhima, and now the Pandava hurled as many back at the
    Rakshasa.
The combat with trees between human being and Rakshasa was so terrible
that the region around was soon despoiled of trees.
The Rakshasa shouted out that he was none other than Vaka
and sprang upon the Pandava and seized him with his arms.
In response, Bhima clasped the Rakshasa in his own arms and dragged him
    violently.
Dragged and also dragging, the cannibal was soon overcome by fatigue.
The earth began to tremble, and large trees that stood there broke in pieces.
Bhima saw that the cannibal was tiring, pressed him down on the earth with his
    knees,
and began to strike him with great force. Placing one knee
on the middle of the Rakshasa's back, Bhima seized his neck with his right hand,
and the cloth on his waist with his left, and with great force bent him double.
The cannibal then roared frightfully. He began to vomit blood as he was being
    broken
on Bhima's knee. Then Vaka died, uttering frightful yells.
Terrified by these sounds, the relatives of that Rakshasa came out with their
    attendants.
Bhima saw that they were terrified out of their minds, and he comforted them,
but he made them promise to give up cannibalism.
"Do not ever again kill human beings," he told them. "If you kill men,
you will have to die, just as Vaka did."
                     The Rakshasas said: "So be it." And they gave their promise.
From that day onward, the Rakshasas of the region were peaceful toward
    mankind.
Bhima then dragged the lifeless cannibal to one of the gates of the town,
left him there, and went away observed by no one.
Vaka's kinsmen who had seen him slain by Bhima's might
were frightened enough to flee in different directions.
Bhima then returned to the Brahmana's house and told Yudhishthira what had
    happened.
The next morning, the inhabitants of the town came out
and saw the Rakshasa lying dead on the ground,
his body covered with blood, huge as a mountain cliff but mangled.
The hair of the townsfolk stood erect. Returning to Ekachakra, they spread the
    news.
Then citizens by the thousands and their wives, the young children,
and the old men and women all came to see Vaka's corpse,
and they were all amazed at the superhuman strength of whoever had killed him.

They began to pray to their gods. Then they began to calculate whose turn it
   had been
the day before to carry food to the Rakshasa. Ascertaining this,
they came to the Brahmana to ask him what had happened.
But that bull among Brahmanas, who was concealing the Pandavas, said to the
   citizens:
"A certain high-souled Brahmana, skilled in mantras, saw me weeping with my
   family
after I had been ordered to supply the Rakshasa's food.
I told him why we were grieving, and that foremost among Brahmanas said
   to me:
'I shall carry the food for that wretched Rakshasa. Do not fear for me.'
And he took the food to the forest of Vaka. This deed, so beneficial to us all,
   was his."
The Brahmanas and Kshatriyas of the city, hearing this, wondered greatly.
And the Vaisyas and the Sudras were also glad, and they all established a festival
in which the worship of Brahmanas was the principal ceremony
in remembrance of this Brahmana who had relieved them from their fears of
   Vaka.

Tapati

After this, the Pandavas continued to dwell at Ekachakra
in the abode of that Brahmana, devoting themselves to the study of the Vedas.
Within a few days, there came a Brahmana of rigid vows
to the abode of their host, to take up his quarters there.
Their host, ever hospitable to all guests, welcomed him with due ceremonies
and gave him rooms in his own apartment.
The Pandavas and their mother asked the new lodger to tell them of his
     experiences.
The Brahmana spoke to them of various countries, shrines, and holy rivers,
of kings and many wonderful provinces and cities.
He also spoke of the self-choice of Yajnasena's daughter,
of the princes of Panchala, and of the births of Dhrishtadyumna and Sikhandi,
as well as the birth, without the intervention of a woman, of Krishnā, also called
     Draupadi,
at the great sacrifice of Drupada. Hearing these extraordinary reports
about that illustrious monarch, Drupada, the Pandavas desired to know the
     details
and asked the Brahmana to satisfy their curiosity:
"How, O Brahmana, did the birth of Dhrishtadyumna, the son of Drupada,
take place from the fire? How also did the birth of Krishnā come about?
How also did Drupada's son learn all weapons from the great bowman Drona?
And how and why was the friendship between Drona and Drupada broken off?"
The Brahmana then told them the particulars about the birth of Drona:
"Where the Ganga enters the plains, there lived a great rishi named Bharadwaja
who was devoted to the most austere penances. One day, on coming to the
     Ganga
for his ablutions, the rishi saw the Apsara Ghritachi standing on the bank after
     her bath.
And it happened that a wind arose and disrobed her. The rishi, seeing her naked,
felt the influence of desire. Though practicing the vow of continence from his
     youth,
as soon as he felt that great desire, his vital fluid spurted out. As it came out,
he held it in a *drona*, or pot, and of that fluid thus was born a son
who came to be called Drona, meaning '*Pot-Born*.' Drona studied all the Vedas
                              and their several branches.

Bharadwaja had a friend named Prishata who was the king of the Panchalas.
About the time that Drona was born, Prishata also obtained a son, named
Drupada.
That bull among Kshatriyas, Prishata's son, went every day
to the dwelling of Bharadwaja, where he played and studied with Drona.
And after Prishata's death, Drupada succeeded him on the throne.
Drona about this time heard that the great Brahmana hero, Rama,
before retiring into the woods, had resolved to give away all his wealth.
Hearing this, he hurried to Rama and said to him: 'O best of Brahmanas, I am
Drona,
and I have come to you to obtain your wealth.' Rama replied:
'I have given away everything. All that I now have is this body of mine and my
weapons.
You may ask of me one of these two, either my body or my weapons.'
Drona asked for the weapons and the mysteries of their use.
Rama of Bhrigu's race, said: 'So be it.' And he gave all his weapons to Drona,
who was delighted because he had obtained from Rama
the most exalted of all weapons, called the Brahma weapon.
He had thus acquired a decided superiority over all men.
Then the son of Bharadwaja, endowed with great prowess, went to King Drupada
and said: 'Know me as your friend.' But Drupada said:
'One of low birth can never be the friend of one whose lineage is pure,
nor can one who is not a car warrior have a car warrior for his friend.
So also one who is not a king cannot have a king as his friend.
Why do you, therefore, desire to revive our former friendship?'
Drona was mortified and set his mind on contriving some means
of humiliating the king of the Panchala.
He went to the capital of the Kurus, called after the name of an elephant.
Then Bhishma took his grandsons and presented them to the wise son of
Bharadwaja
as his pupils for instruction, along with various kinds of wealth.
Drona, eager to humiliate King Drupada, called together his disciples and said
to them:
'Sinless ones, it behooves you, after you have become accomplished in arms,
to give me as my preceptorial fee something that I cherish in my heart.'
Arjuna and others said to their preceptor: 'So be it.'
After a time, when the Pandavas became skilled in arms and sure in their aim,
Drona demanded his fee. He told them: 'Drupada is the king of Chhatravati.
Take his kingdom away from him, and give it to me.'
The Pandavas defeated Drupada in battle and took him prisoner along with his
ministers.
They offered him to Drona, who said to the vanquished monarch: 'O king,
I again solicit your friendship; and because none who is not a king
deserves to be the friend of a king, I am resolved to divide your kingdom
between us.
While you are the king of the country to the south of Ganga,
I will rule the country to the north.' "

The Brahmana continued: "The king of the Panchalas answered:
'O high-souled son of Bharadwaja, let it be so, let there be eternal friendship
    between us!'
Thus establishing a permanent bond between themselves,
Drona and the king of Panchala returned to the places from which they had
    come.
But the thought of that humiliation did not leave the king's mind even for a
    moment.
Sad at heart, the king began to waste away." Hearing these words of the
    Brahmana,
the sons of Kunti were pierced as if with darts. Kunti, seeing their expression,
addressed Yudhishthira: "We have now lived many nights in the abode of this
    Brahmana.
We have passed our time pleasantly in this town, living on alms
obtained from many honest and illustrious persons.
But as we have now seen often all the agreeable woods and gardens of the
    countryside,
seeing them again would no longer give any pleasure.
Alms also are not obtainable now as easily here as before.
It would be well for us now to go to Panchala; we have not seen that country.
It will no doubt prove delightful to us. It is said that alms are obtainable
in the country of the Panchalas, and that Yajnasena, their king, is devoted to
    Brahmanas.
I am of the opinion that it is not good to live long in one place.
Therefore, O son, if you agree, I think it is good for us to go there."
Yudhishthira answered: "It is our duty to obey your command,
which is for our good. But I do not know whether my younger brothers are
    willing to go."
Then Kunti spoke to Bhimasena and Arjuna and the twins about the journey to
    Panchala.
                    They all said: "So be it."
Then Kunti and her sons saluted the Brahmana in whose house they had
    dwelled
and set out for the delightful town of the illustrious Drupada.

✦

While the Pandavas were living in the abode of the Brahmana,
Vyasa, the son of Satyavati, once went to see them.
Those chastisers of foes rose up and stepped forward to receive him.
Saluting him, and worshipping him with joined palms, the Pandavas stood in
    silence.
The sage was gratified and asked them to be seated.
He asked: "Are you living in the path of virtue and according to the scriptures?
Do you worship the Brahmanas? Do you pay homage to those who deserve it?"
After discoursing upon many topics of great interest, Vyasa said:
"An illustrious rishi, living in a certain hermitage, had a daughter

of slender waist, fair lips and fine eyebrows, and possessing every accomplishment.
But as a consequence of her acts in a past life, the maiden was very unfortunate.
Though chaste and beautiful, the damsel could not obtain a husband.
With a sorrowful heart, she began to practice ascetic penances,
with the object of finding a husband. She soon gratified by her severe asceticism
the god Sankara, called Mahadeva, who became propitious to her
and said: 'Ask the boon you desire of me! Blessings upon you!
I am Sankara and am prepared to give you what you ask.'
Over and over, the maid said to the god: 'Give me a husband
endowed with every accomplishment.' And Sankara answered:
'You shall have five husbands from among the Bharata princes.'
To this the maiden replied: 'O lord, I desire to have only one husband.'
But the god said: 'You have said five times, "Give me a husband."
You shall, therefore, in another life have five husbands!'
You princes of Bharata's line, that damsel of celestial beauty has been born
in the line of Drupada. The faultless Krishnā of Prishata's line
has been appointed to be the wife of you all.
Go, therefore, to the capital of the Panchalas, and dwell there.
There is no doubt that, having obtained her as wife, you shall be very happy."
Having said this to the Pandavas, their illustrious and blessed grandsire
bade them farewell and returned whence he had come.

✦

The Pandavas proceeded toward Panchala with joyous hearts,
and with their mother walking before them. To reach their destination,
they traveled due north, walking day and night until they reached a sacred
    shrine of Siva.
Then they arrived at the banks of the Ganga. Dhananjaya walked before them,
torch in hand, to show them the way and guard against wild animals.
It so happened that at that time the proud king of the Gandharvas and his wives
were sporting in that solitary region in the waters of the Ganga.
The king heard the tread of the Pandavas as they approached the river,
and at the sound of their footsteps the Gandharvas were inflamed with wrath.
As the Pandavas approached the king with their mother, he drew his bow to a
    circle
and said: "It is known that, excepting the first forty seconds,
the grey twilight preceding nightfall has been appointed
for the wandering of the Yakshas, the Gandharvas, and the Rakshasas,
all of whom are capable of going everywhere at will.
The rest of the time has been appointed for man to do his work.
If men, wandering during those moments from greed of gain, come near us,
both we and the Rakshasas slay them. Persons acquainted with the Vedas
never applaud those men—not even kings at the head of their troops—
who approach any pools of water at such a time.
Stay at a distance, and do not approach me any closer.
Do you not know that I am bathing in the waters of the Ganges?

I am Angaraparna the Gandharva, ever relying on my own strength!
I am proud and haughty and am the friend of Kuvera.
This is my forest, on the banks of the Ganga, where I sport to gratify all my senses.
It is named after me and is called Angaraparna.
Here neither gods nor Kapalikas nor Gandharvas nor Yakshas can come.
How dare you approach me, the brightest jewel on the diadem of Kuvera?"
Hearing these words of the Gandharva, Arjuna answered: "Blockhead,
whether it be day, night, or twilight, who can bar others from the ocean,
the sides of the Himalayas, or this river? Whether the stomach be empty or full,
whether it be night or day, there is no special time for anybody to come to the
    Ganga.
We don't care if we are disturbing you. Only those who are weak worship you.
These great waters, issuing from the golden peaks of Himavat,
fall into the waters of the ocean, distributed into seven streams.
They who drink the waters of these seven streams—
Ganga, Yamuna, Saraswati, Vitashtha, Sarayu, Gomati, and Gandaki—
are cleansed of all their sins. O Gandharva, this sacred Ganga,
flowing as it does through the celestial region, is called there the Alakananda.
In the region of the Pitris, it becomes the Vaitarani
and is difficult for sinners to cross. Krishna-Dwaipayana himself has said so.
This celestial river is capable of leading to heaven those who touch its waters.
It is open to all and should be free from dangers. Why do you desire to bar us
    from it?
This act of yours is not in consonance with eternal virtue.
Why should we not disregard your words and touch the sacred waters of the
    Ganges?"
Hearing these words of Arjuna, Angaraparna became inflamed with wrath,
drew his bow to a circle, and shot arrows like venomous snakes at the Pandavas.
Arjuna, the son of Pandu, wielding a good shield and a torch he held in his hand,
warded off all those arrows and he addressing the Gandharva:
"Do not seek to terrify those who are skilled in weapons, for weapons hurled at
    them
vanish like froth. I think, O Gandharva, that you are superior to men in prowess.
Therefore shall I fight with you, using celestial weapons and not with any unfair
    means.
This fiery weapon that I shall hurl at you Vrihaspati, the revered preceptor of
    Indra,
gave to Bharadwaja, from whom it was obtained by Agnivesya,
and from Agnivesya by my preceptor, Drona, who gave it to me."
With these words, Arjuna hurled at the Gandharva that blazing weapon made of
    fire,
which burned the Gandharva's chariot in an instant. Knocked senseless,
the mighty Gandharva fell head downward from his chariot.
Dhananjaya seized him by the hair of his head, adorned with garlands of flowers,
and dragged the unconscious king toward his brothers.
The Gandharva's wife, Kumbhinasi, eager to save her husband, ran toward
    Yudhishthira

and sought his protection. The Gandharva said: "O exalted one,
extend your protection to me! Set my husband free! I am Kumbhinasi,
wife of this Gandharva, and I beg you!"
Beholding her so afflicted, the mighty Yudhishthira addressed Arjuna and said:
"O slayer of foes, who would slay a foe who has been vanquished in fight,
and deprived of fame, who is protected by a woman, and who has no prowess?"
Arjuna replied, saying: "Keep your life, O Gandharva! Go hence, and do not
    grieve!
Yudhishthira, the king of the Kurus, commands me to show you mercy."
The Gandharva answered: "You have vanquished me.
I shall therefore abandon my former name Angaraparna, meaning '*Blazing
    Vehicle.*'
My name should not be boastful when my pride in my strength has been
    overcome.
I have been fortunate in that I have met you. O Arjuna, wielder of celestial
    weapons,
I should like to impart to you the power of producing illusions,
that power which *Gandharvas* alone possess. My excellent chariot has been burned
by your fiery weapon. I who had formerly been called after my excellent chariot
shall now be called after my burned chariot. The science of producing illusions
I obtained long ago by ascetic penances. That science I will today impart
to the giver of my life! What good luck does he not deserve who, after
    overcoming a foe,
gives him life when that foe asks for it? This science is called Chakshushi.
It was communicated by Manu to Soma, and by Soma to Viswavasu,
and lastly by Viswavasu to me. Communicated to me by my preceptor,
that science, because I am without energy, is gradually becoming fruitless.
I have spoken to you about its origin and transmission. Listen now to its power!
With it one may see whatever one wishes to see, and in whatever way he likes,
generally or particularly. One can acquire this science only after standing on
    one leg
for six months. I shall, however, communicate to you this knowledge
without your being obliged to observe any such rigid vow.
It is for this knowledge that we are superior to men
and, as we are capable of seeing everything by spiritual sight, equal to the gods.
I intend to give you and each of your brothers a hundred steeds
born in the country of the Gandharvas. Of celestial color,
and endowed with the speed of the mind, those horses are employed
in bearing the celestials and the Gandharvas. They may be lean-fleshed,
but they never tire. In days of yore, the thunderbolt was created
for the chief of the celestials in order that he might slay Vritra, the Asura, with it.
But, hurled at Vritra's head, it broke into a thousand pieces.
The celestials worship those fragments of the thunderbolt.
What is known in the three worlds as glory is but a portion of the thunderbolt.
The hand of the Brahmana with which he pours libations on the sacrificial fire,
the chariot upon which the Kshatriya fights, the charity of the Vaisya,
and the service of the Sudra rendered to the three other classes

are all fragments of the thunderbolt. It has been said that these horses,
forming as they do a portion of the Kshatriya's chariot, are on that account
  unslayable.
Moreover, horses that form a portion of the Kshatriya's chariot
are the offspring of Vadava. Those among them that are born
in the region of the *Gandharvas* can go everywhere and assume any hue
and speed at their owners' will. These horses of mine that I give you
                will always gratify your wishes."
Arjuna replied: "O *Gandharva*, if, from satisfaction for having obtained your life
at my hands in a situation of danger, you give me your science and these horses,
                I will not accept your gift."
The *Gandharva* answered: "A meeting with an illustrious person
is always a source of gratification. Besides, you have given me my life.
Grateful to you, I will give you my science. But that the obligation
may not all be on one side, I will take from you, O bull in Bharata's race,
                your excellent and eternal weapon of fire!"
Arjuna said: "I will accept your horses in exchange for my weapon.
Let our friendship last forever. But tell us, O friend, what we human beings have
  to fear
from the Gandharvas. Chastisers of foes that we are, and virtuous,
and conversant with the Vedas, explain to us, O Gandharva,
why in traveling in the nighttime we have deserved your censure."
The Gandharva said: "You are without wives. You are without a particular *asrama*,
or mode of life. Finally, you are without a Brahmana walking before you.
Therefore, you sons of Pandu, you have deserved censure.
The Yakshas, Rakshasas, Gandharvas, Pisachas, Uragas, and Danavas
are possessed of wisdom and intelligence and are acquainted with the history
of the Kuru race. I have heard, too, from Narada and other celestial rishis
about the good deeds of your ancestors. I myself have witnessed
the prowess of your great race. I have personal knowledge of your preceptor,
the illustrious son of Bharadwaja, celebrated throughout the three worlds
for his knowledge of the Vedas and the science of arms.
I also know Dharma, Vayu, Sakra, the twin Aswins, and Pandu—
these six perpetuators of Kuru race, these excellent celestials
and human progenitors of you all. I also know that you five brothers
are learned and magnanimous, that you are foremost among wielders of
  weapons,
that you are brave and virtuous and observant of vows.
Your understanding and your hearts are excellent, and your behavior is faultless.
Still, I have censured you, for no man endowed with might of arms
should bear with patience any ill usage in the sight of his wife.
This is especially true because our might increases during the hours of darkness.
In the company of my wife, I was filled with wrath.
I have, however, been vanquished by you in battle.
Listen to me as I tell you the reasons that have led to my discomfiture.
The *Brahmacharya* is a very superior mode of life, and as you are in that mode now,
it is for this that I have been defeated by you in battle.

If any married Kshatriya fight with us at night, he can never escape with his life.
But a married Kshatriya who is sanctified with Brahma,
and who has assigned the cares of his state to a priest,
might vanquish all wanderers in the night. O child of Tapati,
men should therefore always employ learned priests
possessing self-command for the acquisition of every good luck they desire.
That Brahmana is worthy of being the king's priest
who is learned in the Vedas and the six branches thereof, who is pure and
    truthful,
and who is of virtuous soul and possessed of self-command.
The monarch becomes ever victorious and finally earns heaven
who has for his priest a Brahmana conversant with the rules of morality,
who is a master of words, and who is pure and of good behavior.
The king should always select an accomplished priest
in order to acquire what he does not have and protect what he does have.
He who desires his own prosperity should ever be guided by his priest,
for he may then obtain forever the whole earth, surrounded by her belt of seas.
O son of Tapati, a king who is without a Brahmana
can never acquire any land by his bravery or glory of birth alone.
Know, therefore, O perpetuator of Kuru's race,
that the kingdom lasts forever in which Brahmanas have power."

✦

Arjuna said: "You have addressed me more than once as Tapatya.
What is the precise significance of this word, O virtuous Gandharva?
Being sons of Kunti, we are indeed Kaunteyas.
But who is Tapati, that we should be called Tapatyas?"
To answer this question, the Gandharva related to Arjuna the following story:
"That Surya, or Vivaswat, in heaven who pervades the whole firmament by his
    light
had a daughter named Tapati. Tapati, the daughter of the god,
was the younger sister of Savitri, and was celebrated throughout the three worlds
and devoted to ascetic penances. No woman among the celestials,
the Asuras, the Yakshas, the Rakshasas, the Apsaras, and the Gandharvas
was equal to her in beauty. Of perfectly faultless features, of black and large eyes,
and in beautiful attire, the girl was chaste and of perfect conduct.
And seeing her, Surya, the sun, thought that there was none in the three worlds
who deserved for his beauty, behavior, and learning to be her husband.
When she attained the age of puberty and was worthy of being bestowed on a
    husband,
her father knew no peace of mind, always thinking of the person he should
    select.
At that time, Riksha's son, the mighty King Samvarana, was worshipping Surya
with offerings of Arghya and flower garlands and scents, and with vows and fasts
and ascetic penances. Indeed, Samvarana worshipped Surya constantly
in all his glory, with humility and piety. And Surya, beholding Samvarana

conversant with all rules of virtue and unequalled for beauty,
regarded him as the fit husband for his daughter, Tapati,
and resolved to bestow his daughter on Samvarana, that best of kings,
                              the scion of a race of worldwide fame.
As Surya himself in the heavens fills the firmament with his splendor,
so did King Samvarana on earth fill every region with the splendor of his good
    deeds.
All men except Brahmanas worshipped Samvarana.
Blessed with good luck, King Samvarana surpassed Soma in soothing the hearts
    of friends
and Surya in scorching the hearts of foes.
One day, King Samvarana went hunting in the woods on the mountain breast.
While wandering in quest of deer, on his excellent steed, he saw her.
He stood motionless, gazing at Tapati. For her beauty, the monarch first believed
that she was the goddess Sri herself. She was the embodiment of Surya's rays.
In the splendor of her person she resembled a flame of fire,
though in gentleness and loveliness she embodied the perfection of the moon.
Standing on the mountain breast, the black-eyed maiden appeared
like a bright statue of gold. The mountain itself, with its creepers and plants,
because of the beauty and attire of that damsel, seemed to have been
    transformed into gold.
The sight of the maiden inspired the monarch with contempt for all other
    women.
The king regarded his eyesight as truly blessed for the good fortune of having
    seen her.
Nothing the king had looked upon from the day of his birth could equal her
    beauty.
His heart and eyes were captivated as if they had been bound with a cord,
and he remained rooted to that spot. The monarch thought
that the artificer of so much beauty had created it only after churning the whole
    world
of gods, Asuras, and human beings. And that monarch of pure descent,
beholding the beautiful maiden, was pierced with Kama's shafts
and lost his peace of mind. Burned with the strong flame of desire,
the king asked that charming maiden, still innocent though in her full youth:
'Who are you and whose? Why do you tarry here? Why do you wander alone
in these solitary woods? You seem to be the coveted ornament
of these ornaments themselves! You seem not to be of celestial or Asura or Yaksha
or Rakshasa or Naga or Gandharva or human origin. O excellent lady,
the best of women that I have ever seen or heard of would not compare with you
in beauty! At the sight of you, lovelier than the moon and with eyes like lotus
    petals,
                              the god of desire is grinding me.'
King Samvarana thus addressed that damsel, but she spoke not a word in return.
Instead, like lightning in the clouds, that large-eyed maiden quickly vanished
    from sight.
The king then wandered through the forest like one out of his senses,

in search of that girl of eyes like lotus petals. Failing to find her, he lamented long and loud and stood motionless with grief."

The Gandharva continued: "When that maiden disappeared, the king, deprived of his senses by Kama, fell down on the earth. And as he fell, that maiden of sweet smiles and prominent and round hips appeared again before him

and said these honeyed words: 'Rise, rise, O chastiser of foes! Blessings upon you. Do not lose your reason, celebrated as you are throughout the world.'

The king opened his eyes and saw before him that same girl of swelling hips. Weak with emotion, the monarch then addressed her: 'Blessings upon you, O excellent woman of black eyes! I am burning with desire and paying you court. Accept me! My life is ebbing away. It is for your sake that Kama is piercing me with his keen shafts, without a moment's pause! I have been bitten by Kama, who is like a venomous viper. Have mercy upon me! O girl of faultless features, O girl of face like the lotus petal and of voice sweet as that of singing Kinnaras, my life now depends on you! Without you, O timid one, I am unable to live! Be merciful to me! It does not become you, O black-eyed maid, to cast me off. It behooves you to relieve me from such affliction by giving me your love! At first sight, you have attracted my heart. I cannot imagine casting my eyes on any other woman! I am your obedient slave! Accept me! The flame of desire burns within me! Extinguish that flame with the water of your love!

Marry me according to the Gandharva form, for of all forms of marriage, the Gandharva is said to be the best.'"

The Gandharva continued: "Hearing those words of the monarch, Tapati answered:

'O king, I am not the mistress of myself! I am a maiden under the control of my father.

If you really feel an affection for me, demand me of my father.

You say, O king, that your heart has been robbed by me.

But you also have, at first sight, robbed me of mine.

I am not the mistress of my body, and therefore I do not approach you.

Women are never independent. What girl is there in the three worlds who would not desire you for her husband, as you are kind to all your dependents,

and as you are born in a pure race? Therefore, when the opportunity comes, ask my father for my hand with worship, ascetic penances, and vows.

If my father bestows me upon you, then, O king, I shall ever be your obedient wife.

My name is Tapati, and I am the younger sister of Savitri, and the daughter of the sun, the illuminator of the universe.'"

The Gandharva continued: "Saying this, Tapati of faultless features ascended the skies.

The monarch again fell down on the earth, where his ministers and followers, searching for him throughout the forest, found him still lying in that solitary spot, like a rainbow dropped from the firmament. His minister-in-chief became like one burned by a fire. Advancing hastily, with affection and respect

the minister raised that best of monarchs lying prostrate on the ground,
and deprived of his senses by desire. Old in wisdom as in age,
old in achievements as in policy, the minister, after having raised the king,
grew easier in his mind. He said to the king: 'Blessings upon you, O sinless one!
It will be all right now.' The minister thought the monarch had been lying on
    the ground
                            overcome with hunger, thirst, and fatigue.
The old man then sprinkled over the crownless head cold water fragrant with
    lotus petals.
Regaining his consciousness, the monarch sent all his attendants away
with the exception of his minister. Having duly purified himself,
the king sat upon that chief of mountains and began to worship Surya.
King Samvarana thought also of his chief priest, Vasishtha, that best of rishis.
The king sat there day and night. The Brahmana sage Vasishtha came on the
    twelfth day—
that great rishi knew at once that the monarch had lost his senses because of
    Tapati.
And that virtuous and best of munis, as soon as he knew this,
addressed the monarch and gave him every assurance.
The illustrious rishi, in sight of that monarch, ascended upward to interview
    Surya.
With joined hands, the Brahmana approached the god of a thousand rays
and introduced himself cheerfully: 'I am Vasishtha.' Then Surya said to the rishi:
'Welcome, O great rishi! Tell me what is in your mind.
Whatever you demand of me, O foremost among eloquent men, I will confer
    on you,
however difficult it may be for me!' The rishi bowed to the god of light and
    answered:
'O Surya, this your daughter, Tapati, the younger sister of Savitri,
I ask of you for Samvarana, that monarch of mighty achievements.
He is conversant with virtue and magnanimity. He will make a worthy husband
for your daughter.' Surya resolved to bestow his daughter upon Samvarana,
saluted the rishi, and replied: 'O! Samvarana is the best of monarchs,
you are the best of rishis, and Tapati is the best of women.
What should we do, then, but bestow her on Samvarana?'
With these words, the god made over his daughter, Tapati, to the illustrious
    Vasishtha
to bestow upon Samvarana. The great rishi accepted the girl, took leave of
    Surya,
and returned to where that bull among the Kurus waited.
King Samvarana, possessed by love, and with his heart fixed on Tapati,
saw that celestial maiden of sweet smiles led by Vasishtha and was exceedingly
    glad.
Tapati of fair eyebrows came down to the firmament like lightning from the
    clouds,
dazzling the ten points of the heavens. The illustrious rishi, Vasishtha of pure
    soul,

approached the monarch after the latter's twelve nights' vow was over.
It was thus that King Samvarana obtained a wife."

✦

Arjuna, that mighty bowman, that foremost one in Kuru's race,
his curiosity aroused by what he had heard of Vasishtha's ascetic power,
said to the Gandharva: "I desire to hear of the rishi you have mentioned,
that Vasishtha. Tell me more about him! Who was this illustrious rishi
who was the priest of our forefathers?" The Gandharva replied:
"Vasishtha is Brahma's spiritual son and Arundhati's husband.
Desire and Wrath are always difficult even for the immortals to conquer,
but by Vasishtha's ascetic penances he vanquished them, and they used to wash
    his feet.
Though his wrath was excited by Viswamitra's offense,
that high-souled rishi did not yet exterminate the Kusikas,
the tribe over whom Viswamitra was king. Look therefore for some accomplished
and desirable Brahmana, conversant with the Vedas and in whose heart virtue
    prevails,
to appoint as your priest. A Kshatriya of good lineage, desirous of conquering
    the earth,
should have a Brahmana before him. Therefore, Arjuna, let some Brahmana
who has his senses under control and is conversant with religion, profit, and
    pleasure
be your priest." Arjuna said: "O Gandharva, how did the hostility between
    Viswamitra
and Vasishtha arise? Tell us about it." The Gandharva replied:
"The story of Vasishtha is regarded as a legend in all the three worlds.
Listen as I recite it fully. By means of arduous penances,
and with the help of Vasishtha's ascetic power, Samvarana had obtained
the beautiful Tatapi as his wife, with due rites on that mountain breast
frequented by the celestials and the Gandharvas.
With the permission of Vasishtha, he desired to sport with his wife on that
    mountain,
and he proclaimed Vasishtha as his regent in his capital and kingdom.
He sported on that mountain like a celestial, dwelling with his wife in the woods
and in the underbrush of the mountain for twelve full years.
For those twelve years, the god of a thousand eyes poured no rain on the capital
or on the kingdom. In that season of drought, the people of that kingdom,
and also trees and animals, began to die. As the drought continued,
not even a drop of dew fell from the skies, and no corn grew.
The inhabitants were in despair and afflicted with hunger and the fear of
    hunger.
They left their homes and fled in all directions.
The famished people of the country began to abandon their wives and children,
and they grew reckless of one another. Without a morsel of food,
the people were reduced to skeletons so that the capital looked like the city

of the king of the dead, full of ghostly beings. With the capital reduced to such a
    state,
Vasishtha, the illustrious and virtuous and best of rishis, decided upon a remedy,
and he brought King Samvarana and his wife back to the city after their long
    seclusion.
When the king entered his capital and came back to his own,
the god of a thousand eyes, the slayer of Asuras, poured rain in abundance
and caused corn to grow. The capital and the country were animated with great joy.
The monarch and his wife, Tapati, once more performed sacrifices
like the lord Indra, god of rain, performing sacrifices with his wife, Sachi."
The Gandharva continued: "This is the history of Tapati of old, the daughter of
    Vivaswat.
It is for her that you are called Tapatya, for King Samvarana begot upon Tapati
a son named Kuru, who was foremost among ascetics. Born in the race of Kuru,
you are, O Arjuna, to be called Tapatya." Arjuna, hearing these words of the
    Gandharva,

                    was inspired with feelings of devotion and stood quite still.

                                    ✦

The Gandharva continued: "Once upon a time, while out hunting, King
    Viswamitra
grew tired and thirsty and realized that he was near the home of Vasishtha,
which he decided to visit. The blessed and illustrious rishi paid him reverence,
saluted the king, and offered him water to wash his face and feet
and also Arghya and wild fruits and clarified butter.
The illustrious rishi had a cow yielding anything that was desired of her.
When she was addressed with the words *O give*, she always gave whatever was
    sought.
She gave various fruits and corn, wild or grown in gardens and fields, and milk,
    of course,
and many excellent foods full of different kinds of tastes, and other enjoyable
    things,
including precious gems and robes of various cloths. The rishi presented the
    monarch
with these desirable objects in profusion, and the king, his minister, and his
    troops
were highly pleased. And the king was amazed by that cow, with four elevated
    limbs
and beautiful flanks and hips that were broad and eyes as prominent as those of
    the frog,
beautiful in size with high udders and straight uplifted ears, handsome horns,
and a strong head and neck. The son of Gadhi applauded the cow named
    Nandini
and spoke to the rishi, saying: 'O Brahmana, give me your Nandini
in exchange for ten thousand cattle, or my kingdom. Enjoy my kingdom
by giving me this cow.' Vasishtha answered: 'I have kept this cow

for the sake of the gods, guests, and the Pitris, and also for my sacrifices.
I cannot give Nandini in exchange even for your kingdom.'
Viswamitra replied: 'I am a Kshatriya, but you are a Brahmana
devoted to asceticism and study. Is there any energy in Brahmanas who are peaceful
and who have their souls under perfect command?
If you do not give me what I desire in exchange even for ten thousand cows,
I will not abandon the practice of my order, and I will take the cow, even by force!'
Vasishtha said: 'You are a Kshatriya endowed with might of arms.
You are a powerful monarch. Do whatever you want.
Do not pause to consider the propriety of your action.'"
The Gandharva continued: "Viswamitra then forcibly seized Nandini,
that cow as white as a swan, and attempted to take her away, whipping and beating her.
The innocent Nandini began to moo piteously. She approached Vasishtha
and stood before him with uplifted face. Though she was treated very cruelly,
she refused to leave the rishi's estate. Moved by her plight, Vasishtha said:
'O amiable one, you are lowing repeatedly, and I hear your cries.
But King Viswamitra is taking you by force. What can I do as a forgiving Brahmana?'"
The Gandharva continued: "Then Nandini, alarmed by the sight of Viswamitra's troops,
and terrified by Viswamitra himself, approached the rishi still closer and said:
'Why are you so indifferent to me, afflicted as I am by the cruel troops of Viswamitra
and crying so piteously, as if I were masterless?' The great rishi was saddened,
but he did not lose his patience or turn from his vow of forgiveness. He said to the cow:
'The Kshatriya's might lies in physical strength; the Brahmana's, in forgiveness.
Because I cannot give up forgiveness, go, O Nandini, if you choose to do so.'
Nandini answered: 'Do you cast me away, O illustrious one?
If you do not cast me off, I cannot be taken away by force.'
Vasishtha said: 'O blessed one, I do not cast you off! Stay if you can!
Over there is your calf, tied with a stout cord, and even now being weakened by it!'"
The Gandharva continued: "Then the cow of Vasishtha, hearing the word *stay*,
raised her head and neck upward and became terrible to behold.
With eyes red with rage, and bellowing repeatedly, she attacked Viswamitra's troops.
Her wrath increased as, afflicted with their stripes, she ran this way and that with those red eyes of hers
blazing with rage. She became terrible to behold,
like the sun in his midday glory. From her tail she began to rain showers of burning coals,
and also from her tail she brought forth an army of Palhavas;
and from her udders, an army of Dravidas and Sakas;

from her womb, an army of Yavanas; from her dung, an army of Savaras;
from her urine, an army of Kanchis; and from her sides, another army of
    Savaras.
And from the froth of her mouth came hosts of Paundras and Kiratas,
Yavanas and Sinhalas, and the barbarous tribes of Khasas and Chivukas
and Pulindas and Chinas and Hunas with Keralas, and numerous other
    Mlechchhas.
That vast army, deployed in the sight of Viswamitra,
attacked that monarch's soldiers. So numerous was that Mlechchha host
that each of the soldiers of Viswamitra was attacked by a band of six or seven of
    their enemies.
Assailed with a mighty shower of weapons, Viswamitra's troops broke and fled,
panic-stricken, in all directions, before his eyes. But the troops of Vasishtha,
although excited with wrath, did not take the life of any of Viswamitra's troops.
Nandini simply caused the monarch's army to be routed and driven off.
They were driven from the rishi's estate and ran a full twenty-seven miles,
    panic-stricken
and shrieking aloud, and they tried to find anyone who could protect them.
Viswamitra, seeing this wonderful feat that resulted from Brahmana prowess,
became disgusted with Kshatriya prowess and said: 'Never mind Kshatriya
    prowess!
Brahmana prowess is true prowess! In judging of strength and weakness,
I see that asceticism is true strength.' Saying this, the monarch
abandoned his large domains and regal splendor and turned his back upon all
    pleasures.
Instead, he set his mind on asceticism. Crowned with success in asceticism
and filling the three worlds with the fervor of his ascetic penances,
he finally became a Brahmana and at last drank soma with Indra himself in
    heaven."

12

Vasishtha

The Gandharva continued: "There was a king in this world named Kalmashapada,
of the race of Ikshvaku, and he was unequaled on earth for prowess.
One day this king went into the woods to hunt, and he pierced with his arrows
many deer and wild boars. In those deep woods the king also slew many rhinoceroses.
Engaged in sport for some length of time, the king became fatigued
and gave up the chase, desiring to rest awhile.
The great Viswamitra had previously decided to make Kalmashapada his disciple.
As that monarch, hungry and thirsty, was traveling through the woods,
he came across that best of rishis, the illustrious son of Vasishtha, on the same path.
The king saw the muni named Saktri, the eldest of Vasishtha's hundred sons,
coming from opposite direction. The king said: 'Stand out of our way.'
The rishi, in a conciliatory manner, answered sweetly: 'O king, this is my way.
This is the eternal rule of morality indicated in every treatise on duty and religion—
that a king should always make way for Brahmanas.'
Thus did they speak to each other, saying: 'Stand aside, stand aside.'
The rishi, who was in the right, did not yield, and neither did the proud and angry king.
Instead, enraged by the rishi, and refusing to yield him the way, he acted like a Rakshasa,
striking him with his whip. That best of rishis, the son of Vasishtha, was angered,
and he cursed that monarch, saying: 'O worst of kings,
since you persecute an ascetic like some Rakshasa, you shall from this day became one
and subsist on human flesh! Go hence, worst of kings! You shall wander the earth,
disguised in human form!' Thus did the rishi Saktri speak to King Kalmashapada.
At this time, Viswamitra approached the place. Between him and Vasishtha
there was a dispute about the discipleship of Kalmashapada.
And Viswamitra, a rishi of severe ascetic penances, approached the pair,
knowing by his spiritual insight that they had been quarreling with each other.

After the curse had been pronounced, the king knew that rishi to be
Vasishtha's son
and equal to Vasishtha in energy. Hoping to benefit himself, Viswamitra
remained there,
concealed from both of them. Then the monarch whom Saktri had cursed,
eager to propitiate the rishi, besought him.
Viswamitra, fearing that the difference might thus be made up,
ordered a Rakshasa to enter the body of the king.
A Rakshasa of the name of Kinkara then entered the monarch's body,
in obedience to Saktri's curse and Viswamitra's command.
And Viswamitra, that best of rishis, knowing that the Rakshasa had possessed
himself of the monarch,
was satisfied and departed.
Soon thereafter, terribly afflicted by the Rakshasa, the king lost all his senses.
At this time, a Brahmana beheld him in the woods and, hungry, begged the king
for some food with meat. Kalmashapada answered: 'Stay here for a moment.
On my return, I will give you whatever food you desire.'
The monarch went away while the Brahmana stayed.
The high-minded king roved for some time and at last entered his inner
apartment.
But, waking at midnight and remembering his promise, he summoned his cook,
told him of his promise to the Brahmana in the forest, and commanded him:
'Hurry to that forest. A Brahmana waits for me in the hope of food.
Go and provide him with food and meat.'
The cook went out in search of meat but could not find any,
and he informed the king of his failure.
The monarch, possessed as he was by the Rakshasa, said without scruple of any
kind:
'Feed him with human flesh.' The cook said: 'So be it.'
And he went to the place where the king's executioners were, took some human
flesh,
washed and cooked it, and covered it with boiled rice.
That was what he brought to the hungry Brahmana. With his spiritual sight,
the Brahmana saw that the food was unholy and unworthy of being eaten.
Red with anger, he said: 'Because that worst of kings offers me food that is unholy
and unworthy of being taken, he shall develop a fondness for such food
for himself. And, as cursed by Saktri of old, the wretch shall wander the earth,
alarming and otherwise troubling all creatures.'
The curse on that king, thus repeated a second time, became doubly strong,
and the king, possessed by a Rakshasa disposition, soon lost all his senses.
A little while after, the king encountered Saktri, who had cursed him, and said:
'Because you pronounced upon me this extraordinary curse,
I shall begin my life of cannibalism by devouring you.'
The king forthwith slew Saktri and ate him, like a tiger eating an animal.
Seeing that Saktri had thus been slain and devoured, Viswamitra urged the
Rakshasa
within the monarch against the other sons of Vasishtha.

Like a wrathful lion preying upon small animals,
the Rakshasa soon devoured the other sons of the illustrious Vasishtha junior to
    Saktri.
When Vasishtha learned that all his sons had been slain at Viswamitra's urging,
he bore his grief like the great mountain that bears the earth.
That best of munis was resolved rather to sacrifice his own life
than to exterminate in anger the race of Kusikas.
The rishi threw himself from the summit of Meru but landed upon the stony
    ground
as though onto a heap of cotton. When he found that death had not resulted
    from his fall,
he kindled a huge fire in the forest and strode into the middle of it,
but the fire, though burning brightly, did not consume him.
Rather, the blazing fire seemed cool to him. Then the great muni, grief-stricken,
went to the seashore, tied a stony weight to his neck, and threw himself into the
    water.
But the waves soon cast him ashore. At last, having failed to kill himself
by any means that he had tried, the Brahmana returned, in distress of heart, to
    his estate.
His estate, however, was without any of his children,
and the muni was afflicted with great grief. Therefore, he left it again.
And in his wandering he saw a river swollen with the waters of the rainy season,
sweeping away numberless trees and plants that had grown on its margin.
The distressed muni thought he would certainly be drowned if he fell into that
    river,
so he tied himself securely with cords and flung himself into the current.
But the stream cut the cords and cast the rishi ashore. He rose from the riverbank
and, because his cords had thus been broken off by the violence of the current,
the rishi called the stream Vipasa, meaning '*Cord Breaker.*'
Because of his grief, the muni could not from that time stay in one place.
He began to wander over mountains and along rivers and lakes.
And beholding once again a river named Haimavati, flowing from Himavat,
of terrible aspect and full of crocodiles and other monsters, the rishi threw
    himself in,
but the river mistook the Brahmana for a great ball of unquenchable fire
and immediately flew in a hundred different directions.
Since then it has been known by the name of the Satadru, meaning '*River of a
    Hundred Courses.*'
On dry land again, he exclaimed: 'I cannot die by my own hand!'
Once more he bent his steps toward home, crossing numberless mountains.
As he was about to reenter his estate, he was met by his daughter-in-law,
    Adrisyanti.
As she neared him, he heard the sound of a very intelligent recitation of the
    Vedas,
with the six graces of elocution. The rishi asked: 'Who is that?'
His daughter-in-law answered: 'I am Adrisyanti, the wife of Saktri.
I am helpless, though devoted to asceticism.'

Vasishtha said: 'But whose is this voice that I heard, repeating the Vedas and the
    Angas
with a voice like that of Saktri?' Adrisyanti answered: 'I bear in my womb
a child by your son Saktri. He has been there a full twelve years.
The voice you hear is that of the unborn child, who is reciting the Vedas.'

Hearing this, the illustrious Vasishtha was very glad.
He said to himself: *Oh! there is a child of my race!*
And he refrained from further attempts at self-destruction.
Accompanied by his daughter-in-law, he returned to his estate.
One day in the solitary woods, Vasishtha and Adrisyanti encountered
    Kalmashapada.
Possessed by the fierce Rakshasa, the king, as he saw the rishi, was filled with
    wrath
and rose up to devour him. Adrisyanti, terrified, addressed her father-in-law:
'Illustrious one, the cruel Rakshasa, like death himself armed with a fierce club,
comes toward us! No one else on earth is conversant enough with the Vedas
to restrain him today. Protect me from this cruel wretch of terrible visage.'
Vasishtha answered: 'Fear not, O daughter, there is no need to fear any Rakshasa.
This is no Rakshasa but is King Kalmashapada endowed with great energy
and celebrated on earth. That terrible man dwells in these woods.'
As the king was approaching, Vasishtha restrained him
by uttering the sound *hum.* Sprinkling the king with water sanctified with
    incantations,
the rishi freed the monarch from that terrible curse.
For twelve years the monarch had been overwhelmed by the energy of
    Vasishtha's son,
as Surya is seized by the planet Rahu during the season of an eclipse.
But, freed now from the Rakshasa, the monarch lit that large forest with his
    splendor,
like the sun illuminating the evening clouds.
Recovering his power of reason, the king saluted that best of rishis
and with joined palms said: 'Illustrious one, I am the son of Sudasa, and your
    disciple.
Best of munis, tell me what is your pleasure and what I am to do.'
Vasishtha replied: 'My desire has already been accomplished.
Return to your kingdom and rule your subjects. And never insult Brahmanas
    anymore.'
The monarch replied: 'O illustrious one, I shall never again insult Brahmanas.
In obedience to your command, I shall always worship Brahmanas.
But I desire to obtain from you that by which I may be freed
from the debt I owe to the race of Ikshvaku!
O best of men, grant me, for the perpetuation of the Ikshvaku race,
a desirable son possessing beauty and accomplishments and good behavior.'
Vasishtha replied to that mighty bowman of a monarch:
'I will give this to you.' After some time, Vasishtha and the king
went to the latter's capital, known all over the earth by the name of Ayodhya.

The citizens came out in great joy to receive the sinless and illustrious one,
like the dwellers in heaven coming out to receive their chief.
The monarch, accompanied by Vasishtha, reentered his capital after a long
    absence.
He was superior to everyone in beauty and filled the town of Ayodhya with his
    splendor,
as the autumn moon fills the whole firmament with his splendor.
And the excellent city, with its streets watered and swept,
and with rows of banners and pendants everywhere, gladdened the monarch's
    heart.
After the royal sage had entered his capital, the queen, at the king's command,
approached Vasishtha. The great rishi made a covenant with her
and united himself with her according to the ordinance.
And after a little while, when the queen conceived,
Vasishtha, that best of rishis, received the reverential salutations of the king
and went back to his estate. The queen bore the embryo in her womb for a long
    time.
When she saw that she did not bring forth anything,
she tore open her womb with a piece of stone.
It was then, in the twelfth year of her pregnancy, that Asmaka was born,
that bull among men, the royal sage who founded the city of Paudanya."

✦

The Gandharva continued: "Adrisyanti, who had been residing in Vasishtha's
    estate,
at last brought forth a son who was the perpetuator of Saktri's race.
Vasishtha himself performed the usual after-birth ceremonies of his grandson.
And because the rishi Vasishtha had decided to kill himself, but had changed his
    mind
when he learned of the existence of that child, the child was called Parasara,
meaning '*Vivifier of the Dead.*' From the day of his birth, Parasara knew Vasishtha
    for his father
and behaved toward him as if that were their relationship.
One day, the child addressed Vasishtha as his *father*
in the presence of his mother, Adrisyanti. Adrisyanti addressed him with tearful
    eyes
and said: 'O child, do not address your grandfather as your *father*.
Your father has been devoured by a Rakshasa. This is not your father
but the father of your father.' Parasara gave way to sorrow, but the sorrow soon
    changed
to anger, and he resolved to destroy the whole of creation.
But Vasishtha, that foremost among persons conversant with Brahma,
addressed his grandson with arguments that drove that resolution from his
    mind.

✦

"What Vasishtha said," the Gandharva continued, "was this:

'There was a celebrated king named Kritavirya, a bull among the kings of the
  earth.

He was the disciple of the Veda-knowing Bhrigus.

After performing the soma sacrifice, that king gratified the Brahmanas

with great presents of rice and wealth. But after that monarch had ascended to
  heaven,

an occasion came when his descendants were in want of wealth.

Knowing that the Bhrigus were rich, those princes went to those Brahmanas

in the guise of beggars. Some among the Bhrigus buried their wealth to protect it.

Some, from fear of the Kshatriyas, gave their wealth to other Brahmanas.

And some gave the Kshatriyas whatever they wanted.

It happened, however, that some Kshatriyas, digging at the house of particular a
  Bhargava,

came upon a large treasure, which was seen by all of them.

Enraged by what they regarded as the deceitful behavior of the Bhrigus,

the Kshatriyas insulted the Brahmanas, though the latter asked for mercy,

and those mighty bowmen slaughtered the Bhrigus with their sharp arrows.

The Kshatriyas wandered the earth, slaughtering even embryos in wombs.

And while the Bhrigu race was being exterminated, the frightened women of
  that tribe

fled to the inaccessible mountains of Himavat. One among them,

desiring to perpetuate her husband's race, held in one of her thighs an embryo

endowed with great energy. A certain Brahmana woman, however,

who learned of this, went from fear to the Kshatriyas and reported to them.

The Kshatriyas then went to destroy that embryo.

When they arrived at the place where the woman was hiding,

they beheld the would-be mother blazing with inborn energy,

and the child in her thigh came out, tearing up the thigh

and dazzling the eyes of those Kshatriyas, like the midday sun.

Deprived of their eyesight, the Kshatriyas wandered over those inaccessible
  mountains.

The blind princes were afflicted with woe and, eager to regain the use of their
  eyes,

resolved to seek the protection of that faultless woman.

The grieving Kshatriyas addressed that illustrious lady, saying:

"By your grace, dear lady, we wish to be restored to sight.

We shall then return together to our homes and abstain forever from our sinful
  practice.

O beautiful one, it behooves you and your child to show us mercy."

The Brahmana lady, thus addressed, said:

"I have not robbed you of your eyesight, nor am I angry with you.

This child, however, of the Bhrigu race is certainly angry with you.

You have been robbed of your sight by this illustrious child,

whose wrath has been aroused by his remembrance of your slaughter of his race.

While you were destroying even the embryos of the Bhrigu race,

I held this child in my thigh for a hundred years!

And in order that the prosperity of Bhrigu's race might be restored,
the entire *Vedas*, with their branches, came to this one even while he was in the
  womb.
It is plain that this scion of the Bhrigu race, enraged by the slaughter of his
  fathers,
desires to slay you! It is by his celestial energy that your eyes have been scorched.
Pray, therefore, to this excellent child born of my thigh.
Propitiated by your homage, he may perhaps restore your eyesight."
Hearing those words of the Brahmana lady,
the princes addressed the thigh-born child, saying: "Be propitious!"
And the child was propitious to them. That best of Brahmana rishis,
because he had been born tearing open his mother's thigh,
came to be known throughout the three worlds by the name of Aurva, meaning
  "*Thigh-Born.*"
The princes regained their eyesight and went away,
but Aurva of the Bhrigu race was still resolved upon overcoming the whole world.
The high-souled rishi set his heart upon the destruction of every creature in the
  world.
And that scion of the Bhrigu race, to pay homage to his slaughtered ancestors,
devoted himself to the most austere of penances, with the object of destroying
  the world.
In order to gratify his ancestors, the rishi afflicted with his severe asceticism
the three worlds of the celestials, the Asuras, and human beings.
The Pitris, learning what the child of their race was doing,
all came from their own region to the rishi and said: "Aurva,
you have been fierce in your asceticism. We have witnessed your power.
Be propitious to the three worlds, and control your wrath.
O child, it was not from incapacity that the Bhrigus were indifferent
to their destruction at the hands of the murderous Kshatriyas.
Rather, it was when we grew weary of the long periods of life allotted to us
that we desired our own destruction through the instrumentality of the
  Kshatriyas.
The wealth that the Bhrigus had placed in their house underground
was only with the object of enraging the Kshatriyas and picking a quarrel with
  them.
We were desirous of heaven. Of what use, then, could wealth be to us?
The treasurer of heaven, Kuvera, had kept a large treasure for us.
When we found that death could not overtake us all,
we decided that this was the best means of achieving our desire.
They who commit suicide never attain to regions that are blessed.
We abstained therefore from self-destruction. What you plan to do is not
  agreeable to us.
Restrain your mind, then, from the sinful act of destroying the whole world.
Kill this wrath of yours that stains your ascetic energy."
To these words of the Pitris, Aurva replied:
"You Pitris, the vow I have made from anger for the destruction of all the worlds
must not be in vain. I cannot consent to be one whose anger and vows are futile.

Like fire consuming dry woods, this rage of mine will consume me
if I do not accomplish my vow. The man who represses wrath excited by just
cause
becomes incapable of compassing the three ends of life—religion, profit, and
pleasure.
The wrath of kings who desire to subjugate the whole earth is not without its uses.
It serves to restrain the wicked and protect the honest. While lying unborn
within my mother's thigh, I heard the doleful cries of my mother
and other women of the Bhrigu race, who were being exterminated by the
Kshatriyas.
You Pitris, when those wretches of Kshatriyas began to exterminate the Bhrigus
and even the unborn children of their race, it was then that wrath filled my soul.
My mother and the other women of our race, each in an advanced state of
pregnancy,
and my father and the other fathers could not find in all the worlds a single
protector.
My mother held me in one of her thighs. If there were punishers of crimes in
the worlds,
no one in all the worlds would dare commit a crime.
If they do not find punishers, the number of sinners becomes large.
The man who has the power to prevent or punish sin and does not do so,
knowing that a sin has been committed, is himself defiled by that sin.
When kings and others capable of protecting my fathers fail to protect them,
postponing that duty and preferring the pleasures of life, I have just cause
to be enraged by them. I am the lord of creation, capable of punishing its
iniquity.
I am incapable of obeying your command. I have the power to punish this
crime,
and if I abstain from doing so, men will once more have to undergo a similar
persecution.
The fire of my wrath is ready to consume the worlds,
but if it is repressed, it will certainly consume me.
You masters, I know that you always seek the good of the worlds.
Direct me, then, regarding what may benefit both myself and the three worlds."
The Pitris replied: "Throw this fire that is born of your wrath,
and that desires to consume the worlds, into the waters. That will do you good.
The worlds are all dependent on water. Every juicy substance contains water,
and indeed the whole universe is made of water. Cast this fire of your wrath,
therefore,
into the waters. If you like, O Brahmana, let this fire born of your wrath
abide in the great ocean, consuming its waters. In this way, O sinless one,
your word will be rendered true, and the worlds, with the gods, will not be
destroyed."
Then Aurva cast the fire of his wrath into the abode of Varuna.
And that fire which consumed the waters of the great ocean
became like a large horse's head, which persons conversant with the Vedas
call by the name of Vadavamukha. And with its mouth it consumes

the waters of the mighty ocean. Blessings upon you!
You do not need to destroy the worlds, Parasara!'
The Brahmana Parasara, thus addressed by Vasishtha,
restrained his wrath from destroying the worlds.
But the rishi Parasara, son of Saktri, endowed with great energy,
performed a Rakshasa sacrifice. And remembering the slaughter of his father,
  Saktri,
he began to consume the Rakshasas, young and old, in the sacrifice he
  performed.
Vasishtha did not restrain him from this slaughter of the Rakshasas,
not wanting to obstruct this second vow of his grandson.
In that sacrifice, Parasara sat before three blazing fires, and he was like a fourth
  fire.
The son of Saktri, like the sun just emerging from the clouds,
illuminated the whole firmament by that stainless sacrifice of his,
into which were poured large libations of clarified butter.
Then Vasishtha and the other rishis beheld that muni blazing with his own
  energy
as if he were a second sun. The great rishi Atri, of liberal soul,
hoping to end that sacrifice, came to Parasara. And there also came Pulastya and
  Pulaha
and Kratu, the performer of many great sacrifices, all desiring to save the
  Rakshasas.
Pulastya, seeing that many Rakshasas had already been slain,
said these words to Parasara: 'There is no obstruction, I hope, to this sacrifice of
  yours!
But do you take pleasure, O child, in this slaughter of all those innocent
  Rakshasas,
who know nothing of your father's death? You must not destroy any creatures
  thus.
This is not the occupation of a Brahmana devoted to asceticism.
Peace is the highest virtue. Therefore, O Parasara, establish peace.
How have you engaged yourself in such a sinful practice?
It does not behoove you to transgress against Saktri himself,
who was well acquainted with all rules of morality. What befell your father
was brought about by his own curse. It was his fault that Saktri was taken into
  heaven.
No Rakshasa was capable of devouring Saktri. He himself provided for his own
  death.
Viswamitra was only a blind instrument in that matter.
Both Saktri and Kalmashapada, having ascended to heaven, are enjoying great
  happiness.
And the younger sons of the great rishi Vasishtha
are also enjoying themselves with the celestials.
You, O child, offspring of Vasishtha's son, have been, in this sacrifice,
only an instrument in the destruction of these innocent Rakshasas.
Blessings upon you! Abandon this sacrifice. Let it come to an end.'

After listening to the words of Pulastya
and of the intelligent Vasishtha, that mighty muni, the son of Saktri,
brought the sacrifice to an end. He cast the fire he had ignited
for the purpose of the Rakshasas' sacrifice deep into the woods
on the north of the Himavat. And there the fire may be seen to this day,
consuming Rakshasas and trees and stones in all seasons."

13

Draupadi

Arjuna asked: "O Gandharva, tell us which Veda-knowing Brahmana
is worthy to be appointed as our priest." The Gandharva replied:
"Dhaumya, the younger brother of Devala, is engaged in the woods in ascetic
   penances.
                    Appoint him, if you like, as your priest."
Arjuna, pleased with all that had happened, gave that Gandharva his weapon of
   fire
with befitting ceremonies. And he said: "Let the horses remain with you for a time.
When the occasion comes, we will take them from you. Blessings upon you."
The Gandharva and the Pandavas then saluted each other and parted ways.
The Pandavas went to Utkochaka, the ashram of Dhaumya, to install him as their
   priest.
He received them with wild fruits and edible roots and consented to their
   request.
The Pandavas and their mother then regarded their sovereignty as already
   regained,
and the daughter of the Panchala king as already obtained.
Those bulls of the Bharata race, with the master Dhaumya as their priest,
also regarded themselves as under a powerful protector. And the high-souled
   Dhaumya
made the Pandavashis Yajamanas, or spiritual disciples, and considered them
already restored, by their own accomplishments, to their sovereignty and
   kingdom.
Those kings of men accepted the benedictions of the Brahmana and resolved
   to go
to the Swayamvara of the princess of Panchala. They set out for Panchala
to see that country and Draupadi and the festivities in expectation of her
   marriage.
Those tigers among men met on the way numerous Brahmanas proceeding
   together
who inquired of the Pandavas: "Whither are you going? From whence have you
   come?"
Yudhishthira replied: "We are brothers traveling with our mother,
coming from Ekachakra." The Brahmanas then said:
"Go this very day to the abode of Drupada in the country of the Panchalas.

A great Swayamvara takes place there. That is where we also are going.
Let us go together. Extraordinary festivities will take place at Drupada's palace.
He has a daughter, risen from the center of the sacrificial altar, with eyes like
    lotus petals
and of faultless features, endowed with youth and intelligence.
She is extremely beautiful. And the slender-waisted Draupadi,
whose body emits a fragrance like that of the blue lotus for two full miles around,
is the sister of the strong-armed Dhrishtadyumna—the would-be slayer of Drona—
who was born with natural mail and sword and bow and arrows from the blazing
    fire,
himself like a second fire. And that daughter of Drupada will select a husband
from among the invited princes. We are going there to see her and the
    festivities,
                        which will be like the festivities of heaven.
To that Swayamvara there will come from various lands kings and princes,
who are performers of sacrifices in which the presents to the Brahmanas are large;
who are devoted to study, are holy and illustrious and of rigid vows;
who are young and handsome; and who are mighty car warriors, accomplished
    in arms.
Hoping to win the hand of the maiden, those monarchs will give away much
    wealth,
cattle and food, and other articles of value. And taking all they will give away,
and witnessing the Swayamvara, and enjoying the festivities,
we shall go wherever we like. There will also be coming to that Swayamvara
from various countries actors and charanas singing the panegyrics of kings,
and dancers, and reciters of Puranas, and heralds, and powerful athletes.
You can see all these sights and receive what will be given away to illustrious ones,
and then you can return with us. You are all handsome as the celestials!
When she sees you, Draupadi may perhaps choose one of you
as superior to the rest. Your brother here, of mighty arms and handsome
and endowed with prowess in athletic encounters, may by chance earn great
    wealth."
To these words, Yudhishthira replied: "Brahmanas, we will go with you
to witness that maiden's Swayamvara, that excellent jubilee."
The Pandavas then proceeded toward the country of the southern Panchalas,
ruled over by King Drupada. On their way, they encountered the illustrious
    Dwaipayana,
a muni of pure soul and perfectly sinless. Saluting that rishi and saluted by him,
they conversed together and were commanded by him to proceed to Drupada's
    palace.
They traveled by slow stages, staying for some time within those beautiful woods
and by fine lakes that they beheld along their way. Devoted to study,
pure in their practices, amiable, and well spoken, the Pandavas at last entered
the country of the Panchalas. They reached the capital, which was also a fortress,
and they took up their quarters in the house of a potter.
Adopting the Brahmanical profession, they led a mendicant life,
and no one recognized them during their stay in Drupada's capital.

✦

Drupada had always cherished the desire of bestowing his daughter on Arjuna,
the son of Pandu. But he had never spoken of this to anybody.
And the king of Panchala, with Arjuna in mind, had ordered a very stiff bow to
be made
that no one else could bend. He ordered a device to be erected in the sky,
and he attached to a target that machinery.
Drupada said: "He who can string this bow and with these arrows hit the target
that hangs from the device shall obtain my daughter."
With these words, King Drupada proclaimed the Swayamvara.
On hearing of this, the kings of many other lands came to his capital.
There also came many illustrious rishis who wanted to behold the Swayamvara.
Duryodhana and the Kurus attended, accompanied by Kama,
and there were many superior Brahmanas from every country.
The citizens, roaring like the sea, all took their seats on the platforms
around the amphitheater. The monarch entered by the northeastern gate.
The amphitheater, erected on an auspicious and level plain to the northeast of
the capital,
was surrounded by beautiful mansions, enclosed on all sides
by high walls and surrounded by a moat, with arched doorways here and there.
It was shaded by a canopy of various colors, scented with black aloes,
sprinkled all over with water mixed with sandalwood paste, and decorated with
flowers.
Those mansions that surrounded it were perfectly white
and resembled the cloud-kissing peaks of Kailasa.
The windows of those palaces were covered with networks of gold;
the walls were set with diamonds and hung with precious carpets and tapestries,
and they too were adorned with garlands of flowers and fragrant with excellent
aloes.
The palaces were as white and spotless as the necks of swans,
and their fragrance could be perceived from eight miles, the distance of a *yojana*.
Each was furnished with a hundred doors wide enough to admit a large crowd.
Furnished with costly beds and carpets, and beautified with various metals,
they resembled the peaks of the Himavat. In those seven-storied houses of
various sizes
dwelled the monarchs Drupada had invited, their persons adorned
with every ornament, who desired to surpass one another.
The amphitheater resounded with the notes of thousands of trumpets as the
inhabitants
of the city and the country who had come to behold Krishnā took their seats.
They looked about them, and they could see seated within those mansions
those lions among kings, all adorned with the fragrant paste of black aloe.
Of great liberality, the kings were all devoted to Brahma;
they protected their kingdoms against all foes,
and for their good deeds they were loved by the whole world.
The Pandavas, too, entered the amphitheater

and sat with the Brahmanas. They beheld the unrivaled wealth
of the king of the Panchalas as well as that concourse of princes, Brahmanas,
and others looking festive for the occasion. There were actors and dancers
performing for the generous crowd, which swelled day by day.
The festivities lasted until the sixteenth day,
when the daughter of Drupada, having washed herself clean,
entered the amphitheatre, richly attired and adorned with every ornament
and bearing in her hand a dish of gold with usual offerings of Arghya and
    flowers.
Then the priest ignited the sacrificial fire and poured upon it libations of
    clarified butter.
Gratifying Agni, the god of fire, by these libations and making the Brahmanas
    utter
the auspicious formula of benediction, he silenced the musical instruments.
And when the vast amphitheater became perfectly still, Dhrishtadyumna,
with a voice as deep as the sound of the kettledrum, took hold of his sister's arm,
stood in the midst of that concourse, and said these words: "Hear, O assembled
    kings!
This is the bow; that is the mark; and these are the arrows.
Shoot the mark through the orifice of the machine with these five sharpened
    arrows.
Whoever achieves this great feat shall obtain today my sister, Krishnā, called
    Draupadi,
as his wife." Drupada's son then addressed his sister,
reciting to her the names, lineages, and achievements of those assembled lords.
Dhrishtadyumna said: "Duryodhana, Durvisaha, Durmukha and
    Dushpradharshana,
Vivinsati, Vikarna, Saha, and Duhsasana; Yuyutsu and Vayuvega and
    Bhimavegarava;
Ugrayudha, Valaki, Kanakayu, and Virochana, Sukundala, Chitrasena, Suvarcha,
and Kanakadhwaja; Nandaka, and Vahusali, and Tuhunda, and Vikata:
these, O sister, and many other mighty sons of Dhritarashtra—all heroes,
accompanied by Karna—have come for your hand.
Innumerable other illustrious monarchs, all bulls among Kshatriyas,
have also come for you: Sakuni, Sauvala, Vrisaka, and Vrihadvala,
these sons of King Gandharva, have come. Foremost among wielders of
    weapons,
the illustrious Aswatthaman and Bhoja, adorned with every ornament,
have also come for you. Vrihanta, Manimana, Dandadhara, Sahadeva,
Jayatsena, Meghasandhi, Virata with his two sons Sankha and Uttara,
Vardhakshemi, Susarma, Senavindu, Suketu with his two sons Sunama and
    Suvarcha,
and the powerful Jarasandha—these and many other great kings,
all Kshatriyas celebrated throughout the world, have come, O blessed one, for you.
These will shoot at the mark. And you shall choose for your husband
                              whoever among these will hit it."
Then those youthful princes—adorned with earrings, vying with one another,

and each regarding himself accomplished in arms and gifted with might—
stood up, brandishing their weapons. Intoxicated with pride of beauty, prowess,
lineage, knowledge, wealth, and youth, they were like Himalayan elephants in rut,
with crowns split from excess of temporal juice.
And glaring at each other with jealousy, and influenced by the god of desire,
they rose up from their royal seats, exclaiming: "Draupadi shall be mine!"
Each of the Kshatriyas in the amphitheater desired to win the daughter of
    Drupada.
They looked like the celestials standing round Uma,
the daughter of the king of mountains. Afflicted with the shafts
of the god of the flowery bow, and with hearts utterly lost
in the contemplation of Krishnā, the princes descended into the amphitheater
and regarded even their best friends with jealousy.
There also came the celestials on their cars, with the Rudras and the Adityas, the
    Vasus
and the twin Aswins, the Swadhas and all the Marutas, and Kuvera,
with Yama walking ahead. And the Daityas came and the Suparnas,
the great Nagas and the celestial rishis, the Guhyakas and the charanas, and
    Viswavasu,
and Narada, and Parvata, and the principal Gandharvas with Apsaras.
And Halayudha, called Valadeva, and Janardana, called Krishna,
and the chief of the Vrishni, Andhaka, and Yadava tribes, who obeyed Krishna.
Beholding those elephants in rut—the five Pandavas,
attracted by Draupadi as mighty elephants are drawn to a lake overgrown with
    lotuses,
or like fire covered with ashes—Krishna, foremost among Yadu heroes, began to
    reflect,
and he said to Rama: "That is Yudhishthira; that is Bhima with Arjuna;
                           and those are Nakula and Sahadeva, the twin
    heroes."
Rama surveyed them slowly and cast a glance of satisfaction at Krishnā.
Biting their lower lips in wrath, the other heroes there, sons and grandsons of
    kings,
with their eyes and hearts and thoughts set on Krishnā,
looked with widened eyes on her alone without noticing the Pandavas,
who also stared at her, and all were struck by the shafts of Kama.
Crowded with celestial rishis and Gandharvas
and Suparnas and Nagas and Asuras and siddhas,
and filled with celestial perfumes, and scattered over with celestial flowers,
and resounding with the kettledrum and the deep hum of infinite voices,
and echoing with the softer music of the flute, the vina, and the tabor,
the cars of the celestials could scarcely find a passage through the firmament.
Then those princes, Karna, Duryodhana, Salwa, Salya, Aswatthaman, Kratha,
    Sunitha,
and many other sons and grandsons of kings, one after another, exhibited their
    prowess
to win that maiden. But, adorned as they were with crowns, garlands, bracelets,

and other ornaments, and bursting with energy, none of those princes,
even in imagination, could string that bow of extraordinary stiffness.
Some among those kings, as they tried with swelling lips to string that bow,
were tossed on the ground and lay motionless for some time.
Their strength spent, and their crowns and garlands loosened from their
    persons,
they panted for breath. Their ambition of winning the maiden was cooled.
Tossed by that tough bow, and with their garlands and bracelets disordered,
they uttered exclamations of woe. Seeing the plight of those monarchs,
Karna, that foremost among bowmen, went to where the bow was,
raised it, strung it, and placed the arrows on the string.
As they watched the son of Surya—Karna of the Suta tribe—preparing to shoot
    the target,
the sons of Pandu regarded the mark as already shot and brought down to the
    ground.
But Draupadi said loudly: "I will not choose a Suta for my lord!"
Karna, laughing in vexation and casting a glance at his father, the sun,
threw aside the bow he had already drawn to a circle.
When all the Kshatriyas had given up the task, the heroic king of the Chedis,
as mighty as Yama himself, the illustrious and determined Sisupala,
the son of Damaghosa, in endeavoring to string the bow, fell to his knees.
Then King Jarasandha approached the bow and stood there for a moment,
fixed and motionless as a mountain. Tossed by the bow, he also fell to his knees
and then rose up and left the amphitheater to return to his kingdom.
Then the great Salya, the king of Madra, did just the same.
At last, when all the monarchs had become subjects of derisive talk,
Arjuna arose from among the Brahmanas and advanced toward the bow.
The principal Brahmanas raised a loud clamor.
Some were displeased, while others were delighted.
Some, possessed of intelligence and foresight,
said to one another: "How can a Brahmana stripling, unpracticed in arms
and weak in strength, string that bow that such celebrated Kshatriyas as Salya
    and others,
powerful and accomplished in the science and practice of arms, could not string?
If he does not achieve success in this untried task, undertaken in boyish
    impulsiveness,
the entire body of Brahmanas here will look ridiculous.
Therefore, forbid this Brahmana to attempt to string the bow as he wants to do
from vanity, childish daring, or mere impulsiveness."
Others said: "We shall not look ridiculous, nor shall we incur disrespect
or the displeasure of the sovereigns." And some said: "This handsome youth
is like the trunk of a mighty elephant. His shoulders and arms and thighs are
    massive;
in patience, he looks like the Himavat. He is so resolute that he may accomplish
    this feat.
Besides, there is nothing in the three worlds that Brahmana men cannot
    accomplish.

Abstaining from all food and living upon air, or eating only fruits
to persevere in their vows, even emaciated and weak, Brahmanas are strong.
Therefore, let this youth bend the bow and string it." Many then said: "So be it."
Arjuna approached the bow and stood there like a mountain.
He walked around the bow and bent his head to the sun god,
and he remembered Krishna also. He took up the bow.
And that bow, which many kings accomplished in the science and practice of
     arms
could not string, even with great exertion, Arjuna, son of Indra, strung
in the twinkling of an eye. He then took up the five arrows, shot the mark,
and brought it down to fall on the ground. The crowd resounded with a great
     clamor.
The gods showered celestial flowers on the head of Arjuna, slayer of foes.
And thousands of Brahmanas waved their upper garments in joy.
All around, the monarchs who had been unsuccessful uttered exclamations
of grief and despair. The musicians struck up in concert.
Charanas and heralds began to chant in sweet tones the praises of the hero
who had accomplished the great feat. And Drupada was filled with joy.
The monarch offered to assist the hero with his soldiers if the need arose.
When the uproar was at its height, Yudhishthira, accompanied by the twins,
hastily left the amphitheater to return to his temporary home.
Draupadi, seeing that the mark had been shot, and gazing at Arjuna, was filled
     with joy.
Wearing a white robe and carrying a garland of flowers, she approached the son
     of Kunti.
Arjuna, having won her by his success, was saluted with reverence by all the
     Brahmanas
and left the lists, followed closely by the maiden who thus became his wife.

◆

When King Drupada expressed his desire to bestow his daughter
on that Brahmana who had shot the mark, all those monarchs who had been
     invited
to the Swayamvara were filled with wrath. They said: "Passing us by,
and treating the monarchs as straw, this Drupada desires to bestow his daughter
on a Brahmana! Having planted the tree, he cuts it down when it is about to
     bear fruit.
The wretch does not hold us in high regard; therefore, let us slay him and his
     son, too.
The Vedic declaration is well known: that the Swayamvara is for the Kshatriyas.
The Brahmanas have no claim in respect of a selection of husband by a
     Kshatriya damsel.
If this damsel does not desire to select any one of us as her lord,
let us cast her into the fire and return to our kingdoms.
As regards this Brahmana, although he has done this injury to the monarchs,
he should not yet be slain; for our kingdoms, lives, and treasures,

our sons, grandsons, and whatever other wealth we have, all exist for Brahmanas.
Still, something must be done to him so that, from fear of disgrace
and desire to maintain what properly belongs to each order,
other Swayamvaras may not terminate in this way."
Those monarchs then took up their weapons and rushed at Drupada
to slay him then and there. Drupada saw them rushing toward him in anger
with bows and arrows, and in fear he sought the protection of the Brahmanas.
But Bhima and Arjuna, those mighty bowmen of the Pandavas, chastisers of all
    foes,
advanced to oppose those monarchs The monarchs with gloved fingers
and upraised weapons advanced toward the Kuru princes to slay them,
but mighty Bhima tore up a large tree and stripped it of its leaves.
With that tree, he stood like the mace-bearing king of the dead.
Near him was Arjuna, who stood with his bow ready to receive those assailants.
Beholding those feats of both Bhima and his brother Arjuna,
Krishna addressed his elder brother Valadeva and said:
"That hero there, with the tread of a mighty lion, who draws the large bow in his
    hand
four full cubits in length, is Arjuna! That other, who has torn up the tree
and is ready to drive off the monarchs, is Bhima! No one else in the world
could perform such feats in the field of battle.
And that other youth, with eyes like lotus petals and a gait like that of a mighty
    lion,
of fair complexion and prominent and shining nose, who left the amphitheater,
was Dharma's son Yudhishthira. The two other youths are the sons of the twin
    Aswins.
The sons of Pandu along with their mother, Kunti, had all escaped from the
    conflagration

                      of the house of lac."
Then Halayudha, with a complexion like that of clouds uncharged with rain,
said to his younger brother Krishna: "I am happy to hear that our father's sister
    Kunti
and the foremost among Kaurava princes have all escaped death!"

✦

The Brahmanas shook their deerskins and water pots made of coconut shells
and exclaimed: "Fear not, we will fight them!" Arjuna answered the Brahmanas:
"Stand aside! You can be spectators of the fight. Showering hundreds of arrows
with straight points, I shall stop all those angry monarchs."
The mighty Arjuna took up the bow he had obtained as dowry
and stood beside his brother Bhima, immovable as a mountain.
The Kshatriyas were furious, with Karna in the lead, but the brothers rushed at
    them
like two elephants rushing against another, hostile elephant. Those monarchs,
    eager for the fight,
exclaimed: "The slaughter in battle of one desiring to fight is permitted!"

They rushed at the Brahmanas. Karna approached Arjuna to fight,
and Salya, the mighty king of Madra, confronted Bhima
while Duryodhana and others engaged with the Brahmanas.
The illustrious Arjuna drew his tough bow and pieced Karna with his sharp
    arrows.
The impetus of those whetted arrows made Karna faint.
When he recovered consciousness, he attacked Arjuna with greater care than
    before.
Karna and Arjuna fought in a frenzy. Such was the lightness of hand they both
    displayed
that each was enveloped by the other's shower of arrows,
and they both became invisible to the spectators of their encounter.
"Behold the strength of my arms." "See how I have countered that feat."
Those words were intelligible only to the heroes as they addressed each other.
Incensed at finding the strength and energy of Arjuna's arms unequaled on the
    earth,
Karna, the son of Surya, fought with greater vigor. And parrying all those arrows
shot at him by Arjuna, Karna sent up a loud shout. This feat of his was
    applauded
by all the warriors. Karna shouted to his antagonist: "O foremost among
    Brahmanas,
I am gratified to observe the energy of your arms and weapons, fit for achieving
    victory.
Are you the embodiment of the art of weapons, or are you Rama, that best of
    Brahmanas,
or Indra himself, or Indra's younger brother Vishnu, who to disguise himself
has assumed the form of a Brahmana and mustered such energy to fight with me?"
Arjuna replied: "I am neither the personification of the science of arms
nor Rama endowed with superhuman powers.
I am only a Brahmana who is foremost among wielders of weapons.
By the grace of my preceptor, I have become accomplished
in the Brahma and the Paurandara weapons. I am here to vanquish you in battle."
Karna, the adopted son of Radha, then desisted from the fight,
for that mighty chariot fighter thought that Brahma energy was invincible.
Meanwhile, on another part of the field, the mighty heroes Salya and Bhimasena
were engaged in a fight. They struck each other with their clenched fists and
    knees,
sometimes pushing each other away and sometimes dragging each other closer,
sometimes throwing each other down, face downward, and sometimes on their
    sides.
They fought, striking and encountering each other's blows,
which were as hard as the clash of two masses of granite.
Bhima, foremost among Kuru heroes, took Salya up in his arms
and hurled him a considerable distance, surprising everyone by the dexterity of
    this feat,
for though he had thrown Salya to the ground, he did it without hurting him
    much.

When Salya was thus thrown down, and Karna was struck with fear,
the other monarchs grew alarmed. Hastily they surrounded Bhima and exclaimed:
"Surely these bulls among Brahmanas are excellent warriors!
To what race have they been born, and where do they live?
Who can encounter Karna, the son of Radha, in fight
except Rama or Drona, or Arjuna, the son of Pandu?
Who can encounter Duryodhana in battle except Krishna, the son of Devaki,
and Kripa, the son of Saradwan? Who can overthrow Salya, mightiest of warriors,
except the hero Valadeva or Bhima, the son of Pandu, or the heroic
    Duryodhana?
Let us, therefore, desist from this fight with the Brahmanas.
Indeed, Brahmanas, however grievously they may offend, should always be
    protected.
But first let us ascertain who they are. Then we may cheerfully fight with them."
Krishna saw that feat of Bhima and believed him and Arjuna to be the sons of
    Kunti.
Gently addressing the assembled monarchs, Krishna said:
"This maiden has been justly acquired by the Brahmana,"
and he induced them to abandon the fight.
The kings then returned to their respective kingdoms, puzzled and confused.
The spectators went away, saying: "The scene has ended in the victory of the
    Brahmanas.
The princess of Panchala has become the bride of a Brahmana."
Surrounded by Brahmanas dressed in skins of deer and other wild animals,
Bhima and Arjuna passed with difficulty through the throng
and looked like the full moon and the sun emerging from the clouds.

✦

Kunti, meanwhile, was worried that her sons were late in returning from their
    begging.
She thought of various evils that might have overtaken her sons.
Had the sons of Dhritarashtra recognized her sons and slain them?
Had some cruel Rakshasas, endowed with powers of deception, fallen upon them
and killed them? She asked herself: "Could the illustrious Vyasa,
who directed my sons to Panchala, have been guided by perverse intelligence?"
But then, in the stillness of the late afternoon, Arjuna and a body of Brahmanas
entered the house of the potter, like the sun breaking through clouds.
On their return, they approached their mother and presented Draupadi to her
as the alms they had obtained that day. Without looking, Kunti replied:
"Enjoy together what you have obtained." But then she saw the princess
and exclaimed: "Oh! what have I said?" Anxious about the possibility of sin,
and contemplating a way in which everyone could be extricated
from this awkward situation, she took the cheerful Draupadi by the hand
and, approaching Yudhishthira, said: "The daughter of King Draupada
was presented to me by your younger brothers as the alms they had obtained.
Out of ignorance, I said: 'Enjoy together what you have obtained.'

Tell me how my speech may not become untrue,
how sin may not touch the daughter of the king of Panchala,
and how she may not be humiliated or embarrassed."
King Yudhishthira, reflecting for a moment, consoled Kunti, and addressed
    Arjuna:
"By you, O brother, has the maiden been won. You, therefore, should wed her.
Ignite the sacred fire, and take her hand with due rites."
Arjuna replied: "Do not make me a participant in sin.
Your recommendation is not conformable to virtue. That is the path of the
    sinful.
You should wed first, then the strong-armed Bhima, then myself, then Nakula,
and, last of all, Sahadeva. Both Vrikodara and myself, and the twins and this
    maiden also,
await your commands. What, after reflection, would seem proper,
conformable with virtue, productive of fame, and beneficial to the king of
    Panchala?
All of us are obedient to you."
The Pandavas all cast their eyes on the princess of Panchala, who looked back at
    them.
And the princes looked at one another. Then, taking their seats,
they began to think of her alone. Indeed, after they had looked at Draupadi,
the God of Desire invaded their hearts and crushed their senses.
Her ravishing beauty was superior to that of all other women on earth.
Yudhishthira, observing his younger brothers, understood what was in their minds
and immediately recollected the words of Vyasa.
Fearing a division among the brothers, the king addressed them all:
"The auspicious Draupadi shall be the common wife of us all."
At those words of their eldest brother, the sons of Pandu felt relief and great
    cheerfulness.

✦

Krishna suspected that the five persons he had seen at the Swayamvara
were none other than the heroes of the Kuru race, and he came with his elder
    brother
Valadeva to the house of the potter, where the Pandavas had taken up their
    quarters.
Krishna and Valadeva saw Yudhishthira in that potter's house with his younger
    brothers
sitting around him. Krishna approached and touched the feet of that prince.
"I am Krishna," he said. Valadeva also approached Yudhishthira and did the same.
The Pandavas expressed great delight at seeing Krishna and Valadeva.
Those Yadu heroes then touched the feet of Kunti, who was their father's sister.
Yudhishthira inquired after Krishna's well-being and asked:
"How, O Vasudeva, have you been able to trace us, as we are living in disguise?"
And Krishna answered: "O king, fire, even if it is covered, can be known.
Who other than the Pandavas could exhibit such might? You sons of Pandu

by sheer good fortune have escaped from that fierce fire. And it is by sheer good
fortune
that the wicked son of Dhritarashtra and his counselors have not succeeded
in accomplishing their wishes. Blessings upon you! Thrive and prosper,
like a fire in a cave that gradually grows and spreads.
And lest any of the monarchs recognize you, let us return to our tent."
Then, by Yudhishthira's leave, Krishna and Valadeva hastily left the potter's abode.
As Bhima and Arjuna were making their way toward the home of the potter,
Dhrishtadyumna, the Panchala prince, followed them. He sent all his attendants
away
and, without the knowledge of the Pandavas, concealed himself in the potter's
house.
Bhima, Arjuna, and the illustrious twins, upon returning from their evening
begging,
cheerfully gave everything to Yudhishthira. Then the kindhearted Kunti
addressed the daughter of Drupada: "O amiable one, you take first a portion
from this,
devote it to the gods, give it away to Brahmanas, feed those who desire to eat,
and give to those who have become our guests. Divide the rest into two halves.
Give one of these to Bhima, for this strong youth of fair complexion always eats
a lot.
Then divide the other half into six parts, four for these youths, one for me,
and one for you." The princess cheerfully did as she had been directed to do.
And the heroes all ate of the food Krishnā had prepared.
Then Sahadeva, the son of Madri, spread a bed of *kusa* grass on the ground.
The heroes each spread their deerskins on these beds and lay down to sleep,
with heads toward the south. Kunti lay down along the line of their heads,
and Krishnā along that of their feet. And though she lay with the sons of Pandu
on that bed of *kusa* grass along the line of their feet, as if she were their nether
pillow,
Krishnā did not grieve or think disrespectfully of those bulls among the Kurus.
The heroes began to converse with one another,
and their conversation was extremely technical as they discussed celestial cars
and weapons
and elephants, and swords and arrows, and battle-axes.
In his hiding place, the son of the Panchala king listened to all they said.
When morning came, Prince Dhristadyumna set out with great haste
to report to Drupada in detail what he had seen and heard
at the potter's abode.
The king of Panchala had been sad because he had not known that
they were the Pandavas who had taken away his daughter.
The illustrious monarch asked Dhristadyumna: "Where has Krishnā gone?
Who has taken her away? Has any Sudra or anyone of mixed descent,
or has a tribute-paying Vaisya merchant taken my daughter away
and thus placed his dirty foot on my head? O son, has that wreath of flowers
been thrown away on a graveyard? Has any Kshatriya of high birth,
or any one of the superior Brahmana order obtained my daughter?

I would not, O son, grieve if my daughter had been united with Arjuna,
that foremost among men! Was it he who took up the bow and shot the mark?"
Dhrishtadyumna replied cheerfully to his father and told him all that had
    happened
and by whom Krishnā had been won. The prince said: "With large red eyes,
attired in deerskin, and resembling a celestial in beauty,
the youth who strung that foremost among bows and brought down the mark set
    on high
was soon surrounded by the foremost among Brahmanas, who offered him their
    homage
for the feat he had achieved. Surrounded by the Brahmanas, he resembled
the thunder-wielding Indra standing in the midst of the celestials and the rishis.
And like a she-elephant following the leader of a herd,
Krishnā cheerfully followed that young man, catching hold of his deerskin.
Then, when the assembled monarchs rose up in wrath
and advanced to fight, another hero appeared who tore up a large tree
and rushed at the kings, felling them right and left like Yama himself
smiting down creatures endowed with life.
Then the assembled kings stood motionless and stared at those two heroes,
who resembled the sun and the moon as they and Krishnā left the amphitheater.
They went to the house of a potter at the outskirts of town,
where there was a lady who, I think, is their mother.
Around her also sat three other impressive men. The two heroes approached her
and paid homage at her feet, and they directed Krishnā to do the same.
Leaving Krishnā with her, they went on their round of mendicant visits.
Afterward, when they returned, Krishnā took from them what they had obtained
    as alms,
devoted a portion thereof to the gods, and gave another portion as gifts to
    Brahmanas.
Of what remained, she gave a portion to that venerable lady
and distributed the rest among those five men. She took a little for herself.
Then, O monarch, they all lay down to sleep.
Krishnā was along the line of their feet, as if she were their nether pillow.
The bed on which they lay was of *kusa* grass, upon which was spread their
    deerskins.
Before going to sleep, they talked about diverse subjects in voices deep as those
    of black clouds.
Their talk indicated that they were neither Visas nor Sudras nor Brahmanas.
Without doubt they are Kshatriyas, their discourse having been on military
    subjects.
It seems, O father, that our hope has been fulfilled, for we have heard
that the sons of Kunti all escaped from the conflagration of the house of lac.
From the way in which the target was shot down by that youth,
and from the strength with which he strung the bow,
and from the manner in which I heard them talk with one another,
I am convinced, O monarch, that they are the sons of Pritha, wandering in
    disguise."

King Drupada was delighted to hear this, and he sent his priest to them,
directing him to ascertain who they were and whether they were indeed
the sons of the illustrious Pandu. The king's priest went to them as he had been
     ordered
and, applauding them all, delivered the king's message:
"Drupada, the boon-giving king of the earth, wants to know who you are.
Give us all the particulars of your family and tribe, place your feet on your foes'
     heads,
and gladden the hearts of the king of Panchala, of his men and mine also.
King Pandu was the dear friend of Drupada, who considered him as another self.
Drupada had long desired to bestow his daughter upon Pandu as his
     daughter-in-law.
You faultless heroes, King Drupada all along hoped Arjuna might wed his
     daughter.
If that has now become possible, nothing could please him more."
The priest fell silent and waited for an answer.
King Yudhishthira commanded Bhima, who sat near him: "Let water be brought
with which to wash his feet, and let the Arghya be offered to this Brahmana.
He is king Drupada's priest and worthy of great respect.
We should worship him with more than ordinary reverence." Bhima did this.
With a joyous heart, the Brahmana accepted the worship offered him and sat at
     his ease.
Yudhishthira then said: "The king of the Panchalas has given away his daughter
according to the practice of his order, and not freely.
This hero has satisfied that requirement and has won the princess.
King Drupada, therefore, has nothing now to say in regard to the race, tribe,
family, and disposition of the man who has performed that feat.
Indeed, all his questions have been answered by the stringing of the bow
and the shooting down of the mark. It is by doing what the king had directed
that this hero has brought away Krishnā from among the assembled monarchs.
In these circumstances, King Drupada should not indulge in any regrets.
The desire that he has all along cherished will be accomplished for his
     handsome princess
who bears, I think, every auspicious mark. None who is weak in strength
could string that bow, and none of mean birth or unaccomplished in arms
could have shot down the mark. Therefore, the king of the Panchalas should not
     grieve
for his daughter today. No one can undo that act of shooting down the mark."
While Yudhishthira was saying this, another messenger came from the king
to say that the nuptial feast was ready. The messenger said:
"In view of his daughter's nuptials, King Drupada has prepared a banquet
for the bridegroom's party. After finishing your daily rites, come to him.
Krishnā's wedding will take place there. Do not delay.
These cars adorned with golden lotuses drawn by excellent horses
are worthy of kings. Riding on them, come to the palace of the king of the
     Panchalas."
Those bulls among the Kurus dismissed the priest.

Kunti and Krishnā rode together on one of those cars.

The brothers ascended other splendid vehicles and proceeded toward
    Drupada's palace.

Meanwhile, having heard from his priest the words of Yudhishthira,

King Drupada, so as to ascertain the order to which those heroes belonged,

assembled a large collection of articles that were required by the ordinance

for weddings of each of the four orders. He had ready fruits, sanctified garlands

and coats of mail, and shields, and carpets, and cattle, and seeds,

and other articles of agriculture. The king also collected articles

appertaining to other arts, and various implements and apparatus of every kind
    of sport.

He had excellent coats of mail and shining shields, swords and fine scimitars,

beautiful chariots and horses, first-class bows and well-adorned arrows,

and various kinds of missiles ornamented with gold. And he also had darts and
    rockets

and battle-axes and various utensils of war. Of course there were beds and
    carpets

and various fine things, and fabrics of various sorts.

When the party arrived at Drupada's palace, Kunti and the virtuous Krishnā

entered the inner apartments of the king. With joyous hearts,

the ladies of the king's household worshipped the queen of the Kurus.

The king and his ministers, and the king's son, and the king's friends and
    attendants,

beholding those foremost among men—each possessing the gait of the lion,

eyes like those of mighty bulls, broad shoulders, and long-hanging arms

like the bodies of enormous snakes—were exceedingly glad.

With perfect fearlessness, the Pandavas sat on excellent seats, furnished with
    footstools,

one after another according to the order of their ages.

After they were seated, well-dressed servants male and female

and skillful cooks brought excellent and costly viands on gold and silver plates.

Those foremost among men ate from those dishes with greatest pleasure.

And after the dinner, those heroes, passing over all other articles,

focused their interest on the various utensils of war.

Drupada's son and Drupada himself along with all his chief ministers of state

inferred from this that the sons of Kunti were of royal blood and were happy
    indeed.

The illustrious king of Panchala then addressed Prince Yudhishthira

in the form applicable to Brahmanas and cheerfully inquired

of that illustrious son of Kunti: "Are we to know you as Kshatriyas or Brahamanas

or are we to know you as celestials, disguising themselves as Brahmanas

and ranging the earth, who have come here for the hand of Krishnā?

Tell us, for we have great doubts! We shall be glad when our doubts have been
    removed.

Have the fates been propitious to us? Truth becomes monarchs better than
    sacrifices.

Therefore, do not tell us what is untrue. You have the beauty of a celestial

and, hearing your reply, I shall make arrangements for my daughter's wedding
              according to the order to which you belong."

Yudhishthira answered: "Do not be downcast, O king. Let joy fill your heart!

Your desire has been fulfilled. We are Kshatriyas, O king, sons of the illustrious
    Pandu.

Know me to be the eldest of the sons of Kunti, and these to be Bhima and
    Arjuna.

By these, O king, was your daughter won in the midst of that concourse of
    monarchs.

The twins, Nakula and Sahadeva, and Kunti wait where Krishnā is.

Let grief be driven from your heart. Your daughter, O monarch,

has been transferred like a lotus from one lake into another.

O king, you are our revered superior and chief refuge. I have told you the whole
    truth."

King Drupada's eyes rolled in ecstasy. For some moments the king

could not answer Yudhishthira. At last he found words with which to reply

to Yudhishthira, and he asked how the Pandavas had escaped

from the town of Varanavata. The son of Pandu told the monarch every detail
              of their escape from the burning palace of lac.

Hearing what the son of Kunti said, King Drupada censured Dhritarashtra,

and he gave every assurance to Yudhishthira, the son of Kunti.

That eloquent man then and there vowed to restore Yudhishthira to his paternal
    throne.

Then the king commanded Kunti and Krishnā and Bhima and Arjuna and the
    twins

to reside with him, where they would be treated with due respect.

King Drupada and his sons approached Yudhishthira and said:

"Let the Kuru prince Arjuna take the hand of my daughter on this auspicious day,

and let him perform the usual rites of marriage."

Yudhishthira replied: "O great king, I also shall have to marry."

King Drupada said: "If it please you, you may take the hand of my daughter
    yourself

or give her in marriage to whichever of your brothers you choose."

Yudhishthira said: "Your daughter, O king, shall be the common wife of us all!

Our mother has ordered it so. I am unmarried still, and so is Bhima.

Your jewel of a daughter has been won by Arjuna. This, O king, is the rule with us:

always to enjoy equally a jewel that we may obtain.

O best of monarchs, that rule of conduct we cannot now abandon.

Krishnā, therefore, shall become the wedded wife of us all.

Let her take our hands, one after another before the fire."

Drupada answered: "It has been directed that one man may have many wives.

But it has never been heard of that one woman may have many husbands!

O son of Kunti, as you are pure and acquainted with the rules of morality,

it behooves you not to commit an act that is sinful and opposed to usage and the
    Vedas."

Yudhishthira replied: "O monarch, morality is subtle.

We do not know its course. Let us follow the way trodden by the illustrious ones.

My tongue has never uttered an untruth. My heart also never turns to what is
  sinful.
My mother commands so, and my heart also approves of it.
Therefore, O king, it is quite conformable to virtue. Accept it, without any
  scruples.
                    Entertain no fear, O king, about this matter."
Drupada said: 'O son of Kunti, your mother, my son Dhrishtadyumna, and you
must settle among yourselves what should be done.
Tell me the result of your deliberations, and tomorrow I will do what is proper."

✦

Yudhishthira, Kunti, and Dhrishtadyumna then discussed the matter.
Just at that time, however, the island-born Vyasa came there in the course of his
  wanderings.
All the Pandavas and the illustrious king of the Panchalas and all others there
  present
stood up and saluted with reverence the illustrious rishi.
The high-souled rishi saluted them in return, asked after their welfare,
and sat down on a carpet of gold. Commanded by Vyasa, those foremost
  among men
all sat down on costly seats. At the first opportunity, Drupada, in sweet accents,
asked the illustrious rishi about the wedding of Krishnā.
"How," he asked, "can one woman become the wife of many men
without being defiled by sin? O! tell me truly."
Vyasa replied: "This practice, opposed to usage and the Vedas, has become
  obsolete.
I desire, however, to hear what the opinion of each of you is upon this matter."
Drupada spoke first, saying: "The practice is sinful, in my opinion,
and opposed to both usage and the Vedas. Nowhere have I seen many men with
  one wife.
The illustrious ones also of former ages never had such a usage among them.
The wise should never commit a sin. I, therefore, cannot decide to act in this way."
Dhrishtadyumna then spoke, saying: "Bull among Brahmanas,
how can the elder brother, of a good disposition, approach the wife of a younger
  brother?
The ways of morality are ever subtle, and therefore we cannot know them
or say what is conformable to morality and what is not.
We therefore cannot do such a deed with a safe conscience.
Indeed, I cannot say: 'Let Draupadi become the common wife of five brothers.'"
Yudhishthira then spoke: "My tongue never utters an untruth,
and my heart never inclines to what is sinful. When my heart approves of it,
it cannot be sinful. I have heard in the Purana that a lady named Jatila,
foremost among virtuous women belonging to the race of Gotama,
married seven rishis. Also an ascetic's daughter, born of a tree,
in former times united herself in marriage with ten brothers,
all bearing the same name of Prachetas, and all of souls exalted by asceticism.

It is said that obedience to a superior is ever meritorious.
Among all superiors it is well understood that the mother is foremost.
It is she who has commanded us to enjoy Draupadi, sharing her
as we share anything obtained as alms. For this reason, O best of Brahmanas,
     I regard the proposed act as virtuous."
Kunti then said: "The act is exactly as the virtuous Yudhishthira has said.
I greatly fear, lest my speech become untrue. How shall I be saved from untruth?"
When they had all had their say, Vyasa pronounced his judgment.
"How," he asked, "shall you be saved from the consequence of untruth?
This is eternal virtue! I will not, O king of the Panchalas, discourse on this
 before you all.
But you alone shall listen to me when I disclose how this practice has been
 established
and why it is to be regarded as old and eternal. There is no doubt
that what Yudhishthira has said is quite conformable to virtue."
Then Vyasa arose, took hold of Drupada's hand, and led him to a private
 apartment.
The Pandavas and Kunti and Dhrishtadyumna of Prishata's race sat there,
waiting for their return. Meanwhile, Vyasa began explained to the king
how the practice of polyandry could not be regarded as sinful.
"In days of yore," he began, "the celestials once commenced a grand sacrifice
in the forest of Naimisha. At that sacrifice, O king, Yama, the son of Vivaswat,
became the slayer of the dedicated animals. Yama, thus employed in that
 sacrifice,
did not, during that period, kill a single human being.
Death having been suspended, the number of human beings increased very
 greatly.
Then Soma and Sakra and Varuna and Kuvera, the Sadhyas, the Rudras, the
 Vasus,
the twin Aswins, these and other celestials went to Prajapati, the creator of the
 universe.
Struck with fear for the increase of the human population of the world,
they addressed the master of creation and said: 'We are alarmed, O lord,
at the increase of human beings on earth, and we come to you for relief.
We plead for your protection.' The grandfather answered:
'You have little cause to be frightened at this increase of human beings.
You all are immortal. Do not take fright at human beings.'
The celestials replied: 'The mortals have become immortal.
There is no distinction now between us and them. Vexed at the blurring of all
 distinction,
we come to you in order that you may distinguish us from them.'
The creator then said: 'The son of Vivaswat is even now engaged in the grand
 sacrifice.
It is for this reason that men are not dying. But when Yama's work is done,
men will again die as before. Yama will, when that time comes,
sweep away by thousands the inhabitants on earth,
     who will scarcely have then any energy left in them.' "

Vyasa continued: "Hearing these words of the first-born deity,
the celestials returned to the spot where the grand sacrifice was being
     performed.
And the mighty one sitting by the side of the Bhagirathi River saw a golden lotus
being carried along by the current. Beholding that lotus, they marveled much.
And among them, Indra, that foremost among celestials, eager to know where it
     came from,
proceeded up the Bhagirathi to the place from which the goddess Ganga issues.
There he saw a woman possessing the splendor of fire.
The woman had come there to take water and was washing herself in the stream,
weeping all the while. The teardrops she shed, falling on the stream,
were being transformed into golden lotuses.
The wielder of the thunderbolt, observing that wonderful sight, approached the
     woman
and asked: 'Who are you, amiable lady? Why do you weep? O! tell me everything.'"
Vyasa continued: "The woman answered: 'O Sakra, you may know who I am,
     and why,
unfortunate that I am, I weep, if only you come with me as I lead the way.
You shall then see what it is I weep for.' Indra followed her as she led the way.
And soon he saw, not far off, a handsome youth with a young lady seated upon a
     throne,
placed upon one of the peaks of Himavat, and playing at dice.
To that youth, the chief of the celestials said: 'Know that this universe is under
     my sway.'
But the young man was so engrossed in dice that he took no notice of what he
     said.
Indra, possessed by anger, repeated: 'I am the lord of the universe.'
The youth, who was none other than the god Mahadeva, the god of the gods,
saw that Indra was filled with wrath, but he only cast a brief glance at him and
     smiled.
By that glance, however, the chief of the celestials was at once paralyzed,
                         and he stood there like a stake.
When the game at dice was over, Mahadeva addressed the weeping woman and
     said:
'Bring Indra to me, for I shall deal with him so that pride may not again enter
     his heart.'
As soon as the woman touched Indra, the chief of the celestials, with his limbs
     paralyzed,
fell down upon the earth. The primordial Mahadeva, of fierce energy, then said
     to him:
'Do not ever again act in this way. Remove this huge stone,
for your strength and energy are immeasurable, and enter the hole it will
     disclose,
where there await some others with the splendor of the sun and who are all
     like you.'
Indra then removed that stone and saw a cave in the breast of that king of
     mountains,

within which were four others who resembled himself.

Beholding their plight, Indra was seized with grief and exclaimed: 'Shall I be like these?'

Then the god glared at Indra with expanded eyes and said in anger:

'Enter this cave without loss of time, for you have foolishly insulted me.'

The chief of the celestials was deeply pained and, with limbs weakened by fear, he trembled like the wind-shaken leaf of a Himalayan fig.

And Indra, cursed unexpectedly by the god who has a bull for his vehicle, addressed that fierce deity of multiform manifestations,

with joined hands and shaking from head to foot, saying: 'You are, O Bhava, the overseer of the universe!' Hearing these words, the god of fiery energy smiled and said:

'Those who are of disposition like yours never obtain my grace.

These others within the cave were once like you.

Enter this cave, then, and lie there awhile. The fate of you all shall certainly be the same.

All of you shall have to take your birth in the world of men,

where, having achieved many difficult feats, and slaying a large number of men, you shall by the merits of your respective deeds regain the valued region of Indra.

You shall accomplish all I have said and much more besides.'

Then those Indras, shorn of their glory, said: 'We shall go from our celestial regions

to the region of men, where salvation is ordained to be difficult of acquisition.

But let the gods Dharma, Vayu, Maghavat, and the twin Aswins

beget us upon our would-be mother. Fighting with men

by means of both celestial and human weapons, we shall return to the region of Indra.'"

Vyasa continued: "Hearing these words of the former Indras,

the wielder of the thunderbolt once more addressed that foremost among gods, saying:

'Instead of going myself, I shall, with a portion of my energy, create from myself a person for the accomplishment of the task you have assigned

to form the fifth among these!' Vishwabhuk, Bhutadhaman, Sivi of great energy, Santi the fourth, and Tejaswin—these, it is said, were the five Indras of old.

And the illustrious god of the formidable bow, from his kindness,

granted the five Indras the desire they cherished.

He also appointed that woman of extraordinary beauty,

who was none other than Sri, goddess of grace, as their common wife in the world of men.

Accompanied by all those Indras, the god Mahadeva then went to Narayana

of immeasurable energy, the Infinite, the Immaterial, the Uncreated, the Old, the Eternal,

and the Spirit of these universes without limits. Narayana approved of everything.

Those Indras then were born in the world of men.

And Narayana took two hairs from his body, one of which was black and the other white.

And those two hairs entered the wombs of two of the Yadu race, Devaki and
    Rohini.
The white hair became Valadeva. And the black hair was born as Krishna.
And those Indras of old who had been confined in the cave on the Himavat
are none other than the sons of Pandu. Among the Pandavas, Arjuna—
called also Savyasachin, meaning '*Ambidextrous*'—is a portion of Sakra."
Vyasa continued: "Thus these brothers who have been born as the Pandavas
are none other than those Indras of long ago. And the celestial Sri,
who had been appointed as their wife, is this Draupadi of extraordinary beauty.
How could she, whose effulgence is like that of the sun or the moon,
whose fragrance spreads for two miles around, take her birth
in any other than an extraordinary way? She comes from within the earth,
by virtue of the sacrificial rites. To you, O king, I cheerfully grant this gift
in the form of spiritual insight. Behold now the sons of Kunti,
endowed with their sacred and celestial bodies of old!"
That sacred Brahmana Vyasa of generous deeds, by means of his ascetic power,
then granted celestial sight to the king. And the king then beheld all the
    Pandavas
endowed with their former bodies. The king saw them possessed of celestial
    bodies,
with golden crowns and celestial garlands, and each resembling Indra himself,
with complexions radiant as fire or the sun, and decked with every ornament,
handsome and youthful, with broad chests and in stature measuring five cubits,
endowed with every accomplishment, and wearing celestial robes of great beauty
                  and fragrant garlands of excellent making.
The king beheld them as so many Mahadevas, three-eyed gods, or as Vasus, or
    Rudras,
or Adityas. And, observing the Pandavas in the forms of those Indras of old,
and Arjuna also in the form of Indra sprung from Sakra himself,
King Drupada was highly pleased. That monarch wondered much
on beholding this manifestation of celestial power and he looked at his
    daughter,
that foremost among women, like a celestial damsel and possessed of the
    splendor of fire,
and regarded her as the worthy wife of those celestial beings.
Beholding that wonderful sight, the monarch touched the feet of Vyasa and
    exclaimed:
                        "O great rishi, I believe it!"
The rishi then continued: "In an ashram there was an illustrious rishi's daughter,
who, though handsome and chaste, had not obtained a husband.
By severe ascetic penances, the maiden gratified the god Sankara, or Mahadeva.
Sankara told the maiden: 'Ask the boon that you desire.' The maiden repeatedly
    said
to the supreme lord: 'I desire to obtain a husband possessed of every
    accomplishment.'
Sankara, the chief of the gods, pleased with her, gave her what she had asked,
saying: 'You shall have, amiable maiden, five husbands.'

The maiden said: 'O Sankara, I desire to have from you only one husband!'
The god of gods spoke again, saying: 'You have, O maiden, addressed me five
    full times,
repeating: "Give me a husband!" Therefore, it shall be as you have asked.
Blessings upon you. All this, however, will happen in a future life!'"
Vyasa continued: "O Drupada, this daughter of yours is that maiden.
Indeed, the faultless Krishnā, sprung from Prishata's race,
has been preordained to become the common wife of five husbands.
The celestial Sri, having undergone severe ascetic penances,
has had her birth as your daughter for the sake of the Pandavas.
That handsome goddess, waited upon by all the celestials,
as a consequence of her own acts becomes the common wife of five husbands.
It is for this that the self-created created her. Having listened to all this, O King
    Drupada,
do as you desire."
Drupada observed: "O great rishi, now that I know all, I cannot be indifferent
to what has been ordained by the gods. Therefore, I resolve to accomplish
what you have said. Destiny's knot cannot be untied. Nothing in this world
is the result of our own acts. What we had decided about securing only one
    bridegroom
has now changed, and we are in favor of many. Krishnā in a former life
had repeatedly said: 'O! give me a husband.' And the great god gave her what
    she had asked.
The god knows the right or wrong of this. As for me, when Sankara has
    ordained so,
no sin can be in it. Let these with happy hearts take the hand of Krishnā."
Then the illustrious Vyasa addressed Yudhishthira the just and said:
"This is an auspicious day, O son of Pandu! This day the moon
has entered the constellation called Pushya. Take the hand of Krishnā today,
you being first and eldest brother!" When Vyasa had said so,
King Yajnasena and his son made preparations for the wedding.
The monarch kept ready various costly articles as marriage presents.
Then he brought out his daughter, Krishnā, decked, after her bath, with jewels
    and pearls.
Then there came to witness the wedding all the friends and relatives of the king,
ministers of state, and many Brahmanas and citizens.
They all took their seats according to their respective ranks.
King Drupada's palace—adorned with those prominent men, with its yard
    decked with lotuses and lilies,
and embellished with lines of ceremonial troops,
festooned around with diamonds and precious stones—looked like the firmament
studded with brilliant stars. Those princes of the Kuru line, adorned with earrings,
attired in costly robes, and perfumed with sandalwood paste,
bathed and performed the usual religious rites and, accompanied by their
    priest, Dhaumya,
entered the wedding hall one after another in due order,
and with glad hearts, like mighty bulls entering a cowpen.

Then Dhaumya, well conversant with the Vedas, ignited the sacred fire
and poured libations of clarified butter into that blazing element.
Dhaumya, calling Yudhishthira, united him with Krishnā.
Walking around the fire, the bridegroom and the bride took each other's hand.
After their union was complete, the priest Dhaumya took leave of Yudhishthira
and left the palace. Then those Kuru princes, attired in gorgeous robes,
took the hand of that best of women, day by day in succession, aided by that priest.
The wonder was that the illustrious princess of slender waist
regained her virginity each day after the previous marriage.
After the weddings were over, King Drupada gave those mighty car warriors
various kinds of excellent gifts. The king gave them one hundred cars
with golden standards, each drawn by four steeds with golden bridles.
And he gave them one hundred elephants, all possessing auspicious marks
on their temples and faces, and like a hundred mountains with golden peaks.
He also gave them a hundred female servants, all in the prime of youth
and clad in costly robes and ornaments and floral wreaths.
And the monarch, making the sacred fire a witness of his gifts,
gave each of those princes of celestial beauty much wealth and many costly robes
and ornaments of great splendor. The sons of Pandu, after their weddings were
over,
and after they had obtained Krishnā, passed their days in joy and happiness,
like so many Indras in the capital of the king of the Panchalas.

✦

King Drupada, after his alliance with the Pandavas, had his fears dispelled.
Indeed, the monarch no longer even feared the gods.
The ladies of the illustrious Drupada's household approached Kunti
and introduced themselves to her, giving their respective names and
worshipping at her feet.
Krishnā, attired in red silk, her wrists still encircled with the auspicious thread,
saluted her mother-in-law with reverence and stood before her with joined palms.
Kunti, out of affection, pronounced a blessing upon her daughter-in-law, saying:
"Be to your husband as Sachi to Indra, Swaha to Vibhavasu, Rohini to Soma,
Damayanti to Nala, Bhadra to Vaisravana, Arundhati to Vasishtha,
and Lakshmi to Narayana! Be the mother of long-lived and heroic children.
Let luck and prosperity ever wait upon you! Wait upon your husbands
engaged in the performance of grand sacrifices. Be devoted to your husbands,
and pass your days in duly entertaining and reverencing guests and strangers
and the pious and the old, children and superiors.
Be the queen of the kingdom and of the capital of Kurujangala,
                              with your husband Yudhishthira the just!
O daughter, let the whole earth, conquered by the prowess of your husbands,
be given away by you to Brahmanas at the horse sacrifice!
O accomplished one, whatever gems there are on earth possessed of superior
virtues,
obtain them, O lucky one, and be happy for a full hundred years!

And, O daughter-in-law, as I rejoice today beholding you attired in red silk,
so shall I rejoice again when I see you become the mother of a son!"
After the sons of Pandu had been married, Hari, or Krishna,
sent to them as presents various gold ornaments set with pearls and lapis lazuli.
And Madhava, called Krishna as well, also sent them costly robes manufactured
   in various countries,
and many beautiful and soft blankets and hides of great value, and many costly
   beds
and carpets and vehicles. He also sent vessels by the hundreds, set with gems and
   diamonds.
And Krishna gave them female servants by the thousands from various countries,
and endowed with beauty, youth, and accomplishments, and decked with every
   ornament.
He also gave them many well-trained elephants brought from the country of
   Madra,
and many excellent horses in costly harness, and cars drawn by excellent horses.
The slayer of Madhu also sent them coins of pure gold by crores upon crores.
And Yudhishthira the just, desirous of gratifying Govinda, known as Krishna,
                              accepted all those presents with great joy.
The news was carried to all the monarchs who had come to the self-choice of
   Draupadi
that the handsome Draupadi had been united in marriage with the five sons of
   Pandu.
And they were also informed that the hero who had bent the bow and shot the
   target
was none other than Arjuna, that first of all wielders of the bow and arrows.
And it became known that the mighty warrior who had dashed Salya,
the king of Madra, on the ground, and who in wrath had terrified the assembled
   monarchs
with the tree he had uprooted and had taken his stand before all foes in
   fearlessness,
was none other than Bhima, that destroyer of hostile ranks,
whose touch alone was sufficient to take the lives of all foes.
The monarchs, upon being informed that the Pandavas had assumed the guise
of peaceful Brahmanas, were much amazed.
They had heard that Kunti and all her sons had been burned to death in the
   house of lac.
They therefore regarded the Pandavas as having come back from the region of
   the dead.
Duryodhana also heard that Draupadi had selected Arjuna, the owner of white
   steeds,
as her lord, and he became greatly depressed. The prince, accompanied by his
   brothers,
by Aswatthaman, by his uncle Sakuni, and by Karna and Kripa, set out
with a heavy heart for his capital. Then Duhsasana, blushing with shame,
addressed his brother softly, saying: "If Arjuna had not disguised himself as a
   Brahmana,

he could never have succeeded in obtaining Draupadi.

It was because of this disguise that no one could recognize him. Fate is always supreme.

Exertion is fruitless; forget about exertions, O brother! The Pandavas are still alive!"

Speaking to one another thus, and blaming Purochana for his carelessness,

they then entered the city of Hastinapura cheerlessly, and with sorrowful hearts.

Realizing that the mighty Pandavas had escaped from the burning house of lac

and were now allied with Drupada, and thinking of Dhrishtadyumna and Sikhandin

and the other sons of Drupada, all accomplished in fighting, they were struck with fear

and overcome with despair. Then Vidura, having learned that Draupadi had been won

by the Pandavas, and that the sons of Dhritarashtra had come back to Hastinapura

in shame, was filled with joy. Approaching Dhritarashtra, Vidura said:

"The Kurus are prospering by good luck!" Hearing those words, Dhritarashtra exclaimed:

"What good luck, O Vidura! What good luck!"

From ignorance, the blind monarch understood that his eldest son Duryodhana

had been chosen by Drupada's daughter as her lord.

And the king immediately ordered various ornaments to be made for Draupadi.

He commanded that both Draupadi and his son Duryodhana

should be brought with pomp to Hastinapura. It was then that Vidura told the monarch

that Draupadi had chosen the Pandavas for her lords, that they were all alive and well,

and that they had been received with great respect by King Drupada.

He also informed Dhritarashtra that the Pandavas had been united

with the many relatives and friends of Drupada, each having large armies,

and with many others who had come to that self-choice.

Hearing these words of Vidura, Dhritarashtra said: "Those children are to me as dear

as they were to Pandu. No, even more! O, listen to me as I explain

why my affection for them now is even greater! The heroic sons of Pandu

are happy and well. They have obtained many friends.

Their relatives and those whom they have gained as allies are all endowed

with great strength. Who among monarchs, in prosperity or adversity,

would not like to have Drupada with his relatives as an ally?"

Vidura replied: "O king, let your understanding remain so, without change

for a hundred years!" Vidura then returned to his own home,

after which Dhritarashtra, Duryodhana, and the son of Radha, Karna, came to the king

and said: "We cannot speak of any transgression in the presence of Vidura!

We have now found you alone and can say all we like!

What is this that you have desired to do? Do you regard the prosperity of your foes

as if it were your own? Why have you been applauding the Pandavas
in the presence of Vidura? O sinless one, you do not act as you should!
We should now exert ourselves every day so as to weaken the Pandavas.
The time has come, O father, for us to take counsel together
so that the Pandavas may not swallow us all with our children and friends and
relatives."

14

Tilottama

Duhsasana, one of Dhritarashta's hundred sons, blushing with shame,
addressed his brother softly, saying: "If Arjuna had not disguised himself as a
    Brahmana,
he could never have succeeded in obtaining Draupadi.
It was because of this disguise, O king, that no one could recognize him.
Fate, I believe, is always supreme. Exertion is fruitless;
forget about exertions, O brother! The Pandavas are still alive!"
Speaking to one another thus, and blaming Purochana for his carelessness,
they entered the city of Hastinapura with sorrowful hearts.
Realizing that the mighty Pandavas were now allied with Drupada,
and thinking of Dhrishtadyumna and Sikhandin and the other sons of Drupada,
all accomplished in fighting, they were overcome with despair.
Vidura, having learned that Draupadi had been won by the Pandavas,
and that the sons of Dhritarashtra had come back to Hastinapura in shame,
was filled with joy. Approaching Dhritarashtra, Vidura said: "The Kurus are
    prospering
by good luck!" Hearing those words, Dhritarashtra exclaimed: "What good luck,
O Vidura!" Had the blind monarch misunderstood?
Did he think his eldest son, Duryodhana, had been chosen by Drupada's
    daughter?
He ordered various ornaments to be made for Draupadi
and commanded that both Draupadi and his son Duryodhana
should be brought with pomp to Hastinapura.
It was then that Vidura told the monarch that Draupadi had chosen the Pandavas
for her lords, that those heroes were all alive and well,
and that they had been received with great respect by King Drupada.
He also informed Dhritarashtra that the Pandavas
had been united with the relatives and friends of Drupada, each having large
    armies,
and with many others who had come to that self-choice.
Hearing these words of Vidura, Dhritarashtra said:
"Those children are to me as dear as they were to Pandu. No, even more!
O, listen to me as I explain why my affection for them now is even greater.
The heroic sons of Pandu are happy and well. They have obtained many friends.

Their relatives and those they have gained as allies are endowed with great
    strength.
Who among monarchs, in prosperity or adversity,
would not like to have Drupada with his relatives as an ally?"
Vidura replied: "O king, let your understanding remain so, without change for a
    hundred years!"
                    Vidura then returned to his own home.
Dhritarashtra, Duryodhana, and the son of Radha, Karna, then came to the king
and said: "We cannot speak of any transgression in the presence of Vidura!
We have now found you alone and can say all we like!
What is this that you have desired to do? Do you regard the prosperity of your foes
as if it were your own? Why have you been applauding the Pandavas
in the presence of Vidura? O sinless one, you do not act as you should!
We should now exert ourselves every day so as to weaken the Pandavas.
The time has come, O father, for us to take counsel together
so that the Pandavas may not swallow us all with our children and friends and
    relatives."
Dhritarashtra replied, saying: "I desire to do exactly what you recommend.
But I do not wish to inform Vidura of it even by a change of muscle.
That was why I applauded the Pandavas in Vidura's presence:
so that he might not know even by a sign what is in my mind.
Now that Vidura has gone away, this is the time, Duryodhana,
for telling me what you have thought of, and what you, Karna, have thought of."
Duryodhana said. "Let us use trusted, skillful, and adroit Brahmanas
to seek to produce dissension among the sons of Kunti and Madri.
Let King Drupada and his sons and all his ministers be plied with riches
so that they may abandon the cause of Yudhishthira.
Or let our spies induce the Pandavas to settle in Drupada's dominions,
by describing to them, separately, the inconvenience of residing in Hastinapura
so that, separated from us, they may permanently settle in Panchala.
Or let some clever spies, full of resources, sow seeds of dissension among the
    Pandavas
and make them jealous of one another. Or let them incite Draupadi against her
    husbands.
She has many lords, and this will not present any difficulty.
Or let some seek to make the Pandavas themselves dissatisfied with Krishnā,
in which case Draupadi herself will also be dissatisfied with them.
Or let some clever spies go there and secretly contrive the death of Bhimasena.
Bhima is the strongest of them all. Relying upon him, the Pandavas looked down
    on us.
Bhima is fierce and brave and the sole support of the Pandavas.
Deprived of him, they will despair and will no longer try to regain their kingdom.
Arjuna is invincible in battle, but only if Bhima protects him from behind.
Indeed, O king, if the Pandavas were conscious of their own feebleness without
    Bhima
and of our strength, they would never think of recovering the kingdom.
Or if they came here and proved docile and obedient to us,

we would then seek to repress them according to the dictates of political science

Or we could tempt them with beautiful girls so that the princess of Panchala
would get angry.

Or we could send messengers to bring them here

so that, when they arrived, we could have trusted agents slay them.

Strive, O father, to employ any of these methods that may be workable. Time
passes.

Before their confidence in King Drupada is established, we may succeed with
them.

But after their mutual trust has been established, we are sure to fail."

Then Karna spoke, saying: "It does not seem to me that this reasoning is correct.

No method will succeed against the Pandavas. You have before, by various subtle
means,

striven to carry out your wishes. But you have always failed to slay your foes.

They were then living near you, O king! They were then unfledged and of
tender years,

but you could not injure them. They are now living at a distance, and full-fledged.

The sons of Kunti cannot now be injured by any subtle contrivances. This is my
opinion.

As they are aided by the Fates, and as they desire to regain their ancestral
kingdom,

we can never succeed in injuring them by any means in our power.

It is impossible to create disunion among them.

They can never be disunited who have all taken a common wife.

Nor can we succeed in estranging Draupadi from the Pandavas by any spies of
ours.

She chose them as her lords when they were in adversity.

Will she abandon them now that they are in prosperity?

Besides, women always like to have many husbands; Draupadi has obtained her
wish.

The king of Panchala is honest and virtuous; he is not avaricious.

Even if we offer him our whole kingdom, he will not abandon the Pandavas.

Drupada's son also possesses every accomplishment and is attached to the
Pandavas.

Therefore, I do not think the Pandavas can now be injured by any subtle means.

What is good and advisable for us now is to attack and smite them

until they are exterminated. Let this be the course you choose.

As long as our party is strong and that of the king of the Panchalas is weak,

you may strike them without any scruple. As long as their vehicles and animals,

friends, and friendly tribes are not mustered together, you may exhibit your
prowess.

As long as the king of the Panchalas and his sons do not set their hearts

upon fighting with us, so long you may, O king, exhibit your prowess.

And, O king, you should do this before Hari Krishna comes with the Yadava host

to the city of Drupada, carrying everything before him, to restore the Pandavas

to their paternal kingdom. Wealth, luxury, or power—

there is nothing that Krishna may not sacrifice for the sake of the Pandavas.

The illustrious Bharata acquired the whole earth by his prowess alone.

Indra has acquired sovereignty of the three worlds by prowess alone.

O king, prowess is always applauded by the Kshatriyas.

Prowess is the cardinal virtue of the brave.

Let us, therefore, with our large army consisting of four kinds of forces,

grind Drupada down without any loss of time, and bring the Pandavas here.

They cannot be discomfited by any policy of conciliation, of gift, of wealth and
bribery,

or of disunion. Vanquish them, therefore, with your strength.

And having conquered them, you may then rule this wide earth.

I see no other means by which we may accomplish our end."

Hearing these words of Karna, Dhritarashtra applauded him.

The monarch then said: "O son, you are gifted with wisdom and accomplished
in arms.

This speech, therefore, favoring the use of force, suits you well.

But let Bhishma and Drona and Vidura and you two take counsel together

and adopt whatever proposal may lead to our benefit."

King Dhritarashtra summoned all those celebrated ministers and took counsel
with them.

Asked to give his opinion, Bhishma replied: "O Dhritarashtra,

I can never approve of a quarrel with the Pandavas. As you are to me, so was
Pandu.

And the sons of Gandhari are to me as those of Kunti.

I should protect them as well as I should your sons!

Under these circumstances, a quarrel with them would be detestable.

Conclude a treaty with those heroes, and let half the land be given to them.

This is the paternal kingdom of those foremost members of the Kuru race.

And as you look upon this kingdom as your paternal inheritance,

the Pandavas also look on it as their paternal legacy.

If the renowned sons of Pandu do not obtain the kingdom, how can it be yours

or that of any other descendant of the Bharatas?

If you regard yourself as one who has lawfully come into possession of the
kingdom,

I think they too may be regarded as having come into possession of the kingdom,

and before you. Give them half the kingdom. This, O tiger among men, is
beneficial to all.

If you act otherwise, evil will befall us all. You, too, shall be covered with dishonor.

O Duryodhana, strive to maintain your good name.

A good name is the source of one's strength.

It has been said that one lives in vain whose reputation has gone.

A man does not die so long as his fame lasts.

Follow, then, the practice that is worthy of the Kuru race.

We are fortunate that the Pandavas have not perished. We are fortunate that
Kunti lives.

We are fortunate that the wretch Purochana, unable to accomplish his wicked
purpose,

has himself perished. From that time, when I heard that the sons of Kunti had been burned to death, I was unable to meet any living creature.

The world, hearing of the fate that overtook Kunti, did not regard Purochana as
guilty

but did so regard you, O king. Your evil reputation is erased, therefore, by the
escape of Pandu's sons from that conflagration and by their reappearance.

Know that as long as those heroes live, the wielder of the thunder himself
cannot deprive them of their ancestral share in the kingdom.

The Pandavas are virtuous and united. They are being wrongly kept out of their
share

in the kingdom. If you act rightly, and if you do what I recommend,
if you seek the welfare of all, then give half the kingdom to them."

When Bhishma had concluded, Drona spoke, saying:

"O King Dhritarashtra, we have heard that friends summoned for consultation
should always speak what is right, what is true, and what is conductive to fame.

Sire, I am of the same mind in this matter as the illustrious Bhishma.

Let a share of the kingdom be given to the Pandavas. This is virtuous.

Send to Drupada, without loss of time, some messenger of agreeable speech
who carries with him a large treasure for the Pandavas.

And let the man go to Drupada as well, with presents for the bridegrooms and
the bride,

and let him speak to that monarch of your increase of power and dignity that
arises

from this new alliance with him. And let the man know that both you and
Duryodhana

are most happy about what has happened. Let him say this repeatedly
to Drupada and Dhrishtadyumna. And let him speak also about the alliance
as having been altogether proper and agreeable to you, and of your being
worthy of it.

And let the man propitiate the sons of Kunti and those of Madri.

At your command, O king, let plenty of ornaments of pure gold be given to
Draupadi.

And let proper presents be given to all the sons of Drupada.

Let the messenger then propose the return of the Pandavas to Hastinapura.

After Drupada has permitted the heroes to come here, let Duhsasana and
Vikarna go out

with a handsome train to receive them. And when they have arrived at
Hastinapura,

receive those men with affection. Let them then be installed on their paternal
throne,

agreeably to the wishes of the people of the realm.

This is how you should treat the Pandavas, who are to you even as your own sons."

When Drona had finished, Karna spoke again: "Both Bhishma and Drona
have been pampered with your wealth and have received favors from you!

You have always regarded them as trusted friends!

What can be more amusing than for them to give you advice that is not for your
good?

How can the wise approve the advice of a person speaking with wicked intent

but taking care to conceal the wickedness of his heart?
Indeed, in a season of distress, friends can neither benefit nor injure.
Everyone's happiness or misery depends on destiny.
He who is wise and he who is foolish, he who is young and he who is old,
he who has allies and he who has none—all become happy or unhappy at times.
We have heard of a king who lived long ago, named Amvuvicha.
His capital was at Rajagriha, and he was the king of all the Magadha chiefs.
He never attended to his affairs. His only exertion consisted in inhaling the air.
All his affairs were in the hands of his minister. And the minister, named
　　Mahakarni,
became the supreme authority in the state. Regarding himself as all powerful,
he began to disregard the king and appropriated everything belonging to the king:
his queens and his treasure and his sovereignty. But the possession of all these,
instead of satisfying his avarice, served only to inflame him all the more.
Having taken everything that belonged to the king, he even coveted the throne.
But with all his best efforts, he did not succeed in acquiring the kingdom
of the monarch, his master, even though the latter was inattentive to business
and content with only breathing the air. What else can be said, O king,
than that this monarch's sovereignty was dependent on destiny?
If, therefore, this kingdom be established in you by destiny, it will continue in you,
even if the whole world were to become your enemy! If destiny has ordained
　　otherwise,
however much you may strive, it will not remain with you!
O learned one, remembering all this, judge of the honesty or otherwise of your
　　advisers.
Ascertain also who among them are wicked and who have spoken wisely and well."
To these words of Karna, Drona replied: "As you are wicked, you say these things
from the wickedness of your own heart. To injure the Pandavas, you find fault
　　with us.
But know, O Karna, that what I have said is for the good of all
and the prosperity of the Kuru race. If you regard all this as productive of evil,
tell us what would be productive of good. If the advice I have given be not
　　followed,
　　　　　　　　　I think the Kurus will be exterminated."
After Drona had finished, Vidura said: "O monarch, your friends are saying
what is for your good. But as you are unwilling to listen to what they say,
their words scarcely find a place in your ears. What Bhishma has said is excellent
and wise and is for your benefit. But you do not listen to him.
Drona has also said much that is for your good, although Karna does not think so.
But, on reflection, I do not find anyone who is better a friend to you
than either of these two lions among men, or anyone who exceeds them in
　　wisdom.
These two—old in years, in wisdom, and in learning—always regard you, O king,
and the sons of Pandu with equal eyes. In virtue and truthfulness,
neither one is in any way inferior to Rama.
Never before have they given you evil advice. And you have never done them any
　　injury.

Why then should these men, always truthful, give you wicked or unsound
    counsel,
especially when you have never done them harm? O scion of Kuru's race,
this is my firm conviction: that these two, acquainted with all rules of morality,
will never utter a word that betrays a spirit of partisanship.
What they have said I regard as highly beneficial to you.
Without doubt, the Pandavas are your sons, as much as Duryodhana and others.
Those ministers who give you advice fraught with evil to the Pandavas
do not really look to your interests. If there is any partiality in your heart
for your own children, those who by their counsel seek to bring it out
certainly do you no good. Therefore, O king, these illustrious persons
have not said anything that leads to evil. But you do not understand this.
What these two have said regarding the invincibility of the Pandavas is perfectly
    true.
Do not doubt it. Blessings upon you! Can the handsome Arjuna, the son of
    Pandu,
using the right and the left hand with equal agility, be vanquished in battle
even by Maghavat himself? Can Bhimasena, with the might of ten thousand
    elephants,
be vanquished in battle by the immortals themselves?
And what man who wants to stay alive can overcome in battle the twins,
Nagula and Sahadeva, who are like the sons of Yama himself?
How can the eldest of the Pandavas, in whom patience, mercy, forgiveness,
truth, and strength live together, be vanquished?
They who have Rama as their ally and Krishna as their counselor
and Satyaki as their partisan have already defeated everybody in war.
They who have Drupada for their father-in-law
and Drupada's sons—Dhristadyumna and others of Prishata's race—
for their brothers-in-law are certainly invincible. Remembering this,
and considering that their claim to the kingdom is even stronger than yours,
behave virtuously toward them. The stain of calumny is on you, O monarch,
because of that act of Purochana. Wash yourself of it now
by kindly behavior toward the Pandavas, which will be an act of great benefit to us,
protecting the lives of us all who belong to Kuru's race,
and will lead to the growth of the whole Kshatriya order!
The Dasarhas, O king, are numerous and strong.
Where Krishna is, all of them must be, and where Krishna is, there victory also
    must be!
Who, unless cursed by the gods, would seek to achieve by means of war
what can be brought about by negotiation? Hearing that the sons of Pritha are
    alive,
the citizens and other subjects of the realm rejoice and are eager to see them.
O monarch, act in a way that is agreeable to them.
Duryodhana and Karna and Sakuni, the son of Suvala, are sinful, foolish and
    young;
do not listen to them. You are possessed of every virtue,
but remember how I told you long ago that for Duryodhana's fault

the subjects of this kingdom would be exterminated."

After listening to these various speeches, Dhritarashtra said:

"The learned Bhishma, the son of Santanu, and the illustrious rishi Drona,

and you, too, O Vidura, have said the truth, and what also is most beneficial to me.

Indeed, as those mighty car warriors, the heroic sons of Kunti, are the children
   of Pandu,

so are they my children, according to the ordinance.

And as my sons are entitled to this kingdom, so are the sons of Pandu entitled
   to it.

Therefore, hasten to bring the Pandavas here along with their mother,

treating them with affection and consideration.

And also bring Draupadi of celestial beauty along with them.

From sheer good fortune, the sons of Kunti are alive;

and from good fortune, those mighty car warriors have obtained the daughter of
   Drupada.

It is from good fortune alone that our strength has increased,

and it is from good fortune that Purochana has perished.

Finally, it is from good fortune that my great grief has been lifted from me!"

Vidura, at Dhritarashtra's command, repaired to Yajnasena and the Pandavas.

And he carried with him numerous jewels and various kinds of wealth

for Draupadi and the Pandavas and Yajnasena also. When he reached Drupada's
   palace,

Vidura, conversant with every rule of morality and deep in every science,

properly approached the monarch and waited upon him.

Drupada received Vidura in proper form, and they inquired after each other's
   welfare.

Vidura then saw the Pandavas and Krishna, and he embraced them
   affectionately

and asked after their well being. The Pandavas and Krishna, in due order,

worshipped Vidura of immeasurable intelligence. Vidura, in the name of
   Dhritarashtra,

repeatedly asked after their welfare and gave to the Pandavas and Kunti and
   Draupadi,

and to Drupada and Drupada's sons, the gems and various kinds of wealth

the Kauravas had sent with him. The modest Vidura then,

in the presence of the Pandavas and Keshava, addressed Drupada thus:

"With your ministers and sons, O monarch, listen to what I say.

King Dhritarashtra, with ministers, sons, and friends, has with a joyous heart

repeatedly inquired after your welfare. And he is pleased with this alliance
   with you.

So also Bhishma of great wisdom, the son of Santanu, with all the Kurus,

inquired after your welfare in every respect. Drona too, your dear friend,

embracing you mentally, asked after your happiness. Dhritarashtra and all the
   Kurus,

because of this alliance with you, regard themselves as supremely blessed.

The establishment of this alliance with you has made them happier

than if they had acquired a new kingdom. In light of all this, O monarch,

permit the Pandavas to return to their ancestral kingdom.
The Kurus are eager again to behold the sons of Pandu, who have been long
    absent.
They as well as Kunti must be eager to see their city.
And all the Kuru ladies and the citizens and our subjects are eager to see
    Draupadi,
the Panchala princess. This, then, is my opinion, O monarch:
that you should, without delay, permit the Pandavas to go there with their wife."
To these words of Vidura, Drupada replied: "It is as you have said, O Vidura.
I too have been exceedingly happy in consequence of this alliance.
It is proper that these illustrious princes should return to their ancestral
    kingdom.
But it is not proper for me to say this myself. If the brave Yudhishthira and Bhima
and Arjuna and the twins desire to go, and if Rama and Krishna are of the same
    mind,
                              then let the Pandavas go home."
When Yudhishthira was asked the question, he said: "We are now, O monarch,
with all our younger brothers, dependent on you.
We shall cheerfully do what you are pleased to command."
Then Krishna said: "I am of the opinion that the Pandavas should go.
But we should abide by the opinion of King Drupada,
                          conversant with every rule of morality."
King Drupada then spoke: "I agree with what this foremost among men thinks.
For the illustrious sons of Pandu now are to me as they are, without doubt, to
    Krishna.
Kunti's son Yudhishthira himself does not seek the welfare of the Pandavas
                          more earnestly than he."
Commanded by the illustrious Drupada, the Pandavas and Kunti
journeyed toward the city called after the elephant.
King Dhritarashtra, when he heard that those heroes had neared the capital,
sent out the Kauravas to receive them. Those who were thus sent
were Vikarna of the great bow, and Chitrasena, and Drona that foremost among
    warriors,
and Kripa of Gautama's line. Surrounded by these, the heroes
entered the city of Hastinapura, which was radiant with the gay throng of
    sightseers.
The Pandavas gladdened the hearts of all who beheld them,
and as they proceeded, they heard various cheers and exclamations.
Some called out: "Here come those tigers among men,
who always protect us as if we were their nearest relatives."
Others agreed, saying: "It seems that the beloved King Pandu returns today
to do what is agreeable to us." And some said: "What good is not done to us
    today,
when the heroic sons of Kunti come back to our town? If we have ever given in
    charity,
if we have ever poured libations of clarified butter upon the fire, if we have
    ascetic merit,

then let the Pandavas stay in our city for a hundred years."

At last the Pandavas arrived at the palace and worshipped at the feet of
    Dhritarashtra

and at those of the illustrious Bhishma. They also worshipped at the feet of
    everyone else

who deserved that honor. They inquired after the welfare of every citizen
    present.

At last, at the command of Dhritarashtra, they entered the apartments assigned
    to them.

They rested there for some time and then were summoned to the court.

When they appeared, King Dhritarashtra said to Yudhishthira: "Listen, O son of
    Kunti,

to what I say. You and your brothers may repair to Khandavaprastha

so that no difference may arise again between you and your cousins.

If you take up your quarters there, no one will be able to do you any injury.

Protected by Arjuna as the celestials are protected by the thunderbolt,

you may reside safely at Khandavaprastha, taking half of the kingdom."

The Pandavas agreed to what Dhritarashtra had said and set out from
    Hastinapura.

They traveled to Khandavaprastha, which was an unreclaimed desert;

but, arriving there, they beautified the place and made it a second heaven.

With Dwaipayana's assistance, they selected a sacred and auspicious region,

performed propitiatory ceremonies, and measured out a piece of land for their
    city.

They surrounded it with a trench as wide as the sea and walls reaching up to the
    heavens

and white as the fleecy clouds or the beams of the moon

so that their city looked as resplendent as Bhogavati, the capital of the nether
    kingdom.

It was adorned with palatial mansions and numerous gates,

each furnished with panels resembling the outstretched wings of Garuda.

And it was protected with gateways that looked like the clouds

and were as high as the Mandara mountains.

The missiles of the foes could not make the slightest impression upon these walls.

They were almost covered with darts and other missiles like double-tongued
    snakes.

The turrets were filled with armed men, and the walls were lined along their
    entire length

with numerous warriors. There were thousands of sharp hooks and fiery missiles,

those machines slaying a century of warriors, and there were other armaments
    on the battlements.

There were also large iron wheels planted on them.

The streets were all wide, well laid out, and decked with innumerable mansions

so that the city was like Amaravati. Thus it came to be called Indraprastha,

meaning "Like Indra's City." In a delightful part of the city rose the palace of the
    Pandavas.

Filled with richness and like the mansion of the celestial treasurer Kuvera,

it looked like a mass of clouds charged with lightning.
When the city was built, there came numerous Brahmanas,
well acquainted with all the Vedas and knowing every language, wishing to dwell
    there.
There also came to that town numerous merchants from every direction
and numerous persons skilled in all the arts and crafts.
Around the city were many gardens, with many trees bearing both fruits and
    flowers.
There were mango trees, known as *amras*, and amaratakas, kadamvas and asokas,
and champakas; and punnagas and nagas and lakuchas and panasas;
and salas and palm trees, called *talas*. There were also tamalas and vakulas,
and ketakas with their fragrant burdens, and there were beautiful blossoming
    amalakas,
branches bent low with the weight of fruits, and lodhras and flowering ankolas;
and blackberry trees, called *jamvus*, and patalas and kunjakas and a profusion of
    other trees
alive with feathery creatures of various species.
Those groves resounded with the shrill cries of peacocks and blackbirds.
And there were various pleasure houses, bright as mirrors, and many bowers
covered over with creepers, and charming, artificial hillocks,
and many lakes full of crystal water as well as tanks fragrant with lotuses and lilies
and adorned with swans and ducks and geese.
And there were many pools full of rare aquatic plants, and large ponds of great
    beauty.
The joy of the Pandavas increased from day to day in their residence
in that large kingdom peopled with pious men.
Having settled the Pandavas there, Krishna obtained their leave to return
with Rama to Dwaravati. The Pandavas passed their days in joy and happiness
at Khandavaprastha with Draupadi. And Yudhishthira ruled the land virtuously,
helped by his brothers, seated on royal seats, as they discharged the duties of
    government.

✦

One day there came to them the celestial rishi named Narada.
Yudhishthira offered him his own handsome seat and gave him the Arghya
with his own hands. The king informed the rishi of the state of his kingdom.
In delight, the rishi accepted this worship, complimented the king,
and gave him his benedictions. He commanded the king to take his seat.
Then the king sent word to Draupadi, in the inner apartments, of the arrival of
    the rishi.
Draupadi purified herself properly and came with a respectful attitude
to Narada and the Pandavas. The virtuous princess of Panchala,
properly veiled, worshipped at the celestial rishi's feet and stood before him
with joined hands. Narada pronounced various benedictions on her
and commanded her to retire. He then addressed in private all the Pandavas,
with Yudhishthira at their head, saying: "The renowned princess of Panchala

is the wedded wife of you all. Establish a rule among yourselves
so that disunion may not arise among you.
In former days, there were two brothers named Sunda and Upasunda living
    together,
celebrated throughout the three worlds,
and both incapable of being slain unless each were to slay the other.
They ruled the same kingdom, lived in the same house, slept on the same bed,
sat on the same seat, and ate from the same dish. And yet they killed each other
for the sake of Tilottama. Therefore, O Yudhishthira, preserve your friendship
for one another, and do what will not produce disunion among you."
Of course Yudhishthira asked: "O great muni, who were Sunda and Upasunda?
How did that dissension arise between them? Why did they slay each other?
And whose daughter was this Tilottama, for whose love the maddened brothers
killed each other? Was she an Apsara or the daughter of a celestial?
We desire, O Brahmana, to hear in detail everything as it happened."
Narada replied: "Listen to me as I recite this old story, O Yudhishthira.
In the old days, a mighty Daitya named Nikumbha, of great energy and strength,
was born in the race of Hiranyakasipu, the great Asura.
To this Nikumbha were born two sons, called Sunda and Upasunda.
Both of them were mighty Asuras of great energy and terrible prowess.
The brothers were both fierce and possessed of wicked hearts.
And those Daityas were both of the same resolution
and always engaged in undertaking the same tasks and achieving the same ends.
They shared with each other in happiness as well as in woe.
Each spoke and did what was agreeable to the other.
The brothers were always together, and neither went anywhere without the other.
Of exactly the same disposition and habits, they seemed to be one individual
divided into two parts. The brothers gradually grew up, always with the same
    purpose,
desirous of subjugating the three worlds. These brothers went
to the mountains of Vindhya to perform severe ascetic penances.
Exhausted with hunger and thirst, with matted locks on their heads,
and attired in barks of trees, they acquired at length sufficient ascetic merit.
Smearing themselves with dirt from head to foot, living upon air alone,
standing on their toes, they threw pieces of the flesh of their bodies into the fire.
With arms upraised and eyes fixed straight ahead, they observed their vows
for a long time. During the course of their penances, a wonderful thing happened.
The mountains of Vindhya, heated for long years by the power of their ascetic
    austerities,
began to emit vapor from every part of their slopes.
The celestials became alarmed and caused numerous obstructions
to impede the progress of the brothers' asceticism. The celestials repeatedly
    tempted the brothers
with every luxury and with the most beautiful girls. The brothers did not break
    their vows.
Then the celestials manifested before the illustrious brothers their powers of
    illusion:

it seemed as if their sisters, mothers, wives, and other relatives, with disheveled hair

and ornaments and robes, were running toward them in terror,

pursued by a Rakshasa with a lance in hand.

It seemed as if the women were imploring the help of the brothers, crying: 'Oh, save us!'

But all this went for nothing, for the brothers still did not break their vows.

And when it was found that all this produced not the slightest impression on either one,

both the women and the Rakshasa vanished from sight.

At last the grandsire himself, the supreme lord, always seeking the welfare of all,

came to those great Asuras and asked them to solicit any boon they desired.

The brothers, Sunda and Upasunda, beheld the grandsire,

rose from their seats, and with joined palms said to the god: 'O grandsire,

if you have been pleased with our ascetic austerities and are kindly disposed to us,

let us have knowledge of all weapons and of all powers of illusion.

Let us be endowed with great strength, and let us be able to assume any form at will.

And let us also be immortal.'

Brahman said: 'Except the immortality you ask for, you shall be given all that you desire.

But you may ask for a form of death by which you may still be equal to the immortals.

Since you have undergone these ascetic austerities from desire of sovereignty alone,

I cannot confer immortality upon you.'"

Narada continued: "Hearing these words of Brahman, Sunda and Upasunda said:

'O grandsire, let us have no fear, then, of any created thing,

mobile or immobile, in the three worlds, but only of each other!'

The grandsire then said: 'I grant you what you have asked for.'

The grandsire allowed them to desist from their asceticism

and returned to his own region. Then the brothers, having received those boons,

could no longer be slain by anybody in the universe. They returned home.

All their friends and relatives happily welcomed those Daityas,

crowned as they were with success in the matter of the favors they had obtained.

Sunda and Upasunda cut off their matted locks and instead wore coronets.

Attired in costly robes and ornaments, they looked handsome indeed.

They caused the moon to rise over their city every night, even out of his season.

And friends and relatives gave themselves up to joy and merriment.

Eat, feed, give, make merry, sing, drink—these were the words heard every day in every house.

Here and there could be heard uproars of hilarity mixed with the clapping of hands

that filled the whole city of the Daityas, who, capable of assuming any form at will,

were engaged in every kind of amusement and scarcely noticed the flight of time,

even regarding a whole year as a single day."

Narada continued: "As soon as those festivities came to an end,
Sunda and Upasunda, hoping to attain the sovereignty of the three worlds,
took counsel and commanded their forces to be arrayed.
With the assent of their friends and relatives, and of the elders of the Daitya race
and of their ministers of state, they performed the rites of departure
and set out in the night, when the constellation Magha was in the ascendant.
The brothers had with them a large Daitya force clad in mail and armed
with maces and axes and lances and clubs. The Daitya heroes set out with joyous
    hearts,
the charanas chanting auspicious panegyrics indicative of their future triumphs.
Furious in war, the Daitya brothers, who were capable of going everywhere at will,
ascended the skies and went to the region of the celestials.
The celestials knew that they were coming and were acquainted with the boons
granted to them by the supreme deity. They therefore left heaven and sought
    refuge
in the region of Brahman. The Daitya brothers soon subjugated the region of
    Indra
and vanquished the diverse tribes of Yakshas and Rakshasas and every sky creature.
Then the mighty car warriors subjugated the Nagas of the nether region,
and then the inmates of the ocean and then all the tribes of the Mlechchhas.
Their next undertaking was the subjugation of the whole earth,
and those heroes summoned their soldiers and issued these cruel commands:
'Brahmanas and royal sages on earth, with their libations
and other food offered at grand sacrifices, increase the energy and strength of
    the gods
as well as their prosperity. Engaged in such acts, they are the enemies of the
    Asuras.
We should therefore slaughter all of them and wipe them from the face of the
    earth!'
Ordering their soldiers thus on the eastern shore of the great ocean,
the Asura brothers set out in all directions. Those who were performing
    sacrifices,
and the Brahmanas who were assisting at those sacrifices, the mighty brothers
instantly and violently slew. Then they departed for some other place.
While their soldiers threw into the water the sacrificial fires in the estates of munis,
the curses the angry rishis uttered were rendered nugatory
by the boons granted by Brahman and did not at all affect the Asura brothers.
When the Brahmanas saw that their curses had produced not the slightest effect,
like arrows shot at stones, they fled in all directions, forsaking their rites and vows.
Even those rishis on earth who were crowned with ascetic success,
and who had their passions under complete control and were engrossed in
    meditation on the deity,
from fear of the Asura brothers fled like snakes at the approach of Vinata's son,
Garuda the snake eater. The sacred precincts were all trodden down and
    broken.
The sacrificial vessels were broken, and their sacred contents were scattered on
    the ground.

The whole universe became empty, as if its creatures had all been stricken down
during the season of general dissolution. And, O king, after the rishis had all
   disappeared
and made themselves invisible, both the great Asuras, resolved upon their
   destruction,
began to assume various forms. Like maddened elephants, the Asura pair
searched out the rishis who had sheltered themselves in caves
and sent them to the region of Yama. Sometimes becoming lions or tigers
and then disappearing the next moment, the cruel pair sought out the rishis
and slew them instantly. Sacrifice and study ceased, and kings and Brahmanas
were exterminated. The earth became utterly destitute of sacrifices and festivals.
And the terrified people uttered cries of "Oh!" and "Alas!" All buying and selling
   stopped.
Religious rites ceased, and the earth saw no more sacred ceremonies or
   marriages.
Agriculture was neglected, and cattle were no longer tended.
Towns and religious precincts fell into desolation. Scattered over with bones,
the earth assumed a frightful aspect. Ceremonies in honor of the Pitris were
   suspended,
and the sacred sound of Vashat and the whole circle of auspicious rites ceased.
The sun and the moon, the planets and stars and constellations
and the other occupants of the firmament witnessed these acts of Sunda and
   Upasunda
and grieved deeply. Subjugating all the points of heaven by means of such cruel
   acts,
the Asura brothers took up their abode in Kurukshetra, without a single rival."
Narada continued: "Then the celestial rishis and the siddhas,
possessing the attributes of tranquillity and self-restraint
and beholding that act of universal slaughter, were afflicted with great grief.
With their passions and senses and souls under complete control,
they went to the abode of the grandsire, moved by compassion for the universe.
They beheld the grandsire, seated with gods and siddhas and Brahmarshis
   around him.
There was present that god of gods, Mahadeva, and also Agni, accompanied by
   Vayu,
and Soma and Surya and Sakra, and rishis devoted to the contemplation of
   Brahma,
and the Vaikhanasas, the Valakhilyas, the Vanaprasthas,
the Marichipas, the Ajas, the Avimudas, and other ascetics of great energy.
All those rishis were sitting with the grandsire,
when the celestial and other rishis approached Brahman with sorrowful hearts
and told him of all the acts of Sunda and Upasunda and of how they had
   committed them.
Then all the celestials and the great rishis pressed the matter before the
   grandsire.
The grandsire reflected for a moment and settled in his mind what he should do.
Resolving to compass the destruction of the Asura brothers,

he summoned Viswakarman, the celestial architect, and commanded him,
      saying:
'Create a damsel capable of captivating all hearts.'
Bowing low to the grandsire and receiving his command with reverence,
the great artificer of the universe created a celestial maiden
with the greatest care. Viswakrit first collected all handsome features for the body
of the damsel he created. The maiden he created was almost a mass of gems
and in beauty was unrivaled among the women of the three worlds.
There was not even a minute part of her body which, by its wealth of beauty,
could not attract the helpless gaze of beholders. Like the embodied Sri herself,
that damsel captivated the eyes and hearts of every creature.
Because she had been created with portions of every gem taken in minute
      measures,
the grandsire bestowed upon her the name of Tilottama.
And as soon as he launched it into life, the damsel bowed to Brahman
and with joined palms said: 'Lord of every created thing, what task am I to
      accomplish?'
The grandsire answered: 'Go, Tilottama, to the Asuras, Sunda and Upasunda.
Tempt them with your captivating beauty. And conduct yourself in such a way
that the Asura brothers may quarrel as soon as they cast their eyes on you.'"
Narada continued: "Bowing to the grandsire, the damsel said: '*So be it.*'
And she walked around the celestial conclave.
The illustrious Brahman was then sitting with face turned eastward,
and Mahadeva with face also toward the east,
and all the celestials with faces northward,
and the rishis with faces toward all directions.
While Tilottama walked around the conclave of the celestials, Indra and
      Mahadeva
were the only ones to succeed in preserving their tranquillity of mind.
But, eager as Mahadeva was of beholding Tilottama,
when the damsel in her progress around the celestial conclave was at his side,
another face like a full-blown lotus appeared on the southern side of his body.
And when she was behind him, another face appeared on the west.
And when the damsel was on the northern side of the great god,
a fourth face appeared on the northern side of his body.
Mahadeva, who was eager to behold the damsel, came thus to have a thousand
      eyes,
each large and slightly reddish, before, behind, and on his sides.
The mass of the celestials and the rishis turned their faces toward her
as Tilottama walked around them. The glances of all those illustrious
      personages,
except those of the divine grandsire himself, fell upon Tilottama's beauty.
When she set out for the city of the Asuras, all regarded the task as already
      accomplished.
After Tilottama had gone away, the great god who was the first cause of the
      universe
                  dismissed all the celestials and the rishis."

Narada continued: "Meanwhile, the Asura brothers, having subjugated the earth,
were without a rival. The fatigue of their exertion was gone
and, having brought the three worlds under equal sway,
they regarded themselves as persons who had nothing more to do.
Having won for themselves all the treasures of the gods,
the Gandharvas, the Yakshas, the Nagas, the Rakshasas, and the kings of the earth,
the brothers passed their days in great happiness. They had no rivals in the three
worlds,
and they gave up all exertion to devote their time to pleasure, as celestials do.
They gave themselves up to every kind of enjoyment, such as women,
and perfumes and floral wreaths and viands and drinks and many other amusing
objects.
In houses and woods and gardens, on hills and in forests, wherever they liked,
they passed their time in pleasure and jollity, like the immortals.
One day they went for purposes of pleasure to a mountain meadow
in the Vindhya range, perfectly level and stony and overgrown with blossoming
trees.
After every object of desire, all of the most agreeable kind, had been brought,
the brothers sat on excellent seats with happy hearts, accompanied by handsome
women.
Those damsels, intent on pleasing the brothers, commenced a dance
and chanted many songs in praise of the mighty pair.
Meanwhile, Tilottama, attired in a single piece of red silk that exposed all her
charms,
came wandering by, plucking wildflowers on her way.
She advanced to where those mighty Asuras were seated.
Both the brothers, intoxicated by the many potions they had imbibed,
were smitten upon beholding that maiden of transcendent beauty.
Rising from their seats, they went quickly to the damsel; and each, being moved
by lust,
sought the maiden for himself. Sunda seized her right hand.
Intoxicated with the boons they had obtained, with physical might,
with the wealth and gems they had gathered from every quarter, with the wine
they had drunk,
and maddened with all these and influenced by limitless desire, they addressed
each other
in anger. 'She is my wife, and therefore your superior,' said Sunda.
'She is my wife, and therefore your sister-in-law', replied Upasunda.
And they said to each other: 'She is mine, not yours.' Soon they were altogether
enraged.
Maddened by the beauty of the damsel, they forgot their love for each other.
Both of them, deprived of reason by passion, took up their maces.
Each repeated: 'I was first.' And they struck each other.
The fierce Asuras fell down upon the ground, their bodies bathed in blood,
like two suns dislodged from the firmament.
Beholding this, the women who had come there and the other Asuras who were
present

all fled, trembling in grief and fear, and took refuge in the nether regions.
The grandsire then appeared, accompanied by the celestials and the great rishis,
to applaud Tilottama and express his wish of granting her a boon.
Before Tilottama had a chance to speak, the supreme deity said:
'Beautiful damsel, you shall roam the region of the Adityas in splendor so great
that no one will ever be able to look at you for any length of time!'
The grandsire of all creatures granted this boon to her,
established the three worlds in Indra as before, and returned to his own region."
Narada continued: "It was thus that the Asuras, ever united
and inspired by the same purpose, slew each other in wrath for the sake of
     Tilottama.
From affection, therefore, I tell you, foremost members of Bharata's line,
that if you desire to do anything agreeable to me, make some such arrangement
by which you may not quarrel with one another for the sake of Draupadi."
The illustrious Pandavas, thus addressed by the great Narada,
consulted with one another and established a rule among themselves
in the presence of the rishi. Their rule was that when one of them
was lying with Draupadi, any of the other four who might intrude
must retire into the forest for twelve years, passing his days as a Brahmacharin.
After the virtuous Pandavas had established that rule among themselves,
the great muni Narada was pleased by what they had done, and he traveled on.
Thus did the Pandavas establish a rule in regard to their common wife.
And it was for this reason that no dispute ever arose among them.

15

Subhadra

The Pandavas, having established a just and benevolent government,
lived and ruled there and, by their prowess of arms, brought many kings under
  their sway.
Draupadi became obedient to all five sons of Pritha.
Like the river Saraswati, full of elephants that take pleasure in that stream,
Draupadi took great delight in her five husbands, and they took delight in her.
In consequence of the virtue of the Pandavas, the whole race of Kurus,
happy and free from sin, grew in prosperity.
But it came to pass that certain robbers stole the cattle of a Brahmana,
and while they were carrying away the booty, the Brahmana, out of his senses
  with anger,
repaired to Khandavaprastha to complain to the Pandavas in accents of woe:
"From this your dominion, my cattle are being taken away by force by wicked men!
Alas, the sacrificial butter of a peaceful Brahmana is being stolen by crows!
The wretched jackal invades the empty cave of a lion!
A king who takes the sixth part of the produce of the land without protecting
  the subjects
has been called by the wise the most sinful person in the world.
The property of a Brahmana is stolen! Virtue itself suffers a diminution!
Pursue them. Take me up by the hand, you Pandavas, for I am plunged in grief!"
Arjuna heard those words of the Brahmana. Loudly he assured him: "Have no
  fear!"
But it so happened that the chamber where the Pandavas had their weapons
was then occupied by Yudhishthira and Draupadi.
Arjuna, therefore, was incapable of entering it, and he was reluctant to go
  unarmed
with the Brahmana. Arjuna reflected: "Alas, this innocent Brahmana's wealth
is being robbed! I should dry his tears. He has come to our gate and weeps
  even now.
If I do not protect him, the king will be touched with sin for my indifference,
our impiety will be cited throughout the kingdom, and we shall incur a great sin.
But if, disregarding the king, I enter the chamber, I shall be behaving badly
to the monarch without a foe. By entering the chamber, I shall incur the penalty
of an exile in the woods. But I do not care if I have to incur sin by disregarding
  the king,

and I do not care if I have to go to the woods and die there.
Virtue is superior to the body and lasts after the body has perished!"
Arjuna decided to enter the chamber and talk with Yudhishthira.
Coming out with the bow, he cheerfully told the Brahmana:
"Proceed with haste, O Brahmana, so that the robbers may not get too far ahead
    of us.
I shall go with you and restore your wealth that has fallen into the hands of the
    thieves."
Then Arjuna, riding in his war-chariot decked with his standard,
pursued the thieves, pierced them with his arrows, and forced them to give up
    the booty.
He returned the cattle to the Brahmana and, winning great renown,
went back to the capital. Bowing to all the elders, and congratulated by
    everybody,
he at last approached Yudhishthira and said: "Give me leave, O lord, to observe
    my vow.
In beholding you with Draupadi, I have violated the rule we established.
I shall therefore go into the woods, for this was our understanding."
But Yudhishthira, afflicted with grief, said in an agitated voice: "Why?"
Then the king said: "If I am an authority worthy of regard, listen to what I say.
I know why you entered my chamber and did what you regard as disagreeable
    to me.
But there is no displeasure in my mind. The younger brother may enter without
    fault
the chamber where the elder brother is with his wife. It is only the elder brother
who acts against the rules of propriety entering the room
where the younger brother is with his wife. Therefore, desist.
                    Your virtue has sustained no diminution."
Arjuna, replied: "I have heard you say yourself that quibbling is not permitted
in the discharge of duty. I cannot waver from truth. Truth is my weapon."
With the king's permission, Arjuna prepared himself for a forest life
and went to the forest, to live there for twelve years.

✦

When the strong-armed Arjuna set out for the forest,
Brahmanas conversant with the Vedas walked for some distance behind him.
Followed as he was by Brahmanas devoted to the contemplation of the supreme
    spirit,
by persons skilled in music,
by ascetics devoted to the deity, by reciters of Puranas,
by narrators of sacred stories, by devotees leading celibate lives, by Vanaprasthas,
by Brahmanas reciting celestial histories, and by various other persons of
    eloquence,
Arjuna journeyed like Indra followed by the Maruts.
And the Bharatas saw, as he journeyed, many delightful forests, lakes, rivers, and
    seas.

At length he arrived at the source of the Ganges and thought of settling there.
When he and the Brahmanas who had followed him took up their residence in
 that region,
the latter performed innumerable Agnihotras, the sacrificial rites of lighting the
 sacred fire.
Because those illustrious Brahmanas, who never deviated from the right path,
daily established and ignited fires for their sacrifices with mantras
on the banks of that sacred stream after the performance of their ablutions,
and poured libations of clarified butter onto them, and worshipped those fires
with offerings of flowers, that region where the Ganges enters the plains
       became exceedingly beautiful.
One day Arjuna descended into the Ganges to perform his ablutions.
Then, after he had offered oblations of water to his deceased ancestors
and was about to leave the stream to perform his sacrificial rites before the fire,
he was dragged into the water by Ulupi, daughter of the king of the Nagas.
She had been urged to do this thing by the god of desire.
She carried the son of Pandu to the beautiful mansion of Kauravya, the king of
 the Nagas.
Arjuna saw there a sacrificial fire that had been lit for him,
and he performed his sacrificial rites there with all devotion. The god Agni
was much gratified with Arjuna for his fearlessness in performing these rites.
Arjuna then addressed the daughter of the king of the Nagas and said:
"O handsome girl, what an act of rashness you have committed!
Whose beautiful region is this? And who are you, and whose daughter are you?"
Ulupi answered: "There is a Naga named Kauravya, born in the line of Airavata.
I am his daughter, and my name is Ulupi.
Seeing you perform your ablutions, I was deprived of reason by the god of desire.
I am still unmarried. Afflicted as I am by the god of desire on your account,
I ask you to gratify me today by giving yourself to me."
Arjuna replied: "At the command of King Yudhishthira,
I am undergoing the vow of Brahmacharin for twelve years. I am not free to act
 as I like.
But I will serve your pleasure if I can. I have never spoken an untruth in my life.
Tell me then, O Naga maid, how I may act so that while serving your pleasure
I may not be guilty of any untruth or breach of duty."
Ulupi answered: "I know why you wander the earth,
and why you have been commanded to lead the life of a Brahmacharin.
This was the understanding to which all of you had agreed:
that he who would enter the room where one of you would be with Draupadi
should lead the life of a Brahmacharin in the woods for twelve years.
The exile of any one of you, then, is only for her sake. You are only observing
 your vow.
But your virtue will not be diminished if you accede to my request.
It is a duty to relieve the distressed. And by this act you will acquire great merit
for saving my life. Know me as your worshipper and yield yourself to me!
It is the opinion of the wise that one should accept a woman who woos.
If you do not, I will destroy myself. I seek your aid, O best of men!

You always protect, O son of Kunti, the afflicted and the masterless.

Weeping in sorrow, I seek your protection, and it behooves you to gratify my wish

and yield yourself to me." The mighty Arjuna did as she desired, with virtue his
motive.

After spending the night in the mansion of the Naga, he rose with the sun in the
morning.

And, accompanied by Ulupi, he came back from the palace of Kauravya

to the region where the Ganges enters the plains.

Ulupi took her leave there and returned to her own abode, but before she left,

she granted Arjuna a boon, making him invincible in water:

"Every amphibious creature shall be conquerable by you."

✦

Arjuna told the Brahmanas who were with him what had happened,

and he set out for the breast of Himavat.

He reached the spot called Agastyavata and went next to Vasishtha's peak.

Thence he proceeded to the peak of Bhrigu. Purifying himself with ablutions,

he gave away to Brahmanas many thousands of cows and horses.

From there, that best of men proceeded to the sacred asylum called
Hiranyavindu

and performed his ablutions there. He then descended from those heights,

accompanied by the Brahmanas, and journeyed eastward,

where he saw many regions of sacred waters one after another.

In the forest of Naimisha he saw the river Utpalini, meaning "Full of Lotuses,"

and the Nanda and the Apara Nanda, the far-famed Kausiki,

and the mighty rivers Gaya and Ganga, and in all the regions of sacred water

he purified himself with the usual rites and gave away many cows to Brahmanas.

Whatever regions of sacred waters and whatever other holy palaces there were

in Vanga and Kalinga, Arjuna visited all of them.

At last all those Brahmanas following the son of Pandu

bade him farewell at the gate of the kingdom of Kalinga and went with him no
further.

Obtaining their leave, Arjuna went toward the ocean with only a few attendants.

Crossing the country of the Kalingas, the mighty one proceeded,

visiting on his way diverse countries and sacred spots, delightful mansions and
houses.

Beholding the Mahendra mountain adorned with the ascetics residing there,

he went to Manipura, proceeding slowly along the seashore.

He saw all the sacred waters and other holy places in that province

and at last went to the virtuous Chitravahana, the ruler of Manipura.

The king of Manipura had a daughter of great beauty named Chitrangada.

And it so happened that Arjuna saw her in her father's palace, roving at pleasure.

Stricken by her beauty, Arjuna desired to possess her.

He went to the king and told him what he sought:

"Give me your daughter, O king! I am an illustrious Kshatriya's son."

The king asked him: "Whose son are you?" And he replied: "I am Arjuna,

the son of Pandu and Kunti." The king then said these words:
"There was in our race a king named Prabhanjana who was childless.
To obtain a child, he underwent severe ascetic penances.
By his asceticism, he gratified Mahadeva, that supreme lord
holding the mighty bow called Pinaka. The illustrious lord granted him the boon
that each successive descendant of his race should have one child only.
Therefore, only one child is born to every successive descendant of this race.
All my ancestors, one after another, have had one male child.
I, however, have only a daughter to perpetuate my race.
But I look upon this daughter of mine as my son. I have made her a Putrika.
Therefore, one among the sons that may be begotten upon her by you
shall be the perpetuator of my race. That son is the dower
for which I may give away my daughter. O son of Pandu, if you agree, you can
   take her."
                         Arjuna agreed and said: "So be it."
Taking Chitravahana's daughter as his wife, the son of Kunti lived in that city
for three years. When Chitrangada at last gave birth to a son,
Arjuna embraced that handsome princess affectionately.
And taking leave of the king, her father, he set out on his wanderings again.

✦

Then that bull of Bharata's race went to the sacred waters
on the banks of the southern ocean, all adorned with the ascetics residing there.
There were scattered five such regions where many ascetics dwelled.
But those five waters were shunned by all of them.
Those sacred waters were called Agastya, and Saubhadra, and Pauloma of great
   holiness,
and Karandhama of great propitiousness yielding the fruits of a horse sacrifice
to those that bathed there, and Bharadwaja, that great washer of sins.
Arjuna, finding those five sacred waters uninhabited,
and ascertaining that they were shunned by the virtuous ascetics,
asked those pious men with joined hands: "Why do you shun these five sacred
   waters?"
They replied: "There dwell in these waters five large crocodiles
that take away any ascetics that may happen to bathe in them."
Although they tried to dissuade him, Arjuna went to inspect those waters.
At Saubhadra, after a great rishi plunged into it to have a bath, an enormous
   crocodile
seized him by the leg. But Arjuna took hold of the beast and dragged it to the
   shore,
where the crocodile was transformed into a beautiful damsel.
Arjuna, startled at this metamorphosis, asked her: "Who are you, O beautiful one?
Why have you been a crocodile? What dreadful sins have you committed?"
The damsel replied, saying: "I am an Apsara that sported in the celestial woods.
I am Varga, dear to the celestial treasurer, Kuvera. I have four companions, all
   handsome

and able to go anywhere at will. With them I was going to the home of Kuvera.
On the way we beheld a Brahmana, exceedingly handsome, studying the Vedas.
The whole forest in which he was sitting seemed to be lit with his ascetic
    splendor
as if by the sun himself. We alit there in order to disturb his meditations.
Saurabheyi and Samichi and Vudvuda and Lata and I approached that Brahmana
at the same time. We began to sing and smile and otherwise tempt him.
But the youth was not even once distracted by us.
His mind was fixed on pure meditation, and his heart never wavered.
Instead, the glance he cast upon us was one of wrath. And he said, staring at us:
'Become crocodiles, and range the waters for a hundred years.'"
Varga continued: "We were deeply distressed and sought to propitiate the
    Brahmana.
We said: 'Inflated with a sense of our beauty and youth, and urged by the god of
    desire,
we have acted very improperly. Pardon us, O Brahmana!
Grow in virtue. You are conversant with virtue and are the friend of every creature.
The eminent always protect those who seek protection at their hands.
We seek your protection. Grant us your pardon.'
The Brahmana of virtuous soul and good deeds became propitious to us.
And he said: 'The words *hundred* and *hundred thousand* are all indicative of
    eternity.
The word *hundred*, however, as I have used it, is to be understood
as a limited period and not an infinite period. You shall, therefore, become
    crocodiles
and seize and take away men for only a hundred years.
And at the end of that period, an exalted individual will drag you all from water
to the land, where you will resume your real forms. Never have I spoken an
    untruth,
even in jest. Therefore, all that I have said must come to pass.
And those sacred waters within which I assign you your places
will, after you have been delivered by that individual,
become known all over the world by the name of Nari-tirthas,
meaning "Sacred Waters Connected with Sufferings and Deliverance of Females,"
and all of them shall be sacred and sin-cleansing in the eyes of the virtuous and
    the wise.'"
Varga finished her discourse, saying: "We saluted the Brahmana with reverence,
walked around him, and came away with heavy hearts, thinking as we proceeded:
Where shall we meet that man who will give us back our own shapes?
Almost at that very moment, we beheld the eminent celestial rishi Narada.
Saluting him with reverence, we stood before him with blushing faces.
He asked of us the cause of our sorrow, and we told him all.
The rishi said: 'In the lowlands bordering the southern ocean,
there are five regions of sacred water. They are delightful and eminently holy.
Go there without delay. Arjuna, the son of Pandu of pure soul,
will soon deliver you from this sad plight.' Hearing those words, we all came here.
O sinless one, I have today been delivered. But those four friends of mine

are still within the waters here. Do a good deed by delivering them also."
Then, that foremost among the Pandavas delivered all of them from that curse.
Rising from the waters, they regained their own forms and looked as they had
    before.
Freeing those sacred waters from the danger for which they had been notorious,
and giving the Apsaras leave to go where they chose, Arjuna desired once more
to behold Chitrangada. He, therefore, proceeded toward the city of Manipura,
where he saw on the throne the son he had begotten upon Chitrangada,
who was called by the name of Vabhruvahana.
Seeing Chitrangada once more, Arjuna proceeded toward the spot called Gokarna
and then visited all the sacred waters and other holy places on the western ocean.
He reached the sacred spot called Prabhasa.
To that delightful region, the slayer of Macho, or Krishna, came to see his friend.
Krishna and Arjuna met, embraced each other, and inquired after each other's
    welfare.
Those dear friends, who were the rishis Nara and Narayana of old, sat down to
    talk.
Krishna asked Arjuna about his travels: "Why are you wandering over the earth,
visiting all the sacred waters and other holy places?" Arjuna told him what had
    happened.
Krishna answered: "This is as it should be." And together, having spent some time
at Prabhasa, they went on to the Raivataka mountain to pass some days there.
Before they arrived at Raivataka, that mountain, at Krishna's command,
had been well adorned by many craftsmen. Much food, too, had been collected
    there.
Enjoying everything that had been laid out there for him,
Arjuna sat with Krishna to see the performances of the actors and the dancers.
Then the high-souled Pandava dismissed them all with proper respect,
lay down on a well-adorned and excellent bed, and described to Krishna
everything about the sacred waters, the lakes and the mountains
and the rivers and the forests he had seen.
While he was speaking of these things, sleep stole upon him.
Arjuna rose in the morning to sweet songs and melodious notes of the guitar
and to the panegyrics and benedictions of the charanas. Krishna greeted him
    affectionately.
Riding upon a golden car, Arjuna then set out for Dwaraka, the capital of the
    Yadavas.
And to honor the son of Kunti, the city of Dwaraka was handsomely adorned,
with all the gardens and houses decorated. The citizens of Dwaraka poured
    eagerly
into the public thoroughfares by hundreds of thousands to see Arjuna,
hundreds and thousands of women mixing with the men to swell the great crowd
of the Bhojas, the Vrishnis, and the Andhakas collected there.
Arjuna was welcomed with respect by all the sons of Bhojas, Vrishnis, and
    Andhakas.
He in his turn worshipped those who deserved his worship, and he received
    their blessings.

He embraced all who were equal to him in age. Proceeding then to Krishna's
   mansion,
which was filled with gems and articles of enjoyment, he took up his abode there
   for many days.

✦

Within a few days, a grand festival of the Vrishnis and the Andhakas began
on the Raivataka mountain. The Bhojas, the Vrishnis, and the Andhakas
gave away much wealth to thousands of Brahmanas.
The region was adorned with mansions decked with gems and artificial trees
of bright hues. Musicians struck up in concert, and dancers danced and singers
   sang.
The citizens came on foot or in excellent cars with their wives and followers
by the hundreds and thousands. There was the lord Haladhara, or Valarama,
roving at will, hilarious with drink, accompanied by his wife, Revati,
and followed by many musicians and vocalists.
Ugrasena also came, the powerful king of the Vrishni race, with his thousand wives
and followed by sweet singers. And Raukmineya and Shamva also, ever furious in
   battle,
roved there, excited with drink and adorned with floral wreaths of great beauty
and with costly attire, and they disported themselves like a pair of celestials.
Akrura and Sarana and Gada, and Vabhru, and Nisatha,
and Charudeshna, and Prithu, Viprithu, and Satyaka, and Satyaki,
and Bhangakara, and Maharava, and Hardikya, and Uddhava and many others
whose names are not given, accompanied by their wives and followed by bands
   of singers,
came to adorn the mountain-festival. When it began, Krishna and Arjuna went
   about together
and, as they wandered, they saw Subhadra, the handsome daughter of Vasudeva,
decked with every ornament and surrounded by her maids.
As soon as Arjuna beheld her, he was possessed by the god of desire.
Krishna noticed Arjuna's rapt stare and said with a smile: "How is this?
Can the heart of one who ranges the woods be agitated by the god of desire?
This is my sister. Her name is Subhadra, and she is my father's favorite daughter.
Tell me if your heart is fixed upon her, for I will then speak to my father on your
   behalf."
Arjuna answered: "She is your sister? Whom can she not fascinate?
Tell me how I may obtain her. To get her, I will accomplish anything achievable
   by man."
Krishna answered: "Self-choice has been ordained for the marriage of Kshatriyas.
But that is doubtful in its consequences, as we do not know this girl's disposition.
In the case of Kshatriyas that are brave, a forcible abduction for purposes of
   marriage
is applauded, as the learned have said. Therefore, carry away my beautiful sister
   by force,
for who knows what she may do at a ceremony of self-choice?"

Then Krishna and Arjuna, having thus settled what should be done,
sent some speedy messengers to Yudhishthira at Indraprastha,
informing him of everything. Yudhishthira gave his assent.
Arjuna, informed of this and ascertaining that the maiden had gone to the
    Raivataka hill,
obtained the permission of Vasudeva, her father. Then, with Krishna's assent,
riding in his well-built car of gold equipped with rows of small bells
and with every kind of weapon and clattering wheels
that resembled the roar of the clouds and with a splendor like that of a blazing fire
that struck terror into the hearts of all foes,
and to which were yoked the steeds Saivya and Sugriva, Arjuna, accoutered in mail
and armed with a sword and with his fingers encased in leather gloves,
                  set out as if on a hunting expedition.
Meanwhile, Subhadra, having paid homage to Raivataka, that prince of hills,
and having worshipped the deities and made the Brahmanas utter benedictions
    upon her,
and having also walked around the hill, was coming toward Dwaravati.
The son of Kunti, afflicted with the shafts of the god of desire,
rushed toward that girl of faultless features, forcibly took her into his car,
and proceeded in his car of gold toward his own city, Indraprastha.
Meanwhile, the armed attendants of Subhadra, seeing her thus seized and taken
    away,
all ran crying toward the city of Dwaraka, where they reported everything
about Arjuna's prowess to the chief officer of the court. When he had heard
    everything,
he blew his gold-trimmed trumpet, calling all to arms.
The Bhojas, the Vrishnis, and the Andhakas poured in from all sides.
Those who were eating left their food, and those who were drinking left their
    drink.
Those great warriors took their seats upon their thousand thrones of gold
covered with excellent carpets and variegated with gems and corals
and possessed of the luster of blazing fire,
and when were seated in what was like a conclave of the celestials,
the chief officer of the court and those at his back spoke of the conduct of
    Arjuna.
The Vrishni heroes, their eyes bloodshot with wine, rose up from their seats,
angry at what Arjuna had done. Some among them said: "Yoke our cars."
And some said: "Bring our weapons." And some said: "Bring our costly bows
and strong coats of mail." Some called to their charioteers to harness their cars,
and some, impatient, yoked their gold-bedecked horses themselves to their cars.
And while their cars and armor and standards were being brought,
the uproar of those heroes grew loud indeed.
But then Valadeva, white and tall as the peak of Kailasa,
wearing garlands of wild flowers and attired in blue robes,
and proud and intoxicated with drink, said these words:
"You senseless men, what are you doing? Krishna sits silent!
Without knowing what is in his mind, why do you roar in wrath?

Let the high-souled Krishna tell us what he proposes. Do as he desires you to do."
All of them, hearing those words, exclaimed: "Excellent! Excellent!"
And they hushed and took their seats once more.
Rama, that oppressor of foes, spoke then to Vasudeva, saying:
"Why, O Krishna, do you sit gazing silently?
It was for your sake that Arjuna was welcomed and honored by us all.
It seems, however, that this wretch did not deserve our homage.
What man is there of a respectable family who would break the plate
after having dined from it? Even if one desires to make such an alliance,
still, remembering all the kindnesses he has received,
who is there desirous of happiness who would act so rashly?
That Pandava insults us, and you too, and he has today outraged Subhadra.
Does he desire his own death? He has placed his foot on the crown of my head.
How shall I bear it? Shall I not resent it, even as a snake would that is trodden
    upon?
I shall today make the earth destitute of Kauravas!
Never shall I put up with this transgression of Arjuna's."
Then all the Bhojas, Vrishnis, and Andhakas present approved of what Valadeva
    had said
and roared deeply like a kettledrum or the clouds' thunder.
Then Vasudeva uttered these words:
"By what he has done, Arjuna has not insulted our family. He has rather
enhanced our respect. He knows that we of the Satwata race are never mercenary.
The son of Pandu also regards a self-choice as doubtful in its results.
And who would approve of accepting a bride as a gift as if she were an animal?
And what man on earth would sell his offspring?
I think that Arjuna, seeing these faults in all the other methods, took the maiden
    by force
according to the ordinance. This alliance is very proper. Subhadra is a renowned
    girl.
Arjuna, too, possesses renown. Who would not desire to have Arjuna for a friend?
He is born in the race of Bharata and the renowned Santanu
and is the son also of the daughter of Kuntibhoja.
I do not see in all the worlds the person that can vanquish him in battle
except the three-eyed god Mahadeva. His car is well known.
Yoked to it are those steeds of mine. As a warrior, Arjuna is famous,
and his lightness of hand is famous. Who is his equal? This is my opinion.
Go after him, then, and by conciliation stop him and bring him back.
If he goes to his city after having vanquished us by force, our fame will be gone.
There is no disgrace, however, in conciliation."
Hearing those words of Vasudeva, they did as he had directed.
They caught up with Arjuna, and he returned to Dwaraka,
where he was united in marriage with Subhadra. He passed a whole year in
    Dwaraka.
The last year of his exile the exalted one passed at the sacred region of
    Pushkara.
After the twelve years were complete, he came back to Khandavaprastha.

He approached the king first and then worshipped the Brahmanas.

At last he went to Draupadi. Jealous, she spoke unto him, saying:

"Why do you tarry here, O son of Kunti? Go to the daughter of the Satwata race!
A second tie always relaxes the first one upon a bundle of sticks."

She lamented much in this strain. But Arjuna pacified her and asked for her
forgiveness.

Then he returned to where Subhadra, attired in red silk, was staying,

and he sent her into the inner apartments dressed not as a queen

but in the simple garb of a cowherd. Still, the renowned Subhadra

looked even more handsome in that dress. The young woman first worshipped
Kunti,

who in affection smelled her head and pronounced infinite blessing upon her.

Then that girl hastily went to Draupadi and worshipped her, saying: "I am your
maid!"

Draupadi rose hastily, embraced her, and said: "Let your husband be without
a foe!"

Delighted, Subhadra said to Draupadi: "So be it!"

And from that time, the Pandavas lived happily, and Kunti also was very happy.

When Krishna heard that Arjuna had reached Indraprastha,

he traveled there, accompanied by Rama and the other heroes

and great warriors of the Vrishni and the Andhaka tribes,

and by his brothers and sons and many other brave warriors.

And Saurin came, accompanied by a large army that protected him.

And with Saurin came Akrura of great intelligence and renown,

the generalissimo of the brave Vrishni host. And there came also Anadhrishti

of great prowess; and Uddhava of great renown, of great intelligence, and of
great soul;

and also Satyaka and Salyaka and Kritavarman and Satwata;

and Pradyumna and Samva and Nisatha and Sanku; and Charudeshna;

and Jhilli of great prowess; and Viprithu also; and Sarana of mighty arms;

and Gada, foremost among learned men. These and many other Vrishnis

and Bhojas and Andhakas came to Indraprastha, bringing many nuptial presents.

King Yudhishthira, hearing that Krishna had arrived, sent the twins to receive him.

The Vrishni host entered Khandavaprastha, which was well adorned with flags
and ensigns.

The streets were well swept and watered and decked with floral wreaths and
bunches.

They were sprinkled with sandalwood water that was fragrant and cooling.

Every part of the town was filled with the sweet scent of burning aloes.

And the city was full of joyous people and crowded with merchants and traders.

When they entered the city, Krishna of mighty arms, Rama, and many of the
Vrishnis,

Andhakas, and Bhojas were worshipped by the citizens and Brahmanas by the
thousands.

At last Krishna entered the palace of the king, which was like the celestial
mansion

of Indra himself. Yudhishthira received him with due ceremonies.

The king smelled the head of Krishna and embraced him.

Krishna, gratified by this reception, humbly worshipped Yudhishthira.

He also paid homage to Bhima. Yudhishthira then received the other principal men

of the Vrishni and the Andhaka tribes with due ceremonies.

Yudhishthira worshipped some as his superiors and welcomed others as equals.

Some he received with affection, and by some he was worshipped with reverence.

Then Krishna gave to the party of the bridegroom much wealth,

and to Subhadra he gave the nuptial presents that had been given her by her relatives.

Krishna gave the Pandavas a thousand cars of gold furnished with rows of bells,

to each of which were hitched four steeds driven by well-trained charioteers.

He also gave them ten thousand cows belonging to the country of Mathura

and yielding much milk of excellent color. He also gave them a thousand mares

with gold harnesses and of a color as white as the beams of the moon,

and a thousand mules, all well trained and possessing the speed of the wind,

white with black manes. And he gave them a thousand damsels well skilled

in assisting at bathing and at drinking, young in years and virgins

all before their first season, well attired and of fine complexion,

each with a hundred pieces of gold around her neck, and of skin perfectly polished,

decked with every ornament and adept at every kind of personal service.

Also he gave hundreds of thousands of draft horses from the country of the Valhikas

as Subhadra's excellent dower, and ten carrier loads of first-class gold,

some purified and some in a state of ore. And as a nuptial present, Rama gave Arjuna a thousand elephants

with secretions flowing in three streams from the three parts of their bodies—

the temple, the ears, and the anus—each as large as a mountain summit,

irresistible in battle, decked with coverlets and bells and other golden ornaments,

and all equipped with excellent howdahs on their backs.

And there was a sea of wealth and gems that the Yadavas presented,

together with the cloths and blankets that represented its foam,

and the elephants its alligators and sharks, and the flags its floating weeds,

swelling into large proportions to mingle with the Pandu ocean and fill it to the brim.

Yudhishthira accepted all those presents and worshipped all those great warriors

of the Vrishni and the Andhaka races, who passed their days in pleasure there

like virtuous men after their deaths in the celestial regions.

The Kurus and the Vrishnis amused themselves there, setting up at times loud shouts

and clapping of hands in sports and merriment.

The Vrishni heroes then returned to the city of Dwaravati.

And the great warriors of the Vrishni and Andhaka races set out

with Rama in the van, carrying with them those gems that had been given them

by those of Kuru's race. But the high-souled Krishna remained there with Arjuna

in the delightful city of Indraprastha. They wandered over the banks of the Yamuna
in search of deer and sported together, piercing with their shafts deer and wild boars.
Then Subhadra gave birth to an illustrious son,
as Puloma's daughter, the queen of heaven, had brought forth Jayanta.
And the son Subhadra brought forth was of long arms, broad chest,
and eyes as large as those of a bull. That hero and oppressor of foes
came to be called Abhimanyu because he was fearless and wrathful.
Upon the birth of this child, Yudhishthira gave away to Brahmanas
ten thousand cows and coins of gold. The child from his earliest years
became the favorite of Krishna and of his father;
and upon his birth, Krishna performed the usual rites of infancy.
The child grew like the moon in the bright fortnight
and soon was conversant with the Vedas.
He acquired from his father the science of weapons both celestial and human,
consisting of four branches and ten divisions. The child also acquired
the knowledge of counteracting the weapons hurled at him by others,
and great lightness of hand and fleetness of motion forward and backward and sideways.
Abhimanyu became like his father in knowledge of the scriptures and the rites of religion.
And Arjuna was filled with joy. Abhimanyu possessed the power of slaying every foe
and bore on his person every auspicious mark.
He was invincible in battle and broad-shouldered as the bull.
With a face as broad as the hood of the cobra, he was as proud as a lion.
Wielding a large bow, he had strength like that of an elephant in rut.
His voice was as deep as the sound of the drum or the clouds,
and he was equal to Krishna in bravery and energy, in beauty and in features.
The auspicious Draupadi also, from her five husbands,
obtained five sons, all of whom were heroes of the foremost rank
and as immovable in battle as the hills: Prativindhya by Yudhishthira,
Sutasoma by Vrikodara, Srutakarman by Arjuna, Satanika by Nakula,
and Srutasena by Sahadeva. And the Brahmanas, from their foreknowledge,
said to Yudhishthira that as his son would be capable of bearing
like the Vindhya mountains the weapons of the foe, he should be called Prativindhya.
And because the child that Draupadi bore to Bhimasena was born after Bhima
had performed a thousand soma sacrifices, he should be called Sutasoma.
And because Arjuna's son was born upon his return from exile, that child should be called
Srutakarman. Nakula named his son Satanika, after a royal sage of that name.
And the son Draupadi bore to Sahadeva was delivered under the constellation
called Vahni-daivata, or Krittika, and thus was called after the leader of the celestial host,
Srutasena or Kartikeya. The sons of Draupadi were born at intervals of one year,
and all became renowned and much attached to one another.

All their rites of infancy and childhood, such as Chudakarana and Upanayana—
the first shave of the head and investiture with the sacred threads—
were performed by Dhaumya according to the ordinance.
All of them, after having studied the Vedas, acquired from Arjuna
a knowledge of all the weapons, celestial and human.
And the Pandavas, having obtained sons who were equal to the children of the
     celestials,
and who all became great warriors, were filled with joy.

16

Agni

The Pandavas began to bring other kings under their sway.
The subjects of the kingdom lived in peace and contentment
under the rule of Yudhishthira the just, who paid homage
to virtue, pleasure, and profit, in judicious proportion, as if each were a dear
  friend.
It seemed as if those three pursuits had become personified on earth in him.
Because of Yudhishthira's influence, the good fortune of all the monarchs of the
  earth
grew strong and stable, and their hearts turned to the meditation of the
  supreme spirit. Virtue itself grew in every way and, assisted by his four
  brothers,
the king was even more resplendent than he would have been if he had been
  alone.
The people delighted in him not only because he was their king
but also from sincere affection. The best of monarchs passed his days
as much concerned for the welfare of all as for his own.
He and his brothers were happy, without a foe to disturb their peace.
Arjuna said one day to Krishna: "Summer days have come! Let us therefore go
to the banks of the Yamuna to sport there in the company of friends.
We can return in the evening." Krishna answered: "This is also my wish."
Then, by Yudhishthira's leave, they set out and arrived at a fine spot
on the banks of the Yamuna, overgrown with numerous tall trees
and covered with several lofty mansions that made the place look like the
  celestial city,
and within which had been collected for Krishna and Arjuna
numerous costly and delicate viands and drinks as well as wreaths and various
  perfumes.
The party entered the inner apartments and began to sport, each according to
  his pleasure.
The women of the party, all of full round hips, deep bosoms, and handsome eyes,
and their gait unsteady with wine, sported there also,
at the command of Krishna and Arjuna. Some among the women played in the
  woods,
some in the waters, and some inside the mansions. Draupadi and Subhadra,
exhilarated with wine, gave these women costly robes and ornaments.

Some among them danced in joy, and some sang; and some laughed and joked;
and some drank of the excellent wines. Some fought with one another
or discoursed with one another in private. The mansions and the woods
were filled with the music of flutes and guitars in a scene of prosperity personified.
Arjuna and Krishna went to a quiet spot in the woods and sat down on two costly
seats
to discuss their many past achievements.
While they were sitting there,
a certain Brahmana came who looked like a tall sala tree.
His complexion was like molten gold; his beard was bright yellow tinged with
green.
With matted locks and dressed in rags, he nonetheless resembled the morning sun
in splendor. As he approached them, both Arjuna and Krishna rose from their
seats
and awaited his commands. "You," he said, "are the two foremost heroes on earth.
I am a voracious Brahmana who always eats much. I solicit you to gratify me
by giving me sufficient food." Krishna and Arjuna asked:
"What kind of food will gratify you?"
The Brahmana replied: "I do not desire ordinary food. Know that I am *Agni*, god
of fire!
Give me the food that suits me. This forest of Khandava is protected by Indra,
and therefore I fail to consume it. In that forest a Naga named Takshaka dwells
with his followers and family. He is the friend of Indra.
It is for him that the wielder of the thunderbolt protects this forest.
Many other creatures also are thus protected here for the sake of Takshaka.
When Indra sees me blazing forth, he pours water upon me from the clouds.
Therefore, I have come to you, who are both skilled in weapons!
If you help me, I will be able to consume this forest, for this is the food that I
desire!
You are conversant with excellent weapons, and I pray you to prevent those
showers
from descending and any creatures from escaping when I begin to devour the
forest!"

✦

And why did the illustrious Agni desire to consume the forest of Khandava,
filled as it was with various living creatures and protected by the chief of the
celestials?
The story of the conflagration of Khandava is told by rishis in the Purana:
There was a celebrated king named Swetaki
who was endowed with strength and was the equal of Indra himself.
No one on earth surpassed him in sacrifices, charity, and intelligence.
King Swetaki, assisted by his priests, performed sacrifices for many long years
until those sacrificial priests' eyes were afflicted by the continued smoke
and they became very weak. They left that monarch, wishing to assist no longer
at his sacrifices. The king, however, repeatedly asked those ritwiks to come to him.

But they refused because of the painful state of their eyes.

The king, therefore, invited others like them to complete the sacrifice he had
 begun.

After some days had elapsed, he desired to perform yet another sacrifice,

which should extend for a hundred years. But the monarch could not obtain
 any priest

to assist him in it. Angry, he addressed those Brahmanas sitting in their ashrams:

"If I were a fallen person, or if I were wanting in homage and service to you,

I should then deserve to be abandoned without scruple.

I seek your protection! It behooves you to be propitious to me.

But, you foremost among Brahmanas, if you abandon me from enmity alone,

I shall go to other priests for their assistance."

Unwilling to assist him, the Brahmanas pretended to be angry and said: "O best
 of kings,

your sacrifices are incessant! We have been wearied by these labors.

Go to Rudra, the god of storms and winds! He will assist at your sacrifice!"

At those words, King Swetaki grew angrier, and he went to the mountains of
 Kailasa

to devote himself to asceticism there. With fixed attention, he worshipped
 Mahadeva,

observing the most rigid vows. He ate only fruits and roots at the twelfth hour

and sometimes at the sixteenth hour. He stood for six months, rapt in attention,

with arms upraised and eyes unmoving, like the trunk of a tree

or a column rooted to the ground. And at last, gratified by that tiger among
 kings,

the god showed himself and spoke to him in a grave voice, saying:

"I have been pleased with you for your asceticism! Ask the boon that you desire."

Hearing these words, the royal sage bowed and replied: "Illustrious one,

worshipped by the three worlds, if you have been pleased with me,

then assist me yourself in my sacrifice!" The god replied:

"We do not ourselves assist at sacrifices. But as you have undergone severe
 penances,

I will assist on one condition. If, for twelve years, you can pour without intermission

libations of clarified butter into the fire, leading all the while the life of a
 Brahmacharin,

then you shall obtain what you ask."

King Swetaki did all that he was directed to do and, after twelve years had
 elapsed,

came again to Rudra, who said: "I have been gratified, O best of kings!

But the duty of assisting at sacrifices properly belongs to Brahmanas.

Therefore, I will not myself assist at your sacrifice.

There is on earth, however, an exalted Brahmana who is a part of my self.

He is known by the name of Durvasa, and he will assist you. Let preparations be
 made."

The king returned to his capital and collected all that was necessary.

Then he presented himself before Rudra once more and said:

"All my preparations are complete, O god of gods!

Let me, therefore, be installed at the sacrifice tomorrow."
Rudra then summoned Durvasa before him and said: "This is that best of
    monarchs.
At my command, assist him in his sacrifice." Durvasa said to Rudra: "So be it."
Then the sacrifice took place and was performed according to the ordinance
and in proper season. And the gifts to the Brahmanas were large.
After the sacrifice had come to an end, all the other priests who had come to
    assist at it
went away, by Durvasa's leave. The monarch then entered his palace,
worshipped by Brahmanas, eulogized by chanters of panegyric hymns,
and congratulated by the citizens. Such was the history of that best of monarchs,
the sage Swetaki, who, in time, ascended to heaven, having won great renown on
    earth.

✦

At that sacrifice of Swetaki, Agni had been required to drink
clarified butter for twelve years in a continuous stream.
Having drunk so much butter, Agni desired never to drink butter again
from the hand of anyone else at any other sacrifice.
He became pale, and he could not shine as before.
He felt a loss of appetite, his energy decreased, and sickness afflicted him.
Therefore, he went to the sacred abode of Brahman, who is worshipped by all,
and said to the deity: "Exalted one, Swetaki by his sacrifice has gratified me to
    excess.
I suffer from a surfeit I cannot dispel. I am being reduced both in splendor and
    strength.
                    I desire to regain my own permanent nature."
Hearing these words, the illustrious creator of all things replied:
"You have eaten, for twelve years, a continuous stream of sacrificial butter
poured into your mouth! But do not grieve, Agni. I shall dispel this surfeit of
    yours.
The dreadful forest Khandava, that abode of the enemies of the gods,
which you once consumed to ashes at the gods' request,
has now become the home of numerous creatures.
When you will have eaten the fat of those creatures, you shall regain your own
    nature.
Proceed there, and consume that forest with its living population. You will then
    be cured."
Hearing these words from the lips of the supreme deity,
Agni went speedily to the forest of Khandava. There he blazed forth in anger.
Beholding Khandava on fire, the dwellers in the forest
made great efforts to extinguish the conflagration.
Hundreds of thousands of elephants brought water in their trunks and poured it
    on the fire.
Thousands of angry hooded snakes scattered upon the fire water from their
    hoods.

And the other creatures dwelling in that forest, by various means and methods,
soon extinguished the fire. In this way, Agni blazed forth in Khandava
   repeatedly,
even seven times. And the blazing fire was extinguished there as often
by the denizens of that forest. Then Agni, in anger and disappointment,
with his ailment uncured, went back to the grandsire and told him what had
   happened.
The deity reflected for a moment and said: "Sinless one, I see a way
by which you may consume the forest of Khandava in the very sight of Indra.
Those old deities Nara and Narayana have become incarnate in the world of men
to accomplish the business of the celestials. They are called on earth Arjuna and
   Krishna
and are now staying in the forest of Khandava. Solicit their aid in consuming the
   forest.
You shall then be able to do this, even if the forest be protected by the celestials.
They will prevent the population of Khandava from escaping
and will thwart Indra also so that he cannot aid anyone in the escape."
Agni hurried to Krishna and Arjuna. Hearing the words of the fire god, Arjuna
   said:
"I have numberless celestial weapons with which I can fight wielders of the
   thunderbolt.
But I have no bow suited to the strength of my arms and capable of bearing
the might I may put forth in battle. Because of the lightness of my hands,
I also require arrows that may never be exhausted.
My car is scarcely able to bear the load of arrows I would desire to keep by me.
I want celestial steeds of pure white with the speed of the wind,
and a car possessing the splendor of the sun
and with a clatter of wheels that resembles the roar of the clouds.
Then there is no weapon suited to Krishna's energy and with which he can slay
Nagas and Pisachas. It behooves you to give us the means
by which success may be achieved and by which we may thwart Indra
in pouring his showers upon the forest. We are ready to do whatever prowess
   can do.
                              But you must give us the means."
The smoke-bannered Hutasana, or Agni, summoned Varuna, the ruler of the
   waters,
who immediately appeared before him. The smoke-bannered celestial welcomed
   Varuna
and said to that god: "Give me without loss of time that bow and quiver,
and that ape-bannered car also, which were obtained from King Soma."
At once Varuna gave that wonderful jewel of a bow endowed with great energy.
That bow was the enhancer of fame and achievements
and was incapable of being injured by any weapon.
It was alone equal to a hundred thousand bows.
It was well adorned and beautiful to behold and was worshipped
by the celestials and the Gandharvas alike. Varuna also gave two inexhaustible
   quivers,

and a car furnished with celestial weapons and with a banner that showed a
   large ape.
Yoked to that car were steeds white as silver of the fleecy clouds,
and decked with golden harness. In fleetness it was like the wind or the mind.
It was incapable of being vanquished by the celestials or the Asuras.
Its splendor was so great that no one could gaze at it, and the sound of its wheels
was tremendous. It had been made by Viswakarman, the architect of the
   universe
and one of the lords of creation, after severe ascetic meditation.
Then Arjuna, accoutered in mail and armed with a sword,
and with his fingers encased in leather gloves, walked around that excellent car
and, bowing to the gods, ascended it like a virtuous man riding in the car
that bears him to heaven. Taking up that celestial bow created by Brahman of old
and called the Gandiva, Arjuna was filled with joy. Bowing to Varuna, he strung it
   forcibly.
Those who heard the noise that the bow made while the mighty Pandava strung it
quaked with fear. And having obtained that car and that bow,
and the two inexhaustible quivers, the son of Kunti was glad
and thought himself competent to assist at the task.
Varuna then gave Krishna a discus with an iron pole attached to a hole in the
   center.
It was a fiery weapon and became his favorite.
With that weapon, Krishna was sure he was equal to the task.
Varuna said: "With this you shall be able to vanquish even foes that are not
   human,
Rakshasas and Pisachas, and Daityas and Nagas. You shall be able with this to
   smite all.
And when you hurl it at foes, this weapon will slay them and come back to your
   hands."
Varuna then gave Krishna a mace named Kaumodaki, capable of slaying every
   Daitya
and producing, when hurled, a roar like that of thunder.
Then Arjuna and Krishna, filled with joy, said to Hutasana: "O lord, blaze forth
and surround this forest on every side. We are now able to help you."
The illustrious god then assumed his most energetic form
and prepared to consume the forest. Surrounding it with his seven flames,
he began to devour the forest of Khandava.
Catching it from all sides with a roar like that of the clouds,
Agni made every creature within it tremble.
And that burning forest then looked as resplendent as Meru, the king of
   mountains,
blazing with the rays of the sun. Krishna and Arjuna, riding in their cars
and placing themselves on opposite sides of the forest, began a great slaughter
of the creatures dwelling in it. Wherever any of them attempted to escape,
those heroes rushed to prevent its flight. Indeed, those two excellent cars
seemed to be but one, and the two warriors but one.

Some had limbs burned, some were scorched with excessive heat, and some came out,
and some ran about from fear. And some clasping their children,
and some their parents and brothers, died calmly without abandoning those dear to them.
Many there were who bit their nether lips, rose upward, and soon fell back,
whirling into the blazing element below. Some rolled on the ground
with wings, eyes, and feet scorched and burned. These creatures all perished soon enough.
The lakes and ponds within that forest, heated by the fire, began to boil;
the fishes and the tortoises in the lakes and ponds all perished.
During that great slaughter of living creatures in that forest,
the burning bodies of various animals looked like fire itself assuming many forms.
The birds that took wing to escape from that conflagration
Arjuna pierced with his shafts and cut into pieces,
and they fell into the burning element below, uttering loud cries.
The clamor was like the frightful uproar of the churning ocean.
Flames of the blazing fire reached the skies and caused great anxiety to the celestials.
The illustrious dwellers in heaven went in a body to Indra of a hundred sacrifices
and a thousand eyes to ask: "Why, O lord of immortals, does Agni burn these creatures?
Has the time come for the destruction of the world?"
Indra, the chief of the celestials, covered the sky with masses of clouds
and began to shower upon the burning forest.
The massed clouds by the hundreds and thousands poured rain upon Khandava
in downpours thick as the flagstaffs of battle cars.
But the showers all dried because of the heat of the fire and could not reach the flames!
Arjuna, wielding his excellent weapons, prevented that rainfall by Indra
with an upward shower of his own weapons. He soon covered the forest of Khandava
with innumerable arrows, like the moon covering the atmosphere with a thick fog.
When the sky above the forest was thus covered, no living creature could then escape.
The winds made a loud roar and agitated all the oceans
to bring together masses of clouds in the sky, charged with torrents of rain.
But Arjuna hurled his excellent weapon called Vayavya
to dispel those clouds, and the energy of Indra's thunderbolts and clouds was destroyed.
The torrents of rain all dried up, and the lightning died down.
Within a moment the sky cleared, and a delicious, cool breeze began to blow.
The disc of the sun resumed its normal state. Then Agni, the eater of clarified butter,
assumed various forms and, sprinkled over with the fat from the bodies of creatures,

blazed forth, filling the universe with his roar. Numerous birds of the Garuda
   tribe
with excellent feathers, seeing that the forest was protected by Krishna and
   Arjuna,
descended from the upper skies, hoping to strike those heroes
with their thunderlike wings, beaks, and claws. Innumerable Nagas also,
with faces emitting fire, descending from high, approached Arjuna
and vomited the most virulent poison. But Arjuna cut them into pieces
with arrows steeped in the fire of his own wrath.
Those birds and snakes then fell into the burning element below.
There also came innumerable Asuras with Gandharvas,
and Yakshas and Rakshasas and Nagas, sending forth terrific yells.
Armed with machines, vomiting iron balls and bullets from their throats
and catapults for propelling huge stones and rockets,
they approached to strike Krishna and Arjuna, their energy increased by wrath.
But Arjuna struck off their heads with his sharp arrows.
Krishna, also, made a great slaughter of the Daitya and the Danava with his discus.
Many Asuras of immeasurable might, pierced by Krishna's arrows
and smitten by the force of his discus, became motionless like waifs and strays
stranded on the bank by the violence of the waves.
Then Indra, the lord of the celestials, riding on his white elephant, rushed at
   those heroes,
took up his thunderbolt, which could never be loosed in vain,
and hurled it. The slayer of Asuras said to the gods: "These two are dead."
With the fierce thunderbolt about to be hurled by their chief,
the celestials all took up their respective weapons:
Yama, the death-dealing mace; and Kuvera, his spiked club; and Varuna, his
   noose;
and Skanda, or Kartikeya, his long lance, motionless like the mountain of Meru.
The Aswins stood there with huge trees in their hands. Dhatri had a bow;
and Jaya, a thick club. Tvashtri of great strength took up a whole mountain;
and Surya, a bright dart. Mrityu armed himself with a battle-ax.
Aryaman stalked about with a bludgeon furnished with sharp spikes.
Mitra held a discus sharp as a razor. And Pusha and Bhaga and Savitri
rushed at Krishna and Arjuna with bows and scimitars in hand.
And Rudras and the Vasus, the mighty Maruts and the Viswedevas
and the Sadhyas, all resplendent with their own energy,
and many other celestials, armed with various weapons,
rushed against those exalted men, intent on smiting them down.
Then were seen wonderful portents all around that robbed every creature of his
   sense
and resembled those that appear at the time of the universal dissolution.
But Arjuna and Krishna, fearless and invincible in battle, saw Indra
and the other celestials prepared for fight and calmly waited, bows in hand.
Those heroes assailed the advancing host with their own thunderlike arrows.
The celestials were repeatedly routed by Krishna and Arjuna and at last left the
   battlefield

to seek the protection of Indra. The munis who witnessed the battle from the skies
saw the celestials defeated by Krishna and Arjuna and were filled with wonder.
Indra was exceedingly gratified and again rushed to the assault with a shower of
    stones.
He wanted to ascertain the prowess of Arjuna, who was able to draw the bow
even with his left hand. Arjuna dispelled with his arrows that shower of stones.
Then Indra produced a thicker shower, but the son gratified his father
by baffling that one also. Then Indra, intending to smite the son of Pandu,
tore up a large peak from Mandara with tall trees on it and hurled it at Arjuna.
But Arjuna divided the mountain peak into a thousand pieces with his fire-
    mouthed arrows.
The fragments fell through the skies, and it looked as if the sun and the moon
    and the planets,
displaced from their positions, were plummeting to earth.
That huge peak fell on that forest, killing numerous creatures that dwelled in
    Khandava.
Then the inhabitants of the forest, the Danavas and Rakshasas and Nagas
and wolves and bears and other wild animals, the elephants, and tigers,
and lions with manes, and deer and buffalo by hundreds, and birds, and other
    creatures,
frightened at the falling stones, fled in all directions. They saw the forest
    burning
and Krishna and Arjuna ready with their weapons.
They set up a frightful roar and the whole firmament rang. To complete their
    destruction,
Krishna hurled his discus at them. The forest dwellers were cut into hundreds of
    pieces
and fell into the mouth of Agni. Mangled by Krishna's discus,
the *Asuras* were besmeared with blood and fat and looked like evening clouds.
And he of the Vrishni race moved like death itself, slaying Pisachas and birds
    and Nagas
and other creatures by thousands. The discus he repeatedly hurled came back to
    his hands
after slaughtering numberless creatures. The face and form of Krishna,
that soul of every created thing, was fierce to behold as he was employed in the
    slaughter.
No one among the celestials could vanquish Krishna and Arjuna.
When they saw that they could not protect the forest or extinguish the
    conflagration,
                         they retired from the scene.
Then Indra, filled with joy, applauded Krishna and Arjuna.
When the celestials gave up the fight, an incorporeal voice, deep and loud,
addressed Indra and said: "Your friend Takshaka, that chief of snakes,
has not been slain! Before the fire started in Khandava, he had journeyed to
    Kurukshetra.
Therefore, it behooves you to go with all the celestials. The destruction of
    Khandava

has been ordained by fate!" Then the chief of the immortals abandoned his wrath
and went back to heaven. Seeing that Indra had abandoned the fight,
the dwellers of heaven followed him with all their soldiers,
and Krishna and Arjuna, when they saw the celestials retreat, set up a leonine roar.
Cut off by Arjuna's arrows, none of the innumerable creatures
could escape the burning forest. Sometimes piercing a hundred creatures with
    one shaft
and sometimes a single creature with a hundred shafts, Arjuna moved about in
    his car.
The creatures fell into the mouth of Agni, struck down as it were by death itself.
Hosts of them roared in pain as elephants and deer and wolves set up cries of
    affliction.
At that sound, Hutasana, with blazing and coppery eyes
and flaming tongue and large mouth, and the hair on the crown of his head all
    fiery,
drank that nectarlike stream of animal fat and was gratified greatly.

◆

It happened that Arjuna saw an Asura named Maya escaping from the abode
of his brother Takshaka. Agni had Vayu, the wind god, as his car driver,
and he assumed a body with matted locks on head, roared like the clouds,
and pursued the Asura, eager to consume him.
Krishna stood with his weapon upraised, ready to smite him down.
But, seeing the discus uplifted and Agni in pursuit, Maya called out for help:
"Run to me, O Arjuna, and protect me!" Arjuna answered: "Fear not!"
Those words seemed to give Maya his life, for when he said to Maya
that there was nothing to fear, Krishna no longer desired to slay Maya,
and Agni also relented. Protected from Indra by Krishna and Arjuna,
Agni burned that forest for fifteen days. Agni spared only six of its dwellers:
Takshaka's son Aswasena, his brother Maya, and four birds called Sarngakas.
When the fire blazed forth in the forest of Khandava, those birds were much
    distressed.
They saw no means of escape. Their mother, the helpless Jarita,
knowing that they were too young to fly, wept aloud and said:
"A terrible conflagration illuminating the whole universe and burning the forest
    down
approaches us. These infants, without feathers and feet,
and the sole refuge of our deceased ancestors, afflict me.
This fire spreads fear all around, licks with its tongue the tallest trees, and comes
    nearer.
But my unfledged children cannot escape. I cannot flee and take them with me.
Nor can I abandon them. Whom among them shall I leave behind,
and whom shall I carry with me? What should I do now that is consistent with
    duty?
My dear children, what do you think? I shall cover you with my wings and die
    with you.

Your cruel father left me some time before, saying:
'Upon Jaritari, because he is the eldest son, will my race depend.
My second, Sarisrikka, will beget progeny for the expansion of my ancestors' race.
My third, Stamvamitra, will be devoted to asceticism,
and my youngest, Drona, will become foremost among those acquainted with
   the Vedas.'
But this terrible calamity has overtaken us! Whom shall I take with me?
As I am deprived of judgment, what should I do that is consistent with duty?"
To their lamenting mother the little birds said: "O mother,
relinquish your affection for us, and go to a place where there is no fire.
If we are killed here, you may have other children. Do what is beneficial to our
   race.
Do not be influenced by love for your offspring, which promises to destroy
both us and you." Jarita replied: "There is a hole here in the ground near this
   tree,
belonging to a mouse. Enter this hole without loss of time. You shall have then
no fear of fire. After you have entered it, I shall cover its mouth with dust.
This is the only means of escape I can see from the blazing fire. When the fire
   is out,
I shall return to remove the dust. Follow my advice if you are to escape."
The infant birds replied: "Without feathers, we are but so many balls of flesh.
If we enter the hole, it is certain that the mouse will eat us all.
Alas, we do not see any means by which we may escape from the fire or from the
   mouse.
We do not see how our father's act of procreation may be prevented
from becoming futile, and how also our mother may be saved.
A death by fire is preferable to a death by being devoured. If we are eaten by the
   mouse,
that death would be ignoble, whereas the destruction of the body in fire
is approved by the wise." To those words of her sons Jarita replied:
"The little mouse that had come out of this hole
was seized by a hawk with his claws and carried away. Therefore, you may enter
   the hole."
But the young ones replied: "We cannot be certain that the mouse was taken by
   the hawk.
And there may be other mice living here. From them we have everything to fear.
Meanwhile, it is doubtful whether fire will approach us here.
Already we see how the wind may be blowing the flames away.
If we enter the hole, death is certain, but if we remain where we are, death is
   uncertain.
O mother, a position in which death is uncertain is better than that in which it is
   certain.
It is your duty, therefore, to escape, because if you live you may obtain other
   children
just as good." Their mother said: "I myself saw the mighty hawk swoop down
and fly away with the mouse from the hole. And while he flew, I followed behind
and pronounced my blessing on him for his having taken away the mouse.

I said to him: 'O king of hawks, because you are flying away with our enemy, the mouse,

in your claws, may you, without a foe, live in heaven with a golden body.'

Afterward, when the hawk had devoured the mouse, I returned, by his leave.

Therefore, you may enter this hole trustfully. You have nothing to fear."

The young ones again said: "Why do you strive to protect us at so much cost to yourself?

Who are we to you? You are young and beautiful and capable of seeking your husband.

Go to him. Let us, by entering the fire, attain to regions of felicity.

If the fire does not consume us, you may come back for us."

The mother then left them in Khandava and went to a spot where there was no fire

and there was safety. Then Agni, in haste and with fierce flames,

approached the spot where the young birds were. They saw the fire coming toward them.

Then Jaritari, the eldest of the four, in Agni's hearing, began to speak.

He said: "The person who is wise remains wakeful in the face of death.

Accordingly, when the hour of death approaches, he feels no pangs.

But the person of perplexed soul, who does not remain awake

when the hour of death comes, feels the pangs of death and never attains salvation."

The second brother, Sarisrikka, said: "You are patient and intelligent.

The time has come when our lives are threatened.

Only one among many becomes wise and brave."

The third brother, Stamvamitra, said: "The eldest brother is called the protector.

It is the eldest brother who rescues the younger ones from danger.

If the eldest fails to rescue them, what can the younger ones do?"

The fourth and youngest brother, Drona, said:

"The cruel god of fire with seven tongues and seven mouths hastens toward our home,

blazing forth in splendor and licking up everything in his path."

Having addressed one another thus, the birds each addressed a eulogistic hymn to Agni.

Jaritari said: "You are, O fire, the soul of air! You are the body of the earth's vegetation!

Water is your parent as you are the parent of water!

Your flames, like the sun's rays, extend above, below, behind, and on each side."

Sarisrikka said: "O smoke-bannered god, our mother is not to be seen,

and we do not know our father! Our feathers have not grown yet.

We have no one to protect us but you. Therefore, O Agni, infants that we are, protect us!

O Agni, as we are distressed, protect us with that auspicious form you have

and with those seven flames of yours! We seek protection at your hands.

You alone, O Agni, are the giver of heat in the universe.

O lord, there is none else but you who gives heat to the rays of the sun.

O, protect us who are young, rishis. O Havyavaha, carrier of sacrificial butter, be pleased to go elsewhere and to take some other route."

Stamvamitra said: "You alone, O Agni, are everything!
This whole universe is established in you!
You sustain every creature, and you support the universe!
You are the carrier of the sacrificial butter, and you are the butter itself!
The wise know you to be both one and many!
Having created the three worlds, you will again destroy them when the time
    comes,
swelling yourself forth! You are the productive cause of the whole universe,
and you also are the essence in which the universe dissolves itself!"

Drona said: "O lord of the universe, growing in strength
and remaining within their bodies, you cause the food that living creatures eat
to be digested. Everything, therefore, is established in you. You are the one
who assumes the form of the sun and, sucking up the waters of the earth
and every liquid juice that the earth yields, gives them back in time in the form
    of rain
and causes everything to grow! From you come these plants and creepers
with green foliage! From you have sprung these pools and the great ocean also!
Our body depends on Varuna, the water god, for we are unable to bear your heat.
Be our auspicious protector! Save us by taking a remote route,
and spare us as the ocean spares the house on its shore!"

Thus addressed, Agni, well pleased at what he heard, replied: "You are a rishi, O
    Drona!
For what you have said is Brahma, Vedic truth. I shall do your pleasure. Fear not!
O best of Brahmanas, I have been pleased by your hymn. Say what I am to do."

Drona said: "O Agni, these cats trouble us every day.
Consume them with their friends and relatives."

Agni did what the Sarngakas asked him to do.
And, growing in strength, he continued to consume the forest of Khandava.
Meanwhile, the birds' father, the rishi Mandapala, grew anxious about his
    children,
although he had spoken of them to the god of fierce rays.
Distressed on account of his sons, he addressed Lapita, his second wife,
with whom he was then living, and he said: "My children are incapable of moving.
When the fire grows in strength and the wind begins to blow violently,
my children will not be able to save themselves. How will their mother rescue
    them?
Unable to save her offspring, that innocent woman will be afflicted with great
    sorrow.
How is Jaritari, my son, and how are Sarisrikka, and Stamvamitra, and Drona,
                        and how is their helpless mother?"

To the weeping Mandapala the jealous Lapita replied: "You need not worry
for your children, who are all rishis endowed with energy and prowess!
They can have no fear of fire. Did you not speak to Agni in my presence,
on their behalf? Has not the illustrious deity promised to save them?
One of the regents of the universe, Agni will never falsify his speech.
It is only by thinking of my rival Jarita that you are so distracted!

The love you bear me is not equal to what you had at first for her.

Go to Jarita, for whom your heart sorrows! As for myself, I shall wander alone as a fit reward for my having attached myself to a wicked person."

Mandapala replied: "I do not wander the earth with such intentions as you imagine.

It is only for the sake of progeny that I am here. And those that I have are in danger.

He who casts off what he has for the sake of what he may acquire is a wicked person.

The world disregards and insults him. Therefore, I must go.

As for yourself, you are free to do as you choose.

This fire that licks the trees brings sorrow to my heart and raises evil presentiments."

Meanwhile, after the fire had left the spot where the Sarngakas dwelled, Jarita hastily returned there to see how they were.

She found that all of them had escaped from the fire and were perfectly well.

Seeing their mother, they began to weep, although they were safe and sound.

She too shed tears upon finding them alive. And she embraced them one by one.

Just at that time, Mandapala arrived. But none of his sons expressed joy at seeing him.

He spoke to them one after another and to Jarita also.

But neither his sons nor Jarita said anything to him in return.

Mandapala then said: "I am speaking to you woefully. Why do you not reply?

I left you, it is true, but I was not happy where I was."

Jarita then said: "What have you to do with these children?

Go to that Lapita of sweet smiles to whom you went before

because you thought me deficient in everything!"

Mandapala replied: "As regards females, there is nothing so destructive of their happiness,

whether in this or the other world, as a co-wife and a clandestine lover.

There is nothing like these two that inflames the fire of hostility.

Even the auspicious and well-behaved Arundhati was jealous of the illustrious Vasishtha.

Arundhati insulted the wise muni among the celestial seven.

In consequence of such insulting thoughts of hers, she has become a little star,

like fire mixed with smoke, sometimes visible and sometimes invisible,

like an omen portending no good among the constellation of seven bright stars

representing the seven rishis. I look to you for the sake of children.

I never wronged you, as Vasishtha never wronged his wife.

Men should never trust women, even if they be wives.

Women, when they have become mothers, should not mind serving their husbands."

After this, all his children came forward to worship him.

And he also spoke gently toward them: "I had spoken to Agni for the safety of you all.

The illustrious deity had assured me that he would grant my wish.

At those words of Agni, and knowing the virtuous disposition of your mother

as well as the great energy that is in you, I did not come here earlier.
Therefore, do not harbor in your hearts any resentment toward me."
Having given such assurances to his sons, the Brahmana Mandapala
took with him his wife and sons, left that region, and went to some other
    country.

✦

It was thus that the illustrious god of fire consumed the forest of Khandava,
with the help of Krishna and Arjuna, for the good of the world.
And having drunk several rivers of fat and marrow, Agni was highly gratified
and showed himself to Arjuna and Krishna. Then Indra, surrounded by the
    Maruts,
descended from the firmament and addressed Arjuna and Krishna:
"You have achieved a feat that even a celestial could not.
Ask each a boon that is not obtainable by any man."
Arjuna asked for all of Indra's weapons. At this, the god of great splendor said:
"When the illustrious Madhava becomes pleased with you, then, O son of Pandu,
I will give you all my weapons! I shall know when the time comes.
I will give you all my weapons of fire and all my Vayavya weapons,
                            and you will accept them all from me."
Then Krishna asked that his friendship with Arjuna might be eternal.
The chief of the celestials granted Krishna the boon he desired.
And, having granted these boons to Krishna and Arjuna, Indra ascended to
    heaven.
Agni, having burned that forest with its animals and birds for fifteen days,
was satisfied and ceased to burn. Addressing Krishna and Arjuna, he said:
"I have been gratified by you two. At my command, you heroes shall be able to go
wherever you choose!" Thus addressed, Arjuna and Krishna,
and the *Danava* Maya also, having wandered a little,
at last sat down on the delightful banks of a river.

✦

Then, in the presence of Krishna, Maya Danava, having worshipped Arjuna,
repeatedly spoke to him with joined hands: "O son of Kunti, I have been saved
    by you
from Krishna and from Agni, who desired to consume me. What may I do for
    you?"
Arjuna said: "You have already done enough, just by this offer. Blessings upon you.
Go wherever you like. Be kind and well disposed toward me,
as we are friendly to and well pleased with you!"
Maya said: "What you have said is worthy of you. But I desire to do something
    for you.
I am a great artist, a Viswakarman among the Danavas.
O son of Pandu, as an artist, I desire to do something for you."
Arjuna said: "You think of yourself as having been saved by me from death.

Even if it were so, I should not make you do anything for me.

At the same time, O Danava, I do not wish to frustrate your intentions.

Do something for Krishna. That will be sufficient repayment for my services."

Krishna reflected for a moment and then commanded Maya:

"Build a palatial *sabha,* or meeting hall, if you desire to do good to Yudhishthira
the just.

Indeed, build such a palace that persons belonging to the world of men

may not be able to imitate it even after examining it with care.

Build a mansion in which we may behold a combination

of godly, Asuric, and human designs." At those words, Maya became exceedingly
glad.

And he built a palace for the son of Pandu like that of the celestials themselves.

Then Krishna and Arjuna explained everything to King Yudhishthira

and introduced Maya to him. Yudhishthira received Maya with respect,

offering him the honor he deserved. And Maya accepted that honor, thinking
highly of it.

Having performed on an auspicious day the initial propitiatory rites of the
foundation,

and having also gratified thousands of well-versed Brahmanas

with sweetened milk and rice and with rich presents of various kinds,

he measured out a plot of land five thousand cubits square,

exceedingly handsome to behold, favorable for construction of a building,

and well suited to the exigencies of every season.

17

Narada

Maya Danava said to Arjuna: "I now go, by your leave, but I shall come back soon.
On the north of the Kailasa peak, near the mountains of Mainaka,
while the Danavas were engaged in a sacrifice on the banks of Lake Vindu,
I gathered a huge quantity of the delightful and variegated rough material
    called *vanda*,
composed of jewels and gems. This was placed in the mansion of Vrishaparva.
If it is still there, I shall return with it. I shall then begin construction of the
    palace,
which is to be adorned with all opulence and celebrated all over the world.
There is also a fierce club that was placed in Lake Vindu by the King of the
    Danavas
after he slaughtered all his foes in battle with it. Besides being heavy and strong
and variegated, with golden knobs, it is capable of bearing great weight
and of slaying all foes and is equal in strength to a hundred thousand clubs.
It is a fit weapon for Bhima, even as the Gandiva is for you.
There is also in that lake a large conch shell called Devadatta of loud sound
that came from Varuna. I shall give all these to you."
The Asura then went away in a northeasterly direction.
On the north of Kailasa, in the mountains of Mainaka,
there is a huge peak of gems and jewels called Hiranya-sringa.
Near that peak is Lake Vindu, on the shore of which King Bhagiratha dwelled
    for years.
He desired to behold the goddess Ganga, since called Bhagirayou, after that
    king's name.
And there, on its shore, Indra, the illustrious lord of every created thing,
performed one hundred great sacrifices. There, for the sake of beauty,
although it was not required by the ordinance, he placed sacrificial stakes
made of gems and altars of gold. There, after performing those sacrifices,
the thousand-eyed lord of Sachi was crowned with success. The fierce Mahadeva,
the eternal lord of every creature, has taken up his abode
after having created all the worlds, and there he dwells, worshipped with
    reverence
by thousands of spirits. Nara and Narayana, Brahma and Yama and Sthanu
perform sacrifices there at the expiration of a thousand *yugas*.
There, for the establishment of virtue and religion,

Vasudeva performed his sacrifices extending for many, many long years.
Maya went there and fetched the club and the conch shell
and the various crystalline articles that had belonged to King Vrishaparva.
Maya also possessed himself of all the great wealth
that was guarded by Yakshas and Rakshasas.
Bringing them back, the Asura constructed a peerless palace of great beauty,
composed entirely of gems and precious stones and celebrated through the
    three worlds.
He gave Bhimasena that best of clubs, and Arjuna the most excellent conch shell
at whose sound all creatures trembled in awe. And the palace that Maya built
consisted of columns of gold and occupied an area of five thousand cubits.
It shone in great splendor, with a brilliance that seemed to darken even the sun's
    rays.
Its effulgence was a mixture of both celestial and terrestrial light,
and it looked to be on fire. Like a mass of new clouds in the sky it rose up into
    view.
The palace was so delightful and refreshing and composed of such excellent
    materials
and furnished with such golden walls and archways and adorned with so many
    pictures,
and was so rich and well built, that it surpassed the mansion of Brahma himself.
Eight thousand Rakshasas—called Kinkaras, fierce, huge-bodied, and with great
    strength,
of red coppery eyes and arrowy ears, well armed and capable of ranging through
    the air—
guarded the palace. Within, Maya placed a tank in which were lotuses
with leaves of dark-colored gems and stalks of bright jewels
and other flowers of beaten gold. Aquatic fowls of various species sported on it.
Besides the full-blown lotuses, it was stocked with fishes and tortoises of golden
    hue.
Its bottom was without mud and its water transparent.
There was a flight of crystal stairs leading from the banks to the edge of the
    water.
The gentle breezes that swept along its bosom softly tousled the flowers that
    studded it.
The banks of that tank were overlaid with slabs of costly marble set with pearls.
And many kings who came there mistook it for land and fell into it with their
    eyes open.
Tall trees of various kinds, of green foliage and cool shade and ever blossoming,
all charming to behold, were planted around the palace.
Artificial woods were laid out that always emitted a delicious fragrance.
And there were many tanks stocked with swans
and the Brahminy ducks known as Karandavas and Chakravakas. The breeze,
    with a lotus fragrance,
complemented the pleasures and the happiness of the Pandavas.
Having constructed such a palatial hall within fourteen months,
Maya reported its completion to Yudhishthira, who entered the palatial *sabha*,

having first fed ten thousand Brahmanas with preparations of milk and rice
mixed with clarified butter and honey, with fruits and roots, and with pork and
    venison.
The king gave those superior Brahmanas from various countries
food seasoned with sesame and prepared with vegetables called *jibanti,*
and rice mixed with clarified butter, as well as different preparations of meat
along with various kinds of other foods, and numberless viands and innumerable
    drinks.
He gave them brand-new robes and clothes and excellent floral wreaths.
The king also provided each of those Brahmanas with a thousand cows.
And the Brahmanas' praises—"What an auspicious day is this!"—
became so loud that they seemed to reach heaven itself.
When the Kuru king entered the *sabha,* having worshipped the gods with music
and varieties of excellent perfumes, the athletes, mimes, prizefighters, and
    charanas
performed and exhibited their skills. Thus Yudhishthira and his brothers
sported within the palace like Sakra himself in heaven.
Upon the seats in that palace sat, along with the Pandavas and rishis,
kings from various countries, all well skilled in the Vedas and Vedangas
and conversant with rules of morality and pure and spotless in behavior.
All these waited on Yudhishthira like the celestials in heaven waiting upon
    Brahma.

✦

One day there appeared before the assembly of Pandavas
the celestial rishi Narada, conversant with the Vedas and Upanishadas,
worshipped by the celestials, acquainted with histories and Puranas,
well versed in all that occurred in ancient aeons,
conversant with the logic known as Nyaya and with the truth of moral science,
and possessing a complete knowledge of the six Angas:
pronunciation, grammar, prosody, etymology, religious rites, and astronomy.
He was a perfect master in reconciling contradictory texts
and in applying general principles to particular cases,
and also in interpreting contraries by reference to differences in situation.
He was eloquent, resolute, intelligent, and possessed of a powerful memory.
He was, moreover, acquainted with the science of morals and politics,
proficient in distinguishing inferior things from superior ones,
skilled in drawing inferences from evidence,
and competent to judge of the correctness or incorrectness of syllogisms.
He was able to answer questions about religion, wealth, pleasure, and salvation
and about the whole universe—above, below, and around—as if it were all
    before his eyes.
He was master of both the Sankhya and Yoga systems of philosophy,
always eager to humble the celestials and Asuras by fomenting quarrels among
    them,
and conversant with the sciences of war and treaty making,

military campaigns, maintenance of posts against the enemy,
and stratagems of ambuscades. He was a master of every branch of learning
and possessed of numberless other accomplishments.
The rishi, having wandered over the different worlds, came to the *sabha*,
accompanied by Parijata and the intelligent Raivata and Saumya and Sumukha.
Possessing the speed of the mind, the rishi came there
and was filled with gladness upon beholding the Pandavas.
The Brahmana paid homage to Yudhishthira by uttering blessings on him
and wishing him victory. The eldest of the Pandavas quickly stood up
with his younger brothers. Bending low with humility, the monarch saluted the
  rishi
and gave him a befitting seat. The king also gave him cattle
and the usual offerings of the Arghya, including honey and the other ingredients.
The monarch also worshipped the rishi with gems and jewels.
The rishi was most pleased and said to Yudhishthira the following words:
"Is the wealth you are earning being spent in proper ways?
Does your mind take pleasure in virtue? Are you enjoying the pleasures of life?
Does your mind sink under their weight? Do you continue in the noble conduct,
consistent with religion and wealth, practiced by your ancestors
toward good, bad, and indifferent subjects? Do you injure religion
for the sake of wealth, or both religion and wealth for the sake of pleasure?
Conversant as you are with the timeliness of everything,
do you follow religion, wealth, pleasure, and salvation, dividing your time
  judiciously?
O sinless one, the six attributes of kings are cleverness of speech,
readiness in providing means, intelligence in dealing with the foe,
memory, acquaintance with morals, and an understanding of politics.
Do you attend to the seven ways of governing: the sowing of dissension,
  chastisement,
conciliation, gifts, incantations, medicine, and magic?
Do you examine, after a survey of your own strength and weakness,
the fourteen possessions of your foes? These are the country, forts, cars,
  elephants,
cavalry, foot soldiers, the principal officials of state, the zenana, food supply,
computations of the army and income, the religious treatises in force,
the accounts of state, the revenue, and wine shops and other secret enemies.
Do you attend to the eight occupations, having examined your own
and your foe's resources? Your seven principal officers of state are
the governor of the citadel, the commander of forces, the chief judge,
the general in interior command, the chief priest, the chief physician,
and the chief astrologer. None of these, I hope, is under the influence of your
  foes,
nor have they, I hope, become idle in consequence of the wealth they have
  earned.
Are they all obedient to you? Your counsels, I hope, are never divulged
by your trusted spies in disguise, by yourself or by your ministers?
You ascertain, I hope, the desires of your friends, foes, and strangers.

Do you make peace and war at proper times?

Do you observe neutrality toward strangers and persons who are neutral
toward you?

And have you made persons like yourself—persons who are old,

prudent in behavior, capable of understanding what should be done and what
should not,

pure as regards birth and blood, and devoted to you—your ministers?

O Bharata, the victories of kings can be attributed to good counsels.

Is your kingdom protected by ministers versed in Sastras, who keep their
counsels close?

Are your foes unable to injure you? You have not become the slave of sleep?

Do you wake at the proper time? Do you think, during the small hours of night,

about what you should do and what you should not do the next day?

You settle nothing alone, I hope, nor do you take counsel with too many.

The plans you have resolved upon do not, I trust, become known all over your
kingdom.

Do you begin immediately to accomplish measures of great utility

that are easy of accomplishment? Are such measures ever obstructed?

Do you keep the farmers out of your sight so that they fear to approach you?

Do you carry out your plans with persons you trust who are incorruptible

and possessed of practical experience? And I hope that your subjects

only know the measures already accomplished and partially accomplished

and awaiting completion, but not those that are only in contemplation.

Have experienced teachers, capable of explaining the causes of things

and learned in the science of morals and every branch of learning,

been appointed to instruct the princes and the chiefs of the army?

Would you trade a thousand ignorant individuals for a single learned man?

The man who is learned confers the greatest benefit in seasons of distress.

Are your forts always filled with treasure, food, weapons, water,

engines, and instruments as also with engineers and bowmen?

Even a single minister who is intelligent and brave,

with his passions under complete control and possessed of wisdom and judgment,

is capable of conferring the highest prosperity on a king or a king's son.

I ask you, therefore, whether there is even one such minister with you.

Do you seek to know everything about the foe's eighteen *tirthas*, those places of
pilgrimage,

and fifteen of your own, by means of spies unacquainted with one another?

Do you watch all your enemies with care and attention, and in a way unknown to
them?

Is the priest you honor possessed of humility and purity of blood

and renown, and is he without jealousy and illiberality?

Has any intelligent and guileless Brahmana, knowledgeable in the ordinances,

been employed by you in the performance of your daily rites before the sacred
fire?

And does he remind you in proper time as to when your Homa should be
performed?

Is your astrologer skilled in reading physiognomy, capable of interpreting omens,

and competent to neutralize the effect of the disturbances of nature?
Have respectable servants been employed in offices that are respectable,
indifferent ones in indifferent offices, and low ones in offices that are low?
Have you appointed to high offices ministers who are without guile,
of good conduct for generations, and above the common run?
Do you oppress your people with cruel and severe punishment?
And do your ministers rule your kingdom under your orders?
Do your ministers ever slight you, like sacrificial priests slighting men who are
    fallen
and incapable of performing any more sacrifices,
or like wives slighting husbands who are proud and self-indulgent in their
    behavior?
Is the commander of your forces possessed of sufficient confidence,
brave, intelligent, patient, well conducted and of good birth, devoted to you and
    competent?
Do you treat with consideration and regard the chief officers of your army
who are skilled in every kind of welfare and who are forward, well behaved,
and endowed with prowess? Do you give your troops their sanctioned rations
and pay at the appointed time? Or do you oppress them by withholding these?
Do you know that the misery caused by arrears of pay and irregularity in rations
drives troops to mutiny, and that this is called by the learned
one of the greatest of mischiefs? Are all the principal high-born men devoted
    to you
and ready with cheerfulness to lay down their lives in battle for your sake?
I hope no one of uncontrolled passions is ever permitted to rule as he likes
in matters appertaining to the army. Is any servant of yours,
who has succeeded in a particular business by the employment of special ability,
disappointed in obtaining from you a little more regard and an increase of food
    and pay?
I hope you reward persons of learning, humility, and skill in every kind of
    knowledge
with gifts of wealth and honor proportionate to their qualifications.
Do you support the wives and children of men who have given their lives for you?
Do you cherish with paternal affection the foe that has been weakened,
or him who has sought your shelter, having been vanquished in battle?
O lord of earth, are you equal to all men? Can everyone approach you, then,
    without fear,
as if you were their mother and father? And do you march without loss of time
against your foe when you hear that he is in distress?
Do you begin your march when the time comes, having taken into consideration
all the omens you might see, the resolutions you have made,
and that the ultimate victory depends upon the twelve mandalas?
Do you give gems and jewels to the principal officers of your enemy, as they
    deserve,
without your enemy's knowledge? Do you seek to conquer your incensed foes
who are slaves to their passions, having first conquered your own soul
and having obtained mastery over your own senses?

Before you march out against your foes, do you properly employ
the four arts of reconciliation, gifts of wealth that produce disunion,
and application of force? Do you go out against your enemies
after having strengthened your own kingdom? And, having gone out against them,
do you exert yourself to the utmost to obtain victory? And, having conquered
    them,
do you then protect them with care? Does your army have all four kinds of
    forces—
regular troops, allies, mercenaries, and irregulars—each with the eight
    furnishings:
cars, elephants, horses, officers, infantry, camp followers, spies who know the
    country,
and well-trained ensigns sent out against your enemies?
I hope you slay your foes without regard to their seasons of reaping and of famine.
I hope your servants and agents in your own kingdom and in the kingdoms of
    your foes
continue to look after their respective duties and to protect one another.
I hope trusted servants have been employed to look after your food, your robes,
and your perfumes. I hope your treasury, barns, stables, arsenals,
and women's apartments are all protected by servants devoted to your welfare.
I hope you protect yourself first from your domestic and public servants
and then from the servants of your relatives.
Do your servants ever speak to you of your extravagant expenditures on drink,
sports, and women? Are your expenditures a fourth, a third, or a half your
    income?
Do you always cherish, with food and wealth, relatives, superiors, merchants,
the aged, and other protégés and the distressed? Do your accountants and clerks
who look after your income and expenditures apprise you every day in the
    forenoon
of your finances? Do you dismiss blameless servants who are accomplished in
    business
and are devoted to your welfare? Do you employ in your business thievish persons
or those who are open to temptation, or hostile? Do you persecute your
    kingdom
with the help of thievish or covetous men or women?
Are your kingdom's farmers contented? Are large lakes and irrigation ponds
constructed all over your kingdom at proper distances so that agriculture in your
    realm
is not entirely dependent on the showers of heaven? Are the farmers in your
    kingdom
wanting in either seed or food? Do you grant with kindness loans of seed grains
to the tillers of the soil, and at reasonable interest?
Are the four professions of agriculture, trade, cattle rearing, and lending at
    interest
carried on by honest men? Upon these depends the happiness of your people.
O king, do the five brave and wise men employed in the five offices
of protecting the city, the citadel, the merchants, and the agriculturists

and punishing the criminals always benefit the kingdom by working with one
    another?
For the protection of your city, have the villages been made like towns,
and the hamlets and outskirts of villages like villages?
Are all these entirely under your supervision and rule?
Are thieves and robbers who sack your towns pursued by your police
over the even and uneven parts of your kingdom?
Do you console women, and are they protected in your realm?
I hope you do not place any confidence in them or divulge any secret before any
    of them.
And, O monarch, having heard of any danger and having reflected on it,
do you lie in the inner apartments enjoying yourself?
Having slept during the second and the third divisions of the night,
do you think of religion and profit in the fourth division wakefully?
Rising from bed at the proper time, and dressing yourself well,
do you show yourself to your people, accompanied by ministers
conversant with the auspiciousness or otherwise of the time?
Do men dressed in red and armed with swords and adorned with ornaments
stand by your side to protect your person? Do you behave like the god of justice
    himself
to those who deserve punishment and those who deserve worship, to those dear
    to you
and those whom you dislike? Do you seek to cure bodily diseases by medicines
    and fasts,
and mental illness with the advice of the aged? I hope that your physicians
are conversant with the eight kinds of treatment and are attached and devoted
    to you.
Does it ever happen, O monarch, that from covetousness or folly or pride
you fail to decide between the plaintiff and the defendant who have come
    before you?
Do you deprive of their pension, through covetousness or folly,
the people who have sought your protection from trustfulness or love?
Do the people of your realm, bought by your foes, ever seek to raise disputes
    with you,
uniting themselves with one another? Are those among your foes who are feeble
repressed by the help of troops that are strong, or by the help of both counsels
    and troops?
Are all the principal chieftains of your empire devoted to you?
Are they ready to lay down their lives for your sake and at your command?
Do you worship Brahmanas and wise men according to their merits
in respect of various branches of learning? Do you have faith in the religion
based on the three Vedas and practiced by men who have gone before you?
Are accomplished Brahmanas entertained in your house and in your presence
with nutritive and excellent food, and do they also obtain gifts at those feasts?
Do you strive to perform the sacrifices called Vajapeya and Pundarika
with their full complement of rites? Do you bow to your relatives and superiors,
to the aged, the gods, the ascetics, the Brahmanas, and the tall trees in villages

that are of so much benefit to people? Do you ever cause grief or anger in anyone?
Do priests capable of granting you auspicious favors always stand at your side?
He who conducts himself in this way never finds his kingdom distressed or
    afflicted;
and that monarch, subjugating the whole earth, enjoys a high degree of felicity.
I hope no well-behaved, pure-souled, and respected person is ever ruined
and has his life taken on a false charge of theft by your ministers ignorant of
    Sastras
and acting from greed! And I hope your ministers from greed never set free a
    real thief,
knowing him to be such and having apprehended him with the booty in his
    possession!
I hope your ministers are never won over by bribes, or wrongly decide disputes
that arise between the rich and the poor. Do you keep yourself free
from the fourteen vices of kings: atheism, untruthfulness, anger, rashness,
procrastination, avoidance of the wise, idleness, restlessness of mind,
taking counsels with only one man, consultation with persons ignorant
of the science of profit, abandonment of a settled plan, divulgence of counsels,
failure to accomplish beneficial projects, and undertaking imprudent projects?
By these, O king, even monarchs firmly seated on their thrones are ruined.
Have your study of the Vedas, your wealth, your knowledge of the Sastras,
                      and your marriage been fruitful?"
When the rishi had finished, Yudhishthira asked:
"How do the Vedas, wealth, wife, and knowledge of the Sastras bear fruit?"
The rishi answered: "The Vedas are said to bear fruit when he who has studied
    them
performs the Agnihotra and other sacrifices. Wealth is said to bear fruit
when he who has enjoyed it himself gives it away in charity.
A wife is said to bear fruit when she is useful and when she bears children.
Knowledge of the Sastras is said to bear fruit
                when it results in humility and good behavior."
The great ascetic Narada again asked Yudhishthira: "Do the officers of your
    government
who are paid from taxes levied on the community take only their just dues
from the merchants who come to your territories from distant lands,
impelled by the desire of gain? Are the merchants treated with consideration
in your capital and kingdom, and are they able to bring their goods here
without being deceived by the unfair practices of the buyers
and of the officers of government? Do you always give to all your artisans
the materials of their works and their wages for periods of not more than four
    months?
Do you examine the works executed by them and applaud them before good men
and reward them, having shown them proper respect?
Are you acquainted with all mysterious incantations
and with the secrets of poisons destructive of all foes?
Do you protect your kingdom from the fear of fire, of snakes
and other animals destructive of life, of disease, and of Rakshasas?

Acquainted as you are with every duty, do you cherish like a father the blind, the dumb,

the lame, the deformed, the friendless, and the ascetics who have no homes?

Have you banished these six evils, O monarch: sleep, idleness, fear, anger,
weakness of mind, and procrastination?"

Having heard these words of that best of Brahmanas, the monarch bowed down to him

and worshipped at his feet. Gratified by everything he had heard, the king said to Narada:

"I shall do as you have directed, for my knowledge has been expanded by your advice!"

The king then acted according to that advice and gained in time the whole earth
bounded by her belt of seas.

Narada again spoke, saying: "That king who is thus employed

in the protection of four orders—Brahmanas, Kshatriyas, Vaishyas, and Sudras—

passes his days here happily and attains hereafter to the heavenly region of Sakra."

The Quarrel

Sakuni

Duryodhana stayed on in the Pandavas' assembly house
and with Sakuni explored the mansion. He found in it many celestial designs
he had never seen before. One day King Duryodhana came upon a crystal
    surface,
which from ignorance he mistook for a pool of water.
He drew up his clothes as if to wade across it. But it was not water,
and, realizing his mistake, he wandered about the mansion in great sorrow and
    chagrin.
On the other hand, sometime later the king mistook a lake of crystal water
adorned with lotuses of crystal petals for land and fell into it with all his clothes on.
Seeing that Duryodhana had fallen into the lake, the mighty Bhima laughed
    aloud
as did also the servants of the palace. Other servants, at the command of the
    king,
brought him dry and handsome clothes. But Bhima and Arjuna and both the
    twins
laughed aloud. Duryodhana was not used to putting up with insults
and could not bear their laughter. Concealing his emotions,
he avoided looking at them. But later on, seeing Duryodhana again draw up his
    clothes
to cross a piece of dry land that he had mistaken for water, they all laughed again.
Another time, the king mistook a closed door made of crystal as open.
And as he was about to pass through it, his head struck against it,
and he stood with his brain reeling. And then, mistaking as closed another door
made of crystal that was really open, the king tried to open it with outstretched
    hands
and tumbled down to the ground. And, coming upon another door that was
    really open,
                    the king, thinking it closed, went away from it.
King Duryodhana, seeing that vast wealth in the Rajasuya sacrifice,
and having become the victim of those numerous errors within the assembly
    house,
at last returned, by leave of the Pandavas, to Hastinapura.
Afflicted by the Pandavas' prosperity, the heart of King Duryodhana inclined to sin
as he proceeded toward his city, reflecting on all he had seen and suffered.

At the Pandavas' happiness and the spectacle of kings of the earth paying them
    homage,
and everybody, young and old, engaged in doing good to them,
and at the recollection of their splendor and prosperity, Duryodhana,
the son of Dhritarashtra, became pale. Proceeding to his city with a troubled
    heart,
the prince thought of nothing but that assembly house and the prosperity of
    Yudhishthira.
And Duryodhana, the son of Dhritarashtra, was so taken up with his thoughts
that he spoke no word to Sakuni, Suvala's son,
even though the latter addressed him repeatedly. Sakuni asked: "O Duryodhana,
why are you proceeding in this dejected way?" Duryodhana replied:
"O uncle, beholding this whole earth under the sway of Yudhishthira
in consequence of the might of Arjuna's weapons, and beholding also that sacrifice
of the son of Pritha like the glorious sacrifice of Sakra himself among the
    celestials,
I am filled with jealousy and burn day and night.
I am dried up like a shallow tank in the summer season
and my heart burns with jealousy, although I know I ought not to be jealous."
After a moment of silence, Duryodhana continued:
"I shall throw myself upon a flaming fire or swallow poison or drown myself in
    water.
I cannot live. What man is there in the world possessed of vigor and self-esteem
who can bear to see his foes in the enjoyment of prosperity and himself in
    destitution?
I see that accession to prosperity and good fortune in my foes,
and I bear it, which means that I am neither a woman nor one who is not a
    woman,
nor a man nor one who is not a man. I see their sovereignty over the world
and their vast affluence, as demonstrated by that sacrifice,
and I wonder, who is there like me who would not smart under all that?
I am incapable of acquiring such royal prosperity on my own,
but I do not see allies to whom I can turn for help.
It is for this reason that I am thinking of self-destruction.
That great and serene prosperity of the son of Kunti
drives me to regard fate as supreme and exertions as fruitless.
O son of Suvala, formerly I strove to compass his destruction,
but despite all my efforts he has grown in prosperity, like the lotus in a pool of
    water.
The sons of Dhritarashtra are decaying, and the sons of Pritha are growing day
    by day.
I think of the prosperity of the Pandavas and that assembly house of theirs,
and I remember those menials laughing at me, and my heart burns as if it were
    on fire.
Therefore, know me now as deeply grieved and filled with jealousy,
                and speak of it to King Dhritarashtra."
Sakuni said: "O Duryodhana, you should not be jealous of Yudhishthira.

The sons of Pandu are enjoying what they deserve because of their own good
    fortune.
You could not destroy them by repeatedly devising numberless plans,
some of which you even put into practice. Those tigers among men out of sheer
    luck
escaped all your machinations. They have obtained Draupadi as their wife
and Drupada with his sons and Krishna too as allies
capable of helping them in subjugating the whole world.
And having inherited the paternal share of the kingdom, they have grown
in consequence of their own energies. What is there to make you sorry for this?
Having gratified Hustasana, Arjuna has obtained the bow Gandiva
and inexhaustible quivers and many celestial weapons.
With that unique bow and by the strength of his own arms
he has brought all the kings of the world under his sway.
What is there to make you sorry for this?
Having saved the Asura Maya from a conflagration, Arjuna caused him to build
that assembly house. And it is for this also that, commanded by Maya,
those grim Rakshasas called Kinkaras erected that assembly house.
What is there in this to make you sorry? You have said that you are without allies.
This is not true. Your brothers are obedient to you.
Drona of great prowess and wielding the large bow, Radha's son Karna,
the great warrior Gautama, or Kripa, myself with my brothers and King
    Saumadatti—
these are your allies. Uniting yourself with these, you can conquer the earth."
Duryodhana said: "O king, with you and these other great warriors
I shall subjugate the Pandavas. If I can now conquer them, the world will be mine,
and all the monarchs, and that assembly house so full of wealth."
Sakuni replied: "Dhananjaya and Vasudeva, Bhimasena and Yudhishthira,
Nakula and Sahadeva and Drupada with his sons cannot be vanquished in battle
by even the celestials, for they are all great warriors wielding the largest bows,
accomplished in weapons, and delighting in battle.
But, O king, I know the means by which Yudhishthira may be vanquished.
                    Listen to me, and adopt my plan."
Duryodhana asked: "Without danger to our friends and other illustrious men?
O uncle, tell me how I may vanquish him." Sakuni said: "Yudhishthira is fond of
    dice,
even though he does not know how to play. If he is invited to play,
he will be unable to refuse. I am skillful at dice. There is none equal to me on
    earth,
not even in the three worlds. O son of Kuru, therefore, ask him to play at dice.
Skilled as I am, I will win his kingdom and all his splendid prosperity for you.
But discuss all this with King Dhritarashtra. At his command, I will win without
    doubt
                the entirety of Yudhishthira's possessions."
Duryodhana said: "You are the one who should discuss all this with
    Dhritarashtra.
I shall not be able to do so."

Sakuni, the son of Suvala, approached Dhritarashtra, seated on his throne, and
    said to him:
"Know, O great king, that Duryodhana has become pale and emaciated
and depressed and prey to anxiety. Why do you not ascertain the grief
that is in the heart of your eldest son, grief that is caused by your foe?"
Dhritarashtra spoke then to Duryodhana and said:
"What is the reason for your great affliction?

If it is fit for me to hear it, then explain it to me. Sakuni says that you have
    become pale
and emaciated. What is the cause of your sorrow? My vast wealth is at your
    command.
None of your brothers or our relatives ever does anything disagreeable to you.
You wear the best apparel and eat the best food that is prepared with meat.
The best of horses carries you. What then has made you pale and depressed?
Costly beds, beautiful damsels, mansions decked with excellent furniture,
and sport of the most delightful kind all wait at your command,
as is the case with the gods themselves. Therefore, why do you grieve, O son,
as if you were destitute?"

Duryodhana replied: "I eat and dress like a wretch and pass my time
as prey to fierce jealousy. Contentment and pride are destructive of prosperity,
as are compassion and fear. One who acts under the influence of these
never obtains anything worthwhile. In light of Yudhishthira's prosperity,
whatever I enjoy brings me no pleasure. He has such splendor as to make me pale.
Even though his affluence is not now before me, yet I see it as if it were.
I have therefore lost color and become melancholy and emaciated.
Yudhishthira supports eighty-eight thousand Snataka Brahmanas,
giving to each of them thirty slave girls. Besides this, a thousand other Brahmanas
daily eat at his palace the best of food on golden plates.
The king of Kambhoja sent to him as tribute innumerable skins—black, darkish,
    and red—
of the Kadali deer, as also numberless blankets of excellent textures.
And hundreds and thousands of she-elephants and thirty thousand she-camels
wander within the palace, for the kings of the earth brought them all as tribute
to the capital of the Pandavas. And the kings also brought to this foremost of
    sacrifices
heaps upon heaps of jewels and gems for the son of Kunti.
And beholding that enormous collection of wealth belonging to them,
I cannot enjoy any peace of mind. Hundreds of Brahmanas
supported by the grants from Yudhishthira waited at the palace gate
with three millions of tribute but were prevented by the doorkeepers
from entering the mansion. Bringing with them clarified butter in *kamandalus*,
    or water pots, of gold,
they did not obtain admission into the palace, and Ocean himself brought to him
in vessels of white copper the nectar that is generated within his waters
and is much superior to that of Sakra's flowers and annual plants.

And Krishna at the conclusion of the sacrifice bathed the son of Pritha with
    seawater
brought in a thousand jars of gold, all adorned with numerous gems.
Seeing all this, I became feverish with jealousy.
There is another wonderful incident also which I will relate to you.
When a hundred thousand Brahmanas were fed,
it had been arranged that every day conchs would be blown in a chorus.
But I continually heard conchs blown almost repeatedly.
And when I heard those notes, my hair stood on end. And that palatial compound,
filled with innumerable monarchs who came there as spectators,
looked like the cloudless firmament with its multitude of stars.
Monarchs came to that sacrifice of the wise son of Pandu
bringing with them every kind of wealth. The kings that came there became like
    Vaisyas,
the distributors of food to the Brahmanas who were fed.
And the prosperity that I beheld of Yudhishthira was such
that neither the chief of the celestials himself, nor Yama nor Varuna,
                    nor the lord of the Guhyakas owns as much.
Beholding that prosperity of the son of Pandu, I feel my heart burning and
    cannot enjoy peace."
Sakuni replied: "Hear how you may obtain this unrivaled prosperity
that you see in the son of Pandu. I am an adept at dice, superior to all in the world.
I can ascertain the success or otherwise of every throw,
and I know when to stake and when not. I have special knowledge of the game.
Yudhishthira also is fond of dice playing, though he possesses little skill in it.
Summoned to play or battle, he is sure to come forward,
and I will defeat him repeatedly at every throw by practicing deceptions.
I promise to win all that wealth of his,
                and you, O Duryodhana, shall then enjoy it."
King Duryodhana, thus addressed by Sakuni, without a moment's pause
said to Dhritarashtra: "This Sakuni, an adept at gambling,
is ready to win the wealth of the sons of Pandu. You should permit him to do so."
Dhritarashtra replied: "I always follow the counsels of Vidura, my wise minister.
Having consulted with him, I will inform you of my judgment in respect of this
    affair.
Endowed with great foresight, he will tell us what is good and proper for both
    parties
                and what should be done in this matter."
Duryodhana said: "If you consult with Vidura, he will tell you to refuse.
And if you refuse, I will kill myself. And when I am dead,
you will be happy with Vidura. You will then enjoy the whole earth.
                What need have you of me?"
Dhritarashtra, hearing these words of sorrow from Duryodhana,
had mixed feelings but was ready to do what Duryodhana had asked of him.
He commanded his seneschal: "Let artificers erect a delightful and spacious
    palace
with a hundred doors and a thousand columns and, with carpenters and joiners,

set jewels and precious stones all over the walls. Make it handsome and easy of
  access,

and report to me when everything is complete."

✦

King Dhritarashtra, having made this resolution to pacify Duryodhana,
sent messengers to summon Vidura, for he never made decisions without his
  counsel.
But as regards this matter, the king, although he knew the evils of gambling,
was yet attracted to it. The intelligent Vidura, however,
as soon as he heard of it, knew that the arrival of Kali was at hand.
And seeing that the way to destruction was about to open, he hurried to
  Dhritarashtra.
He approached his illustrious eldest brother, bowed down to his feet,
and said: "O exalted king, I do not approve of this decision you have made.
You should have acted in such a way that no dispute would arise
among your children on account of this gambling match."
Dhritarashtra replied: "O Vidura, if the gods be merciful unto us,
no dispute will ever arise among my sons.
Therefore, auspicious or otherwise, let this friendly challenge at dice proceed.
This is what fate has ordained for us. And when I am near,
and Drona and Bhishma and you too are present,
nothing evil that fate may have ordained is likely to happen.
Go, therefore, on a car with horses that have the speed of the wind, to
  Khandavaprastha
and bring Yudhishthira back with you. This is my decision. Say no more about it."
Hearing these words, Vidura concluded that his race was doomed.

✦

And how did that game at dice take place, fraught with such evil
and through which the sons of Pandu were plunged into such sorrow?
What kings were present, and who approved of the gambling match, and who
  forbade it?
What was indeed the cause of the destruction of the world?
Having ascertained the opinion of Vidura, Dhritarashtra told Duryodhana in
  private:
"Have nothing to do with dice. Vidura does not speak well of it.
He never gives me advice that is not for my good.
Do as he says, O son, for I regard it all as for your good also.
Indeed, Vidura knows, with all its mysteries, the science of political morality
that the illustrious and learned and wise Vrihaspati,
the celestial rishi who is the spiritual guide of Vasava, unfolded
to the wise chief of the immortals. I always accept what Vidura advises.
It is evident that gambling sows dissension. And dissension is the ruin of the
  kingdom.

You have obtained from us what a father and a mother should give to their son:
ancestral rank and possessions. You are educated in every branch of knowledge
and have been brought up with affection in your paternal dwelling.
The eldest among all your brothers, living within your own kingdom,
why are you unhappy? You have food and attire of the very best kind,
which ordinary men do not have. Why do you still grieve?
Ruling your large ancestral kingdom full of people and wealth,
you shine as splendidly as the chief of the celestials in heaven.
You must tell me, then, what can be the root of this grief."
Duryodhana answered: "I am a sinful wretch because I eat and dress well
but think of the prosperity of my foes.
It has been said that he is a wretch who is not filled with jealousy
at the sight of his enemy's prosperity. This prosperity of mine does not gratify me.
I compare it to that blazing prosperity of the son of Kunti, and I am much pained.
I see the whole earth having to acknowledge Yudhishthira's superiority.
The Nipas, the Chitrakas, the Kukkuras, the Karaskaras,
and the Lauha-janghas are living in the palace of Yudhishthira like bondsmen.
The Himavat, the ocean, the regions on the seashore,
and the numberless other regions that yield jewels and gems
have all acknowledged the hegemony of the house of Yudhishthira.
And regarding me as the eldest and entitled to respect,
Yudhishthira received me respectfully and appointed me as keeper
of the jewels and gems that had been brought as tribute.
The like of the invaluable jewels that were brought there had never before been
     seen.
My hands were fatigued from receiving that wealth.
And when I was tired, those who brought the valuable articles from distant
     regions
had to stand and wait until I was able to resume my labor.
Bringing jewels from Lake Vindu, the Asura architect Maya constructed for the
     Pandavas
a lakelike surface made of crystal. I looked at the artificial lotuses it was filled with
and I mistook it for water. And seeing me draw up my clothes while about to
     cross it,
Bhima laughed at me, regarding me as having lost my head at the sight of such
     affluence.
If I had had the ability, I would have slain him for that.
But if we endeavor to slay him now, ours will be the fate of Sisupala.
O king, that insult burns me. Once again, beholding a similar lake
that was really full of water, but which I mistook for a crystal surface, I fell into it.
At that, Bhima and Arjuna both laughed derisively, and Draupadi and other
     females
joined in the laughter. That pained my heart exceedingly.
My apparel having been wet, the menials at the command of the king
gave me other clothes. That also is my great sorrow.
And hear now of another mistake I made.
In attempting to pass through what was exactly the shape of a door,

but through which there was really no passage,
I struck my forehead against stone and injured myself.
The twins Nakula and Sahadeva, seeing from a distance that I was hit on the head,
came and supported me in their arms, expressing great concern for me.
And Sahadeva told me, as if with a smile: 'This is the door. Go this way!'
And Bhima laughed aloud and said: 'O son of Dhritarashtra, this is the door.'
And I had not even heard of the names of many of the gems I saw in that mansion.
          And it is for these reasons that my heart aches so."
Duryodhana continued: "Listen now about all the costly articles I saw,
belonging to the sons of Pandu and brought one after another by the kings of
     the earth.
Seeing all that wealth, I lost my reason and scarcely knew myself.
The king of Kambhoja gave innumerable skins of the best kind
and blankets made of wool, of the soft fur of rodents and other burrowers,
and of the hair of cats, all inlaid with threads of gold.
And he also gave three hundred horses of the Titteti and Kalmasha species,
with noses like those of parrots. And he also gave three hundred camels
and an equal number of she-asses, all fattened with olives.
And innumerable Brahmanas, engaged in rearing cattle
and occupied in low offices for the gratification of King Yudhishthira,
waited at the gate with three hundred millions of tribute,
but they were denied admission into the palace.
And hundreds upon hundreds of Brahmanas, rich in cattle
and living upon the lands that Yudhishthira had given them,
came with their handsome golden *kamandalus* filled with clarified butter.
And though they had brought such tribute, they were refused admission to the
     palace.
And the Sudra kings from the regions on the seacoast
brought with them hundreds of thousands of serving girls of the Karpasika
     country,
all of beautiful features and slender waist and luxuriant hair
and decked in golden ornaments, and also many skins of the antelope,
worthy even of Brahmanas, as tribute to the king.
And the Vairama, Parada, and Tunga tribes, with the Kitavas
who live upon crops that depend on water from the sky or of the river,
and they who were born in regions on the seashore, in woodlands,
or countries on the other side of the ocean,
waited at the gate and were refused permission to enter,
with goats and cattle and asses and camels and vegetables, honey and blankets
and jewels and gems of various kinds.
And that great warrior King Bhagadatta, the brave ruler of Pragjyotisha
and the mighty sovereign of the Mlechchhas, at the head of a large number of
     Yavanas,
waited at the gate, unable to enter, even with a considerable tribute of horses
of the best breed with the speed of the wind. And King Bhagadatta,
seeing the concourse, had to go away from the gate,
making over a number of swords with handles of the purest ivory

and adorned with diamonds and every kind of gem.
And many tribes from different regions—of whom some possess two eyes
and some three, and some having eyes on their foreheads,
and those also called Aushmikas and Nishadas and Romakas,
some cannibals, and many possessing only one leg—stood at the gate
but were refused permission to enter.
And these rulers brought as tribute ten thousand asses of diverse hues
and black necks and huge bodies and great speed and much docility.
And these asses were all of goodly size and delightful color.
There were many kings that gave Yudhishthira much gold and silver.
And having given much tribute, they obtained admission into the palace.
The people that came possessing only one leg gave Yudhishthira many wild horses,
some of which were as red as the cochineal, and some white,
and some possessing the hues of the rainbow, and some looking like evening
    clouds,
and some that were of variegated color. And they were all endowed
with the speed of the wind. They also gave the king gold of superior quality.
I also saw numberless Chins and Sakas and Uddras,
and many barbarous tribes living in the woods, and many Vrishnis and
    Harahunas,
and the dusky tribes of the Himavat, and many Nipas and people from the
    seacoast
waiting at the gate and being refused permission to enter.
The people of Valhika gave him ten thousand asses of goodly size
with black necks that could run two hundred miles every day.
And those asses were of many shapes and were well trained.
Celebrated all over the world, they had symmetrical proportions and excellent
    color,
with their skins pleasant to the touch. And the Valhikas also presented
    numerous blankets
of woolen texture manufactured in the region of Chin, and numerous skins of
    the Ranku deer,
and clothes manufactured from jute, and others woven with the threads spun by
    insects.
They also gave thousands of other clothes not made of cotton, in the color of
    the lotus
and of smooth texture. They gave soft sheepskins by the thousands
as well as many sharp swords and scimitars, and hatchets and fine-edged
    battle-axes.
And they presented perfumes and jewels and gems of various kinds
by the thousands as they waited at the gate, having been refused admission to
    the palace.
Beholding these kings of the earth giving to our foes such excellent presents,
I wished for death. I do not see the least good in continuing to live!
O ruler of men, a yoke tied to a bullock's shoulders by a blind man becomes
    loosened.
Such is the case with us. The younger ones are growing

while the elder ones are decaying. And beholding all this, I cannot enjoy peace,

even with the aid of reflection. And it is for this, O king, that I am plunged into grief."

To this Dhritarashtra replied: "You are my eldest son and born also of my eldest wife.

Therefore, do not be jealous of the Pandavas.

He who is jealous is always unhappy and suffers the pangs of death.

Yudhishthira is innocent of deception, possesses wealth equal to yours,

has your friends for his, and is not jealous of you. Why should you be jealous of him?

In respect of friends and allies, you are equal to Yudhishthira.

Why should you, therefore, covet foolishly the property of your brother?

If you covet the dignity attaching to the performance of a sacrifice,

let the priests arrange for you the great sacrifice called the Saptatantu.

The kings of the earth will then cheerfully, and with great respect,

bring for you also much wealth and gems and ornaments.

Envying others' possessions is exceedingly mean.

But he enjoys happiness who is content with what he has

and is engaged in the practices of his own order.

Never striving to obtain the wealth of others, persevering in one's own affairs,

and protecting what has been earned—these are the indications of true greatness.

He who is unmoved in calamity, skilled in his own business,

and ever vigilant and humble always prospers. The sons of Pandu are like your arms.

Do not lop them off. Do not plunge into internal dissension

for the sake of the wealth of your brothers.

There is great sin in quarreling with friends. Your grandsires are theirs also.

Give away in charity on occasions of sacrifices, gratify every dear object of your desire,

disport in the company of women freely, and enjoy peace."

To this, Duryodhana said: "Like the spoon that has no idea of the taste of soup,

he who is devoid of intellect cannot understand the real import of the scriptures.

Like a boat fastened to another, you and I are tied together.

Are you unmindful of your own interests? Or do you have hostile feelings toward me?

Your sons and allies are doomed to destruction because they have you for their ruler,

for you describe as attainable in the future what is to be done at the present moment.

O king, you are mature in wisdom, you have the opportunity to listen to the ancient teachings,

and your senses are under your control. Do not confound us who seek our own interests.

Vrihaspati, the priest of the celestials, has said that the usages of kings

are different from those of common people.

Kings, therefore, should always attend to their own interests with vigilance.
The attainment of success is the sole criterion to guide the conduct of a
 Kshatriya.
Whether the means is virtuous or sinful, what scruples can there be
in the duties of one's own order? He who desires to snatch the prosperity of his foe
should bring every direction under his subjection,
like the charioteer taming the steeds with his whip.
Those used to handling weapons say that a weapon is not simply an instrument
 that cuts
but is a means that can defeat a foe.
Who is a foe and who a friend does not depend on looks or size.
Whoever pains another is to be regarded as a foe by him who is pained.
Discontent is the root of prosperity. Therefore, I desire to be discontented.
Whoever strives after the acquisition of prosperity is a truly politic person.
Nobody should be attached to wealth and affluence,
for the wealth that has been earned and hoarded may be plundered.
The usages of kings are even such. It was during a period of peace
that Sakra cut off the head of Namuchi after having given a pledge to the
 contrary,
and he did so because he approved of this eternal usage toward the enemy.
Like a snake that swallows up frogs and other creatures living in holes,
the earth swallows up a king who is peaceful
and a Brahmana who does not stir from his home.
O king, none can by nature be anyone's foe. He is a foe if he is a competitor.
He who foolishly neglects a growing foe has his vitals cut off as by an untreated
 disease.
An enemy, however insignificant, if suffered to grow in prowess,
swallows one like the white ants at the root of a tree eating the tree itself.
Let not the prosperity of a foe be acceptable.
He who wishes for the increase of his wealth grows in the midst of his relatives
like the body naturally growing from the moment of birth.
Prowess confers speedy growth. Coveting as I do the prosperity of the Pandavas,
I have not yet made it my own. I have doubts about my ability, but I shall resolve
 them.
I will either obtain the prosperity of the Pandavas or lie down, having perished
 in battle.
When the state of my mind is such, what do I care for life,
for the Pandavas are growing every day while our possessions know no increase?"
Then Sakuni said: "I will snatch this prosperity of Yudhishthira for you.
O king, let Yudhishthira be summoned. By throwing dice, a skillful man,
risking nothing, may vanquish one who has no skill.
Betting is my bow, the dice are my arrows, the marks on them my bowstring,
       and the diceboard my car."
Duryodhana agreed and said: "This Sukuni, skilled at dice, is ready
to snatch the prosperity of the son of Pandu. You must give him permission."
Dhritarashtra was silent for some moments and then said:
"I am obedient to the counsels of my brother, the illustrious Vidura.

Consulting with him, I shall tell what should be done in this matter."
But Duryodhana objected. "Vidura," he said, "is always engaged in doing good
to the sons of Pandu, while his feelings toward us are otherwise.
He will without doubt dissuade you from what we propose.
No man should set himself to any task depending upon the counsels of another,
for the minds of two persons seldom agree in any particular act.
Neither sickness nor Yama waits until one is in prosperity.
So long as there is life and health, one should not wait for prosperity
     but act to accomplish his purpose."
Dhritarashtra said: "Hostility with those who are strong never recommends itself
 to me.
Hostility brings about a change of feelings, and that itself is a weapon,
although not made of steel. You regard as a great blessing what will bring in its
 train
the terrible consequences of war. Fraught with mischief, if it once begins,
    it creates sharp swords and pointed arrows."
Duryodhana replied: "Men of the most ancient times invented the use of dice.
There is no destruction in it, nor is there any striking with weapons.
Let the words of Sakuni, therefore, be acceptable,
and let your command be issued for the speedy construction of the assembly
 house.
The door of heaven, leading us to such happiness, will be opened to us by
 gambling.
Indeed, they who gamble, with such help as we have, deserve good fortune.
The Pandavas will become your equals instead of your superiors.
    Gamble therefore with the Pandavas."
King Dhritarashtra said: "Your words do not recommend themselves to me.
Do what is agreeable to you. But you shall repent for acting according to these
 words."

✦

The weak-minded Dhritarashtra regarded fate as supreme and unavoidable;
and, deprived of reason by fate, and obedient to the counsels of his son,
he commanded his men in a loud voice, saying:
"Construct, without loss of time, an assembly house of the most beautiful
 description
to be called the Crystal-Arched Palace, with a thousand columns,
decked with gold and lapis lazuli, furnished with a hundred gates,
and a full two miles in length and in breadth."
Thousands of artificers endowed with intelligence and skill erected the palace
with the greatest speed and brought to it every kind of luxurious article.
Soon afterward, they reported to the king that the palace had been finished
and that it was delightful and handsome and furnished with every kind of gem
and covered with many-colored carpets inlaid with gold.
King Dhritarashtra then summoned Vidura, the chief of his ministers, and said:
"Go to Khandavaprastha, and bring King Yudhishthira here without loss of time.

Let him come with his brothers to behold this handsome assembly house of mine,
furnished with countless jewels and gems and costly beds and carpets,
                   and let a friendly match at dice commence here."
Vidura, that foremost among intelligent men, disapproved of his brother's words
    and said:
"I do not like this command of yours. Do not do this.
I fear that this will bring about the destruction of our race.
When your sons lose their unity, dissension will ensue.
This is what I fear from this match at dice."
Dhritarashtra said: "The whole universe moves at the will of its creator,
under the controlling influence of fate. It is not free.
Therefore, O Vidura, go to King Yudhishthira, and bring that invincible son of
    Kunti."
Against his will, Vidura set out with horses of high mettle and great speed and
    strength
for the abode of the wise sons of Pandu.
Vidura arrived at the city of King Yudhishthira, entered it, and, coming to the
    palace,
the virtuous Vidura approached Yudhishthira. He saluted Vidura
and asked him about Dhritarashtra and his sons.
And Yudhishthira said: "Your mind seems cheerless. Do you come here in
    happiness and peace?
The sons of Dhritarashtra, I hope, are obedient to their old father.
The people also, I hope, are obedient to Dhritarashtra's rule."
Vidura said: "The illustrious king and his sons are well and happy
and, surrounded by his relatives, he reigns even like Indra himself.
The king is happy with his sons, who are all obedient to him, and he has no grief.
But the illustrious monarch is bent on his own aggrandizement.
He has commanded me to inquire after your peace and prosperity
and to ask you to come to Hastinapura with your brothers and to say,
after beholding King Dhritarashtra's newly erected palace, if it is equal to
    your own.
Come there with your brothers, enjoy the mansion, and sit if you will
to a friendly match at dice. The Kurus have already arrived there, and you will
    see there
those gamblers and cheats that King Dhritarashtra has already brought.
                  It is for this, O king, that I have come."
Yudhishthira said: "O Vidura, if we sit to a match at dice, we may quarrel.
What man is there who, knowing all this, will consent to gamble?
What do you think? We all are obedient to your counsels."
Vidura said: "Gambling is the root of misery, and I strove to dissuade the king
    from it.
But the king sent me to you. O learned one, do what is right."
Yudhishthira said: "Besides the sons of Dhritarashtra,
what other dishonest gamblers are there ready for play?
Tell us who they are and with whom we shall have to play,
staking hundreds upon hundreds of our possessions."

Vidura said: "O monarch, Sakuni, the king of Gandhara,
an adept at dice with great skill of hand and knowing the odds,
Vivingati, King Chitrasena, Satyavrata, Purumitra and Jaya—
                              all of these are there."
Yudhishthira said: "It would seem then that some of the most desperate
and terrible gamblers who always depend upon deceit are there.
This whole universe, however, is at the will of its maker, under the control of fate.
I do not desire, at the command of King Dhritarashtra, to engage in gambling.
The father always wishes to benefit his son. You are our master, O Vidura.
Tell me what is proper for us. Unwilling as I am to gamble,
if the wicked Sakuni summons me to it in the *sabha* and challenges me,
I will never refuse. For that is my eternal vow."
King Yudhishthira commanded that preparations for his journey might be made
     quickly.
And the next day, accompanied by his relatives and attendants,
and taking with him also the women of the household, with Draupadi in their
     midst,
the king set out for the capital of the Kurus.
He said: "Like some brilliant body falling before the eyes, fate deprives us of
     reason,
and man, tied as it were with a cord, submits to the sway of Providence."
And, saying this, King Yudhishthira set out with Vidura,
riding upon the car that had been given him by the king of Valhika.
Blazing with royal splendor, with Brahmanas walking before him,
he set out from his city, summoned by Dhritarashtra
and impelled by what has been ordained by *kala*, or time.
Arriving at Hastinapura, Yudhishthira went to the palace of Dhritarashtra.
The son of Pandu approached the king, and then Bhishma and Drona
and Karna, and Kripa, and the son of Drona, and embraced and was embraced
     by them all.
He then approached Somadatta, and Duryodhana and Salya, and the son of
     Suvala,
and those other kings also who had arrived before him.
Yudhishthira then went to the brave Dusshasana and then all his other brothers
and then to Jayadratha and next to all the Kurus, one after another.
And then, surrounded by his brothers, he entered the apartment of King
     Dhritarashtra.
Yudhishthira there beheld the reverend Gandhari, ever obedient to her lord,
and surrounded by her daughters-in-law like Rohini by the stars.
Saluting Gandhari and blessed by her in return, Yudhishthira beheld his old uncle,
that illustrious monarch whose wisdom was his eye. King Dhritarashtra smelled
     Yudhishthira's head
and the heads of those four other princes of the Kuru race.
And the handsome Pandavas became exceedingly glad. Commanded by the
     Dhritarashtra,
the Pandavas retired to the chambers allotted to them, furnished with jewels and
     gems.

And when they had retired into the chambers, the women of Dhritarashtra's
    household,
with Dussala taking the lead, visited them. And the daughters-in-law of
    Dhritarashtra,
beholding the blazing beauty and prosperity of Yajnasena,
became cheerless and filled with jealousy.
Those tigers among men, having conversed with the ladies,
went through their daily physical exercises and performed the religious rites of
    the day.
Then they decked their persons with fragrant paste of sandalwood.
And, desiring good luck and prosperity, they gave gifts to the Brahmanas
so they might utter benedictions. They ate food that was of the best taste
and retired to their chambers for the night, where they were put to sleep
with music by beautiful females and obtained from them what came in due
    course,
passing with cheerful hearts a delightful night of pleasure and sport.
In the morning, awakened by charanas with sweet music,
they rose from their beds at dawn, went through the usual rites,
and entered into the assembly house to be saluted by those already there for
    gambling.

19

The Jackal

The Pandavas, with Yudhishthira at their head, entered the assembly house,
approached the kings who were there, worshipped those who deserved to be
   worshipped,
and saluted others as each merited, according to age.
Then, when they were seated, Sakuni, the son of Suvala, addressed Yudhishthira:
"O king, the assembly is full. We have been waiting for you.
Let the dice be cast and the rules of play be fixed."
Yudhishthira said: "Deceitful gambling is sinful. There is no Kshatriya prowess
   in it.
There is certainly no morality in it. Why, then, do you praise gambling so?
The wise do not applaud the pride that gamesters take in deceitful play.
O Sakuni, if you vanquish us, let it not be as a wretch would do, by deceitful
   means."
Sakuni said: "That high-souled player who knows the secrets of winning and
   losing,
who is skilled in baffling the deceitful arts of his fellow players
and is alert to the diverse operations of which gambling consists, truly knows the
   game,
and he deals with all of it. It is the staking at dice, which may be lost or won,
that may injure us. And it is for this reason that gambling is regarded as a fault.
Let us, therefore, begin the play. Fear not! Let the stakes be fixed."
Yudhishthira said: "Devala, that best of munis, who always instructs us
about all those acts that may lead to heaven, hell, or the other regions,
has said that it is sinful to play deceitfully with a gamester.
To obtain victory in battle without cunning or stratagem is the best sport.
Gambling, however, is a sport in which this is not so.
Still, those who are respectable never use the language of the Mlechchhas,
nor do they adopt deceitfulness in their behavior.
War carried on without crookedness and cunning is the act of honest men.
Do not, O Sakuni, play desperately to win that wealth with which you may
   benefit the Brahmanas.
Even enemies should not be vanquished by desperate stakes or deceitful play.
I do not desire either happiness or wealth by means of cunning.
At any rate, the conduct of a gamester, even if it be without deceitfulness,
                         should not be applauded."

Sakuni said: "It is from a desire of winning, which is not a very honest motive,
that one learned person approaches another in a contest of learning.
Such a motive, however, is hardly regarded as dishonest.
So also a person skilled at dice approaches one less skilled from a desire of
    winning.
So also one who is skilled in weapons approaches one less skilled.
This is the practice in every contest. The motive is always victory, O Yudhishthira.
If, therefore, you regard me as actuated by dishonest motives,
or if you are suspicious or afraid, desist from play."
Yudhishthira said: "Summoned, I do not withdraw. This is my vow.
We all are under the control of destiny. With whom in this assembly am I to play?
Who is there that can stake equally with me? Let the play begin."
Duryodhana said: "I shall supply jewels and gems and every kind of wealth.
And it is for me that my uncle Sakuni will play."
Yudhishthira said: "Gambling with the agency of another
seems to me contrary to the rule. Still, if you insist, let the play begin."

◆

All those kings with Dhritarashtra at their head took their seats.
Bhishma and Drona and Kripa and the high-souled Vidura with cheerless hearts
sat behind. Those kings with leonine necks and great power took their seats
separately and in pairs upon many elevated seats of beautiful colors.
The mansion was resplendent with those assembled potentates,
like heaven itself with a conclave of the celestials.
Yudhishthira said: "This excellent trove of pearls of great value,
so beautiful and decked with pure gold, this, O king, is my stake.
What is your counterstake with which you wish to play ?"
Duryodhana said: "I have many jewels and much wealth. But I am not vain of
    them.
                                    Here is my stake."
Then Sakuni, well skilled at dice, took up the dice and cast them.
And he said to Yudhishthira: "Lo, I have won!"
Yudhishthira said: "You won this bet by unfair means. Do not be so proud of
    yourself.
Let us play again, staking thousands upon thousands. I have many beautiful jars,
each full of a thousand nishkas, in my treasury,
inexhaustible gold, and much silver. This is the wealth with which I will bet!"
Sakuni cast the dice a second time. And a second time he said to King
    Yudhishthira:
"Lo, I have won!" Yudhishthira said: "This my sacred and victorious royal car,
which gladdens the heart and has carried us here, and which is equal in value
to a thousand cars. It is of symmetrical proportions and covered with tigerskin,
and furnished with excellent wheels and flagstaffs, and decked with strings of
    little bells
whose clatter is like the roar of the clouds or of the ocean,
and it is drawn by eight noble steeds white as moonbeams

from whose hooves no terrestrial creature can escape—this is what I will stake
  with you!"
Sakuni, ready with the dice, cast them.
He looked at the table and said to Yudhishthira for the third time: "Lo, I have
  won!"
Yudhishthira said: "I have a hundred thousand serving girls,
all young, and decked with golden bracelets on their wrists and upper arms,
and with nishkas around their necks and other ornaments
adorned with costly garlands, and attired in rich robes,
daubed with sandalwood paste, wearing jewels and gold,
and well skilled in the four and sixty elegant arts, especially in dancing and
  singing,
and who serve at my command the celestials, the Snataka Brahmanas, and kings.
                    With this wealth I will bet!"
Sakuni threw the dice down and said yet again to Yudhishthira: "Lo, I have won!"
Yudhishthira said: "I have thousands of servingmen,
skilled in waiting upon guests, always attired in silken robes,
endowed with wisdom and intelligence, their senses under control though
  young,
and decked with earrings, who serve all guests night and day
with plates and dishes in hand. With this wealth I will bet!"
Sakuni, ready with the dice, cast them and said yet again to Yudhishthira: "Lo, I
  have won!"
Yudhishthira said: "I have one thousand elephants with golden girdles,
decked with ornaments, with the mark of the lotus on their temples and necks,
adorned with golden garlands, with fine white tusks long and thick as plowshafts,
worthy of carrying kings on their backs, capable of bearing every kind of noise
on the field of battle, with huge bodies that can batter down the walls of hostile
  towns,
of the color of new-formed clouds, and each possessing eight she-elephants.
                    With this wealth I will bet."
Sakuni threw the dice, laughed, and said yet again to Yudhishthira: "Lo, I have
  won!"
Yudhishthira then said: "I have as many cars as elephants,
all furnished with golden poles and flagstaffs, and well-trained horses,
and warriors that fight wonderfully and each of whom receives a thousand coins
as his monthly pay whether he fights or not. With this wealth I will bet!"
The wretch Sakuni, with enmity in his heart, cast the dice and said once more:
                    "Lo, I have won."
Yudhishthira said: "I have steeds of the Tittiri, Kalmasha, and Gandharva breeds,
decked with ornaments, which Chitraratha, having been vanquished in battle,
cheerfully gave to Arjuna, the wielder of the Gandiva. With this wealth I will bet."
Sakuni was not reluctant. He cast the dice and all but crowed: "Lo, I have won!"
Yudhishthira said: "I have ten thousand cars and vehicles to which are yoked
draft animals of the foremost breed. And I have sixty thousand warriors
picked from each order who are all brave and have the prowess of heroes,
                    With this wealth I will bet."

Sakuni cast the dice, glanced at the pips, and said quietly to Yudhishthira:
"Lo, I have won!"

✦

During the course of this gambling, certain to bring utter ruin down on
　　Yudhishthira,
Vidura said to Dhritarashtra: "O great king, attend to what I say,
although my words may not be agreeable to you.
They are like medicine to one who is ill and about to breathe his last.
When this Duryodhana of sinful mind had, immediately after his birth, cried
　　like a jackal,
it was interpreted as a sign that he had been ordained
to bring about the destruction of the Bharata race.
Know, O king, that he will be the cause of the death of all of you.
A jackal is living in your house, O king, in the form of Duryodhana.
Listen to the words of the poet Sukra, which I will quote:
'They who collect honey in the mountains, having found what they were seeking,
do not notice that they are about to fall. Ascending dangerous heights,
concentrated on the pursuit of what they seek, they fall down and meet with
　　destruction.'
Thus Duryodhana also, maddened with the play at dice, like the collector of
　　honey,
concentrating on what he seeks, does not mark the consequences.
Making enemies of these great warriors, he does not see the precipice before him.
You know that among the Bhojas, they abandoned, for the good of the citizens,
　　　　　　　　　　　a son who was unworthy of their race.
The Andhakas, the Yadavas, and the Bhojas, uniting together, abandoned Kansa.
And afterward—when, at the command of the tribe, Kansa had been slain by
　　Krishna—
all the men of the tribe were exceedingly happy for a hundred years.
So, at your command, let Arjuna slay Duryodhana,
and let the Kurus be glad and pass their days in happiness.
In exchange for a crow, O great king, buy these peacocks, the Pandavas;
and in exchange for a jackal, buy these tigers.
For the sake of a family, a member may be sacrificed; for the sake of a village,
a family may be sacrificed; for the sake of a province, a village may be sacrificed;
and for the sake of one's soul, the whole earth may be sacrificed.
This was what the omniscient Kavya himself, acquainted with the thoughts
of every creature and a source of terror to all foes, said to the great Asuras
to induce them to abandon Jambha at the moment of his birth.
It is said that a certain king, having caused a number of wild birds that vomited
　　gold
to take up their quarters in his house, afterward killed them from temptation.
O slayer of foes, blinded by temptation and the desire of enjoyment,
for the sake of gold the king destroyed at the same time both his present and
　　future gains.

Therefore, O king, do not prosecute the Pandavas from the desire for profit.
Do not behave like the king in that story, for then, blinded by folly,
you will have to repent afterward. Like a flower seller who plucks many flowers
in the garden from trees that he cherishes with affection, continue to pluck
   flowers
day by day from the Pandavas. Do not scorch them to their roots,
like a fire-producing breeze that reduces everything to charcoal.
Do not go to the region of Yama with your sons and troops,
for who is there capable of fighting with the sons of Pritha, together?
Not to speak of others, is the chief of the celestials capable of doing so?"
Vidura continued: "Gambling is the root of dissension and brings about disunion.
Its consequences are frightful. Yet Duryodhana, by gambling, creates for himself
   enmity.
The descendants of Pratipa and Shantanu, with their troops and their allies the
   Valhikas,
will for the sins of Duryodhana meet with destruction.
Duryodhana, in this intoxication, drives luck and prosperity from his kingdom,
like an infuriated bull breaking his own horns.
That brave and learned person who disregards his own foresight
and follows the inclination of another man's heart sinks in terrible affliction,
like one who goes to the sea in a boat steered by a child.
Duryodhana is gambling with the son of Pandu, and you are glad that he is
   winning.
But it is such success that begets war, which ends in the death of men.
Do not enter into the terrible fire that has blazed forth from this wretch.
When Yudhishthira, the son of Pandu, intoxicated with dice, gives way to his
   wrath,
and Vrikodara and Arjuna and the twins do the same,
who in that hour of confusion will prove your refuge?
O great king, you are yourself a mine of wealth and can earn by other means
as much wealth as you seek to earn by gambling.
What do you gain by winning from the Pandavas their riches?
Win the Pandavas themselves, who will be more to you than all the wealth they
   have.
We know the skill of Suvala in play. This hill king has nefarious methods in
   gambling.
Let Sakuni return to where he came from. Do not war with the sons of Pandu!"
Duryodhana said: "You are always boasting of the fame of our enemies
and deprecating the sons of Dhritarashtra. We know, O Vidura, of whom you are
   fond.
You always disregarded us as children. A man is likely to wish for success
for those who are near to him and defeat for those who are not his favorites.
His praise and blame are applied accordingly. Your tongue and mind betray
   your heart.
But the hostility you show in speech is even greater than what is in your heart.
You have been cherished by us like a serpent on our lap.
Like a cat, you wish evil to him who cherishes you.

The wise have said that there is no sin graver than that of injuring one's master.
How is it that you do not fear this sin?
Having vanquished our enemies, we have obtained great advantages.
Do not use not harsh words to us. You are always willing to make peace with the
    foes.
And it is for this reason that you hate us. A man becomes a foe
by speaking words that are unpardonable. Then again, in praising the enemy,
the secrets of one's own party should not be divulged. But you transgress this
    rule.
Therefore, O parasite, why do you obstruct us so? You say whatever you wish.
Do not insult us. We know your mind. Go and learn, sitting at the feet of the old.
Do not meddle in the affairs of other men. Do not imagine that you are our
    chief.
Say no more harsh words to us, O Vidura. We do not ask you what is for our
    good.
Cease then, and do not irritate those who have already borne too much from you.
There is only one controller, no second.
He controls even the child that is in the mother's womb. I am controlled by him.
Like water that always flows downward, I am acting in the way he is directing me.
Whoever breaks his head against a stone wall, and whoever feeds a serpent,
must be guided in those acts of theirs by their own intellect.
In this matter, therefore, I am guided by my own intelligence.
One should not give shelter to one who is the friend of one's foes,
or to another who is ever jealous of his protector, or to another who is
    evil-minded.
               Therefore, O Vidura, go where you please."
Vidura said to Dhritarashtra: "O monarch, tell us objectively what you think
of the conduct of those who abandon their servingmen thus for giving advice to
    them.
The hearts of kings are fickle. First granting protection, they then strike with
    clubs.
Duryodhana, you regard yourself as mature in intellect, and you consider me a
    child.
But he is a child who, having first accepted someone for a friend, then finds
    fault with him.
After this, O king, if you wish to hear words that are agreeable to you,
ask women and idiots and cripples or persons of that description.
A sinful man speaking words that are agreeable is easy to find in this world.
But a speaker of words that are disagreeable though sound is very rare.
A king's true ally disregards what is agreeable or disagreeable to his master
and bears himself virtuously and utters what may be disagreeable but is
    necessary.
O great king, drink what the honest drink and the dishonest shun—
humility, which is like a medicine that is bitter, pungent, burning, unintoxicating,
disagreeable, and revolting. But drinking it, O king, you will regain sobriety.
I always wish Dhritarashtra and his sons affluence and fame.
Come what may, I bow to you and take my leave. Let the Brahmanas wish me well.

O son of Kuru, the lesson I impart is that the wise should never enrage vipers
that have venom in their very glances!"

✦

Sakuni said: "Yudhishthira, you have lost much wealth of the Pandavas.
If you still have anything that you have not yet lost, tell us what it is!"
Yudhishthira said: "I have untold wealth. But why is it that you ask?
Wager tens of thousands and millions, and millions and tens of millions
and hundreds of millions, and tens of billions and hundreds of billions, and
    trillions
and tens of trillions and hundreds of trillions, and tens of quadrillions
and hundreds of quadrillions and even more wealth. I have as much.
          With that wealth I will play with you."
Sakuni threw the dice and yet again said to Yudhishthira:
                 "Lo, I have won!"

Yudhishthira said: "I have immeasurable cattle and horses and milk cows with
    calves
and goats and sheep in the country from the Parnasa to the eastern bank of the
    Sindu.
With this wealth I will play with you."And again Sakuni cast the dice, counted the
    pips,
and said to Yudhishthira: "Lo, I have won!"
Yudhishthira said: "I have my city, the country, land, the wealth of all dwelling
    therein
except of the Brahmanas. With this wealth I will play with you."
Yet again Sakuni cast the dice, counted the pips, and said: "Lo, I have won!"
Yudhishthira said: "These princes here, O king, who look resplendent in their
    ornaments,
and their earrings and nishkas and the ornaments on their persons are now my
    wealth.
          With this wealth I will play with you."
Again Sakuni cast the dice and said to Yudhishthira: "Lo, I have won them!"
Yudhishthira said: "Nakula here, of mighty arms and leonine neck,
of red eyes and endowed with youth, is now my one stake. He is my wealth."
Sakuni said: "O King Yudhishthira, Prince Nakula is dear to you.
But he is already under our subjection. With whom as stake will you now play?"
Saying this, Sakuni cast the dice and said to Yudhishthira: "Lo, he has been won
    by us!"
Yudhishthira said: "Sahadeva administers justice. He has also a reputation for
    learning.
However wrong it is for him to be to be staked in play, with him as stake I will play,
         betting such a dear object as if, indeed, he were not so!"
Hearing this, Sakuni cast the dice. "Lo, I have won," he said.
Sakuni then said: "O king, the sons of Madri, dear to you, have both been won
    by me.

It would seem, however, that you also have high regard for Bhimasena and
  Dhananjaya."
Yudhishthira said: "Wretch! You create disunion among us who are all of one
  heart."
Sakuni said: "A man who is drunk falls into the pit of hell and stays there,
deprived of the power of motion. You are, O king, senior to us in age
and possessed of the highest accomplishments. I beg your pardon and bow to you.
You know that gamblers, while excited with play, utter such ravings
as they would never say in their waking moments nor even in dreams."
Yudhishthira said: "Arjuna takes us like a boat to the other shore of the sea of
  battle,
he is ever victorious over foes. That prince, the one hero in this world, is here.
With Arjuna as stake, I will now play with you."
Hearing this, Sakuni cast the dice once more, waited for them to settle,
                    and said to Yudhishthira: "Lo, I have won!"
And he repeated: "I have won this foremost among bowmen.
Oh, play now with the wealth still left to you—with Bhima, your brother, as your
  stake."
Yudhishthira said: "However undeserving he may be of such treatment,
I will now play with you by staking Bhimasena, that prince who is our leader,
who is the foremost in fight, even like the wielder of the thunderbolt,
the high-souled one with leonine neck and arched eyebrows
and eyes looking askance, who is incapable of putting up with an insult,
who has no equal in might in the world, who is foremost among wielders of the
  mace,
                    and who grinds all foes."
Hearing this, Sakuni, ready with the dice, cast them and said to Yudhishthira:
"Lo, I have won!" He continued: "You have lost much wealth,
horses and elephants and your brothers as well.
Say if you have anything that you have not lost."
Yudhishthira said: "I alone, the eldest of all my brothers and dear to them,
am yet unwon. Won by you, I will do what he who is won will have to do."
Hearing this, Sakuni nodded, cast the dice, and said to Yudhishthira: "Lo, I have
  won!"
Sakuni continued: "You have permitted yourself to be won. This is very sinful.
There is wealth still left to you, O king. Therefore, your having lost yourself is
  sinful."
Sakuni then spoke to all the brave kings present of his having won, one after
  another,
                    all the Pandavas.
The son of Suvala then, addressing Yudhishthira, said:
"O king, there is still one stake dear to you that I have yet to win.
Stake Draupadi, the princess of Panchala. By her you may win yourself back."
Yudhishthira said: "With Draupadi at stake, I will now play.
Possessed of eyes like the leaves of the autumn lotus, and fragrant as the autumn
  lotus,
equal in beauty to Lakshmi, who delights in autumn lotuses,

and to Sri herself in symmetry and every grace,
she is such a woman as a man may desire for a wife.
She is possessed of every accomplishment, and compassionate,
well spoken, and fit for the acquisition of virtue, pleasure, and wealth.
Retiring to bed last and waking up first, she looks after all,
down to the cowherds and the shepherds.
Her face, too, when covered with sweat, looks like the lotus or the jasmine.
Of slender waist like that of the wasp, of long flowing locks, of red lips
and body without down is the princess of Panchala.
O king, making the slender-waisted Draupadi my stake, I will play with you."
When King Yudhishthira had spoken thus, the aged persons in the assembly
    called out:
"Fie! Fie!" The whole conclave was agitated, and the kings all gave way to grief.
Bhishma and Drona and Kripa were covered with a cold sweat.
And Vidura, holding his head between his hands, sat like one who has lost his
    reason.
He sat with face downward, giving way to his reflections and sighing like a snake.
But Dhritarashtra, glad at heart, asked repeatedly: "Has the stake been won?
Has the stake been won?" And he could not conceal his emotions.
Karna, Dussasana, and others laughed aloud while tears flowed
from the eyes of all the others in the assembly.
And the son of Suvala, proud of success and flurried with excitement, repeated:
"You have one more stake, one more stake, one more stake." And he took up the
    dice.

✦

Duryodhana said: "Come, Vidura, bring Draupadi here,
the dear and beloved wife of the Pandavas. Let her sweep the chambers
and let her stay where our servingwomen stay."
Vidura said: "Do you not know that by uttering such harsh words
you are tying yourself with cords? Do you not understand
that you are hanging on the edge of a precipice?
Do you not know that, being a deer, you provoke many tigers to rage?
Snakes of deadly venom, angered and vengeful, are coiled on your head!
Do not provoke them further, lest you find yourself in the region of Yama.
In my judgment, slavery does not attach to Draupadi,
inasmuch as she was staked by the king after he had lost himself
and ceased to be his own master. Like the bamboo that bears fruit
only when it is about to die, the son of Dhritarashtra wins this treasure at play.
Intoxicated, he fails to perceive in these his last moments
that dice bring about enmity and frightful terrors.
No man should utter harsh speeches and pierce the hearts of others.
No man should subjugate his enemies by dice.
No one should utter such words as are disapproved by the Vedas
and that lead to hell and enrage others. Someone utters words that are harsh.
Stung by them, another burns day and night. These words pierce his very heart.

The learned, therefore, never utter them.
It is only low men who are like dogs and use harsh words
toward all classes of people. Alas! The son of Dhritarashtra does not know
that dishonesty is one of the frightful doors of hell.
Regrettably, many of the Kurus, with Dussasana among them, have followed him
on the path of dishonesty in the matter of this dice game.
Even gourds may sink and stones may float, and boats also may sink in water,
but this foolish king, the son of Dhritarashtra, does not listen not to my words
that are as a prescription for him. He will be the cause of the destruction of the
    Kurus."
Intoxicated with pride, Duryodhana spoke: "Shame on Vidura!"
Casting his eyes upon Pratikamin, in attendance, he commanded him,
in the midst of all those reverend seniors: "Go, Pratikamin, and bring Draupadi
    here.
You need not have any fears of the sons of Pandu. Vidura alone raves in fear."
Then Pratikamin, of the Suta caste, proceeded with haste
and entered the abode of the Pandavas, like a dog in a lion's den.
He approached the queen of the sons of Pandu and said:
"Yudhishthira was intoxicated with dice, and Duryodhana has won you.
Come, then, to the abode of Dhritarashtra.
I will take you, O Draupadi, and assign you to some menial work."
Draupadi said: "Why, O Pratikamin, do you say this?
What prince is there who plays, betting his wife?
The king was certainly intoxicated with dice. Or he could not find anything else
    to bet."
Pratikamin said: "The king had first staked his brothers, then himself,
and then you, O princess."
                    Draupadi said: "Son of the Suta race,
go and ask the gamblers in the assembly whom he lost first, himself or me.
When you have the answer, then take me with you."
The messenger returned to the assembly and repeated the words of Draupadi.
And he spoke to Yudhishthira, sitting in the midst of the kings, saying:
"Draupadi has asked you: 'Whose lord were you at the time you lost me in play?
                    Did you lose yourself first or me?'"
Yudhishthira sat there like one demented and deprived of reason, and he gave
    no answer.
Duryodhana then said: "Let the princess of Panchala come and put her question
    herself.
Let everyone in this assembly hear the words that pass between her and
    Yudhishthira."
The messenger went again to the palace, much distressed, and said to Draupadi:
"O princess, they in the assembly are summoning you.
It seems that the end of the Kauravas is at hand.
When Duryodhana, O princess, is for taking you before the assembly,
this weak-brained king will no longer be able to protect his prosperity."
Draupadi said: "The great ordainer of the world has indeed decreed it so.
Happiness and misery pay their court to both the wise and the unwise.

But morality, it has been said, is the highest of all objects in the world.

If cherished, it will dispense blessings to us. Let that morality not abandon the
 Kauravas.

Go back to those in that assembly, and repeat my words, which are consonant
 with morality.

I am ready to do whatever those elderly and virtuous persons tell me to do."

The Suta went back to the assembly and repeated what Draupadi had said.

But all sat with faces downward, uttering not a word,

knowing the eagerness and resolution of Dhritarashtra's son.

Yudhishthira, however, hearing of Duryodhana's intentions,

sent a messenger to Draupadi to say that although she was attired in one piece
 of cloth

with her navel itself exposed, in consequence of her season having come,

she should appear before her father-in-law weeping bitterly.

The illustrious Pandavas, meanwhile, distressed and sorrowful, and bound by
 promise,

         could not settle what they should do.

King Duryodhana, glad at heart, said to the Suta: "O Pratikamin, bring her here.

Let the Kauravas answer her question before her face."

The Suta, then, obedient to his commands, but terrified at the possible wrath

of the daughter of Drupada, once again asked those in the assembly:

      "What shall I say to her?"

Duryodhana, hearing this, said to Dussasana: "This Suta fears Draupadi.

Therefore, go yourself and forcibly bring her here.

Our enemies are now subject to our will. What can they do to you?"

Prince Dussasana rose with blood-red eyes, entered the Pandavas' apartment,

and said to the princess: "Come, come, O princess of Panchala,

you have been won by us. Come now, and accept the Kurus as your lords."

In great affliction Draupadi rose up, rubbed her pale face with her hands,

and ran to the ladies' quarters of Dhritarashtra's household.

Dussasana, roaring in anger, ran after her and seized her by her long wavy hair.

Alas! Those locks that had been sprinkled with water sanctified with mantras

in the great Rajasuya sacrifice were now tugged by the son of Dhritarashtra.

And Dussasana dragged Draupadi into the presence of the assembly

and made her tremble like a banana plant in a storm.

With body bent, she cried faintly: "Wretch! It ill behooves you

to take me before the assembly. My season has come, and I am now clad

in one piece of attire." But even as she was praying piteously to Krishna and
 Vishnu,

who were Narayana and Nara on earth, Dussasana said to her:

"Whether your season has come or not, whether you are attired in one piece of
 cloth

or entirely naked, you have been won at dice and made our slave,

      and you are to live among our servingwomen."

With her hair disheveled and her attire loosened, all the while dragged by
 Dussasana,

the modest Draupadi, consumed with anger, said:

"In this assembly are persons conversant with all the branches of learning
devoted to the performance of sacrifices and other rites, and all equal to Indra,
persons some of whom are really my superiors and who deserve respect.
I cannot stay before them in this state. O wretch of wicked deeds!
Do not drag me so; do not uncover me so. The princes who are my lords
will not pardon you, even if you have the gods themselves with Indra as your allies.
The illustrious son of Dharma is bound by the obligations of morality.
Morality, however, is subtle. Only those possessed of clearness of vision can
    ascertain it.
In speech I am unwilling to admit an atom of fault in my lord for forgetting his
    virtues.
You drag me in my season before these Kuru heroes. This is an unworthy act.
But no one here rebukes you. All these men are apparently of the same mind
    as you.
Shame! Truly has the virtue of the Bharatas been extinguished,
and the usage of those acquainted with the Kshatriya practice has disappeared!
Otherwise these Kurus in this assembly would never have looked silently on
    this act
that transgresses the limits of their practices. Drona and Bhishma have lost their
    energy,
and so has the high-souled Vidura, and so also has the king.
Why else would these foremost among the Kuru elders look silently on this great
    crime?"
Thus did Draupadi of slender waist cry in distress in that assembly.
And casting a glance on her enraged lords, the Pandavas, who were filled with
    wrath,
she inflamed them further with that glance of hers.
They were not so distressed by having been robbed of their kingdom,
their wealth, and their costliest gems as they were by that glance of Draupadi,
                  moved by modesty and anger.
Dussasana dragged her still more forcibly and mocked her—"Slave, slave!"—
and laughed aloud. At those words, Karna became very glad and laughed also.
And Sakuni, the son of Suvala, the Gandhara king, similarly applauded Dussasana.
Among all those in the assembly except these three and Duryodhana,
everyone was filled with sorrow at seeing Draupadi thus dragged before that
    assembly.
Bhishma said: "Morality is subtle. I therefore am unable to decide this point,
considering that on the one hand a person with no wealth
cannot stake wealth belonging to others, while on the other hand
wives are always under the orders and at the disposal of their lords.
Yudhishthira can abandon the whole world full of wealth,
but he will never sacrifice morality. The son of Pandu admitted that he was won,
and I am unable to decide this matter. Sakuni has no equal among men at dice.
The son of Kunti still voluntarily gambled with him.
The illustrious Yudhishthira does not himself believe Sakuni played with him
    deceitfully.
              Therefore, I cannot decide this point."

Draupadi said: "The king was summoned to this assembly
and, though possessing no skill at dice, was made to play
with skillful, wicked, deceitful, desperate gamblers.
How can he be said, then, to have staked voluntarily?
The chief of the Pandavas was deprived of his senses
by deceitful wretches acting together, and then vanquished.
He could not understand their tricks, but he has now done so.
Here in this assembly there are Kurus who are the lords
of both their sons and their daughters-in-law!
Let all of them, reflecting upon my words, decide the question I have raised."
To Draupadi, who was weeping and crying piteously,
Dussasana spoke many disagreeable and harsh words.
And he dragged her upper garments that were loosened.
Beholding her in that condition, which she little deserved, Bhima,
afflicted beyond endurance, with his eyes fixed upon Yudhishthira, gave way to
    wrath.
He said: "Yudhishthira, gamblers have in their houses prostitutes and such
    women,
but they do not stake those women, having kindness for them.
Whatever wealth and other excellent articles the king of Kasi gave—
whatever, gems, animals, wealth, coats of mail, and weapons that other kings
    gave—
our kingdom, yourself, and ourselves have all been won by the foes.
At all this my wrath was not excited, for you are our lord.
This, however, I regard as highly improper—this staking of Draupadi.
This innocent girl does not deserve such treatment.
Having obtained the Pandavas as her lords, it is for you alone
that she is being thus persecuted by the low, cruel, and mean-minded Kauravas.
It is for her sake, O king, that my anger falls on you. I shall burn those hands of
    yours.
                    Sahadeva, bring some fire."
Arjuna said: "You have never before this uttered such words as these.
Your high morality has been destroyed by these cruel foes.
But you should not fulfill the wishes of the enemy. Practice the highest morality.
Whom does it serve for you to threaten your virtuous eldest brother?
The king was summoned by the foe and, remembering the usage of the
    Kshatriyas,
he played at dice against his will. That is certainly conducive to our great fame."
Bhima said: "If I had not known that the king was acting according to Kshatriya
    usage,
then I would have taken his hands together by sheer force and burned them in
    a fire."
With the Pandavas thus distressed and the princess of Panchala thus afflicted,
Vikarna the son of Dhritarashtra said: "You kings, answer Draupadi's question.
If we do not judge a matter referred to us, all of us will assuredly go to hell.
How is it that Bhishma and Dhritarashtra, both of whom are the oldest of the
    Kurus,

and also the high-souled Vidura do not say anything?

Why do these best of men not answer the question? Let those other kings assembled here

answer the question according to their judgment, leaving aside motives of gain and anger,

and declare, after reflection, on which side each of them stands."

Thus did Vikarna repeatedly appeal to those in the assembly.

But those kings answered him not a word, good or ill.

And Vikarna, having repeatedly appealed to all the kings, rubbed his hands

and sighed like a snake. At last the prince said: "You kings of the earth, you Kauravas,

whether you answer this question or not, I will say what I regard as just and proper.

It has been said that hunting, drinking, gambling, and women are the four vices of kings.

The man who is addicted to these forsakes virtue.

And people do not regard the acts done by a person who is thus improperly engaged

as of any authority. This son of Pandu, deeply engaged in vicious acts,

urged thereto by deceitful gamblers, made Draupadi a stake.

The innocent Draupadi is, besides, the common wife of all the sons of Pandu.

And the king, having first lost himself, offered her as a stake.

Suvala, desirous of a wager, prevailed upon Yudhishthira to stake her.

Reflecting upon all these circumstances, I regard Draupadi as not having been won."

At these words, a loud uproar rose from among those in the assembly.

They all applauded Vikarna and censured the son of Suvala.

And at that sound, the son of Karna, deprived of his senses by anger, said:

"O Vikarna, many inconsistent conditions are evident in this assembly.

These personages here have not uttered a word, for they all regard Draupadi

as having been properly won. You alone are bursting with wrath.

Though a boy, you speak in the assembly as if you were old.

You do not know what morality truly is, for you say like a fool that Draupadi,

who has been fairly won, was not won at all. How can you say this

when the eldest of the Pandavas staked all his possessions?

Draupadi is included in all the possessions of Yudhishthira. Why do you regard her

who was justly won as not won? Or, if you think that bringing her here

attired in a single piece of cloth is an action of impropriety,

listen to the justification I will offer.

The gods have ordained only one husband for one woman.

This Draupadi, however, has many husbands. She is, therefore, an unchaste woman.

To bring her, then, into this assembly, attired though she be in one piece of cloth,

and even to uncover her is not at all an act that may cause shock or surprise.

Whatever wealth the Pandavas had, she and the Pandavas themselves have all been justly won by the son of Suvala.

Dussasana, this Vikarna speaking words of apparent wisdom is but a boy.

Take off the robes of the Pandavas and also the attire of Draupadi."

At once the Pandavas took off their upper garments and threw them to the floor.

Then Dussasana forcibly seized Draupadi's attire before the eyes of all
>
>and began to pull it off her person.

She thought of Hari, and cried aloud: "O Govinda, O Krishna, O Kesava,

do you not see that the Kauravas are humiliating me? O Lord, husband of
Lakshmi,

O Lord of Vraja, O destroyer of all afflictions,

O Janarddana, rescue me, I who am sinking in the Kaurava Ocean.

O Krishna, O Krishna, O you great Yogin, soul of the universe,

you creator of all things, save me. I am losing my senses in the midst of the Kurus."

Thus did that afflicted lady, covering her face, cry aloud.

Hearing Draupadi's words, Krishna was deeply moved and, leaving his seat,
>
>the benevolent arrived there on foot.

And while Draupadi had been crying aloud to Krishna,

she had also called on Vishnu and Hari and Nara for protection.

The illustrious Dharma, remaining unseen, covered her

with excellent clothes of many hues.

And as the attire of Draupadi was being pulled, and one after another was
taken off,

a new one of the same kind appeared and covered her.

And thus did it continue until many garments were piled at her feet.

Owing to the protection of Dharma, hundreds upon hundreds of robes of many
hues

came off Draupadi's person. There arose then a deep uproar of many, many
voices.

And the kings present in that assembly, beholding that most extraordinary sight,

began to applaud Draupadi and censure the son of Dhritarashtra.

Bhima then, squeezing his hands, and with his lips quivering in rage,

swore in the midst of all those kings a terrible oath in a loud voice:

"Hear these words of mine, you Kshatriyas of the world!

Words such as these were never before uttered by other men,

nor will anybody in the future ever utter them.

You lords of earth, if having spoken these words I do not accomplish them
hereafter,

let me not obtain the region of my deceased ancestors.

Tearing open in battle, by sheer force, the breast of this wretch,

this wicked-minded scoundrel of the Bharata race,

if I do not drink his lifeblood, let me not obtain the region of my ancestors!"

These words of Bhima made the down of the hearers' arms horripilate,

and everybody applauded him and censured the son of Dhritarashtra.

When a mass of clothes had been gathered in that assembly, all dragged from
Draupadi,
>
>Dussasana, tired and ashamed, sat down.

Beholding the sons of Kunti in that state, those in that assembly hall

uttered the word *shame* on Dussasana. The voices of all raised together were so loud
that they made the hair on everybody's head stand on end.
All the honest men in the assembly said: "Alas!
The Kauravas cannot answer the question Draupadi put to them."
Then Vidura, that master of morality, waved his hands and silenced everyone.
He said: "You who are in this assembly, Draupadi put her question
and is now weeping helplessly. You are not answering her.
Virtue and morality are being persecuted by such conduct.
An afflicted person approaches an assembly of good men
and is like one who is being consumed by fire.
They who are in the assembly quench that fire and cool him with truth and morality.
The afflicted person asks the assembly about his rights as sanctioned by morality.
Those in the assembly, unmoved by interest and anger, should answer the question.
Vikarna has answered the question, according to his own knowledge and judgment.
You should also answer it as you think proper.
Knowing the rules of morality, and having attended an assembly,
he who does not answer a query that is put shall incur half the demerit that attaches to a lie.
He, on the other hand, who knows the rules of morality and, having joined an assembly,
answers falsely shall assuredly incur the sin of a lie.
The learned quote as an example in this connection
        the history of Prahlada and the son of Angirasa."

✦

Vidura then told that story: "There was a chief of the Daityas of the name Prahlada,
who had a son named Virochana. Competing for a bride, he quarreled with Sudhanwan,
the son of Angiras. They mutually wagered their lives, saying,
'I am superior' and 'No, I am superior.' And to resolve their quarrel, they chose Prahlada
to decide between them, asking him: 'Which of us is superior to the other?'
Frightened by this quarrel, Prahlada cast his eyes upon Sudhanwan,
who in rage, burning like the mace of Yama, said to him: 'If you answer falsely,
or do not answer at all, your head will be split into a hundred pieces
        by the wielder of the thunderbolt.'
The Daitya, trembling like a leaf of the fig tree, went to Kasyapa of great energy
to take counsel with him. And Prahlada said: 'You are, O illustrious and exalted one,
fully conversant with the rules of morality that should guide both the gods and the Asuras

and the Brahmanas as well. Here, however, is a situation of great difficulty.
Tell me, I beg you, what regions are obtainable by those who,
upon being asked a question, do not answer it or answer it falsely.'
Kasyapa replied: 'He who knows but does not answer a question,
from temptation, anger, or fear, casts upon himself a thousand nooses of Varuna.
And the person who is cited as a witness and speaks carelessly
casts a thousand nooses of Varuna upon himself.
On the completion of one full year, one such noose is loosened.
Therefore, he who knows should speak the truth without any subterfuge.
If virtue, pierced by sin, repairs to an assembly for aid,
it is the duty of everybody in the assembly to remove the dart.
Otherwise, they themselves would be pierced by it.
In an assembly where a truly censurable act is not rebuked,
half the demerit of that act attaches to the head of that assembly,
a fourth to the person acting censurably, and a fourth to the others who are
    there.
In that assembly, on the other hand, when he who deserves censure is rebuked,
the head of the assembly is freed from all sins, and the other members incur
    no sin.
It is only the perpetrator himself of the act who is held responsible for it.
O Prahlada, they who answer falsely people who have asked them about morality
destroy the meritorious acts of their seven preceding and seven succeeding
    generations.
The grief of one who has lost all his wealth, of one who has lost a son,
of one who is in debt, of one who is separated from his companions,
of a woman who has lost her husband, of one who has lost his all
in consequence of the king's demand, of a woman who is sterile,
of one who has been devoured by a tiger, of one who is a co-wife,
and of one who has been deprived of his property by false witnesses
have been said by the gods to be uniform in degree.
All these different sorts of grief are his who speaks falsely.
A person becomes a witness in consequence of his having seen, heard,
and understood a thing. Therefore, a witness should always tell the truth.
A truth-telling witness never loses his religious merits or earthly possessions.'
Hearing these words of Kasyapa, Prahlada told his son:
'Sudhanwan is superior to you, as indeed his father, Angiras, is superior to me.
The mother also of Sudhanwan is superior to your mother.
Therefore, O Virochana, this Sudhanwan is now the lord of the woman
for whom you two contend.' At these words of Prahlada, Sudhanwan said:
'Since you are unmoved by affection for your child, you have adhered to virtue.
I command, let this son of yours live for a hundred years' "
Vidura continued: "Let all the persons, therefore, present in this assembly
reflect upon what should be the answer to the question asked by Draupadi."
The kings heard these words of Vidura but did not respond.
Karna alone spoke to Dussasana, saying: "Take away this servingwoman
into the inner apartments." And thereupon Dussasana dragged before all the
    spectators

the helpless and modest Draupadi, trembling and crying to her lords, the
    Pandavas.
Draupadi said: "Wait a little, wicked-minded Dussasana.
I have an act to perform, a high duty that has not yet been performed by me.
Dragged forcibly by this wretch's strong arms, I was deprived of my senses.
I salute these reverend seniors in this assembly of the Kurus.
                That I could not do so before cannot be my fault."
Dragged with greater force than before, the helpless Draupadi fell upon the
    ground
and wept in that assembly of the Kurus, saying: "Only once before,
on the occasion of the Swayamvara, was I beheld by the assembled kings
in the amphitheater, and never afterward. I am today brought before this
    assembly.
She whom even the winds and the sun had never before seen in her palace
is today before this assembly and exposed to the gaze of the crowd.
Alas, she whom the sons of Pandu could not, while in her palace, suffer to be
    touched,
even by the wind, is today suffered by the Pandavas to be seized by this wretch.
These Kauravas also suffer their daughter-in-law, so unworthy of such treatment,
to be thus afflicted before them. The times are out of joint.
What can be more distressing to me than that, although highborn and chaste,
I should yet be compelled to enter this public court?
Where is that virtue for which these kings were noted?
Kings of ancient days never brought their wedded wives into the public court.
That eternal usage has disappeared from among the Kauravas.
Otherwise, how is it that the chaste wife of the Pandavas,
the sister of Prishata's son, the friend of Vasudeva, is brought before this
    assembly?
I am the wedded wife of King Yudhishthira, and I come from the same dynasty
as that to which the king belongs. Tell me now if I am a servingmaid or
    otherwise.
I will cheerfully accept your answer. This wretch, this destroyer
of the name of the Kurus, is hurting me. I cannot bear it any longer.
I desire you to answer whether you regard me as won or unwon.
                I will accept your verdict, whatever it may be."
Hearing these words, Bhishma answered: "I have already said, O blessed one,
that the course of morality is subtle. Even the wisest fail to understand it always.
What in this world a strong man calls morality is regarded as such by others,
even though it may really be otherwise, but what a weak man calls morality
is scarcely regarded as such, even if it be absolutely correct.
From the importance of the issue involved, from its intricacy and subtlety,
I am unable to answer your question with certitude.
However, it is certain that, as all the Kurus have become the slaves of folly,
the destruction of this our race will happen on no distant date.
The family into which you have been admitted as a daughter-in-law
is such that those who are born into it, however much they might be afflicted by
    calamities,

never deviate from the paths of virtue and morality.
O princess of Panchala, this conduct of yours, although sunk in distress,
is assuredly worthy of you. These persons, Drona and others of mature years,
and conversant with morality, sit with their heads downward like men who are
    dead,
with bodies from which life has departed. It seems to me, however, that
    Yudhishthira
is an authority on this question. It behooves him to declare whether you are won
    or not."
The kings present in that assembly, from fear of Duryodhana, spoke not a word,
although they saw Draupadi crying piteously in affliction, like a female osprey.
And the son of Dhritarashtra, seeing those kings and sons and grandsons of
    kings
all remaining silent, smiled a little and addressed the daughter of the king of
    Panchala.
"O Draupadi," he said, "the question you have put depends on your husbands—
on Bhima of mighty strength, on Arjuna, on Nakula, on Sahadeva.
Let them answer your question and for your sake declare
in the midst of these respectable men that Yudhishthira is not their lord.
Let them thereby make King Yudhishthira the Just a liar.
You shall then be freed from the condition of slavery.
Let the illustrious son of Dharma, always adhering to virtue, who is even like
    Indra,
himself declare whether he is not your lord. At his words, accept the Pandavas
    or us
without delay. Indeed, all the assembled Kauravas float in the ocean of your
    distress.
Endowed with magnanimity, they are unable to answer your question."
Hearing these words of the Kuru king, all in the assembly loudly applauded
and, shouting approvingly, made signs to one another.
Among some, sounds of distress were heard, such as "O!" and "Alas!"
And at these words of Duryodhana, the Kauravas became exceedingly glad.
The kings, with faces turned sideways, looked at Yudhishthira,
curious to hear what he would say. Everyone was curious to hear
what Arjuna and Bhimasena and the twins would say.
When the hum of many voices stilled, Bhimasena, waving his strong arms
smeared with sandalwood paste, spoke these words:
"If this high-souled king Yudhishthira the Just, our eldest brother,
had not been our lord, we would never have forgiven the Kuru race for all this.
He is the lord of all our religious and ascetic merits, the lord of even our lives.
If he regards himself as won, we too have all been won.
If this were not so, who is there among creatures touching the earth with their
    feet
who would escape from me with his life after having touched those locks
of the princess of Panchala? Behold these mighty, well-formed arms of mine,
like maces of iron. Having once come within them, even he of a hundred
    sacrifices

is incapable of escape. Bound by the ties of virtue and the reverence
due to our eldest brother, and repeatedly urged by Arjuna to remain silent,
I am not doing anything terrible. If, however, I am commanded by King
  Yudhishthira,
I will slay these wretched sons of Dhritarashtra, punches doing the work of
  swords,
                          like a lion slaying a number of little animals."
To Bhima who had spoken these words, Bhishma and Drona and Vidura said:
"Forbear, O Bhima. Everything is possible with you."
Then Karna said: "Of all the persons in the assembly,
only Bhishma, Vidura, and Drona appear to be independent,
for they speak of their master as wicked, censure him, and never wish for his
  prosperity.
The slave, the son, and the wife are always dependent—
they cannot earn wealth, for whatever they earn belongs to their master.
You are the wife of a slave, incapable of possessing anything on his own account.
Repair now to the inner apartments of King Dhritarashtra, and serve the king's
  relatives.
That is now your proper business. The sons of Dhritarashtra
rather than the sons of Pritha are now your masters. Select another husband,
one who will not make you a slave by gambling.
It is well known that women, especially those who are slaves,
are not censurable if they achieve freedom by electing husbands.
Therefore, let it be done by you. Nakula has been won, as also Bhimasena,
and Yudhishthira also, and Sahadeva, and Arjuna. And you are now a slave.
Your husbands are slaves and cannot continue to be your lords.
Does the son of Pritha regard life, prowess, and manhood
as of no use, so that he offers a daughter of Drupada, the king of Panchala,
                    in the presence of all this assembly as a stake at dice?"
The wrathful Bhima breathed hard and was the very picture of woe.
Obedient to the king and bound by the tie of virtue and duty,
and with his eyes inflamed by anger, he said: "O king, I cannot be angry
at these words of this son of a Suta, for we have entered the state of servitude.
But, O king, could our enemies have said these things to me
                    if you had not staked this princess?"
King Duryodhana addressed Yudhishthira, who was silent and deprived of his
  senses,
saying: "O king, both Bhima and Arjuna and the twins also are under your sway.
Answer the question that Draupadi has asked. Say whether you regard her as
  unwon."
And having spoken thus, Duryodhana uncovered his left thigh,
which was like the stem of a plantain tree or the trunk of an elephant
and was graced with auspicious signs and endowed with the strength of thunder,
and he showed it to Draupadi. Seeing this, Bhimasena expanded his red eyes
and said to Duryodhana in the midst of all those kings,
as if piercing them with his dartlike words:
"Let me not attain to the regions obtained by my ancestors

if I do not break that thigh of yours in the great conflict!"
Sparks of fire radiated from every sense organ of the wrathful Bhima,
like those that come out of every crack and orifice in the body of a blazing tree.
Vidura then said: "Behold the great danger that arises from Bhimasena.
Know for certain that this great calamity that threatens to overtake the Bharatas
has been sent by destiny itself. The sons of Dhritarashtra have gambled,
disregarding every proper consideration. They are even now disputing in this
    assembly
about a lady of the royal household. The prosperity of our kingdom is at an end.
Alas, the Kauravas are even now engaged in sinful consultations.
You Kauravas, take to heart this high precept that I declare.
If virtue is persecuted, the whole assembly becomes polluted.
If Yudhishthira had staked her before he had himself been won,
he would certainly have been regarded as her master.
If, however, a person stakes anything at a time when he himself is incapable
of holding any wealth, then to win is very like obtaining wealth in a dream.
Listen to the words of the king of Gandhara and do not swerve from this truth."
Duryodhana replied to Vidura: "I am willing to abide by the words of Bhima,
of Arjuna, and of the twins. Let them say that Yudhishthira is not their master.
Draupadi will then be freed from her state of bondage."
Arjuna then spoke up: "King Yudhishthira the Just was certainly our master
before he began to play. But he lost himself.
Let all the Kauravas judge whose master he could be after that."
Just then a jackal began to cry loudly in the Homa chamber
of King Dhritarashtra's palace. And, answering the jackal that howled so,
the asses began to bray responsively. Terrible birds also, from all sides,
joined in with their cries. Vidura and the daughter of Suvala both understood
the meaning of those sounds. Bhishma and Drona and the learned Gautama
    cried:
"*Swashti! Swashti!* Amen! Amen!" Then Gandhari and Vidura explained it to the
    king:
"Wicked Duryodhana, destruction has already overtaken you when you insult
in such language the wife of these bulls among the Kurus, especially their wife,
    Draupadi."
The wise Dhritarashtra, reflecting with the aid of his wisdom,
and desirous of saving his relatives and friends from destruction,
began to console the princess of Panchala, and the monarch said to her:
"Ask of me any boon that you desire, O princess.
Chaste and devoted to virtue, you are first among all my daughters-in-law."
Draupadi said: "If you will grant me a boon, I ask that the handsome
    Yudhishthira,
obedient to every duty, be freed from slavery. Let not unthinking children
call my child Prativindhya the child of a slave."
Dhritarashtra said: "Let it be as you say. And ask another boon, for I will give it.
My heart inclines to give you a second boon. You deserve more than one."
Draupadi said: "I ask, O king, that Bhimasena and Dhananjaya and the twins
    also,

with their cars and bows, freed from bondage, regain their liberty."

Dhritarashtra said: "Let it be as you desire. And ask a third boon,

for you have not been sufficiently honored with two boons.

Virtuous in your behavior, you are foremost among my daughters-in-law."

But Draupadi said: "O best of kings, covetousness always brings about the loss of
virtue.

I do not deserve a third boon. Therefore, I dare not ask any.

It has been said that a Vaisya may ask one boon; a Kshatriya lady, two boons;

a Kshatriya male, three; and a Brahmana, a hundred.

O king, my husbands, freed from the wretched state of bondage,

will be able to achieve prosperity by their own virtuous acts!"

20

Exile

Karna said: "We have never heard of such a thing.
When the sons of both Pandu and Dhritarashtra were excited with wrath,
a woman, this Draupadi, was the salvation of the sons of Pandu.
The princess of Panchala was a boat for the sons of Pandu,
who were sinking in an ocean of distress.
It was she who brought them safely to shore."
Hearing these words of Karna, who was telling the Kurus how the sons of Pandu
were saved by their wife, the angry Bhimasena in great affliction told Arjuna:
"It has been said that there are three lights in every person—
offspring, acts, and learning—for from these three, creation sprang.
When life becomes extinct and the body becomes impure and is cast off by
     relatives,
these three are of service to every person. But the light in us has been dimmed
by this insult to our wife. How, O Arjuna, can a son born from this insulted wife
     of ours

                                    prove serviceable to us?"
Arjuna replied: "Superior persons never mind the harsh words uttered by
     inferior men.
Persons who have earned respect for themselves, even if they are able to retaliate,
do not remember acts of hostility of their enemies,
but, on the other hand, treasure up only their good deeds."
Bhima asked: "Shall I slay right now all these foes assembled together,
or shall I destroy them by the roots, outside this palace?
Or what need is there of words, or of commands?
I shall slay them all now, and you will rule the whole earth."
Bhima and his younger brothers, like lions in the midst of a herd of inferior
     animals,
cast angry glances around them. But Arjuna with appealing looks
tried to pacify his elder brother. Still, the mighty-armed hero
burned with the fire of his wrath. And this issued out of his ears and other orifices
with smoke and sparks and flames. His face became terrible to behold,
with his brows furrowed like those of Yama at the time of the universal
     destruction.
Then Yudhishthira forbade the mighty hero, embracing him with his arms
and telling him: "Control yourself. Stay in silence and peace."

And having pacified the mighty-armed one, the king approached his uncle
    Dhritarashtra,
with hands joined in entreaty. "O king," he said, "you are our master.
Command us as to what we shall do. We desire to remain always obedient to you."
Dhritarashtra replied: "Go in peace and safety. Go, rule your own kingdom
with your wealth. And take to heart this command of an old man,
this wholesome advice I give that is even a nutritive regimen.
O Yudhishthira, you know the subtle path of morality. You are also humble,
and you wait upon the old. Where there is intelligence, there is forbearance.
Follow, therefore, the counsels of peace. The ax falls upon wood, not upon
    stone:
you are open to advice, not Duryodhana. They are the best of men who do not
    remember
acts of hostility of their foes, who behold only the merits of their enemies,
and who never enter into hostilities themselves.
The good do good to others without expectation of any good in return.
O Yudhishthira, it is only the worst of men who utter harsh words in quarreling,
while those who are indifferent reply to such words when spoken by others.
But those who are good and wise never think of or remember such words
and do not care when they have been uttered by their foes.
Those who are good, aware of their own feelings, can understand the feelings of
    others
and therefore remember only good deeds and not those of hostility.
You have acted as good men of prepossessing countenance do
who do not transgress the limits of virtue, wealth, pleasure, and salvation.
Look at your mother, Gandhari, and at me if you wish to remember only what is
    good.
Look at me, a father to you, old and blind and still alive.
It was for seeing our friends and examining the strengths and weaknesses of my
    children
that I allowed this match at dice to proceed. Those among the Kurus
who have you for their ruler and the intelligent Vidura for their counselor
have nothing to grieve for. In you is virtue; in Arjuna, patience; in Bhima, prowess;
and in the twins, reverence for superiors. Blessings upon you.
Return to Khandavaprastha, and let there be brotherly love
between you and your cousins. Let your heart always be fixed on virtue."
Then, having gone through every ceremony of politeness,
King Yudhishthira, accompanied by his brothers and Draupadi,
ascended their cars, which were all of the hue of the clouds,
and with cheerful hearts set out for that best of cities called Indraprastha.

✦

Learning that the Pandavas had been commanded by the wise Dhritarashtra
to return to their capital, Dussasana went immediately to his brother
    Duryodhana
and, afflicted with grief, said: "That which we won after so much trouble

the old man has thrown away. He has made over the whole of that wealth to the
    foes."
At these words, Duryodhana and Karna and Sakuni, the son of Suvala,
united together and approached King Dhritarashtra in haste to speak to him.
Duryodhana said: "Have you not heard, O king, what Vrihaspati,
the preceptor of the celestials, said in the course of counseling Sakra
about mortals and politics? 'Those enemies who always do wrong by stratagem
    or force
should be slain by every means.' If, therefore, with the wealth of the Pandavas
we gratify the kings of the earth and then fight with the sons of Pandu,
what reverses can overtake us? When one has placed his foot on the neck of
    venomous vipers,
is it possible for him to take his foot off? The angry sons of Pandu,
like wrathful snakes, will annihilate us. Even now Arjuna proceeds,
encased in mail and furnished with his pair of quivers,
frequently taking up the Gandiva and breathing hard and casting angry glances
    around.
Bhima rides on his car, whirling his heavy mace.
Nakula is with him, with the sword in his grasp and the semicircular shield in his
    hand.
And Sahadeva and Yudhishthira have made clear signs of their intentions.
In their cars, which are full of all kinds of arms, they are whipping their horses
and assembling their forces. Persecuted as they have been by us,
they are incapable of forgiving us for those injuries.
Who is there among them that will forgive that insult to Draupadi?
We must again gamble with the son of Pandu and send them all into exile.
We are competent to bring them under our sway in this way.
Either we or they, defeated at dice, shall dress in skins
and repair to the woods for twelve years.
The thirteenth year shall have to be spent in some inhabited country,
    unrecognized;
and, if recognized, an exile for another twelve years shall be the consequence.
Either we or they shall have to live so. Let the play begin, casting the dice.
O king, this is our highest duty. Sakuni knows well the whole science of dice.
Even if they succeed in observing this vow for thirteen years,
we shall be in the meantime firmly rooted in the kingdom,
making alliances and assembling a vast and invincible host
so that we shall be able to defeat the sons of Pandu if they reappear."
Dhritarashtra said: "Bring the Pandavas back, then.
                  Let them return at once, again to cast dice."
Then Drona, Somadatta and Valhika, Gautama, Vidura, the son of Drona,
and the son of Dhritarashtra by his Vaisya wife, Bhurisravas,
and Bhishma, and Vikarna all said: "No, let the play not resume. Let there be
    peace."
But Dhritarashtra, partial to his sons, disregarded the counsels of all his wise
    friends
               and relatives and summoned the sons of Pandu.

It was then that the virtuous Gandhari, afflicted with grief
on account of her affection for her sons, addressed King Dhritarashtra and said:
"When Duryodhana was born, Vidura said: 'It is well to send this disgrace of the race
to the other world.' He cried repeatedly and dissonantly, like a jackal.
Take this to heart, O king of the Kurus. Do not sink us all into an ocean of
    calamity.
Do not give your approbation to the counsels of the wicked.
Do not be the cause of the destruction of our line.
Who is there who would break an embankment that has been completed
or rekindle a conflagration that has been extinguished?
Who is there who will provoke the peaceful sons of Pritha?
The scriptures can never control the wicked-minded, for good or evil.
And a person of immature understanding will never act as one of mature years.
Let your sons follow you as their leader.
Let them not be separated from you forever by losing their lives.
O king, abandon this wretch of our race.
You could not, from parental affection, do it before.
But recognize that the time has now come for the destruction of our race
    through him.
Do not flinch, O king. Let your mind be guided by counsels of peace and
    virtue.
That prosperity acquired by wicked acts is soon destroyed,
while that which is won by just and peaceful means takes root
                    and descends from generation to generation."
The king replied: "If the destruction of our race is come, let it come.
I am unable to prevent it. Let it be as my sons desire. Let the Pandavas return.
And let my sons again gamble with the sons of Pandu."

✦

At Dhritarashtra's command, the royal messenger caught up with Yudhishthira,
who had by that time gone a great way, and he said to that monarch:
"These are the words of your fatherlike uncle that I deliver to you:
'The assembly is ready. O king Yudhishthira, come and cast the dice.'"
Yudhishthira replied: "Creatures obtain fruits good and ill
according to the dispensation of the ordainer of the creation.
Those fruits are inevitable, whether I play or not. This is a summons to dice;
it is, besides, the command of the old king.
                    Although I know that it will prove destructive to me, I cannot
    refuse."
Even though a living animal made of gold was an impossibility,
Rama nevertheless allowed himself to be tempted by a golden deer.
The minds of men over whom calamities hang become deranged.
Yudhishthira and his brothers retraced their steps.
And, knowing full well the deception practiced by Sakuni,
the sons of Pritha sat again at dice with him at the risk of their destruction.

The Pandavas again entered that assembly, which afflicted the hearts of all their
  friends.
Sakuni said: "The old king has given you back all your wealth.
That is well. But listen to me. There is a stake of great value.
Whichever of us is defeated at dice shall dress in deerskins, enter the great
  forest,
live there for twelve years, and then pass the whole of the thirteenth year
in some inhabited region, unrecognized. And if the losers are then recognized,
they shall return to an exile of another twelve years.
On the expiration of the thirteenth year, that losing party is then to have his
  kingdom
surrendered by the other. O Yudhishthira, with this resolution, play, casting the
  dice."
At these words, those in the assembly raised up their arms
and said: "Shame on the friends of Duryodhana,
that they do not apprise him of his great danger.
Whether Dhritarashtra understands or not, it is your duty to tell him plainly."
King Yudhishthira from shame and a sense of virtue again sat at dice.
And even though possessed of great intelligence and fully knowing the
  consequences,
he played as if he knew that the destruction of the Kurus was at hand.
Yudhishthira said: "How can a king like me, observant of the uses of his own order,
refuse when summoned to dice? I will therefore play with you."
Sakuni said: "We have many cattle and horses, and milk cows,
and an infinite number of goats and sheep, and elephants and treasures and gold
and slaves both male and female. All these we staked before,
but now let this be our one stake—exile into the woods.
Whoever may be defeated, either you or we, will dwell in the woods for twelve
  years
and the thirteenth year, unrecognized, in some inhabited place.
                        With this determination, we will play."
The son of Pritha accepted the bet, and Sakuni took up the dice.
He cast them, read the pips, and said to Yudhishthira: "Lo, I have won!"

✦

Then the vanquished sons of Pritha prepared for their exile in the woods.
One after another, they cast off their royal robes and attired themselves in
  deerskins.
And Dussasana, seeing them ready to go into exile, exclaimed:
"The absolute sovereignty of illustrious King Duryodhana has commenced!
The sons of Pandu have been vanquished and plunged into great affliction.
Now have we attained the goal, by either strait or winding paths,
for today we become superior to our foes in prosperity and in the duration of
  our rule.
We have become praiseworthy men. We have plunged the sons of Pritha into
  eternal hell.

They have been deprived of happiness and kingdom forever and ever.
Proud of their wealth, they laughed in derision at the son of Dhritarashtra.
Now they will have to go into the woods, defeated. Let them put aside
their variegated coats of mail and their resplendent robes of celestial make,
and let them dress themselves in deerskins
according to the stake they accepted from the son of Suvala.
They always used to boast that they had no equals in all the world,
but they will now regard themselves as grains of sesame without the kernel.
Although in this dress of theirs the Pandavas may seem wise and powerful,
they still look like persons unentitled to perform sacrifices.
The wise Drupada, having bestowed his daughter on the sons of Pandu,
acted most unfortunately, for her husbands are as eunuchs.
What joy will be hers upon beholding in the woods her husbands dressed in skins
and threadbare rags, deprived of their wealth and possessions?"
Then to Draupadi he said: "Elect a husband, whomever you like,
from among all these present, so that these calamities may not drag you to
    wretchedness.
Why should you wait any longer upon the fallen sons of Pandu?
Vain is the effort to press the sesame grain for oil when it is devoid of the kernel!"
Thus did Dussasana utter harsh words; and, hearing them, Bhima approached
    him,
like a Himalayan lion bearing down upon a jackal, and rebuked him:
"Villain, your raving is sinful ! You pierce our hearts with these arrowy words.
So shall I pierce your heart in battle, remembering this day.
And those also who, from anger or covetousness, walk behind you as your
    protectors
I shall also send to the abode of Yama along with their descendants and
    relatives."
Dussasana responded to this by abandoning all sense of shame,
and he danced around the Kurus, loudly calling: "O cow! O cow!"
Bhima said: "Wretch, dare you use such words as these?
Whom does it behoove to boast, having won your wealth by foul means?
I tell you that if I do not drink your lifeblood, piercing open your breast in
    battle,
let me not attain to the regions of blessedness.
I tell you truly that only by slaying the sons of Dhritarashtra in battle,
before the eyes of all these warriors, shall I pacify this wrath of mine."
As the Pandavas were going away from the assembly
the wicked Duryodhana, from excess of joy, mimicked with his own steps
the leonine tread of Bhima. Bhima, half turning toward him, said:
"Do not think, fool, that by this you gain any ascendancy over me.
I shall soon slay you, with all your followers, and that will be my answer to you."
The mighty and proud Bhima suppressed his rage, rose,
and followed the steps of Yudhishthira, but his parting words, leaving the
    Kaurava court,
were: "I will slay Duryodhana, and Arjuna will slay Karna,
and Sahadeva will slay Sakuni, that gambler with dice.

I repeat in this assembly these proud words, which the gods will assuredly make
    good
if ever we engage in battle with the Kurus. I will slay this wretched Duryodhana
in battle with my mace, and, prostrating him on the ground, will place my foot
    on his head.
And as regards Dussasana, who is audacious in speech, I will drink his blood like
    a lion."
Arjuna said: "O Bhima, the resolutions of superior men are not known in words
    only.
On the fourteenth year from this day, they shall see what happens."
Bhima again said: "The earth shall drink the blood of Duryodhana,
and Karna, and the wicked Sakuni, and Dussasana, who makes the fourth."
Arjuna said: "O Bhima, I will slay this Karna in battle, so malicious and vain.
To do what is agreeable to Bhima, Arjuna vows that he will slay in battle
with his arrows this Karna, with all his followers.
And I will send to the regions of Yama those other kings so foolish as to fight
    against me.
The mountains of Himavat might be removed from where they are,
the maker of the day lose his brightness, the moon his coldness, but this vow of
    mine
will be kept. All this shall assuredly happen if, on the fourteenth year from this,
Duryodhana does not, with proper respect, return our kingdom to us."
After Arjuna had said this, Sahadeva, the handsome son of Madri,
desirous of slaying Sakuni, waved his mighty arms and sighed like a snake,
exclaiming: "You disgrace of the Gandhara kings, those whom you think of as
    defeated
are not really so! Those are sharp-pointed arrows of which you run the risk.
I shall accomplish all that Bhima has said about you and all your followers.
If therefore you have anything to do, do it before that day comes."
Then Nakula, the handsomest of men, spoke these words:
"I shall send all those wicked sons of Dhritarashtra to the abode of Yama.
They are eager for death, impelled by fate,
and moved also by the wish of doing what is agreeable to Duryodhana.
They have used harsh and insulting speech at the gambling match.
Soon enough, at the command of Yudhishthira, and remembering the wrongs to
    Draupadi,
I shall make the earth destitute of the sons of Dhritarashtra."
              Having made these virtuous promises,
those tigers among men approached King Dhritarashtra.
Yudhishthira said: "I bid farewell to all the Bharatas, to my old grandsire
    Bhishma,
King Somadatta, great King Valhika, Drona, Kripa, all the other kings,
Aswathaman, Vidura, Dhritarashtra, all the sons of Dhritarashtra, Yayutsu,
Sanjaya, and all the courtiers. I bid you farewell . One day I shall see you again."
Overcome with shame, none could say anything to Yudhishthira.
Within their hearts, however, they prayed for the welfare of that intelligent
    prince.

Vidura then said: "The reverend Pritha is a princess by birth.
It is not right for her to go into the woods. Delicate, old, and accustomed to comfort,
that blessed one will live, respected by me, in my abode.
Know this, you sons of Pandu. And may you be safe always."
The Pandavas said: "Let it be as you say. You are our uncle, and almost like a father.
We are all obedient to you. You are our most respected superior.
Order whatever else there is that remains to be done."
Vidura answered: "O Yudhishthira, you should know what I think:
that one who is vanquished by sinful means need not be pained by such defeat.
You know every rule of morality; Arjuna is ever victorious in battle;
Bhimasena is the slayer of foes; Nakula is the gatherer of wealth;
Sahadeva has administrative talents; Dhaumya is learned in the Vedas;
and the well-behaved Draupadi is conversant with virtue and economy.
You are attached to one another and feel delight at one another's company,
and enemies cannot separate you from one another. You are contented.
Therefore, who will not envy you? O Bharata, this separation
from the concerns of the world will be of great benefit to you.
Formerly you were instructed on the mountains of Himavat by Meru Savarni;
in the town of Varanavata, by Krishna Dwaipayana; on the cliff of Bhrigu, by Rama;
and on the banks of the Dhrishadwati, by Sambhu himself.
You have also listened to the instruction of the great rishi Asita on the hills of Anjana,
and you became a disciple of Bhrigu on the banks of the Kalmashi.
Narada and your priest Dhaumya will now become your instructors.
In regard to the next world, do not abandon these excellent lessons
you have obtained from the rishis. O son of Pandu, you surpass, in intelligence
and in strength, all other monarchs, and in virtue even the rishis.
Resolve, therefore, to win victory, which belongs to Indra;
to control your wrath, which belongs to Yama;
to give in charity, which belongs to Kuvera;
and to control all passions, which belongs to Varuna.
And obtain the power of gladdening from the moon,
the power of sustaining all from water, forbearance from the earth,
energy from the solar disc, strength from the winds,
and affluence from the other elements. Welfare and immunity to ailment be yours.
I hope to see you return. Act properly and duly in all seasons,
in those of distress and in those of difficulty. O son of Kunti, by our leave go hence.
                    Blessings upon you."
Thus addressed by Vidura, Yudhishthira, the son of Pandu, said:
"So be it." And, bowing low to Bhishma and Drona, he went away.

◆

When Draupadi was about to set out, she went to the illustrious Kunti
to take her leave. She asked leave also of the other ladies of the household,
who had all been plunged into grief. Saluting and embracing every one of them
as each deserved, she turned to go. But there arose within the inner apartments
of the Pandavas a loud wail of woe. Kunti was afflicted at seeing Draupadi depart
and uttered these words in a voice choked with grief:
"O child, grieve not that this great calamity has overtaken you.
You are conversant with the duties of the female sex,
and your behavior and conduct are as they should be.
I need not instruct you as to your duties toward your lords.
You are chaste and accomplished, and your qualities have adorned the race of
    your birth
as well as the race into which you have been admitted by marriage.
Fortunate are the Kauravas that they have not been burned by your wrath.
Travel safely, blessed by my prayers. Good women never suffer in their hearts
at what is inevitable. Protected by virtue that is superior to everything,
you shall soon obtain good fortune. While in the woods, keep your eye on my
    child
Sahadeva. See that his heart does not sink under this great calamity."
Princess Draupadi said: "So be it!" And, bathed in tears and clad in one piece of
    cloth
stained with blood, with her hair disheveled, she left her mother-in-law.
As Draupadi went away, weeping and wailing, Pritha, grieving, followed her.
Pritha had not gone far when she saw her sons shorn of their ornaments and
    robes,
their bodies clad in deerskins, and their heads down with shame.
And she saw them surrounded by rejoicing foes and pitied by friends.
She approached her sons, embraced them all, and, choked by woe, said:
"You are virtuous and good-mannered and adorned with all excellent qualities.
    You are
all high-minded and engaged in the service of your superiors.
And you are devoted to the gods and the performance of sacrifices.
Why, then, has this calamity overtaken you? Why this reversal of fortune?
Alas, I brought you forth. All this must be due to my misfortune.
It is for this that you have been overtaken by this disaster.
How shall you lose your wealth and possessions and live poor in the pathless
    woods?
If I had known that you were destined to live in the woods,
I would not, on Pundit's death, have come from the mountains to Hastinapura.
Fortunate was your father, for he truly reaped the fruit of his asceticism,
and he was gifted with foresight as he entertained the wish of ascending to
    heaven
without having to feel any pain on account of his sons.
Fortunate also was the virtuous Madri, who had, it seems,
foreknowledge of what would happen and who on that account
obtained the high path of emancipation and every blessing.
Madri relied upon me, and her mind and her affections were always fixed on me.

You children are all excellent and dear to me. I obtained you after much
    suffering.
I will go with you. Everything that lives is sure to perish.
Has Brahma forgotten to ordain my death? Perhaps it is so,
and, therefore, life does not quit me. O Krishna, O you who dwell in Dwaraka,
O younger brother of Sankarshana, where are you?
Why do you not deliver me and these best of men from this woe?
My sons are always attached to virtue and nobility and good fame and prowess.
They do not deserve to suffer affliction. Show them mercy!
O Pandu, where are you? Why do you allow your good children to be thus sent
into exile, defeated at dice? O Sahadeva, do not go. You are my dearest child,
dearer than my body itself. Do not forsake me.
Have some kindness for me. Bound by the ties of virtue, let your brothers go.
        You can earn the virtue that springs from waiting upon me."
The Pandavas then consoled their weeping mother
and with hearts plunged in grief set out for the woods.
Vidura, also much afflicted, consoled the distressed Kunti and led her to his
    house.
The ladies of Dhritarashtra's house, hearing of everything that had happened,
wept loudly and censured the Kauravas. The ladies of the royal household
sat silent for a long time, covering their lotuslike faces with their fair hands.
King Dhritarashtra, thinking of the dangers that threatened his sons,
fell prey to anxiety and could not enjoy peace of mind.
Anxiously meditating on everything, and with mind deprived of its equanimity,
he sent a messenger to Vidura, saying: "Come to me without a moment's delay."
As soon as he came, the monarch asked him with great anxiety how the Pandavas
had left Hastinapura: "How does it go with Yudhishthira? And with Arjuna?
And the twin sons of Madri? And how is Dhaumya? And the illustrious Draupadi?
        I desire to hear everything."
Vidura replied: "Yudhishthira, the son of Kunti, has gone away, covering his face
with his clothes. Bhima has gone, stretching forth his mighty arms.
Arjuna scatters sand as he progresses And Sahadeva, the son of Madri,
has besmeared his face, while Nakula, the handsomest of men,
has stained himself with dust, and in his heart there is great affliction.
The large-eyed and beautiful Draupadi has gone,
covering her face with her disheveled hair and following in the wake of the king,
in tears. Dhaumya, too, goes along the road
with *kusa* grass in hand and uttering the mantras of Sama Veda that relate to
    Yama."
Dhritarashtra asked: "Why are the Pandavas leaving Hastinapura in such varied
    guises?"
Vidura replied: "Although he is persecuted by your sons and robbed of kingdom
    and wealth,
the mind of wise King Yudhishthira the Just has not yet deviated
from the path of virtue. King Yudhishthira is always kind to your children.
Filled as he is with wrath, he does not open his eyes.
He says: 'I should not burn the people by looking at them with angry eyes.'

Therefore, the royal son of Pandu covers his face.
Bhima believes there is none equal to him in strength of arms,
and he goes repeatedly stretching forth those mighty arms of his,
desiring to do to his enemies deeds worthy of them.
Arjuna, capable of using both his hands in wielding the Gandiva,
scatters sand grains emblematic of the arrows he would shower in battle.
O Bharata, he indicated that as the sand grains are scattered by him with ease,
so will he rain arrows with perfect ease on the foe in time of battle.
And Sahadeva besmears his face, that none may recognize him in this day of
    trouble.
And, O exalted one, Nakula stains himself with dust, thinking that otherwise
he may steal the hearts of ladies who may look at him.
And Draupadi goes attired in one piece of stained cloth, her hair disheveled,
and weeping, signifying that the wives of those by whom she has been reduced
to such a plight shall in the fourteenth year hence be deprived of their husbands,
sons, and relatives and, smeared all over with blood, with hair disheveled
and all in their feminine seasons, they shall enter Hastinapura,
having offered oblations of water to the names of those they will have lost.
And the learned Dhaumya, with passions under full control,
holds the *kusa* grass in his hand and points it toward the southwest
as he walks ahead, singing the mantras of the Sama Veda that relate to Yama.
This signifies that when the Bharatas shall be slain in battle,
the priests of the Kurus will thus sing the Soma mantras for the benefit of the
    dead.
The citizens, afflicted with great grief, repeatedly cry out: 'Alas, alas,
behold our masters are going away! Shame on the Kuru elders,
who have acted like children in banishing the heirs of Pandu, from sheer
    covetousness.
Separated from the son of Pandu, we all shall be masterless.
What love can we bear to the wicked and avaricious Kurus?'
Thus have the sons of Kunti gone away, indicating, by manner and signs,
the resolutions in their hearts. And as those foremost among men left
    Hastinapura,
flashes of lightning appeared in the sky, although there were no clouds,
and the earth began to tremble.
Rahu came to devour the sun, although it was not the day of an eclipse.
Meteors fell, keeping the city to their right. And jackals and vultures and ravens
and other carnivorous beasts and birds shrieked and cried aloud from the
    temples
and the tops of sacred trees and walls and housetops.
These extraordinary calamitous portents, O king, were seen and heard,
indicating the destruction of the Bharatas as the consequence of your evil
    counsels."
While King Dhritarashtra and Vidura were talking, there appeared in that
    assembly
the best of the celestial rishis. And he uttered these terrible words:
"On the fourteenth year hence, the Kauravas, because of Duryodhana's fault,

will all be destroyed by the might of Bhima and Arjuna."
And having said this, that best of celestial rishis, with Vedic grace,
                    ascended through the skies and disappeared.
Then Duryodhana and Karna and Sakuni, the son of Suvala,
regarding Drona as their sole refuge, offered the kingdom to him.
Drona said: "The Brahamanas have said that the Pandavas, being of celestial
    origin,
are incapable of being slain. The sons of Dhritarashtra, however,
having heartily and with reverence sought my protection,
I shall look after them to the best of my power. Destiny is supreme.
I cannot abandon them. The sons of Pandu, defeated at dice,
will live in the woods for twelve years, practicing the Brahmacharya mode of life.
Then they will return in anger and, to our grief, take vengeance on their foes.
I had formerly deprived Drupada of his kingdom in a friendly dispute.
Robbed of his kingdom by me, the king performed a sacrifice for obtaining a son
who should slay me. Aided by the ascetic power of Yaja and Upayaja,
Drupada obtained from the sacrificial fire a son named Dhrishtadyumna
and a daughter, the faultless Draupadi, both risen from the sacrificial platform.
Dhrishtadyumna is the brother-in-law of the sons of Pandu and is dear to them.
It is from him, then, that I have much to fear. Of celestial origin and resplendent
    as fire,
he was born with bow and arrows, and encased in mail. I am a mortal being.
That slayer of all foes, the son of Parshatta, has taken the side of the Pandavas,
and I shall have to lose my life if he and I ever encounter each other in battle.
What grief can be greater to me in this world than this:
that Dhrishtadyumna is the destined slayer of Drona? I know that he was born
    to slay me,
and it is widely known throughout the world. For your sake, O Duryodhana,
that terrible season of destruction is almost come. Do what may be beneficial
    to you.
Do not think that everything has been accomplished by sending the Pandavas
    into exile.
Your happiness will last for but a moment, even as in winter the shadow
of the top of the palm tree rests only for a short time at its base.
Perform various kinds of sacrifices, and enjoy, and give everything you like.
On the fourteenth year hence, a great calamity will overwhelm you."
Hearing these words, Dhritarashtra said: "The preceptor has uttered what is
    true.
Go, Vidura, and bring back the Pandavas. If they do not come back,
let them go, treated with respect and affection.
Let my sons go with weapons and cars and infantry and every other good thing."
Sanjaya approached Dhritarashtra and said: "O lord of the earth,
having now obtained the whole earth with all its wealth,
and having sent the sons of Pandu into exile, why do you grieve so?"
Dhritarashtra said: "Why should they not grieve who will have to encounter in
    battle
those bulls among warriors, the sons of Pandu, fighting with the aid of allies?"

Sanjaya said: "All this great hostility is inevitable on account of your mistaken
    action,
and this will bring about the wholesale destruction of the world.
Forbidden by Bhishma, by Drona, and by Vidura, your wicked-minded son
sent his Suta messenger to bring into court the beloved and virtuous wife of the
    Pandavas.
The gods first deprive that man of his reason to whom they send defeat and
    disgrace.
It is for this that such a person sees things in a strange light. When destruction is
    at hand,
evil appears good to the understanding polluted by sin, and man adheres to it
    firmly.
That which is improper appears proper, and that which is proper appears
    improper
to the man about to be overwhelmed by destruction, and evil is what he prefers.
The time that brings destruction does not come with upraised club to smash
    one's head.
On the other hand, the peculiarity of such a time is that it makes a man
behold evil in good, and good in evil. The wretches have brought on themselves
this terrible destruction by dragging the helpless princess of Panchala into the
    court.
Who else than Duryodhana, that false player of dice, could bring into the
    assembly
with insults the daughter of Drupada, sprung not from any woman's womb
but from the sacred fire? That handsome woman, then in her season,
attired in one piece of stained cloth, was brought into the court
and cast her eyes upon the Pandavas. She saw them robbed of their wealth,
of their kingdom, and even of their attire as well as of their beauty and every
    enjoyment
and plunged into a state of bondage. Bound by the tie of virtue,
they were then unable to exert their prowess. Before all the assembled kings,
Duryodhana and Karna spoke cruel and harsh words
to the distressed and enraged Draupadi, who was undeserving of such treatment.
O monarch, all this appears to me as foreboding fearful consequences."
Dhritarashtra said: "Sanjaya, the glances of the distressed daughter of Drupada
might consume the whole earth. Can it be possible that a single son of mine will
    live?
The wives of the Bharatas, uniting with Gandhari, upon beholding the virtuous
    wife
of the Pandavas dragged into the court, set up a frightful wail.
Even now, along with all my subjects, they weep every day.
Enraged at the ill treatment of Draupadi, the Brahmanas did not perform that
    evening
their Agnihotra sacrifice. The winds blew mightily as they did
at the time of the universal dissolution. There was a terrible thunderstorm also.
Meteors fell, and Rahu swallowed the sun unseasonably, alarming the people.
Our war chariots were suddenly ablaze, and all their flagstaffs fell down,

foreboding evil to the Bharatas. Jackals cried frightfully
from within the sacred fire chamber of Duryodhana, and asses from all
    directions brayed.
Then Bhishma, Drona, Kripa, Somadatta, and the high-souled Valhika left the
    assembly.
It was then, at the advice of Vidura, that I addressed Draupadi and said:
'I will grant you boons—indeed, whatever you ask.'
The princess of Panchala begged of me the liberation of the Pandavas.
I set the Pandavas free and commanded them to return to their capital
on their cars and with their bows and arrows.
It was then that Vidura told me: 'Nevertheless, this will prove the destruction
of the Bharata race. This daughter of the king of Panchala is the faultless Sri
    herself.
Of celestial origin, she is the wedded wife of the Pandavas.
The wrathful sons of Pandu will never forgive this insult to her.
Nor will the mighty bowmen of the Vrishni race or the mighty Panchala warriors
suffer this in silence. Supported by Bhima of unequaled prowess,
Arjuna will come back, surrounded by the Panchala host.
And Bhimasena with his unsurpassed strength will also come back,
whirling his mace like Yama himself with his club.
These kings will scarcely be able to bear the force of Bhima's mace.
Therefore, O king, not hostility but peace with the sons of Pandu is what seems
    best.
The sons of Pandu are always stronger than the Kurus.
You know, O king, that mighty King Jarasandha was slain in battle by Bhima
with his bare arms. Make peace, therefore, with the sons of Pandu. Unite the two
    parties.
And if you act in this way, you are sure to obtain good luck.'
It was thus that Vidura addressed me; but, moved by love for my son, I did not
    listen."

21

Saunaka

When day broke, the Brahmanas set out with the Pandavas toward the forest.
The Brahmanas, who supported themselves by mendicancy,
stood before the Pandavas, and there King Yudhishthira addressed them, saying:
"Robbed of our prosperity and kingdom, robbed of everything,
we are about to enter the deep woods in sorrow,
depending for food on fruits and roots and the yield of the chase.
The forest is full of dangers and abounds with reptiles and beasts of prey.
It appears to me that you will have to suffer much privation and misery there.
The sufferings of Brahmanas could overpower even the gods.
That they will overwhelm me is certain. Therefore, O Brahmanas, go back!"
The Brahmanas replied: "O king, your path is ours! It is not right for you to
    forsake us,
who are your devoted admirers! The gods take compassion upon their
    worshippers,
                        especially upon Brahmanas of regulated lives!"
Yudhishthira said: "I too am devoted to the Brahmanas!
But this destitution overwhelms me with confusion!
My brothers, who are to procure fruits and roots and deer, are stupefied with
    grief
on account of the distress of Draupadi and the loss of our kingdom!
                    I cannot employ them in painful tasks!"
The Brahmanas said: "Do not be anxious about us. Find a place for us in your
    heart!
We shall provide our own food as we follow you, and by meditation and prayer
we shall look after your welfare while with pleasant conversation we entertain you."
Yudhishthira said: "I am always pleased with the company of the spiritual ones!
But my fallen condition makes me see myself as an object of reproach!
How shall I be with you all, who do not deserve to bear our trouble
but, out of love for me, are painfully subsisting upon food procured by your own
    toil?"
The weeping king sat down upon the ground. Then a learned Brahmana,
Saunaka by name, versed in self-knowledge and skilled in the Sankhya system of
    Yoga,
addressed the king: "Causes of grief by the thousands and causes of fear by the
    hundreds

day after day overwhelm the ignorant but not the wise.
Surely, sensible men like you never suffer themselves to be deluded
by acts opposed to true knowledge, fraught with every kind of evil,
and jeopardizing salvation. O king, in you dwells that understanding
furnished with the eight attributes capable of providing against all evil
and resulting from a study of the Vedas and scriptures!
Men like you are never stupefied by the accession of poverty
or by an affliction overtaking their friends through bodily or mental unease!
Listen, I shall recite the couplets that were chanted of old by the illustrious Janaka
on the subject of self-control! This world is afflicted with bodily and mental
    suffering.
Listen now to the means of allaying it: Disease, contact with painful things,
toil, and want of desired objects are the four causes that induce bodily suffering.
As regards disease, it may be allayed by the application of medicine,
while mental ailments are cured by seeking to forget them and by Yoga
    meditation.
For this reason, sensible physicians first seek to allay mental suffering
by agreeable conversation and the offer of desirable objects.
And as a hot iron bar thrust into a jar makes the water in it hot,
so does mental grief bring on bodily agony. As water quenches fire,
so does true knowledge allay mental disquiet. And when the mind attains ease,
the body finds ease also. It seems that affection is the root of all mental sorrow.
Affection makes every creature miserable and brings on every kind of woe.
Affection is the root of all misery and fear, of joy and grief and every kind of pain.
From affection springs all ambition and the love of worldly goods!
Both of these are sources of evil, though the first is worse than the second.
And as a small fire thrust into the hollow of a tree consumes the whole tree to its
    roots,
even so affection, ever so small, destroys both virtue and profit.
He cannot be regarded as having renounced the world
who has merely withdrawn from worldly possessions.
But he who is in actual contact with the world and sees its faults
may be said to have renounced the world.
When he has been freed from every evil passion, and with his soul dependent on
    nothing,
his is a true renunciation of the world. Therefore, no one should place affection
either on friends or on the wealth one has earned. Even affection for one's own
    person
may be extinguished by knowledge. Like the lotus leaf that is never drenched by
    water,
the souls of men capable of distinguishing between the ephemeral and the
    everlasting,
devoted to the pursuit of the eternal, conversant with the scriptures,
and purified by knowledge can never be moved by affection.
The man influenced by affection is tortured by desire; and from the desire
that springs up in his heart, his thirst for worldly possessions increases.
Those find happiness who can renounce this thirst,

which can never be renounced by the wicked, for it does not decay
with the decay of the body and is truly a fatal disease!
It has neither beginning nor end. Dwelling within the heart, it destroys creatures
like a fire of incorporeal origin. And as kindling is consumed by the fire
that is fed by itself, so does a person of impure soul find destruction
from the covetousness born of his own heart. As creatures endowed with life
have a dread of death, so men of wealth are in constant apprehension
of the king and the thief, of water and fire and even of their relatives.
As a morsel of meat, if in air, may be devoured by birds,
and if on ground, by beasts of prey, and if in water, by the fishes,
even so is the man of wealth exposed to dangers wherever he may be.
To many, the wealth they own is their bane, and he who sees happiness in wealth
becomes wedded to it and does not know happiness.
These are the miseries of men that the wise see in riches!
Men undergo infinite misery in the acquisition and retention of wealth.
Its expenditure, meanwhile, is fraught with grief.
Sometimes life itself is lost for the sake of wealth!
The abandonment of wealth produces misery,
and even those who are cherished because of their wealth can become enemies
for the sake of that wealth! If the possession of wealth is fraught with such
    misery,
one should not mind its loss. It is the ignorant alone who are discontented;
the wise are always content, and this contentment is the highest object of pursuit.
The wise know the instability of youth and beauty, of life and treasure hoards,
of prosperity and the company of loved ones and never covet them.
One should refrain from the acquisition of wealth
and the pain incident to it.
As regards those who pursue wealth for purposes of virtue,
it is better for them to refrain altogether from such pursuit,
for it is better not to touch mire at all than to wash it off
after having been besmeared with it. O Yudhishthira, for these reasons
you should not covet anything! If you would have virtue,
                emancipate yourself from the desire of worldly possessions!"
Yudhishthira answered: "O Brahmana, my desire for wealth
is not to enjoy it when I have obtained it. Only for the support of the Brahmanas
do I desire it, not because I am actuated by avarice!
For what purpose, O Brahmana, does a person like me lead a domestic life
if he cannot cherish and support those who follow him?
All creatures divide the food they procure among those who depend on them.
So should a person leading a domestic life give a share of his food to Yatis
and Brahmacharins who have renounced cooking for themselves.
The houses of the good men can never be in want of grass on which to sit,
space in which to rest, water with which to wash and to assuage thirst,
and, fourthly, sweet words. To the weary, a bed; to one fatigued with standing, a
    seat;
to the thirsty, water; and to the hungry, food should be given.
To a guest are due pleasant looks, a cheerful heart, and sweet words.

The host, rising up, should advance toward the guest, offer him a seat, and
    worship him.

This is morality. They who do not perform the Agnihotra sacrifice, do not wait
    upon bulls,

and do not cherish their kinsmen and guests and friends,

and sons and wives and servants are consumed with sin for such neglect.

None should cook his food for himself alone, and none should slay an animal

without dedicating it to the gods, the Pitris, and guests.

Nor should one eat of that food that has not been duly dedicated to the gods
    and Pitris.

By scattering food on the earth, morning and evening, for the benefit of dogs
    and birds,

one performs the Viswedeva sacrifice. What remains in a sacrifice

after dedication to the gods and the Pitris is regarded as ambrosia;

and what remains after feeding guests is called Vighasa and is equivalent to
    ambrosia.

Feeding a guest is equivalent to a sacrifice, and the pleasant looks the host casts
upon the guest,

the attention he gives him, the sweet words with which he addresses him,

the respect he shows by serving him first, and the food and drink he provides him

are the five Dakshinas, or offerings, in that sacrifice.

He who gives, without stint, food to a fatigued wayfarer he has never seen before
                    obtains great merit. O Brahmana, what is your opinion on this?"

Saunaka said: "Alas, this world is full of contradictions!

What shames the good gratifies the wicked!

Moved by ignorance and passion, and slaves of their own senses,

even fools perform many acts of apparent merit to gratify their appetites in the
    afterlife!

With eyes open, these men are led astray by their seducing senses,

even as a charioteer who has lost his grip is led by restive and wicked steeds!

When any of the six senses finds its particular object,

the desire springs up in the heart to enjoy that particular object.

And thus when one's heart proceeds to enjoy the object of any particular sense,

a wish is entertained, which in its turn gives birth to a resolve.

And, finally, like an insect falling into a flame from love of light, the man falls

into the fire of temptation, pierced by the shafts!

Like a wheel that is incessantly rolling, every creature, from ignorance and desire,

falls into various states in this world, wandering from one birth to another,

and ranging the entire circle of existences from a Brahma to the point of a blade
    of grass,

now in water, now on land, and now in the air! Listen now to the course of the
    wise,

who are intent on profitable virtue and desirous of emancipation!

The Vedas enjoin one to act but renounce interest in action.

Therefore, you should act, renounce self-interest, perform sacrifices,

study the Vedas, give gifts, do penance, seek truth in both speech and action,

practice forgiveness, subdue the senses, and renounce desire.

Those who wish to subdue the world for purposes of salvation
should always act, fully renouncing motives, subduing their senses,
rigidly observing vows, devotedly serving their preceptors, austerely regulating
    their diets,
diligently studying the Vedas, and restraining their hearts.
By renouncing desire and aversion, the gods have attained prosperity.
You have already achieved such success, so far as your debts to your ancestors,
both male and female, are concerned, and that success which is derived from
    sacrifices.
For serving the holy ones, endeavor to attain success in penances.
Those who are crowned with ascetic success can do whatever they like;
therefore, practicing asceticism you may realize all your wishes."
Yudhishthira the son of Kunti, thus addressed by Saunaka,
turned to Dhaumya, his priest, and in the midst of his brothers said:
"The Brahmanas versed in the Vedas are following me as I depart for the forest.
Afflicted with many calamities, I am unable to support them.
I cannot abandon them, nor have I the power to offer them sustenance.
Tell me, O holy one, what I should do in such a pass."
After reflecting for a moment, Dhaumya said:
"In days of old, all living beings that had been created were sorely afflicted with
    hunger.
And like a father to all of them, Savita, the sun, took compassion upon them.
Going first into the northern declension, the sun drew up water by his rays,
and coming back to the southern declension, he stayed over the earth
with his heat centered in himself. And while the sun so stayed over the earth,
the lord of the vegetable world, the moon, converted the vapors into clouds
and poured them down in the shape of water, causing plants to spring up.
Thus it is the sun himself who, drenched by the lunar influence, is transformed
upon the sprouting of seeds into the holy vegetables furnished with the six tastes.
And it is these that constitute the food of all creatures upon the earth.
Thus inherent in the food that supports the lives of creatures is solar energy,
and the sun is therefore the father of all creatures. Take refuge in him,
    Yudhishthira.
All illustrious monarchs of pure descent and deeds
are known to have delivered their people by practicing high asceticism.
Therefore, do likewise: enter upon a regimen of austerities,
                and you may support the spiritual ones."
And how did King Yudhishthira, for the sake of the Brahmanas, adore the sun?
Dhaumya disclosed to him the one hundred and eight names of the sun, saying:
"Surya; Aryaman; Bhaga; Twastri; Pusha; Arka; Savitri; Ravi;
Gabhastimat; Aja; Kala; Mrityu; Dhatri; Prabhakara; Prithibi;
Apa; Teja; Kha; Vayu, the sole stay; Soma; Vrihaspati;
Sukra; Angaraka; Indra; Vivaswat; Diptanshu;
Suchi; Sauri; Sanaichara; Brahma; Vishnu; Rudra; Skanda;
Vaisravana; Yama; Vaidyutagni; Jatharagni; Aindhna;
Dharmadhwaja; Veda-karttri; Vedanga; Vedavahana;
Krita; Treta; Dwapara; Kali, full of every impurity; Kastha;

Muhurtta; Kshapa; Kshana; Samvatsara-kara; Aswattha; Kalachakra;
Bibhavasu; Purusha; Saswata; Yogin; Vyaktavyakta; Sanatana; Kaladhyaksha;
Prajadhyaksha; Viswakarman; Tamounda; Varuna; Sagara;
Ansu; Jimuta; Jivana; Arihan; Bhutasraya; Bhutapati; Srastri;
Samvartaka; Vanhi; Sarvadi; Ananta; Kapila; Bhanu;
Kamada; Sarvatomukha; Jaya; Visala; Varada; Manas; Suparna;
Bhutadi; Sighraga; Prandharana; Dhanwantari; Dhumaketu;
Adideva; Aditisuta; Dwadasatman; Aravindaksha; Pitri; Matri;
Pitamaha; Swarga-dwara; Prajadwara; Mokshadwara; Tripistapa;
Dehakarti; Prasantatman; Viswatman; Viswatomukha;
Characharatman; Sukhsmatman; and the merciful Maitreya.
These are the hundred and eight names of Surya, as told by Brahma, the
    self-created.
For the acquisition of prosperity, I bow down to you,
blazing like gold or fire, who are worshipped by the gods and the Pitris
and the Yakshas, and who are adored by Asuras, Nisacharas, and siddhas.
He who, with fixed attention, recites this litany at sunrise
obtains a wife and offspring and riches and the memory of his former existence;
and by reciting this litany, a person attains patience and memory.
Let a man concentrate his mind and recite this hymn.
By doing so, he shall be proof against grief and forest fire and ocean flood,
                        and every object of desire shall be his."
Having heard these words suitable to the occasion, Yudhishthira,
with heart concentrated and purified, began to engage in austere meditation,
moved by the desire of supporting the Brahmanas.
Worshipping the maker of day with offerings of flowers and other articles,
the king performed his ablutions. Standing in the stream, he turned his face
toward the god of day. And touching the water of the Ganges, the virtuous
    Yudhishthira,
with senses under complete control and depending upon air alone for his
    sustenance,
stood there with rapt soul engaged in the Yoga of air
and began to sing the hymn of praise to the sun:
"You are, O sun, the eye of the universe.
You are the soul of all corporeal existences. You are the origin of all things.
You are the embodiment of the acts of all religious men.
You are the refuge of those versed in the Sankhya philosophy,
the mysteries of the soul, and you are the support of the Yogins.
You are a door open and unbolted.
You are the refuge of those wishing for emancipation.
You sustain and discover the world and sanctify and support it from pure
    compassion.
Brahmanas versed in the Vedas appearing before you adore you in due time,
reciting the hymns from the respective branches of the Vedas.
You are adored by all the rishis.
The siddhas and the charanas and the Gandharvas and the Yakshas
and the Guhyakas and the Nagas, desirous of obtaining boons, follow your car

coursing through the skies. There is nothing that I know of in all the seven worlds,

including that of Brahma, that is beyond you.

There are other beings both great and endowed with energy, but none has your luster.

All light is in you. In you are the five elements and all intelligence,

and knowledge and asceticism and the ascetic properties.

The discus by which the wielder of the Saranga humbles the pride of Asuras

was forged by Viswakarman with your energy.

In summer you draw, by your rays, moisture from all corporeal existences and plants

and liquid substances and pour it down in the rainy season.

Your rays warm and scorch and then cool as clouds roar and flash with lightning

and pour down showers when the season comes.

Neither fire nor shelter nor woolen clothes give greater comfort

to one suffering from chilling blasts than do your rays.

You illuminate the whole earth with her thirteen islands.

You alone are engaged in the welfare of the three worlds.

If you do not rise, the universe becomes blind and the learned cannot employ themselves

in the attainment of virtue, wealth, and profit.

Those versed in chronology say that you are the beginning and you are the end

of a day of Brahma, which consists of a full thousand *yugas*.

When the time of universal dissolution comes,

the fire Samvartaka, born of your wrath, will consume the three worlds.

And clouds of various hues, begotten of your rays, accompanied by the elephant Airavata

and the thunderbolt, will bring about the appointed deluges.

Dividing yourself into twelve parts and becoming as many suns,

you drink up the ocean once more with your rays.

You are called Indra, you are Vishnu, you are Brahma, you are Prajapati.

You are fire and you are the subtle mind. And you are lord and the eternal Brahma.

You are Hansa, you are Savitri, you are Bhanu, Ansumalin, and Vrishakapi.

You are Vivaswan, Mihira, Pusha, Mitra, and Dharma.

You are thousand-rayed, you are Aditya, and Tapana, and the lord of rays.

You are Martanda, and Arka, and Ravi, and Surya and Saranya and maker of day,

and Divakara and Suptasaspti, and Dhumakeshin and Virochana.

You are spoken of as swift of speed and as the destroyer of darkness

and the possessor of yellow steeds. He who adores you on the sixth or seventh lunar day,

with humility and tranquillity of mind, obtains the grace of Lakshmi.

O lord of all food, grant food in abundance to me with which to entertain all my guests.

I bow also to all those followers of yours who have taken refuge at your feet:

Mathara and Aruna and Danda and others, including Asani and Kshuva and the others.

And I bow also to the celestial mothers of all creatures: Kshuva and Maitri.
                    Let them deliver me, their suppliant."
Pleased with this hymn, the maker of day, self-luminous and blazing like fire,
showed himself to the son of Pandu. And Vivaswan said: "You shall obtain
all that you desire. I shall provide you with food for five and seven years together.
And, O king, accept this copper vessel which I give you.
As long as Draupadi holds this vessel without partaking of its contents, fruits and
     roots
and meat and vegetables cooked in your kitchen shall from this day be
     inexhaustible.
And, in the fourteenth year, you shall regain your kingdom."
                    Having said this, the god vanished.
The virtuous son of Kunti, rising from the water, took hold of Dhaumya's feet.
And he then went to the kitchen with Draupadi and was adored by her.
The son of Pandu thereupon set himself to cook their day's food,
and the food, however little, dressed and furnished with the four tastes,
increased and became inexhaustible. With it Yudhishthira fed the spiritual ones.
After the Brahmanas had been fed and his younger brothers also,
Yudhishthira himself ate of the Vighasa that was left.
After Yudhishthira had eaten, the daughter of Prishata took what was left.
And after she had taken her meal, the day's food was exhausted.
So the son of Pandu, as resplendent as that celestial, entertained the Brahmanas.
And after the sacrifices, the sons of Pandu, blessed by the rites performed by
     Dhaumya,
and accompanied by him and also by the Brahmanas, set out for the woods of
     Kamyaka.

22

Shiva

One day, Bhima came to Yudhishthira and said:
"O king, you are like froth, unstable as a ripe fruit that is about to fall from the
	tree,
mortal, and dependent on time, which is infinite and immeasurable,
quick as a shaft or flowing like a stream and carrying everything before it.
How can you take time for granted?
How can one wait whose life is shortened every moment?
Only he whose life is unlimited, or who knows with certitude
what the span of his life will be, and who knows the future
as if it were before his eyes, can wait with assurance for the arrival of an expected
	time.
If we wait, O king, for thirteen years, that period, shortening our lives,
will bring us nearer to death. Therefore, we should strive to possess our kingdom
before we die. He who fails to achieve fame by failing to chastise his foes
is like an unclean thing. He is a useless burden on the earth, like an incapacitated
	bull,
and he perishes ingloriously. The man who is destitute of strength and courage,
and who fails to punish his foes, lives in vain. Your hand can rain gold;
your fame is spread over the whole earth. Therefore, slay your foes in battle,
and enjoy the wealth acquired by the might of your arms.
O king, if a man slays his injurer and goes that very day into hell,
then hell becomes heaven to him. O king, the pain one feels in suppressing
	one's wrath
burns like fire itself. Even now I burn with it and cannot sleep in the day or the
	night.
Arjuna is foremost in drawing the bowstring. He burns with grief,
though he lives here like a lion in his den. He represses the wrath that rises in
	his breast.
Nakula, Sahadeva, and old Kunti, the mother of heroes, are all dumb,
desiring to please you. Only Draupadi and I speak to you, burning with grief.
Whatever I speak to you is agreeable to all of them, however,
for all of them are plunged in distress and eagerly wish for battle.
What more wretched calamity can overtake us
than that our kingdom should be wrested from us by contemptible foes
and enjoyed by them? From the weakness of our disposition,

you feel shame in violating your pledge.
But, O slayer of foes, no one applauds you for thus suffering such pain
because of the kindliness of your disposition. Your intellect does not always see
     the truth—
you are like an ignorant person of high birth who has memorized the words of
     the Vedas
without understanding their sense. You are kind like a Brahmana.
How have you been born in the Kshatriya order? Those born in the Kshatriya
     order
are generally of crooked heart. You have heard recited to you the duties of kings
as promulgated by Manu. They are fraught with crookedness and unfairness
and are precepts opposed to tranquillity and virtue. Why do you then forgive
the wicked sons of Dhritarashtra? You have intelligence, prowess, learning,
and high birth. Why do you act like a huge motionless snake that suns itself on a
     rock?
O son of Kunti, he who desires to conceal us is trying to conceal Himavat
with of a handful of grass. Known as you are over the whole earth,
you will not be able to live unknown, like the sun that can never course through
     the sky
unnoticed by men. Like a large tree in a well-watered region with spreading
     branches
and flowers and leaves, or like Indra's elephant, how will you live unknown?
How also will the brothers Nakula and Sahadeva, a couple of young lions, live in
     secret?
How will Draupadi, a princess and mother of heroes, and known over all the
     world,
live unknown? Everybody knows me from my boyhood. How can I go incognito?
The mighty mountains of Meru could as well seek to be concealed.
We expelled many kings from their kingdom who will all follow
the bad son of Dhritarashtra. Desiring to do good to Dhritarashtra,
they will certainly seek to injure us. They will set against us numerous spies.
If any of these discover us and report their discovery, great danger will overtake us.
We have already lived in the woods a full thirteen months.
Regard those months as thirteen years. The wise have said that a month is like a
     year,
like the pot herb that is a substitute for the Soma.
Or, if you break your pledge, you may free yourself from this sin by offering food
to a quiet bull carrying sacred burdens. Therefore, resolve to slay your enemies.
          For any Kshatriya, there is no virtue higher than fighting!"
Yudhishthira sighed heavily and reflected in silence. And he thought:
I have heard the duties of kings recited to me and also the duties of the different orders.
He is said to observe those duties truly who keeps them before his eyes
so as to regulate his conduct both in the present and in the future.
Knowing as I do the true course of virtue, how can I grind it down
as if I were grinding the mountains of Meru?
Having reflected so for a moment, he replied to Bhima: "It is as you have said.
But listen now to what I say. Whatever sinful deeds one seeks to achieve

that depend on courage alone will always be a source of pain.
But whatever is begun with deliberation, with well-directed prowess
and much previous thought is likely to succeed. The gods themselves favor such
    designs.
Hear from me something about what you think should be done.
Bhurisravas, Sala, the mighty Jarasandha, Bhishma, Drona,
Karna, the mighty son of Drona, Dhritarashtra's sons, Duryodhana, and others
so difficult to vanquish are all accomplished in arms and always ready for battle
    with us.
Those kings and chiefs of the earth also who have been injured by us
have all adopted the side of the Kauravas and are bound by ties of affection to
    them.
O Bharata, they are engaged in seeking the good of Duryodhana and not of us.
With full treasures and aided by large forces, they will certainly strive in battle.
All the officers of the Kuru army, together with their sons and relatives,
have been honored by Duryodhana with wealth and luxuries.
Those heroes are also much regarded by Duryodhana.
This is my conclusion—that they will sacrifice their lives for Duryodhana in
    battle.
Although the behavior of Bhishma, Drona, and the illustrious Kripa is the same
toward us as toward them, yet I believe that in order to pay off the royal favors
    they enjoy,
they will throw their very lives into battle. All of them are masters of celestial
    weapons
and devoted to the practice of virtue. I think they are incapable of being
    vanquished
even by gods led by Vasava himself. There is again among them the mighty
    Karna—
impetuous, and ever wrathful, master of all weapons, invincible,
and encased in impenetrable mail. Without first vanquishing in battle all
    those men,
unaided as you are, how can you slay Duryodhana?
I cannot sleep, thinking of the lightness of hand of that Suta's son,
           whom I regard as the foremost of all wielders of the bow!"
The impetuous Bhima forbore from speaking anything more.
And while the sons of Pandu were thus conversing with each other,
there came to that spot the great ascetic Vyasa, the son of Satyavati.
And as he came, the sons of Pandu worshipped him.
Then that foremost among speakers, addressing Yudhishthira, said:
"Knowing by spiritual insight what is passing in your heart, I have come to you.
The fear in your heart, arising from Bhishma, and Drona, and Kripa, and Karna,
and Drona's son, and prince Duryodhana, and Dussasana, I will dispel
by means of an act enjoined by the ordinance. Hearing it from me,
accomplish it with patience, and having accomplished it, O king,
           quell this fever of yours."
Taking Yudhishthira to a corner, Vyasa addressed him in words of deep import:
"O best of the Bharatas, the time is come for your prosperity,

when Arjuna will slay your foes in battle.
Accept from me this knowledge called Pratismriti that I impart to you.
Receiving it from you, Arjuna will be able to accomplish his desire.
Let Arjuna go to Mahendra and Rudra, and Varuna, and Kuvera, and Yama,
to receive weapons from them. He is competent to behold the gods
for his asceticism and prowess. He is a rishi of great energy, the friend of
  Narayana—
ancient, eternal, a god himself, invincible, ever successful, and knowing no
  deterioration.
With mighty arms, he will achieve mighty deeds,
having obtained weapons from Indra, and Rudra, and the Lokapalas.
Think also of going from this to some other forest that may, O king, be fit for
  your abode.
To reside in one place for any length of time is scarcely pleasant.
In your case, it might also cause anxiety among the ascetics.
And as you maintain numerous Brahmanas, continued residence here
might exhaust the deer of this forest and destroy the creepers and plants."
Glad of Vyasa's advice, Yudhishthira left the wood of Dwaitavana
and went to the forest of Kamyaka on the banks of the Saraswati.
And the Brahmanas of ascetic merit, versed in spelling and pronunciation,
followed him like the rishis following the chief of the celestials.
The Bharatas took up their residence there along with their friends and
  attendants.
And those heroes lived there for some time,
devoted to the exercise of the bow and hearing all the while the chanting of the
  Vedas.

✦

After some time, Yudhishthira remembered the command of Vyasa,
and he summoned Arjuna and addressed him in private:
"The whole science of arms dwells in Bhishma, and Drona, and Kripa,
and Karna, and Drona's son. They know all sorts of Brahma and celestial
and human and Vayavya weapons, and modes of using them in offense and
  defense.
All of them are conciliated and honored and gratified by Dhritarashtra's son,
who behaves toward them as one should behave toward one's preceptor.
Toward all these warriors Dhritarashtra's son behaves with great affection;
and all the chiefs, honored and gratified by him, seek his good in return.
Thus honored by him, they will not fail to put forth their might.
The whole earth is now under Duryodhana's sway,
with all the villages and towns, and all the seas and woods and mines!
You alone are our refuge. On you rests a great burden.
I shall, therefore, tell you what to do now. I have obtained a science from Vyasa.
That science will expose the whole universe to you.
Attentively receive that science now from me,
and in due time, by its aid, you may attain the grace of the celestials.

Devote yourself to fierce asceticism. Armed with the bow and the sword, and
    cased in mail,
undertake austerities and good vows, and go northward without giving way to
    anybody.
All celestial weapons are with Indra, gathered together in one place.
Go to Indra, and he will give you all his weapons.
              Take your bow and set out this very day in order to behold
    Purandara."
Taking up the Gandiva and his inexhaustible quivers,
and accoutered in mail and gauntlets and finger protectors made of the skin of
    the guana,
and having poured oblations into the fire and made the Brahmanas utter
    benedictions,
Arjuna set out from Kamyaka to behold Indra. The hero heaved a sigh and
    looked up,
imagining the death of Dhritarashtra's sons.
Beholding Kunti's son thus armed and about to set out,
the Brahmanas and siddhas and invisible spirits addressed him, saying:
"O son of Kunti, obtain soon what you seek." And the Brahmanas uttered
    benedictions
              and said: "Let victory be yours!"
Draupadi said to him: "Let all that Kunti desired at your birth, and all that you
    desire,
be accomplished! It is my great grief that the wretch Duryodhana
in the assembly of princes mockingly called me a cow and said many other hard
    things.
But the grief I experience at parting with you is far greater than any I felt at
    those insults.
Certainly, in your absence, your brothers will while away their waking hours
in talking of your heroic deeds! But if you stay away for any length of time,
we shall derive no pleasure from our enjoyments. Life itself will be distasteful to us.
Our welfare and woe, our life and death, our kingdom and prosperity all
    depend on you.
I bless you. Let triumph be yours. Go, and win success with speed.
I bow to Dhatri and Vidhatri! Let Hri, Sree, Kirti, Dhriti, Pushti, Uma, Lakshmi,
and Saraswati protect you on your way. I bow to the Vasus, the Rudras and Adityas,
the Manilas, the Viswadevas, and the Sadhyas for procuring your welfare.
              Be safe from all spirits of mischief of the sky, the earth, and the heaven."
The strong-armed son of Pandu then walked around his brothers
              and around Dhaumya also, took up his handsome bow, and set out.
All creatures made way for Arjuna along the path he took.
He passed over many mountains inhabited by ascetics and reached the sacred
    Himavat,
the resort of the celestials. The high-souled one reached the sacred mountain in
    one day,
for like the winds he had the speed of the mind because of his ascetic austerities.
Having crossed the Himavat and then the Gandhamadana,

he passed over many uneven and dangerous spots, walking night and day
    without fatigue.
And having reached Indrakila, Arjuna heard a voice in the skies saying: "Stop!"
The son of Pandu looked all around and beheld, under the shade of a tree, an
    ascetic
blazing with Brahma brilliancy, of a tawny color with matted locks, and thin.
The mighty ascetic addressed Arjuna, saying: "Who are you, O child,
coming here with bow and arrows, and cased in mail and accoutered
in scabbard and gauntlet, and evidently wedded to the customs of the Kshatriya?
There is no need of weapons here. This is the abode of peaceful Brahmanas,
devoted to ascetic austerities, without anger or joy. There is no use for the bow
    here,
for there is no dispute in this place of any kind. Therefore, throw away your bow.
You have obtained a pure state of life by coming here.
O hero, there is no man who is like you in energy and prowess."
But that Brahmana with a smiling face did not succeed in persuading Arjuna.
The holy man smilingly addressed Arjuna once more, saying:
"Slayer of foes, blessings upon you! I am Indra—ask of me the boon you desire."
The heroic Arjuna bent his head, joined his hands, and replied
to him of a thousand eyes: "Grant me this boon, O illustrious one—
              I desire to learn all the weapons from you."
The chief of the celestials replied to him cheerfully, saying:
"When you have reached this region, what need is there of weapons?
You have already obtained a pure state of life. Ask for the regions of bliss you
    desire."
Arjuna replied to him: "I do not desire regions of bliss or objects of enjoyment
or the state of a celestial. What is this talk of happiness?
I do not desire the prosperity of all the gods. Having left my brothers in the forest,
and without avenging myself, I shall incur opprobrium for all ages of all the
    world."
Indra consoled him with gentle words, saying:
"When you are able to behold the three-eyed trident-bearing Shiva, lord of all
    creatures,
it is then, O child, that I will give you all the celestial weapons.
Therefore, strive to obtain the sight of the highest of the gods,
for it is only after you have seen him that you will obtain all your wishes."
              Having spoken thus, Indra disappeared.

✦

Alone, Arjuna continued northward toward the summit of the Himavat.
He entered that terrible forest abounding with thorny plants and trees and
    flowers
and fruits of various kinds, inhabited by winged creatures of various species,
swarming with animals of diverse kinds and also with siddhas and charanas.
When he entered that forest, destitute of human beings, there sounded in the
    heavens

conchs and drums. A thick shower of flowers fell upon the earth.
The clouds spreading over the firmament cast a thick shade.
Passing over those difficult and woody regions at the foot of the great mountains,
Arjuna soon reached the breast of the Himavat.
He stayed there for some time and beheld there numerous trees with expansive
  verdure
and resounding with the notes of warblers. He saw rivers with currents of lapis
  lazuli,
broken by fierce eddies here and there, and echoing with the notes of swans
and ducks and cranes. Delighted, Arjuna devoted himself to rigid austerities
in that pleasant woody region. Clad in rags made of grass,
and furnished with a black deerskin and a stick, he ate withered leaves
fallen upon the ground. He passed the first month eating fruits every three nights;
and the second, eating at intervals of six nights; and the third, eating every
  fortnight.
When the fourth month came, that best of the Bharatas subsisted on air alone.
With arms upraised, and leaning on nothing, and standing on the tips of his toes,
he continued his austerities. The illustrious hero's locks, because of frequent
  bathing,
took on the hue of lightning or the lotus. Then all the great rishis went together
to the god of the Pinaka to tell him about the fierce asceticism of Pritha's son.
Bowing to that god of gods, they informed him of Arjuna's austerities, saying:
"This son of Pritha is engaged in the most difficult of austerities
on the breast of the Himavat. Heated by his asceticism, the earth is smoking all
  around.
We do not know what his object is for these austerities. But he is causing us pain.
                        You must stop him!"
Hearing the words of those munis with souls under perfect control,
Shiva, the lord of all creatures, the husband of Uma, said: "Do not indulge in grief
on account of Arjuna! Return cheerfully to the places from which you have come.
I know the desire that is in Arjuna's heart. His wish is not for heaven,
nor for prosperity, nor for long life. I will accomplish this day all that he desires."
The truth-speaking rishis heard these words of Shiva, were delighted,
and returned to their respective abodes. After all those illustrious ascetics had
  gone away,
that wielder of the Pinaka and cleanser of all sins, assuming the form of a Kirata
resplendent as a golden tree, and with a huge and stalwart form like a second
  Meru.
Taking in hand a bow, and arrows like snakes of virulent poison,
and looking like an embodiment of fire, he came quickly down on the breast of
  Himavat.
That handsome god of gods was accompanied by Uma in the guise of a Kirata
  woman,
and also by a swarm of merry spirits of various forms and garb,
and by thousands of women in the form and attire of Kiratas.
And that region suddenly blazed up in beauty because of the arrival of the god
  of gods

in such company. A solemn stillness pervaded the place. The sounds of springs
and brooks and of birds ceased. And as the god of gods approached Pritha's son,
he saw a Danava named Muka, seeking, in the form of a boar, to slay Arjuna.
Arjuna took up the Gandiva and arrows resembling snakes of virulent poison.
He strung his bow, filled the air with its twang, and addressed the boar:
"I have not injured you. But as you seek to slay me, I shall send you to Yama's
    abode."
Seeing that Arjuna was about to slay the boar, Shiva in the guise of a Kirata
bade him stop: "I was the first to aim at the boar, the color of the mountain of
    Indrakila."
Arjuna, however, disregarded these words and struck the boar.
The Kirata, also blazing with splendor, let fly an arrow like flaming fire
and resembling a thunderbolt, at the same beast.
And at the same instant the arrows shot by both reached the wide body of Muka,
which was as hard as adamant. The two shafts hit the boar with a loud sound,
like that of Indra's thunderbolt or the rumble of the clouds crashing together
upon the breast of a mountain. Muka, thus struck by two shafts
resembling snakes of blazing mouths, yielded up his life
and assumed once more his terrible Rakshasa form.
Arjuna then beheld before him that person, blazing as a god,
attired in the dress of a Kirata and accompanied by many women.
The son of Kunti said: "Who are you, wandering in these solitary woods
and surrounded by women? Being of the splendor of gold, are you not afraid of
    this forest?
Why did you shoot the boar at which I had first aimed?
This Rakshasa came here with the object of slaying me, and I had aimed at it.
You shall not, therefore, escape from me alive.
Your behavior toward me is not consistent with the customs of the chase.
                    Therefore will I take your life."
The Kirata, smiling, replied: "You need not be anxious on my account.
This forest is the proper abode for us who always dwell in the woods.
But may I inquire why you are here in the midst of such difficulties?
Why do you, so delicate and brought up in luxury and possessed of the splendor
    of fire,
                    dwell in such a solitary region?"
Arjuna answered: "Relying on the Gandiva and arrows blazing like fire,
I live in this great forest, like a second Pavaki.
You have seen how this Rakshasa came here in the form of an animal and how I
    slew it."
The Kirata replied: "This Rakshasa was first struck with the shot from my bow
and was killed and sent to the regions of Yama by me. He was first aimed at by me.
And it was with my shot that he was deprived of life.
Proud of your strength, you should not impute your own fault to others.
You are at fault; and, therefore, you shall not escape from me with your life.
I will shoot shafts like thunderbolts at you. Try your best to shoot your arrows
    at me."
Arjuna became angry at the Kirata and attacked him with arrows.

The Kirata, however, received all those shafts upon himself,
repeatedly saying: "Wretch, shoot the best arrows capable of piercing into the
    vitals."
Arjuna showered arrows upon him. Both of them then became angry
and engaged in fierce conflict, shooting at each other showers of arrows,
each of which resembled a snake of virulent poison.
Shiva bore that downpour on him with a cheerful heart and stood unwounded,
immovable as a hill. Arjuna saw that his hail of arrows was futile and marveled,
saying to himself: *Excellent! Excellent!*
This mountaineer of delicate limbs, dwelling on the heights of the Himavat,
bears without wavering the shafts of the Gandiva! Who is he?
Is he Rudra himself, or some other god, or a Yaksha, or an Asura?
Except for the god who wields the Pinaka,
there is none who can bear the thousands of arrows shot from the Gandiva.
Whether he is a god or a Yaksha—in fact, anybody except Rudra—
I shall soon send him to the regions of Yama.
Arjuna then began to shoot arrows by the hundreds,
and they resembled in splendor the rays of the sun.
The illustrious creator of the worlds bore the downpour of shafts cheerfully,
like a mountain bearing a shower of rocks. When Arjuna's arrows were
    exhausted,
he became greatly alarmed and thought of the god Agni
who had, during the burning of the Khandava, given him his two inexhaustible
    quivers.
But the quivers were empty now, and the arrows had all been shot.
He asked himself: *What shall I shoot now from my bow? Who is this person*
who swallows up my arrows? I shall slay him with the end of my bow,
as elephants are killed with lances, and shall send him to the domain
                                of the mace-bearing Yama.
The illustrious Arjuna then took up his bow and, dragging the Kirata with his
    bowstring,
struck him with fierce blows that descended like thunderbolts.
But the mountaineer snatched the celestial bow from his hands.
Arjuna then took up his sword and, to end the conflict, rushed at his foe.
With the whole might of his arms, the Kuru prince struck upon the head of the
    Kirata
that sharp blade, a weapon incapable of being resisted
even by solid rocks. But as it touched the Kirata's crown, the sword broke into
    pieces.
Arjuna then continued the conflict with trees and stones.
The illustrious god in the form of the Kirata bore that shower of trees and rocks
with patience and even indifference. The mighty son of Pritha,
his mouth smoking with wrath, then struck the invincible god with clenched
    fists.
His blows descended like thunderbolts. The god returned Arjuna's blows
with fierce counterblows, and there arose loud and terrifying sounds.
That exchange of blows resembled the conflict of ancient times

between Vritra and Vasava, but it lasted only a moment.
The mighty Arjuna clasped the Kirata and pressed him against his breast,
but the Kirata, possessed of great strength, pressed the son of Pandu with equal
  force.
And with the pressure of their arms and their breasts, their bodies began to emit
  smoke,
like charcoal in fire. Then the great god, smiting the already smitten son of
  Pandu,
and attacking him in anger with his full might, deprived him of his senses.
Arjuna, pressed by the god of gods, with his limbs bruised and mangled,
was incapable of motion and was all but reduced to a ball of flesh.
Struck by the illustrious god, he became breathless and fell down on the earth,
unable to move, and looking like one who was dead. He regained consciousness
and rose up again, his body covered with blood. Prostrating himself
before a clay image he had made of the gracious god of gods,
he worshipped it with floral offerings. Shiva was pleased with Arjuna
and, seeing that his body had been emaciated with ascetic austerities,
spoke to him in a voice as deep as the roaring of the clouds, saying:
"I have been pleased with you, for your act is without parallel.
There is no Kshatriya equal to you in courage and determination.
Your strength and prowess are almost equal to mine. Behold me,
O bull of the Bharata race! O large-eyed one! I will grant you eyes to see me
in my true form. You were a rishi before. You will vanquish all your foes,
even the dwellers of heaven. I will grant you an irresistible weapon.
          Soon you shall be able to wield that weapon of mine."
Arjuna then beheld him—Mahadeva, Shiva, Bhava—
that god of blazing splendor, that wielder of the Pinaka,
that one who had his abode on the mountains of Kailasa, accompanied by Uma.
Bending down on his knee and bowing with his head, the son of Pritha
worshipped him and asked for his grace. Arjuna said:
"O chief of all gods, O destroyer of the eyes of Bhaga, O god of gods,
O Mahadeva, O god of blue throat, O god of matted locks,
I know you as the cause of all causes. O lord of three eyes!
You are the refuge of all the gods! This universe has sprung from you.
You are incapable of being vanquished by the three worlds of the celestials,
the Asuras, and men. You are Shiva in the form of Vishnu,
and Vishnu in the form of Shiva. You destroyed long ago the great sacrifice of
  Daksha.
O Hari, O Rudra, I bow to you. You have an eye in your forehead.
You rain down objects of desire, O bearer of the trident, O wielder of the Pinaka,
O Surya. O god of pure body, creator of all, I bow to you, I worship you to obtain
  grace.
You are the source of universal blessing, the cause of the causes of the universe.
You are beyond the foremost of male beings, the highest, the subtlest!
Pardon my faults. It was to obtain a sight of yourself that I came to this great
  mountain,
which is dear to you and the abode of ascetics. Let not this rashness of mine

be regarded as a fault, this combat in which I was engaged with you from
ignorance.

O Shiva, I seek your protection. Pardon me for all I have done."
The god whose sign was the bull took the handsome hands of Arjuna into his
and replied to him: "I have pardoned you." He clasped Arjuna with his arms
and said: "In your former life you were Nara, the friend of Narayana.
In Vadari you were engaged in fierce ascetic austerities for several thousands of
years.
In you as well as in Vishnu—that first of male beings—dwells great might.
Taking up that fierce bow whose twang resembles the deep roar of the clouds,
you as well as Krishna chastised the Danavas during the coronation of Indra.
Your Gandiva is that bow, fit for your hands. I snatched it from you,
helped by my powers of illusion. This pair of quivers, fit for you,
will again be inexhaustible! And your body will be free from pain and disease.
Your prowess is incapable of being overcome. I have been pleased with you.
Ask of me the boon that you desire. Not even in heaven is there any male equal
to you,

nor any Kshatriya who is your superior."
Arjuna said: "O illustrious god, if you will grant me my desire,
I ask of you, O lord, that fierce celestial weapon wielded by you called the
Brahmasira—
that weapon of terrific prowess which destroys at the end of the *yuga* the entire
universe,
and that weapon by the help of which, O god of gods, I may obtain victory
in the terrible conflict that shall take place between myself on one side
and Karna and Bhishma and Kripa and Drona on the other.
I desire that weapon which, when hurled with mantras, produces darts by the
thousands
and fierce-looking maces and arrows like snakes of virulent poison,
and by means of which I may fight with Bhishma, Drona, Kripa, and Karna
of ever-abusive tongue. O illustrious destroyer of the eyes of Bhaga,
this is my foremost desire—that I may be able to fight with all of them and
succeed."
Shiva replied: "I will give you that favorite weapon of mine called the
Pashupatastra.
You are capable of holding, hurling, and withdrawing it.
Neither Indra, the chief of the gods, nor Yama nor the king of the Yakshas nor
Varuna
nor Vayu knows this weapon. How could men know anything of it?
But it should not be hurled without adequate cause; for, if hurled at any foe of
little might,
it could destroy the whole universe. In the three worlds,
with all their mobile and immobile creatures, there is none this weapon cannot
slay.
And it may be hurled by the bow, by words, by the eye, or by the mind."
Arjuna purified himself and approached the lord of the universe with rapt
attention:

"Instruct me!" Mahadeva then imparted to him the knowledge of that weapon
together with all the mysteries about hurling and withdrawing it.
And that weapon thence waited upon Arjuna as it did upon Shiva, the lord of
    Uma.
Arjuna accepted it gladly. At that moment the whole earth,
with its mountains and woods and trees and seas and forests and villages
and towns and mines, trembled. Hurricanes and whirlwinds began to blow.
And the gods and the Danavas beheld that terrible weapon in its embodied form
next to Arjuna. And whatever evil there had been in his body was dispelled
by the touch of the three-eyed deity. He then commanded Arjuna: "Go into
    heaven."
Arjuna then worshipped the god with bent head and gazed at him with joined
    hands.
The lord of all the dwellers of heaven, the deity of blazing splendor
having his abode on mountain breasts, the husband of Uma,
the god of passions under complete control, and the source of all blessings
then gave back to Arjuna the great bow called the Gandiva,
                            destructive of Danavas and Pisachas.
Then the god of gods, leaving that blessed mountain with snowy plateaus and
    valleys,
the favorite resort of the sky-ranging great rishis, ascended to the skies.

✦

Thus Shiva disappeared as the son of Pandu watched,
like the sun setting in the sight of the world.
Arjuna marveled at this, saying: "I have seen the great god of gods.
I am fortunate indeed and much favored, for I have both beheld and touched
the three-eyed Hara, the wielder of the Pinaka. I shall win success.
I am already great. I have already vanquished my enemies.
                            My purposes are already achieved."
While he was thinking these things, there appeared Varuna,
the god of waters, handsome and of the splendor of lapis lazuli,
accompanied by all kinds of aquatic creatures
and filling all the points of the horizon with a blazing effulgence.
Accompanied by rivers both male and female,
and by Nagas and Daityas and Sadhyas and inferior deities, Varuna arrived
with the lord Kuvera, of body resembling pure gold, seated on his car of great
    splendor
and accompanied by numerous Yakshas. And the lord of treasures,
possessed of great beauty, came there to see Arjuna, as did Yama
of great beauty, the powerful destroyer of all the worlds,
accompanied by the Pitris, both embodied and disembodied.
And the god of justice, of inconceivable soul, the son of Surya,
the destroyer of all creatures, with mace in hand came there on his car,
illuminating the three worlds with regions of the Guhyakas, the Gandharvas,
and the Nagas, like a second Surya as he rises at the end of the *yuga.*

There, from the summits of the great mountain, they beheld Arjuna
engaged in ascetic austerities. And at that moment the illustrious Sakra also came,
accompanied by his queen, seated on the back of the celestial elephant, Airavata,
and surrounded by all the deities. Because of the white umbrella held over his
    head,
he looked like the moon in the midst of fleecy clouds.
Praised by Gandharvas and by rishis endowed with the wealth of asceticism,
the chief of the celestials alit on a summit of the mountain, like a second sun.
Then Yama, from a summit on the south, said in a voice as deep as that of the
    clouds:
"Arjuna, behold us, the protectors of the worlds! We will grant you spiritual
    vision,
for you deserve to behold us. You were in your former life a rishi of
    immeasurable soul,
known as Nara. At the command of Brahma, you have been born among men!
You shall vanquish in battle the highly virtuous grandsire of the Kurus—
Bhishma of great energy, who is born of the Vasus.
You shall also defeat all the Kshatriyas of fiery energy
commanded by the son of Bharadwaja in battle.
You shall also defeat those Danavas of fierce prowess that have been born
    among men,
and those Danavas also that are called Nivatakavachas.
And you shall also slay Karna, who is even a portion of my father Surya.
And you shall slay as well all the portions of celestials, Danavas, and Rakshasas
that have been incarnated on earth. And these shall then attain to the regions
their acts have earned. The fame of your achievements will last forever in the
    world—
you have gratified Mahadeva himself in conflict. You shall, with Vishnu,
lighten the burden of the earth. Accept this weapon of mine—
the mace I wield, incapable of being resisted by anybody.
                    With this weapon you will achieve great deeds."
The son of Pritha then received from Yama that weapon
along with the mantras and the rites and the mysteries of hurling and
    withdrawing it.
Then Varuna, the lord of all aquatic creatures, blue as the clouds,
from a summit he had occupied in the west, uttered these words:
"O son of Pritha, you are foremost among the Kshatriyas. Behold me! I am
    Varuna,
the lord of waters. Hurled by me, my nooses are incapable of being resisted.
Accept from me these Varuna weapons along with the mysteries
of hurling and withdrawing them. Even if Yama himself be your foe,
with these in your hands he will not be able to escape from you.
With these, you will range over the field, and the land will be destitute of
    Kshatriyas."
The lord of treasures then spoke: "O son of Pandu of great might and wisdom,
I too have been pleased with you. And this meeting with you
gives me as much pleasure as a meeting with Krishna. You were a god before,

eternal as other gods. I grant you celestial vision.
You will defeat even invincible Daityas and Danavas.
Accept from me an excellent weapon with which you will be able
to consume the ranks of Dhritarashtra. Take then this favorite weapon of mine,
called the Antarddhana. It is capable of sending the foe to sleep.
When the illustrious Sankara slew Tripura, this was the weapon he shot
and by which many mighty Asuras were consumed. I take it up to give to you.
With the dignity of the Meru, you are competent to hold this weapon."
After these words had been spoken, Arjuna duly received from Kuvera
that celestial weapon. Then the chief of the celestials said
in a voice as deep as the kettledrum: "O mighty-armed son of Kunti,
you are an ancient god. You have already achieved the highest success.
But you have yet to accomplish the purposes of the gods.
You must ascend to heaven. Therefore, prepare, O hero of great splendor!
My own car, with Matali as charioteer, will soon descend to the earth.
I will take you to heaven and will grant you there all my celestial weapons."
The celestials then went away, returning to the places from which they had
come.

23

Arjuna Visits Heaven

As Arjuna thought of the car of Indra, it came down, dividing the clouds,
illuminating the firmament, and filling the welkin with its rattle,
deep as the roar of thunderheads, swords, missiles of terrible forms,
maces of frightful description, winged darts of celestial splendor,
lightning of the brightest effulgence, and thunderbolts, and enormous pinwheels
producing deafening sounds. There were also fierce and huge-bodied Nagas
with fiery mouths, and heaps of stones as white as the fleecy clouds.
The car was drawn by ten thousand horses of golden hue, with the speed of the
    wind—
indeed, with such speed that the eye could hardly mark its progress.
Arjuna saw on that car the flagstaff called Vaijayanta,
of blazing radiance, emerald in color or the dark-blue of the lotus,
and decked with golden ornaments straight as bamboo.
There was a charioteer decked in gold seated on that car,
Matali, who descended from the car, bowed, and addressed him, saying:
"O lucky son of Indra! Indra himself wishes to see you. Ascend this car he has
    sent.
Your father, the chief of the immortals, that god of a hundred sacrifices,
has commanded me, saying: 'Bring the son of Kunti here. Let the gods
    behold him.'
Indra himself, surrounded by the celestials and rishis and Gandharvas and
    Apsaras,
waits for you. At the command of the chastiser of Paka, ascend with me
                            from this region to that of the celestials."
The delightful city of Indra which Arjuna saw was the resort of siddhas and
    charanas.
It was adorned with the flowers of every season, and with sacred trees of all kinds.
And there were also celestial gardens, called Nandana, the favorite resort of
    Apsaras.
Fanned by the fragrant breezes charged with the aroma of sweet-scented flowers,
the trees with celestial blossoms seemed to welcome him. The region was such
that none could behold it who had not gone through ascetic austerities
or who had not poured libations on fire. It was a place for the virtuous alone.
None was competent to see it who had not performed sacrifices
or had not observed rigid vows, or who was without knowledge of the Vedas

or had not bathed in sacred waters or was not distinguished for sacrifices and gifts.
And none was competent to see it who was a disturber of sacrifices, or who was low,
or who drank intoxicating liquors, or who was a violator of his preceptor's bed,
or who was an eater of unsanctified meat, or who was wicked.
Having beheld those celestial gardens resounding with celestial music,
the strong-armed son of Pandu entered the favorite city of Indra.
He beheld there celestial cars by the thousands, capable of going everywhere
    at will.
There were tens of thousands of such cars moving in every direction.
And, fanned by pleasant breezes charged with the perfumes of flowers,
the son of Pandu was praised by Apsaras and Gandharvas.
The celestials, accompanied by the Gandharvas and siddhas and great rishis,
then reverenced Pritha's son of white deeds. Benedictions were poured upon him,
accompanied by the sounds of celestial music of conchs and drums.
At the command of Indra, Arjuna went to that extensive starry way
called by the name of Suravithi, where he met with the Sadhyas,
the Viswas, the Marutas, the twin Aswins, the Adityas, the Vasus,
the Rudras, the Brahmarshis of great splendor,
and numerous royal sages with Dilipa at their head,
and Tumvura and Narada, and those two Gandharvas named Haha and Huhu.
Having met and duly saluted them all, he beheld last of all the chief of the
    celestials,
the god of a hundred sacrifices. Then the strong-armed son of Pritha,
alighting from the car, approached the lord himself of the gods, his father.
A beautiful white umbrella with a golden staff was held over the chief of the
    celestials.
And he was fanned with a yak tail perfumed with celestial scents.
And the son of Kunti approached Indra and saluted him, bending his head to
    the ground.
Indra thereupon embraced him with his round plump arms and, taking his hand,
made him sit beside him on his own sacred seat.
The lord of the celestials smelled the head of Arjuna, bending in humility,
and even took him upon his lap. Pritha's son blazed in splendor, like a second
    Indra.
The wielder of the thunderbolt patted gently again and again
with his own hands, which bore the marks of the thunderbolt,
the handsome and huge arms of Arjuna, which resembled a pair of golden
    columns
and were hard in consequence of drawing the bowstring.
The more Indra gazed upon him, the more he delighted to gaze.
And, seated on one seat, father and son enhanced the beauty of the assembly,
like the sun and the moon beautifying the firmament together.
A band of Gandharvas headed by Tumvuru, skilled in music sacred and profane,
sang many verses in melodious notes. And Ghritachi and Menaka and Rambha
and Purvachitti and Urvasi and Misrakesi and others by the thousands,
possessed of eyes like lotus leaves, danced there. With slim waists and fair large
    hips,

they began to perform various routines, shaking their deep bosoms,
casting their glances around, and exhibiting other attractive attitudes
capable of stealing the hearts and resolutions and minds of the spectators.
The gods and the Gandharvas then, at Indra's direction, procured an excellent
   Arghya
and reverenced the son of Pritha, giving him water to wash both his feet and his
   face.
Then they caused the prince to enter Indra's palace, where he took up residence.
There the son of Pandu acquired celestial weapons and the means of
   withdrawing them.
And he received from the hands of Sakra his favorite weapon of irresistible force,
the thunderbolt, and those other weapons also of tremendous roar,
the lightnings of heaven, whose flashes are predictable from the appearance of
   clouds
and the dances of peacocks. The son of Pandu, after he had obtained those
   weapons,
remembered his brothers. But at the command of Indra, he lived for a full five
   years
                     in heaven, surrounded by every comfort and luxury.
After Arjuna had obtained all the weapons, Indra addressed him, saying: "O son
   of Kunti,
you must learn music and dancing from Chitrasena.
Learn the instrumental music that is current among the celestials and does not
   exist
in the world of men, for it will be to your benefit."
And Indra gave Chitrasena as a friend to Arjuna.
And the son of Pritha lived happily in peace with Chitrasena, who instructed him
in music, vocal and instrumental, and in dancing. But Arjuna's mind was not at
   peace,
for he remembered his brothers and his mother and the play at dice of Sakuni,
   the son of Suvala.

✦

One day, noticing that Arjuna's glances were cast upon Urvasi,
Indra summoned Chitrasena and said: "O king of Gandharvas, I am pleased;
go as my messenger to that foremost among Apsaras, Urvasi,
and let her wait upon that tiger among men, Arjuna. Tell her:
'Through my instrumentality, Arjuna has learned all the weapons and other arts.
You should make him conversant with the arts of acquitting oneself
in female company.'" In obedience to that command of Vasava,
Chitrasena went to Urvasi, that foremost among Apsaras.
Seated at ease, he addressed Urvasi, saying: "Let it be known that I come here
dispatched by the sole lord of heaven, who asks a favor of you.
You know Arjuna, who is known among gods and men for his many inborn
   virtues;
who is endowed with genius and splendid energy, is of a forgiving temper

and without malice of any kind; who has studied the four Vedas with their
  branches,
and the Upanishads, and the Puranas also. O Urvasi, know that this hero
is to be made to taste the joys of heaven. Commanded by Indra,
let him today obtain your favors. Do this, O amiable one, for Arjuna is inclined
  to you."
Urvasi smiled and answered with a glad heart: "Hearing of the virtues
that should adorn men, I would bestow myself upon anyone who possessed
  them.
Why should I not then choose Arjuna for a lover?
At the command of Indra, and for my friendship with you,
and moved also by the numerous virtues of Arjuna, I am already under the
  influence
                    of the god of love. I shall gladly go to Arjuna."
Moved by the desire of possessing Arjuna, Urvasi took a bath and decked herself
in charming ornaments and splendid garlands of celestial odor.
And inflamed by the god of love, her heart pierced through by the shafts
shot by Manmatha, keeping in view the beauty of Arjuna,
and her imagination wholly taken up by thoughts of Arjuna,
she imagined sporting with him on an excellent bed laid over with celestial sheets.
When the twilight had deepened and the moon was up, that Apsara of high hips
set out for the mansion of Arjuna. In that mood, and with her crisp, soft, and
  long braids
decked with bunches of flowers, she looked extremely beautiful.
As she proceeded, her deep, finely tapering bosom, decked with a chain of gold,
adorned with celestial unguents, and smeared with fragrant sandalwood paste,
  began to tremble.
And because of the weight of her breasts, she was forced to lean slightly forward,
bending her exceedingly beautiful waist. And her loins of faultless shape,
the elegant abode of the god of love, furnished with fair and high and round hips
and wide at their lower part, and decked with chains of gold,
and capable of shaking the saintliness of anchorites, clothed with filmy attire,
appeared highly graceful. Her feet, with fair shapely ankles, and with flat soles
and straight toes the color of burnished copper, their upper surfaces high and
  curved
like tortoiseback and marked by ornaments furnished with rows of little bells,
looked exceedingly handsome. Exhilarated with a little liquor which she had
  taken,
and excited by desire, she looked even more beautiful than usual.
And though heaven abounded with many wonderful objects, yet when Urvasi
proceeded in this manner, the siddhas and charanas and Gandharvas regarded her
as the most wonderful object they had cast their eyes upon.
With the upper half of her body clad in an attire of fine texture and cloudy hues,
she looked as resplendent as the moon in the firmament shrouded by fleecy
  clouds.
Endowed with the speed of the winds or the mind, she of luminous smiles
soon reached the mansion of Arjuna, sent word through the keeper in attendance,

and soon entered that brilliant and charming palace.

But beholding her at night in his mansion, Arjuna, with a fear-stricken heart,
stepped up to receive her with respect. As soon as he saw her, he closed his eyes.
Saluting her, he offered her such worship as is offered to a superior.

Arjuna said: "O foremost among Apsaras, I reverence you by bending my head
    down.

Let me know your commands. I wait upon you as your servant."

Hearing these words, Urvasi became deprived of her senses.

And she said: "I shall tell you all that has passed between me and Chitrasena,
and why I have come here. On account of your arrival here in heaven,
Indra had convened a large and charming assembly with celestial festivities.
To that assembly came the Rudras and the Adityas and the Aswins and the Vasus.
And there came also numbers of great rishis and royal sages and siddhas and
    charanas

and Yakshas and great Nagas. And when the members of the assembly
had taken their seats according to rank, honor, and prowess,
the Gandharvas began to strike the vinas and sing charming songs of celestial
    melody.

The principal Apsaras commenced to dance, but you looked only on me
with steadfast gaze. When that assembly of the celestials broke up,
the gods dispersed to their respective palaces. And the principal Apsaras also
returned to their abodes. It was then that Indra sent Chitrasena to me,
and he addressed me, saying: 'I have been sent by the chief of the celestials.
Do something that would be agreeable to Indra and myself and to yourself as well.
Seek to please Arjuna, who is brave in battle and is always possessed of
    magnanimity.'

These, O son of Pritha, were his words.

Thus commanded by him and by your father also, I come to you to wait upon you.
My heart has been attracted, and I am under the influence of the god of love."

Hearing her speak in this strain, Arjuna was overcome with bashfulness.

Shutting his ears with his hands, he said: "O blessed lady, shame on my sense of
    hearing

when you speak thus, for you are equal in my estimation to the wife of a superior.
That I had gazed particularly at you is true. There was a reason for it,
which I shall explain to you. In the assembly I gazed at you
with eyes expanded in delight, thinking: *This blessed lady*
is the mother of the Kaurava race. O blessed Apsara,
you must not entertain other feelings toward me, for you are superior to my
    superiors,

being the parent of my race."

Urvasi answered: "O son of the chief of the celestials, we Apsaras are free
and unconfined in our choice. You must not think of me as your superior.
The sons and grandsons of Puru's race who have come here because of ascetic
    merit

all sport with us without incurring any sin. Relent, therefore, and do not send
    me away.

I am burning with desire. I am devoted to you. Accept me!"

Arjuna replied: "Let the four directions and the transverse directions
and let the gods also listen. As Kunti, or Madri, or Sachi is to me,
so are you, the parent of my race, an object of reverence to me.
Return, O lady of the fairest complexion. I bend my head to you
and prostrate myself at your feet. You deserve my worship as my own mother;
and you must protect me as a son."
Urvasi was deprived of her senses by wrath.
Trembling with rage, and contracting her brows, she cursed Arjuna,
saying: "Since you disregard a woman who has come to your mansion
at the command of your father and of her own will, a woman who is pierced
by the shafts of Kama, therefore shall you have to pass your time among females
unregarded, and as a dancer, destitute of manhood and scorned as a eunuch."
Urvasi's lips quivered in anger, and she was breathing heavily
as she departed and returned to her own abode.
Arjuna immediately sought Chitrasena and told him all that had passed
between him and Urvasi in the night, including the curse she had pronounced
upon him.
And Chitrasena then reported to Indra, who called his son and in private
consoled him:
"You have now vanquished even rishis by your patience and self-control.
But the curse Urvasi pronounced on you must stand and will be to your benefit.
You will have to pass the thirteenth year of your exile unknown to all.
It is then that you shall suffer the curse of Urvasi. And having passed one year
as a dancer without manhood, you shall regain your power at the end of that
term."
Thus addressed by Indra, Arjuna was relieved and ceased to think of the curse.
He sported in regions of heaven with the Gandharva Chitrasena of great
celebrity.
One day, the great rishi Lomasa in the course of his wanderings
went to the abode of Indra, desiring to behold the lord of the celestials.
The great muni approached the chief of the gods and bowed to him respectfully.
He saw the son of Pandu occupying half of Indra's seat,
and he began to wonder how Arjuna, who was a Kshatriya, had deserved
the seat of Indra himself. What acts of merit had he performed
and what regions had he conquered by ascetic merit so that he had obtained a
seat
worshipped by the gods themselves? And as the rishi was occupied these thoughts,
Indra came to know of them and addressed Lomasa with a smile:
"Listen, O Brahmarshi, about what is now passing in your mind.
This is no mortal, although he has taken his birth among men.
This mighty-armed hero is my son, born of Kunti.
He has come hither in order to acquire weapons he needs.
Do you not recognize him as an ancient rishi of the highest merit?
Listen to me, O Brahmana, as I tell you who he is and why he has come to me.
Those ancient and excellent rishis named Nara and Narayana
are none other than Hrishikesa and Dhananjaya.
Those rishis, celebrated throughout the three worlds, have been born on earth

for the acquisition of virtue. That sacred asylum,
which even gods and illustrious rishis are not competent to behold,
is known throughout the world by the name of Vadari
and is situated at the source of the Ganga,
which is worshipped by the siddhas and the charanas. It was the abode, O
    Brahmana,
of Vishnu and Jishnu, those rishis of blazing splendor who have at my desire
been born on earth and endowed with mighty energy.
Besides this, there are certain Asuras known as Nivatakavachas,
who, proud of the boon they have acquired, are employed in doing us injuries.
Those fierce and mighty Danavas live in the nether regions.
All the celestials together are incapable of fighting with them.
The blessed Vishnu, the slayer of Madhu, is known on earth as Kapila,
and his glance alone destroyed the illustrious sons of Sagara
when they approached him with loud sounds in the bowels of the earth.
That illustrious and invincible Hari is capable of doing us a great service.
Either he or Partha or both may do us that great service.
As the illustrious Hari slew the Nagas in the great lake,
he by sight alone is capable of slaying those Asuras called the Nivatakavachas
along with their followers. But the slayer of Madhu should not be urged
when the task is insignificant. He is a mighty concatenation of energy.
It swells to increasing proportions, and it may consume the whole universe.
This Arjuna also is competent to encounter them all, and the hero,
having slain them in battle, will go back to the world of men.
Go, at my request, back to earth. You will behold the brave Yudhishthira
living in the woods of Kamyaka. Tell him for me that he should not be anxious
on account of Arjuna—that hero will return to earth a thorough master of
    weapons,
for without sanctified prowess of arms, and without skill in weapons,
he would not be able to encounter Bhishma and Drona and others in battle.
You will also report to Yudhishthira that the illustrious and mighty-armed Arjuna
has also mastered the science of celestial dancing and music both instrumental
    and vocal.
And also tell him that he and his brothers should see the various sacred shrines.
For, having bathed in different sacred waters, he will be cleansed of his sins,
and the fever of his heart will abate. Then he will be able to enjoy his kingdom,
happy in the thought that his sins have been washed away.
And, O foremost among Brahmanas, you must protect Yudhishthira
during his wandering over the earth. Fierce Rakshasas live in mountain fastnesses.
                  Protect the king from those cannibals."
After Indra had spoken thus unto Lomasa, Arjuna also addressed that rishi, saying:
"Take care of Yudhishthira, the son of Pandu. Let the king, under your protection,
visit the various places of pilgrimage and give to Brahmanas in charity."
The mighty ascetic Lomasa answered both: "So be it." And he set out for the
    earth,
where he found King Yudhishthira surrounded by ascetics and his younger
    brothers.

✦

What did Dhritarashtra say when he heard of the great feats of Arjuna
from Dwaipayana, that foremost among rishis?
He said to Sanjaya: "O charioteer, do you know the acts of the intelligent Arjuna,
of which I have heard from beginning to end? My wretched and sinful son
is even now engaged in a policy of the most vulgar kind.
He will certainly depopulate the earth.
The illustrious person whose words even in jest are true, and who has Arjuna
to fight for him, is sure to win the three worlds.
Who, even beyond the influence of death and decay, can stand before Arjuna
when he scatters his barbed and sharp-pointed arrows whetted on stone?
My wretched sons who have to fight with the invincible Pandavas are all doomed.
Reflecting day and night, I do not see the warrior among us
who is able to stand in battle before the wielder of the Gandiva.
If Drona, or Karna, or even Bhishma should advance against him in fighting,
a great calamity is likely to befall the earth.
But even in that case, I do not see the way to our success. Karna is kind and
    forgetful.
The preceptor Drona is old. Arjuna, however, is wrathful, and strong, and proud,
and of firm and steady prowess. As all these warriors are invincible,
a terrible fight will take place among them. All of them are heroes
skilled in weapons and of great reputation. They would not wish
for the sovereignty of the world if it were to be purchased by defeat.
Indeed, peace will be restored only on the death of these or of Arjuna.
The slayer of Arjuna, however, does not exist, nor does one who can vanquish him.
How shall that wrath of his, which has me for its object, be pacified?
O Sanjaya, the thunderbolt falling on the mountaintop may leave a portion
    unconsumed,
but the shafts shot by Arjuna leave nothing behind.
As the rays of the sun heat this mobile and immobile universe, so will the shafts
shot by Arjuna's hands scorch my sons.
Vidhatri, the formless soul of the universe, has created Arjuna
as an all-consuming destroyer. He stands in battle as a foe,
vomiting and scattering swarms of arrows. Who can defeat him?"

24

Karna

What was Yudhisthira's great fear in respect to Karna,
and why did he never express it to anyone? After twelve years of their exile had
    passed
and the thirteenth year had begun, Indra, ever friendly to the sons of Pandu,
resolved to beg of Karna his earrings. When he discovered the plan
of the chief of the celestials about the earrings, Surya, the sun,
having effulgence for his wealth, appeared to Karna.
And while that hero was lying down at night, at his ease on a rich bed
overlaid with costly sheets, the effulgent deity, filled with affection for his son,
showed himself in Karna's dreams in the form of a handsome Brahmana
versed in the Vedas. Surya said these words for Karna's benefit: "O son, listen!
I tell you today what is for your great good to know!
With the object of obtaining your earrings, Indra, to benefit the sons of Pandu,
will come to you, disguised as a Brahmana!
He knows your character and realizes that when you are solicited by pious people
you give gifts but never take any in return!
You give to Brahmanas wealth or anything they ask of you and never refuse
anything to anybody. Knowing how you are, Indra will come to beg of you
your earrings and coat of mail. But do not give them away.
Put him off, if you can, with sweet speeches. I tell you this for your supreme
    benefit!
When he asks for the earrings, you must refuse, offering instead other kinds of
    wealth,
such as gems and women and cows, and citing various precedents.
If you give away the earrings you were born with, your life will be shortened.
You will meet with death! Arrayed in your mail and earrings,
you will be incapable of being slain by foes in battle!
Both these jeweled ornaments have sprung from Amrita, the stuff of immortality.
Therefore, if your life is at all dear to you, preserve them."
Hearing these words, Karna said: "Who are you, showing me such kindness?"
The Brahmana thereupon said: "My son, I am he of a thousand rays!
                    Out of affection, I point out to you the right path!"
Karna replied: "This is most fortunate—that the god of splendor addresses me
    today,
seeking my welfare. Listen, however, to these words of mine!

May it please you, it is only from affection that I tell you this!
If I am dear to you, I should not be dissuaded from the observance of my vow,
which the whole world knows: that I am prepared to give away life itself
to superior Brahmanas! If Indra comes to me disguised as a Brahmana
to beg for the benefit of the sons of Pandu, I will give him the earrings and the
    mail
so that my fame, which has spread over the three worlds, may not suffer
    diminution!
For persons like us, it is not correct to save life by a blameworthy act.
On the contrary, it is proper for us to meet death with the approbation of the
    world,
and under circumstances bringing fame. If the slayer himself of Vala and Vritra
comes to ask for the mail and the earrings for the benefit of the sons of Pandu,
that will conduce to my fame and to *his* infamy!
I wish for fame in this world, even if it is to be purchased with life itself,
for those who have fame enjoy the celestial regions, while those who do not,
    do not.
Fame keeps people alive in this world, even like a mother, while infamy kills men,
even though they may move about with bodies undestroyed.
O lord of the worlds, that fame is the life of men is evidenced by an ancient
    couplet
sung by the creator himself: 'In the next world fame is the chief support of a
    person,
while in this world fame lengthens life.' Therefore, by giving away
the earrings and mail with which I was born, I will win eternal fame!
And by offering up my body as a gift to the gods in the sacrifice of war,
by achieving feats difficult of performance, and by conquering my foes in fight,
I will acquire renown. And by dispelling on the field of battle the fears of the
    frightened
who may beg for their lives, and relieving old men and boys and Brahmanas
from terror and anxiety, I will win excellent fame and the highest heaven.
My fame is to be protected with the sacrifice even of my life. This is my vow!"
Surya said: "Never do anything that is harmful to yourself and your friends,
your sons, your wives, your father, and your mother.
People may desire renown in this world and lasting fame in heaven
without wishing to sacrifice their bodies.
But as you desire undying fame at the expense of your life,
fame will, without doubt, snatch away your life!
O bull among men, in this world the father, the mother, the son, and other
    relatives
are only of use to him who is alive. As regards kings, it is only when they are alive
that prowess can be of any use to them. Do you understand this?
Fame is only for the good of those who are alive!
The fame of a dead man is like a garland of flowers around the neck of his corpse.
As you revere me, I tell you this for your benefit.
Those who worship me are always protected by me. Act, then, according to my
    words!

There is, besides, some profound mystery in all this ordained by fate.

It is for this that I tell you so. Act without mistrust of any kind!

It is not fit for you to know what is a secret to the very gods, and I cannot reveal
    it to you.

You will, however, understand it in time.

When the wielder of the thunderbolt asks you for them, do not give him your
    earrings!

With your handsome earrings, you look beautiful, even like the moon himself

in the clear firmament in the Visakha constellation!

You and Arjuna also will surely encounter each other in battle.

But if you are furnished with your earrings, Arjuna will never be able to vanquish
    you,

                even if Indra himself comes to his assistance."

Karna said: "As you know me for your worshipper,

so also you know that there is nothing I cannot give away in charity.

Neither my wives nor my sons nor my own self nor my friends are as dear to me

as you, because of the veneration I feel for you! You can say with all confidence:

'Karna reveres me and is dear to me. He knows no other deity in heaven.'

And it is in light of this certainty that you have said to me what is for my benefit.

Yet again do I beseech you with bended head, again do I place myself in your
    hands.

I will repeat the answer I have already given. You must forgive me!

Death itself is not fraught with such terrors for me as untruth!

As regards especially the Brahmanas, I do not hesitate to yield up my life for them!

And, O divine one, respecting what you have said to me of Arjuna, the son of
    Pandu,

let your grief born of your anxiety of heart be dispelled touching him and myself,

for I shall surely conquer Arjuna in battle! You know that I have great strength

of weapons obtained from Jamadagnya, Satyavati's son, and from the high-
    souled Drona.

Permit me to observe my vow so that to him of the thunderbolt coming to beg
    of me

                I may give away even my life!"

Surya said: "If you give away your earrings to the wielder of the thunderbolt,

you should also, for the purpose of securing victory, speak to him, saying:

'O you of a hundred sacrifices, I shall give you the earrings on one condition.'

Furnished with the earrings, you cannot be slain by any being.

Indra wants your earrings because he wants to see you slain in battle by Arjuna.

You must beseech him, saying: 'Give me an infallible dart capable of slaying all
    foes,

and I will, O thousand-eyed deity, give the earrings along with my excellent coat
    of mail!'

Only on this condition should you give the earrings to Indra.

With that dart, O Karna, you will slay foes in battle, for that dart of the chief

of the celestials does not return to the hand that hurls it without slaying enemies
                by the hundreds and thousands!"

Having said this, the thousand-rayed deity suddenly vanished.

The next day, after having said his prayers, Karna related his dream to the sun.
And Surya, resplendent and divine, said to him with a smile: "It is even so!"
Then Karna, eager to obtain the dart, waited in expectation of Indra's arrival.

✦

What was that secret which was not revealed to Karna by the deity of warm rays?
And of what kind were those earrings, and of what sort was that coat of mail?
From where did that mail and those earrings come?
Once on a time, there appeared before King Kuntibhoja a Brahmana of fierce
    energy
and tall stature, bearing a beard and matted locks and carrying a staff in his hand.
Agreeable to the eye and of faultless limbs, he blazed forth in splendor.
He was possessed of a yellow-blue complexion like that of honey.
His speech was mellifluous, and he was adorned with ascetic merit
and a knowledge of the Vedas. That person addressed the king and said:
"O you who are free from pride, I wish to live as a guest in your house,
feeding on the food obtained as alms from you! Neither your followers nor you
    yourself
shall ever act in such a way as to produce my displeasure!
If, O sinless one, it please you, I would then live in your house thus:
I shall leave your abode when I wish and come back when it should please me.
          And no one shall offend me in respect of my food or bed."
Then Kuntibhoja said: "Be it so, and more. I have an illustrious daughter named
    Kunti.
She has an excellent character and is observant of vows, chaste, and of subdued
    demeanor.
She shall attend on you and minister to you. You will be pleased with her
    disposition!"
Having said this to that Brahmana, the king went to his daughter Kunti
and told her: "This eminently pious Brahmana wants to dwell in my house!
I have accepted his proposal, saying: 'So be it.' And I rely on your aptitude and
    skill
in ministering to him. Therefore, you must act in such a manner
that my words may not be untrue. Give him whatever he may want.
A Brahmana is the embodiment of preeminent energy and the highest ascetic
    merit.
It is because of the virtuous practices of Brahmanas that the sun shines in the
    heavens.
This is a highly virtuous member of that order who is entrusted to your care.
You should tend this Brahmana with concentrated mind.
O daughter, I know that from childhood upward you have been attentive to
    Brahmanas
and superiors and relatives and servants and friends, to your mothers and myself.
I know you bear yourself well, bestowing proper regard upon everyone.
And, O you of faultless limbs, in the interior of my palace there is not one,
even among the servants, who is dissatisfied with you.

I have therefore thought you fit to wait upon all Brahmanas of wrathful temper.
You are, O Kunti, a girl I have adopted as my daughter.
You are born in the race of the Vrishnis and are the favorite daughter of the
river Suraya.
You were given to me by your father himself. The sister of Vasudeva by birth,
you are by adoption foremost among my children. Having promised me with
these words—
'I will give you my firstborn'—your father gave you to me while you were yet an
infant.
It is for this reason that you are my daughter. Born and reared so, you have come
from one happy state to another, like a lotus transferred from one lake to
another.
Women, especially those of mean extraction, although they may be kept under
restraint,
become in consequence of their unripe age generally deformed in character.
But you, O Kunti, are born in a royal race, and your beauty also is extraordinary.
Therefore, renouncing pride and haughtiness and a sense of self-importance,
wait upon the boon-giving Brahmana, and thereby attain to an auspicious state!
But if, on the contrary, you stir up the anger of this best of the twice-born ones,
my entire race will be consumed by him!"
Kunti said: "According to your promise, I will, O king, with concentrated mind,
serve that Brahmana. I do not say this falsely. It is my nature to worship
Brahmanas.
Whether that worshipful one comes in the evening or in the morning
or at night or even at midnight, he will have no reason to be angry with me!
You may rely on me! I shall be always attentive to what is agreeable to this
Brahmana
and to what also brings good to you. I know that Brahmanas are eminently
virtuous.
When propitiated they bestow salvation, and when displeased
they are capable of bringing destruction upon the offender.
You will not come to any grief from that spiritual person because of any act of
mine."
When she had thus spoken, the king embraced her and instructed her as to what
to do.
The illustrious Kuntibhoja then made over the girl Kunti to that Brahmana,
saying: "This is my daughter, O Brahmana. She is of tender age
and brought up in luxury. If she transgresses at any time, do not take that to heart!
Illustrious Brahmanas are never angry with old men, children, and ascetics,
even if these transgress. In respect of even a great wrong,
forgiveness is due from the spiritual. The worship offered to the best of one's
power
should be acceptable to you!" And the Brahmana said: "So be it!"
Thereupon the king assigned him apartments that were white as swans.
And in the room intended for the sacrificial fire, the king placed a brilliant seat
especially constructed for him. The food and other things that were offered the
Brahmana

were of the same excellent kind. And casting aside idleness and self-importance,
the princess addressed herself with goodwill to waiting upon the Brahmana.
By serving him with careful attention and a pure heart, she succeeded in
    pleasing him.
He sometimes returned in the evening or late at night, having said to her:
"I will come back in the morning." But she was ready at all hours with sumptuous
    food and drink
and a well-made bed. And as day after day passed, her attentions to him increased
instead of undergoing any diminution. Even when the Brahmana reproved her,
found fault, or addressed her in harsh words, she never did anything
    disagreeable to him.
On many occasions the Brahmana came back after the appointed hour had long
    passed
and in the middle of the night said: "Give me food!"
But on all those occasions Kunti said: "All is ready." And she held the fare
    before him.
Like a disciple, daughter, or sister, that blameless gem of a girl
with a devoted heart served that foremost of Brahmanas, who was well-pleased
with her conduct and ministrations. He received those attentions of hers,
valuing them rightly. And her father asked her every morning and evening:
"O daughter, is the Brahmana satisfied with your ministrations?"
She would reply: "Exceedingly well." And the high-souled Kuntibhoja
                            experienced the greatest delight.
When, after a full year, the ascetic was unable to find any fault whatever in Kunti,
he said to her: "O gentle maid, I have been well pleased with your attentions!
Ask me for such boons as are difficult of being obtained by mortals,
obtaining which you may surpass in fame all the women in this world."
Kunti answered: "Everything has already been done on my behalf
since you and my father have been pleased with me!
I consider the boon as already obtained, O Brahmana!"
The Brahmana thereupon said: "If you do not wish to obtain boons from me,
then take from me this mantra for invoking the celestials!
Any among the celestials whom you may invoke by uttering this mantra
will appear before you and be under your power. Willing or not, by virtue of this
    mantra
that deity in gentle guise, and assuming the attitude of a slave, will be under
    your power!"
That faultless maiden could not, from fear of a curse, refuse a second time
to comply with the wishes of that best of the twice-born.
The Brahmana then imparted to that girl those mantras
which are recited in the beginning of the Atharvan Veda.
And, having imparted those mantras to her, he said to Kuntibhoja:
"I have, O monarch, dwelled happily in your house,
always worshipped with due regard and gratified by your daughter.
                            I shall now depart."
The maiden, of course, began to ponder and said to herself:
What is the nature of those mantras that have been bestowed on me

by that high-souled one? I shall test their power.

And as she was thinking in this way, she suddenly perceived the approach of her season.

Because it arrived while she was yet unmarried, she blushed in shame.

It happened that as she was seated in her chamber on a rich bed, she beheld the sun

rising in the east. And both the mind and the eyes of that maiden of excellent waist

were riveted upon its bright circle. She gazed and gazed on that orb

without being satiated with the beauty of the morning sun.

And she suddenly became gifted with celestial sight and beheld that god of divine form,

accoutered in mail and adorned with earrings.

At the sight of the god, she became curious as to the powers of the mantras,

and she resolved to invoke him. With recourse to Pranayama,

she invoked the maker of day, who speedily presented himself.

He was of a yellowish hue like honey and was possessed of mighty arms.

His neck was marked with lines like those of a conch shell.

Furnished with armlets and decked with a diadem, he came smiling,

illuminating all the directions. It was by Yoga power that he divided himself in twain

and in one part continued to give heat while the other appeared before Kunti.

He addressed Kunti in words most sweet: "O gentle maiden,

overpowered by the mantras, I come here obedient to you. What shall I do, O queen?

I shall do whatever you may command." Hearing these words of the deity, Kunti said:

"O worshipful one, go you back to where you came from!

I invoked you from curiosity alone. Pardon me, I beseech you!"

Surya then said: "I will return to the place I have come from!

But it is not proper for you, having called a celestial, to send him away in vain.

Your intention, O blessed one, is to have from Surya a son, furnished with a coat of mail

and earrings, who in prowess would be beyond compare in this world!

Therefore, O damsel of elephantine gait, surrender yourself to me!

You shall then have a son according to your wish! I will go back

after having known you! If you do not gratify me today, I shall in anger curse you,

your father, and that Brahmana also. For your fault I will surely consume them all,

and I shall inflict terrible punishment on that foolish father of yours,

who does not know this transgression of yours,

and on that Brahmana who bestowed the mantras on you

without knowing your disposition and character!

Yonder all the celestials in heaven, with Purandara at their head, are looking at me

with derisive smiles for my having been deceived by you, O lady!

Look at them, for you are now possessed of celestial sight!

Before this I endowed you with celestial vision so that you could see me!"

The princess beheld the celestials in the firmament, each in his proper sphere,

even as she saw before her that highly resplendent deity furnished with rays.
And beholding them all, the girl became frightened and blushed in shame.
She addressed Surya, saying: "O lord of rays, go you back to your own region.
On account of my maidenhood, this outrage of yours is fraught with woe to me!
It is only one's father, mother, and other superiors who can give away a
    daughter's body.
Virtue I shall never sacrifice, seeing that in this world keeping one's person
    inviolate
is deemed as the highest duty of women and is held in high regard!
It was only to test the power of my mantras and from childishness that I
    summoned you.
Considering that this was done by a girl of tender years, you must, O lord,
    forgive me!"
Then Surya said: "It is because you are a girl that I am speaking to you so mildly.
To one not so young, I would not concede this. Surrender yourself, Kunti!
You shall surely attain happiness thereby. Since you have invoked me with mantras,
it is not proper for me to go away without the accomplishment of any purpose,
for if I do so, I shall be the object of laughter in the world
and a byword with all the celestials. Yield to me! You shall obtain a son like me,
                  and you shall also be much praised in all the world."
Although that noble girl addressed him in sweet words,
she was unable to dissuade that deity of a thousand rays.
At last, from fear of a curse, she reflected for a long time:
How may my innocent father and that Brahmana escape the angry Surya's curse
for my sake? Although energy and asceticism are capable of destroying sins,
even honest persons, if they are of unripe age, should not foolishly court them.
By acting foolishly in the way I have today, I have been placed in a frightful situation.
I am entirely within the grasp of this deity.
Yet how can I do what is sinful by taking it on myself to surrender my person to him?
She was so confounded that she could not decide what to do.
Afraid, on the one hand, of the reproach of friends if she obeyed the deity
and, on the other, of his curse if she disobeyed him, the damsel at last said to
    the god:
"O god, as my father and mother and friends are still living, this violation of my
    duty
should not take place. If I commit this unlawful act with you,
the reputation of this race shall be ruined in this world on my account.
But if you deem this to be a meritorious act, I shall fulfill your desire,
even though my relatives may not have bestowed me on you!
May I remain chaste after having surrendered my person to you!
Surely the virtue, reputation, fame, and life of every creature are established
    in you!"
Hearing these words of hers, Surya replied:
"Neither your father nor your mother nor any other superior of yours
is competent to give you away! May good betide you. Listen to my words!
You shall not by any means be guilty of any sin by complying with my request.
How can I, desirous of the welfare of all creatures, commit an unrighteous act?

You shall remain a virgin after having gratified me.
And your son shall be mighty-armed and illustrious."
To this Kunti said: "If I obtain a son from you, may he be furnished with a coat of mail
and earrings, and may he be mighty-armed and endowed with great strength!"
Surya answered: "O gentle maiden, your son shall be mighty-armed
and decked with earrings and a celestial coat of mail.
And both his earrings and coat of mail will be made of Amrita,
and his coat will also be invulnerable."
Kunti then said: "If the excellent mail and earrings of the son you will beget on me
be made of Amrita, then, O worshipful deity, let your purpose be fulfilled!
May he be powerful, strong, energetic, and handsome, even like you,
and may he also be endowed with virtue!"
Surya answered: "O princess, these earrings had been given to me by Aditi.
I will bestow them, as also this excellent mail, on your son!"
Kunti then said: "Very well, O worshipful one, I will, as you say, gratify you!"
Surya said: "So be it!"
And that ranger of the skies entered into Kunti and touched her on the navel.
At this, that damsel, on account of Surya's energy, became stupefied.
And the reverend lady fell down on her bed, deprived of her senses.
Surya then addressed her, saying: "I will now depart, O girl of graceful hips!
You shall bring forth a son who will become foremost among wielders of weapons.
At the same time you shall remain a virgin."
Then, as the highly effulgent Surya was about to depart,
the girl bashfully said to him: "So be it!"
And it was thus that the daughter of King Kuntibhoja,
importuned by Surya, had fallen down on that excellent bed like a broken
creeper.
And it was thus that the deity of fierce rays, stupefying her,
entered into her by virtue of Yoga power and placed himself within her womb.
The deity, however, did not sully her by deflowering her in the flesh.
It was on the first day of the lighted fortnight during the tenth month of the year
that Kunti conceived a son like the lord himself of the stars in the firmament.
From fear of her friends, she concealed her pregnancy.
And as the damsel lived entirely in the apartments assigned to the maidens
and carefully hid her condition, no one but her nurse knew the truth.
In due time that beauteous maiden, by the grace of the deity,
brought forth a son resembling a very god.
And like his father, the child was equipped in a coat of mail and decked with
earrings.
He was possessed of leonine eyes and shoulders like those of a bull.
No sooner was the girl delivered of her child than she consulted with her nurse
and placed the infant in a commodious and smooth box made of wickerwork
and spread over with soft sheets and furnished with a costly pillow.
Its surface was laid over with wax, and it was encased in a rich cover.
With tears in her eyes, she carried the infant to the river Aswa
and consigned the basket to its waters. Although she knew it to be improper

for an unmarried girl to bear offspring, yet from maternal affection she wept
   piteously.
While consigning the basket to the waters of the river Aswa, Kunti said:
"O child, may good betide you at the hands of all who inhabit the land,
the water, the sky, and the celestial regions. May all your paths be auspicious!
May no one obstruct your way! And may all who come across you
have their hearts divested of hostility toward you. May the lord of waters, Varuna,
protect you in water! And may the deity who ranges the skies protect you in the sky.
And may Surya, your father, from whom I have obtained you as ordained by
   destiny,
protect you everywhere! Even in foreign lands I shall be able to recognize you
by this mail of yours! Surely your sire, the divine Surya, is blessed,
for he will with his celestial sight behold you going down the current!
Blessed also is that lady who will take you for her son
and who will give you suck when you are thirsty!
O son, she who will behold you crawl on the ground,
begrimed with dust and sweetly uttering inarticulate words, is surely blessed!
And she who will behold your arrival at your youthful prime,
like a maned lion born in Himalayan forests, is surely blessed!"
Having thus bewailed piteously, Kunti laid the basket on the waters of the river
   Aswa
in the dead of night and, though desirous of beholding her son again and again,
returned to the palace, fearing lest her father learn of what had happened.
Meanwhile, the basket floated from the river Aswa to the river Charmanwati,
and from the Charmanwati it passed to the Yamuna, and so on to the Ganga.
Carried by the waves of the Ganga, the child in the basket came to the city of
   Champa,
ruled by a person of the Suta tribe. The coat of mail and those earrings of Amrita
that were born with his body, as also the ordinance of destiny, kept the child alive.
It came to pass that at this time a Suta named Adhiratha, a friend of Dhritarashtra,
came to the river Ganga accompanied by his wife, Radha,
who was unparalleled on earth for beauty. That highly blessed woman
had made great efforts to obtain a son, but she had failed to conceive.
And on coming to the river Ganga, she beheld a box drifting along the current,
containing articles capable of protecting from dangers and decked with unguents.
The box was brought before her by the current of the river.
Curious, the lady ordered that it be seized.
And she then related all to Adhiratha of the charioteer caste.
Hearing this, Adhiratha took away the box from the riverside and opened it.
He beheld a boy resembling the morning sun.
The infant was furnished with golden mail and looked exceedingly beautiful,
with a face decked in earrings. Thereupon the charioteer and his wife were
   astonished,
and their eyes expanded in wonder. Taking the infant on his lap, Adhiratha said:
"Not since I was born have I ever seen such a wonder.
This child that has come to us must be of celestial birth.
Sonless as I am, it is the gods who have sent him to me!"

Saying this, he gave the infant to Radha, and she adopted,
according to the ordinance, that child of celestial form and divine origin
and possessed of the splendor of the filaments of the lotus.
Duly reared by her, the child endowed with great prowess grew up.
After Karna's adoption, Adhiratha had other sons begotten by himself.
Seeing the child furnished with bright mail and golden earrings,
the twice-born ones named him Vasusena.
Thus did that child, endowed with great splendor and immeasurable prowess,
become the son of the charioteer and come to be known as Vasusena and Vrisha.
And Kunti learned through spies that her own son, clad in celestial mail,
was growing up among the Angas as the eldest son of Adhiratha, a charioteer.
After the passage of time, Adhiratha sent him to the city named after the
    elephant.
And there Karna resided with Drona for the purpose of learning arms.
There that powerful youth contracted a friendship with Duryodhana;
and, having acquired all the four kinds of weapons from Drona, Kripa, and Rama,
he became famous in the world as a mighty bowman.
As a friend of Dhritarashtra's son, he became intent on injuring the sons of Kunti.
He was always eager to fight with the high-souled Arjuna.
From the time they first saw each other, Karna would challenge Arjuna,
and Arjuna, for his part, would challenge Karna.
This secret was without doubt known to the sun:
that Karna, begot by himself on Kunti, was being reared in the race of the Sutas.
And Yudhishthira, beholding Karna decked with his earrings and mail,
and thinking him to be unslayable in fight, was exceedingly pained.

◆

When Karna, after rising from the water, used at midday to worship the effulgent
    Surya
with joined hands, the Brahmanas would solicit him for wealth.
At that time there was nothing that he would not give away to the twice-born.
Indra assumed the guise of a Brahmana, appeared before him at such a time,
and said: "Give me!" And Radha's son replied to him: "You are welcome!"
Not knowing his intention, Karna addressed the Brahmana, saying:
"A necklace of gold, or beauteous damsels, or villages with plenty of cows—
which shall I give you?" The Brahmana replied: "I do not ask for a necklace of
    gold
or fair damsels or any other agreeable object. Those you give
to people who ask for them. If you are sincere in your vow, you will cut from
    your person
this coat of mail born with your body, and these earrings also,
and bestow them upon me, for this one gain of mine will be superior to every
    other gain!"
Hearing these words, Kama, said: "O Brahmana, I will give you homestead land
and fair damsels and cows and fields. But my mail and earrings I am unable to
    give."

Although thus addressed by Karna, still that Brahmana did not ask for any other
  boon.
And although Karna sought to pacify him and worshipped him duly,
yet that best of Brahmanas would not ask for any other present.
Radha's son again spoke to him with a smile: "My mail, O holy one,
was born with my body, and this pair of earrings has arisen from Amrita.
It is because of these that I am unslayable in the three worlds. I cannot part with
  them.
Accept from me the entire kingdom of the earth, rid of enemies and full of
  prosperity!
But if I am deprived of my earrings and the mail born with my body,
            I shall be liable to be vanquished by foes!"
When Indra again refused to ask for any other boon, Karna addressed him,
  saying:
"O god of gods, even before this I had recognized you!
It is not proper for me to confer on you any unprofitable boon,
for you are the very lord of the celestials! On the contrary, it is you, being the
  creator
and lord of all beings, who should confer boons on me!
If I give you this coat of mail and earrings, then I am sure to meet with
  destruction,
and you shall also undergo ridicule! Therefore, take my earrings and excellent
  mail
in exchange for something conferred by you! Otherwise, I will not bestow them
  on you!"
Indra replied: "Even before I came to you, Surya knew of my purpose
and without doubt has unfolded everything to you! O Karna, be it as you wish!
Except the thunderbolt alone, tell me what it is that you desire to have!"
Karna was delighted and, seeing that his purpose was about to be accomplished,
he proposed to Indra: "In exchange for my coat of mail and earrings,
give me a dart, incapable of being resisted, that can destroy hosts of enemies
arrayed in order of battle!" Indra replied to Karna:
"You give me your earrings and the coat of mail born with your body,
and in return take this dart!
When I encounter the Daitya in battle, this dart is incapable of being eluded.
Hurled by my hand, it destroys enemies by the hundreds
and comes back to my hand after achieving its purpose.
In your hand, however, this dart will slay only one powerful enemy.
And having achieved that feat, it will, roaring and blazing, return to me!"
To this Karna replied: "I desire to slay in fierce fight one enemy of mine
who roars fiercely and is hot as fire, and of whom I am in fear!"
To this Indra answered: "You shall slay such a roaring and powerful foe in battle.
But that one whom you seek to slay is protected by an illustrious personage.
Even he whom persons versed in the Vedas call the invincible boar
and the incomprehensible Narayana—even Krishna himself is protecting him!"
Thereupon Karna replied: "Nevertheless, give me the weapon that will destroy
only one powerful foe! I shall, for my part, bestow on you my mail and earrings,

cutting them off my person. Grant, however, that my body thus wounded
may not be unsightly!"
Indra said: "As you are bent upon observing the truth, your person shall not be
　unsightly,
nor shall any scar remain on it. You shall be possessed of the complexion
of your father himself. But if, maddened by wrath, you hurl this dart
while there are still other weapons with you, and when your life is not in
　imminent peril,
it will fall on yourself."
Karna answered: "As you direct, O Indra, I shall hurl this Vasavi dart
only when I am in imminent peril!" Taking the blazing dart, Karna peeled off his
　mail.
And watching Karna cutting his own body,
the entire host of celestials and men and Danavas set up a leonine roar.
Karna betrayed no contortions of face while peeling his mail.
As they watched that hero among men thus cutting his body with a weapon,
and always smiling, celestial kettledrums began to be played,
and celestial flowers were showered on him. Karna gave to Vasava the mail
still dripping blood. And, cutting off his earrings also, he handed them over to
　Indra.
It is for this reason that he came to be called Karna, meaning "*Peeler of His Own
　Covering.*"
Indra, having thus beguiled Karna, thought with a smile
that the business of the sons of Pandu had already been completed.
And having done all this, he ascended to heaven.

25

Virata

The son of the god of justice, the royal Yudhishthira,
called together all his younger brothers and said to them:
"Exiled from our kingdom, we have passed twelve years.
The thirteenth year, harder than the first twelve, has now come.
Therefore, O Arjuna, select some spot where we may pass our days
undiscovered by our enemies."Arjuna replied: "I shall mention some spots
that are both delightful and secluded, and you must select one of them.
Surrounding the kingdom of the Kurus are many countries beautiful and rich in
  corn,
such as Panchala, Chedi, Matsya, Surasena, Pattachchara, Dasarna, Navarashtra,
Malla, Salva, Yugandhara, Saurashtra, Avanti, and the spacious Kuntirashtra.
Which of these, O king, would you choose for us to spend the year?"
Yudhishthira said: "The aged Virata, king of the Matsyas,
is virtuous, powerful, charitable, and liked by all. Also he is attached to the
  Pandavas.
In the city of Virata, then, we shall spend this year, entering his service.
Tell me, in what capacities will you present yourselves before the king of the
  Matsyas?"
Arjuna said: "What service will you take in Virata's kingdom? You are mild,
  charitable,
modest, virtuous, and firm in promise. What will you do, O king,
afflicted as you are with calamity? A king is not qualified to bear trouble
like an ordinary person. How will you overcome this misfortune that has
  overtaken you?"
Yudhishthira replied: "You bulls among men, hear what I shall do
on appearing before King Virata. Presenting myself as a Brahmana, Kanka by
  name,
skilled in dice and fond of play, I shall become a courtier of that high-souled
  king.
And, moving upon chessboards beautiful pawns made of ivory
of blue and yellow and red and white hue, and by throws of black and red dice,
I shall entertain the king with his courtiers and friends.
Nobody will succeed in discovering me. Should the monarch ask me, I shall say:
'Formerly I was the bosom friend of Yudhishthira.' Thus shall I pass my days in
  that city.

What office will you fill in the city of Virata, Bhima?"
Bhima said: "I intend to present myself as a cook bearing the name of Vallava.
I am skilled in culinary art, and I shall prepare curries for the king,
surpassing all those skillful cooks who hitherto provided his food,
and I shall gratify the monarch. I shall carry mighty loads of wood.
And the monarch, seeing that mighty feat, will be pleased.
And when they behold such superhuman feats of mine, the servants of the
household
will honor me as a king. And I shall have entire control over viands and drinks.
Commanded to subdue powerful elephants and mighty bulls, I will do as I am
bidden.
And if any combatants will fight with me in the lists, then will I vanquish them
and thereby entertain the monarch. But I shall not take the life of any of them.
I shall only bring them down in such a way that they may not be killed.
And on being asked as regards my antecedent I shall say:
'Formerly I was the wrestler and cook of Yudhishthira.' Thus shall I maintain
myself."
Yudhishthira said: "And what office will be performed by Arjuna,
that mighty descendant of the Kurus?
Even as the sun is foremost among heat-giving bodies,
as the Brahmana is the best of all bipeds, as the cobra is foremost among
serpents,
as fire is the first of all things possessed of energy,
as the thunderbolt is foremost among weapons,
as the humped bull is foremost among animals of the bovine breed,
as the ocean is foremost among watery expanses,
as clouds charged with rain are foremost among clouds,
as the son is foremost among beloved objects,
and as the wife is the best of all friends,
so is Arjuna foremost among bowmen.
What office will the wielder of the Gandiva perform, whose car is drawn by white
horses
and who is not inferior to Indra or Vasudeva himself?
What office will be performed by one who is among men as is Himavat among
mountains,
the ocean among expanses of water, the tiger among beasts,
and Garuda among feathery tribes?"
Arjuna replied: "O lord of the Earth, I will declare myself as one of the neuter sex.
It is indeed difficult to hide the marks of the bowstring on my arms.
But I will cover both my scarred arms with bangles.
Wearing brilliant rings on my ears and conch bangles on my wrists,
and with a braid hanging down from my head,
I shall appear as one of the third sex, Vrihannala by name.
And living as a female I shall entertain the king and the inmates of the inner
apartments
by reciting stories. I shall also instruct the women of Virata's palace in singing
and in delightful modes of dancing and in musical instruments of diverse kinds.

I shall also recite the various excellent acts of men and thus
conceal myself.
And should the king ask, I will say: 'I lived as a waiting maid of Draupadi
in Yudhishthira's palace.' And concealing myself this way, as fire is concealed by
ashes,
I shall pass my days agreeably in the palace of Virata."
Then the king addressed another brother of his: "Tender, possessed of a graceful
presence,
and deserving of every luxury as you are, what office will you discharge, Nakula,
while living in the dominions of that king?" Nakula said:
"Under the name of Granthika, I shall become the keeper of the horses of King
Virata.
I have thorough knowledge of this work and am skillful in tending horses.
Besides, the task is agreeable to me, and I possess great skill in training horses.
In my hands, even colts and mares become docile and never vicious
in bearing a rider or drawing a car. To those persons in the city of Virata
who may inquire of me, I shall say: 'Formerly I was employed by Yudhishthira,
in charge of his horses.' Thus disguised, I shall spend my days in the city of Virata."
Yudhishthira then asked: "How will you, Sahadeva, bear yourself before that king?
What will you do to live in disguise?" Sahadeva replied:
"I will become a keeper of the cattle of Virata's king.
I am skilled in milking cows as well as in taming their fierceness.
Passing under the name of Tantripal, I shall perform my duties deftly.
Let your heart's fever be dispelled. Formerly I was frequently employed
to look after your cattle, and I have particular knowledge of that work.
I am well acquainted with the tending of herds and with auspicious marks of cows.
I can also discriminate bulls with auspicious marks,
the scent of whose urine may make even the barren bring forth calves.
Thus will I live, taking delight in work of this kind.
No one will then be able to recognize me, and I will please the king."
Yudhishthira said: "This is our beloved wife, dearer to us than our lives.
She deserves to be cherished by us like a mother, and regarded like an elder sister.
Unacquainted as she is with any kind of work, what office will Draupadi perform?
Delicate and young, she is a princess of great repute.
Devoted to her lords, and eminently virtuous, how will she live?
Since her birth, she has enjoyed only garlands and perfume, ornaments and
costly robes."
Draupadi replied: "There is a class of persons called Sairindhris,
who enter the services of others. Respectable women do not do this.
But I shall give myself out as a Sairindhri, skilled in dressing hair.
And on being questioned by the king, I shall say: 'I served as a waiting woman
of Draupadi in Yudhishthira's household.' I shall thus pass my days in disguise
and serve the famous Sudeshna, the wife of the king.
Surely, obtaining me, she will appreciate me. Do not grieve, O king."
Yudhishthira said: "You speak well.
But O! fair girl, you were born in a respectable family.
Chaste as you are and always engaged in observing virtuous vows,

you do not know what sin is. Therefore, conduct yourself in such a way
that sinful men of evil hearts may not be gladdened by gazing at you."
Yudhishthira continued: "You have all said what offices you will perform.
I have said what I will do. Let our priest, accompanied by charioteers and cooks,
repair to the abode of Drupada and there maintain our Agnihotra fires.
And let Indrasena and the others, taking with them the empty cars, proceed to
  Dwaravati.
And let all these maidservants of Draupadi go to the Panchalas
with our charioteers and cooks. And let all of them say:
'We do not know where the Pandavas have gone, leaving us at the lake of
  Dwaitavana.'"

✦

Having thus told one another the offices they would discharge,
the Pandavas sought Dhaumya's advice. And Dhaumya the priest said:
"Sons of Pandu, the arrangements you have made regarding the Brahmanas,
your friends, cars, weapons, and the sacred fires are excellent.
But it behooves you—Yudhishthira and Arjuna especially—
to make provision for the protection of Draupadi.
You are with the characters of men. Yet whatever may be your knowledge,
friends may from affection be permitted to repeat what is already known.
I shall, therefore, venture a further word. To dwell with a king is, alas, difficult.
But I shall tell you how you may reside in the royal household, avoiding every
  fault.
In this world, that cherisher and protector of all beings, the king,
is a deity in embodied form and is as a great fire sanctified with all the mantras.
One should present oneself before the king, having obtained his permission at
  the gate.
No one should desire a seat another may covet. He who regards himself as a
  favorite—
occupying the king's car, or coach, or seat, or vehicle, or elephant—
is unworthy of dwelling in a royal household. Only one who never takes a seat
the occupation of which is likely to raise alarm in the minds of malicious people
is worthy of dwelling in a royal household.
No one should offer counsel to a king that has not been asked for.
Paying homage in season to the king, one should silently sit beside the king,
for kings take umbrage at babblers. A wise person should not contract friendship
with the king's wife, or with the occupants of the inner apartments,
or with those who are objects of royal displeasure.
One near the king should perform even the most unimportant actions
with the king's knowledge. Behaving thus with a sovereign, one does not come
  to harm.
Even if an individual attain the highest office, he should consider himself as if
  born blind
in respect to the king's dignity, for the rulers of men do not forgive even their sons
and grandsons and brothers when they tamper with the royal dignity.

Kings should be served with scrupulous care, even as are Agni and other gods,
and he who is disloyal to his sovereign will certainly be destroyed by him.
Renouncing anger, and pride, and negligence, it behooves a man
to follow the course directed by the monarch. After carefully deliberating on all
    things,
a person should set forth before the king topics that are both profitable and
    pleasant;
but should a subject be profitable without being pleasant, he should still
    communicate it,
despite its disagreeableness. One should be well disposed toward the king
in all his interests and not indulge in speech that is alike unpleasant and profitless.
Always thinking *The king does not like me*, one should banish negligence
and be intent on bringing about what is agreeable and advantageous to him.
Only he who never swerves from his place, who is not friendly
to those hostile to the king, and who strives not to do wrong to the king
is worthy to dwell in a royal household. A learned man should sit
on either the king's right or his left; he should not sit behind him,
for that is the place appointed for armed guards, and to sit before him is
    forbidden.
Let none, when the king is engaged in doing anything in respect to his servants,
come forward pressing himself zealously before others, for even if the aggrieved
be very poor and desperate, such conduct would still be inexcusable.
No man should reveal to others any lie the king may have told,
inasmuch as the king bears ill will to those who report his falsehoods.
Kings also always disregard persons who think of themselves as learned.
No man should be proud, thinking *I am brave* or *I am intelligent*;
but a person obtains the good graces of a king and enjoys the good things of life
by behaving agreeably to the king's wishes.
What man who is respected by the wise can even think of doing mischief
to one whose anger is a great impediment, and whose favor is productive of
    mighty fruits?
No one should move his lips, arms, and thighs before the king.
A person should speak and spit before the king only mildly.
In the presence of even laughable objects, a man should not break out into loud
    laughter
like a maniac, nor should he show unreasonable gravity by containing himself.
One should smile modestly to show his interest in what is before him.
He who is ever mindful of the king's welfare and is neither exhilarated by reward
nor depressed by disgrace is alone worthy of dwelling in a royal household.
That learned courtier who always pleases the king and his son
with agreeable speeches succeeds in dwelling in a royal household as a favorite.
The courtier who has lost the royal favor for just reason,
but does not speak evil of the king, regains his prosperity.
The man who serves the king or lives in his domains, if he is sagacious,
should speak in praise of the king, both in his presence and in his absence.
The courtier who attempts to obtain his end by employing force against the king
cannot keep his place long and incurs the risk of death.

None should, for self-interest, open communications with the king's enemies.
Nor should one distinguish oneself above the king in matters requiring ability
    and talents.
Only he who is always cheerful and strong, brave and truthful, and mild,
and who follows his master like his shadow, is worthy to dwell in a royal household.
Only he who, on being entrusted with a project, comes forward and says, 'I will
    do this'
is worthy of living in a royal household. Only he who, on being entrusted with a
    task
either within the king's dominion or out of it, and who never fears to undertake it,
is fit to reside in a royal household. Only he who leaves his home on the king's
    business
without worrying about his dear ones, and who undergoes present misery
in expectation of future happiness, is worthy of dwelling in a royal household.
Commissioned to a task, one should not take bribes,
for by such appropriation one becomes liable to fetters or death.
The robes, ornaments, cars, and other things that the king may be pleased to
    bestow
should always be used, for by this one wins the royal favor.
Controlling your minds, spend this year, you sons of Pandu, behaving in this way.
            Later, regaining your own kingdom, you may live as you please."
Yudhishthira said: "We have been well taught by you. Blessings upon you.
There is none who could say these things to us except our mother Kunti, and
    Vidura."
Dhaumya, that best of Brahmanas, performed the rites of departure
and, lighting up their fires, offered with mantra oblations on them
for the prosperity and success of the Pandavas and for their reconquest of the
    whole world.
After they had walked around those fires and around the Brahmanas of ascetic
    wealth,
the six set out, placing Draupadi in their front.
Dhaumya took up their sacred fires and set out for the Panchalas.
Indrasena, the majordomo, and others already mentioned
went to the Yadavas, and they looked after the horses and the cars of the Pandavas
            and passed their time happily and in privacy.

✦

Looking wan, and wearing beards and equipped with swords,
they entered Matsya's dominions still dressed as hunters.
When they arrived in that country, Draupadi said to Yudhishthira:
"We see footpaths here and various fields. But it appears that Virata's metropolis
is still at a distance. Let us pass here what part of the night is still left,
            for my fatigue is great."
Yudhishthira answered: "Arjuna, take up Draupadi and carry her.
As soon as we emerge from this forest, we shall arrive at the city."
Thereupon, like the leader of a herd of elephants, Arjuna took Draupadi up

and, on coming to the vicinity of the city, let her down again.

Yudhishthira said to Arjuna: "Where shall we deposit our weapons
before entering the city? If we enter with our weapons about us,
we shall surely excite the alarm of the citizens.
Further, your tremendous bow, the Gandiva, is known to all men
so that people will, without doubt, recognize us. And if even one of us is
   discovered,
we shall have to pass another twelve years in the forest."
Arjuna said: "We are close to a cemetery, and near its inaccessible peak
is a mighty sami tree, throwing about its gigantic branches and difficult to climb.
No human being will see us as we are depositing our arms there.
That tree is in the middle of an out-of-the way forest abounding in beasts and
   snakes
and is near a dreary cemetery. Stowing away our weapons on the sami tree,
let us go to the city and live there, free from anxiety!"
Arjuna then prepared to put the weapons on the tree.
Nakula ascended the tree, deposited on it the bows and the other weapons,
and tied them fast onto those parts of the tree that he thought would not break,
and where the rain would not penetrate. And the Pandavas hung up a corpse on
   the tree,
knowing that people smelling the stench of the corpse would avoid the tree
and keep their distance. They explained to the shepherds and cowherds:
"This is our mother, aged one hundred and eighty years. We have hung up her
   dead body
in accordance with the custom observed by our forefathers."
And they went on toward the city where, for purposes of concealment,
Yudhishthira kept these five names for himself and his brothers:
Jaya, Jayanta, Vijaya, Jayatsena, and Jayatvala.

✦

While Yudhishthira was on his way to the city of Virata,
he prayed to the Divine Durga, the supreme goddess of the universe,
born in the womb of Yasoda and fond of the boons bestowed on her by Narayana,
sprung from the race of the cowherd Nanda and the giver of prosperity,
the enhancer of the glory of the family, the terrifier of Kansa
and the destroyer of Asuras. He saluted the goddess who is always decked
in celestial garlands and attired in celestial robes and who rescues the
   worshipper sunk in sin.
The king, desirous of obtaining a sight of the goddess, invoked her
and praised her by reciting various names derived from hymns.
Yudhishthira said: "Salutations, O giver of boons.
Identical with Krishna, O maiden, you have observed the vow of Brahmacharya.
Your body is as bright as the newly risen sun. Your face is as beautiful as the full
   moon.
Salutations, goddess of eight hands and four faces, of fair round hips and deep
   bosom,

and wearing bangles made of emeralds and sapphires and fine bracelets
on your upper arms. You shine, O goddess, as Padma, the consort of Narayana.
Sable as the black clouds, your face is as beautiful as that of Sankarshana.
You bear two large arms as long as a pair of poles raised in honor of Indra.
In your six other arms you bear a vessel, a lotus, a bell, a noose,
a bow, a large discus, and various other weapons.
You are the only female in the universe who possesses the attribute of purity.
You are decked with a pair of well-made ears graced with excellent rings.
With an excellent diadem and beautiful braid, with robes made of the skins of
    snakes,
and with the brilliant girdle around your hips, you shine like the Mandara
    mountain
encircled with snakes. You shine also with peacock plumes standing erect on
    your head,
and you have sanctified the celestial regions by vowing perpetual maidenhood.
O foremost among deities, extend to me your grace, show me your mercy,
and be the source of blessings to me. You are Jaya and Vijaya,
and it is you who give victory in battle. Grant me victory, O goddess,
and give me boons also at this hour of distress. O Kali, O Kali, you are the great
    Kali,
ever fond of wine and meat and animal sacrifice.
You are able to go everywhere at will and to bestow boons on your devotees,
and you are always followed in your journeys by Brahma and the other gods.
By them who call upon you for the relief of their burdens, and by them also
who bow to you at daybreak on earth, there is nothing that cannot be attained.
And because you rescue people from difficulties,
whether they are afflicted in the wilderness or sinking in the great ocean,
you are called Durga. You are the sole refuge of men when attacked by robbers
or while afflicted in crossing streams and seas or in wilderness and forests.
Those men who remember you are never prostrated, O great goddess.
You are fame, you are prosperity, you are steadiness, and you are success;
you are the wife, you are men's offspring, you are knowledge, and you are the
    intellect.
You are the two twilights, the night sleep, light—both solar and lunar—
beauty, forgiveness, mercy, and every other thing.
You dispel your devotees' fetters, ignorance, loss of children and loss of wealth,
disease, death, and fear. I, who have been deprived of my kingdom, seek your
    protection.
Be kind as you are to all who seek your protection;
                    be affectionate to all your devotees, watch over us!"
Thus praised, the goddess showed herself to the son of Pandu,
and she addressed him in these words: "O mighty king, listen to what I say.
You have vanquished and slain the ranks of the Kauravas through my grace,
and victory in battle will soon be yours. You shall again lord it over the entire
    earth,
                    having cleared your dominions of thorns.

Through my grace, joy and health shall be yours, and they who recite my
    attributes
shall be freed from their sins and made happy.
I will bestow upon them kingdom, long life, beauty of person, and offspring.
As for those who invoke me, as you did—in exile or in the city, in the midst of
    battle
or in forests or in inaccessible deserts, in seas or in mountain fastnesses—
there is nothing that they will not obtain in this world.
And he will achieve success in every business who listens to, or recites with
    devotion,
this excellent hymn. Through my grace neither the Kuru's spies
nor those who dwell in the country of the Matsyas
will succeed in recognizing you all as long as you reside in Virata's city!"
And having said these words to Yudhishthira, the goddess disappeared.

◆

Tying up in his clothing dice made of gold and set with lapis lazuli,
and holding them under his arm, King Yudhishthira made his appearance
before King Virata, who was seated in his court.
And beholding this stranger, who looked like the moon hidden in clouds,
King Virata addressed his counselors and the twice-born Brahmanas and the
    charioteers
and the Vaisyas and others: "Find out who it is, so much like a king,
who visits my court for the first time. He cannot be a Brahmana.
My guess would be that he is a man of men, and a lord of earth.
He has neither slaves nor cars nor elephants, and yet he shines like Indra himself.
The marks on his person show him to be one whose locks
have undergone the sacred investiture. This is my belief.
He approaches me without hesitation, even as an elephant in rut
                      approaches a collection of lotuses!"
As the king was pondering these thoughts, Yudhishthira came before Virata
and addressed him: "O king, I am a Brahmana who has lost his all,
and I come to you for the means of subsistence.
I desire to live here with you, acting under your commands."
The king replied: "You are welcome. Accept the appointment you ask for!"
King Virata then addressed him with a glad heart: "I ask you, in affection,
from the dominions of what king do you come here?
Tell me also your name and family, and what knowledge or skills you have."
Yudhishthira said: "My name is Kanka, and I am a Brahmana of the Vaiyaghra
    family.
I am skilled in casting dice, and formerly I was a friend of Yudhishthira."
Virata replied: "I will grant you whatever boon you may desire.
I like even cunning gamblers. But you are like a god, and you deserve a
    kingdom."
Yudhishthira said: "I ask, O lord of earth, that I may not be involved in any dispute

on account of dice with low people. Further, anyone I defeat at dice shall pay me
and not be permitted to retain what I have won."
Virata replied: "I shall slay anyone who may happen to displease you,
and should he be one of the twice-born ones, I shall banish him from my
　　dominions.
Let the assembled subjects listen! Kanka is as much lord of this realm as I myself.
You, Kanka, shall be my friend and shall ride the same vehicles as I.
And there shall be at your disposal apparel in plenty, and various viands and
　　drinks.
And you shall look into my affairs, both internal and external.
And for you all my doors shall be open. When men out of employment
or of strained circumstances apply to you, bring their words to me, day or night,
and I will give them whatever they desire. No fear shall be yours while you reside
　　here."
Having thus had an interview with Virata's king, and having received boons
　　from him,
that bull among men lived happily, highly regarded by all.
Nor could anyone discover his identity as he lived there.

✦

Then another approached King Virata. With the playful gait of a lion,
and holding in hand a cooking ladle and a spoon,
and also an unsheathed sword of sable hue and without a spot on the blade,
he came in the guise of a cook, illumining all around him by his splendor,
like the sun discovering the whole world. Attired in black,
he approached the king of the Matsyas.
　　　　　　　　　　　　　Beholding that kinglike person before him,
Virata addressed his assembled subjects: "Who is that youth,
with shoulders broad like those of a lion, and so exceedingly handsome?
Revolving the matter in my mind, I cannot ascertain who he is,
nor can I with even serious thought guess his intention in coming here.
It seems to me that he is either the king of the Gandharvas or Purandara himself.
Ascertain who stands before my eyes. Let him have what he seeks."
Swift-footed messengers went up to the son of Kunti
and informed the younger brother of Yudhishthira of everything the king had
　　said.
He approached Virata and said: "O foremost among kings, I am a cook, Vallava
　　by name.
I am skilled in preparing dishes. Employ me in your kitchen!"
Virata said: "I do not believe that cooking is your office.
You resemble the deity of a thousand eyes; and in grace and beauty and prowess,
　　　　　　　　　　　　you shine among these all as a king!"
Bhima replied: "O king of kings, I am your cook and servant.
It is not only curries that I know about, O monarch,
although King Yudhishthira always used to approve the taste of my dishes.
I am also a wrestler, and there is no one who is equal to me in strength.

Even in fights with lions and elephants, I shall contribute to your entertainment."
Virata said: "You will do what you wish, as you describe yourself as having skill.
I do not, however, think that this office is worthy of you,
for you deserve this entire earth girt round by the sea. But do as you like.
Be the superintendent of my kitchen, where you will be placed at the head
of those I have appointed there." Bhima soon became the favorite of King
    Virata,
and he lived there recognized neither by the other servants of Virata nor by
    anyone else.

✦

Binding her long, black, soft, fine, and faultless tresses into a knotted braid,
Draupadi of black eyes and sweet smiles threw it upon her right shoulder
and concealed it under a cloth. She wore a single piece of dirty though costly
    fabric.
And dressing herself as a Sairindhri, she wandered in seeming affliction.
Men and women asked her: "Who are you? And what do you seek?"
She replied: "I am a king's Sairindhri. I desire to serve anyone who will
    maintain me."
But considering her beauty and dress, and hearing her speech that was so sweet,
the people could not believe she was a maidservant in search of subsistence.
But it came to pass that Virata's beloved queen, daughter of the king of Kekaya,
while looking out from the terrace saw Draupadi,
forlorn and clad in a single piece of cloth. The queen addressed her, saying:
"O beautiful one, who are you, and what do you seek?"
Draupadi said: "O queen, I am Sairindhri. I will serve anyone who will
    maintain me."
Then Sudeshna, the queen, said: "What you say of your calling is hardly
    compatible
with so much beauty. You might rather be the mistress of servants.
Your heels are not prominent, and your thighs touch each other.
Your intelligence is great, and your navel deep, and your words solemn.
And your toes, bust, hips, back, sides, and toenails and palms are all well
    developed.
Your speech is sweet as the song of the swan.
Like a Kashmiri mare, you are furnished with every auspicious mark.
Your eyelashes are beautifully curled, and your nether lip is like the ruddy
    ground.
Your waist is slender, your neck bears lines that resemble those of the conch,
and your veins are scarcely visible. Indeed, your countenance is like the full
    moon,
and your eyes are like leaves of the autumnal lotus, and your body is fragrant as
    the lotus.
In beauty you resemble Sri herself. Tell me, beautiful damsel, who you are."
Draupadi replied: "I am a maidservant of the Sairindhri class.
I know how to dress hair, to pound fragrant substances for preparing unguents,

and also how to make garlands of jasmines and lotuses and blue lilies and
    champakas.
Formerly I served Krishna's favorite queen, Satyabhama,
and also Draupadi, the wife of the Pandavas and the foremost beauty of the
    Kuru race.
I wander about alone, earning good food and dress; and as long as I get these,
I live wherever they are obtainable. Draupadi called me Malini, meaning '*Maker
    of Garlands.*'"
Hearing this, Sudeshna said: "I would retain you myself
if the doubt did not cross my mind that the king would be attracted to you.
Attracted by your beauty, the females of the household and my maids are
    looking at you.
What male person can resist you? Surely, beholding your superhuman beauty,
King Virata is sure to forsake me and will turn to you with his whole heart.
With your faultless limbs and your large eyes casting quick glances,
anyone you look upon is sure to be stricken with desire.
He who sees you often will surely catch the flame. Even as the crab conceives
for her own ruin, I may bring destruction upon myself by harboring you."
Draupadi replied: "Neither Virata nor any other person
will be able to have me, for my five youthful husbands,
who are Gandharvas and sons of a Gandharva king of exceeding power,
always protect me. None can do me a wrong.
It is the wish of my Gandharva husbands that I should serve
only such persons as will not give me to touch food already partaken of by another,
or tell me to wash their feet. Any man who attempts to have me like any
    common woman
meets with death that very night, for those Gandharvas always protect me secretly."
Sudeshna said: "You bring delight to my heart.
If it is as you say, I will take you into my household.
You shall not have food that has been partaken of by another, or wash anyone's
    feet."
Thus addressed by Virata's wife, Draupadi began to live in that city.

✦

Then, clad in a cowherd's dress, and speaking the dialect of cowherds,
Sahadeva came to the cattle pen of Virata's city.
The king was struck with amazement at that splendid bull among men
and told his men to summon Sahadeva. When he came, the king addressed him:
"To whom do you belong? From where do you come? And what work do you
    seek?
I have never seen you before. Tell me about yourself."
Sahadeva answered in accents as deep as the roar of a cloud:
"I am a Vaisya, Arishtanemi by name. People used to call me Tantripal.
I was a cowherd for the sons of Pandu.
I intend now to live beside you, for I do not know where those lions among
    kings are.

I cannot live without service and should not like to enter the service of anyone
    but you."
Virata replied: "You must either be a Brahmana or a Kshatriya.
You look as if you were the lord of the earth. The office of a Vaisya is not fit
    for you.
Tell me from the dominions of what king you come,
and what you know, and in what capacity you would remain with us,
                        and also what pay you would accept."
Sahadeva answered: "Yudhishthira, the eldest of the five sons of Pandu,
had one division of cattle numbering eight hundred and ten thousand;
and another, ten thousand; and another again, twenty thousand; and so on.
I was employed in keeping those cattle.
I know the present, the past, and the future of all cattle living within ten *yojanas*.
The Kuru king, Yudhishthira, was well pleased with me.
I am also acquainted with the means that aid cattle in multiplying within a short
    time,
and by which they may enjoy immunity from disease.
I can also single out bulls having auspicious marks for which men worship them
and, by smelling their urine, those by which the barren may conceive."
Virata said: "I have a hundred thousand cattle divided into distinct herds.
All those, together with their keepers, I place in your charge."
Then, undiscovered by that monarch, Sahadeva began to live happily.
Nor did anyone besides his brothers recognize him.

✦

There next appeared at the gates a person of enormous size and exquisite
    beauty,
decked in the ornaments of women and wearing large earrings
and beautiful conch bracelets overlaid with gold.
That mighty-armed individual with long and abundant hair floating about his
    neck
resembled an elephant in gait. Shaking the very earth with his tread,
he approached Virata and stood before him. Beholding the son of the great Indra,
shining with exquisite luster and having the gait of a mighty elephant,
whose true form was concealed in disguise, the king addressed his courtiers,
    saying:
"From where does this person come? I have never heard of him before."
The men present spoke of the newcomer as one unknown to them,
and the king wonderingly said to the stranger: "Possessed of great strength,
you are like a celestial. Wearing conch bracelets overlaid with gold,
a braid, and earrings, you shine like one who rides on chariots,
wandering about equipped with mail and bow and arrows,
and decked with garlands and fine hair.
I am old and desirous of relinquishing my burden.
Consider yourself my son, and rule all the Matsyas.
It seems to me that such a person as you cannot possibly be of the neuter sex."

Arjuna said: "I sing, dance, and play on instruments.
Assign me to Princess Uttara. I shall be dancing master to the royal maiden.
As to how I have come by this form, what will it avail you to hear the account,
which will only augment my pain? Know me to be Vrihannala,
a son or daughter without father or mother."
Virata said: "Vrihannala, I give you what you desire.
Instruct my daughter and those like her in dancing.
To me, however, this office seems unworthy of you.
You deserve the dominion of the entire earth girt round by the ocean."
The king of the Matsyas then tested Vrihannala in dancing, music, and other
    fine arts
and, consulting with his various ministers, forthwith had him examined by women.
Learning that his impotence was of a permanent nature,
he sent him to the maiden's apartments. There the mighty Arjuna gave lessons
in singing and instrumental music to the daughter of Virata, her friends, and
    her maids,
and he soon won their good graces. In this manner, Arjuna lived there in
    disguise,
taking pleasure in their company and unknown to the people within and
    without the palace.

✦

After a while, another son of Pandu was seen making his way toward King Virata.
As he advanced, he seemed to everyone like a solar orb emerged from the clouds.
He observed the horses around him and, seeing this, the king of the Matsyas said:
"I wonder where this man comes from. He looks intently at my steeds.
He must be proficient in horsemanship. Let him be ushered into my presence
    quickly.
                         He is a warrior and looks like a god!"
That destroyer of foes then went up to the king and said to him:
"Victory to you, O king, and blessings upon you. As a trainer of horses,
I have always been highly esteemed by kings. I will be a clever keeper of your
    horses."
Virata said: "I will give you vehicles, wealth, and spacious quarters.
You shall manage my horses. But first tell me where you come from, who you are,
and how you happen to come here. Tell us also all the arts of which you are
    master."
Nakula replied: "As you know, Yudhishthira is the eldest of the five sons of Pandu.
I was formerly employed by him to keep his horses.
I am acquainted with the temper of steeds and know the art of breaking them.
I know also how to correct vicious horses and all the methods of treating their
    diseases.
No animal in my hands becomes weak or ill.
Even mares in my hands are never vicious. People call me Granthika."
Virata said: "Whatever horses I have, I consign to your care.
And all the keepers of my horses and all my charioteers will be subordinate to you.

If this suits you, say what remuneration you desire.

But you resemble a celestial, and the office of groomsman is not worthy of you.

Your appearance here pleases me as much as if Yudhishthira himself were here.

How does that blameless son of Pandu dwell in the forest, destitute of servants?"

Like a chief of the Gandharvas, Nakula was treated thus respectfully by King
  Virata.

And he conducted himself there in such a manner

as to make himself dear and agreeable to all in the palace.

No one recognized him while he lived under Virata's protection.

It was in this manner, then, that the sons of Pandu lived in the country of the
  Matsyas.

And, true to their pledge, they passed their days incognito with great composure.

✦

By the grace of the sage Trinavindu and of the high-souled lord of justice,

the Pandavas lived unrecognized by others in the city of Virata.

Yudhishthira made himself agreeable as a courtier to Virata

and to Virata's sons and to all the Matsyas. An adept in the mysteries of dice,

the son of Pandu caused them to play according to his pleasure

and made them sit together in the dice hall like a row of birds bound on a string.

And King Yudhishthira, unknown to the monarch, distributed among his
  brothers

the wealth he won from Virata. Bhimasena, for his part, sold to Yudhishthira for
  a price

meat and viands of various kinds, which he obtained from the king.

And Arjuna distributed among all his brothers the proceeds of worn-out clothes,

which he earned in the inner apartments of the palace.

Sahadeva, too, disguised as a cowherd, gave his brothers milk, curds, and
  clarified butter.

And Nakula shared the money the king gave him for managing the horses.

Draupadi, herself in a pitiable condition, looked after all those brothers

and behaved in such a way as to remain unrecognized.

And those lords of men, apprehensive of danger from the son of Dhritarashtra,

continued to dwell there in concealment, watching over their wife, Draupadi.

After three months had passed, there was a grand festival in honor of the divine
  Brahma,

which was celebrated with pomp in the country of the Matsyas.

To this there came athletes from all quarters by the thousands,

like hosts of celestials to the abode of Brahma or of Shiva, to witness that festival.

And they were endowed with huge bodies and great prowess.

Proud of their strength, they were highly honored by the king.

Their shoulders and waists and necks were like those of lions,

and their bodies were very clean, and their hearts were quite at ease.

Many times they had won success in the lists in the presence of kings.

Among them was one who towered above the rest and challenged them all to a
  combat.

None dared to approach him as he proudly stalked the arena.
When all the athletes stood sad and dispirited,
the king of the Matsyas made him fight with his cook.
Urged by the king, Bhima made up his mind reluctantly, for he could not disobey
a royal command. That tiger among men then, having worshipped the king,
entered the spacious arena, pacing with the wary steps of a tiger.
The son of Kunti then girded up his loins, to the great delight of the spectators.
Bhima then summoned to the combat that athlete known by the name of Jimuta,
who was like the Asura Vritra, whose prowess was widely known.
Both of them were possessed of great courage and formidable prowess.
They were like a couple of infuriated elephants, each sixty years old.
The two men then engaged in a wrestling combat, each eager to vanquish the
    other.
Terrible was the encounter that then took place between them,
like the clash of a thunderbolt against a stony mountainside.
Each of them, exceedingly powerful, delighted in the other's strength,
and each stood eager to take advantage of his adversary's lapse.
Various were the modes of attack and defense as each dashed against the other
and flung his adversary far away. Each cast the other down
and pressed him to the ground. And each got up again and squeezed the other
    in his arms.
Each threw the other violently off his feet by boxing him on the breast.
And each caught the other by the legs, whirled him around, and threw him to
    the ground.
Each slapped the other with his palms,
and each struck the other with outstretched fingers,
which were like spears as each thrust his fingernails into the other's body.
They gave each other violent kicks and struck knee and head against head,
producing the crash of one stone against another. In this manner, the furious
    combat
between those warriors raged on without weapons,
sustained mainly by the power of their arms and their physical and mental
    energy,
to the infinite delight of the spectators. All the people took deep interest in that
    encounter
between those powerful wrestlers, who fought like Indra and the Asura Vritra,
and they cheered both of them with loud acclamations and applause.
The broad-chested and long-armed experts in wrestling pulled and pressed and
    whirled
and hurled each other down and struck each other with their knees,
expressing all the while their scorn for each other in loud voices.
In this way they fought with their bare arms, which were like spiked maces of iron.
And at last the powerful and mighty-armed Bhima, shouting aloud,
seized the vociferous athlete by the arms, even as the lion seizes the elephant,
and, taking him up from the ground and holding him aloft,
began to whirl him around, to the great astonishment of the assembled athletes
and the people of Matsya. Having whirled him around and around

a hundred times, until he was insensible, Bhima finally dashed him to death
on the ground. The brave and renowned Jimuta was thus killed.
Virata and his friends were filled with great delight.
In the exuberance of his joy, the noble-minded king rewarded Vallava then and
there.
Killing numerous athletes and many others of great strength, he pleased the king.
When no one else could be found to encounter him in the lists,
the king made him fight with tigers and lions and elephants.
The king also made him battle with furious and powerful lions in the harem,
for the entertainment of the ladies. And Arjuna, too, pleased the king
and all the ladies of the inner apartments by singing and dancing.
And Nakula pleased Virata, that best of kings, by showing him well-trained steeds
that followed him wherever he went. And the king rewarded him with ample
presents.
And seeing around Sahadeva a herd of well-trained bullocks,
Virata bestowed upon him also wealth of diverse kinds.
Thus did those eminent persons live there in disguise, serving King Virata.

26

Kichaka

It came to pass that as the year was about to expire, the redoubtable Kichaka,
the commander of Virata's forces, chanced to see Draupadi.
And beholding that lady endowed with the splendor of a daughter of the
celestials,
treading the earth like a goddess, Kichaka, afflicted with the shafts of Kama,
desired to possess her. Burning with desire's flame,
Virata's general came to Sudeshna, his sister,
and said to her: "I have never before seen this beautiful lady in King Virata's
palace.
This damsel maddens me with her beauty, even as a new wine
maddens one with its fragrance. Tell me, who is this graceful and captivating lady
with the beauty of a goddess? Whose is she, and whence has she come?
It seems to me that there is no other medicine for my illness but her.
One like her is ill suited to serve you. Let her instead rule over me and whatever
is mine.
Let her grace my spacious and beautiful palace,
decked with various ornaments of gold, full of viands and drinks in profusion,
with excellent plates and every kind of plenty, besides elephants, horses and cars."
Having thus consulted with Sudeshna, Kichaka went to Princess Draupadi
and, like a jackal in the forest accosting a lioness, spoke these words:
"Who and whose are you, O beautiful one? And whence have you come
to the city of Virata? Your beauty and gracefulness are of the very first order,
and the comeliness of your features is unparalleled.
With its loveliness, your face shines like the resplendent moon.
Your eyes are like lotus petals. Your speech resembles the notes of the kanka
bird.
Never before have I beheld a woman possessed of beauty like yours.
Are you Lakshmi herself, having her abode in the midst of lotuses,
or are you called Bhuti? With beauty like Rati's, are you she who sports
in the embraces of the god of love?
Who is there in the whole world who will not succumb to the influence of desire,
beholding your face? Endowed with unrivaled beauty and celestial grace
of the most attractive kind, that face of yours is like the full moon,
its celestial effulgence resembling his radiant face and its smile resembling his
soft light.

Your breasts, so beautiful and well developed and endowed with unrivaled
     gracefulness,
and deep and well rounded and without any space between them,
are worthy of being decked with necklaces of gold. They are the whips of Kama
urging me forward. O damsel of slender waist,
as I behold that waist of yours, marked with four wrinkles and measuring but a
     span,
and as I see you slightly stooping forward because of the weight of your breasts,
and as I look on those graceful hips of yours, broad as the banks of a river,
the incurable fever of desire afflicts me sorely.
Quench that fire kindled by Kama. Union with you is a rain-charged cloud,
and your surrender is the shower that the cloud may drop.
You must relieve me of my agony by favoring me with your embraces
and sporting with me to satiety.
Do not dwell here in misery. Let unrivaled delight be yours.
This beauty of yours and this prime of your youth are now without their use.
You do not shine and are like a graceful garland lying unused and unworn.
I will forsake all my old wives. Let them become your slaves.
And I will stay by you as your slave, ever obedient to you."
Draupadi replied: "In desiring me, a female servant of low extraction
employed in the despicable office of dressing hair,
you desire one who does not deserve that honor. Then again, I am the wife of
     others.
Therefore, I thank you and wish that good betide you,
but this conduct of yours is not proper. Remember the precept of morality:
that persons should take delight only in their wedded wives.
Abstaining from improper acts is always the study of those who are good.
Overcome by ignorance, sinful men under the influence of desire
come either to extreme infamy or to dreadful calamity."
But the wicked Kichaka, losing control over his senses and overcome by lust,
although aware of the numerous evils of fornication condemned by everybody
and sometimes leading to the destruction of life itself,
then spoke to Draupadi: "You must not disregard me. I am under the power of
     Kama.
If you disregard me, you will repent of it afterward.
The real lord of this entire kingdom, dear lady, is myself. I am the one
upon whom the people of this realm depend. In energy and prowess
I am unrivaled on earth. Why it is that, having it in your power to enjoy here
every object of desire and every luxury and comfort without its equal,
you prefer servitude? Become the mistress of this kingdom, which I shall confer
     on you."
But that chaste daughter of Drupada answered him reprovingly:
"Do not act foolishly, and do not throw away your life.
I am protected by my five husbands. You cannot have me.
I have Gandharvas for my husbands. Enraged, they will slay you.
Do not bring destruction on yourself. You intend to tread a path inaccessible
     to men.

You are like a foolish child that stands on one shore of the ocean
and intends to cross over to the other side. Why do you solicit me so persistently,
even as a sick person wishes for the night that will put a stop to his existence?
Why do you desire me like an infant lying on its mother's lap and wishing to
    catch the moon?
For you, who thus solicit those Gandharvas' beloved wife, there is no refuge
    either on earth or in the sky.
Have you no sense? You should seek what is good for you and what will save your
    life."
Rejected thus by the princess, Kichaka was afflicted with maddening lust
and, forgetting all sense of propriety, he addressed his sister Sudeshna:
"Do whatever you have to do so that your Sairindhri may come into my arms.
Find some means by which the damsel of the gait of an elephant may accept me.
                    I am dying of absorbing desire."
That gentle lady, the intelligent queen of Virata, was touched with pity.
And, having reflected on Kichaka's purpose and on the anxiety of her
    Sairindhri,
Sudeshna answered her brother: "On the occasion of some festival,
procure viands and wines for me. I shall then send my Sairindhri to you
on the pretense of fetching wine. And when she arrives in solitude, free from
    interruption,
you may humor her as you like. Thus soothed, she may incline her mind to you."
He left his sister's apartments. And he soon procured wines well filtered
and worthy of a king. And employing skilled cooks, he prepared choice viands
and delicious drinks and many kinds of meat of the highest excellence.
And when all this had been done, that gentle lady Sudeshna said to her
    Sairindhri:
"Go to Kichaka to fetch wine, for I am afflicted with thirst."
The Sairindhri replied: "Princess, I shall not be able to repair to Kichaka's
    apartments.
You know how shameless he is. I shall not lead a lustful life in your palace,
faithless to my husbands. You remember the conditions I set, entering your
    service.
The foolish Kichaka, afflicted by the god of desire, will offer me insult.
Therefore, I cannot go to his quarters. You have many maids. Send one of them."
Sudeshna said: "If you are sent by me, surely he will not harm you."
And she handed over a golden vessel furnished with a cover.
Filled with apprehension, and weeping, Draupadi prayed for the protection of
    the gods
and set out for Kichaka's abode to fetch the wine.
She then adored Surya for a moment. And Surya, having considered what she
    urged,
commanded a Rakshasa to protect her invisibly.
From that time the Rakshasa attended upon that blameless lady under all
    circumstances.

✦

In Kichaka's presence she was like a frightened doe.

He, meanwhile, experienced the joy of a person who wishes to cross to the other shore

when he at last obtains a boat. Kichaka said: "You are welcome.

Surely the night that is gone has brought me an auspicious day,

for I have got you today as the mistress of my house. Do what is agreeable to me.

Let golden chains, and conchs and bright earrings made of gold,

and beautiful rubies and gems, and silken robes and deerskins be brought for you.

I have also an excellent bed prepared for you.

Come, sit upon it and drink with me the wine prepared from the honey flower."

Draupadi said: "I have been sent to you by the princess to fetch wine.

Bring me wine quickly, for she told me that she is exceedingly thirsty."

To this Kichaka said: "Others will carry what the princess wants."

      And he caught hold of Draupadi's right arm.

Draupadi exclaimed: "As I have never been unfaithful to my husbands,

even in thought, I swear, O wretch, that I shall see you dragged

and lying powerless on the ground!" As that large-eyed lady reproved him in that strain,

Kichaka seized the end of her upper garment as she attempted to run away.

The beautiful princess was unable to tolerate this, and, trembling with wrath,

she dashed him to the ground. He tumbled down like a tree whose roots had been cut.

And, still trembling, she rushed to the court where King Yudhishthira was,

for protection. While she ran with all her speed,

Kichaka followed her, seized her by the hair, and threw her down to the ground.

In the presence of the king, he kicked her. The Rakshasa that had been sent by Surya

to protect Draupadi then gave Kichaka a shove with a force mighty as that of the wind.

And, overpowered by the force of the Rakshasa, Kichaka reeled and fell down senseless.

Both Yudhishthira and Bhimasena, who were seated there, saw that outrage on Draupadi.

Eager for the destruction of the wicked Kichaka, the illustrious Bhima gnashed his teeth,

and his forehead was covered with sweat. A smoky exhalation shot forth from his eyes,

and his eyelashes stood on end. That slayer of hostile heroes

pressed his forehead with his hands. And, in fury, he was on the point of starting up,

but King Yudhishthira, apprehensive of discovery, squeezed his thumbs

and commanded him to forbear. He said: "Look for trees for fuel.

If you are in need of kindling, then go out and fell trees."

The weeping Draupadi approached the entrance of the court

and saw her melancholy lords, still desirous of keeping up their disguises.

With eyes afire, she spoke these words to the king of the Matsyas:

"Alas, the son of a Suta has kicked today the proud and beloved wife

of those whose foe can never sleep in peace even if four kingdoms intervene
between him and them.
Alas, the son of a Suta has kicked today the proud and beloved wife
of those truthful personages who are devoted to Brahmanas
and who always give away without having been asked anything at all in gift.
Alas! the son of a Suta has kicked today the proud and beloved wife
of those who travel with the continual sounds of kettledrums and bowstrings.
Alas, the son of a Suta has kicked today the proud and beloved wife
of those who are possessed of abundant energy and might
and who are liberal in gifts and proud of their dignity.
Alas, the son of a Suta has kicked today the proud and beloved wife
of those who, if they had not been fettered by ties of duty, could destroy this
　　entire world.
Where, alas, are those mighty warriors today who, though living in disguise,
have always granted protection to those who solicit it?
Why do those heroes today, endowed as they are with strength and immeasurable
　　energy,
quietly suffer, like eunuchs, as their dear and chaste wife is thus insulted by a
　　Suta's son?
What can I, a weak woman, do when Virata, deficient in virtue, permits me
to be thus wronged by a villain? You do not, O king, act like a king toward this
　　Kichaka.
Your behavior is like that of a robber and does not shine in a court.
That I should thus be insulted in your very presence, O Matsya, is highly
　　improper.
Let all the courtiers here look at this violence of Kichaka.
He is ignorant of duty and morality, and Matsya is equally so.
These courtiers, too, who wait upon such a king, are destitute of virtue."
With these and other words of the same kind,
the beautiful Draupadi with tearful eyes rebuked the king of the Matsyas.
And Virata said: "I do not know what your dispute has been out of our sight.
Not knowing the true cause, how can I show my discrimination?"
Then the courtiers, having learned everything, applauded Draupadi,
and they all exclaimed: "Well done! Well done!" And they censured Kichaka.
The courtiers said: "The person who owns this large-eyed lady for his wife
possesses what is of exceeding value, and he has no occasion to indulge in any
　　grief.
Surely a damsel of such transcendent beauty and perfectly faultless limbs
is rare among men. Indeed, it seems to us that she is a goddess."
While the courtiers were thus applauding Draupadi, Yudhishthira's forehead,
from ire, became covered with sweat. That bull of the Kuru race addressed his
　　spouse:
"Do not stay here, O Sairindhri, but retire to the apartments of Sudeshna.
The wives of heroes bear affliction for the sake of their husbands,
and, undergoing toil in ministering unto their lords, they attain to a region
where their husbands may go. Your Gandharva husbands, effulgent as the sun,
do not, I imagine, consider this an occasion for manifesting their wrath,

for otherwise they would rush to your aid. O Sairindhri,

you are ignorant of the timeliness of things, and it is for this that you weep like
an actress,

interrupting the play of dice in Matsya's court. Retire, O Sairindhri!

The Gandharvas will do what is agreeable to you and

take the life of him who has wronged you."

Then that Sairindhri replied: "They of whom I am the wedded wife are
extremely kind.

And as the eldest of them all is addicted to dice, they are liable to be oppressed
by all."

Having said this, the fair-hipped Draupadi, with disheveled hair and eyes red in
anger,

ran toward the apartments of Sudeshna. Because she had wept so long,

her face looked like the lunar disc in the firmament, emerged from the clouds.

Seeing her in that condition, Sudeshna asked: "Who has insulted you? Why do
you weep?

Who has done you wrong? What has caused your grief?"

Draupadi answered: "As I went to fetch wine for you, Kichaka struck me in the
court

in the presence of the king, as if in the midst of a solitary wood."

Hearing this, Sudeshna said: "As Kichaka, maddened by lust, has insulted you,

who are incapable of being possessed by him, I shall cause him to be slain if you
wish it."

But Draupadi replied: "Others will slay him, even they whom he has wronged.

I think it is clear that he will go to the abode of Yama this very day!"

✦

Drupada's daughter of dark hue and slender waist,

eagerly wishing for the destruction of Virata's general, went to her quarters

and performed her ablutions. Washing her body and clothes, she wept

and pondered the means of dispelling her grief. She said to herself:

What am I to do? Where shall I go? And, thinking thus, she remembered Bhima

and thought: *No one but Bhima can accomplish the purpose on which my heart is set!*

She rose up at night, left her bed, and speedily proceeded toward Bhimasena's
quarters

to ask him how he could sleep while that wretched commander of Virata's forces,

who was her foe, yet lived, having perpetrated that day an act so foul.

Draupadi of sweet smiles, finding Bhimasena in the cooking apartments,

approached him with the eagerness of a three-year-old cow brought up in the
woods

approaching a powerful bull in her first season, or of a she-crane living by the
water's side

approaching her mate in the pairing season. The princess of Panchala

embraced the second son of Pandu, even as a creeper embraces a huge and
mighty sala tree

on the banks of the Gomati. Embracing him with her arms,

she awakened him as a lioness awakens a sleeping lion in a trackless forest.
And, embracing Bhimasena even as a she-elephant embraces her mighty mate,
the faultless Draupadi addressed him: "Arise, arise!
Why do you lie down like one who is dead?
Surely no living man suffers a wretch to live who has disgraced his wife!"
Bhima then rose up and sat upon his couch overlaid with rich bedding.
And he said: "Why have you come here in such a hurry? Your color is gone,
and you look lean and pale. Tell me everything in detail.
Having heard everything, I shall apply the remedy.
I alone am entitled to your confidence in all things,
for it is I who deliver you from perils again and again!
Tell me quickly your wish, and your purpose,
                    and then return to your bed before others awake."
Relating her woes to Bhimasena, Draupadi began to weep silently,
and with words choked in tears, and sighing repeatedly, she said to Bhima:
"Great must have been my offense of old for, unfortunate as I am,
I am yet alive, when it is clear that I should die."
Then Bhima covered his face with those delicate hands of his wife,
marked as they were with corns, and he began to weep. Full of woe, he said:
"Shame on the might of my arms, and shame on the Gandiva of Arjuna,
inasmuch as your hands, red before, now are covered with corns.
I would have caused carnage in Virata's court
but for the fact that Yudhishthira eyed me and forbade it.
Otherwise, like a mighty elephant, I would, without hesitation,
                    have crushed the head of Kichaka
intoxicated with the pride of sovereignty.
When I saw him kick you, I imagined at that instant a wholesale slaughter of the
    Matsyas.
Yudhishthira, however, forbade me; and, understanding his intention,
I have kept quiet. That we have been deprived of our kingdom,
that I have not yet slain the Kurus, that I have not yet taken the heads of
    Suyodhana
and Karna, and Suvala's son Sakuni, and the wicked Duhsasana—
these acts and omissions are consuming every limb of mine.
The thought of them pains my heart, as if a javelin were implanted in it.
If King Yudhishthira hears your rebukes, he will surely put an end to Kichaka's life.
There remains only a short while more, even half a month,
and when the thirteenth year is complete, you will again become the queen of a
    king."
Draupadi said: "It is from grief alone that I have shed these tears.
I do not censure Yudhishthira, nor is there any use in dwelling on the past.
But come forward to the work of the hour. Jealous of my beauty, Sudeshna the
    sister of Kichaka,
pains me by her efforts to prevent the king from taking a fancy to me.
And the wicked-souled Kichaka of immoral ways constantly solicits me.
Angry with him for this, but suppressing my wrath, I answered that wretch,
    saying:

'Kichaka, protect yourself. I am the beloved queen and wife of five Gandharvas.
Those heroes will slay you who are so rash.' But Kichaka replied: 'I have no fear
of the Gandharvas, O Sairindhri of sweet smiles.
I will slay a hundred thousand Gandharvas in battle. Therefore, O timid one,
    consent!'
I again addressed him, saying: 'You are no match for those illustrious Gandharvas.
Of respectable parentage and good disposition, I always adhere to virtue
and never wish for the death of anyone. It is for this reason that I warn you, O
    Kichaka!'
At this, that man of wicked soul burst into loud laughter.
And then it happened that Sudeshna, urged by her brother,
moved by affection for him, and wanting to do him a favor,
dispatched me to him to fetch wine from his quarters!
At first he addressed me in sweet words, and when that failed, he became enraged
and intended to use violence. I rushed toward the palace where the king was.
Knocking me to the ground, that wretch then kicked me in the presence of the
    king,
and before the eyes of Kanka and many others,
including charioteers, royal favorites, elephant riders, and citizens.
I rebuked the king and Kanka again and again.
The king, however, neither restrained Kichaka nor punished him.
The principal ally of King Virata in war, the cruel Kichaka, bereft of virtue,
is loved by both the king and the queen. Brave, proud, sinful, adulterous,
and engrossed in all objects of enjoyment, he earns immense wealth from the king
and robs the possessions of others, even if they cry out in distress.
He never walks the path of virtue or performs any virtuous act.
Of wicked soul and vicious disposition, haughty and villainous,
and always afflicted by the shafts of Kama, though repulsed repeatedly,
if he sees me again, he will violate me. I shall then surely renounce my life.
Although you are striving to acquire virtue, your highly meritorious acts will
    come to naught.
You are now obeying your pledge, but you will lose your wife.
By protecting one's wife, one protects one's offspring,
and by protecting one's offspring, one protects oneself.
It is because one begets oneself in one's wife that the wise call the wife *jaya*.
The husband also should be protected by the wife,
who should be thinking: *How else will he take his birth in my womb?*
I have heard it from Brahmanas expounding the duties of the several orders
that a Kshatriya has no other duty than subduing enemies.
Alas, Kichaka kicked me in the presence of Yudhishthira the Just
and also of yourself, Bhimasena. Slay this wretch who has insulted me.
Smash this lustful man like an earthenware pot dashed upon a stone.
If tomorrow's sun sheds his rays upon him who is the source of many griefs of
    mine,
I shall surely mix poison in a drink and consume it,
                    for I never shall yield to Kichaka."
Draupadi then hid her face in Bhima's breast and began to weep.

Bhima embraced her and consoled her to the best of his power.
He wiped with his hands her tear-streaked face.
Then, thinking of Kichaka, and licking with his tongue the corners of his mouth,
Bhima, filled with wrath, spoke to that distressed lady:
"I will do as you say. I will slay Kichaka with all his friends tomorrow evening.
Renounce sorrow and grief, and arrange a meeting with Kichaka.
The dancing hall that the king of the Matsya has erected
is used by the girls for dancing during the day.
They repair, however, to their homes at night.
In that hall is an excellent and well-placed wooden bedstead
where I will make him see the spirits of his deceased grandsires.
But when you converse with him, you must manage it so that others may not
   hear you."

✦

When the night had passed, Kichaka went to the palace and accosted Draupadi,
saying: "Throwing you down in the court, I kicked you in the presence of the king.
And you could not obtain protection. Virata is the king of the Matsyas in name
   only.
Commanding the forces of this realm, it is I who am the real lord of the Matsyas.
Therefore, accept me cheerfully. I shall become your slave.
And I will immediately give you a hundred nishkas
and engage a hundred male and a hundred female servants to attend you
and will also bestow on you cars yoked with she-mules.
                    O timid lady, let our union take place."
Draupadi replied: "Kichaka, this is my condition.
Neither your friends nor your brothers should know your union with me.
I am in terror of detection by those illustrious Gandharvas.
Promise me this, and I yield to you." Kichaka said: "I will do as you say.
Afflicted by the god of love, I will repair alone to your abode for union with you
so that those Gandharvas may not learn of this act of yours."
Draupadi said: "When it is dark, go to the dancing hall erected by the king,
where the girls dance during the day. The Gandharvas do not know that place.
We shall then escape all eyes and all censure."
That half day seemed to Draupadi as long as a whole month.
And Kichaka returned home experiencing the greatest delight,
not knowing that he faced death in the form of a Sairindhri.
Deprived of his senses by lust, Kichaka became engaged in embellishing his
   person
with unguents and garlands and ornaments. While he was doing all this,
thinking of that damsel of large eyes, the day seemed to him to be without end.
And the beauty of Kichaka, about to forsake beauty forever, seemed to heighten,
like the wick of a burning lamp about to expire.
Absorbed in the contemplation of the expected meeting, he did not even see
how the day had departed. Meanwhile, Draupadi approached her husband Bhima
and stood before him in the kitchen. She said to him: "Just as you directed,

I have given Kichaka to understand that our meeting will take place in the
   dancing hall.
He will come alone at night to the empty hall. Slay him there.
Lift him up from the earth even as Krishna lifted up the Naga from the Yamuna.
Afflicted as I am with grief, wipe my tears, and protect your honor and that of
   your race."
Bhima said: "Except for the glad tidings you bring me, I need no other aid
   whatever.
The delight I feel on hearing from you about my coming encounter with Kichaka
is equal to what I felt in slaying Hidimva. I swear to you by truth,
by my brothers, and by morality that I will slay Kichaka,
even as the lord of the celestials slew Vritra.
I will crush Kichaka, and if the Matsyas fight for him, then I will slay them, too.
And slaying Duryodhana afterward, I shall win back the earth.
Let Yudhishthira continue to pay homage to the king of Matsya."
Draupadi said: "In order that you may not have to renounce the truth
already pledged to me, slay Kichaka in secret."
Bhima, assuring her, said: "I shall slay Kichaka together with his friends,
unknown to others during the darkness of the night.
I shall crush, even as an elephant crushes a vela fruit, the head of the wicked
   Kichaka,
                  who wishes for what is unattainable by him!"
Repairing to the place of assignation at night, Bhima sat down, disguising himself.
And he waited there in expectation of Kichaka like a lion lying in wait for a deer.
Kichaka, having embellished his person, came to the dancing hall at the
   appointed time.
Thinking of the assignation, he entered the chamber, which was enveloped in
   gloom.
Then that wretch came upon Bhima of incomparable prowess,
who had come a little before and had been waiting in a corner.
And as an insect approaches a flame, or a puny animal a lion,
so did Kichaka approach Bhima, who was lying on the bed and burning in anger
at the thought of the insult offered to Draupadi. And having approached Bhima,
Kichaka, possessed by lust, and with his heart and soul filled with ecstasy, said:
"I have already given many and various kinds of wealth to you
as well as a hundred maids and many fine robes, and also a mansion
adorned with beauteous and youthful maidservants
and embellished by every kind of sports and amusements.
And having set all those apart for you, I have come hither.
All of a sudden, women have begun to praise me, saying:
'There is not any other person like you in beauty and dress!' "
Hearing this, Bhima said: "It is well that you are handsome and that you praise
   yourself.
I think, however, that you have never before enjoyed such a pleasurable touch!
You know the ways of gallantry. Skilled in the art of lovemaking,
you are a favorite with women. There is none like you in this world!"
Saying this, the mighty-armed Bhima suddenly rose up and laughingly said:

"Your sister, O wretch, shall today behold you dragged by me to the ground,
like a mighty elephant, huge as a mountain, dragged to the ground by a lion.
When you are slain, that Sairindhri will live in peace, and we her husbands also."
Saying this, the mighty Bhima seized Kichaka by the hairs of his head,
which were adorned with garlands. Although seized with force by the hair,
Kichaka quickly freed his hair and grasped the arms of Bhima.
Then, between those lions among men, fired with wrath,
between that chief of the Kichaka clan and that best of men,
there ensued a hand-to-hand encounter like that between two powerful elephants
for a female elephant in the season of spring.
Both equally infuriated, and both eager for victory, both combatants raised their
    arms,
resembling snakes furnished with five hoods, and attacked each other
with their nails and teeth, wrought up to a frenzy of wrath.
Assailed by the powerful Kichaka, the resolute Bhima did not waver a single step.
Locked in each other's embrace, and dragging each other, they fought like
    mighty bulls.
With nails and teeth for their weapons, they had between them a fierce encounter,
like that of two furious tigers. The mighty Bhima then seized Kichaka,
and Kichaka, that foremost among strong persons, threw Bhima down with
    violence.
And as those mighty combatants fought on, the crash of their arms produced a
    loud noise,
like the clatter of splitting bamboos. Then Bhima threw Kichaka down by force
within the room and began to toss him about furiously,
even as a hurricane tosses a tree. Attacked thus by the powerful Bhima,
Kichaka grew weak and began to tremble. For all that, he tugged at the Pandava
to the best of his power. Attacking Bhima, and making him waver a little,
the mighty Kichaka struck him with his knees and brought him down to the
    ground.
But, overthrown by the powerful Kichaka, Bhima quickly rose up like Yama himself
with mace in hand. And thus that powerful Suta and the Pandava,
intoxicated with strength and challenging each other, grappled at midnight
in that solitary place. As they roared at each other in wrath,
that excellent and strong edifice began to shake. Slapped on the chest
by the mighty Bhima, Kichaka, fired with wrath, moved not a single step.
Bearing for a moment only that onslaught incapable of being borne on earth,
the Suta, overpowered by Bhima's might, became enfeebled.
And seeing him waning and weakening, Bhima endowed with great strength
forcibly drew Kichaka toward his breast and pressed hard.
And breathing hard again and again in wrath,
that best of victors forcibly seized Kichaka by the hair.
The mighty Bhima roared like a hungry tiger that has killed a large animal.
Finding him exhausted, Bhima bound him fast with his arms, as one binds a beast.
Then Bhima began to whirl the senseless Kichaka, who roared like a broken
    trumpet.
To pacify Draupadi's fury, Bhima grasped Kichaka's throat with his arms

and began to squeeze it. Assailing with his knees the waist of that worst of the
Kichakas,
all the limbs of whose body had been broken into fragments and whose eyes
were closed,
Bhima slew him, as one would slay a beast.
Then the son of Pandu began to roll him about on the ground.
And Bhima said: "Slaying this wretch who intended to violate our wife,
I am freed from the debt I owed to my brothers and have attained perfect peace."
And having said this, that foremost among men, his eyes red with wrath,
relinquished his hold on Kichaka, whose dress and ornaments had fallen from
his person,
whose eyes were still rolling, and whose body was still trembling.
That foremost among mighty persons, biting his lips in rage, again attacked
and thrust his arms and legs and neck and head into Kichaka's lifeless body,
crushing all its limbs and reducing it to a ball of flesh.
The mighty Bhimasena then showed Kichaka to Draupadi and said:
"Come, princess of Panchala, and see what has become of that lustful wretch!"
Saying this, Bhima pressed his feet upon the body of that wicked person.
Bhima then bade farewell to Draupadi and went back to the kitchen.
And Draupadi, having caused Kichaka to be slain, had her grief removed
and experienced the greatest delight. To the keepers of the dancing hall she said:
"Come and behold Kichaka, who had violated other people's wives,
lying down here, slain by my Gandharva husbands."
And hearing these words, the guards of the dancing hall
came by the thousands to that spot, torches in hand, and they beheld the lifeless
Kichaka
on the ground, drenched with blood.
And they were struck with amazement.
And seeing the overthrow of Kichaka, they said: "Where are his neck and his legs?"
And they all concluded that he had been killed by a Gandharva.

✦

Then all the relatives of Kichaka arrived and saw him there,
and they wailed aloud, surrounding him on all sides.
Beholding Kichaka with every limb mangled,
lying like a tortoise dragged to dry ground from the water,
they were overcome with fright, and the bristles of their bodies stood on end.
Seeing him crushed like a Danava by Indra, they took him for his funeral
obsequies.
Thus assembled, those persons of the Suta clan spied Draupadi,
who stood leaning on a nearby pillar, and exclaimed: "Let this unchaste woman
be slain
for whom Kichaka has himself lost his life. Or, without slaying her here,
let us cremate her with him who had lusted after her,
for it behooves us to accomplish what is agreeable to that deceased son of Suta."
Then they addressed Virata, saying: "It is for her sake that Kichaka has lost his life.

Let her, therefore, be cremated along with him.
It is right and just for you to grant this permission."
King Virata, knowing the prowess of the Suta, gave his assent
to the Sairindhri's being burned along with the Suta's son.
And at this, the Kichakas approached the stupefied Draupadi and seized her.
Binding her and placing her upon the bier, they set out for the cemetery.
The blameless Draupadi wailed aloud for the help of her husbands,
saying: "O! let Jaya and Jayanta and Vijaya and Jayatsena and Jayadvala hear me.
The Sutas are taking me away. Let those illustrious Gandharvas
listen to my words. The Sutas are taking me away!"
Hearing those lamentations, Bhima, without a moment's reflection,
started up from his bed and said: "I have heard your words, O Sairindhri.
You have, therefore, no more cause for fear at the hands of the Sutas."
The mighty-armed Bhima began to swell his body.
Carefully changing his attire, he went out of the palace by a wrong egress
and, climbing over a wall with the aid of a tree, he proceeded to the cemetery
to which the Kichakas had gone. Hurrying toward the funeral pyre, he saw a
    large tree,
tall as palmyra palm, with gigantic shoulders and a withered top.
Grasping with his arms that tree measuring ten fathoms around, that mighty hero
rushed, mace in hand, like Yama himself toward the Sutas.
Impelled by his rush, banyans and peepals and kinsukas
fell on the earth and lay in clusters. Seeing that Gandharva approach them
like a lion in fury, all the Sutas trembled with fear and said to each other:
"The powerful Gandharva comes here filled with rage, and with a tree in hand.
Let the Sairindhri, therefore, from whom this danger of ours has arisen, be set
    free."
And they set Draupadi free and ran breathlessly toward the city.
But seeing them run away, Bhima, that mighty son of the wind god,
dispatched by means of that tree a hundred and five of them to the abode of
    Yama,
like the wielder of the thunderbolt slaying the Danavas.
And setting Draupadi free from her bonds, he comforted her.
Bhima then addressed the distressed princess of Panchala, whose face was
    bathed in tears,
saying: "Thus are they slain that wrong you without cause. Return to the city.
You have no longer any cause for fear. I will go to Virata's kitchen by another
    route."
It was thus that a hundred and five of those Kichakas were slain.
Their corpses lay on the ground, making the place look like a great forest
overspread with uprooted trees after a hurricane.
Including Virata's general, slain before, the slaughtered Sutas were one hundred
    and six.
The citizens went to the king and told him what had happened.
Virata replied: "Perform the last rites, and let all the Kichakas be burned on one
    blazing pyre,
with gems and fragrant unguents in profusion."

Delivered by Bhimasena, Draupadi was relieved of her fears.
She washed her limbs and clothes in water and proceeded toward the city,
like a doe that had been frightened by a tiger.
But beholding her, the citizens, in fear of the Gandharvas, fled in all directions.
Some of them went so far as to shut their eyes.
And then, at the gate of the kitchen, the princess of Panchala saw Bhimasena
standing like an infuriated elephant of gigantic proportions.
Looking at him with widened eyes, Draupadi, in words intelligible to the two of
     them alone, said:
"I bow to that prince of the Gandharvas who rescued me."
At these words of hers, Bhima said: "Those persons who were living in the city in
     debt
will now gather here, regarding themselves as freed from their debt."
Then Draupadi beheld the mighty-armed Arjuna in the dancing hall,
instructing King Virata's daughters in dancing.
And issuing with Arjuna from the dancing hall, all those damsels came to
     Draupadi,
who had been persecuted so sorely, innocent though she was.
And they said: "By good luck you have been delivered from your dangers.
By good luck you have returned safely.
And by good luck those Sutas have been slain who had wronged you."
Then Draupadi, with those girls, entered the royal abode to appear before
     Sudeshna.
When Draupadi came before the queen, the king's wife addressed her at his
     command,
saying: "Go speedily wherever you like. The king has been filled with fear
by this discomfiture at the hands of the Gandharvas.
You are young and unparalleled on earth in beauty. You are, besides,
an object of desire with men. The Gandharvas are exceedingly wrathful."
To this the Sairindhri said: "Beauteous lady, let the king suffer me to live here
for only thirteen days more. Without doubt, the Gandharvas also will be obliged
     by this.
They will then convey me hence and do what would be agreeable to Virata.
By doing this, the king will reap great benefit."

✦

Meanwhile, the spies employed by Dhritarashtra's son,
having searched various villages and towns and kingdoms,
and having done all that they had been commanded to do,
and having completed their examination, in the manner directed,
of the countries indicated in their orders,
returned to Nagarupa, pleased with at least one thing that they had learned.
Dhritarashtra's son King Duryodhana was seated in his court
with Drona and Karna and Kripa, with the high-souled Bhishma, his own brothers,
and those great warriors, the Trigartas.
The spies addressed the king, saying: "Lord of men, great has been our care

in the search after the sons of Pandu in that mighty forest.
We have searched in arbors of matted woods and plants of every species,
but we have failed to discover that track by which Kunti's sons may have gone.
We have searched for their footprints on mountaintops and in inaccessible
   fastnesses,
in various kingdoms and provinces teeming with people, in encampments and
   cities.
We have found no trace of the sons of Pandu.
It seems that they have perished without leaving a trace.
We followed in their track but soon lost their footprints,
and we do not know their present residence. O lord of men,
for some time we followed in the wake of their charioteers.
And, making our inquiries, we truly ascertained what we desired to know.
The charioteers reached Dwaravati without the sons of Pritha among them.
Neither the sons of Pandu nor the chaste Draupadi are in that city of Yadavas.
We have not been able to discover their present abode.
We are acquainted with the disposition of the sons of Pandu
and know something of the feats they have achieved.
Give us instructions as to what we should next do in the search for the sons of
   Pandu.
Listen also to these agreeable words of ours, promising great good to you:
King Matsya's commander, Kichaka of wicked soul,
by whom the Trigartas were repeatedly vanquished, now lies on the ground
with all his brothers, slain by invisible Gandharvas during the hours of darkness.
Having heard this delightful news about the discomfiture of our enemies,
we have been most pleased. Tell us now what should next be done."

27

The Yaksha

Once upon a time, as a deer was butting about a tree at an ashram,
it chanced that there stuck fast in its antlers the two sticks for making fire
along with the churning staff belonging to a Brahmana devoted to ascetic
    austerities.
And with long bounds that powerful deer left the ashram,
taking with it the Brahmana's sticks and churning staff.
Seeing his sticks and churning staff gone, the Brahmana,
anxious on account of his Agnihotra sacrifice, came before the Pandavas
in great distress, said what had happened,
and asked the sons of Pandu to track the deer by its footprints
and bring back his sticks and churning staff
so that his Agnihotra would not be stopped.
Yudhishthira was sympathetic and, taking up his bow,
sallied forth with his brothers on the trail of the deer.
They soon found it at no great distance and discharged barbed arrows, javelins,
and darts at it, but they could not pierce it with any of these.
They struggled to pursue and slay it, but the deer became suddenly invisible.
The noble-minded sons of Pandu, fatigued and disappointed
and afflicted with hunger and thirst, approached a banyan tree and sat down in
    its shade.
There Nakula, stricken with sorrow and urged by impatience,
addressed his eldest brother, saying: "In our family, O king,
virtue has never been sacrificed, nor has there been loss of wealth from insolence.
And having been asked, we have never said no to any creature.
Why then in the present case have we met with this disaster?"
Yudhishthira said: "There is no limit to calamities.
It is the lord of justice alone who distributes the fruits of both virtue and vice."
Thereupon Bhima said: "Surely this calamity has befallen us because I did not
    slay
Pratikamin on the very spot when he dragged Draupadi as a slave into the
    assembly."
And Arjuna said: "Surely this calamity has befallen us
because I did not resent those insulting words of the Suta's son, piercing the
    very bones!"
And Sahadeva said: "Surely this calamity has befallen us

because I did not slay Sakuni when he defeated you at dice!"

Then King Yudhishthira addressed Nakula, saying: "Climb this tree and look around the ten points of the horizon. See whether there is water near us or such trees as grow on watery grounds. Your brothers are all fatigued and thirsty."

At once Nakula climbed the tree, looked around, and said to his eldest brother: "I see many trees that grow by the water's side and I hear the cries of cranes.
Water must be near here."

Yudhishthira then said: "Go then and fetch water in these quivers."

Nakula said: "So be it." And he hurried toward where there was water and soon found it.

He saw a crystal lake inhabited by cranes and he desired to drink of it, but he heard these words from the sky: "Child, do not commit this rash act! This lake is in my possession. You must first answer my questions, and only then may you drink of this water and take away as much as you require."

Nakula, however, exceedingly thirsty, disregarded these words and drank of the cool water.
Having drunk of it, he dropped down dead.

Seeing Nakula's delay, Yudhishthira said to Sahadeva: "It is long since our brother left.

Go and bring back your twin brother, with water." Sahadeva said: "So be it." And he set out.

Arriving at the water, he beheld his brother lying dead on the ground.

Afflicted by the death of his brother, and suffering severely from thirst, he advanced toward the water but heard these words: "Child, do not commit this rash act!

This lake is in my possession. First answer my question, and only then may you drink of the water and take away as much as you may require."

Sahadeva, however, was extremely thirsty and, disregarding these words, drank of the water, and having drunk of it,
dropped down dead.

Then Yudhishthira said to Arjuna: "It is long since your two brothers have left us.

Go and bring them back, with water. You are our refuge when we are in distress!"

Thus addressed, Arjuna took his bow and arrows and his naked sword and set out.

Reaching the water, he beheld his two younger brothers lying dead.

And seeing them as if asleep, that lion among men, much aggrieved, raised his bow and looked around that wood but found no one in that mighty forest.

Fatigued, he rushed in the direction of the water, but he heard a voice from the sky: "Why do you approach this water? You shall not be able to drink of it by force.

If you can answer the question I will put to you, only then shall you drink of the water and take away as much as you require." Arjuna said: "Forbid me by appearing before me!

And when you shall be sorely pierced with arrows, you will not again speak this way!"

Having said this, he showered arrows on all sides, inspired by mantras.

And he also displayed his skill in shooting at an invisible mark by sound alone.
Sorely afflicted with thirst, he discharged barbed darts and javelins and iron
arrows,
showering into the sky innumerable shafts incapable of being resisted.
Thereupon the invisible Yaksha said: "What is the need of all this trouble?
Drink only after answering my questions! If you drink, however, without
answering,
you shall die immediately." Arjuna disregarded those words, drank of the water,
and immediately after dropped down dead.
Seeing Arjuna's delay, Yudhishthira addressed Bhimasena, saying:
"It is a long while since Nakula and Sahadeva and Arjuna have gone to fetch water.
Go and bring them back, together with water!" Bhimasena said: "So be it." And
he set out
for that place where his brothers lay dead. Finding them, Bhima,
afflicted though he was with thirst, was exceedingly distressed.
That mighty hero thought this to have been the act of some Yaksha or Rakshasa.
And he thought: *I shall surely have to fight today. But let me first appease my thirst.*
He rushed forward with the intention of drinking, but the Yaksha said:
"Child, do not commit this rash act! This lake is in my possession.
First answer my questions; then you may drink and take as much water as you
require!"
Addressed by the Yaksha, Bhima, without answering his questions, drank of the
water.
And as soon as he drank, he dropped dead on the spot.
Then Yudhishthira, perceiving that his brothers had left him a very long time
ago, thought:
Why is it that the two sons of Madri and the wielder of the Gandiva are delaying?
And why does Bhima, too, delay? I shall go to search for them!
Yudhishthira then rose up, his heart burning in grief. And he said within himself:
Is this forest under some malign influence? Or is it infested by some wicked beasts?
Or have they all fallen, in consequence of having disregarded some mighty being?
Or, not finding water in the spot to which those heroes had first repaired,
have they spent all this time searching through the forest? Why have they not returned?
Yudhishthira entered the forest, where no human sound was heard,
and which was inhabited by deer and bears and birds and adorned with bright
green trees
and echoing with the hum of the black bee and the notes of winged warblers.
After a short while, he beheld that beautiful lake, which looked as if it had been
made
by the celestial artificer himself. It was adorned with flowers of a golden hue
and with lotuses and sindhuvars. And it abounded with canes and ketakas and
karaviras
and pippalas. Fatigued from walking, Yudhishthira saw the lake and, struck with
wonder,
saw his brothers, lying dead like the regents of the world
dropped from their spheres at the end of the *yuga.*
That virtuous lord of men, immersed in an ocean of sorrows,

attempted to ascertain the cause of the catastrophe.

Having bewailed much, Yudhishthira reflected on who could have slain those
    heroes:

There are no strokes of weapons upon them, nor is anyone's footprint here.

The being must be mighty by whom my brothers have been slain.

I shall ponder this, but let me first drink of the water and then try to reason it out.

It may be that the crooked-minded Duryodhana has caused this water

to be secretly placed here by the king of the Gandharvas.

What man can trust that person of evil passions, to whom good and evil are alike?

Or perhaps this is an act of that wicked-souled one through secret messengers.

Thus did that highly intelligent one give way to diverse reflections.

He did not believe the water to have been tainted with poison,

for though his brothers were dead, no corpselike pallor was upon them:

The color on the faces of these my brothers has not faded!

He continued: *Each of these foremost among men was like a mighty cataract.*

Who but Yama himself, who brings the end of all things, could have thus undone them?

And he began to perform his ablutions in that lake. But while he descended into it,

he heard these words of the Yaksha from the sky: "I am a crane, living on tiny
    fish.

By me have your brothers been brought under the sway of the lord of departed
    spirits.

If you do not answer the questions put by me, O prince, yours shall be the fifth
    corpse.

Do not, O child, act rashly! This lake is mine. Only having answered my
    questions first

may you drink and carry away as much as you require."

Yudhishthira answered: "Are you foremost among the Rudras, or the Vasus,

or the Marutas? What god are you? This could not have been done by a bird!

Who has overthrown the four mighty mountains—the Himavat, the Paripatra,
    the Vindhya,

and the Malaya? Great is your feat!

Those whom neither gods nor Gandharvas nor Asuras nor Rakshasas could
    withstand,

you have slain! Therefore, your deed is exceedingly wonderful!

I do not know what your business may be, nor do I know your purpose.

Therefore, my curiosity is great, and also my fear!

I ask you, therefore, O worshipful one, who are you?"

Hearing these words the Yaksha said: "I am a Yaksha and not an amphibious bird.

It is by me that all these brothers of yours have been slain."

✦

Yudhishthira approached the speaker of these harsh words and beheld that Yaksha

of unusual eyes and huge body, tall as a palmyra palm and looking like the sun,

irresistible and gigantic like a mountain, and uttering a roar deep as that of the
    clouds.

The Yaksha said: "These your brothers, repeatedly forbidden by me,

forcibly took away my water. It is for this that I slew them!
If you first answer my questions, you may then take away as much as you like."
Yudhishthira said: "I do not covet what is in your possession.
Virtuous persons never applaud themselves or boast.
I shall therefore answer your questions, according to my intelligence. Ask away!"
The Yaksha then asked: "What makes the sun rise? Who keeps him company?
Who causes him to set? And in whom is he established?"
Yudhishthira answered: "Brahma makes the sun rise, the gods keep him company,
Dharma causes him to set, and he is established in truth."
The Yaksha asked: "By what does one become learned?
By what does he attain what is very great? How can one have second sight?
And how can one acquire intelligence?"
Yudhishthira answered: "It is by study of the Srutis that a person becomes learned.
It is by ascetic austerities that one acquires what is very great.
It is by intelligence that a person acquires second sight.
And it is by serving the old that one becomes wise."
The Yaksha asked: "What constitutes the divinity of the Brahmanas?
What in their practice is like that of the pious?
What is the human attribute of the Brahmanas?
And what practice of theirs is like that of the impious?"
Yudhishthira answered: "The study of the Vedas constitutes their divinity.
Their asceticism constitutes behavior that is like that of the pious.
Their liability to death is their human attribute. And slander is their impiety."
The Yaksha asked: "What constitutes the divinity of the Kshatriyas?
What in their practice is like that of the pious? What is their human attribute?
And what practice of theirs is like that of the impious?"
Yudhishthira answered: "Arrows and weapons are their divinity.
Celebration of sacrifices is their act which is like that of the pious.
Liability to fear is their human attribute.
And refusal of protection is that act of theirs which is like that of the impious."
The Yaksha asked: "What constitutes the Sama Veda of the sacrifice?
What constitutes the Yajur Veda of the sacrifice? What is the refuge of a sacrifice?
And what is that which sacrifice cannot do without?"
Yudhishthira said: "Life is the Sama Veda of the sacrifice.
The mind is the Yajur Veda of the sacrifice. The Rig Veda is the refuge of the
    sacrifice.
And it is the Rig Veda alone which sacrifice cannot do without."
The Yaksha asked: "What is weightier than the earth itself?
What is higher than the heavens? What is fleeter than the wind?
And what is more numerous than blades of grass?"
Yudhishthira answered: "The mother is weightier than the earth.
The father is higher than the heavens. The mind is fleeter than the wind.
And our thoughts are more numerous than blades of grass."
The Yaksha asked: "What does not close its eyes while asleep?
What does not move after birth? What is without heart?
And what swells with its own impetus?"
Yudhishthira answered: "A fish does not close its eyes while asleep.

An egg does not move after birth. A stone is without heart.

And a river swells with its own impetus."

The Yaksha asked: "Who is the friend of the exile? Who is the friend of the householder?

Who is the friend of him that ails? And who is the friend of one about to die?"

Yudhishthira answered: "The friend of the exile in a distant land is his companion.

The friend of the householder is the wife. The friend of him that ails is the physician.

And the friend of him about to die is charity."

The Yaksha asked: "Who is the guest of all creatures? What is the eternal duty?

What is Amrita? And what is this entire universe?"

Yudhishthira answered: "Agni is the guest of all creatures. The milk of cows is Amrita.

Homa is the eternal duty. And this universe consists of air alone."

The Yaksha asked: "What sojourns alone? What is reborn after its birth?

What is the remedy against cold? And what is the largest field?"

Yudhishthira answered: "The sun sojourns alone. The moon takes birth anew.

Fire is the remedy against cold. And the earth is the largest field."

The Yaksha asked: "What is the highest refuge of virtue? what of fame?

what of heaven? and what of happiness?"

Yudhishthira answered: "Liberality is the highest refuge of virtue; gift, of fame;

truth, of heaven; and good behavior, of happiness."

The Yaksha asked: "What is the soul of man? Who is the friend the gods bestow on man?

What is man's chief support? And what is his chief refuge?"

Yudhishthira answered: "The son is a man's soul.

The wife is the friend bestowed on man by the gods.

The clouds are his chief support. And giving is his chief refuge."

The Yaksha asked: "What is the best of all laudable things?

What is the most valuable of all possessions? What is the best of all gains?

And what is the best of all kinds of happiness?"

Yudhishthira answered: "The best of all laudable things is skill.

The best of all possessions is knowledge. The best of all gains is health.

And contentment is the best of all kinds of happiness."

The Yaksha asked: "What is the highest duty in the world?

What is that virtue which always bears fruit?

What is that which, if controlled, does not lead to regret?

And who are they with whom an alliance cannot break?"

Yudhishthira answered: "The highest of duties is to refrain from injury.

The rites ordained in the Three Vedas always bear fruit.

The mind, if controlled, does not lead to regret.

And an alliance with the good never breaks."

The Yaksha asked: "What is it which, if renounced, makes one agreeable?

What is it which, if renounced, leads to no regret?

What is it which, if renounced, makes one wealthy?

And what is it which, if renounced, makes one happy?"

Yudhishthira answered: "Pride, if renounced, makes one agreeable.

Wrath, if renounced, leads to no regret. Desire, if renounced, makes one wealthy. And avarice, if renounced, makes one happy."

The Yaksha asked: "Why does one give to Brahmanas? why to mimes and dancers? why to servants? and why to kings?"

Yudhishthira answered: "It is for religious merit that one gives to Brahmanas; for fame that one gives to mimes and dancers; for supporting them that one gives to servants; and for obtaining relief from fear that one gives to kings."

The Yaksha asked: "In what is the world enveloped? Owing to what can a thing not discover itself? For what are friends forsaken? And for what does one fail to go to heaven?"

Yudhishthira answered: "The world is enveloped in darkness. Darkness does not permit a thing to show itself. It is from avarice that friends are forsaken. And it is connection with the world for which one fails to go to heaven."

The Yaksha asked: "For what may one be considered as dead? For what may a kingdom be considered as dead? For what may a Sraddha be considered as dead? for what, a sacrifice?"

Yudhishthira answered: "For want of wealth may a man be regarded as dead. A kingdom for want of a king may be regarded as dead. A Sraddha performed with the aid of a priest with no learning may be regarded as dead. And a sacrifice in which there are no gifts to Brahmanas is dead."

The Yaksha asked: "What constitutes the way? What has been spoken of as water? what as food? what as poison? Tell us also what is the proper time of a Sraddha rite, and then drink and take away as much as you like!"

Yudhishthira answered: "They who are good constitute the way. Space has been spoken of as water. The cow is food. A request is poison. And a Brahmana is regarded as the proper time of a Sraddha. I do not know what you may think of all this, O Yaksha."

The Yaksha asked: "What has been said to be the sign of asceticism? And what is true restraint? What constitutes forgiveness? And what is shame?"

Yudhishthira answered: "Staying in one's own religion is asceticism. The restraint of the mind is of all restraints the true one. Forgiveness consists in enduring enmity; and shame, in withdrawing from all unworthy acts."

The Yaksha asked: "What is said to be knowledge? what, tranquillity? What constitutes mercy? And what has been called simplicity?"

Yudhishthira answered: "True knowledge is that of divinity. True tranquillity is that of the heart. Mercy consists in wishing happiness to all. And simplicity is equanimity of heart."

The Yaksha asked: "What enemy is invincible? What constitutes an incurable disease for man? What sort of man is called honest; and what sort, dishonest?"

Yudhishthira answered: "Anger is an invincible enemy. Covetousness constitutes an incurable disease. He is honest who desires the welfare of all creatures;

and he is dishonest who is unmerciful."

The Yaksha asked: "What is ignorance? And what is pride?
What also is to be understood by idleness? And what has been spoken of as grief?"

Yudhishthira answered: "True ignorance consists in not knowing one's duties.
Pride is one's consciousness of being oneself an actor or sufferer in life.
Idleness consists in not discharging one's duties. And ignorance is grief."

The Yaksha asked: "What do the rishis say is steadiness; and what, patience?
What also is a real ablution? And what is charity?"

Yudhishthira answered: "Steadiness consists in one's staying in one's own religion.
True patience consists in the subjugation of the senses.
A true bath consists in washing the mind clean of all impurities.
And charity consists in protecting all creatures."

The Yaksha asked: "What man should be regarded as learned,
and who should be called an atheist? Who should be called ignorant?
What is called desire, and what are the sources of desire? And what is envy?"

Yudhishthira answered: "He is to be called learned who knows his duties.
An atheist is one who is ignorant, and one who is ignorant is an atheist.
Desire is due to objects of possession. And envy is nothing else but grief of heart."

The Yaksha asked: "What is pride? What is hypocrisy?
What is the grace of the gods? And what is wickedness?"

Yudhishthira answered: "Stolid ignorance is pride.
The setting up of a religious standard is hypocrisy.
The grace of the gods is the fruit of our gifts.
And wickedness consists in speaking ill of others."

The Yaksha asked: "Virtue, profit, and desire are opposed to one another.
How could things thus antagonistic to one another exist together?"

Yudhishthira answered: "When a wife and virtue agree with each other,
then all the three you have mentioned may exist together."

The Yaksha asked: "Who is condemned to everlasting hell?
It behooves you to answer quickly the question that I ask!"

Yudhishthira answered: "He who summons a poor Brahmana, promising him a gift,
and then tells him that he has nothing to give goes to everlasting hell.
He also must go to everlasting hell who imputes falsehood to the Vedas,
the scriptures, the Brahmanas, the gods, and the ceremonies in honor of the Pitris.
He also goes to everlasting hell who, though in possession of wealth,
never gives away or enjoys himself from avarice and says he has nothing."

The Yaksha asked: "Is it by birth, behavior, study, or learning
that a person becomes a Brahmana? Tell us with certitude!"

Yudhishthira answered: "Listen, O Yaksha! It is neither birth nor study nor learning
that is the cause of becoming a Brahmana. It is behavior that achieves this.
One's behavior should always be well guarded, especially that of a Brahmana.
He who maintains his conduct unimpaired is never impaired himself.
Professors and pupils—in fact, all who study the scriptures—
are to be regarded as illiterate wretches if they are addicted to wicked habits.

Only he is learned who performs his religious duties.

Even he who has studied the four Vedas is to be regarded as a wicked wretch,
scarcely distinguishable from a Sudra, if his conduct be incorrect.

Only he who performs the Agnihotra sacrifice and has his senses under control
  is a Brahmana."

The Yaksha asked: "What does one gain by speaking agreeable words?

What does one gain by always acting with judgment?

What does one gain by having many friends; and what, by being devoted to virtue?"

Yudhishthira answered: "He who speaks agreeable words becomes agreeable to all.

He who acts with judgment obtains whatever he seeks.

He who has many friends lives happily.

And he who is devoted to virtue obtains a happy state in the next world."

The Yaksha asked: "Who is truly happy? What is most wonderful? What is the path?

And what is the news? Answer these questions, and your dead brothers will revive."

Yudhishthira answered: "O amphibious creature, a man who cooks in his own
  house

at the fifth or the sixth part of the day with scanty vegetables,

but who is not in debt and who does not stir from home, is truly happy.

Day after day, countless creatures are going to the abode of Yama,

yet those who remain behind believe themselves to be immortal.

What can be more wonderful than this? Argument leads to no certain conclusion,
the Srutis are different from one another,

there is not even one rishi whose opinion can be accepted by all,

and the truth about religion and duty is hidden in deep caves.

Therefore, the path is the one along which the great have trodden.

This world full of ignorance is like a pan. The sun is fire, the days and nights are
  fuel.

The months and the seasons are the wooden ladle.

Time is the cook that is cooking all creatures in that pan: this is the news."

The Yaksha said: "You have truly answered all my questions!

Tell us now who is truly a man, and what man truly possesses every kind of wealth."

Yudhishthira answered: "The report of one's good action reaches heaven
and spreads over the earth. As long as that report lasts,

so long is a person to whom the agreeable and the disagreeable, weal and woe,
the past and the future are the same is said to possess every kind of wealth."

The Yaksha said: "You have truly answered who is a man,

and what man possesses every kind of wealth. Therefore, let one only of your
  brothers,

whom you may choose, get up with life!"

Yudhishthira answered: "Let this one that is of darkish hue, whose eyes are red,
who is tall like a large sala tree, whose chest is broad and whose arms are long—
                    let this Nakula get up with life!"

The Yaksha rejoined: "But Bhimasena is dear to you,

and Arjuna is one on whom all of you depend!

Why, then, O king, do you wish a stepbrother to get up with his life?

How can you forsake Bhima, whose strength is equal to that of ten thousand
  elephants,

and instead choose life for Nakula?"
Yudhishthira said: "If virtue is sacrificed, he who sacrifices it is himself lost.
So virtue also cherishes the cherisher.
Therefore, taking care that virtue, by being sacrificed, may not sacrifice us,
I never forsake virtue. Abstention from injury is the highest virtue,
even higher than the highest object of attainment. I endeavor to practice that
    virtue.
Let men know that the king is always virtuous! Let Nakula, therefore, revive!
My father had two wives, Kunti and Madri. Let both of them have children.
This is what I wish. As Kunti is to me, so also is Madri.
There is no difference between them in my eye. Therefore, let Nakula live!"
The Yaksha said: "Since abstention from injury is regarded by you
as higher than both profit and pleasure, therefore all your brothers may live!"

✦

Then, in obedience to the words of the Yaksha, the Pandavas rose up,
and in a moment their hunger and thirst left them. Thereupon Yudhishthira said:
"I ask you, who are incapable of being vanquished, and who stand on one leg in
    the lake,
what god you are, for I cannot take you for a Yaksha! Are you the foremost
    among the Vasus
or the Rudras, or are you the chief of the Maruts?
Or are you the lord of the celestials, wielder of the thunderbolt?
Each of my brothers is capable of fighting as many as a hundred thousand
    warriors,
and I do not know of a warrior who can slay them all.
I see that their senses have refreshed, as if they have sweetly awakened from
    slumber.
Are you a friend of ours, or even our father himself?"
To this the Yaksha replied: "Child, I am your father, the lord of justice,
possessed of great prowess. Know that I came here desiring to behold you!
Fame, truth, self-restraint, purity, candor, modesty,
steadiness, charity, austerities and the qualities of the Brahmanas are my body!
And abstention from injury, impartiality, peace, penances,
sanctity, and freedom from malice are the doors through which I am accessible.
You are always dear to me! By good luck, you are devoted to the Five—
tranquillity of mind, self-restraint, abstention from sensual pleasures,
resignation, and Yoga meditation. And also by good luck, you have conquered
    the Six—
hunger, thirst, sorrow, bluntness of mortal feeling, decrepitude, and death.
Of the Six, two appear in the first part of life, two in the middle part,
and the remaining two at the end in order to make men repair to the next world.
I am the lord of justice! I came to test your merit.
I am well pleased to witness your harmlessness, and I will confer boons upon you.
Ask of me, and surely I shall confer them. Those who revere me are never in
    distress!"

Yudhishthira said: "A deer was carrying away a Brahmana's fire sticks.
Therefore, the first boon that I shall ask is that the Brahmana's adorations to Agni
be not interrupted!" The Yaksha said: "It was I who, to examine you,
carried away, in the guise of a deer, the Brahmana's fire sticks.

I give you this boon! But ask for another."
Yudhishthira said: "We have spent these twelve years in the forest,
and the thirteenth year is come. May no one recognize us this year."
The god replied: "I give this boon to you!
Even if you range this entire earth in your proper forms,
none in the three worlds shall recognize you.
You perpetuators of the Kuru race, through my grace,
will spend this thirteenth year secretly and unrecognized in Virata's kingdom!
And every one of you will be able at will to assume any form he likes!
Go now, and present the Brahmana with his fire sticks.
But ask for another boon that you may like. I will confer it.
I have not yet been satisfied by granting boons to you.
Accept a third boon, my son, that is great and incomparable."
Yudhishthira said: "It is enough that I have beheld you with my senses, god of
    gods!
O father, whatever boon you will confer on me I shall surely accept gladly!
May I always conquer covetousness and folly and anger,
and may my mind be ever devoted to charity, truth, and ascetic austerities!"
The lord of justice said: "Even by nature have you been endowed with these
    qualities,
for you are the lord of justice himself! Again attain what you asked for!"
Having said these words, the worshipful lord of justice vanished.
And the high-souled Pandavas, after they had slept sweetly, were reunited.
Those heroes returned to the hermitage
                    and gave the fire sticks back to the Brahmana.
That man who contemplates this illustrious and fame-enhancing story
of the revival of the Pandavas and the meeting of father and son,
Dharma and Yudhishthira, obtains perfect tranquillity of mind, and sons and
    grandsons,
and also a life extending over a hundred years!
And the mind of that man who takes this story to heart
will never delight in unrighteousness, or in disunion among friends,
or in misappropriation of another's property,
or in staining other people's wives,
or in foul thoughts!

28

Susarman

Having listened to his spies, King Duryodhana reflected
and then addressed his courtiers, saying:
"It is difficult to ascertain the course of events.
We must discover where the sons of Pandu have gone
in this thirteenth year in which they are to pass unrecognized.
The greater part of that year has already expired.
If they pass undetected in what remains of this year, they will have fulfilled their
    pledge
and will then return like mighty elephants, or like snakes of virulent poison.
Filled with wrath, they will inflict terrible chastisement on the Kurus.
You must, therefore, make all efforts to induce the sons of Pandu
to reenter the woods, suppressing their rage.
Indeed, you should adopt such means as may remove all causes of quarrel
and anxiety from the kingdom, making it tranquil and unthreatened by foes
and incapable of sustaining a diminution of territory."
To these words of Duryodhana, Karna said: "Let other spies, abler and more
    cunning,
and capable of accomplishing their object, set out at once.
Let them, in disguise, wander through swelling kingdoms and populous provinces,
prying into assemblies of the learned and delightful retreats of all provinces.
In the inner apartments of palaces, in shrines and at holy spots, in mines and
    other regions,
the sons of Pandu should be sought with all eagerness."
After Karna had spoken, Duryodhana's second brother, Dussasana, of sinful
    disposition,
said: "O monarch, let only those spies in whom we have confidence,
receiving their rewards in advance, go again to search.
Of this and whatever else has been said by Karna we fully approve.
It is my belief, however, that neither the track the Pandavas have followed
nor their present abode or occupation will be discovered.
Perhaps the Pandavas are closely concealed; perhaps they have gone to the other
    side of the ocean.
Or, perhaps, proud as they are of their strength and courage,
they have been devoured by wild beasts or have been overtaken by some unusual
    danger

and have perished. Therefore, O prince, dispelling all anxieties from your heart, achieve what you will, always acting according to your instincts."

Drona then said: "Persons like the sons of Pandu never perish or undergo discomfiture.

Brave and skilled in every science, intelligent, and with senses under control, virtuous and grateful and obedient to the virtuous Yudhishthira, they could never perish in this way. Why, then, should not Yudhishthira, possessing a knowledge of policy, be able to restore the prosperity of his brothers who are so obedient and devoted and high-souled?

It is for this that they await their opportunity.

Do, therefore, what should now be done.

Let also the abode which the sons of Pandu are to occupy be now settled.

The son of Pritha is capable of consuming his foes by a mere glance of his eyes.

Knowing all this, do what is proper. Let us, therefore, once more search after them,

sending Brahmanas and charanas, ascetics crowned with success, and others of this kind who may have a knowledge of those heroes."

Then that grandsire of the Bharatas, Bhishma the son of Shantanu, conversant with the Vedas, acquainted with the proprieties of time and place, and possessing a knowledge of every duty of morality, applauded Drona's words and spoke his views, which were consistent with virtue and expressive of his attachment to the virtuous Yudhishthira. He said:

"I approve of the words of the admirable Drona. I have no hesitation in saying so.

Aided by their own energy, the sons of Pandu, who are now leading a life of concealment

in obedience to virtue, will never perish. Therefore, I am for employing honest counsel

in our behavior toward the sons of Pandu. It would not be the policy of any wise man

to cause them to be discovered now by means of spies.

What we should do to the sons of Pandu I shall say,

reflecting with the aid of the intellect. I shall say nothing to you from ill will.

People like me should never give such counsel to one who is dishonest,

for good counsel should be offered only to those who are honest.

Evil advice should never be offered. He who is devoted to truth and obedient to the aged—

he, indeed, who is wise—while speaking in an assembly should always speak the truth.

I should, therefore, say that I think differently from all those people here about the abode of Yudhishthira in this thirteenth year of his exile.

The ruler, O child, of the city or the province where King Yudhishthira resides cannot have any misfortune. Charitable and liberal and humble and modest must be the people of the country where King Yudhishthira resides.

Agreeable in speech, with passions under control; observant of truth; cheerful, healthy, pure in conduct, and skillful in work must be the people of the country where King Yudhishthira resides.

The people of that place cannot be envious or malicious, or vain, or proud

but must all adhere to their respective duties.
Indeed, in the place where Yudhishthira resides, Vedic hymns will be chanted,
sacrifices will be performed, the last full libations will always be poured,
and gifts to Brahmanas will always be in profusion.
There the clouds pour abundant rain, and the country, furnished with good
 harvest,
will be without fear. There the paddy will not be without grain,
fruits will not lack juice, floral garlands will not be without fragrance,
and the conversation of men will always be full of agreeable words.
There where King Yudhishthira resides the breezes will be delicious,
the meetings of men will always be friendly, and there will be no cause for fear.
There cattle will be plentiful, with none lean-fleshed or weak,
and milk and curds and butter will all be savory and nutritious.
Where King Yudhishthira resides, every kind of corn will be full of nutrition
and every comestible full of flavor. Where he resides, the objects of the senses—
 taste,
touch, smell, sight, and hearing—will be endowed with excellent attributes.
Indeed, in the country where the sons of Pandu may have taken up their abode
during this thirteenth year of their exile, the people will be contented and
 cheerful,
pure in conduct and without misery of any kind.
Devoted to gods and guests, and to the worship of these with their whole soul,
they will be fond of giving away and filled with great energy.
The people will eschew all that is evil and will be desirous of achieving only what
 is good.
Always observant of sacrifices and pure vows, and hating untruth in speech,
the people of the place where King Yudhishthira may reside
will always be desirous of obtaining what is good, auspicious, and beneficial.
That son of Pritha, now that he has concealed himself, is incapable of being
 found out
even by Brahmanas, let alone ordinary persons. He is living in close disguise
in a region whose characteristics I have described.
Regarding his excellent mode of life, I dare not say anything more.
Reflecting upon all this, do what you may think to be beneficial, if indeed you
 have faith in me."
Then Kripa, Saradwata's son, said: "What the aged Bhishma has said
concerning the Pandavas is reasonable, suited to the occasion,
consistent with virtue and profit, agreeable to the ear,
fraught with sound reason, and worthy of him.
Listen also to what I would say on this subject.
By means of spies, you must ascertain the track the Pandavas have followed
and adopt that policy which may bring about your welfare.
He who is solicitous of his welfare should not disregard even an ordinary foe.
What shall I say then of the Pandavas, who are thorough masters of all weapons
 in battle?
When the time comes for the reappearance of the high-souled Pandavas,

you should ascertain your strength both in your own kingdom and in those of
  other kings.
Without doubt, the return of the Pandavas is at hand.
When their promised term of exile is over, the mighty sons of Pritha will come
  here,
bursting with energy. In order to conclude an advantageous treaty with them,
you should have recourse to sound policy
and address yourself to increasing your forces and improving your treasury.
Reckon your strength, compared to that of all your allies weak and strong.
Having recourse to the arts of conciliation, disunion, chastisement,
bribery, presents, and fair behavior, attack your foes and subdue the weak by
  might,
and win over your allies and troops by soft speeches.
When you have by these means strengthened your army and filled your treasury,
success will be yours. When you have done all this, you will be able to fight
powerful enemies, let alone the sons of Pritha, who are deficient
in troops and animals of their own. By adopting all these expedients
according to the customs of your order, you will attain enduring happiness in
  due time."

✦

Discomfited many times before by Matsya's Suta Kichaka,
aided by the Matsyas and the Salyas, the mighty king of the Trigartas, Susarman,
who owned innumerable cars, regarding the opportunity to be a favorable one,
spoke the following words to Duryodhana, while eyeing Karna askance:
"My kingdom has many times been forcibly invaded by the king of the Matsyas.
The mighty Kichaka was that king's generalissimo. Crooked and wrathful
and of prowess famed over all the world, sinful in deeds and highly cruel,
that wretch has been slain by the Gandharvas.
Now that Kichaka is dead, King Virata, shorn of pride and his refuge gone,
will lose all courage. I think, therefore, that we ought now to invade that kingdom.
The accident that has happened is a favorable one for us. Let us repair
to Virata's kingdom, which is abounding in corn. We will appropriate his gems
and other wealth. Let us go to share with each other his villages and kingdom.
Or, invading his city by force, let us carry off by the thousands his excellent
  cattle.
Uniting the forces of the Kauravas and the Trigartas, let us take his admirable
  herds.
Uniting our forces well, we will check his power and force him to sue for peace.
Having brought him under subjection by just means, we will live in our kingdom
  happily,
while your power also will be enhanced." Hearing the words of Susarman, Karna
  said:
"Susarman has spoken well; the opportunity is favorable and promises to be
  profitable.

Therefore, if it please you, let us draw up our forces in battle array and set out at
once.
Or let the expedition be managed as Saradwata's son Kripa, the preceptor
Drona,
and the wise and aged Bhishma may think best. What business have we
with the sons of Pandu, destitute as they are of wealth, might, and prowess?
They have either disappeared for good or gone to the abode of Yama.
We will proceed without anxiety to Virata's city to plunder his cattle and other
wealth."
Accepting these words of Karna, King Duryodhana commanded his brother
Dussasana:
"Consulting with the elders, array our forces without delay.
We will, with all the Kauravas, go to the appointed place.
Let also that mighty warrior, King Susarman, set out with the Trigartas
for the dominions of the Matsyas. And let Susarman proceed first, concealing his
intention.
Following in their wake, we will set out the day after in close array
for the prosperous dominions of King Matsya. Let the Trigartas, however,
suddenly repair to the city of Virata and seize that immense wealth of cattle.
Marching in two divisions, we also will seize thousands of excellent cattle."
Then those warriors, the Trigartas, accompanied by their infantry of terrible
prowess,
marched toward the southeast to wage war with Virata and seize his herds.
Susarman set out on the seventh day of the dark fortnight.
And on the eighth, the Kauravas and all their troops began to seize cattle by the
thousands.

✦

In King Virata's service, dwelling in disguise in his excellent city,
the high-souled Pandavas were completing the promised period of living in
disguise.
And after Kichaka had been slain, the mighty King Virata rested his hopes
on the sons of Kunti. It was on the expiration of the thirteenth year of their exile
that Susarman seized Virata's cattle by the thousands.
The herdsman of Virata came with great speed to the city and to the king of the
Matsyas,
seated on the throne with the sons of Pandu and surrounded by brave warriors.
The herdsman bowed down to him and addressed him: "O foremost among kings,
the Trigartas, defeating and humiliating us in battle, are seizing your cattle
by the hundreds and thousands. Rescue them! See that they are not lost to you."
Hearing these words, the king arrayed the Matsya force for battle,
abounding in cars and elephants and horses and infantry and standards.
And kings and princes speedily put on their shining and beautiful armor,
worthy of being worn by heroes. Virata's beloved brother, Satanika, put on a coat
of mail
made of the hardest steel and adorned with burnished gold.

And Madirakshya, next in birth to Satanika, put on a strong coat of mail
plated with gold and capable of resisting every weapon.
And the coat of mail that the king himself put on was invulnerable
and decked with a hundred suns, a hundred circles, a hundred spots, and a
hundred eyes.
And the coat of mail that Suryadatta put on was as bright as the sun,
plated with gold, and as broad as a hundred lotuses of the fragrant kahlara
species.
And the coat of mail that Virata's eldest son, the heroic Sanksha, put on
was impenetrable and made of burnished steel and decked with a hundred eyes
of gold.
It was thus that each of those godlike warriors, furnished with weapons and
eager for battle,
donned his corselet. Then they all yoked to their excellent cars white steeds in
mail.
Then Matsya's glorious standard was hoisted on his excellent car,
decked with gold and resembling the sun in its effulgence. Other Kshatriya
warriors also
raised on their respective cars gold-decked standards of various shapes and
devices.
King Matsya then addressed his brother Satanika, saying:
"Kanka and Vallava and Tantripal and Damagranthi of great energy
will surely fight. Give them cars furnished with banners, and let them have on
their bodies
coats of mail that are invulnerable and easy to wear. Let them also have fine
weapons."
Hearing these words of the king, Satanika immediately ordered cars
for those sons of Pritha—the royal Yudhishthira, and Bhima, and Nakula, and
Sahadeva.
Commanded by the king, the charioteers got cars ready for them.
And those grinders of foes donned the beautiful coats of mail, invulnerable and
easy to wear,
that Virata had ordered for them. Mounted on cars yoked to good steeds,
the sons of Pritha set out with cheerful hearts, following in Virata's wake.
Infuriated elephants of terrible mien, fully sixty years of age,
with shapely tusks and mounted by trained warriors skilled in fight, followed the
king
like moving hills. The principal warriors of Matsya who cheerfully followed the
king
had eight thousand cars, a thousand elephants, and sixty thousand horses.
The force of Virata, marching forth and marking the footprints of the cattle,
looked splendid.
The Matsyas overtook the Trigartas when the sun had just passed the meridian.
Both excited to fury, the mighty Trigartas and the Matsyas sent up loud roars.
The terrible elephants, ridden by the skilful mahouts of both sides, were urged on
with spiked clubs and hooks. And when the sun was low on the horizon
the encounter that took place between the infantry and the cavalry

and the chariots and elephants of both parties was like that of old
between the gods and the Asuras—terrible, sufficient to make one's hair prickle,
and calculated to increase the population of Yama's kingdom.
As the combatants rushed against one another, smiting and slashing,
such thick clouds of dust began to rise that nothing could be seen.
Covered with the dust raised by the contending armies, birds dropped down on
    the earth.
The sun himself disappeared behind the thick cloud of arrows, and the firmament
looked bright as if with myriads of fireflies. Shifting their bows,
the staves of which were decked with gold, from one hand to another,
those heroes began to strike each other down, discharging arrows right and left.
Cars encountered cars, as foot soldiers fought with foot soldiers, horsemen with
    horsemen,
and elephants with mighty elephants. Furiously they encountered one another
with swords and axes, bearded darts and javelins, and iron clubs.
Yet neither party succeeded in prevailing over the other. Severed heads,
some with beautiful noses, some with upper lips deeply gashed,
some decked with earrings, and some divided with wounds about the well-
    trimmed hair,
were seen rolling on the ground, covered with dust. Soon the field of battle
was overspread with the limbs of Kshatriya warriors cut off by arrows
and lying like trunks of sala trees. Scattered over with heads decked in earrings
and sandalwood paste–besmeared arms looking like the bodies of snakes, the
    field of battle
became exceedingly beautiful. The frightful dust soon became drenched
with torrents of blood. Some began to swoon away, and the warriors fought,
reckless of consideration of humanity, friendship, and relationship.
Vultures descended to the ground, their view obstructed by the thick shower of
    arrows.
But although those strong-armed combatants fought one another furiously,
the heroes of neither party succeeded in routing their antagonists.
Satanika having slain a full hundred of the enemy and Visalaksha a full four
    hundred,
both those mighty warriors penetrated into the heart of the great Trigarta host.
Those heroes began to deprive their antagonists of their senses in closer combat
in which the combatants seized one another's hair and tore one another with
    their nails.
Eyeing that point where the cars of the Trigartas had been mustered in strong
    numbers,
those heroes directed their attack toward it. That foremost among car warriors,
    King Virata,
with Suryadatta in his van and Madiraksha behind, having destroyed five
    hundred cars,
eight hundred horses, and five warriors on great cars, displayed various skillful
    maneuvers
on that field of battle. At last the king came upon the ruler of the Trigartas,
mounted on a golden chariot. And those high-souled and powerful warriors

rushed against each other like two bulls in a cowpen.

Then Susarman, the king of the Trigartas, challenged Matsya to a single combat
on cars.

Those warriors rushed against each other on their cars and showered arrows on
each other,

like clouds pouring torrents of rain. Enraged, those warriors, both skilled in
weapons

and both wielding swords and darts and maces, moved about on the battlefield,

assailing each other. King Virata pierced Susarman with ten shafts

and each of his four horses with five shafts. And Susarman pierced the king of
Matsya

with fifty whetted shafts. Then, because of the dust on the battlefield,

the soldiers of both Susarman and Matsya's king could not distinguish one
another.

When the world was enveloped in dust and the gloom of night, the warriors of
both sides,

without breaking the order of battle, desisted for a while.

But soon the moon arose, dispelling the darkness, illuminating the night,

and gladdening the hearts of the Kshatriya warriors. When everything was visible
again,

the battle resumed and raged on so furiously that the combatants

could not distinguish one another. Susarman, with his younger brother,

and accompanied by all his cars, rushed toward the king of Matsya.

Descending from their cars, the royal brothers, maces in hand, rushed toward
the foe.

The hostile hosts assailed each other with maces, swords, scimitars, battle-axes,

and bearded darts with keen edges and points of excellent temper.

King Susarman, having by his energy oppressed and defeated the army of the
Matsyas,

impetuously rushed toward Virata himself. And the two brothers

having slain Virata's two steeds, his charioteer, and those soldiers protecting his
rear,

took him captive. Then, afflicting him sorely, like a lustful man afflicting a
damsel,

Susarman placed Virata on his own car and rushed off the field.

When the powerful Virata was taken captive, the Matsyas fled in fear in all
directions.

Seeing them panic-stricken, Kunti's son, Yudhishthira, addressed Bhima, saying:

"Virata has been taken captive. Rescue him. As we have lived happily in Virata's
city,

having every desire of ours gratified, you must discharge that debt by liberating
him."

To this, Bhimasena replied: "I will. Mark the feat I will achieve in battling with
the foe,

relying solely on the might of my arms. Stand aside and witness my prowess.

Uprooting this mighty tree and using it as a mace, I will rout the enemy."

King Yudhishthira, however, said to his brother: "Do not commit such a rash act.

Let the tree stand there. You must not achieve such feats in a superhuman manner
by means of that tree, for if you do, the people will recognize you
and say: 'This is Bhima.' Take some human weapon, such as a bow and arrows,
or a sword, or a battle-ax, and liberate him without letting anyone know who
you are.
The twins will defend your wheels. Fighting together, liberate the king of the
Matsyas!"
Bhimasena took up an excellent bow and shot from it a shower of arrows
thick as the downpour of a rain-charged cloud. And he then rushed furiously
toward Susarman and said to the lord of the Trigartas: "Stay! Stay!"
Susarman—seeing Bhima, like Yama himself, saying, "Stay! Stay! Witness this feat.
This combat is at hand!"—considered the situation. Taking up his bow,
he turned back, along with his brothers. In the twinkling of an eye,
Bhima destroyed those cars that sought to oppose him.
Soon hundreds of thousands of cars and elephants and horses and horsemen
and brave and fierce bowmen were overthrown by Bhima as Virata watched.
And the infantry also began to be slaughtered by the illustrious Bhima, mace in
hand.
Beholding that onslaught, Susarman thought: *My brother seems to have succumbed
in the midst of this mighty host. Is my army going to be annihilated?*
Drawing his bowstring to his ear, Susarman turned back and shot keen-edged
shafts.
The Matsya warriors, seeing the Pandavas charging on their car, urged their
steeds on
and shot excellent weapons, wounding the Trigarta soldiers.
Virata's son also, exceedingly exasperated, began to perform prodigious feats of
valor.
Kunti's son Yudhishthira slew a thousand of the foe,
and Bhima showed the abode of Yama to seven thousand.
Nakula sent seven hundred to their deaths by means of his arrows. And Sahadeva
as well,
commanded by Yudhishthira, slew three hundred brave warriors.
Having slain such numbers, Yudhishthira, with weapons upraised,
rushed against Susarman and assailed him with volleys of arrows.
Susarman, enraged, pierced Yudhishthira with nine arrows, and each of his four
steeds
with four. Then Bhima approached Susarman and crushed his steeds.
And having slain the soldiers who protected his rear,
Bhima dragged his antagonist's charioteer to the ground.
Seeing that the king of Trigarta's car was without a driver, the defender of his car
wheels,
the famous and brave Madiraksha, came to his aid.
The powerful Virata, leaping down from Susarman's car and securing the latter's
mace,
ran in pursuit of him. And Virata, though old, moved on the field, mace in hand,
like a lusty youth. Bhima, seeing Susarman flee, addressed him, saying:
"Desist, O prince! This flight of yours is not proper!

With this prowess of yours, how could you wish to carry off the cattle by force?
How also, forsaking your follower, do you droop so in the midst of foes?"
The mighty Susarman, that lord of countless cars, answered Bhima, saying:
"Stay! Stay!" And he suddenly turned around and rushed at him.
Bhima, leaping down from his car as he alone could do, rushed forward with
      coolness,
desiring to take Susarman's life. The mighty Bhimasena rushed toward him
like a lion rushing at a small deer. And Bhima seized Susarman by the hair,
lifted him up in anger, and dashed him to the ground.
As Susarman lay crying in agony, Bhima kicked him in the head
and, placing his knee on Susarman's breast, dealt him several severe blows. The
      king of the Trigartas
became senseless. And the whole Trigarta army, stricken with panic, broke and
      fled.
The mighty sons of Pandu, having vanquished Susarman, rescued the cattle
and other wealth and, having dispelled Virata's anxiety, stood together before
      that king.
Bhimasena then said: "This wretch given to wicked deeds
does not deserve to escape from me with his life. But what can I do? The king is
      so lenient!"
Then, taking Susarman by the neck as the king of the Trigartas lay insensible
and covered with dust, and binding him fast, Bhima placed Susarman on his car
and went to Yudhishthira in the middle of the field. Bhima showed him Susarman.
King Yudhishthira said: "Let this worst of men be set free."
Bhima then said to the mighty Susarman: "If you wish to live, listen to my words.
You must say in every court and assembly of men: 'I am a slave.'
On this condition only will I grant you your life. This is the law pertaining to the
      vanquished."
Thereupon Bhima's elder brother addressed Bhima, saying: "If you regard us as
      an authority,
liberate this wicked person. He has already become King Virata's slave."
And turning then to Susarman, he said: "You are freed.
Go as a free man, and never act again in this way."
Susarman was overwhelmed with shame and hung down his head.
Liberated from slavery, he went to King Virata, saluted the monarch, and
      departed.

✦

The Pandavas, having slain their enemies and liberated Susarman,
passed that night happily on the field of battle. And Virata gratified those mighty
      warriors
with wealth and honor. Virata said: "All these gems are now as much yours as
      mine.
According to your pleasure, live here happily.
Delivered from perils today by your prowess, I am now crowned with victory.
I invite you to become the lords of the Matsyas."

The Pandavas, with Yudhishthira at their head, joining their hands, replied to
    the king:
"We are well pleased with all that you say. We are gratified that you have been
    freed
from your foes." Virata, the lord of the Matsyas, again addressed Yudhishthira,
    saying:
"Come, we will install you in sovereignty over the Matsyas. And we will bestow
    on you
things that are rare objects of desire, for you deserve everything in our hands.
I will bestow on you gems and cattle and gold and rubies and pearls. I bow to you.
It is through your prowess that I have not succumbed to the foe."
Yudhishthira answered: "We are well pleased with your delightful words.
May you be ever happy, always practicing humanity toward all creatures.
Let messengers be sent into the city to tell the glad tidings and proclaim your
    victory."
The king ordered that the messengers be dispatched, adding:
"And let damsels and courtesans, decked in ornaments, come out of the city
with every kind of musical instrument." The men all departed then with cheerful
    hearts.
And they proclaimed at sunrise, all about the city gates, the victory of the king.

29

Uttara

When Virata, king of the Matsyas, had set out in pursuit of the Trigartas
to recover his cattle, Duryodhana and his forces invaded his dominions.
Bhishma and Drona, and Karna and Kripa, acquainted with the best of weapons;
Aswatthaman, and Suvala's son, and Dussasana, and Vivingsati and Vikarna
and Chitrasena, endowed with great energy; and Durmukha and Dussaha—
these and many other great warriors drove off the cowherds of King Virata
and took away the cattle. The Kauravas seized sixty thousand head.
And loud was the cry of woe set up by the cowherds smitten by those warriors.
The chief of the cowherds mounted a chariot and set out for the city, wailing in
    affliction.
It was to Prince Uttara, proud son of King Virata, that he reported on the royal
    cattle:
"Rise, therefore, and bring back your cattle, O prince, for the kingdom's good.
Your father, the king of the Matsyas, left you in the empty city.
He boasts of you in court, saying: 'My son, equal to me, is a hero
and is the supporter of the glory of my race. My son is a warrior
skilled in arrows and weapons and has great courage.'
Let his words now be true! Bring back the cattle after vanquishing the Kurus.
Your bow is like a vina. Its two ends represent the ivory pillows;
its string, the main cord; its staff, the fingerboard; and the arrows shot from it
are musical notes. Strike in the midst of the foe that vina of musical sound.
Vanquishing all the Kurus in battle, return to the city after having achieved great
    renown.
Son of the Matsyas' king, you are the sole refuge of this kingdom.
We subjects of this realm have our protector in you."
Thus addressed by the cowherd in the presence of the females,
the prince boasted within the women's apartments: "Firm as I am in the use of
    the bow,
I would set out this very day on the trail of the cattle
if only someone skilled in the management of horses became my charioteer.
I do not know the man who may be my charioteer. Find one for me.
My own was slain in the great battle that was fought from day to day
for a whole month, or at least for eight and twenty nights.
As soon as I get another conversant with the management of the steeds,
I will set out and will bring back the cattle,

affrighting in battle Duryodhana and Bhishma and Karna and Kripa and Drona
and other mighty bowmen assembled for fight.
The assembled Kurus shall witness my prowess and shall say to one another:
'Is it Arjuna himself who is opposing us?' "
Having heard these words spoken by the prince, Arjuna cheerfully spoke in
    private
to his wife of faultless beauty, Draupadi, the princess of Panchala:
"Say to Uttara without delay: 'This Vrihannala was formerly the resolute charioteer
of Pandu's son, Arjuna. Tried in many a great battle, he will be your charioteer.' "
Draupadi stepped out from among the women
and said: "The handsome youth known by the name of Vrihannala
was formerly the charioteer of Arjuna. While I lived with the Pandavas,
I knew him to be a disciple of that illustrious warrior, and inferior to none in use
    of the bow.
He held the reins of Arjuna's steeds when Agni consumed the forest of Khandava.
It was with him as charioteer that Arjuna conquered all creatures at
    Khandava-prastha.
In fact, there is no charioteer equal to him." Prince Uttara said: "You know this
    youth.
You know what this one of the neuter sex may or may not be.
I cannot, however, request that Vrihannala hold the reins of my horses."
Draupadi said: "O hero, Vrihannala will obey the words
of your younger sister, that damsel of graceful hips.
If he consents to be your charioteer, you will without doubt
vanquish the Kurus and rescue your cattle."
Thus addressed by that Sairindhri, Prince Uttara spoke to his sister: "Go and
    fetch Vrihannala."
Princess Uttara repaired to the dancing hall, where Vrihannala, that strong-
    armed son of Pandu,
was staying in disguise. That far-famed daughter of King Virata,
adorned with a golden necklace and ever obedient to her brother,
repaired to the dancing hall like a flash of lightning rushing toward dark clouds
                    and saluted Arjuna.
Arjuna asked her: "What brings you here, a damsel decked in a necklace of gold?
Why are you in such a hurry, O gazelle-eyed maiden?"
The princess, standing among her female attendants and displaying proper
    modesty,
said: "The cattle of this realm, O Vrihannala, are being driven away by the Kurus,
and it is to conquer them that my brother will set out with bow in hand.
Not long ago his own charioteer was slain in battle,
and there is none equal to the one slain who can act as my brother's charioteer.
The Sairindhri has spoken to him about your skill in the management of steeds.
You were formerly the favorite charioteer of Arjuna.
Will you, therefore, O Vrihannala, act as the charioteer of my brother?
By this time, our cattle have surely been driven away by the Kurus.
If you do not act, I who ask you to perform this service out of affection will give
    up my life!"

Thus addressed, Vrihannala, that oppressor of foes, went to Prince Uttara, who
    said:

"With you as his charioteer, Arjuna gratified Agni at the Khandava forest!

The Sairindhri has spoken of you to me. She knows the Pandavas.

Will you, therefore, O Vrihannala, hold, as you did for him,

the reins of my steeds, desirous as I am of fighting with the Kurus

and rescuing my bovine wealth?" Vrihannala replied:

"What ability have I to act as a charioteer in the field of battle?

If it is song or dance or musical instruments or such other things, I can
    entertain you,

but where is my skill for becoming a charioteer?"

Uttara said: "Singer or dancer, mount my car, and hold the reins of my excellent
    steeds!"

Although Arjuna was acquainted with everything having to do with chariots,

in the presence of Uttara he began to make many mistakes for the sake of fun.

When he sought to put the coat of mail on his body by raising it upward,

the large-eyed maidens burst into loud laughter. And seeing him ignorant of
    armor,

Uttara himself equipped Vrihannala with a costly coat of mail.

Then the prince, encasing his own person in an excellent armor of solar
    effulgence,

and hoisting his standard, bearing the figure of a lion,

caused Vrihannala to become his charioteer. And the hero Vrihannala set out,

taking with him many costly bows and a large number of beautiful arrows.

Princess Uttara and her maidens said to Vrihannala: "Bring us dolls when you
    come back,

and various kinds of fine clothes, after vanquishing the Kurus!"

Arjuna, the son of Pandu, in a voice as deep as the roar of the clouds, answered
    the maidens:

"If Uttara can vanquish those warriors, I will certainly bring back dolls and fine
    clothes."

The heroic Arjuna then urged the steeds toward the Kuru army,

over which floated innumerable flags.

The elderly dames and maidens and Brahmanas of rigid vows stared at Uttara,

seated on his car with Vrihannala as charioteer, and they walked around the car

to bless the hero Vrihannala. The women said: "Let the victory that Arjuna
    achieved of old

during the burning of the forest of Khandava be yours, O Vrihannala,

when you encounter the Kurus today with Prince Uttara."

The son of King Virata addressed his charioteer, saying: "Proceed toward the
    Kurus.

I will defeat those assembled Kurus who have come here to win victory.

I will rescue my cattle from them. I will then return to the capital."

At these words of the prince, Arjuna urged those excellent steeds onward.

They seemed to fly through the air. Heading toward the cemetery,

they came upon the Kurus and beheld their army arrayed in order of battle.

Uttara, seeing that mighty host abounding in elephants, horses, and chariots

and protected by Karna and Duryodhana and Kripa and Shantanu's son
and that intelligent bowman Drona, with his son Aswatthaman,
became agitated with fear, with the hairs on his body standing on end,
and said to Arjuna: "I dare not fight with the Kurus. I am incapable of battling
　　with this host,
abounding in heroic warriors who are difficult to vanquish, even for the celestials.
I do not venture to penetrate into their army consisting of formidable bowmen
and abounding in horses and elephants and cars and foot soldiers and banners.
I am fainting with fear at the very sight of them."
The base and foolish Uttara, bewailing his fate in the presence of the high-
　　spirited Arjuna
disguised as his charioteer, said: "My father has gone out to meet the Trigartas,
taking his whole army and leaving me in the empty city. There are no troops to
　　assist me.
Alone, a mere boy who has not undergone much exercise in arms,
I am unable to encounter these innumerable warriors skilled in weapons.
　　　　　　　　Therefore, O Vrihannala, cease to advance!"
Vrihannala said: "Why do you show fear, which enhances the joy of your foes?
As yet you have done nothing on the field of battle with the enemy.
It was you who ordered me: 'Take me toward the Kauravas.' I will, therefore,
　　take you
there where those flags are, into the midst of the hostile Kurus,
who are prepared to fight for the cattle as hawks are for meat.
Having talked so highly of your manliness before both men and women,
why would you now desist from the fight?
If you should return home without recapturing the cattle, brave men and even
　　women
will laugh at you in derision. As regards myself, I cannot return to the city
without having rescued the cattle, praised highly as I have been by the Sairindhri
for my skill in driving. It is for those praises by the Sairindhri and for your words
　　also
that I have come. Why should I not, therefore, give battle to the Kurus?"
Uttara said: "Let the Kurus rob the Matsyas of their wealth. Let men and women
　　laugh.
Let my cattle perish. Let the city be a desert. Let me stand exposed before my
　　father.
Still there is no need of battle." The terrified prince then jumped down from
　　his car,
threw down his bow and arrows, and fled, sacrificing honor and pride.
Vrihannala, however, exclaimed: "This is not the practice of the brave,
this flight of a Kshatriya from the field of battle! Even death in battle
is better than flight from fear." Having said this, Arjuna came down from the car
and, with his long braid and red garments fluttering in the air, chased the
　　fleeing prince.
Some soldiers, not knowing that it was Arjuna who was running with his braid
　　flapping,
burst out into laughter at the sight. The Kurus argued:

"Who is this person thus disguised like fire concealed in ashes?
He is partly a man and partly a woman. Although bearing a neuter form,
he resembles Arjuna. His are the same head and neck, and the same arms,
like a couple of maces. And this one's gait also is like his. He must be Arjuna.
Who else would come alone against us? Virata left a single son of his in the
      empty city.
That son has come out from childishness, not from heroism. It is Uttara—
having, without a doubt, made Arjuna his charioteer—who is now living in
      disguise.
It seems that he is flying in panic. And Arjuna runs after him to bring him back."
Meanwhile, within a hundred steps, Arjuna seized Uttara by the hair.
And that son of Virata lamented: "Listen, good Vrihannala—turn the car
      around.
He who lives meets with prosperity. I will give you a hundred coins of pure gold
and eight pieces of lapis lazuli set with gold, and a chariot with a golden flagstaff
and drawn by excellent steeds, and also ten elephants of great strength. But set
      me free!"
Laughing, Arjuna dragged Uttara toward the car and said: "If you do not venture
      to fight,
come and hold the reins of the steeds as I fight. Protected by the might of my
      arms,
penetrate into that formidable array of cars guarded by mighty warriors.
Fear not! You are a Kshatriya, and foremost among royal princes.
I shall fight the Kurus and recover the cattle. Just be my charioteer."
Having thus comforted the prince, the son of Pritha lifted the trembling Uttara
      onto the car.

✦

All the great car warriors of the Kurus, with Bhishma and Drona at their head,
beholding Vrihannala, that bull among men, seated on the car in the guise of a
      person of the third sex
and driving toward the sami tree, having taken Uttara up,
became worried, suspecting that it might be Arjuna who was coming.
The preceptor Drona, seeing that they were so dispirited, said:
"Violent and hot are the winds that blow, showering gravel in profusion.
The sky also is overcast with a gloom of ashy hue.
The clouds present the strange sight of being dry and waterless.
The jackals are yelling hideously, frightened by the conflagrations on all sides.
The horses, too, are shedding tears, and our banners tremble although moved
      by no one.
With these inauspicious indications, a great danger is at hand. Stay vigilant!
Expect a terrible slaughter, and guard the cattle.
This hero in the habit of a person of the third sex is Arjuna. There is no doubt."
Then, addressing Bhishma, the preceptor continued: "This is Arjuna, who will
      vanquish us
and take away the cattle! Put to great hardship in the forest, he comes in wrath.

Taught by Indra himself, he is like Indra in battle, and I do not see a hero
who can withstand him."
Karna said: "You always censure us by speaking of the virtues of Arjuna,
but he is not equal to even a sixteenth part of myself or Duryodhana!"
Duryodhana said: "If this be Arjuna, then my purpose has already been fulfilled,
for then the Pandavas, if discovered, shall have to wander for another twelve
years.
Or, if this be any other person, I will prostrate him on the earth with keen-edged
arrows."
Duryodhana having said this, Bhishma and Drona and Kripa and Drona's son all
applauded.

✦

Vrihannala, having reached that sami tree, and having ascertained Virata's son
to be delicate
and inexperienced in battle, said to Uttara: "Take down from this tree
some bows that are there, for these bows of yours are unable to bear my strength.
In this tree of thick foliage are tied the bows and arrows and banners and coats
of mail
of the heroic sons of Pandu. There also is Arjuna's bow of great energy, the
Gandiva,
which is equal to thousands of other bows and capable of extending a kingdom's
limits.
The other bows, of Yudhishthira, Bhima, and the twins, are equally mighty and
tough."
Uttara said: "I have heard that a corpse is tied in this tree.
How can I, therefore, being a prince by birth, touch it with my hands?
I was born in the Kshatriya order, the son of a king, and am observant of mantras
and vows.
It is therefore unbecoming for me to do that. Why do you make me an unclean
bearer of corpses
by compelling me to come in contact with a dead body?"
Vrihannala said: "You shall remain clean and unpolluted. Do not fear.
There are only bows in this tree, and not corpses."
Virata's son alit from the car and reluctantly climbed the sami tree.
First cutting off the wrappings of the bows, and then the ropes with which they
were tied,
the prince beheld the Gandiva along with four other bows.
And as the bows were untied, their splendor, radiant as the sun, shone
like the planets at the time of their rising. But Uttara, seeing the bows,
become afflicted with fear, and the hairs of his body again horripilated.
He touched those large bows of great splendor and said to Vrihannala:
"To what warrior of fame does this excellent bow belong with a hundred golden
bosses?
Whose is this excellent bow of good sides, easy to hold,
on the staff of which shine golden elephants of such brightness?

Whose is this excellent bow, adorned with three score of Indragoapkas insects of
   pure gold
at regular intervals? Whose is this excellent bow, with three golden suns
blazing forth with such brilliance? Whose is this bow, variegated with gold and
   gems,
and on which golden insects are set with beautiful stones?
Whose are these arrows with wings, having golden heads and cased in golden
   quivers?
Who owns these large shafts, so thick, furnished with vulturine wings whetted on
   stone,
yellowish in hue, sharp-pointed, well tempered, and entirely made of iron?
Whose is this sable quiver bearing five images of tigers,
which holds shafts intermixed with boar-eared arrows?
Whose are these seven hundred arrows, long and thick,
capable of drinking the enemy's blood and looking like the crescent-shaped
   moon?
Whose are these gold-crested arrows whetted on stones,
the lower halves of which are furnished with wings of the hue of parrots'
   feathers,
and the upper halves of which are of well-tempered steel?
Whose is this sword with the mark of a toad on it, and pointed like a toad's head?
Cased in a variegated sheath of tigerskin, whose is this large sword of excellent
   blade,
variegated with gold, and furnished with tinkling bells?
Whose is this handsome scimitar of polished blade and golden hilt?
Manufactured in the country of the Nishadas, irresistible, incapable of being
   broken,
whose is this sword of polished blade in a scabbard of cowskin?
Whose is this beautiful and long sword, sable as the night sky in hue,
mounted with gold, well tempered, and cased in a sheath of goatskin?
Who owns this well-tempered and broad sword, longer than the breadth of thirty
   fingers,
polished by constant clash with others' weapons and kept in a case of gold bright
   as fire?
Whose is this beautiful scimitar of sable blade covered with golden bosses,
capable of cutting through the bodies of adversaries, whose touch is as fatal
as that of a venomous snake which is irresistible and excites the terror of foes?
Great is my wonder at the sight of all these excellent objects."
Vrihannala said: "The one you first asked about is Arjuna's bow of worldwide
   fame,
called the Gandiva, capable of devastating hostile hosts.
Embellished with gold, this Gandiva is the largest of all weapons belonging to
   Arjuna.
Alone equal to a hundred thousand weapons, it is with this that he vanquishes
                   both men and celestials.
Shiva held it first for a thousand years. Afterward Prajapati held it
for five hundred and three years. After that Sakra, for eighty-five years.

And then Soma held it for five hundred years.
                    After that Varuna, for a hundred years.
And finally Pareha, surnamed Swetavahana, has held it for sixty-five years.
Of high celestial origin, this is the best of all bows. Adored among gods and men,
it has a handsome form. Arjuna obtained this beautiful bow from Varuna.
This other bow, of handsome sides and golden handle, is Bhima's,
with which that son of Pritha has conquered the whole of the eastern regions.
This other excellent bow, of beautiful shape and adorned with images of
    Indragoapkas bugs,
belongs to King Yudhishthira. This weapon with golden suns of blazing splendor
belongs to Nakula. And this last bow, adorned with golden images of insects
and set with gems and stones, belongs to that son of Madri who is called Sahadeva.
These winged arrows, a thousand in number, sharp as razors
and destructive as the poison of snakes, belong to Arjuna. When he shoots them
    in battle,
these arrows blaze forth brilliantly and become inexhaustible.
These long and thick shafts resembling the lunar crescent in shape,
keen-edged and capable of thinning the enemy's ranks, belong to Bhima.
And this quiver bearing five images of tigers, full of yellowish shafts whetted on
    stone,
and furnished with golden wings, belongs to Nakula.
This is the quiver of the intelligent son of Madri,
with which he had conquered in battle the whole of the western regions.
And these arrows, all effulgent as the sun, painted all over with various colors
and capable of destroying enemies by the thousands, are those of Sahadeva.
These short and well-tempered and thick shafts, with long feathers and golden
    heads
and consisting of three knots, belong to King Yudhishthira.
This sword, with blade long and carved with the image of a toad
and head shaped like a toad's mouth, strong and irresistible, belongs to Arjuna.
Encased in a sheath of tigerskin, of long blade, handsome and irresistible,
and terrible to adversaries, this sword belongs to Bhimasena.
This excellent blade in a well-painted sheath, furnished with a golden hilt,
belongs to the wise Kaurava, Yudhishthira the Just. And this sword of strong blade,
irresistible and intended for various modes of fight and sheathed in goatskin,
is Nakula's. The huge, irresistible scimitar in a sheath of cowskin belongs to
    Sahadeva."
Uttara said: "These weapons adorned with gold look exceedingly beautiful.
But where are Arjuna and Yudhishthira and Nakula and Sahadeva and
    Bhimasena?
Having lost their kingdom at dice, the high-souled Pandavas are no longer
    heard of.
Where also is Draupadi, the princess of Panchala, famed as the gem among
    women,
who followed the sons of Pandu to the forest after their defeat at dice?"
Arjuna said: "I am Arjuna. Your father's courtier is Yudhishthira,
and your father's cook, Vallava, is Bhimasena. The groom of horses is Nakula,

and Sahadeva is in the cowpen. And know you that the Sairindhri is Draupadi,
        for whose sake the Kichakas have been slain."
Uttara said: "I will believe all this if you can enumerate the ten names of Arjuna!"
Arjuna said: "I will tell you my ten names.
Listen, and compare them with what you heard before.
They are Arjuna, Falguna, Jishnu, Kiritin, Swetavahana, Vibhatsu, Vijaya, Krishna,
Savyasachin, and Dhananjaya." Uttara said: "Tell me, why are you called Vijaya,
and why Swetavahana? Why are you named Krishna, and why Arjuna
and Falguna and Jishnu and Kiritin and Vibhatsu?
And why are you called Dhananjaya and Savyasachin?
I have heard the origin of the several names of that hero, and I can believe your
    words
if you can tell me all about them." Arjuna said:
"They called me Dhananjaya because I lived in the midst of wealth,
having subjugated all the countries and taken away their treasures.
They called me Vijaya because when I go out to battle with invincible kings,
I never return without vanquishing them.
I am called Swetavahana because, when I am battling with the foe,
white horses decked in golden armor are always yoked to my car.
They call me Falguna because I was born on the breast of the Himavat
on a day when the constellation Uttara Falguna was in the ascendant.
I am named Kiritin after a diadem, resplendent like the sun,
that was placed on my head by Indra during my encounter with the powerful
    Danavas.
I am known as Vibhatsu among gods and men
for my never having committed a detestable deed on the battlefield.
And since both of my hands are capable of drawing the Gandiva,
I am known as Savyasachin among gods and men.
They call me Arjuna because my complexion is very rare and my acts are stainless.
I am known among human beings and celestials by the name of Jishnu
because I am unapproachable and incapable of being kept down,
and because I am a tamer of adversaries and the son of the slayer of Paka.
And Krishna, my tenth appellation, was given to me by my father
out of affection toward his black-skinned boy of great purity."
The son of Virata then saluted Arjuna and said:
"My name is Bhuminjaya, and I am also called Uttara. It is my good luck to
    behold you.
O you with red eyes, and arms that are mighty and each like the trunk of an
    elephant,
I ask you to pardon what I said to you from ignorance.
My fears have been dispelled, and the love I bear you is great."

✦

Uttara said: "Mounted as you are on this large car, with me as driver,
which division of the hostile army would you penetrate?"
Arjuna answered: "I am pleased with you. You have no cause for fear.

Tie all those quivers to my car, and take from among those
the sword of polished blade and adorned with gold."
Uttara climbed down from the tree, bringing with him Arjuna's weapons.
Uttara said: "I know your steadiness in battle; but, reflecting on this, I am
 bewildered.
Foolish as I am, I am incapable of understanding by what distressful
 circumstances
a person of such handsome limbs could become deprived of manhood!
Indeed, you seem to me to be Mahadeva, or Indra,
or the chief of the Gandharvas, but disguised as one of the third sex."
Arjuna said: "I am observing this vow only for one year,
in conformity to the behest of my elder brother.
I am not truly one of the neuter sex, but I have adopted this vow of celibacy
in subservience to another's will, and from desire of religious merit.
But know that now I have completed my vow."
Uttara said: " I have now an ally in battle. What shall I do? Command me.
I will hold the reins of your horses that are capable of breaking the ranks of
 hostile cars!"

✦

Arjuna took off his bracelets. He then tied his black and curling locks
with a piece of white cloth. Seated on that car, with face turned to the east,
the mighty-armed hero, purifying his body and concentrating his soul,
recalled to his mind all his weapons. And the weapons came and, addressing
 Arjuna, said:
"We are here. We are your servants, O son of Indra." And Arjuna, bowing to them,
received them in his hands and replied: "Dwell in my memory."
Quickly stringing his bow, the Gandiva, he twanged it.
And the twang of that bow was as loud as the collision of two mighty bulls.
The birds began to totter in the skies, and large trees began to shake.
It was a loud thunderclap, and the Kurus knew from that sound
that it was Arjuna drawing the string of his best of bows from his car.
Uttara said: "You are alone. These mighty car warriors are many.
How will you vanquish in battle all these who are skilled in every kind of weapon?
You are without a follower, while the Kauravas have many.
It is for this that I stay beside you, stricken with fear."
Bursting out into loud laughter, Arjuna said to him: "Be not afraid, O hero!
What friendly follower did I have while fighting with the mighty Gandharvas?
Who was my ally while I was engaged in conflict at Khandava against so many
 celestials
and Danavas? Trained in arms by the preceptor Drona, by Sakra, and Vaisravana,
and Yama, and Varuna, and Agni, and Kripa, and Krishna of Madhu's race,
and by Shiva, the wielder of the Pinaka, why shall I not fight with these?
Drive the car, and let your heart's fever be dispelled."
Having taken down the banner with the lion's figure,
and having deposited it at the foot of the sami tree, Arjuna hoisted on that car

his own golden banner, bearing the figure of an ape with a lion's tail,
which was a celestial illusion contrived by Viswakarman himself,
for as soon as he had thought of that gift of Agni,
Agni, knowing his wish, ordered those superhuman creatures
to take their place in that banner.
And with the beautiful flag of handsome make, with quivers attached to it
and adorned with gold, that excellent flagstaff of celestial beauty instantly fell
from the firmament onto his car. Beholding it, the hero circumambulated it
    respectfully.
The ape-bannered Arjuna, with fingers encased in gloves of iguana leather,
took up his bow and arrows and set out in a northerly direction.
He blew his large conch shell of thundering sound, and at that sound the steeds
endowed with swiftness dropped down on the ground, upon their knees.
Uttara also, greatly affrighted, sat down on the car.
Thereupon the son of Kunti took the reins himself and, raising the steeds,
placed them in their proper positions. Embracing Uttara, he said: "Fear not, O
    prince.
You are a Kshatriya by birth. Why do you become so dispirited in the midst of foes?
You must have heard before now the blare of many conchs and the notes of
    many trumpets,
and the roar also of many elephants in the midst of ranks arrayed for battle.
Why are you so terrified by the blare of this conch, as if you were an ordinary
    person?"
Uttara said: "I have heard the blare of many a conch and many a trumpet
and the roar of many an elephant in the battle array, but I have never before
    heard
the blare of such a conch, nor have I ever seen a banner like this.
Never before have I heard the twang of a bow such as this.
My mind is bewildered; my perception of direction is confused.
My ears, too, have been deafened by the twang of the Gandiva!
The whole firmament seems to be covered by this banner and hidden from view!"
Arjuna said: "Stand firm on the car, pressing your feet on it,
and hold the bridles tightly, for I shall blow the conch again."
Arjuna then blew his conch again and filled his foes with grief and his friends
    with joy.
The sound was so loud that it seemed to split hills and mountains.
Uttara once again sat down on the car, clinging to it in fear.

✦

Meanwhile, Drona said: "From the rattle of the car
and the manner in which the clouds have enveloped the sky and the earth itself
    trembles,
this warrior can be none else than Savyasachin.
Our weapons do not shine, our steeds are dispirited, and our fires do not flare up.
All this is ominous. Our animals are setting up a frightful howl, gazing toward
    the sun.

Crows perch on our banners. All this is ominous.

Those vultures and kites on our right portend great danger.

That jackal also, running through our ranks, wails dismally. All this portends calamity.

Surely this forebodes a great destruction of Kshatriyas.

Things endowed with light are all pale; beasts and birds look fierce.

O king, your ranks seem to be confounded by these blazing meteors.

Vultures and kites wheel above your troops.

Indeed, our ranks seem already to have been vanquished, for none is eager to fight.

Sending the cattle ahead, we should stand here ready to strike,

with all our warriors arrayed in order of battle."

King Duryodhana then said to Bhishma and Drona and Kripa:

"Both Karna and I had said this to the preceptors.

This was the pledge of the sons of Pandu: that if defeated at dice,

they would reside in the woods for twelve years,

and then one more year somewhere unknown to us. That thirteenth year is yet running.

Arjuna, therefore, who is still to live incognito, has appeared before us.

And if he has come before the term of exile be at its end, the Pandavas

shall have to pass another twelve years in the woods.

Whether his appearance is due to forgetfulness on their part or induced by desire of dominion,

or whether it is a mistake of ours, Bhishma must calculate,

assessing the shortness or excess of the promised period.

Even moralists are puzzled in judging their own acts.

As regards ourselves, we have come hither to fight with the Matsyas and seize their cattle.

If it is Arjuna who has come, what fault can attach to us?

We have come here to fight against the Matsyas on behalf of the Trigartas

for the numerous acts represented to us of oppression committed by the Matsyas.

It was for this that we promised aid to the Trigartas, who were overcome with fear.

It may be that the Trigartas are now bringing away the cattle

or that, being defeated, they are coming toward us to negotiate with the king of the Matsyas.

Or it may be that, having driven the Trigartas off,

the king of the Matsyas, at the head of his people and his whole army of fierce warriors,

appears on the scene and advances to make night attacks upon us.

It may be that some one leader among them is advancing to vanquish us,

or it may be that the king himself of the Matsyas is come.

But whether it be the king of the Matsyas or Arjuna, we must all fight him.

This has been our pledge. Why are all these best of car warriors,

Bhishma and Drona and Kripa and Vikarna and Drona's son,

now sitting on their cars, panic-stricken? At present there is nothing better than fighting.

Therefore, make up your minds.

If, because of the cattle we have seized, an encounter takes place
with the divine wielder himself of the thunderbolt, or even with Yama,
who is there who will be liable to reach Hastinapura? Pierced by the shafts of
    the foe,
how will the foot soldiers, flying through the deep forest with their backs to the
    field,
escape with life, when escape for the cavalry is doubtful?"
Karna replied: "Disregarding the preceptor, make all arrangements.
He knows well the intentions of the Pandavas and strikes terror in our hearts.
His affection for Arjuna is great. Seeing him coming alone, Drona chants his
    praises.
Make such arrangements that our troops may not break.
Everything is in confusion just because Drona heard the neigh of Arjuna's steeds.
The Pandavas are always the special favorites of the preceptor.
The selfish Pandavas have stationed Drona among us. He betrays himself by his
    speech.
Whoever would extol a person upon hearing the neigh of his steeds?
Horses always neigh, whether walking or standing. The winds blow at all times.
And Indra always showers rain. The roar of the clouds may frequently be heard.
What has Arjuna to do with these, and why are these reasons to praise him?
All this on Drona's part is due either to the desire of doing good to Arjuna
or to his wrath and hatred toward us. Preceptors are wise and sinless
and kind to all creatures. But they should never be consulted in times of peril.
In knowing the lapses of others, in studying the characters of men,
in understanding the science of horses and elephants and cars, in treating the
    diseases of asses
and camels and goats and sheep and cattle, in planning buildings and gateways,
and in pointing out the defects of food and drink, the learned are in their
    proper sphere.
But disregard learned men who extol the heroism of the foe.
Place the cattle securely and array the troops and guards in proper places so we
    may fight."
Karna continued: "I see all these blessed ones looking alarmed and panic-stricken,
unresolved and unwilling to fight. Whether he who is coming
is the king of the Matsyas or Arjuna, I will resist him as the banks resist the
    swelling sea.
Shot from my bow, these flying arrows, like gliding snakes,
are all sure of aim. Discharged by my light hands, these keen-edged arrows
furnished with golden wings shall cover Arjuna like locusts shrouding a tree.
Having been engaged in ascetic austerities for the last thirteen years,
Arjuna will strike but mildly in this conflict, and the son of Kunti,
having become a Brahmana endowed with good qualities,
has thus become a fit person to receive my shafts by the thousands.
This bowman is celebrated over the three worlds, but I am in no way inferior
    to him.
With golden arrows furnished with vulturine wings shot on all sides,
let the firmament seem today to swarm with fireflies.

Slaying Arjuna in battle, I will discharge today that debt
difficult of repayment but promised a long time ago by me to Dhritarashtra's son.
Hard though he be as Indra's thunderbolt, and possessed of the energy
of that chief of the celestials, I will surely grind Arjuna down
even as one afflicts an elephant by means of burning brands.
A heroic and mighty car warrior he is, and foremost among wielders of weapons,
but I shall seize the unresisting Arjuna like Garuda seizing a snake.
I will lead many cars, making a great thunder,
and my horses will advance with the speed of the wind.
Discharged from my bow, my arrows, like venomous snakes,
will pierce Arjuna's body like serpents penetrating an anthill.
Covered with arrows that have golden wings, the son of Kunti will be decked like
    a hill
covered with karnikara flowers. Struck with my javelin,
the ape stationed at his banner's top shall fall to the ground, uttering terrible cries.
The firmament will be filled with the cries of the superhuman creatures
stationed on the flagstaff of the foe as I afflict them. They will fly in all directions.
I shall pluck up by the roots the long-existing dart in Duryodhana's heart
by throwing Arjuna down from his car. The Kauravas will today behold Arjuna
with his car broken, his horses killed, his valor gone, and himself sighing like a
    snake.
Let the Kauravas leave here, taking this wealth of cattle,
or, if they wish, let them stay on their cars and witness my combat."

✦

Kripa said to Karna: "Your crooked heart always inclines to war.
You do not know the true nature of things, nor do you reckon their
    consequences.
There are various kinds of lessons we can infer from the scriptures.
Of these, a battle has been regarded by those acquainted with the past
as the most sinful thing possible. It is only when time and place are favorable
that military operations can lead to success. In the present instance, however,
the time being unfavorable, no good can come of fighting.
A display of prowess in proper time and place is beneficial.
Learned men can never act according to the ideas of a car driver.
In consideration of all this, an encounter with Arjuna is not advisable for us.
Alone Arjuna saved the Kurus from the Gandharvas, and alone he satiated Agni.
Alone he led the life of a Brahmacharin for five years on the breast of Himavat.
It is he alone who he has studied the science of weapons for five years under Indra.
Alone, vanquishing all foes, he has spread the fame of the Kurus.
Alone that chastiser of foes vanquished Chitrasena, the king of the Gandharvas.
Alone he overthrew in battle the fierce Nivatakavachas and the Kalakhanchas
that the gods themselves had not been able to slay.
What, O Karna, have you achieved single-handedly like any of the sons of Pandu,
each of whom alone has subjugated many lords of earth?
Whoever desires to fight with Arjuna should take a sedative.

As to yourself, you desire to take out the fangs of an angry snake of virulent
 poison
by stretching forth your right hand and extending your forefinger.
Or, rubbed over with clarified butter and dressed in silken robes, you desire
to pass through the midst of a blazing fire fed with fat and tallow and clarified
 butter.
Who would bind his own hands and feet, tie a huge stone to his neck,
and then try to swim across the ocean? What manliness is there in such an act?
Deceived by us, and liberated from thirteen years' exile, will not the illustrious
 hero
annihilate us? Having ignorantly come to a place where he lay concealed
like fire hidden in a well, we have exposed ourselves to great danger.
But irresistible though he be in battle, we should fight against him.
Let, therefore, our troops, clad in mail, stand here arrayed in ranks and ready to
 strike.
Let Drona and Duryodhana and Bhishma and yourself and Drona's son and
 ourselves
all fight with the son of Pritha. Do not, O Karna, act so rashly as to fight alone.
If we six car warriors be united, we can then be a match for that son of Pritha
who is resolved to fight and who is as fierce as the wielder of the thunderbolt.
Aided by our troops arrayed in ranks, we great bowmen, standing together,
will fight with Arjuna even as the Danavas encounter Vasava in battle."
Aswatthaman, Drona's son, said: "The cattle, O Karna, have not yet been won,
nor have they yet crossed the boundary of their owner's dominions,
nor have they yet reached Hastinapura. Why do you, therefore, boast?
Men of true heroism, having won numerous battles and acquired enormous
 wealth
and vanquished hostile hosts, speak not a word of their prowess.
Fire burns mutely, and mutely does the sun shine.
Mutely also does the earth bear creatures, both mobile and immobile.
The Self-Existent has sanctioned such offices for the four orders,
that each having recourse to them may acquire wealth without being censurable.
A Brahmana, having studied the Vedas, should perform sacrifices himself
and officiate at the sacrifices of others. A Kshatriya, depending upon the bow,
should perform sacrifices himself but should never officiate at the sacrifices of
 others.
And a Vaisya, having earned wealth, should cause the rites enjoined in the Vedas
to be performed for him. A Sudra should always wait upon and serve
the other three orders. Those who live as florists and vendors of meat may earn
 wealth
by expedients fraught with deceit. Acting according to the dictates of the
 scriptures,
the exalted sons of Pandu acquired the sovereignty of the whole earth,
and they always act respectfully toward their superiors, even if the latter are
 hostile.
What Kshatriya ever expressed delight at having obtained a kingdom by means
 of dice,

like this shameless son of Dhritarashtra? Having acquired wealth in this way—
    by deceit,
like a butcher—who that is wise would boast of it?
In what single combat did you vanquish Dhananjaya or Nakula or Sahadeva,
although you have robbed them of their wealth? In what battle
did you defeat Yudhishthira or Bhima ? In what battle was Arjuna bested by you?
What you have done is to drag that princess to court while she was ill
and had but one article of clothing on. You have cut the mighty root,
delicate as the sandalwood, of the Pandava tree.
Remember what Vidura said when you made the Pandavas act as slaves!
We see that men and others, even insects and ants, show forgiveness
according to their power of endurance. The son of Pandu, however,
is incapable of forgiving the sufferings of Draupadi.
Surely Dhananjaya comes here for the destruction of the sons of Dhritarashtra.
Inflamed as Dhananjaya is with wrath, anyone attacked by him will be overthrown
like a tree under the weight of Garuda! In prowess he is superior to you,
and in bowmanship equal to the lord of the celestials, and in battle equal to
    Krishna.
Who then would not praise him? What man is a match for Arjuna,
who counteracts celestial weapons with celestial, and human weapons with
    human?
Those acquainted with the scriptures declare that a disciple is in no way inferior
    to a son,
and it is for this that the son of Pandu is a favorite of Drona.
Employ the means you adopted in the match at dice.
Let Sakuni, that deceitful gambler, fight now!
The Gandiva, however, does not cast dice, unlike the Krita or the Dwapara;
these shoot, by the myriads, blazing and keen-edged shafts at foes.
The fierce arrows from the Gandiva, furnished with vulturine wings, pierce
    mountains.
The destroyers of all, named Yama and Vayu and the horse-faced Agni,
leave some remnant behind, but Arjuna inflamed with wrath never does.
As you had played at dice in the assembly with your uncle's help, so fight in this
    battle
protected by Suvala's son. Let the preceptor, if he chooses, fight.
I shall not, however, fight with Arjuna. We are to fight with the king of the Matsyas,
                    if indeed he comes on the trail of the cattle."
Bhishma said: "Drona's son observes well, and Kripa, too, observes rightly.
As for Karna, it is only out of regard for the duties of the Kshatriya order
that he desires to fight. No man of wisdom can blame the preceptor.
I, however, am of the opinion that, considering both the time and the place, we
    must fight.
Why should not that man be bewildered who has just emerged from adversity?
What Karna said to you was only for raising our drooping spirits.
As regards yourself, O preceptor's son, forgive everything.
When the son of Kunti has come, this is not the time for quarrel.
Everything should now be forgiven by yourself and the preceptor Kripa.

This is not the time for disunion. Let all of us, uniting, fight with Indra's son.
Of all the calamities that may befall an army, as enumerated by the wise,
the worst is disunion among the leaders."
Aswatthaman said: "These just observations need not be uttered in our presence;
the preceptor, however, filled with wrath, spoke of Arjuna's virtues.
The virtues of an enemy should be admitted, even as the faults of even one's
preceptor
may be pointed out. Therefore, one should declare the merits of a son or a
disciple."
Duryodhana said: "Let the preceptor grant his forgiveness, and let peace be
restored.
If the preceptor be at one with us, whatever should be done in the present
emergency
would seem to have been already done."
Then Duryodhana, assisted by Karna and Kripa and the high-souled Bhishma,
pacified Drona, who said: "I was already mollified by the words first spoken by
Bhishma.
Make such arrangements that Arjuna may not be able to approach Duryodhana
in battle,
and that King Duryodhana may not be captured by the foe.
Arjuna has not revealed himself before the expiration of the term of exile,
nor will he pardon this act of ours today, having only recovered the cattle.
I am myself doubtful of the completion of the period of exile, as Duryodhana
said before.
With this in mind, it behooves the son of Ganga to say what is true."
Bhishma said: "The wheel of time revolves with its divisions,
with Kalas and Kasthas and Muhurtas and days and fortnights and months
and constellations and planets and seasons and years.
In consequence of their fractional excesses and the deviations of the heavenly
bodies,
there is an increase of two months in every five years. It seems to me that,
calculating thus,
there would be an excess of five months and twelve nights in thirteen years.
Everything, therefore, that the sons of Pandu had promised, they have exactly
fulfilled.
Knowing this to be certain, Arjuna has made his appearance. All of them are
high-souled
and fully conversant with the meanings of the scriptures.
How would they deviate from virtue who have Yudhishthira as their guide?
The sons of Kunti have achieved a difficult feat.
If they had coveted the possession of their kingdom by unfair means,
then they would have sought to display their prowess at the time of the match at
dice.
Bound in bonds of virtue, they did not deviate from the duties of the Kshatriya
order.
The sons of Pritha would prefer death to falsehood.
When the time comes, however, the Pandavas will not give up what is theirs,

even if it is defended by the wielder of the thunderbolt himself.

We shall have to oppose in battle the foremost among brandishers of weapons.

Therefore, let such advantageous arrangements be made as have the sanction of the good

and the honest so that our possessions may not be appropriated by the foe.

I have never seen a battle in which one of the parties could say: 'We are sure to win.'

When a battle occurs, there must be victory or defeat, prosperity or adversity.

Without doubt, a party to a battle must have either of the two.

Therefore, O king, whether a battle be now proper or consistent with virtue or not, make your arrangements soon, for Arjuna is at hand."

Duryodhana said: "I will not give the Pandavas their kingdom.

Let every preparation, therefore, for battle be made without delay."

Bhishma said: "Listen to what I regard as proper, if it please you.

I should always say what is for your good, O Kaurava.

Proceed toward the capital, taking with you a fourth part of the army.

And let another fourth march, escorting the cattle.

With half the troops we will fight the Pandavas.

Drona and Karna and Aswatthaman and Kripa and I will withstand Arjuna,

or the king of the Matsyas, or Indra himself, if he approaches.

Indeed, we will withstand any of these, as does the shore withstand the surging sea."

These words spoken by the high-souled Bhishma were acceptable to the king of the Kauravas,

and he acted accordingly, without delay.

Bhishma, having sent away the king and then the cattle, began to array the soldiers

in order of battle. Addressing the preceptor, he said: "Stand in the center,

and let Aswatthaman stand on the left, and let the wise Kripa, son of Saradwata,

defend the right wing, and let Karna of the Suta caste, clad in mail, stand in the van.

I will stand in the rear of the whole army, protecting it from that point."

✦

Arjuna advanced toward the Kauravas, who saw his banner and heard the din of his car

as well as the twang of the Gandiva that he stretched repeatedly.

Observing all this, Drona said: "See these two arrows coming together to fall at my feet,

and two others that pass off, barely touching my ears.

Completing the period of exile and having achieved many wonderful feats,

Arjuna salutes me and whispers in my ears.

After a long time, we see again this son of Pandu, blazing with beauty and grace."

Seeing the Kurus ready for battle, Arjuna said to Matsya's son:

"O charioteer, restrain the steeds at a point from which my arrows may reach the enemy.

Meanwhile, let me see where, in the midst of this army, is that wretch of the
    Kuru race.
Singling out that vainest of princes, I will fall upon his head,
for upon the defeat of that wretch the others will regard themselves as also
    defeated.
There stands Drona, and next to him his son. And there are those great
    bowmen,
Bhishma and Kripa and Karna. But I do not see the king there.
I suspect that, anxious to save his life, he retreats, taking the cattle with him.
Leaving this array of car warriors, proceed to the spot where Duryodhana is.
There will I fight, for there the battle will not be fruitless.
Defeating him, I will come back with the cattle."
Uttara, Virata's son, restrained the steeds with an effort and turned them
by a pull at the bridle from the spot where those bulls of the Kuru race were,
urging the steeds on toward the place where Duryodhana was.
As Arjuna went away, leaving that thick array of cars, Kripa guessed his intention
and said to his comrades: "This Vibhatsu desires not to take up his stand
at a spot remote from the king. Let us quickly fall upon the flanks of the
    advancing hero.
Of what use to us would be the cattle or all this vast wealth
if Duryodhana were to sink like a boat in the ocean?"
Meanwhile, Arjuna, having proceeded toward that division of the army,
announced himself by name and covered the troops with his arrows, thick as
    locusts.
The hostile warriors could not see anything, the earth and the sky having been
    blotted out.
The soldiers were so confounded that none could even flee the field.
The light-handedness of Arjuna they all applauded mentally.
Then Arjuna blew his conch, which always made the hairs of the foe stand erect.
Twanging his best of bows, he urged the creatures on his flagstaff
to roar more frightfully. And at the blare of his conch and the rattle of his car
    wheels
and the twang of the Gandiva and the roar of the superhuman creatures on his
    flagstaff,
the earth trembled. And the cattle, shaking their upraised tails and lowing
    together,
turned back, proceeding along the southern road.

✦

Having disorganized the hostile host, and having recovered the cattle,
that foremost among bowmen proceeded toward Duryodhana.
The cattle were running wild toward the city of the Matsyas.
All of a sudden the Kuru warriors fell upon Arjuna, who was advancing
toward Duryodhana. And beholding Kurus' countless divisions arrayed in order
    of battle
with banners waving over them, Arjuna, that slayer of foes, addressing Uttara, said:

"Urge on these white steeds decked with golden bridles.
Do your best, for I would approach this crowd of Kuru lions.
Like an elephant desiring an encounter with another,
the Suta's son of wicked soul eagerly desires a battle with me.
Take me to him who has grown so proud under the patronage of Duryodhana."
The son of Virata with large steeds broke that array of cars
and took the Pandava into the midst of the battlefield.
Seeing this, those mighty car warriors, Chitrasena and Sangramajit
and Satrusaha and Jaya, desirous of aiding Karna, rushed with arrows and long
    shafts
toward Arjuna. Then, inflamed with wrath, Arjuna began to consume
with fiery arrows that array of cars belonging to those bulls among the Kurus,
like a tremendous conflagration consuming a forest.
When the battle was raging furiously, the Kuru hero Vikarna,
mounted on his car, approached that foremost among car warriors, showering
    upon him
terrible shafts thick and long. Arjuna, first cutting Vikarna's bow, then cut off
    Vikarna's flagstaff.
And Vikarna at once took flight.
After Vikarna's flight, Satruntapa, unable to repress his ire, attacked Arjuna
with a perfect shower of arrows. Drowned, as it were, in the midst of the Kuru
    array,
Arjuna, pierced by King Satruntapa, that mighty car warrior,
struck the latter in return with five shafts and then slew his car driver with ten.
Satruntapa fell dead on the battlefield, like a tree on a mountaintop torn up by
    the wind.
Those brave bulls among men, mangled in battle by that braver bull among men,
began to waver and tremble like mighty forests shaken by the violence of the wind
that blows at the time of the universal dissolution.
And those resplendent heroes, deprived of life, measured their lengths on the
    ground.
As the wind ranges at will, scattering masses of clouds and fallen leaves
in the season of spring, so did that foremost among car warriors range in that
    battle,
scattering all his foes before him. Slaying the red steeds yoked to the car of
    Sangramajit,
the brother of Vikatana's son, Arjuna then cut off his antagonist's head
with a crescent-shaped arrow. And when his brother was slain, Vikareana's son,
mustering all his prowess, rushed at Arjuna like a huge elephant with
    outstretched tusks,
or like a tiger at a mighty bull. And the son of Vikarna pierced the son of Pandu
with twelve shafts, and all his steeds also in every part of their bodies,
and Virata's son, too, in his hand. Rushing impetuously against Vikarna's son,
who was advancing against him, Arjuna attacked him fiercely,
like Garuda of variegated plumage swooping down upon a snake.
Both of them were foremost among bowmen, and both were endowed with great
    strength

and capable of slaying foes. Seeing that an encounter was imminent, the Kauravas,
eager to watch it, stood aloof as onlookers. And the son of Pandu, beholding the
    offender Karna,
soon made him, his horses, his car, and his car driver
invisible by means of a frightful shower of countless arrows.
The warriors of the Bharatas, headed by Bhishma, with their horses, elephants,
    and cars,
pierced by Arjuna and rendered invisible by means of his shafts, and their ranks
    scattered,
began to wail in grief. The illustrious and heroic Karna, however,
counteracting with numberless arrows of his own those shafts of Arjuna's,
soon burst into view with bow and arrows like a blazing fire.
Then there arose the sound of loud clapping of hands,
with the blare of conchs and trumpets and kettledrums,
from the Kurus while they applauded Vikareana's son,
who filled the atmosphere with the sound of his bowstring.
Beholding Arjuna filling the air with the twang of the Gandiva,
and the upraised tail of the monkey that constituted his flag,
and that terrible creature yelling furiously from the top of his flagstaff,
Karna sent forth a loud roar. Afflicting Vikareana's son and his steeds, car and
    driver,
Arjuna poured an arrowy shower upon him, casting his eyes on the grandsire
and Drona and Kripa. And Vikareana's son also poured upon Arjuna a shower of
    arrows
like a rain-charged cloud. The diadem-decked Arjuna also covered Karna
with a thick downpour of keen-edged shafts. The two heroes on their cars,
in a combat carried on by means of countless shafts and weapons,
appeared to the spectators to be like the sun and the moon covered by clouds.
The light-handed Karna, unable to bear the sight of the foe, pierced the four
    horses
of the diadem-decked hero with whetted arrows and then struck his car driver
with three shafts, and his flagstaff also with three.
Wielding the Gandiva, Arjuna, like a lion awakened from slumber,
attacked Karna with straight-flying arrows. Karna produced a volley of arrows in
    return
that covered Arjuna's car. Arjuna, taking some keen crescent-shaped arrows
    from his quiver
and drawing his bow to his ear, pierced the Suta's son on every part of his body—
arms, thighs, head, forehead, neck, and everywhere. Kanra, mangled, quit the
    battle
and took flight, like one elephant vanquished by another.

✦

After Karna had fled from the field, other warriors, headed by Duryodhana,
one after another fell upon the son of Pandu with their respective divisions.
Arjuna of white steeds rushed toward the foe, discharging celestial weapons,

and soon covered all the points of the horizon with countless arrows from the
    Gandiva,
like the sun covering the earth with his rays.
Among those who fought on cars and horses and elephants, and among the foot
    soldiers,
there was none that had on his body a space of even two fingers' breadth
unwounded with sharp arrows. For his dexterity in applying celestial weapons,
and for the training of the steeds and the skill of Uttara,
and for the coursing of his weapons and his prowess and light-handedness,
people began to regard Arjuna as the fire that blazes forth
during the time of the universal dissolution to consume all created things.
Mangled by his arrows, the hostile ranks looked like newly risen clouds
on the breast of a hill reflecting the solar rays,
or like groves of asoka trees resplendent with clusters of flowers.
Indeed, the soldiers looked like a beautiful garland whose flowers wither and
    drop away.
The indifferent wind bore on its wings in the sky torn flags and umbrellas
of the hostile host. Frightened by the havoc among their ranks,
the steeds fled in all directions, freed from their yokes by Arjuna's arrows
and dragging after them broken portions of cars.
And elephants, struck on their ears and ribs and tusks and nether lips
and other delicate parts of their bodies, dropped down on the battlefield.
The earth, bestrewn in a short time with the corpses of elephants of the Kauravas,
looked like the sky overcast with masses of black clouds.
By the energy of his weapons and the twang of his bow,
and the preternatural yells of the creatures stationed on his flagstaff,
and the terrible roar of the monkey, and the blast of his conch,
that mighty grinder of foes struck terror into the hearts of all the troops of
    Duryodhana.
Unwilling to commit the sin of slaying the defenseless,
Arjuna fell back and attacked the army from behind with clouds of keen arrows,
proceeding toward their targets like hawks let off by falconers.
He soon covered the entire field with clusters of blood-drinking arrows.
Foes were able to behold Arjuna's car, when near, only once,
for immediately afterward they and their horses were sent to the other world.
As his arrows, unobstructed by the bodies of foes, passed through them,
so his car, unimpeded by hostile ranks, passed through them, too.
The arrows of the Gandiva never fell upon anything except their target,
even as the eye never dwells on anything that is not beautiful.
Dust mixed with blood uplifted by the wind reddened the rays of the sun.
And the sky became so red that it looked as if it were evening.
Indeed, the sun ceases to shed his rays as soon as he sets,
but the son of Pandu did not stop shooting his arrows.
Arjuna then shot three and seventy arrows of sharp points at Drona,
and ten at Dussaha and eight at Drona's son, and twelve at Dussasana,
and three at Kripa, the son of Saradwat. He pierced Bhishma, the son of Shantanu,
with arrows, and King Duryodhana with a hundred.

And last, he pierced Karna in the ear with a bearded shaft.

When that great bowman was thus hit, and his horses and car and driver were
destroyed,

the troops that supported him began to break.

Desiring to know Arjuna's purpose, Uttara addressed him on the field of battle,
and said:

"Toward which division shall I go?" Arjuna replied: "Take me to that warrior
you see

encased in a coat of tigerskin on the car with the blue flag and drawn by red
steeds.

He is Kripa. I shall show that great bowman my swift-handedness in archery.

And that warrior whose flag bears the device of a water pot worked in gold

is the preceptor Drona. He is an object of regard with me, as also with all bearers
of arms.

Therefore, circumambulate that great hero cheerfully.

Let us bend our heads there, for that is the eternal virtue.

If Drona strikes me first, then I shall strike him, for then he will not be able to
resent it.

And there, close to Drona, that warrior whose flag bears the device of a bow

is the preceptor's son, the great car warrior Aswatthaman,

who is also an object of regard with me and with every bearer of arms.

Therefore, stop again and again when you come by his car.

And there, that warrior in golden mail, surrounded by a third part of the army,

and whose flag bears the device of an elephant on a ground of gold,

is the illustrious King Duryodhana, the son of Dhritarashtra.

Take me before him in your car that is capable of grinding hostile cars.

This king is difficult to vanquish in battle and is the first of all of Drona's disciples

in lightness of hand. I shall show him my superior swiftness in archery.

And that warrior whose flag bears the device of a stout cord for binding elephants

is Karna, the son of Vikareana, whom you already know.

When you come before that wicked son of Radha, be very careful,

for he always challenges me to an encounter.

And the warrior whose flag is blue and bears the device of five stars with a sun,

and who holds a huge bow in hand, and over whose head is an umbrella of pure
white,

and whose mail of gold looks as bright as the sun or the moon,

and who with his helmet of gold strikes terror into my heart,

is Bhishma, the son of Shantanu and the grandsire of us all.

Entertained with regal splendor by Duryodhana, he is very partial toward that
prince.

Let him be approached last of all, for he may, even now, be an obstacle to me."

✦

All the celestials and siddhas and all the foremost sages came to behold
that encounter between Arjuna and the Kurus. The sacred fragrance of celestial
garlands

filled the air, like that of blossoming woods in early spring.
The red umbrellas and robes and garlands of the gods
were beautiful. And the dust of the earth soon disappeared in a celestial
    effulgence.
Redolent of divine perfumes, the breeze began to soothe the combatants.
And the firmament seemed ablaze and exceedingly gorgeous,
decked with arrived and arriving cars of handsome and various make,
all illuminated with diverse jewels. Surrounded by the celestials,
and wearing a garland of lotuses and lilies, the powerful wielder of the
    thunderbolt
was magnificent on his car. And the slayer of Vala, although he gazed at his son
on the field of battle, was hardly satiated with such gazing.
With the army of the Kurus arrayed in order of battle, Arjuna said to Uttara:
"Proceed to where Kripa is going by the southern side of that car
whose flag bears the device of a golden altar." Uttara urged those steeds of
    silvery hue
onward and, skilled in guiding vehicles, he sometimes wheeled about,
sometimes performed in circular mazes, and sometimes turned to the left or right,
bewildering the Kurus. At last he approached the car of Kripa,
and Arjuna announced his name and powerfully blew that best of conchs
called Devadatta, the blare of which was like the splitting of a mountain.
Having reached the very heavens, that sound echoed back
like a thunderclap hurled by Maghavat on the mountain breast. Thereupon Kripa,
unable to bear that sound, and eager for the fight,
took up his own sea-begotten conch and blew it vehemently.
Filling the three worlds with the sound, that foremost among car warriors took
    up a large bow
and twanged the bowstring. Those mighty warriors, equal to two suns,
stood opposed to each other, shining like two masses of autumn clouds.
Then Saradwat's son quickly pierced Arjuna with ten swift, whetted arrows
able to enter into the very vitals. Arjuna drew that foremost among weapons, the
    Gandiva,
and shot innumerable iron arrows all capable of penetrating into the body's core.
He enveloped Kripa with hundreds of shafts. Kripa assailed the high-souled Arjuna
with ten thousand arrows, which set up on the field of battle a loud roar.
Then he pierced Kripa's four horses with four fatal arrows from the Gandiva.
Those steeds suddenly reared, and Kripa reeled off his car.
Out of regard for his opponent's dignity, Arjuna ceased to fire arrows at him.
But Kripa remounted his own car and quickly pierced Arjuna with ten arrows
furnished with feathers of the kanka bird.
With a crescent-shaped arrow, Arjuna cut Kripa's bow and then his coat of mail,
but he did not wound his body, which was like that of a serpent
that in season has cast off its skin. As soon as his bow had been cut off,
Kripa took up another and strung that bow, which was also cut off by Kunti's son
with straight shafts. In this way, the son of Pandu cut off other bows
as soon as they were taken up, one after another, by Saradwat's son.
When all Kripa's bows were thus cut off, that mighty hero hurled from his car

a javelin at Arjuna like a blazing thunderbolt. It came whizzing through the air
with the flash of a meteor, but Arjuna cut it off with ten arrows.
And beholding his javelin thus cut off, Kripa quickly took up another bow
and almost simultaneously shot a number of crescent-shaped arrows.
Arjuna immediately cut them into fragments with ten keen-edged shafts
and then discharged thirteen arrows whetted on stone and resembling tongues
 of fire.
With one of these, he cut the yoke of his adversary's car; and with four, pierced
 his steeds;
and with the sixth, severed the head of his antagonist's car driver from his body.
Then, with three, that mighty car warrior pierced the triple bamboo pole of
 Kripa's car;
and with two, its wheels. And with the twelfth arrow, he cut off Kripa's flagstaff.
And with the thirteenth, he pierced Kripa in the breast. Then Kripa—with his
 bow cut off,
his car broken, his steeds slain, and his car driver killed—leaped down,
took up a mace, and hurled it at Arjuna. But that heavy and polished mace was
 repelled
by Arjuna's arrows. Then the warriors of Kripa's division, to rescue the son of
 Saradwat,
assailed Arjuna from all sides and covered him with their arrows.
Uttara turned the steed to the left and began to perform the circuitous maneuver
called the *yamaka* and thus withstood all those warriors.
Those bulls among men led Kripa away from the vicinity of Arjuna.

✦

Then the invincible Drona took up his bow, to which he had already strung an
 arrow,
and rushed toward Arjuna. Seeing the preceptor advancing on his golden car,
Arjuna said to Uttara: "O friend, carry me before that warrior
on whose banner top is seen a golden altar resembling a long flame of fire,
and whose car is drawn by steeds that are red and large and exceedingly
 handsome.
That warrior is Drona, with whom I desire to fight.
Forgiveness, self-control, truth, abstention from injury, rectitude of conduct—
these and countless other virtues always dwell in that spiritual one.
Therefore, take me before the preceptor."
Virata's son urged his steeds toward the car of Bharadwaja's son,
as Drona rushed toward the advancing Arjuna. The son of Bharadwaja blew his
 conch,
whose blare was that of a hundred trumpets. And the whole army became
 agitated
like the sea in a tempest, seeing those excellent steeds red in hue mingling in
 battle
with Arjuna's steeds of swanlike whiteness. That mighty car warrior Arjuna
saluted the preceptor and addressed Drona in humble and sweet tones, saying:

"Having completed our exile in the woods, we now desire to avenge our wrongs.
As we are invincible in battle, it does not behoove you to be angry with us.
I will not strike you unless you strike me first. You may act as you choose."
In reply, Drona discharged at him more than twenty arrows.
But Arjuna cut them off before they could reach him.
At this, the mighty Drona covered Arjuna's car with a thousand arrows.
And to anger him, he then covered his steeds of silvery whiteness
with arrows whetted on stone and winged with kanka feathers.
Drona and Arjuna thus commenced their battle.
All the warriors assembled there were filled with wonder.
They all admired Drona, exclaiming: "Well done! Well done!
Who else but Arjuna is worthy of fighting with Drona in battle?
Surely the duties of a Kshatriya are stern, for Arjuna fights with his own
    preceptor!"
Inflamed with fire, those mighty heroes standing before each other,
each incapable of overcoming the other, covered each other with showers of
    arrows.
The entire sky was covered with arrows and became one wide expanse of shade.
The encounter between them was dreadful and resembled that between Vali and
    Vasava.
A voice was heard in the sky applauding Drona and saying:
"Difficult is the feat performed by Drona
inasmuch as he fights with Arjuna, that conqueror of both celestials and Daityas."
Beholding Arjuna's infallibility, training, fleetness of hand, and the range of his
    arrows,
Drona was amazed. Arjuna drew the Gandiva, now with one hand and now with
    the other,
and shot a hail of arrows resembling a flight of locusts,
and the spectators applauded him, exclaiming: "Excellent! Excellent!"
So intense was the volley that the very air was unable to penetrate the thick array.
The spectators could not perceive any interval.
All at once, hundreds and thousands of straight arrows fell upon Drona's car.
The Kuru army set up exclamations of "Oh!" and "Alas!"
Although enraged with Arjuna, Aswatthaman admired that feat of the son of
    Pritha.
In fury, he rushed toward Arjuna and discharged at him a downpour of arrows.
Turning his steeds toward Drona's son, Arjuna gave Drona a chance to leave the
    field.
And Drona, wounded in that terrible encounter, and with his mail and banner
    gone,
sped away by the aid of swift horses. Then Drona's son rushed toward Arjuna,
coming on like a hurricane, showering arrows like a rain-charged cloud.
Arjuna received him with a cloud of arrows. Aswatthaman's horses, sorely
    afflicted,
became bewildered and could not ascertain which way to go.
But as Pritha's son ranged on the field, the powerful son of Drona, finding an
    opportunity,

cut the string of the Gandiva with an arrow furnished with a horseshoe head.
And beholding that extraordinary feat, the celestials applauded him highly,
                              exclaiming "Well done! Well done!"
Drona and Bhishma, and Karna, and the mighty warrior Kripa all applauded his
     feat.
And the son of Drona, drawing his excellent bow, pierced the breast of Arjuna
with his shafts, furnished with kanka feathers.
Thereupon, with loud laughter, the mighty-armed son of Pritha attached a fresh
     string
to the Gandiva and, moistening his bowstring with the sweat that stood on his
     forehead,
advanced toward his adversary, even as the infuriated leader of a herd of elephants
rushes at another elephant. The encounter that took place between those two
     heroes
made the hair of the spectators stand on end. Arjuna's quivers were inexhaustible,
and thus was that hero able to remain on the field, immovable as a mountain;
but Aswatthaman's arrows, because of his ceaseless discharge, were quickly
     exhausted.
                    It was thus that Arjuna prevailed over his adversary.

◆

Then Karna, drawing his large bow with great force, twanged the bowstring.
Immediately there arose loud exclamations of "Oh!" and "Alas!"
Pritha's son, casting his eyes in the direction of the twang,
beheld before him the son of Radha and was infuriated. Eager to slay Karna,
Arjuna stared at him with rolling eyes, and when he turned away from
     Aswatthaman,
the Kuru warriors discharged thousands of arrows at him.
Leaving Drona's son, he rushed toward Karna and, wanting a single combat
     with him,
said: "The time has now come for making good your boast in the midst of the
     assembly—
that there is none equal to you in fighting. Today, contend with me,
and you shall know the limits of your strength and no longer speak dismissively
     of others.
Fight with me in the sight of the Kurus, and make good what you said before.
You witnessed Panchala's princess outraged by villains in the midst of the court,
and now you shall reap the fruit of that act of yours.
Fettered by the bonds of morality before, I desisted from vengeance then.
But now the fruit of that wrath has ripened, and our conflict is at hand.
O wicked man, we suffered much in that forest for twelve years.
Reap now the reward of our concentrated vengeance, and fight with me in
     battle."
Karna replied: "Accomplish in deed what you say in words.
That you forbore years ago was owing to your inability to do anything.
If we witness your prowess now, we may acknowledge its truth.

If your past forbearance was due to your having been bound by the bonds of
    morality,
you are equally bound now, although you regard yourself as free.
Having passed your exile in the woods in strict accordance with your pledge,
and being therefore weakened by practicing an ascetic course of life,
how can you desire a combat with me now? Your wish is about to be gratified.
Fight with me now, and behold my strength."
Arjuna said: "Even now you fled from me in battle, and only because of this do
    you live,
although your younger brother has been slain. What other person,
having seen his younger brother slain in battle, would himself fly from the field
and then boast, as you do, in the midst of good and true men?"
The invincible Arjuna rushed at him and discharged a volley of shafts
capable of penetrating a coat of mail. But Karna responded with his own arrows.
That fierce exchange of arrows covered all sides and pierced the steeds
and arms and leather gloves of the combatants.
Thus assaulted, Arjuna cut the strings of Karna's quiver with a sharp arrow.
Karna then pierced the Pandava in the hand, which loosened the latter's hold of
    the bow.
Then Arjuna cut Karna's bow into fragments, and Karna replied by hurling a dart
at his adversary, but Arjuna fended it off with arrows.
Then the warriors that followed the son of Radha rushed in crowds at Arjuna,
but he sent them all to the abode of Yama with arrows from the Gandiva.
He also slew Karna's steeds with arrows shot from the bowstring drawn to the ear,
and they dropped to the ground. Taking another arrow, the son of Kunti
pierced the breast of Karna, and that arrow, cleaving through his mail,
penetrated his body. At this, Karna's vision was obscured, and his senses left him.
Regaining consciousness, he felt a great pain, and he fled from the combat.
Arjuna said to Uttara: "Take me toward that division
where you see the device of a golden palmyra. There our grandfather,
    Shantanu's son,
like a celestial waits, eager for an encounter with me."
But Uttara, sorely pierced with arrows, said: "I am no longer able to guide your
    steeds.
My spirits droop, and my mind is bewildered. The directions are whirling before
    my eyes.
I have been deprived of my senses by the stench of fat and blood and flesh.
It is from terror that my mind is cleft in twain. Never before have I seen
such a muster of horses in battle. And at the blare of conchs, the leonine roars
made by the warriors, the shrieks of elephants, and the twang of the Gandiva,
I have been so stupefied that I have been deprived of both hearing and memory.
As I watch you draw the Gandiva to a circle, which becomes a circle of fire,
my sight fails me, and my heart is rent asunder. I have no strength
to hold whip and reins." Arjuna said: "Do not fear. You have performed
    wonderful feats.
You are a prince born in the illustrious line of Matsyas.
Do not feel dispirited in chastising your foes. Muster all your fortitude

and hold the reins of my steeds while I once more engage in battle."
Arjuna again asked: "Take me to the van of Bhishma's division.
I will cut off his bowstring in the battle. You shall behold today
the celestial weapons of blazing beauty, looking like flashes of lightning
sporting in the midst of the clouds in the sky. The Kauravas shall see
the gold-decked back of my Gandiva today, and assembled together the foe shall
    dispute:
'By which hand of his, the right or the left, does he shoot?'
And I shall cause a dreadful river of death to flow toward the other world,
with blood for its waters and cars for its eddies and elephants for its crocodiles.
With my arrows, I shall extirpate the Kuru forest,
having hands and feet and heads and backs and arms for the branches of its trees.
Alone, bow in hand, vanquishing the Kuru host, I shall have a hundred paths
    open before me,
like those of a forest in conflagration. You shall today behold the Kuru army
moving around and around like a wheel. I shall show you today my training
in arrows and weapons. Stay on my car, whether the ground be rough or smooth.
I have obtained from Rudra the Raudra, from Varuna the Varuna, from Agni the
    Agneya,
from the god of wind the Vayava, and from Sakra the thunderbolt and other
    weapons.
I shall certainly exterminate the fierce Dharearashtra forest, even though it is
    protected
by many leonine warriors. Therefore, let your fears be dispelled."
Thus assured, Uttara penetrated into that array of cars protected by Bhishma.
The son of Ganga, however, cheerfully withstood Arjuna
who then, confronting Bhishma, cut his standard at the roots with a gold-decked
    arrow.
The standard fell to the ground. And at this, four mighty warriors, Dussasana
    and Vikarna
and Dussaha and Vivingsati, skilled in weapons and all decked with handsome
    garlands,
rushed toward Arjuna and surrounded him. Dussasana pierced the son of Virata
with a crescent-shaped arrow, and he pierced Arjuna with another arrow in the
    breast.
With a sharp-edged arrow furnished with vulturine wings,
Arjuna cut off his adversary's bow plated with gold and then pierced him in the
    breast
                    with five arrows. Dussasana then fled the combat.
Then Vikarna, the son of Dhritarashtra, pierced Arjuna.
But the son of Kunti at almost the same time hit him in the forehead,
and he fell down from his car. At this, Dussaha, supported by Vivingsati,
covered Arjuna with a cloud of sharp arrows, desiring to rescue his brother.
Arjuna, however, without the least anxiety, pierced both at almost the same
    instant
with a couple of keen-edged arrows and slew the steeds of both of them.
Thereupon both those sons of Dhritarashtra, deprived of their steeds

and with their bodies mangled, were taken away by the warriors behind them,
who had rushed forward with other cars. The unvanquished son of Kunti,
decked with a diadem and sure of his aim, attacked all sides with his arrows.
Then all the great car warriors of the Kurus, united, assailed Arjuna from all sides.
But he completely covered them with clouds of arrows, even as mist covers
    mountains.
Penetrating the bodies of elephants and horses, and steel coats of mail,
the arrows of Arjuna fell by the thousands. Afflicted with fear, the car warriors
began to leap down from their cars, and the horse soldiers from horseback,
while the foot soldiers flew in all directions. And loud was the clatter of Arjuna's
    shafts
as they cleft the mighty warriors' coats of mail made of steel, silver, and copper.
The field was soon covered with the corpses of warriors
mounted on elephants and horses, all mangled by the shafts of Arjuna,
and it seemed as if, bow in hand, he was dancing on the battlefield
that was bestrewn with severed heads decked with turbans, earrings, and necklaces,
so that the earth looked beautiful by being scattered all over
with human trunks mangled by shafts, arms with bows still in their grasp,
                and hands decked with ornaments.
In the presence of Duryodhana, his troops became dispirited and ceased to fight.
The field of battle was a dreadful river of blood with waving billows,
like the river of death that is created by time at the end of the *yuga*,
having the disheveled hair of the dead and dying for its floating moss and straw,
with bows and arrows for its boats, and flesh and animal juices for its mire.
Elephants were its alligators and the cars its rafts. And marrow and fat and blood
constituted its currents. It struck terror into the hearts of the spectators.
And dreadful to behold, and most fearful, keen-edged weapons were its
    crocodiles.
Rakshasas and cannibals haunted it from end to end, strings of pearls were its
    ripples,
and various precious ornaments were its bubbles. And with swarms of arrows for
    its eddies
and steeds for its tortoises, it was incapable of being crossed.

✦

Then, during the great havoc among the Kurus, Bhishma rushed at Arjuna,
taking up an excellent bow adorned with gold and many arrows of keen points
capable of piercing the vitals of the foe. And with the white umbrella over his
    head,
that tiger among men looked as beautiful as a hill at sunrise.
The son of Ganga, blowing his conch, cheered the sons of Dhritarashtra,
and wheeling along his right came upon Arjuna to impede his course.
The son of Kunti received him with a glad heart, like a hill receiving a rain cloud.
Bhishma, however, pierced Arjuna's flagstaff with eight arrows,
which struck the blazing ape and those creatures stationed on the banner top.
Then, with a mighty javelin of sharp edge, Arjuna cut off Bhishma's umbrella,

which fell to the ground. Then he struck his adversary's flagstaff with many shafts,
and then his steeds, and then the couple of drivers who protected Bhishma's
	flanks.
Unable to bear this, Bhishma, though cognizant of the Pandava's might,
attacked him with a powerful celestial weapon, and he in return
hurled a celestial weapon at Bhishma. In the conflict between Bhishma and
	Arjuna,
shafts striking against shafts shone in the air like fireflies in the season of the rains.
Repelling weapons with weapons, those two bulls of the Bharata race
fought on playfully and dazzled the eyes of all created beings.
Those illustrious warriors ranged the field of battle,
using the celestial weapons obtained from Prajapati and Indra and Agni
and the fierce Rudra and Kuvera and Varuna and Yama and Vayu.
Those who were watching exclaimed:
"Bravo, Arjuna! Bravo, Bhishma!"
All the celestials with Indra, stationed in the firmament,
gazed with wonder upon another celestial weapon hurled with great force
by that astonishing archer with clouds of shafts.
The soldiers were incapable even of looking at the son of Pandu,
who was like the midday sun blazing in the sky. And none ventured to look at
	Bhishma.
Both were famous for their achievements, and both were of fierce prowess.
Both were equal in feats of heroism, and both were difficult to vanquish in battle.
The lord of the celestials, therefore, paid proper respect to both
by a shower of celestial flowers. Meanwhile, Bhishma assailed Arjuna on the left
	side,
while that drawer of the bow with either hand was on the point of piercing him.
And at this, Arjuna, laughing aloud, cut off the bow of Bhishma
with an arrow of keen edge and furnished with vulturine wings.
At last Arjuna pierced Bhishma in the breast with ten shafts
although the latter was contending with all his prowess. Sorely afflicted with pain,
Ganga's son of mighty arms, and irresistible in battle, stood for a long time
leaning on the pole of his car. Seeing him deprived of consciousness,
the driver of his steeds, thinking of his instructions about protecting warriors in
	a swoon,
led him away to safety.

✦

After Bhishma had fled, leaving the van of battle, the illustrious son of
	Dhritarashtra,
hoisting high his flag, approached Arjuna, bow in hand. There was a loud roar.
And with a spear-headed shaft shot from his bow stretched to the ear,
he pierced the forehead of Arjuna who, with that keen shaft of golden point
on the forehead, looked resplendent, like a beautiful hill with a single peak.
But Arjuna, cut by that arrow, saw his warm lifeblood gush out profusely
and trickle down his body, shining like a wreath of golden flowers.

Struck thus by Duryodhana, the swift-handed Arjuna of unfailing strength,
swelling with rage, pierced the king in return with arrows like snakes of virulent
poison.
Duryodhana attacked Arjuna, and Arjuna attacked Duryodhana.
And those foremost among men, both born in the same race, struck each other
alike.
Then Vikarna, one of Dhritirashtra's sons, seated on an infuriated elephant as
huge as a mountain,
and supported by four cars, rushed against the son of Kunti.
Seeing that elephant advancing with speed, Arjuna struck it on the head
between the temples with an iron arrow of great impetus shot from the bowstring
stretched to the ear. And like the thunderbolt hurled by Indra splitting a
mountain,
that arrow, furnished with vulturine wings, penetrated up to the very feathers
into the body of that elephant as huge as a hill. That lord of the elephant species
trembled,
deprived of strength. Vikarna alit in terror and ran back a full eight hundred
paces
to ascend the car of Vivingsati. The son of Pritha then smote Duryodhana in the
breast
with another arrow of the same kind. And both the elephant and the king
having thus been wounded, and Vikarna having broken and fled
along with the supporters of the king's car, the other warriors, smitten with the
arrows,
fled the field in panic. Duryodhana, foremost among the Kurus,
turned and ran away from Arjuna, pierced by that arrow and vomiting forth
blood.
Arjuna, still eager for battle, censured him angrily: "Sacrificing your great fame,
why do you turn your back? Why are those trumpets of yours not sounding now,
as they were when you set out from your kingdom? I am an obedient servant
of Yudhishthira, being the third son of Pritha, standing here for battle.
Turn around and show me your face, and bear in mind the behavior of kings.
The name Duryodhana bestowed on you before is now meaningless.
When you run away and leave the battle, where is your persistence in combat?
Nor do I see your bodyguards, O Duryodhana, before or behind.
O foremost among men, fly away and save your life from the hands of
Pandu's son."

✦

Thus summoned by the illustrious hero, Dhritarashtra's son turned back,
stung by those censures, like a mighty elephant pricked by a sharp hook,
but Karna stopped the king on the way and went himself to meet Arjuna in
battle.
And Bhishma also turned back his steeds and rushed, bow in hand,
to protect Duryodhana from Arjuna. And Drona and Kripa and Vivingsati and
Dussasana

and others, too, rushed forward with drawn bows and arrows fixed on the
bowstrings,
to protect Duryodhana. Seeing those divisions advance toward him
like the swelling surges of the ocean, the son of Pritha rushed at them
like a crane rushing at a descending cloud. With celestial weapons in their hands,
they completely surrounded the son of Pritha and rained on him from all sides
a perfect shower of shafts. But warding off all the weapons of the Kurus,
the wielder of the Gandiva employed another irresistible weapon obtained from
Indra,
called Sanmohana. Entirely covering the cardinal directions with keen-edged
arrows
furnished with beautiful feathers, that mighty hero stupefied their senses
with the twang of the Gandiva. Once more Arjuna, taking up that large conch,
blew it with force and filled the whole earth and sky with its noise.
And all those Kuru heroes were deprived of their senses by the sound and stood
still,
their bows dropping from their hands. When the Kuru army became insensible,
Arjuna, calling to mind Uttara's words, addressed Uttara, that son of Virata, the
Matsya king:
"Go among the Kurus as long as they remain insensible, and bring away
the white garments of Drona and Kripa and the yellow and handsome ones of
Karna
as well as the blue ones of the king and Drona's son. I think Bhishma is not
stupefied,
for he knows how to counteract this weapon of mine. So pass him by,
keeping his steeds to your left, for those who are sensible should be avoided."
Uttara jumped down from the car, took those garments off the warriors,
and came back to his place. The son of Virata then urged the four steeds
with flanks adorned with golden armor and took Arjuna away from the battlefield
and the array of the infantry bearing standards in their hands.
Bhishma, seeing that best of men thus going away, struck him with arrows.
And Arjuna, having slain Bhishma's steeds, pierced him with ten shafts.
Abandoning Bhishma on the field of battle, having first slain his car driver,
Arjuna came out of that multitude of cars like the sun emerging from the clouds.
Dhritarashtra's son, that foremost among Kuru heroes,
recovered his senses and saw the son of Pritha standing like the lord of the
celestials
alone on the battlefield. He said to Bhishma: "How has this one escaped from you?"
At this, Shantanu's son, smiling, said: "Where were you, and where was your
prowess?
You were unconscious and unable to use your arrows and handsome bow!
Arjuna is not accustomed to committing atrocious deeds, nor is his soul inclined
to sin.
He does not renounce his principles even for the sake of the three worlds.
It is only because of this that all of us have not been slain in this battle.
O foremost among Kuru heroes, go back to the city of the Kurus
and let Arjuna also go away, having recaptured the cattle."

King Duryodhana, no longer eager for battle, drew a deep sigh and was silent.
He decided that the advice of Bhishma was beneficial
and the other warriors also, seeing that the Pandavas were gaining in strength,
and desiring to protect Duryodhana, resolved to return.
The son of Pritha followed them for a while, to address them and worship them.
Having paid his respects to the aged grandsire, the son of Shantanu, as also to
    the preceptor Drona,
and having saluted with beautiful arrows Drona's son
and Kripa and other venerable ones among the Kurus,
he broke Duryodhana's crown decked with precious gems into fragments
with another arrow. Then, having saluted all the venerable and brave warriors,
he filled the three worlds with the twang of the Gandiva
and blew his conch called Devadatta, piercing the hearts of all his foes.
Arjuna said to Matsya's son: "Turn back your steeds. Your cattle have been
    recovered.
The foe is going away and you can return to your city with a cheerful heart."
And the celestials also, having witnessed that most wonderful encounter
between Arjuna and the Kurus, were highly delighted
and went to their respective abodes, reflecting upon his splendid feats.

✦

Having vanquished the Kurus in battle, Arjuna brought back the cattle of Virata.
And while Dhritarashtra, after their rout, was going away,
a large number of Kuru soldiers appeared from the deep forest with slow steps,
to stand in fear before Arjuna with joined palms and hair disheveled.
Fatigued, hungry, thirsty, arrived in a foreign land, insensible with terror,
and confused, they all bowed down to the son of Pritha and said: "We are your
    slaves."
Arjuna said: "Blessings upon you. You may go away. You have no cause for fear.
I will not take your lives. You have my assurance of protection."
The warriors thanked him with benedictions in praise of his achievements and
    fame
                    and wished him long life.

✦

Approaching the city of Virata, Arjuna respectfully addressed Uttara, the prince
    of Matsya:
"It is known to you alone that the sons of Pritha are all living with your father.
Do not eulogize them upon entering the city, for then the king may hide himself
    in fear.
On the other hand, upon entering the city, proclaim in the presence of your
    father
that the deed was your own, saying: 'By me has the army of the Kurus been
    vanquished,
               and by me have the cattle been recovered!'"

Uttara said: "The feat you have achieved is beyond my power.
I shall not, however, reveal you to my father, as long as you tell me not to do it."
Arjuna returned again to the cemetery and at the same sami tree
stood with his body mangled by the arrows of the enemy.
That terrible monkey blazing like fire ascended to the sky with those other creatures
of the flagstaff. The illusion melted away, and Uttara's banner,
bearing the device of a lion, was again set up on the car.
Having replaced the arrows and quivers of those foremost among the Kuru princes,
and also that other weapon, the Gandiva, the illustrious prince of Matsya
set out for the city with a glad heart, with Arjuna as his charioteer,
again posing as Vrihannala, the car driver of Uttara.
Arjuna said: "O prince, seeing the cattle escorted in advance of us
by the cowherds, we shall enter Virata's metropolis in the afternoon,
having tended the steeds with drink and a bath.
Let the cowherds repair to the city with the good news and proclaim your victory."

✦

The brave King Virata was seated on his throne,
and all his subjects, headed by the Brahmanas, stood before him.
The king asked: "Where has Uttara gone?" And the women and maidens of the palace
and the other females of the inner apartments joyfully said to him:
"Uttara sallied forth alone, with only Vrihannala as his second,
to vanquish the six mighty car warriors—Bhishma, Kripa, Karna, Duryodhana,
Drona, and Drona's son—who had all come with the Kuru army."
King Virata, hearing that his brave son had gone forth with only one car
and with Vrihannala as his driver, was filled with grief and to his chief counselors said:
"Without doubt, the Kauravas and other lords of earth,
learning of the defeat of the Trigartas, will never keep their ground.
Therefore, let those of my warriors who have not been wounded by the Trigartas
go out with a mighty force to protect Uttara." At once the king dispatched horses
and elephants and cars and a large number of foot soldiers with various weapons,
and he said: "Learn without loss of time whether the prince still lives!
I myself think that, with a person of the neuter sex for his car driver, he is not alive."
King Yudhishthira smiled and said to the afflicted King Virata:
"If Vrihannala has been his charioteer, the foe will never be able to take away your cattle.
Protected by that charioteer, your son will be able to vanquish in battle
all the lords of earth allied with the Kurus, indeed, even the gods and the Asuras
and the siddhas and the Yakshas together."

Meanwhile, the swift-footed messengers dispatched by Uttara,
having reached Virata's city, gave tidings of the victory.
And the minister-in-chief informed the king of the great victory that had been won,
the defeat of the Kurus, and the expected arrival of Uttara.
And he said: "All the cattle have been brought back,
the Kurus have been defeated, and Uttara is well, along with his driver."
Yudhishthira said: "It is good luck that the cattle are recovered and the Kurus
    routed.
I do not, however, regard it as strange that your son should have vanquished the
    Kurus,
for his victory was assured if he had Vrihannala for his charioteer."
King Virata was so happy that the hairs of his body stood erect.
And having made presents of raiments to the messengers,
he ordered his ministers, saying: "Let the highways be decorated with flags,
and let all the gods and goddesses be worshipped with flowery offerings.
Let princes and brave warriors and musicians and harlots decked in ornaments
march out to receive my son. And let the crier, speedily riding an intoxicated
    elephant,
proclaim my victory at places where four roads meet."
All the citizens with flags and cymbals and trumpets and conchs,
and beautiful women attired in gorgeous robes, and reciters of sacred hymns
accompanied by bards and minstrels, and drummers and other kinds of
    musicians
issued forth from the city of the mighty Virata to welcome Uttara.
The wise king of the Matsyas cheerfully said: "O Sairindhri, fetch the dice.
                    And let the play commence."
The son of Pandu replied, saying: "We have heard that one whose heart is filled
    with joy
should not play with a cunning gambler. I do not, therefore, dare gamble with you
who are so transported with joy. I am ever desirous of doing what is for your good.
Let the play, however, commence if it please you."
Virata said: "My female slaves and cattle, my gold and whatsoever other wealth I
    have,
nothing of all this shall you be able to protect today even if I do not gamble."
Kanka said in reply: "O monarch, what business have you with gambling,
which is attended with numerous evils? It should, therefore, be shunned.
You may have seen or at least heard of Yudhishthira, the son of Pandu.
He lost his extensive and prosperous kingdom and his godlike brothers at dice.
For this reason, I am averse to gambling. But if you like, O king, I will play."
While the play was going on, Matsya said to the son of Pandu:
"The Kauravas, who are so formidable, have been vanquished in battle by my son."
To this, King Yudhishthira replied: "Why should he not conquer
who has Vrihannala for his charioteer?" King Matsya became angry
and said: "You wretch of a Brahmana, do you compare one of the neuter sex
with my son? Have you no knowledge of what is proper and what improper
for one to say? Without doubt, you disrespect me. Why should not my son
    vanquish

all those with Bhishma and Drona as their leaders?
O Brahmana, for friendship only I pardon you your offense.
You must not, however, say such a thing again if you wish to live."
Yudhishthira answered: "There where Bhishma and Drona and Drona's son
and the son of Vikareana and Kripa and King Duryodhana
and other royal and mighty car warriors are assembled,
or there where Indra himself is surrounded by the Maruts,
what other person than Vrihannala can fight, encountering them all?
None has been, none will be, his equal in strength of arms!
Indeed, it is Vrihannala only whose heart is filled with joy at the sight of conflict.
It is he who has vanquished the celestials and the Asuras and human beings
fighting together. With such a one for his ally, why should your son not conquer
     the foe?"
Virata said: "You do not yet restrain your tongue. If there were none to punish,
no one would practice virtue." Saying this, the king, inflamed with anger,
struck Yudhishthira in the face with a die and reproached him: "Let it not recur!"
Blood began to flow from Yudhishthira's nose.
But the son of Pritha held the blood in his hands before it fell on the ground.
The virtuous Yudhishthira then glanced at Draupadi, who was standing by his side.
Understanding his meaning, the faultless Draupadi brought a golden vessel
filled with water to receive the blood that flowed from his nose.
Meanwhile, Uttara, decked with floral chaplets, entered the city and was received
with respect by the citizens, the women, and the people of the provinces.
Approaching the gate of the palace, he sent the news of his arrival to his father.
The porter approached the king and said: "Your son, Uttara, waits at the gate,
                         with Vrihannala as his companion."
The Matsya king said: "Usher in both, as I am very eager to see them."
Then Yudhishthira gently whispered into the ear of the doorkeeper:
"Let Uttara enter alone. Vrihannala must not come in.
Such is the vow of that hero of mighty arms that whoever causes a wound on my
     person
or sheds my blood, except in battle, shall not live.
Inflamed with rage, Vrihannala will never bear to see me bleeding
but will slay Virata, with his counselors and troops and steeds."
Then Uttara, the eldest son of the king, entered
and, having worshipped the feet of his father, approached Kanka,
who was covered with blood and seated on the ground at one end of the court,
waited upon by the Sairindhri. Seeing this, Uttara asked his father:
"By whom, O king, has this one been struck? Whose is this sinful act?"
Virata said: "This crooked Brahmana has been struck by me.
He deserves even more than this. When I was praising you,
                         he praised that person of the third sex."
Uttara said: "You have committed an improper act.
Propitiate him at once so that the poison of a Brahmana's curse may not
     consume you!"
Virata soothed Kunti's son, who was like a fire hidden in ashes,
and asked his forgiveness. And to the king, who wanted to obtain his pardon,

the Pandava replied: "I have long ago forgiven you. I have no anger.
Had this blood from my nostrils fallen on the ground,
then, without doubt, you and your kingdom would have been destroyed.
I do not blame you, O king, for having struck an innocent person.
Those who are powerful generally act with unreasoning severity."
When the bleeding had stopped, Vrihannala entered the council room
and, having saluted both Virata and Kanka, stood silent.
The king began to praise Uttara in Savyasachin's hearing, saying:
"I never had nor shall have a son equal to you! How, indeed, could you
    encounter Karna,
who leaves not a single mark unhit among even a thousand he may aim at all at
    once?
How could you encounter Bhishma, who has no equal in the whole world of men?
How could you encounter Drona, that foremost among wielders of weapons,
that preceptor of the Vrishnis and Kauravas, the twice-born one
who may be regarded as the preceptor of all the Kshatriyas?
How could you meet in battle the celebrated Aswatthaman?
How could you encounter Duryodhana, the prince capable of piercing even a
    mountain
with his mighty arrows? My foes have all been thrashed. A delicious breeze blows.
And since you have recovered in battle all my wealth that had been seized,
all those mighty warriors were struck with panic. Without doubt, you have routed
    the foe
and snatched away from them my wealth of cattle, as you might have snatched
    his prey from a tiger."
Uttara said: "The cattle have not been recovered by me, nor has the foe
been vanquished by me. All that has been accomplished by the son of a deity.
Capable of striking like a thunderbolt, that youth of celestial origin
saw me running away in fear and stopped me, and he mounted on my car.
It was he who recovered the cattle and vanquished the Kauravas.
                    The deed is that hero's and not mine."
Virata said: "Where is that mighty-armed and famous youth of celestial origin,
that hero who recovered in battle my wealth that had been seized by the Kurus?
I am eager to behold and worship that mighty warrior of celestial origin
                    who saved you and my cattle also."
Uttara replied: "The mighty son of a deity disappeared.
I think, however, that he will show himself either tomorrow or the day after."
Virata remained ignorant of the son of Pandu, whom Uttara had thus described
and who was living in the palace in disguise.

◆

Then, on the third day, attired in white robes after a bath,
and decked in ornaments of all kinds, the five Pandava brothers,
having accomplished their vow, and with Yudhishthira at their head,
looked resplendent as they entered the palace gate like five intoxicated
    elephants.

In the council hall of Virata they took their seats on the thrones reserved for kings
and shone brilliantly, like fires on the sacrificial altar.
Virata then entered to hold his council and discharge other royal offices.
Seeing the illustrious Pandavas, the king reflected for a moment.
Then the Matsya king spoke to Kanka, seated there like a celestial
and looking like the lord of celestials surrounded by the Maruts.
He said: "A player at dice, you were employed by me as a courtier!
How can you occupy a royal seat thus attired in handsome robes and ornaments?"
Wanting to jest with him, Arjuna said in reply:
"This person, O king, deserves to occupy the same seat as Indra himself.
Devoted to the Brahmanas, acquainted with the Vedas, indifferent to luxury
and carnal enjoyments, habitually performing sacrifices, steady in vows,
he is the very embodiment of virtue and superior in intelligence to everybody on
    earth.
He is conversant with various weapons, and there is none even among the gods
or Asuras or men or Rakshasas or Gandharvas or Yaksha chiefs or Kinnaras
or mighty Uragas who is like him. A man of great foresight and energy,
beloved by the citizens and inhabitants of the provinces,
he is the mightiest of car warriors among the sons of Pandu.
Kind to all creatures, he is none other than the bull of the Kuru race,
King Yudhishthira the Just. The achievements of this king resemble the sun
    himself
of blazing effulgence. And his fame has traveled in all directions;
and, like the rays following the risen sun, ten thousand swift elephants followed him
when he dwelt among the Kurus. And thirty thousand cars decked in gold,
and drawn by the best steeds, also used to follow him. And fully eight hundred
    bards
adorned with earrings set with shining gems, and accompanied by minstrels,
recited his praises in those days, like the rishis adoring Indra.
And the Kauravas and other lords of earth always waited upon him like slaves,
as did the celestials upon Kuvera. Eighty-eight thousand high-souled Snatakas
depended for their subsistence upon this king practicing excellent vows.
This illustrious lord protected the aged and the helpless, the maimed and the
    blind,
as if they were his sons, and he ruled over his subjects virtuously.
Steady in morality and self-control, capable of restraining his anger,
bountiful, devoted to the Brahmanas, and truthful, this is the son of Pandu.
Possessed of such attributes, does not this bull among kings deserve a royal seat?"
Virata said: "If he is indeed Yudhishthira, the Kuru king, the son of Kunti,
which among these is his brother Arjuna, and which the mighty Bhima?
Which of these is Nakula, and which Sahadeva, and where is the celebrated
    Draupadi?
Since their defeat at dice, the sons of Pritha have not been heard of by anyone."
Arjuna said: "This one, O king, who is called Vallava and is your cook,
is Bhima of mighty arms and terrible prowess.
He who had been the keeper of your horses is that slayer of foes called Nakula,
and this one is Sahadeva, the keeper of your cattle.

Both these sons of Madri are great car warriors, possessed of much fame and
    beauty.
And this lady of eyes like lotus petals and slender waist and sweet smiles
is Drupada's daughter, your wife's Sairindhri, for whose sake the Kichakas were
    slain.
I am Arjuna, of whom it is evident that you have heard,
that son of Pritha who is Bhima's junior, and senior to the twins!
We have, O king, happily passed in your abode this period of life incognito,
                      like infants in the womb!"
After Arjuna had pointed out those five heroic Pandavas,
the son of Virata then spoke of Arjuna's prowess, saying:
"This is the one who slew the foe, like a lion devastating a flock of deer.
He ranged through crowds of hostile cars, slaying their best of car warriors.
He killed a huge elephant with a single arrow.
That enormous beast, with its flanks adorned with an armor of gold,
fell down, piercing the earth with his tusks.
By him have the cattle been recovered and the Kauravas vanquished in battle.
My ears have been deafened by the blare of his conch.
It was by this hero that Bhishma, Drona, and Duryodhana were vanquished.
                      That achievement is his and not mine."
The king of the Matsyas, considering himself guilty of having offended
    Yudhishthira,
said to Uttara in reply: "I think the time has come for me to propitiate the sons
    of Pandu.
And, if you like, I shall bestow my daughter upon Arjuna."
Vitara continued: "When I was brought under the foe's subjection in battle,
it was Bhimasena who rescued me. My cattle have been recovered by Arjuna.
It is through the might of their arms that we have obtained victory in battle.
Such being the case, all of us, with our counselors, shall propitiate Yudhishthira.
Blessed be you and all your brothers. If we have ever said or done anything in
    ignorance
to offend you, it behooves you to forgive us."
Then the high-souled Virata approached King Yudhishthira,
made an alliance with him, and offered him his whole kingdom
together with the scepter and treasury and metropolis.
Addressing all the Pandavas, and especially Arjuna,
the mighty king of the Matsyas repeatedly said: "It is my great good fortune to
    see you."
And having again and again embraced Yudhishthira and Bhima and the sons of
    Madri,
and having smelled their heads, Virata was not satiated with gazing at them.
He said to King Yudhishthira: "I make over my entire kingdom to the sons of
    Pritha,
and whatever else I have. Let the sons of Pandu accept these without hesitation.
And let Arjuna accept the hand of my daughter, for that best of men is fit to be
    her lord."
King Yudhishthira glanced toward Arjuna. And Arjuna said to the Matsya king:

"I accept your daughter as my daughter-in-law. An alliance of this kind
between the Matsya and the Bharatas is, indeed, desirable."
Virata asked: "Why do you not wish to accept my daughter as your wife?"
Arjuna replied: "Residing in your inner apartments, I had occasion to behold her,
and alone or in company she trusted me as her father.
Well versed in singing and dancing, I was liked and regarded by her,
and, indeed, your daughter always regarded me as her protector.
I lived for a whole year with her, although she had attained the age of puberty.
Under these circumstances, you or other men may, not without reason,
entertain suspicions about her or me. Therefore, O king, I, who am pure
and have my senses under control, beg of you that your daughter
may be my daughter-in-law. Thus do I attest to her purity.
There is no difference between a daughter-in-law and a daughter,
as also between a son and oneself. By adopting this course, her purity will be
    proved.
I accept, therefore, O king, your daughter Uttara as my daughter-in-law.
My son, the mighty-armed Abhimanyu, surpassing all in knowledge of weapons
and resembling in beauty a celestial youth, is the favorite nephew of Krishna,
the wielder of the discus. He, O king, is fit to be your son-in-law
                        and the husband of your daughter."
Virata said: "O son of Pritha, do what you think should be done.
He who has Arjuna for the father of his son-in-law has all his desires gratified."
King Yudhishthira gave his assent to what was thus agreed upon
between the Matsya king and Arjuna. And the son of Kunti sent invitations to
    Krishna
and to all his friends and relatives, and Virata did the same.
Then, after the expiration of the thirteenth year, the five Pandavas took up their
    abode
in one of Virata's towns, called Upaplavya, and Arjuna brought over Abhimanyu
and Janardana and many people of the Dasarha race from the Anarea country.
And the king of Kasi, and also Saivya, being very friendly to Yudhishthira, arrived,
each accompanied by an *akshauhini* of troops. The mighty Drupada,
with the heroic sons of Draupadi and the unvanquished Sikhandin
and that foremost among wielders of weapons, the invincible Dhrishtadyumna,
came there with another *akshauhini* of troops.
As they arrived, the king of the Matsyas adored them duly
and entertained their troops and servants and carriers of burdens.
He was highly pleased to bestow his daughter upon Abhimanyu.
The nuptial festival began between the families of the Matsya king and the
    Pandavas.
Conchs and cymbals and horns and drums and other musical instruments
played in the palace of Virata. And deer of various kinds
and clean animals by the hundreds were slain.
Wines of various kinds and intoxicating juices of trees were collected.
Mimes and bards, versed in singing and legendary lore, waited upon the kings
and chanted their praises and genealogies.
And the matrons of the Matsyas, of symmetrical bodies and limbs

and wearing earrings of pearls and gems, headed by Sudeshna,
came to the place where the marriage knot was to be tied.
Among those beautiful females of fair complexion and excellent ornaments,
Draupadi was foremost in beauty and fame and splendor.
Arjuna accepted Virata's daughter of faultless limbs on behalf of his son by
    Subhadra.
Virata then gave as dowry seven thousand steeds with the speed of the wind
and two hundred elephants of the best kind and much wealth also.
And having duly poured libations of clarified butter on the blazing fire
and paid homage to the twice-born ones, Virata offered the Pandavas his
    kingdom,
his army, his treasury, and himself. After the marriage had taken place,
    Yudhishthira
gave away to the Brahmanas all the wealth that had been brought by Krishna.
And he also gave away thousands of cattle and diverse kinds of robes
and various excellent ornaments and vehicles and beds,
delicious viands of various kinds, and an assortment of wonderful drinks.
The king also made gifts of land to the Brahmanas and also cattle by the
    thousands.
And he gave away thousands of steeds and much gold and much wealth of other
    kinds

                        to persons of all ages.
And the city of the Matsya king shone brightly for the great festival.

The War

30

The Envoys

Yudhishthira consulted with Virata and also with his father-in-law, King Drupada:
What should he do if Duryodhana did not return the kingdom
that they believed still belonged to them?
The return of Indraprastha and their lands had been a part of the terms
to which both parties had agreed. But what were the prospects that Duryodhana
would honor his word? To learn his intentions, King Drupada dispatched his
    priest
to Dhritarashtra's court with instructions to inquire about the Kurus' intentions
and to appraise their mood. Drupada's priest approached the Kaurava chief
and was honored by Dhritarashtra as also by Bhishma and Vidura.
He spoke the following words in the midst of all the leaders of Duryodhana's
    army:
"The eternal duties of kings are known to you all.
But I shall yet recite them as an introduction to what I am going to say.
Both Dhritarashtra and Pandu are sons of the same father.
There is no doubt that the share to each of the paternal wealth should be equal.
The sons of Dhritarashtra have obtained the paternal wealth.
Why did the sons of Pandu not receive their paternal portion?
You are aware of how their paternal property was usurped by Dhritarashtra's sons,
who endeavored in various ways to remove the sons of Pandu from their path,
even by murderous contrivances. But their destined terms of life had not wholly
    run out,
and the sons of Pandu could not be sent to the abode of Yama.
Then again, when those high-souled princes had carved out a kingdom
by their own strength, the mean-minded sons of Dhritarashtra, aided by
    Suvala's son,
robbed them of it by deceit. To this, Dhritarashtra gave his sanction.
And they were sent to sojourn for thirteen years in the wilderness.
In the council hall they were also subjected to indignities of various kinds,
along with their wife, valiant though they were. And great were the sufferings
they had to endure in the woods. In the city of Virata those princes
had also to endure unspeakable woes, such as are endured only by vicious men
when their souls transmigrate into the forms of inferior beings.
But overlooking all these injuries, they now desire nothing but a peaceful
    settlement

with the Kurus! The heroic sons of Pandu are not eager for war with the Kurus.
They desire to get back their own share without involving the world in ruin.
If Dhritarashtra's son proposes a reason in favor of war, it can never be a proper
  reason.
The sons of Pandu are more powerful.
Seven *akshauhinis* of troops have been collected on behalf of Yudhishthira,
all eager to fight with the Kurus, and they are now awaiting his word of
  command.
Others there are, tigers among men, equal in might to a thousand *akshauhinis*,
such as Satyaki and Bhimasena, and the twin brothers of mighty strength.
It is true that these eleven divisions of troops are arrayed on one side,
but these are balanced on the other by the mighty-armed Dhananjaya of
  manifold form.
And as Arjuna exceeds in strength even all these troops together,
so does Vasudeva's son Krishna of great effulgence and powerful intellect.
In view of the magnitude of the opposing force, who is there who would fight
the valor of Arjuna and the wisdom of Krishna? Therefore, I ask you
to give back what should be given, as dictated by morality and the agreement.
                    Do not let the opportunity pass!"
Having heard his words, Bhishma, senior in wisdom, paid honors to him and said:
"How fortunate that they are all well, and Krishna, too!
How fortunate that they have procured aid and are inclined to a virtuous course!
How fortunate that those scions of Kuru's race desire peace with their cousins!
There is no doubt that what you have said is true, but your words are
  exceedingly sharp
because, I suppose, you are a Brahmana. No doubt the sons of Pandu were
  harassed
both here and in the woods. No doubt they are entitled to get the property of
  their father.
Arjuna, the son of Pritha, is well trained in weapons and is a great car warrior.
Who can withstand him in battle? Even the wielder of the thunderbolt cannot,
and other bowmen are hardly worth mentioning. He is a match for all the three
  worlds!"
But while Bhishma was thus speaking, Karna insolently interrupted him
and, looking at Duryodhana, said: "There is no creature in the world, O
  Brahmana,
who is not informed of all these facts. What is the good of repeating them?
On behalf of Duryodhana, Sakuni won in games of dice,
and Yudhishthira went to the woods, according to a stipulation of the wager.
He is now paying no regard to that stipulation but, confident of aid
from the Matsyas and Panchalas, wishes to get back his ancestral throne.
Duryodhana will not yield even a single foot of land if you appeal to his fears,
but if justice required it, he would give up the whole earth even to a foe.
If they wish to get back their ancestral throne, they should pass the specified time
in the forest, as had been stipulated. Afterward let them live
as the dependents of Duryodhana, safe and sound.
From dull-headedness, however, let them not turn their minds

toward an unrighteous course. But if, abandoning the path of virtue, they want war,
then, when they encounter the praiseworthy Kurus, they will remember my
    words."
Bhishma said: "What is the use of your talking? You should remember when
    Arjuna
single-handedly overpowered in battle six car warriors.
If we do not act as this Brahmana has said, we shall be all slain by him in battle!"
Then Dhritarashtra pacified Bhishma with words of entreaty and rebuked Karna.
He said: "What Bhishma has said is salutary for us, as also for the Pandavas,
and likewise for the whole universe. I shall, however, after deliberation,
send Sanjaya to the sons of Pandu. You need not wait. Go to the son of Pandu
    today."
The Kaurava chief honored Drupada's priest and sent him back to the Pandavas.
Then, summoning Sanjaya to the council hall, he said to him: "They say, O
    Sanjaya,
that the Pandavas have arrived at Upaplavya. Go and inquire after them.
You must greet Yudhishthira with the following words: 'It is good luck
that, emerged from the woods, you have reached such a city.'
And to all of them you must say: 'Are you well, having spent that period of
    sojourn,
you who were unworthy of such harassment?' In no time will they be appeased,
for, though treated treacherously by foes, they are righteous and good.
In no case, Sanjaya, have I ever met with any untruthfulness on their part.
It was by their own valor that they won their prosperity. They were always dutiful
    to me.
Though I scrutinized their conduct, I could never find fault with them.
They are always mindful of virtue and wealth. They never give way
to love of sensual enjoyments, or cold, or hunger, or thirst.
They subdue sleep and laziness and wrath and joy and heedlessness.
The sons of Pritha, mindful of both virtue and wealth, are always pleasant to all.
Friendship with them never loses its ardor over time,
and they bestow honors and wealth on everyone, according to his deserts.
Not a soul in the race of our ancestor Ajamida ever entertains hatred for them
excepting this vile, capricious, dull-headed Duryodhana,
and excepting also the still more mean-minded Karna.
It is childish on Duryodhana's part to think that it is possible to rob the Pandavas
of their just share so long as they are alive. It is wise to yield his due share before
    the war
to Yudhishthira, whose steps are followed by Arjuna and Krishna
and Bhima and Satyaki and the two sons of Madri and the warriors of the
    Srinjaya race.
That wielder of the Gandiva, Arjuna, seated on his car, could alone devastate the
    world.
Likewise the victorious and high-souled Krishna, the lord of the three worlds,
is able to do the same. What mortal would stand before the one who discharges
    his arrows
that roar like the clouds, covering all sides, like flights of swift locusts?

Alone on his car, holding the Gandiva, he conquered the northern regions
as also the Kurus of the north and brought away with him all their wealth.
He converted the people of the Dravida land to be a portion of his own army.
It was Arjuna who defeated in the Khandava woods all the gods together with
    Indra
and made offerings to Agni, enhancing the honor and fame of the Pandavas.
Of all wielders of the mace, there is none equal to Bhima,
and there is none also who is so skillful a rider of elephants.
On a car, they say, he yields not even to Arjuna, and as to might of arms,
he is equal to ten thousand elephants. Of great heart and strong,
and endowed with great lightness of hand, the twin brothers, sons of Madri,
trained by Arjuna, would leave not a foe alive. They are like a pair of hawks
preying upon large flocks of birds. Our army, so large, will be nowhere
when it encounters them. On their side will be Dhrishtadyumna,
who is regarded as one of the Pandavas themselves.
The chief of the Somaka tribe, with his followers, is so devoted to the Pandavas
that he is ready to lay down his life for them. Who could withstand Yudhishthira,
who has Krishna, the best of the Vrishni tribe, for his leader? I have heard that
    Virata,
the chief of the Matsyas, with whom the Pandavas lived for some time
and whose wishes were fulfilled by them, is devoted, along with his sons,
to the Pandava cause and has become, though old in years, an adherent of
    Yudhishthira.
All who are valiant among the lords of the earth have been brought together
and are devoted to the Pandava cause. I hear that they are bold, worthy, and
    respectful
who have allied themselves to King Yudhishthira from feelings of attachment
    to him.
And many warriors dwelling on the hills and inaccessible fastnesses,
and many who are high in lineage and old in years, and many Mlechchha tribes
    also,
wielding weapons of various kinds, have assembled together
and are devoted to the cause of the Pandavas.
Go speedily on a car to where the troops of the king of the Panchalas are
    encamped.
Ask Yudhishthira about his welfare. Address him in affectionate terms.
You will also meet Krishna, who is the chief of all brave men,
and who is endowed with a magnanimous soul. Ask on my part as to his welfare
    also,
and tell him that Dhritarashtra desires peace with Pandu's sons.
There is nothing that Yudhishthira would not do at the bidding of Krishna.
Possessed of great learning, he is always devoted to the Panchalas' cause.
You will also inquire about the welfare of all the assembled sons of Pandu
and the Srinjayas and Satyaki and Virata and all the five sons of Draupadi,
making it clear that you are a messenger from me.
And whatever you may deem to be opportune and beneficial for Bharata's race,
everything that may not be unpalatable or provocative of war,

all that, O Sanjaya, must you say in the midst of those kings."

Having heard these words of King Dhritarashtra, Sanjaya went to Upaplavya

to see the Pandavas. He approached King Yudhishthira, made obeisance to him,

and then spoke cheerfully: "What good fortune, O king, that I see you hale, attended by friends

and little inferior to the great Indra. The aged and wise King Dhritarashtra

has inquired about your welfare. I hope that Bhimasena is well and that Arjuna

and the two sons of Madri are well. I hope that Princess Draupadi also is well,

she who never swerves from the path of truth, that lady of great energy, that wife of heroes."

Yudhishthira said: "O Sanjaya, son of Gavalgana, has your journey here been safe?

We are pleased to see you. I ask in return how you are.

I am, O learned man, in excellent health with my younger brothers.

It has been a long while since I have received news of the king of the Kurus, that descendant of Bharata.

Having seen you, O Sanjaya, I feel as if I have seen the king himself, so pleased am I!

Is our aged grandsire Bhishma, endowed with great energy and the highest wisdom

and always devoted to the practices of his own order, in health?

I hope that he still retains all his former habits. I hope that the high-souled King Dhritarashtra,

the son of Vichitravirya, is in excellent health with his sons.

I hope that the great King Valhika, the son of Pratipa, endowed with great learning,

is also in health. I hope that Somadatta is in fine health, and that Bhurisravas, and Satyasandha,

and Sala, and Drona with his son, and the Brahmana Kripa are also well.

I hope that all those mighty bowmen are free from disease.

How happy are they in whose kingdom dwells the mighty and handsome bowman, the well-behaved son of Drona! I hope that Yuyutsu, the intelligent son of Dhritarashtra

by his Vaisya wife, is in good health.

I hope that Karna, who counsels the dull-headed Duryodhana, is in health.

I hope that the aged ladies, the mothers of Bharata's race, the kitchen maidens,

the bondmaids, the daughters-in-law, the boys, the sisters' sons, and the sisters,

and the daughters' sons of Dhritarashtra's house are all free from trouble.

I hope that the king still allows their former subsistence to the Brahmanas.

I hope that Dhritarashtra's son has not seized those gifts I made to the Brahmanas.

I hope that Dhritarashtra and his sons meet in a spirit of forbearance

any overbearing conduct on the part of the Brahmanas.

I hope that Dhritarashtra never neglects to make provision for them, that being the sole highway to heaven.

If, like dull-headed persons, the sons of Kuru do not treat the Brahmanas

in a forbearing spirit, wholesale destruction will overtake them.

I hope that King Dhritarashtra and his sons try to provide for the functionaries of the state.

I hope that there are no enemies of theirs who, disguised as friends, conspire for
their ruin.

I hope that none of these Kurus talk of our having committed any crimes.

I hope that Drona and his son and Kripa do not talk of our having been guilty in
any way.

I hope that all the Kurus look up to King Dhritarashtra and his sons as
protectors of their tribe.

I hope that when they see a horde of robbers, they remember the deeds of Arjuna,
the leader in all fields of battle. I hope that they remember the arrows shot from
the Gandiva,

which course through the air in a straight path, impelled by the stretched
bowstring,

making a noise as loud as that of the thunder. I have not seen the warrior

who excels or even rivals Arjuna, who can shoot by a single effort of his hand

sixty-one whetted and keen-edged shafts furnished with excellent feathers.

Do they remember Bhima also, who with great energy causes hostile hosts

arrayed in battle to tremble in dread, like an elephant with rent temples

agitating a forest of reeds? Do they remember the mighty Sahadeva, the son of
Madri,

who in Dantakura conquered the Kalingas, shooting arrows by the left hand and
the right?

Do they remember Nakula, who was sent, under your eyes, to conquer the Sivis

and the Trigartas and who brought the western region under my power?

Do they remember the disgrace that was theirs when under evil counsels

they came to the woods of Dwaitavana on pretense of taking away their cattle?

Those wicked ones, having been overpowered by their enemies,

were afterward liberated by Bhimasena and Arjuna,

with myself protecting the rear of Arjuna in the fight that ensued,

and with Bhima protecting the rear of the sons of Madri,

and with the wielder of the Gandiva coming out unharmed from the press of
battle,

having made a great slaughter of the hostile host. Do they remember all that?

It is not by a single good deed, O Sanjaya, that happiness can here be attained,

when by all our endeavors we are unable to win over the son of Dhritarashtra!"

Sanjaya said: "It is as you have said, O son of Pandu!

Do you inquire about the welfare of the Kurus, and of those foremost among
them?

Free from illness of every kind and in possession of excellent spirit

are those foremost among the Kurus about whom you ask.

You know that there are certainly righteous and aged men,

as well as men who are sinful and wicked, about Dhritarashtra's son.

Dhritarashtra's son would make gifts even to his enemies.

It is not likely, therefore, that he should withdraw the donations made to the
Brahmanas.

It is customary with you Kshatriyas to follow a rule fit for butchers,

which leads you to do harm to those who bear you no ill will, but the practice is
not good.

Dhritarashtra with his sons would be guilty of the sin of internecine dissension
were he to bear ill will toward you who are righteous.
He does not approve of this injury done to you. He is exceedingly sorry for it.
Dhritirashtra grieves in his heart, for, having communicated with the Brahmanas,
he has learned that provoking internecine dissension is the greatest of sins.
O king of men, they remember your prowess on the field and that of Arjuna,
who takes the lead in battle. They remember Bhima wielding his mace
when the sound of the conch shell and the drum rose to the highest pitch.
They remember those mighty car warriors, the two sons of Madri,
who on the field of battle careered in all directions, shooting incessant showers
    of shafts
on hostile hosts, and who did not know what it is to tremble in fight.
I believe, O king, that what futurity has in store for a particular person cannot be
    known,
since you, O son of Pandu, who are endowed with all the virtues,
have had to suffer troubles of such an unendurable kind.
All this, no doubt, O Yudhishthira, you will again make good through your
    intelligence.
The sons of Pandu would never abandon virtue for the sake of pleasure.
You, O Yudhishthira, will so arrange matters that all the sons of Dhritarashtra
and Pandu and the Srinjayas, and all the kings who have been assembled here,
will attain peace. O Yudhishthira, hear what Dhritarashtra,
having consulted with his ministers and sons, has said. And be attentive to the
    same."
Yudhishthira said: "Here are met the Pandavas and the Srinjayas, and Krishna,
and Yuyudhana and Virata. Tell us all that Dhritarashtra has directed you to say."
Sanjaya said: "I greet Yudhishthira, and Vrikodara and Dhananjaya,
and the two sons of Madri, and Vasudeva the descendant of Sura,
and Satyaki, and the aged ruler of the Panchalas, and Dhrishtadyumna.
Let all listen to the words I say from a desire for the welfare of the Kurus.
King Dhritarashtra eagerly welcomes the chance of peace,
and he hastened the preparation of my car for this journey here.
Let it be acceptable to King Yudhishthira with his brothers and sons and relations.
Let the sons of Pandu prefer peace. The sons of Pritha are endowed with every
    virtue,
with steadiness and mildness and candor. Born into a noble family,
they are humane, liberal, and loath to commit any act which would be a cause
    for shame.
They know what is proper to be done. A base deed is not befitting you,
for you are so high-minded and have such an awesome following of troops.
If you committed a sinful act, it would be a blot on your fair name,
like a drop of collyrium on a white cloth. Who could knowingly be guilty of an act
that would result in universal slaughter, that would be sinful and lead to hell,
an act consisting in the destruction of men, whether through victory or defeat?
Blessed are they who have served their relatives' cause.
They are the true sons and friends and relatives of Kuru's race
who would lay down their lives in order to ensure the welfare of the Kurus.

If you sons of Pritha chastised the Kurus by defeating and slaying all your foes,
your subsequent lives would be equivalent to death,
for what is life after all your kinsfolk have been killed?
Who, even if he were Indra himself with all the gods on his side,
would be able to defeat you, who are aided by Kesava and Chekitanas
and Satyaki and are protected by Dhrishtadyumna's arms?
Who again, O king, can defeat in battle the Kurus, who are protected by Drona
and Bhishma and Aswatthaman and Salya and Kripa and Karna
with a host of Kshatriya kings? Who, without loss to himself,
is able to slay the vast force assembled by Dhritarashtra's son?
Therefore, I do not see any good either in victory or in defeat.
How can the sons of Pritha, like persons of low birth, commit an act of
    unrighteousness?
Therefore, I appease. I prostrate myself before Krishna and the king of the
    Panchalas.
I look to you as my refuge, with joined hands, so that the Kurus as well as the
    Srinjayas
may be benefited. It is not likely that either Krishna or Arjuna will heed my words.
Either of them would lay down his life if asked to do so. Therefore, I say this
for the success of my mission. This is the desire of the king and his counselor
    Bhishma:
that there may be confirmed peace between you and the Kurus."
Yudhishthira said: "What words from me, O Sanjaya, have you heard indicative
    of war?
Peace is preferable to war. Who, having an alternative, would wish to fight?
If a man could have every wish of his heart without having to do anything,
he would be unlikely to do even the least troublesome thing,
and far less would he engage in war. Who is so cursed by the gods
that he would choose to do so? The sons of Pritha desire their own happiness,
but their conduct, always marked by righteousness, is conducive to the world's
    good.
They desire only that happiness which results from righteousness.
He who fondly follows the lead of his senses and desires to obtain happiness
and avoid misery bestirs himself to action that in its essence is nothing but misery.
He who hankers after pleasure causes his body to suffer.
One free from such hankering does not know what misery is.
As a kindled fire blazes the higher the more fuel is put upon it,
so is desire never satiated with the acquisition of its object
but gains force, like a fire when clarified butter is poured upon it.
Compare all this abundant fund of enjoyment that King Dhritarashtra has
with what we possess. He who is unfortunate never wins victories.
He who is unfortunate does not enjoy the voice of music.
He who is unfortunate does not enjoy garlands and scents.
Nor can one who is unfortunate enjoy cool and fragrant unguents.
Finally, he who is unfortunate does not wear fine clothes.
If this were not so, we would never have been driven from the Kurus.
The king is in trouble and seeks protection in the might of others. This is not wise.

Let him receive from others the same behavior that he displays toward them.
Why does King Dhritarashtra now complain, although he has all this prosperity?
It is because he has followed the counsels of his wicked son of vicious soul,
who is addicted to crooked ways and confirmed in folly.
Duryodhana disregarded the words of Vidura, the best of his well-wishers,
as if the latter were hostile to him. King Dhritarashtra, desiring solely to satisfy
    his sons,
would knowingly enter upon an unrighteous course.
Indeed, on account of his fondness for his son, he would not pay heed to Vidura,
who, out of all the Kurus, is the wisest and best of his well-wishers,
possessing vast learning, clever in speech, and righteous in act.
King Dhritarashtra desires to satisfy his son,
who, while seeking honors from others, is envious and wrathful;
who transgresses the rules for the acquisition of power and wealth;
whose tongue is foul, and who always follows the dictates of his wrath;
whose soul is absorbed in sensual pleasures;
who, full of unfriendly feelings toward many, obeys no law;
and whose life is evil, whose heart is implacable, and whose understanding is
    vicious.
For such a son as this, King Dhritarashtra knowingly abandoned virtue and
    pleasure.
Even then, O Sanjaya, when I was engaged in that game of dice,
I thought that the destruction of the Kurus was at hand,
for Vidura, when speaking those wise words, obtained no praise from
    Dhritarashtra.
So long as they had placed themselves under the lead of Vidura's wisdom,
their kingdom was flourishing. Hear from me who are the counselors now
of the covetous Duryodhana: they are Dussasana, and Sakuni the son of Suvala,
and Karna the Suta's son! O son of Gavalgana, look at this folly of his!
So I do not see, though I think about it, how there can be prosperity for the
    Kurus
and the Srinjayas when Dhritarashtra has taken the throne from others,
and when the far-seeing Vidura has been banished elsewhere.
Dhritarashtra and his sons now look for undisputed sovereignty over the whole
    world.
Absolute peace is, therefore, unattainable.
When Arjuna takes up his weapon to fight, Karna believes that Arjuna can be
    withstood.
Formerly there were many great battles. Why could not Karna be of any avail in
    them?
It is known to Karna and Drona and the grandsire Bhishma, as also to many
    other Kurus,
that there is no wielder of the bow comparable to Arjuna.
It is known to all the assembled rulers of the earth how sovereignty was obtained
by Duryodhana, although Arjuna, that repressor of foes, was alive.
Pertinaciously does Dhritarashtra's son believe that it is possible to rob the sons
    of Pandu

of what is their own, although he knows, having himself gone to the place of
   battle,
how Arjuna conducted himself when he had nothing but a bow four cubits long.
Dhritarashtra's sons are alive only because they have not as yet heard the twang
of the stretched Gandiva. Duryodhana believes his object already gained
as long as he does not see the wrathful Bhima. Even Indra would forbear
to rob us of our sovereignty as long as Bhima and Arjuna and the heroic Nakula
and the patient Sahadeva were alive! The old king and his son still entertain the
   notion
that Dhritarashtra's sons will not be killed on the field of battle, consumed by
   the fiery wrath
of Pandu's sons. You know, O Sanjaya, what misery we have suffered!
For my respect to you, I would forgive them all.
You know what transpired between ourselves and those sons of Kuru.
You know how we conducted ourselves toward Dhritarashtra's son.
Let the same state of things continue. I shall seek peace, as you counsel me to do.
Let me have Indraprastha for my kingdom.
Let this be given to me by Duryodhana, the chief of Bharata's race."
Sanjaya said: "O Pandava, the world has heard of your righteous conduct.
I see it also to be so. Life is transient, that may end in great infamy.
But, considering this, you should not perish. If the Kurus will not yield your share
without war, I think it is far better for you to live upon alms
in the kingdom of the Andhakas and the Vrishnis than to obtain sovereignty by war.
Since this mortal existence is for only a short period and subject to constant
   suffering
and unstable, and since it is never comparable in worth to a good name,
therefore one should never perpetrate a sin. It is the desires that adhere to
   mortal men
and are obstructions to a virtuous life. Therefore, a wise man should kill them all
and thereby gain stainless fame in the world. Thirst after wealth is fetters in this
   world.
The virtue of those who seek it is sure to suffer. He is wise, therefore, who seeks
   virtue alone.
A man devoid of virtue and of vicious soul is overtaken by ruin,
even though he may obtain the whole of this earth.
You have studied the Vedas, lived the life of a saintly Brahman,
performed sacrificial rites, and made charities to Brahmanas.
Even remembering the highest position attainable by mortal beings,
you have also devoted your soul for years and years to the pursuit of pleasure.
He who devotes himself excessively to the pleasures and joys of life
and never employs himself in the practice of religious meditation must be
   miserable.
Similarly, he who, never having lived a continent life, forsakes the path of virtue
and commits sin has no faith in the existence of a world to come.
Dull as he is after death, he has torment for his lot.
In the world to come, whether one's deeds have been good or evil, they are not
   annihilated.

Good and evil deeds precede a man on his journey to the world to come.
He is sure to follow in their path. All acts are done so long as this body lasts.
After death, there is nothing to be done.
And you have done mighty deeds that will do good to you in the world to come
and are admired by righteous men. In the next world one is free from death
and decrepitude and fear, and from hunger and thirst.
There is nothing to be done in that place, unless it be to delight one's senses.
Therefore, do not act any longer from desire in this world.
Do not undertake action in this world and thereby take leave of truth and sobriety
and candor and humanity. Possessed of mighty resources, dreaded by all,
having an army, and followed behind by Krishna and Arjuna,
you might have slain the foremost among your foes on the field of battle.
You might have then brought Duryodhana's pride low.
O Pandava, why have you allowed your foes to grow so powerful?
Why have you weakened your friends? Why are you now desirous of fighting,
having let the proper opportunity slip? An unwise or an unrighteous man
may win prosperity by fighting, but a wise and righteous man, were he free from
     pride,
would only fall away from a prosperous path by fighting. Your mind inclines
to an unrighteous course. From wrath you never committed a sinful act.
What, then, is the cause for which you now intend to do this deed
against the dictates of wisdom? Wrath is a bitter drug.
Although it has nothing to do with disease, it brings on a disease of the head,
robs one of fair fame, and leads to sinful acts.
It is sipped by those who are righteous and gulped down by those who are
     unrighteous.
I ask you to put it aside and to desist from war.
Who would incline himself to wrath, which leads to sin?
Forbearance would be more beneficial to you than love of enjoyments
where Bhishma would be slain, and Drona with his son, and Kripa, and
     Somadatta's son,
and Vikarna and Vivingsati, and Karna and Duryodhana.
After you have slain all these, what bliss may there be for you to enjoy?
Even having won the entire sea-girt earth, you will never be free
from decrepitude and death, pleasure and pain, bliss and misery.
Knowing all this, do not be engaged in war. If you take this course
because your counselors desire it, then give up everything to them, and run away.
You should not fall away from the path that leads to the region of the gods!"
Yudhishthira said: "It is true that righteous deeds are foremost among our acts,
as you say. You should, however, assure me, having first ascertained
whether it is virtue or vice that I practice. When vice assumes the aspects of virtue
and virtue wholly seems as vice, they who are learned should discriminate
     between them
by means of reason. So, again, virtue and vice, which are both eternal and
     absolute,
exchange their aspects during seasons of distress. One should follow without
     deviation

the duties prescribed for the order to which one belongs by birth.
But duties in seasons of distress are otherwise. When his means of living are
    totally gone,
the man who is destitute should certainly find other means
by which he may be able to discharge the sanctioned duties of his order.
One who is not destitute of his means of living, as also one who is in distress,
is to be blamed if he acts as if his state were otherwise.
O Sanjaya, you should regard them as worthy who adhere to the practices
of their own order in usual times as also those who do not in times of distress;
you should censure them that act otherwise in usual times,
while adhering to their ordained practices during times of distress.
Whatever wealth there may be on this earth, whatever there may be among the
    gods,
or whatever there may be unattainable by them—the region of the Prajapati,
or heaven, or the region of Brahma himself—I would not seek it by unrighteous
    means.
Here is Krishna, the giver of virtue's fruits, who is clever, politic, intelligent,
who has waited upon the Brahmanas, who knows everything and counsels
    mighty kings.
Let Krishna say whether I would be censurable if I dismissed all ideas of peace,
or whether, if I fought, I should be abandoning the duties of my caste,
for Krishna seeks the welfare of both sides. Him you must know as the great
    judge
of the propriety of all acts. Krishna is dear to us, and is the most illustrious of men.
                      I never disregard what Krishna says."
Krishna said: "I desire, Sanjaya, that the sons of Pandu may not be ruined
and that they may prosper and attain their wishes. Similarly, I pray for the
    prosperity
of King Dhritarashtra whose sons are many.
My desire has always been that I should tell them nothing else
than that peace would be acceptable to King Dhritarashtra.
I also deem it proper for the sons of Pandu.
A peaceful disposition of an exceedingly rare character has been displayed
by Pandu's son in this matter. But if Dhritarashtra and his sons are so covetous,
I do not see why hostility should not run high.
You cannot pretend to be more versed than I am, or than Yudhishthira is,
in the niceties of right and wrong. Why then do you speak words of reproach
about the conduct of Yudhishthira, who is enterprising, mindful of his own duty,
thoughtful of the welfare of his family, and in conformity with treatises of
    morality?
With regard to the topic at hand, the Brahmanas have held opinions of various
    kinds.
Some say that success in the world to come depends upon deeds.
Some declare that action should be shunned, and that salvation is attainable
by knowledge. The Brahmanas say that one may have a knowledge of edible
    things,
but that his hunger will not be appeased unless he actually eats.

Those branches of knowledge that help the doing of work bear fruit,
but not other kinds, for the fruit of work is demonstrative proof.
A thirsty person drinks water, and by that act his thirst is allayed.
This result proceeds, no doubt, from the deed.
If anyone thinks that something is better than deeds,
I say that both his work and his deeds are meaningless.
In the other world, it is by virtue of action that the gods flourish.
It is by action that the wind blows. It is by action that the sleepless Surya rises
    every day
and becomes the cause of day and night, and by deeds that Soma passes through
    the months
and the combinations of constellations. Fire is kindled of itself and burns
by virtue of work, doing good to mankind.
The sleepless earth sustains by force this very great burden.
The sleepless rivers, giving satisfaction to all beings, carry their waters with speed.
The sleepless Indra, possessed of a mighty force, pours down rain from the
    heavens.
Desirous of being the greatest of the gods, he led a life of austerities
such as a holy Brahmana leads. Indra gave up pleasure
and all things agreeable to the heart. He sedulously cherished virtue and truth,
and self-control, and forbearance, and impartiality, and humanity.
It was by deeds that he attained a position as the highest of all the gods.
Following the above course of life, Indra attained high sovereignty over heaven.
Vrihaspati, intently and with self-control, led in a proper manner
that life of austerities that a Brahmana leads. He gave up pleasure and
    controlled his senses
and thereby attained the position of preceptor of the celestials.
Knowing, O Sanjaya, that this is the rule followed by the best of Brahmanas
and Kshatriyas and Vaisyas, and being one of the wisest of men,
why are you making this endeavor on behalf of those sons of Kuru?
You must know that Yudhishthira is constantly engaged in the study of the Vedas.
He is inclined to the horse sacrifice and the Rajasuya.
Again, he rides horses and elephants, is arrayed in armor, mounts a car,
and takes up the bow and all kinds of other weapons.
Now, if the sons of Pritha could see a course of action
not involving the slaughter of the sons of Kuru, they would adopt it.
Their virtue would then be saved, and an act of religious merit also would be
    achieved,
even if they would then have to force Bhima to conduct himself with humanity.
On the other hand, if in doing what their forefathers did they should meet with
    death,
then, in trying their utmost to discharge their duty, they would find such a death
    worthy of praise.
Supposing that you approve of peace alone, I should like to hear what you may
    have to say to this question:
Which way does the injunction of religious law lie—is it proper for the king to
    fight, or not?

You must take into consideration the division of the four castes,
and the scheme of respective duties allotted to each.
You must hear the course of action that the Pandavas are going to adopt.
Then may you praise or censure. A Brahmana should study, offer sacrifices,
make charities, and visit the best of all holy places on earth.
He should teach, minister as a priest in sacrifices offered by others worthy of
    such help,
and accept gifts from known persons. Similarly, a Kshatriya should protect the
    people
in accordance with the injunctions of the law, diligently practice the virtue of
    charity,
offer sacrifices, study the whole Veda, take a wife, and lead a virtuous
    householder's life.
If he be possessed of a virtuous soul, and if he practice the holy virtues,
he may easily attain the region of the supreme spirit.
A Vaisya should study and diligently earn and accumulate wealth
by means of commerce, agriculture, and the tending of cattle.
He should so act as to please the Brahmanas and the Kshatriyas, be virtuous,
                    do good works, and be a householder.
The following are the duties declared for a Sudra from olden times:
He should serve the Brahmanas and submit to them, should not study,
should not sacrifice, and should be diligent in doing all that is for his good.
The king protects all these with proper care and sets all the castes
to perform their respective duties. He should not be given to sensual enjoyments.
He should be impartial and treat all his subjects on an equal footing.
The king should never obey the dictates of such desires as are opposed to
    righteousness.
If there be anybody who is more praiseworthy than he, who is well known
and gifted with all the virtues, the king should instruct his subjects to see him.
A bad king, however, would not understand this.
Growing strong and inhuman, and becoming a mark for destiny's wrath,
he would cast covetous eyes on the riches of others.
Then comes war, for which purpose weapons came into being, and armor, and
    bows.
Indra invented these contrivances for putting the plunderers to death.
He also contrived armor, and weapons, and bows.
Religious merit is acquired through putting the robbers to death.
Many awful evils have manifested themselves on account of the Kurus'
having been unrighteous and unmindful of law and religion. This is not right,
    Sanjaya.
Now, King Dhritarashtra and his sons have seized what belonged to Pandu's son.
He disobeys the immemorial law that should be observed by kings.
All the Kurus are following in his wake. A thief who steals wealth unseen
and one who forcibly seizes the same in open daylight are both to be
    condemned.
What is the difference between them and Dhritarashtra's sons?
From avarice he regards whatever he intends to do as righteous.

The share of the Pandavas is, no doubt, fixed.

Why should that share of theirs be seized by that fool?

This being the state of things, it would be praiseworthy for us even to be killed in
fight.

A paternal kingdom is preferable to sovereignty received from a stranger.

These time-honored rules of law you must propound to the Kurus,

in the midst of the assembled kings—I mean those dull-headed ones

who have been assembled by Dhritarashtra's son and are already in the clutches
of death.'

Look once more at that vilest of all their acts, their conduct in the council hall—

that those Kurus, at whose head stood Bhishma, did not interfere

when the beloved wife of the sons of Pandu, daughter of Drupada,

of fair fame, pure life, and conduct worthy of praise, was seized, while weeping,

by that slave of lust! All the Kurus, including young and old, were present.

If they had then prevented that indignity offered to her,

then I should have been content with Dhritarashtra's behavior.

It would have been for the final good of his sons also.

Dussasana forcibly took Draupadi into the midst of the public hall.

Carried there, expecting sympathy, she found none to take her part except
Vidura.

The kings uttered not a word of protest, solely because they were a set of
imbeciles.

Vidura alone spoke words of opposition from a sense of duty,

words conceived in righteousness that were addressed to Duryodhana of little
sense.

You did not say then what morality was, but now you come to instruct the son of
Pandu!

Draupadi, however, having repaired to the hall at that time, made everything
right,

for like a vessel in the sea, she rescued the Pandavas and herself

from that ocean's rising tide of misfortunes. Then in that hall, while Draupadi
stood,

the charioteer's son addressed her in the presence of her fathers-in-law, saying:

'O daughter of Drupada, you have no refuge. Better become a bondwoman

to the house of Dhritarashtra's son. Your husbands, being defeated, no longer
exist.

You have a loving soul. Choose someone else for your lord.'

This speech, proceeding from Karna, was an arrow of words, sharp,

cutting all hopes, hitting the tenderest parts, and altogether frightful.

It buried itself deep in Arjuna's heart.

When the sons of Pandu were about to adopt garments of the skins of black deer,

Dussasana spoke the following pungent words: 'These all are mean eunuchs,
ruined,

and damned for a long, long time.'

You know, O Sanjaya, all these words of an opprobrious kind

that were spoken at the time of the game of dice.

I desire to go personally to the Kurus to settle this difficult matter.

If without injury to the Pandava cause I succeed in bringing about peace with
   the Kurus,

then an act of religious merit, resulting in very great blessings, will have been
   done by me,

and the Kurus, too, will have been extricated from the meshes of death.

I hope that when I shall speak to the Kurus words of wisdom,

resting on rules of righteousness—words fraught with sense

and free from all tendency to inhumanity—Dhritarashtra's son will pay heed to
   them.

I hope that when I arrive, the Kurus will pay me due respect.

Otherwise you may rest assured that those vicious sons of Dhritarashtra,

already scorched by their own vicious acts, will be burned up by Arjuna and
   Bhima.

When Pandu's sons were defeated at the dice game,

Dhritarashtra's sons spoke to them words that were harsh and rude.

But when the time comes, Bhima will take care to remind Duryodhana of those
   words.

Duryodhana is a big tree of evil passions. Karna is its trunk, Sakuni is its branches,

and Dussasana forms its blossoms and fruits, while the wise King Dhritarashtra is
   its roots.

Yudhishthira is a big tree of righteousness. Arjuna is its trunk, Bhima is its
   branches,

the sons of Madri are its abundant flowers and fruits,

and its roots are myself and religion and religious men.

King Dhritarashtra and his sons constitute a forest, while the sons of Pandu are
   its tigers.

Do not cut down the forest with its tigers, and let the tigers not be driven from
   the forest.

The tiger, out of the woods, is easily slain; the wood without a tiger is easily cut
   down.

Therefore, it is the tiger that protects the forest, and the forest that shelters the
   tiger.

The Dhritarashtras are creepers, while the Pandavas are sala trees.

A creeper can never flourish unless it has a large tree to twine around.

The sons of Pritha are ready to wait upon Dhritarashtra

as, indeed, those grinders of foes are ready for war.

Let King Dhritarashtra now do what may be proper for him to do.

The high-souled sons of Pandu, though competent to fight, are yet now in place

with their cousins. O learned man, represent all this truly to Dhritarashtra."

Sanjaya said: "I bid you farewell, O son of Pandu. Let prosperity be yours.

I hope that I have not been carried away by the feelings of my heart or said
   anything offensive.

I would also bid farewell to Yudhishthira, to Bhima and Arjuna,

to the son of Madri, to Satyaki, and to Chekitana, and take my departure.

Let peace and happiness be yours. Let all the kings look at me with eyes of
   affection."

Yudhishthira said: "Sanjaya, you may take your leave. Peace to you!

O learned man, you never think ill of us. Both they and we know you
to be a person of pure heart in the midst of all in the court of the Kurus.
Besides, being an ambassador now, you are faithful, beloved by us,
of agreeable speech and excellent conduct, and well affected toward us.
You never utter harsh and cutting words, or those that are false or bitter.
We know that your words are always fraught with morality and grave import.
Among envoys, you are the most dear to us.
Besides you, there is another who may come here, and that is Vidura.
Formerly, we always used to see you. You are indeed a friend to us.
And repairing to the priest of King Dhritarashtra, as also to his preceptors and
    Ritwijas,
you should address them and inquire after their welfare.
They should first be informed of my proposal for peace,
and then you should ask after their welfare.
You should also ask after the welfare of those who live in the kingdom,
carrying on trade, and those who fill important offices of state.
Our beloved preceptor Drona, who is fully versed in morality,
who is our counselor, who had practiced the Brahmacharya vow for mastering
    the Vedas,
who once again has made the science of weapons full and complete,
and who is always graciously inclined toward us—greet him in our name.
You should also inquire into the welfare of Aswatthaman
and repair to the abode of Kripa, the son of Saradwat,
that mighty car warrior and foremost among persons having a knowledge of self;
and, repeatedly saluting him in my name, touch his feet with your hand.
You should also, touching his feet, represent me as hale to that foremost among
    Kurus,
Bhishma, in whom are combined bravery, and abstention from injury,
and asceticism, and wisdom and good behavior, and Vedic learning, and firmness.
Salute also the wise, venerable, and blind King Dhritarashtra,
who is possessed of great learning and reverential to the old, and who is leader
    of the Kurus.
You should inquire as well about the welfare of the eldest of Dhritarashtra's sons,
Dhuryodhana, who is wicked and ignorant and deceitful and vicious,
and who now governs the entire world. You should even ask after the welfare
of the wicked Dussasana, that mighty bowman and hero among the Kurus,
who is younger than Duryodhana and who possesses a character like that of his
    brother.
Salute, too, the wise chief of the Valhikas,
who cherishes no other wish save that there should be peace among the Bharatas.
Ask about the welfare of Karna, the son of Vikareana,
that hero who is ready to vanquish, alone and unassisted, the Pandavas
whom no one dares assail in battle, that Karna who is unparalleled
in deluding those who are already deluded.
You must also ask after Vidura, who alone is devoted to us,
who is our instructor, who reared us, who is our father and mother and friend,
whose understanding never finds obstruction, and who is our counselor.

Finally, say to Duryodhana: 'That desire that torments you,
of ruling the Kurus without a rival, is unreasonable. It has no justification.
As for ourselves, we will never do anything that may be disagreeable to you!
O foremost among Bharata heroes, either give me back Indraprastha or fight
   with me!' "

✦

Sanjaya delivered the message to Duryodhana,
but Duryodhana refused to give Indraprastha back to the Pandavas.
When the Pandavas heard of his decision, it was clear to them that war was
   inevitable.
Still, Krishna said that he would try one last time, and that he might be more
   persuasive
than Sanjaya could have been; and that he would speak, not to Duryodhana,
but to King Dhritarashtra, who might be less closed to persuasive arguments.
Krishna traveled to Hastinapura in the company of Narada, the seer,
and spoke to the blind king. Dhritarashtra listened, nodding as if in agreement,
but then he said: "O holy one, it is as you say, Narada.
My wish also is to do precisely as you urge. But, O holy one, I have no power!"
The Kuru king, having said these words to Narada,
then addressed Krishna: "You have told me what leads to heaven
and what is beneficial to the world, as is consistent with virtue and fraught with
   reason.
I am not independent, however. Duryodhana never does what is agreeable to me.
Therefore, Krishna, strive to persuade that foolish and wicked son of mine,
who disobeys my commands. He never listens to the beneficial words of Gandhari,
or of wise Vidura, or of other friends like Bhishma, all of whom seek his good.
Therefore, counsel that crooked, senseless, and wicked-souled prince yourself.
By doing this, you shall have done that noble act which a friend should always do."
Krishna then approached the ever-wrathful Duryodhana and said to him:
"O best of Kurus, listen to these words of mine, uttered especially for your good
as well as for that of your followers. You are born to a race distinguished for
   wisdom.
It behooves you to act righteously, as I indicate. Possessed of learning
and endowed with excellent behavior, you are adorned with every splendid
   quality.
Those who are born into ignoble families, or who are wicked-souled, cruel, and
   shameless,
act in a way that seems acceptable to you.
In this world, only the inclinations of those who are righteous seem to be
   consistent
with the dictates of virtue and profit. The inclinations, however, of the
   unrighteous
seem to be perverse. O bull of Bharata's race, the disposition that you manifest
is of that perverse kind. Persistence in such behavior is sinful, frightful, wicked,
and capable of leading to death itself. It is, besides, without cause.

If, by avoiding that which is productive only of woe, you would achieve your own
    good;

if, O chastiser of foes, you would escape from the sinful and disreputable deeds
of your brothers, followers, and counselors; then, O tiger among men,
make peace with the sons of Pandu, who are all endowed with wisdom and bravery
and with great exertion and great learning, who all have their souls under
    control.

Such conduct will be conducive to the happiness of Dhritarashtra,
who possesses great wisdom; of grandsire Bhishma; of Drona; of the high-souled
    Kripa;

of Somadatta; of wise Valhika; of Aswatthaman, Vikarna, Sanjaya, and Vivingsati;
and of many of your kinsmen, and many of your friends also.
The whole world will benefit from that peace. You are endowed with modesty,
are born in a noble race, and have learning and kindness of heart.
Be obedient, sire, to the commands of your father and also of your mother.
Good sons always regard as beneficial that which their fathers command.
Indeed, when overtaken by calamity, everyone recollects the injunctions of his
    father.

Peace with the Pandavas recommends itself to your father.
Let it, therefore, recommend itself to you and your counselors as well.
That mortal who, having listened to the counsels of friends,
does not act according to them is consumed by the consequences of his disregard,
like the man who swallows the kimpaka fruit. He who from folly
does not accept beneficial counsels, who is unnerved by procrastination
and unable to attain his object, is obliged to repent at last.
He, on the other hand, who, having listened to beneficial counsels,
accepts them at once, abandoning his former opinion, wins happiness in the
    world.

Disregarding the opinions of the righteous, he who abides by the opinions of
    the wicked
soon makes his friends weep for him in consequence of his being plunged into
    distress.

Forsaking superior counselors, he who seeks the advice of inferior ones
soon falls into great distress and does not succeed in saving himself.
That companion of the sinful, who behaves falsely and never listens to good
    friends,
who honors strangers but hates those who are his own, is soon cast off by the
    earth.

Having quarreled with the sons of Pandu, you seek protection from those who
    are sinful,
incapable, and foolish. What other man is there on earth, besides you,
who—disregarding kinsmen who are all mighty charioteers,
each of whom resembles Sakra himself—would seek protection from strangers?
You have persecuted the sons of Kunti from their very birth.
They have not been angry with you, for the sons of Pandu are indeed virtuous.
You must therefore act toward those principal kinsmen of yours with equal
    generosity.

Do not yield yourself to the influence of wrath.

The exertions of the wise are always associated with virtue, profit, and desire.

If, indeed, all these three cannot be attained, men follow at least virtue and
    profit.

If, again, these three are pursued separately, those who have their hearts under
    control

choose virtue; those who are neither good nor bad, but occupy a middle station,

choose profit, which is always the subject of dispute;

while those who are fools choose the gratification of desire.

The fool who from temptation gives up virtue, and pursues profit and desire

by unrighteous means, is soon destroyed by his senses.

He who seeks profit and desire should yet practice virtue at the outset,

for neither profit nor desire is really dissociated from virtue.

It has been said that virtue alone is the cause of the three,

for he who seeks the three may, by the aid of virtue alone, grow like fire

brought into contact with a heap of dry grass.

You seek by unrighteous means this extensive empire,

flourishing and prosperous and well known to all the monarchs of the earth.

O king, he who behaves falsely toward those who conduct themselves righteously

certainly cuts himself down, like a forest with an ax.

One who has his soul under control never disregards anybody in the three
    worlds—

not even the commonest creature, far less those bulls among men, the sons of
    Pandu.

He who surrenders himself to the influence of anger loses his sense of right and
    wrong.

Rank growth must always be cut off. Behold, O Bharata, this is the proof.

At present, O sire, union with the sons of Pandu is better for you

than your union with the wicked. If you make peace with them,

you may obtain the fruition of all your wishes. O best of kings,

while enjoying the kingdom that has been founded by the Pandavas,

you seek protection from others, disregarding the Pandavas themselves.

Reposing the cares of your state on Dussasana, Durvisaha, Karna, and Suvala's son,

you desire the continuance of your prosperity.

These, however, are far inferior to the Pandavas in knowledge, in virtue,

in capacity for acquiring wealth, and in prowess.

Indeed, letting alone the four I have mentioned, all these kings together,

with you at their head, are incapable even of looking at the face of Bhima,

when angry, on the field of battle. This force consisting of all the kings of the
    earth

is at your elbow. There are also Bhishma, and Drona, and this Karna, and Kripa,

and Bhurisrava, and Somadatta, and Aswatthaman, and Jayadratha.

All these together are incapable of fighting against Arjuna.

Indeed, he is incapable of being vanquished in battle even by all the gods,

Asuras, men, and Gandharvas. Do not set your heart on battle.

Do you see in any of the royal races of the earth the man who, having battled
    Arjuna,

has returned home safe and sound? What advantage is there in universal
  slaughter?
Do you hope to vanquish in battle Arjuna, who, when excited with rage,
is invincible, irresistible, ever victorious, and indefatigable?
With myself as his second, when that son of Pritha rushes to the field of battle
against an enemy, who is there competent to challenge him?
Look at your sons, your brothers, your kinsmen and other relatives.
Do not let these chiefs of Bharata's race all perish on your account.
Do not let people say that you are the exterminator of your race
and the destroyer of its achievements. Those mighty car warriors, the Pandavas,
if peace be made, will install you as the Yuvaraja
and your father, Dhritarashtra, as the sovereign of this extensive empire.
Give to the sons of Pritha half the kingdom, and win great prosperity.
Make peace with the Pandavas, act according to the counsels of your friends,
and rejoicing with them, you are sure to obtain what is for your good for ever
  and ever."

✦

Bhishma, hearing these words of Krishna, then said to the vindictive
  Duryodhana:
"Krishna has spoken to you, to bring about peace between kinsmen.
Follow those counsels, and do not yield to the influence of wrath.
If you do not act according to the words of the high-souled Krishna,
you will have neither prosperity nor happiness nor what is for your good.
The mighty-armed Krishna has said to you what is consistent with virtue and
  profit.
Accept that object, and do not exterminate the population of the earth.
This resplendent prosperity of the Bharatas, among all the kings of the earth,
you will destroy through your wickedness
and you will also, through this arrogant disposition of yours,
deprive yourself—with all your counselors, sons, brothers, and kinsmen—of life
if you dismiss the words of Krishna, of your father, and of wise Vidura,
words that are consistent with truth and fraught with benefit to yourself.
Be not the exterminator of your race. Be not a wicked man.
Let not your heart be sinful. Do not tread the path of unrighteousness.
Do not sink your father and mother into an ocean of grief."
After Bhishma had spoken, Duryodhana, filled with wrath,
was breathing heavily, and Drona also spoke to Duryodhana:
"O sire, the words that Krishna has spoken to you are fraught with virtue and
  profit.
Bhishma also has said the same. Both of them are wise and with souls under
  control,
desirous of doing what is for your good, and possessed of great learning.
They have said what is beneficial. Accept their words, O king,
and act according to what both Krishna and Bhishma have said.
Those who are encouraging you are unable to give you victory.

During the time of battle, they will throw the burden of hostility on others' necks.
Do not slaughter the earth's population. Do not slay your sons and brothers.
If you do not accept the truthful words of your friends, Krishna and Bhishma,
then you will surely have to repent. But what use is there in telling you
what is conducive to your happiness and good? Everything has now been said
   to you.
Do as you wish. I cannot say anything more, O foremost of Bharata's race."
After Drona had ceased, Vidura said to that vindictive son of Dhritarashtra:
"O Duryodhana, I do not grieve for you. I grieve, however, for Gandhari and
   your father.
Having you of wicked soul for their protector—you of whom they will shortly be
   deprived—
they will have to wander without anybody to look after them, and deprived of
   friends,
like a pair of birds shorn of their wings. Having begotten such a wicked son,
who is the exterminator of his race, they will have to wander the earth in sorrow."
After this, King Dhritarashtra addressed Duryodhana, seated in the midst of his
   brothers
and surrounded by all the kings: "Listen, O Duryodhana, and accept those words
which are eternal, highly beneficial, and conducive to what is for your highest
   good.
With the aid of this Krishna of faultless deeds, we among all the kings
are sure to have all our cherished objects. Taking his advice, reconcile with
   Yudhishthira.
Through Krishna's agency, bind yourself closely with the Pandavas.
I think the time for that is come. Do not let the opportunity pass away."
Hearing in that assembly of the Kurus these words that were disagreeable to him,
Duryodhana replied to the mighty-armed Krishna, saying:
"It behooves you, O Krishna, to speak after reflecting on all circumstances.
Indeed, uttering such harsh words, without any reason you find fault with me
   alone.
But do you censure me, having surveyed the strength and weakness of both sides?
Indeed, you all reproach me alone, and not any other monarch.
I, however, do not find the least fault in myself. Yet all of you, including the old
   king,
hate me, but I do not behold any fault in myself, however minute.
In the game at dice that was joyfully accepted by them, the Pandavas were
   vanquished,
and their kingdom was won by Sakuni. What blame can be mine in regard to that?
On the other hand, O slayer of Madhu, the wealth that was won from the
   Pandavas
I then ordered to be returned to them. It cannot be any fault of ours
that the invincible Pandavas, defeated once again at dice, had to go to the woods.
Imputing what fault to us do they regard us as their enemies?
Though really weak, why do the Pandavas so cheerfully seek a quarrel with us,
as if they were strong? What have we done to them?
We shall not in consequence of any fierce deed or alarming word of theirs

bow down to them in fear, deprived of our senses.

We cannot bow down to Indra himself, let alone the sons of Pandu.

I do not see the man, observant of Kshatriya virtues, who can conquer us in
  battle.

Never mind the Pandavas—the very gods are not competent to vanquish Bhishma,
Kripa, Drona, and Karna in battle. If we are cut off with weapons in battle,
when our end comes, even that will lead us to heaven.

Who is there, born to a noble race and conforming to Kshatriya practices,
who would from fear bow to an enemy, desirous only of saving his life?

A person like me should bow down only to the Brahmanas, for the sake of piety,
without regarding anybody else. It is my opinion that this is the duty of Kshatriyas.

That share in the kingdom which was formerly given them by my father
shall never again be theirs, as long as I live. As long as King Dhritarashtra lives,
both we and they, sheathing our weapons, should live in dependence on him.

The kingdom—given away formerly from ignorance or fear, when I was a child
and dependent on others—which cannot be given away again, shall not be
  obtainable by the Pandavas.

As long as I live, even that much of our land as may be covered by the point of a
  needle

shall not be given by us to them."

Reflecting for a moment, with eyes red in anger, Krishna said:

"Do you wish for a bed of heroes? You shall have it, along with your counselors.

Wait only a short while, and a great slaughter will come.

You think that you have committed no offense against the Pandavas?

Let the assembled monarchs judge. Who else is there capable of insulting a
  brother's wife

in the way you did, or of dragging her into the assembly and addressing her
in the language you used? Of noble parentage, of excellent behavior,
and dearer to them than their very lives, the queen consort of Pandu's sons
was treated thus by you. All the Kauravas know the words addressed in their
  assembly

by Dussasana to the sons of Kunti when they were about to set out for the woods.

Who is capable of behaving so wretchedly toward his own kinsmen,
who are always engaged in the practice of virtue, are untainted by avarice,
and are always correct in their behavior? Language such as becomes only those
who are heartless and despicable was frequently repeated by Karna and Dussasana
and also by you. You took great pains to burn to death, at Varanavata,
the sons of Pandu with their mother, while they were children,
although that effort of yours was not crowned with success.

After this, the Pandavas with their mother were obliged to live for a long while
concealed in the town of Ekachakra in the abode of a Brahmana.

With poison, with snakes and cords, you sought by every means
the destruction of the Pandavas, although none of your designs was successful.

How can you now say that you have not offended against the high-souled
  Pandavas?

You are unwilling to give them their share in the kingdom, although they beg it
  of you.

You shall have to give it to them when, divested of prosperity, you are laid low.
Great is the advantage in peace, O king, both to yourself and to Yudhishthira.
Peace, however, does not recommend itself to you. To what can it be due
but your loss of understanding? Sinful and disreputable is that act you are about
    to undertake."
While Krishna was saying this, Dussasana addressed the vindictive Duryodhana
in the midst of the Kurus, saying: "If you do not make peace with the Pandavas,
the Kauravas will bind you hand and foot and make you over to the son of Kunti.
Bhishma and Drona and your own father will give the three of us—Dussasana,
    yourself, and me—
                    to them, to the Pandavas!"
Hearing these words of his brother, the wicked, shameless, disobedient,
    disrespectful,
and vain Duryodhana, breathing heavily, like a great snake, rose up from his seat
and—disregarding Vidura, and Dhritarashtra and the great King Valhika,
and Kripa, and Somadatta, and Bhishma, and Drona, and Janardana—left the
    court.
Seeing this, Bhishma said: "The enemies of that person
who, abandoning both virtue and profit, follows the impulses of wrath
will rejoice on beholding him plunged into distress at no distant date.
This fool, wrongly vain of his sovereignty, obeys only the dictates of wrath and
    avarice.
I see that the hour of all the Kshatriyas is arrived,
for all those kings, from delusion, have with their counselors followed
    Duryodhana."
Addressing all those who were still there, headed by Bhishma and Drona,
Krishna said: "This is a great transgression, for which all the elders of the Kuru
    race
are responsible in that they do not forcibly seize and bind this wicked king.
I think the time has come for doing this. It may still be productive of good.
The words I will speak will soon lead to beneficial results
The wicked son, of ill-regulated soul, having usurped his father's sovereignty
during the latter's lifetime, subjects himself to death.
For the sake of a province, a village may be sacrificed.
And for the sake of one's self, the whole earth may be sacrificed.
O monarch, binding Duryodhana fast, make peace with the Pandavas.
Let not the whole Kshatriya race be slaughtered on your account."
Hearing these words of Krishna, King Dhritarashtra lost no time in answering
    Vidura.
The king said: "Go, O child, to Gandhari, possessed of great wisdom and
    foresight,
and bring her here. With her I will solicit this wickedhearted son of mine.
If she can pacify this wretch of evil heart, we may yet be able to act
according to the words of our friend Krishna.
It may be that, speaking words in recommendation of peace, she may yet succeed
in pointing out the right path to this fool. If she can dispel this great and
    dreadful calamity

about to be caused by Duryodhana, it will lead to the attainment
of happiness and peace forever and ever."
Vidura brought Gandhari to the council room. And Dhritarashtra then said to her:
"Your son of wicked soul, who transgresses all my commands,
is about to sacrifice both sovereignty and life because of his lust for sovereignty.
He has left the court with his sinful counselors,
disregarding his superiors
and setting at naught the words of his well-wishers."
Gandhari, that princess of great fame, desirous of what was highly beneficial,
said: "Bring here, without loss of time, that kingdom-coveting, sick son of mine.
He who is of uncultivated heart and sacrifices both virtue and profit
does not deserve to govern. For all that, however, Duryodhana,
who is destitute of humility, has obtained a kingdom.
Indeed, O Dhritarashtra, you are too fond of your son and are much to be
blamed for this,
for, knowing well his sinfulness, you yet follow his counsel.
That son of yours, completely possessed by lust and wrath,
is now the slave of delusion and therefore incapable of being turned back by you.
You are now reaping the fruit, O Dhritarashtra, of having made over the
kingdom
to an ignorant fool of wicked soul, possessed by avarice and having wicked
counselors.
Why is the king indifferent today to that disunion which is about to take place
between persons related so closely? Your enemies will laugh at you.
Who would use force, facing a calamity that can be avoided by conciliation and
gift?"
At Dhritarashtra's command, and at his mother's also, Duryodhana was
summoned.
Anticipating his mother's words, the prince reentered the court
with eyes as red as copper from wrath, and breathing as heavily as a snake.
Beholding her son, who was treading a wrong path, Gandhari rebuked him
severely:
"O Duryodhana, attend to these words of mine that are beneficial to you
as also to all your followers, words that you can obey and that will produce your
happiness.
Obey the words of your well-wishers, which your father and Bhishma and Drona
and Kripa and Vidura have spoken. If you make peace, you will by that
render homage to Bhishma, your father, me, and all your well-wishers, with
Drona at their head. Nobody succeeds by his own desire alone
in acquiring and keeping or enjoying a kingdom. The man without his senses
under control
cannot enjoy sovereignty for any length of time.
Lust and wrath wean a man away from his possessions and enjoyments.
Conquering these foes first, a king brings the earth under his subjection.
Sovereignty over men is a great thing, and who desires to obtain an extensive
empire
must bind his senses to both profit and virtue, for if the senses are restrained,

intelligence increases, like fire that increases when fed with fuel.
If not controlled, these can slay their possessor, like unbroken horses
capable of killing an unskillful driver. He who seeks to conquer his counselors
without conquering himself, and to conquer foes without conquering his
    counselors,
is soon vanquished and ruined. He who conquers himself first, taking the self for
    a foe,
will not seek in vain to conquer his counselors and enemies afterward.
Lust and wrath that dwell in the body are deprived of their strength by wisdom,
like a couple of fish ensnared in a net with close holes.
Uniting yourself with the heroic sons of Pandu, you can enjoy the earth in
    happiness.
What Bhishma and Drona have told you is quite true. Krishna and Arjuna are
    invincible.
Seek, therefore, the protection of this mighty-armed one, for if Krishna is
    gracious,
both sides will be happy. That man who is not obedient to the wishes of learned
    friends,
and who seeks always his prosperity, only gladdens his enemies.
There is no good in battle, no virtue and no profit. How then can it bring
    happiness?
Even victory is not always certain. Do not set your heart on battle.
Half the earth is sufficient to yield the means of support to you and your
    counselors.
By acting according to the words of your well-wishers, you may win great fame,
but a quarrel with the sons of Pandu will only divest you of your great prosperity.
Their persecution for a full thirteen years has been enough.
Quench now that fire augmented by lust and wrath.
You are not a match for the Pandavas, nor is Kripa, who is exceedingly wrathful,
nor is your brother Dussasana. Indeed, when Bhishma and Drona and Kripa
and Karna and Bhimasena and Dhananjaya and Dhrishtadyumna will be enraged,
the population of the earth will be exterminated. Under the influence of wrath,
do not exterminate the Kurus. Of little understanding as you are,
you think that Bhishma and Drona and Kripa and all others will fight for you
with all their might. That will never happen, for these are endowed with
    self-knowledge,
and their affection toward the Pandavas and yourselves is equal.
If, for the sake of the sustenance they have obtained from King Dhritarashtra,
they consent to yield up their lives, they will not yet be angry at King Yudhishthira.
It is never seen in this world that men acquire wealth by avarice.
                Renounce your avarice, then, and desist."

✦

Duryodhana, disregarding these words of his mother, went away in anger.
And, leaving the court behind him, the Kuru prince consulted
with Suvala's royal son, Sakuni, most clever in dice.

And this was the resolution which Duryodhana and Karna and Suvala's son
    Sakuni,
with Dussasana as their fourth, arrived at:
"Krishna seeks, with King Dhritarashtra and Shantanu's son, to seize us first.
We, however, shall forcibly seize this tiger among men first,
as Indra seized Virochana's son Vali. Hearing that this one of Vrishni's race
has been seized, the Pandavas will lose heart and become incapable of exertion,
like snakes whose fangs have been broken. This mighty-armed one
is the refuge and protection of them all. If he is confined,
the Pandavas with the Somakas will despair. Therefore, disregarding
    Dhritarashtra's cries,
we will seize this Krishna, who is quick in action, and only then fight with the foe."
After those sinful men of wicked soul had come to this resolution,
highly intelligent Satyaki, capable of reading the heart by signs, soon came to
    know of it.
And because of that knowledge, he soon issued out of the court,
accompanied by Hridika's son Kritavarman.
Satyaki said to Kritavarman: "Array the troops. And wait at the entrance of the
    court
until I present this matter to Krishna." That hero then reentered the court
and informed the high-souled Krishna, and then Dhritarashtra, and then Vidura,
of the conspiracy. Laughingly, he said: "These wicked men intend to commit an
    act here
that is disapproved by the good, who are mindful of virtue, profit, and desire.
They will, however, never be able actually to achieve it.
These fools of sinful souls are about to perpetrate a highly unbecoming deed.
Those wretches of little understanding are like idiots and children,
desiring to seize a blazing fire by means of their garments."
Hearing these words of Satyaki, Vidura said these words to Dhritarashtra
in the midst of the Kurus: "O king, the hour of all your sons is come,
for they are endeavoring to perpetrate a highly infamous act,
however incapable they may be of actually accomplishing it.
United together, they desire to vanquish this younger brother of Vasava and
    seize him.
Indeed, encountering this invincible and irresistible one,
they will all perish like insects in a blazing fire.
If he wishes, he can send all of them, even if they fight in a body,
to the abode of Yama, like an enraged lion dispatching a herd of elephants.
He will, however, never do any such sinful and censurable act."
After Vidura had said these words, Krishna, looking at Dhritarashtra,
continued to speak in the midst of those well-meaning persons:
"O king, if these men desire to chastise me by using violence, permit them to
    chastise me,
for I dare chastise all of them together.
I will not perpetrate any sinful act. Coveting the possessions of the Pandavas,
your sons will lose their own. If they desire to perpetrate such a deed,
Yudhishthira's object will then be accomplished; for, this very day,

seizing these and all who follow them, I can make them over to the sons of Pritha.
I will not, however, commit in your presence any such censurable deed
that can proceed only from wrath and a sinful understanding.
Let it be as Duryodhana desires. I give permission to all your sons to do it."
Dhritarashtra then said to Vidura: "Quickly bring hither the sinful Duryodhana,
who is so covetous of sovereignty, with his friends, counselors, brothers, and
    followers.
I shall see if, indeed, making one more effort, I can bring him to the right path."
Vidura once more caused the unwilling Duryodhana to enter the court with his
    brothers,
surrounded by the kings who followed him.
King Dhritarashtra then addressed Duryodhana, surrounded by Karna and
    Dussasana,
saying: "O wretch of accumulated sins, having for your allies men of despicable
    acts,
infamous is the deed that you seek to do. Of little understanding, only one like you
can seek to do an act so thoroughly disapproved by the good,
however impossible it may be of being actually achieved.
Uniting with sinful allies, do you wish to chastise this invincible one
of eyes like lotus leaves? Like a child wishing to have the moon, you seek, O fool,
to do what cannot be done by the very gods, headed by Vasava, with all their
    strength!
Do you not know that Krishna is incapable of being withstood in battle
by gods and men and Gandharvas and Asuras and Uragas?
Like the wind, which none can seize with his hands,
like the moon, which no arms can reach,
like the earth, which none can support on his head, Krishna is invulnerable to
    force."
Then Vidura, turning his eyes to Duryodhana, addressed him, saying:
"Listen now to these words of mine. At the gates of Saubha, that foremost
    among monkeys,
known by the name of Dwivida, covered Krishna with a mighty shower of stones.
Desirous of seizing him by putting forth all his prowess and exertion,
he yet did not succeed. Do you seek to apprehend that Krishna by force?
In the city of Nirmochana, six thousand Asuras failed to seize him with their
    nooses.
Do you seek to apprehend that Krishna by force?
While only a child, he slew Putana and two Asuras assuming the shape of birds,
and he held up the mountains of Govardhana on his little finger
to protect the cattle from a continuous rain.
While floating on the vast deep, he slew Madhu and Kaitabha,
and in another birth he slew Hayagriva the Horse-Necked.
He is the maker of everything but is himself made by none. He is the cause of all
    power.
Whatever he wishes, he accomplishes without any effort.
Do you not know sinless Govinda, of terrible prowess and incapable of
    deterioration?

This one, like an angry snake of virulent poison, is the never-ending source of
    energy.
In seeking to use violence toward Krishna, you will, with all your followers,
                    perish like an insect failing into a fire."
After Vidura had said this, Krishna addressed Duryodhana and said:
"From delusion, you think I am alone, and therefore you seek to make me a
    captive
after vanquishing me by violence. Here, however, are all the Pandavas
and all the Vrishnis and Andhakas. Here are all the Adityas, the Rudras, and the
    Vasus,
with all the great rishis." Saying this, Krishna burst into loud laughter.
And as he laughed, from his body that resembled a blazing fire
issued myriads of gods, each of lightning's effulgence but no bigger than a thumb.
On his forehead appeared Brahman, and on his breast Rudra.
And on his arms appeared the regents of the world,
and from his mouth issued Agni, the Adityas, the Sadhyas, the Vasus,
the Aswins, and the Marutas, with Indra and the Viswedevas.
And myriads of Yakshas, and the Gandharvas, and Rakshasas also,
of the same measure and form, issued thence.
And from his two arms issued Sankarshana and Dhananjaya.
And Arjuna stood on his right, bow in hand,
and Rama stood on his left, armed with the plow.
And behind him stood Bhima, and Yudhishthira, and the two sons of Madri,
and before him were all the Andhakas, and the Vrishnis, with Pradyumna
and other chiefs bearing mighty weapons upraised.
And on his diverse arms were seen the conch, the discus, the mace,
the bow called Saranga, the plow, the javelin, the Nandaka,
and every other weapon, all shining with effulgence and upraised for striking.
And from his eyes and nose and ears and every other part of his body
issued fierce sparks of fire mixed with smoke.
And from the pores of his body issued sparks of fire like the rays of the sun.
And beholding that awful form of the high-souled Krishna,
all the kings closed their eyes, with terrified hearts,
except Drona and Bhishma and Vidura, endowed with great intelligence,
and greatly blessed Sanjaya, and the rishis, possessed of the wealth of asceticism,
for the divine Krishna gave them this divine sight on that occasion.
And beholding in the Kuru court that wonderful sight,
they heard celestial drums beat in the sky and saw a floral shower fall upon him.
The whole earth trembled, and the oceans were agitated.
Then that tiger among men withdrew that divine and highly wonderful
and extremely varied and auspicious form.
And arm in arm with Satyaki on one side and Hridika's son Kritavarman on the
    other,
and obtaining permission of the rishis, Krishna left the court,
like a blazing fire mixed with smoke. At the gate he saw his charioteer, Daruka,
waiting with his large white car furnished with rows of tinkling bells,
decked with golden ornaments, and covered all over with white tigerskins

to which were harnessed his steeds Saivya and others.

And there also appeared, mounted on his car, that favorite hero of Vrishnis,
the mighty car warrior Kritavarman, the son of Hridika.

As Krishna, who had his car ready, was about to depart, King Dhritarashtra
addressed him once more and said: "O grinder of foes,
you have seen the power I wield over my sons!

You have indeed witnessed all with your own eyes. Nothing now is unknown to you.
Seeing me endeavor to bring about peace between the Kurus and the Pandavas,
and knowing the state in which I find myself,
it behooves you not to entertain any suspicion regarding me.

You know what words I have spoken to Duryodhana.

The Kauravas and all the kings of the earth also know that I have made every
endeavor

to bring about peace."

Krishna then addressed Dhritarashtra, Drona, the grandsire Bhishma, Vidura,
Valhika, and Kripa, saying: "You have witnessed all that has happened
in the assembly of the Kurus. You have seen how wicked Duryodhana,
like an uneducated wretch, left the court in anger,
and how King Dhritarashtra also describes himself to be powerless.

With the permission of you all, I shall now go back to Yudhishthira."

Saluting them, Krishna then mounted his car and set out.

And Bhishma, Drona, and Kripa, and Vidura, and Aswatthaman and Vikarna,
and that mighty car warrior Yuyutsu all began to follow him.

Krishna, on his large white car furnished with rows of tinkling bells,
proceeded then, in the sight of the Kurus, to the abode of his paternal aunt,
Kunti.

◆

Entering Kunti's abode and worshipping her feet, Krishna told her briefly
all that had happened in the Kuru assembly: "Diverse words, fraught with
reasons,
were said both by myself and the rishis, but Duryodhana would not accept them.

As regards him and his followers, their hour is come. Now, by your leave,
I shall return to the Pandavas. What should I say to them as your instructions?"

Kunti answered: "Say to King Yudhishthira: 'Your virtue, O son, is decreasing
greatly.

Do not act vainly. Like a reader of the Vedas incapable of catching their real
meaning,
cast your eyes on the duties of your own order, as ordained by the self-created.

Do not ask whether the era is the cause of the king or the king the cause of
the era,
for it is certain that the king is the cause of the era. A king of wicked deeds
resides in hell
for countless ages. The king's sins taint the world, and the world's taint him.

Observe your kingly duties that befit your ancestry.

That is not the conduct of a royal sage which you wish to display.

Indeed, he who is stained by weakness of heart and adheres to compassion
and is unsteady never obtains the merit born of cherishing his subjects with love.
That understanding according to which you are now acting was never wished
    for you
by Pandu, or myself, or your grandsire, while we uttered blessings on you.
Sacrifice, gift, merit, and bravery, subjects and children, greatness of soul,
and might, and energy were always what we prayed for you.
The mother and the father, as also the gods, always desire for their children
liberality and generosity and study and sacrifice and sway over subjects.
Whether all this be righteous or unrighteous, you are to practice it because of
    your birth.
Hungry men, approaching a brave and bountiful monarch, are gratified
and live by his side. What virtue can be superior to this?
A virtuous person, upon acquiring a kingdom, should make all persons his own,
attaching some by gift, some by force, and some by sweet words.
A Brahmana should adopt mendicancy, a Kshatriya should protect subjects,
a Vaisya should earn wealth, and a Sudra should serve the other three.
Mendicancy, therefore, is forbidden to you. Nor is agriculture suited to you.
You are a Kshatriya, and therefore the protector of all in distress.
You are to live by the prowess of your arms and recover your paternal share
of the kingdom you lost by conciliation, whether by working disunion among
    your foes,
or by gift of money, or violence, or well-directed policy.
What can be a matter of greater grief than that I, deprived of friends,
should live upon food supplied by others after having brought you forth?
With your merit worn out, do not, with your younger brothers, obtain a sinful
    end.'"

31

Kunti

Kunti said to Krishna: "O chastiser of foes, there is an old story
of the conversation between Vidula and her son. You must tell Yudhishthira
anything that can be gathered from this. There was a highborn lady of great
    intelligence
named Vidula. She was famous, slightly wrathful, of crooked disposition,
but devoted to Kshatriya virtues. She was known to all the kings of the earth.
She had listened to the speeches and instructions of diverse men.
And the Princess Vidula one day rebuked her son
who, after his defeat by the king of the Sindhus, lay prostrate and in despair.
She said: 'You are not my son, O enhancer of the joys of foes.
You could not have been begotten by me and your father! Without wrath as
    you are,
you cannot be counted as a man. Your features betray you to be a eunuch.
If you are desirous of your own welfare, bear your burden on your shoulders.
Do not disgrace your soul. Do not suffer it to be gratified with a trifle.
Set your heart on your welfare, and be not afraid. Abandon your fears.
O coward, do not lie down thus after your defeat, delighting foes and grieving
    friends,
and bereft of honor. Little streams are filled up with only a small quantity of
    water.
The palms of a mouse are filled with only a little.
A coward is soon gratified with small acquisitions.
Rather perish in plucking the fangs of a snake than die miserably like a dog.
Put forth your prowess even at the risk of your life. Like a hawk that ranges the sky,
wander fearlessly. Put forth your prowess, and watch your foes for an
    opportunity.
Why do you lie down like a carcass, or like one smitten by lightning?
Do not slumber after having been vanquished by the foe. Do not disappear from
    sight.
Make yourself known by your deeds. Never occupy the intermediate,
the low, or the lowest station. Blaze up like a torch of tinduka wood, even for a
    moment,
but never smolder from desire like a flameless fire of paddy chaff.
Let no son be born to a royal race who is either exceedingly fierce or
    exceedingly mild.

Repairing to the field of battle and achieving every great feat possible for man to
    achieve,

a brave man is freed from the debt he owes to the duties of the Kshatriya order.

Such a person never disgraces himself. Whether he gains his object or not,

he who is possessed of sense never indulges in grief.

On the other hand, such a person accomplishes what should be done

without caring for his life. Therefore, display your prowess, or obtain that end

which is inevitable. All your religious rites, O eunuch, and all your achievements

are gone. The very root of all your enjoyment is cut off. What then do you live for?

If one must fall and sink, one should seize the foe by the hips and thus fall with
    the foe.

Even if one's roots are cut off, one should not yet give way to despair.

Horses of high mettle put forth all their prowess for dragging or bearing heavy
    weights.

Remembering their behavior, muster all your strength and sense of honor.

Know in what your manliness consists.

He who has not achieved a great feat forming the subject of men's conversation

only increases the population. He is neither man nor woman.

He whose fame is not founded in respect of charity, asceticism, truth, learning,

and acquisition of wealth is only his mother's excreta.

On the other hand, he who surpasses others in learning, asceticism, wealth,

prowess, and deeds is truly a man. It behooves you not to adopt the idle,

wretched, infamous, and miserable profession of mendicancy worthy only of a
    coward.

Friends never derive any happiness from obtaining that weak person for a friend,

at whose sight foes are delighted, who is despised by men, is without robes,

is gratified with small acquisitions, is destitute, has no courage, and is low.

Alas, exiled from our kingdom, driven from home, deprived of all means of
    enjoyment,

and destitute of resources, we shall have to perish from want of the very means
    of life!

You misbehave in the midst of those who are good and are the destroyer of your
    family.

By bringing you forth, O Sanjaya, I have brought forth Kali himself in the shape
    of a son.

Let no woman bring forth such a son as you, who are without wrath,

without exertion, without energy, and the joy of your foes.

Do not smolder. Blaze up! Slay your foes.

For but a moment, for ever so short a time, blaze up on the heads of your
    enemies.

He is a man who cherishes wrath and does not forgive.

He, on the other hand, who is forgiving and without wrath is neither a man nor
    a woman.

Steel your heart, and seek to recover your own.

A brave king of mighty strength who moves like a lion may go the way of all
    creatures.

The subjects, however, who reside in his dominions do not become unhappy.

That king who, disregarding his own happiness and pleasures,
seeks the prosperity of his kingdom succeeds in gladdening his counselors and
    friends.'
Hearing these words, the son said: 'If you do not behold me,
of what use would the whole earth be to you, of what use your ornaments,
of what use all the means of pleasure and even life itself?' The mother said:
'Let those regions be obtained by our foes that belong to those who are low.
Let those again who are friends go to those regions that are obtainable
by persons whose souls are held in respect.
Do not adopt the course of life that is followed by those wretched persons
who, destitute of strength and without servants, live upon the food supplied by
    others.
Like the creatures of the earth that depend on the clouds,
or the gods that depend on Indra, let the Brahmanas and your friends all
    depend on you
for their sustenance. His life, O Sanjaya, is not vain on whom all creatures depend,
like birds repairing to a tree abounding with ripe fruits.
The life of that brave man is praiseworthy by whose prowess friends derive
    happiness,
like the gods deriving happiness through the prowess of Indra.
That man who lives in greatness, depending on the prowess of his own arms,
succeeds in winning fame in this world and a blessed state in the next!'
Vidula continued: 'Alas, like medicine to a dying man,
these words that are fraught with grave import and are proper and reasonable
make no impression on you! It is true, the king of the Sindhus has many
    followers.
They are, however, all to be discounted, from weakness and ignorance of proper
    means.
They wait for the distress of their master, without being able to deliver themselves
by their own exertions. As regards his open enemies, they will come to you
if they behold you putting forth your prowess.
Uniting with them, seek refuge now in a mountain fastness,
waiting for calamity to overtake the foe, for he is not free from disease and death.
By name you are Sanjaya the Victorious. I do not, however, behold
any such indication in you. Be true to your name. Be my son.
Beholding you while a child, a Brahmana of great foresight and wisdom, said:
"This one falling into great distress will again win greatness."
Remembering his words, I hope for your victory.
It is for that, O son, I tell you so and shall tell you again and again.
That man who pursues the fruition of his objects according to the ways of policy,
and for the success of whose objects other people strive cordially, is sure to win.
Engage in war without withdrawing yourself from it.
Samvara has said: "Nothing is more miserable than to be anxious for food
from day to day." A state such as this has been said to be more unhappy
than the death of one's husband and sons. Poverty is a form of death.
I was possessed of every auspicious thing and was worshipped by my husband.
My power extended over all. Our friends beheld me decked in costly garlands

and ornaments, with my body well washed and attired in excellent robes,
and myself always cheerful. When you behold both me and your wife
weakened from want of food, you will then, O Sanjaya, scarcely desire to live.
If I have to say no to a Brahmana, my heart will burst, for neither my husband nor I
ever said no to a Brahmana before. We were the refuge of others,
without ourselves ever having taken refuge with others.
You must be our means of crossing the ocean that is difficult to cross.
In the absence of boats, be our boat. Make a place for us where there is none.
Revive us who are dead. You are competent to encounter all foes
if you do not cherish the desire of life. If, however, you are for adopting this mode of life
fit only for a eunuch, then, with troubled soul, it would be better to sacrifice your life.
A brave man wins fame by slaying even a single foe.
By slaying Vritra, Indra became the great Indra
and acquired the sovereignty of all the gods and the cup for drinking soma,
and the lordship of all the worlds. When a hero wins fame in a fair fight,
his enemies are pained and bow down to him. Cowards become helpless
and by their own conduct bestow every object of desire on those who are skilled and brave
and who fight reckless of their lives. Whether kingdoms be overtaken by mighty ruin,
or whether life itself be endangered, they who are noble never desist
until they exterminate the foes within their reach.
Slay your foes in battle. Let me not behold you cheerless. Let me not see you in misery,
surrounded by our sorrowing selves and your rejoicing foes.
What peace can my heart know if I behold you giving laudatory speeches
in honor of others or walking submissively behind them?
O! never was one born in this race to walk behind another.
I know what the eternal essence of Kshatriya virtues is,
as spoken of by the old and the older ones and by those coming late and later still.
Eternal and unswerving, it has been ordained by the creator himself.
He who has in this world been born as a Kshatriya
and has acquired a knowledge of the duties of that order
will never from fear or the sake of sustenance bow down to anybody on earth.
One should rather break in the joints than yield in this world to anybody.
A high-souled Kshatriya should always roam like an infuriated elephant.
He should, O Sanjaya, bow down to Brahmanas only, for the sake of virtue.
He should rule over all other orders, destroying all evildoers.
Possessed of allies, or destitute of them, he should do this as long as he lives.'"
Kunti continued: "Hearing these words of his mother, the son said:
'O ruthless and wrathful mother, you think highly of martial heroism.
Your heart is surely made of steel beaten into that shape.
To hell with Kshatriya practices, in accordance with which you urge me to battle

as if I were a stranger to you, and for the sake of which you speak to me—your
    only son—
as if you were not my mother. If you are dissociated from me, your son,
of what use then would the whole earth be to you,
of what use all your ornaments and all the means of enjoyment?
Indeed, of what use would life itself be to you?'
The mother said: 'All the acts of those who are wise are undertaken, O son,
for the sake of virtue and profit. Eyeing virtue and profit only, I urge you to
    battle.
If at such a time you do not resort to action, then, disrespected by the people,
you would do that which would be most disagreeable to me.
If, O Sanjaya, you are about to be stained with infamy
and I do not from affection tell you anything, then that affection
would be worthless and unreasonable, like that of the she-ass for her young.
He who takes delight in well-instructed sons and grandsons enjoys a delight that
    is real.
He, on the other hand, who takes delight in a son destitute of exertion,
refractory, and wicked-minded does not have the very thing for which a son is
    desired.
A Kshatriya, O Sanjaya, has been created for battle and victory.
Whether he wins or perishes, he obtains the region of Indra.
The happiness that a Kshatriya obtains by reducing his foes to subjection
is such that the like of it does not exist in heaven in the sacred region of Indra.
Burning with wrath, a Kshatriya of great energy, if vanquished many times,
should wait, desiring to vanquish his foes. How else can he obtain peace of mind?
He who is possessed of wisdom regards anything small as disagreeable.
To that person to whom anything small becomes agreeable,
that little thing ultimately becomes a source of pain.
He becomes wretched, feels every want, and is lost like the Ganga entering the
    ocean.'
The son said: 'You should not say such things to your son.
Show him kindness, staying by his side like a silent and dumb being.'
The mother said: 'Great is my gratification, since you say so.
I, who may be urged by you to my duty, shall therefore urge you to do yours.
I will indeed honor you then, when I behold you crowned with success
after the slaughter of all the Saindhavas.' The son said:
'Without wealth, without allies, how can success and victory be mine?
Conscious of this exceedingly miserable state of mine, I have abstained
from desire for a kingdom, like an evildoer abstaining from desire for heaven.
If, therefore, you see any means by which all this can be effected,
speak of it to me, and I shall do all that you command me to do.'
The mother said: 'Do not disgrace your soul, O son, by anticipations of failure.
In any act, the attainment of success is uncertain. Knowing that success is
    uncertain,
people still act, so that they sometimes succeed and sometimes do not.
But they who abstain from action never obtain success.
In the absence of exertion, there is but one result, which is failure.

That wise king who engages in acts, having performed all auspicious rites
and with the gods and the Brahmanas on his side, soon wins success.
Like the sun embracing the east, the goddess of prosperity embraces him.
I see you have shown yourself fit for my various suggestions and encouraging
    speeches.
Display now your prowess. It behooves you to win, by every exertion,
the object you have in view. Bring to your side those who are angry with your foes,
those who are covetous, those who have been weakened by your foes,
those who are jealous of them, those who have been humiliated by them,
those who always challenge them from an excess of pride, and all others of this
    class.
By this means you will be able to break the mighty host of your enemy,
like an impetuous and fierce-rising tempest scattering the clouds.
Give your would-be allies wealth before it is due. Seek their good,
be up and doing, and speak sweetly to them all.
They will then do the right thing and place you at their head.
When the enemy comes to know that his foe has become reckless of his life,
then is he troubled on the latter's account as from a snake living in his chamber.
If, knowing one to be powerful, one's enemy does not strive to subjugate one,
he should at least make one friendly by the application of the arts of conciliation,
gifts, and the like. Even that would be tantamount to subjugation.
Obtaining respite by means of the art of conciliation, one may see one's wealth
    increase.
And if one's wealth increases, one is worshipped and sought as a refuge by one's
    friends.
If, again, one is deprived of wealth, one is abandoned by friends and relatives
and, more than that, mistrusted and even despised by them.
It is perfectly impossible for him ever to regain his kingdom who,
having united himself with his foe, lives confidently.'
The mother continued: 'Into whatever calamity a king may fall, he should not
    show his distress.
Beholding the king afflicted with fright, the whole kingdom, the army,
and the counselors all yield to fear, and the subjects become disunited.
Some go and embrace the side of the enemy, others simply abandon the king,
and others again, who had been humiliated, strive to strike.
They, however, who are intimate friends wait by his side,
but, though desiring his welfare, from their inability to do anything wait helplessly,
like a cow whose calf has been tethered.
You have many friends whom you once worshipped, friends after your heart
who feel for your kingdom and desire to take your calamities on themselves.
Do not frighten those friends or suffer them to abandon you on seeing you afraid.
If you understand what I have said, and if all I have said appears proper and
    sufficient,
then, O Sanjaya, muster your patience, and gird up your loins for victory.
We have a large number of treasure houses unknown to you.
I alone know of their existence. I will place these at your disposal.
You also have, O Sanjaya, more than one friend who sympathizes with you

in your joys and woes, and who never retreats from the field of battle.
Allies such as these always play the part of faithful counselors
to a person who seeks his own welfare and tries to acquire what is agreeable to
    himself.' "
Kunti continued: "Hearing this speech of his mother fraught with good sense,
Sanjaya felt the despair that had overtaken his heart lift instantly,
and he said: 'When I have you for my guide, who are so concerned about my
    future welfare,
I shall certainly either rescue my paternal kingdom that is sunk in water
or perish in the attempt. During your discourse, I was almost a silent listener.
Now and then only I interposed a word. It was only with the view of drawing
    you out.
I have not been satiated with your words, like a person not satiated with drinking
    Amrita.
With support from allies, I shall gird up my loins to repress my foes and obtain
    victory.' "
Kunti continued: "Pierced by the rhetorical arrows of his mother, the son roused
    himself
like a steed of proud mettle and achieved all that his mother had pointed out.
When a king is afflicted by foes and overcome with despair,
his minister should make him hear this excellent history that enhances energy.
Indeed, this history is called *Jaya* and should be heard by everyone desirous of
    victory.
Having listened to it, one may soon subjugate the whole earth.
This history causes a woman to bring forth a heroic son.
The woman quick with child who repeatedly listens to it gives birth to a hero,
a brave son of irresistible prowess, one who is foremost in learning,
ascetic austerities, and liberality, who is devoted to asceticism,
blazing forth with Brahmanic beauty, radiant with effulgence, endowed with
    great might,
blessed—a mighty car warrior, possessed of great intelligence, ever victorious,
invincible, a chastiser of the wicked, and a protector of all those who practice
    virtue."

✦

Having spoken thus with Kunti, Krishna sought out Karna to talk with him
and try to enlist him to the Pandavas' side. Karna listened respectfully
but, in the end, could not be won over. He said:
"Without doubt, you have said these words from your love and friendship for me,
as also in consequence of your desire of doing me good. I know all that you have
    told me.
Morally, I am the son of Pandu, as also because of the injunctions of the
    scriptures,
as you will agree. My mother, while a maiden, bore me in her womb
through her connection with Surya, the sun god.
And at the command of Surya himself, she abandoned me as soon as I was born.

Thus, O Krishna, I came into the world. Morally, therefore, I am the son of Pandu.
Kunti, however, abandoned me without thinking of my welfare.
The Suta Adhiratha, as soon as he beheld me, took me to his home,
and Radha's breasts, from her affection for me, were filled with milk that very day,
and she cleaned my urine and evacuations. How can one like us, conversant with duties
and ever engaged in listening to scriptures, deprive her of her oblation to her ancestors?
So also Adhiratha of the Suta class regards me as a son, and I too, from affection,
always regard him as my father. Adhiratha, from paternal affection,
caused all the rites of infancy to be performed according to the rules of the scriptures.
When I attained to youth, I married wives according to his selections.
Through them have been born my sons and grandsons.
My heart also, O Krishna, and all the bonds of affection and love, are fixed on them.
From joy or fear, I cannot venture to destroy those bonds
even for the sake of the whole earth or heaps of gold.
Because of my connection with Duryodhana of Dhritarashtra's race, I have, O Krishna,
enjoyed sovereignty for thirteen years without a thorn in my side.
I have performed many sacrifices, always in connection with persons of the Suta tribe.
All my family rites and marriage rites have been performed with the Sutas.
Obtaining me, Duryodhana has thus made preparations for an armed encounter
and provoked hostilities with the sons of Pandu. And it is for this reason that,
in the battle that will ensue, I have been chosen as the great antagonist of Arjuna
to advance against him in a single combat. For the sake of death, or the ties of blood,
or fear, or temptation, I cannot venture to behave falsely toward the son of Dhritarashtra.
If I do not now engage in a single combat with Arjuna, this will be inglorious
for both myself and him. Without doubt, you have told me all this for my benefit.
The Pandavas, obedient as they are to you, will do all that you have said.
You must, however, conceal our discourse for the present.
If King Yudhishthira of virtuous soul comes to know me as the firstborn son of Kunti,
he will never accept the kingdom. If, again, this mighty empire becomes mine,
I shall certainly make it over to Duryodhana only. Let Yudhishthira of virtuous soul
become king forever. He who has Krishna for his advisor
and Arjuna and that mighty car warrior Bhima for his combatants,
as also Nakula and Sahadeva and the sons of Draupadi, is fit to rule the whole earth.
Dhrishtadyumna, the prince of the Panchalas; that mighty car warrior Satyaki;
Uttamaujas; Yudhamanyu, the prince of Somakas who is devoted to truth;
the ruler of the Chedis, Chekitana; the invincible Sikhandin;

the Kekaya brothers, all of the hue of Indragoapka insects;
Bhimasena's uncle Kuntibhoja, possessed of steeds the colors of the rainbow;
the mighty car warrior Syenajit; Sanka the son of Virata; and you, O Krishna,
all make up this great assemblage of Kshatriyas on Yudhishthira's side.
This blazing kingdom, celebrated among all the kings of the earth, is already won
by Yudhishthira. A great sacrifice of arms is about to be celebrated
by Dhritarashtra's son. You will be the Upadrashtri of that sacrifice.
The office of Adhyaryu also will be yours. The ape-bannered Arjuna
accoutered in mail will be the sacrificial bowl, Gandiva will be the sacrificial ladle,
and the prowess of the warriors will be the clarified butter that is to be consumed.
The weapons called Aindra, Pashupatastra, Brahma, and Sthunakarna, applied
    by Arjuna,
will be the mantras of that sacrifice. Resembling his father,
or perhaps surpassing him in prowess, Subhadra's son Abhimanyu
will be the chief Vedic hymn to be chanted. That destroyer of elephant ranks,
that utterer of fierce roars in battle, that tiger among men, the exceedingly
    mighty Bhima
will be Udgatri and Prastotri. King Yudhishthira of virtuous soul,
ever engaged in the Yapa and Homa rites, will himself be the Brahma of that
    sacrifice.
The sounds of conchs, tabors, and drums, and the leonine roaring
rising high in the skies, will be the calls to those invited to eat.
The two sons of Madri, Nakula and Sahadeva of great fame and prowess,
will be the slayers of the sacrificial animals, and rows of bright cars
furnished with standards of variegated hue will be the stakes for their tying.
Barbed arrows, and darts, and long shafts, and arrows with heads like calf's teeth
will play the part of spoons with which to distribute the soma juice,
while Tomaras will be the vessels of soma, and bows will be Pavitras.
The swords will be Kapalas; the heads of slain warriors, the Purodasas;
and the blood of warriors, the clarified butter.
In this sacrifice, the lances and bright maces will be pokers for stirring the
    sacrificial fire
and the corner stakes to keep the firewood from falling down.
The arrows shot by the wielder of Gandiva and by other mighty car warriors
and by Drona and Drona's son will play the part of ladles for distributing the
    soma.
Satyaki will discharge the duties of the chief assistant of the Adhyaryu.
Of this sacrifice, Dhritarashtra's son will be installed as the performer,
while this vast army will be his wife. When the nocturnal rites of sacrifice begin,
Bhima's son, the mighty Ghatotkacha, will play the part of the slayer of victims.
Mighty Dhrishtadyumna, who sprang to life from the sacrificial fire,
having for its mouth the rites celebrated with mantras, will be the Dakshina.
For those harsh words, O Krishna, that I said before to the sons of Pandu
for the gratification of Dhritarashtra's son, for that wicked conduct of mine,
I am consumed with repentance. When you see me slain by Arjuna,
then will the Punachiti of this sacrifice commence.
When the second son of Pandu drinks the blood of the loudly roaring Dussasana,

then will the soma-drinking of this sacrifice have taken place.

When the two princes of Panchala, Dhrishtadyumna and Sikhandin,

overthrow Drona and Bhishma, then will this sacrifice be suspended for an
interval.

When mighty Bhimasena slays Duryodhana, then will this sacrifice be concluded.

When the wives of Dhritarashtra's sons and grandsons, deprived of husbands
and sons

and without protectors, indulge in lamentations on the field of battle

haunted by dogs and vultures and other carrion birds,

then will the final bath of this sacrifice take place.

I pray to you not to let the Kshatriyas, old in learning and old in years, perish
miserably.

O Krishna, let this swelling host of Kshatriyas perish by means of weapons

on that most sacred of all spots in the three worlds, the field of Kurukshetra.

Accomplish on this spot what you have in your mind so that the whole Kshatriya
order

may attain heaven. As long as the hills and the rivers last,

so long will last the fame of these achievements.

The Brahmanas will recite this great war of the Bharatas.

The fame that they achieve in battles is the wealth that Kshatriyas own.

O Krishna, bring Kunti's son Arjuna before me for battle, keeping this discourse
a secret."

Hearing these words of Karna, Krishna, that slayer of hostile heroes, said:

"Do not the means of winning an empire recommend themselves to you?

Do you not wish to rule over the whole earth given by me to you?

The victory of the Pandavas is certain. The triumphal banner of Arjuna,

with the fierce ape on it, seems to be already set up.

The divine artificer, Bhaumana, has applied such celestial illusion in its
construction

that it stands high, displayed like Indra's banner.

Various celestial creatures of terrifying shape, indicating victory, are seen on that
standard.

Extending for a *yojana* upward and all around, that beautiful standard of Arjuna's,

resembling fire in radiance, is never, when set up, obstructed by hills or trees.

When you behold in battle Arjuna on his car, drawn by white steeds and driven
by me,

applying the Aindra, Agneya, and Maruta weapons,

and when you hear the twang of Gandiva piercing the sky like thunder,

then all signs of the Krita, the Treta, and the Dwapara ages will disappear

and instead Kali will be present. When you behold in battle Kunti's son,

the invincible Yudhishthira, resembling the sun in brilliance,

protecting his own mighty army and burning the army of his foes,

then all signs of the Krita, the Treta, and the Dwapara ages will disappear.

When you behold the mighty Bhimasena dancing after drinking the blood of
Dussasana,

like a fierce elephant with rent temples after having killed a mighty antagonist,

then all signs of the Krita, the Treta, and the Dwapara ages will disappear.

When you behold in battle Arjuna checking Drona and Shantanu's son and Kripa
and King Duryodhana and Jayadratha of Sindhu's race, all rushing to the
encounter,
then all signs of the Krita, the Treta, and the Dwapara ages will disappear.
When you behold in battle the two mighty sons of Madri agitating,
then, from the very moment when weapons begin to clash,
all signs of the Krita, the Treta, and the Dwapara ages will disappear.
Returning to the court, O Karna, say to Drona and Shantanu's son and Kripa
that the present month is a delightful one, and that food, drink, and fuel
are abundant now. All plants and herbs are vigorous now, all trees full of fruits,
and there are no flies. The roads are free from mire, and the waters are of
agreeable taste.
The weather is neither very hot nor very cold and is, therefore, highly pleasant.
In seven days there will be a new moon. Let the battle commence then,
for that day, it has been said, is presided over by Indra.
Say also to all the kings that have come for the battle that I will accomplish their
desire.
Indeed, all the kings and princes obedient to the orders of Duryodhana
will obtain death by weapons
                    and therefore may attain to an excellent state in heaven."
Hearing these auspicious words, Karna worshipped Krishna and said:
"Knowing everything, why do you yet seek to beguile me?
The destruction of the whole earth is at hand.
Without doubt, O Krishna, there will be a fierce battle
between the Pandavas and the Kurus which will cover the earth with bloody mire.
All the kings and princes following the lead of Duryodhana,
consumed by the fire of weapons, will proceed to the abode of Yama.
Diverse frightful visions are seen, and many terrible portents, and fierce
disturbances.
All these omens, making the hairs of the observers horripilate,
indicate the defeat of Dhritarashtra's son and the victory of Yudhishthira.
That fierce planet of great effulgence, Sanaischara,
is influencing the constellation called Rohini, in order to afflict the creatures of
the earth.
The planet Angaraka, wheeling toward the constellation Jeshyoura,
approaches Anuradhas, indicating a great slaughter of friends.
Without doubt a terrible calamity approaches the Kurus,
especially when the planet Mahapat afflicts the constellation Chitra.
The spot on the lunar disc has changed its position, and Rahu approaches the sun.
Meteors are falling from the sky. The elephants are sending forth frightful cries
while the horses shed tears without taking any delight in food and drink.
They say that on the appearance of these portents a terrible calamity
approaches.
Among the steeds, elephants, and soldiers, in all the divisions of Duryodhana's
army,
it is seen that, while they take but little food, their excreta are abundant.
The wise have said that this is an indication of defeat.

The elephants and steeds of the Pandavas all seem cheerful,
and all the animals wheel to their right. This is an indication of their success.
The same animals pass to the left in Duryodhana's army,
while incorporeal voices are constantly heard. All this is an indication of defeat.
All auspicious birds, such as peacocks, swans, cranes, chatakas, jivajivas,
and large flights of vakas, follow the Pandavas while vultures, kanka birds, hawks,
Rakshasas, wolves, and bees in flights, herds, and swarms follow the Kauravas.
The drums in the army of Dhritarashtra's son yield no sounds
while those of the Pandavas produce sounds without being struck.
The wells in the midst of Duryodhana's encampment send forth loud roars
like those of huge bulls. All this is an indication of defeat.
The gods are showering flesh and blood on Duryodhana's soldiers.
Vapory edifices of great effulgence, with high walls, deep trenches,
and handsome porches, are suddenly appearing in the skies over the Kuru
    encampment.
A black circle surrounding the solar disc appears in the sky.
Both twilights at sunrise and sunset indicate great terrors.
The jackals yell hideously. All this is an indication of defeat.
Diverse birds, each having but one wing, one eye, and one leg, utter terrible
    screams.
All this is an indication of defeat. Fierce birds with black wings and red legs
hover over the Kuru encampment at nightfall. All this is an indication of defeat.
The soldiers of Duryodhana betray hatred for Brahmanas first,
and then for their preceptors, and then for all their affectionate servants.
The eastern horizon of Duryodhana's encampment appears red,
the southern is of the hue of weapons, and the western is of an earthy hue.
All the quarters around Duryodhana's encampment seem to be ablaze.
In the appearance of all these portents, great is the danger that is indicated.
In a vision, I have beheld Yudhishthira ascending with his brothers to a palace
supported by a thousand columns. All of them appeared with white headgear
and in white robes. And all of them appeared to be seated on white seats.
In the midst of the same vision, you, O Krishna, were employed
in enveloping the blood-dyed earth with weapons.
Yudhishthira at the same time, ascending upon a heap of bones,
was eating *payasa*, sweet buttered rice, from a golden cup, and I beheld him
    swallowing the earth
handed over to him by you. This indicates that he will verily rule the earth.
I beheld Bhima standing on a summit, mace in hand and devouring this earth.
This plainly indicates that he will slay all of us in fierce battle.
It is known to me that victory is where righteousness is.
I saw Arjuna, the wielder of Gandiva, seated on the back of a white elephant
    with you
and blazing forth with great beauty. I have no doubt, O Krishna, that you will
    slay
all the kings headed by Duryodhana. I saw Nakula and Sahadeva and that mighty
    Satyaki
adorned with white bracelets, white cuirasses, white garlands, and white robes.

They were seated upon excellent litters borne on the shoulders of strong men.
I saw umbrellas over the heads of all three. Among the soldiers of Dhritarashtra's
     son,
these three were decked with white headgear: Aswatthaman, Kripa,
and Kritavarman of Satwata's race. All other kings had blood-red headgear.
I saw also Bhishma and Drona ascending on a vehicle drawn by camels,
preceded by myself and Dhritarashtra's son, to the quarter ruled by Agastya.
This indicates that we shall soon have to proceed to Yama's abode.
I have no doubt that the other kings and I, and indeed the entire assemblage of
     Kshatriyas,
shall have to enter into the Gandiva fire."
Krishna said: "The destruction of the earth is at hand when my words
do not become acceptable to your heart. When the destruction of all creatures
     approaches,
                              wrong assumes the semblance of right."
Karna said: "If we come out of this great battle with our lives,
then may we meet here again. Otherwise, O Krishna, we shall certainly meet in
     heaven.
O sinless one, it seems to me now that only there is it possible for us to meet."
Having spoken these words, Karna closely pressed Krishna to his bosom.

32

Councils

In the midst of all those assembled kings, Bhishma said to Duryodhana:
"Once upon a time, Vrihaspati and Sakra went to Brahma.
The Maruts also with Indra, the Vasus with Agni, the Adityas, the Sadhyas,
the seven celestial rishis, the Gandharvas, Viswavasu,
and the beautiful tribes of the Apsaras all approached the ancient grandsire.
And having bowed down to the lord of the universe,
all those dwellers of heaven sat around him. Just then, the two ancient deities,
the rishis Nara and Narayana, as if drawing to themselves by their own energy
the minds and energies of all who were present there, left the place.
Thereupon Vrihaspati asked Brahma: 'Who are these two who leave
without worshipping you? Tell us, O grandsire, who are they?'
Brahma replied: 'These two, endowed with ascetic merit,
blazing with effulgence and beauty, illuminating both the earth and the heaven,
possessed of great might, and pervading and surpassing all, are Nara and
    Narayana,
dwelling now in the region of Brahman, having arrived from the other world.
Endowed with great might and prowess, they shine because of their own
    asceticism.
By their acts they always contribute to the joy of the world.
Worshipped by gods and Gandharvas, they exist only for the destruction of
    Asuras.' "
Bhishma continued: "Having heard these words,
Indra went to the spot where those two were practicing ascetic austerities,
accompanied by all the celestials and having Vrihaspati at their head.
At that time, the dwellers of heaven had been very much alarmed because of a
    war raging
between themselves and the Asuras. Indra asked that couple to grant him a boon.
Thus solicited, those two said: 'Name the boon,' and Indra said: 'Give us your aid.'
They then said to Indra: 'We will do what you wish.'
It was with their aid that Indra subsequently vanquished the Daityas and the
    Danavas.
And Nara slew in battle hundreds and thousands of Indra's foes among the
    Paulomas
and the Kalakhanjas. It was Arjuna who, riding on a whirling car,
severed in battle with a broad-headed arrow the head of the Asura Jambha

while the latter was about to swallow him. It was he who afflicted
the Daitya city of Hiranyapura on the other side of the ocean,
having vanquished in battle sixty thousands of Nivatakavachas.
It was this conqueror of hostile towns, this Arjuna of mighty arms,
who gratified Agni, having vanquished the very gods with Indra at their head.
And Narayana has, in this world, also destroyed in the same way
numberless other Daityas and Danavas. Such are those two of mighty energy
who are now seen united with each other. We have heard that the two heroic car
warriors
Krishna and Arjuna are now united with each other
and that they are those same ancient gods, the divine Nara and Narayana.
Among all on earth, they are incapable of being vanquished by the Asuras
and the gods headed by Indra himself. Narayana is Krishna, and Nara is Arjuna.
Indeed, they are one soul born in twain. These two, by their acts,
enjoy numerous eternal and inexhaustible regions
and are repeatedly born in those worlds when destructive wars are necessary.
For this reason their mission is to fight.
This is what Narada, conversant with the Vedas, said to the Vrishnis.
When you, O Duryodhana, see Krishna with conch shell and discus and mace in
hand,
and that terrible wielder of the bow, Arjuna, armed with weapons—
when you behold those eternal and illustrious ones, the two Krishnas
seated on the same car—then you will remember my words.
Why should such danger not threaten the Kurus, when your intellect has fallen off
from both profit and virtue? If you do not heed my words,
you shall have to hear of the slaughter of many, for all the Kauravas accept your
opinion.
You are alone in holding as true this opinion.
Only three persons—Karna, a low-born Suta's son cursed by Rama;
Sakuni, the son of Suvala; and your sinful brother Dussasana—share your view."
Karna said: "You should not use such words about me,
for I have adopted the duties of the Kshatriya order without failing in those of
my own.
Besides, what wickedness is there in me? I have no sin known to Dhritarashtra's
people.
I have never done any injury to Dhritarashtra's son.
On the other hand, I will slay all the Pandavas in battle.
How can they who are wise make peace again with those who have been injured?
It is always my duty to do all that is agreeable to King Dhritarashtra
and especially to Duryodhana, for he is in possession of the kingdom."
Having listened to these words of Karna, Bhishma addressed King Dhritarashtra:
"Although this one often boasts, saying: 'I shall slay the Pandavas,'
yet he is not equal to even a sixteenth part of the high-souled Pandavas.
The great calamity that is about to overtake your sons of wicked souls
is the act of this wretched son of a Suta! Relying upon him, your foolish son
Duryodhana
has insulted those chastisers of foes. But what difficult feat achieved before

by this wretch is equal to any of those achieved by every one of the Pandavas?
Beholding in the city of Virata his beloved brother slain by Arjuna,
what did this one then do? When Arjuna rushed against all the assembled Kurus,
crushed them, and took away their robes, was this one not there?
When your son was being led away as a captive by the Gandharvas
on the occasion of the taking of the cattle, where was this son of a Suta then,
who now bellows like a bull? There, it was Bhima, and the illustrious Arjuna,
and the twins who encountered the Gandharvas and vanquished them.
Always beautiful, but always unmindful of both virtue and profit,
these are the many false things that this one says."
Then high-souled Drona, son of Bharadwaja,
having paid due homage to Dhritarashtra and the assembled kings,
spoke these words: "Do as Bhishma has said.
You must not act according to the words of those who are covetous of wealth.
Peace with the Pandavas seems much the best. Everything said by Arjuna
and repeated here by Sanjaya will be accomplished by that son of Pandu,
for there is no bowman equal to him in the three worlds!"
Without regarding these words of both Drona and Bhishma, however,
the king asked Sanjaya about the Pandavas.
From that moment, when the king returned a wrong answer to Bhishma and
     Drona,
                         the Kauravas gave up all hope of life.
Duryodhana said: "The whole earth was formerly under the foe's command.
Now, however, the foes are incapable of vanquishing us in battle,
for our enemies, the sons of Pandu, are without allies and destitute of energy.
The sovereignty of the earth now rests in me, and the kings I have assembled
are of the same mind. All these kings can, for my sake, enter into the fire or the sea.
They are all laughing at you, beholding you filled with grief,
lamenting like one out of his wits, and frightened at the praises of the foe.
Not even Indra is capable of vanquishing my vast host.
The self-created Brahma, if he wanted to slay it, could not annihilate it.
Having given up all hope of a city, Yudhishthira craves only five villages,
frightened, O lord, by the army I have assembled and by my power.
The belief you entertain in the prowess of Vrikodara, the son of Kunti, is
     unfounded.
There is none on earth equal to me in an encounter with the mace.
None has ever surpassed me in such an encounter, nor will any do so.
With devoted application, and undergoing many privations,
I have lived in my preceptor's abode. I have completed my exercises there.
It is for this reason that I have no fear either of Bhima or of others.
When I humbly waited upon Sankarshana, my preceptor,
it was his firm conviction that Duryodhana has no equal in the mace.
In battle I am Sankarshana's equal, and in might there is none superior to me.
Bhima will never be able to bear the blow of my mace in battle.
A single blow that I may wrathfully deal to Bhima
will certainly carry him without delay to the abode of Yama.
I wish to see Vrikodara, mace in hand. This has been my long-cherished desire.

Struck in battle with my mace, Vrikodara, the son of Pritha,
will fall dead on the ground, his limbs shattered.
Smitten with a blow of my mace, the mountains of Himavat would split
into a hundred thousand fragments. Vrikodra himself knows this truth,
as also Vasudeva and Arjuna, that there is none equal to Duryodhana
in the use of the mace. Let your fears, therefore, be dispelled.
And after I have slain him, numerous car warriors of equal or superior energy
will speedily throw Arjuna down.
Bhishma; Drona; Kripa, and Drona's son; Karna, and Bhurisravas;
Salya, the king of Pragjyotish; and Jayadratha, the king of the Sindhus—
each is singly capable of slaying the Pandavas. United, they will within a moment
send Arjuna to the abode of Yama. There is no reason why the united army
of all the kings will be incapable of vanquishing Arjuna singly.
A hundred times shrouded by immeasurable arrows shot by Bhishma and Drona
and Drona's son and Kripa, Partha will have to go to Yama's abode.
Our grandsire born of Ganga is superior to Shantanu himself.
There is no slayer of Bhishma on earth, for his father, being gratified,
gave him a boon, saying: 'You shall not die except when it is your own wish.'
And Drona took his birth in a water pot from the saint Bharadwaja.
And from Drona came his son, having knowledge of the highest weapons.
And Kripa, foremost among preceptors, also has taken his birth
from the great rishi Gautama. Born in a clump of heath, this illustrious one
is incapable of being slain. Then again, the father, mother, and maternal uncle
of Aswatthaman are not born of woman's womb. I have that hero also on my side.
All these mighty car warriors can inflict pain on Indra himself in battle.
Arjuna is incapable even of looking at any one of these singly.
United, these tigers among men will certainly slay him.
Karna also, I suppose, is equal to Bhishma and Drona and Kripa.
Rama himself had told him: 'You are my equal.'
Karna had two earrings born with him of great brilliance and beauty.
Indra begged them of that repressor of foes in exchange for an infallible shaft.
How would Arjuna escape with his life from Karna, who is protected by that
    arrow?
My success, therefore, is as certain as a fruit held fast in my own grasp.
The utter defeat also of my foes is already bruited about on earth.
This Bhishma kills every day ten thousand soldiers.
Equal to him are these bowmen, Drona, Drona's son, and Kripa.
The ranks of the Samsaptaka warriors have made this resolution:
'Either we will slay Arjuna or that ape-bannered warrior will slay us.'
Why do you then apprehend danger from the Pandavas?
When Bhimasena is slain, O Bharata, who else among them will fight?
The five brothers, with Dhrishtadyumna and Satyaki—
these seven warriors of the enemy are their chief strength.
Our chief warriors are Bhishma; Drona; Kripa; Drona's son; Karna;
Somadatta; Valhika; Salya, the king of Pragjyotisha;
the two kings, Vindha and Anuvinda, of Avanti; Jayadratha;
your sons Dussasana, Durmukha, Dussaha, Srutayu;

and Chitrasena, Purumitra, Vivingsati, Sala, Bhurisravas, and Vikarna.

I have assembled one and ten *akshauhinis.*

The army of the enemy is less than mine, amounting only to seven *akshauhinis.*

How then can I be defeated? Vrihaspati has said that an army which is less by a third

ought to be encountered. My army exceeds that of the foe by a third.

Besides, the enemy has many defects, while my forces are have many good virtues."

Dhritarashtra said: "Yudhishthira, the son of Pandu, is endowed with Kshatriya energy

and has led the Brahmacharya mode of life from his very youth.

Alas, with him these foolish sons of mine desire to fight, disregarding me,

and thus I complain. I ask you, O Duryodhana, to desist from hostility.

War is never applauded under any circumstances.

Half the earth is quite enough for the maintenance of yourself and all your followers.

Give back to the sons of Pandu their proper share.

All the Kauravas deem it to be consistent with justice that you should make peace

with the high-souled sons of Pandu. Reflect and you will find that your army

will bring you to your own death. You do not understand this because of your own folly.

I do not desire war, nor does Valhika, nor Bhishma, nor Drona, nor Aswatthaman,

nor Sanjaya, nor Somadatta, nor Salya, nor Kripa, nor Satyavrata, nor Purumitra, nor Bhurisravas. In fact, none of these desires war.

Indeed, those warriors on whom the Kauravas will have to rely do not approve of the war.

Let that be acceptable to you. Alas, you do not even seek it of your own will,

but it is rather Karna and the evil-minded Dussasana and Sakuni who are leading you to it."

Duryodhana said: "I challenge the Pandavas to battle without depending upon you

or Drona or Aswatthaman or Sanjaya or Vikarna or Kamvoja

or Kripa or Valhika or Satyavrata or Purumitra or Bhurisravas or others of your party.

But only Karna and I are prepared to celebrate the sacrifice of battle,

with all the necessary rites, making Yudhishthira the victim.

In that sacrifice, my car will be the altar; my sword will be the smaller ladle;

my mace, the larger, for pouring libations; and my coat of mail, the assembly of spectators.

My four steeds will be the officiating priests; my arrows will be the blades of *kusa* grass;

and fame will be the clarified butter.

O king, performing such a sacrifice in battle in honor of Yama,

the ingredients of which will all be furnished by ourselves, we will return victorious

after having slain our foes. Karna and my brother Dussasana and I

will slay the Pandavas in battle. Either I will slay them and hold sway over this earth

or the sons of Pandu, having slain me, will enjoy the earth.

I would sacrifice my life, kingdom, wealth, everything, but would not be able to live
side by side with the Pandavas. I will not surrender to the Pandavas even that much land
which may be covered by the sharp point of a needle."
Dhritarashtra said: "I now abandon Duryodhana forever.
I nevertheless grieve for you all, you kings, who will follow this fool
who is about to proceed to Yama's abode. Like tigers among a herd of deer,
those foremost smiters, the sons of Pandu, will smite down your principal leaders
assembled for battle. The Bharata host, like a helpless woman, will be crushed
and hurled to a distance by Yuyudhana of long arms.
Adding to the strength of Yudhishthira's army, which without him was already sufficient,
Sini's son will take his stand on the field of battle and scatter his arrows
like seeds on a cultivated field. And Bhimasena will take up his position in the van,
and all his soldiers will fearlessly stand in his rear, as behind a rampart.
Indeed, when you, Duryodhana, behold elephants huge as hills
prostrated on the ground with their tusks disabled, their temples crushed,
and their bodies dyed with gore, when you will see them lying on the field of battle
like riven hills, then, afraid of a clash with him, you will remember my words.
Beholding your host, consisting of cars, steeds, and elephants,
consumed by Bhimasena, and presenting the spectacle of a conflagration's track,
you will remember my words. If you do not make peace with the Pandavas,
overwhelming calamity will be yours. Slain by Bhimasena with his mace,
you will rest in peace, and when you see the Kuru host leveled to the ground
like a large forest torn up by the roots, then will you remember my words."
Dhritarashtra said to Sanjaya: "Tell me what Krishna and Dhananjaya said.
I am eager to hear from you all about this."
Sanjaya answered: "With my face bent down and my hands joined together,
I entered the inner apartments to meet with those gods among men.
There I beheld those chastisers of foes, exhilarated with Bassia wine,
and their bodies adorned with garlands of flowers.
Attired in excellent robes and adorned with celestial ornaments, they sat on a golden dais
decked with numerous gems and covered over with carpets of diverse textures and hues.
I beheld Krishna's feet resting upon Arjuna's lap, while those of the high-souled Arjuna
rested upon the laps of Krishna and Satyabhama. Arjuna then invited me
to sit on a footstool made of gold. Touching it with my hand, I sat on the ground.
And when he withdrew his feet from the footstool, I saw auspicious marks on his soles.
Those consisted of two longitudinal lines running from heel to big toe.
As I beheld those youthful heroes, both seated on the same seat, a great fear seized me.
They seemed to me to be Indra and Vishnu seated together.

That very moment, I was convinced that the wishes of Yudhishthira the Just,
who had those two to obey his orders, were certain to succeed.
Entertained with food and drink, and honored with other courtesies,
I conveyed to them your message, placing my joined hands on my head.
Then Arjuna, removing Krishna's auspicious foot from his lap,
with his hand scarred by the flappings of the bowstring, urged him to speak.
Sitting erect like Indra's banner, adorned with every ornament,
Krishna then addressed me in words that were sweet, charming, and mild
though awful and alarming to the son of Dhritarashtra.
Indeed, the words of Krishna, who alone is fit to speak, were of correct emphasis
and accent and pregnant with meaning though heartrending in the end:
'O Sanjaya, say to the wise Dhritarashtra,
and in the hearing of Bhishma, that foremost among the Kurus, and also of
    Drona,
having first saluted at our request all the aged ones,
and having inquired after the welfare of the younger ones:
"Do you celebrate diverse sacrifices, making presents to the Brahmanas,
and rejoice with your sons and wives because a great danger threatens you?
Do you give away wealth to deserving persons,
beget desirable sons, and do agreeable offices to those who are dear to you
because King Yudhishthira is eager for victory?" '
While I was at a distance, Krishna, with tears, said:
'I have not yet paid off that debt that has been accumulating with time.
You have provoked hostilities with Arjuna, who has for his bow the invincible
    Gandiva,
and who has me for his helpmate. He who is capable of vanquishing Arjuna in
    battle
is able to uphold the earth with his two arms, to consume all created things in
    anger,
and to hurl the celestials from heaven. Among the celestials, Asuras, and men,
among Yakshas, Gandharvas, and Nagas, I do not find the person
who can encounter Arjuna in battle. That wonderful story we have all heard
of an encounter in the city of Virata between a single person on one side
and innumerable warriors on the other is sufficient proof of this.
That you all fled in all directions, being routed in the city of Virata
by that son of Pandu singly, is sufficient proof of this.
Such might, prowess, energy, speed, lightness of hand, indefatigability, and
    patience
are to be found in no one but him.' Having heard these words of Krishna,
the diadem-decked Arjuna, of white steeds, also spoke to the same effect."
Having heard these words of Sanjaya, the blind monarch, with the eye of wisdom,
took that speech into his consideration. And having reckoned in detail
the merits and demerits as far as he could, and having ascertained
the strength and weakness of both parties, the learned and intelligent king
began to compare the powers of both sides.
And having at last ascertained that the Kurus were much weaker, Dhritarashtra
    said

to Duryodhana: "This anxiety of mine persists. It seems that I behold it with my eye.
This is not mere inference. All created beings show affection for their offspring
and to the best of their power do what is agreeable and beneficial to them.
This is to be seen also in the case of benefactors.
They who are good always desire to return the good done to them
and to do what is agreeable to their benefactors.
Remembering what was done to him at Khandava,
Agni will render aid to Arjuna in this encounter between the Kurus and the
    Pandavas.
And from parental affection, Dharma and other celestials will aid the Pandavas.
I think that, to save them from Bhishma and Drona and Kripa, the celestials
will be filled with wrath, resembling the thunderbolt in its effects.
Endowed with energy and well versed in the use of weapons, those tigers
    among men,
the sons of Pritha, when united with the celestials, will be incapable
of being even gazed upon by human warriors.
Reflecting day and night on this, I am unhappy and sleepless through anxiety
for the welfare of the Kurus. A terrible destruction is about to overtake the Kurus
if there is no way for peace to end this quarrel. I am for peace and not war."
Hearing these words of his father, the passionate son of Dhritarashtra,
inflamed with great wrath, again said these words of envy:
"You think the Parthas, having the celestials for their allies, cannot be
    vanquished.
Let your fear be dispelled. The gods attained to their divinity
for absence of desire, of covetousness, and of enmity as well as for their
    indifference
to all worldly affairs. Formerly, Dwaipayana-Vyasa and Narada of ascetic
    austerities,
and Rama, the son of Jamadagni, told us this. The gods never engage in work
like human beings, whether from desire or wrath or covetousness or envy.
Indeed, if Agni or Vayu or Dharma or Indra or the Aswins had ever engaged in
    work
from worldly desire, then the sons of Pritha could never have fallen into distress.
Do not, therefore, indulge in such anxiety, because the gods, O Bharata,
always set their eyes on affairs worthy of themselves.
If, however, envy or lust becomes noticeable in the gods because of a yielding to
    desire,
then, according to what has been ordained by the gods themselves,
such envy or lust can never prevail. Charmed by me, Agni will be instantly
    extinguished,
even if he blazes up all around to consume all creatures.
The energy with which the gods are endowed is indeed great, but mine is greater.
If the earth herself cleaves in twain, or if mountain crests split,
I can reunite them by my incantations before the eyes of all.
If, for the destruction of creatures animate and inanimate, mobile and immobile,
a terrific tempest or stony shower of loud roar happens, I can always,
from compassion for created beings, stop it before the eyes of all.

When the waters are solidified by me, even cars and infantry can move over them.
It is I who set into motion all the affairs of both gods and Asuras.
To whatever countries I go with my *akshauhinis* on any mission, my steeds move
wherever I desire. Within my dominions there are no fearful snakes,
and, protected by my incantations, creatures within my territories are never
    injured
by others that are frightful. The very clouds pour in my dominions, showers
as much my subjects desire and when they desire.
The Aswins, Vayu, Agni, Indra with the Maruts, and Dharma will not venture
to protect my foes. If these had been able to protect by their might my
    adversaries,
never would the sons of Pritha have fallen into such distress for three and ten
    years.
I tell you truly that neither gods nor Gandharvas nor Asuras nor Rakshasas
are capable of saving him who has incurred my displeasure.
I have never before been frustrated as regards the reward or punishment
that I intended to bestow or inflict on friend or foe.
If ever I said, 'This is to be,' that has always been.
People, therefore, have always known me as a speaker of truth.
All persons can bear witness to my greatness, the fame of which has spread
    everywhere.
I mention this for your information and not from pride.
Never have I praised myself before, for to praise oneself is mean.
You will hear of the defeat of the Pandavas and the Matsyas,
of the Panchalas and the Kekayas, of Satyaki and Vasudeva, at my hands.
Indeed, as rivers on entering the ocean are entirely lost in it,
so the Pandavas, with all their followers, on approaching me will be annihilated.
My intelligence is superior, my energy is superior, my prowess is superior,
my knowledge is superior, my resources are superior by far to those of the
    Pandavas.
Whatever knowledge of weapons is in the grandsire,
in Drona, in Kripa, in Salya, and in Shalya exists in me as well."
Vidura then said: "We have heard, O sire, from old men
that once upon a time a falconer spread his net on the ground
to catch feathery denizens of the air,
and in that net were ensnared at the same time two birds that lived together.
Taking the net up, the two winged creatures soared together into the air.
Seeing them soar into the sky, the falconer, without giving way to despair,
began to follow them in the direction they flew.
Just then an ascetic living in a hermitage close by, who had finished his morning
    prayers,
saw the falconer running in that manner and hoping still to secure the feathery
    creatures.
Seeing that tenant of the earth quickly pursuing those tenants of the air,
the ascetic said to him: 'O falconer, it appears very strange and wonderful to me
that you, who are a treader of the earth, pursue creatures that are tenants of the
    air.'

The falconer said: 'These two, united together, are taking away my snare.
Up in the air, however, they will quarrel and will come under my control.'"
Vidura continued: "The two birds, doomed to death, soon after quarreled.
And when the foolish pair quarreled, they both fell to earth,
where, ensnared in the meshes of death, they quarreled angrily with each other.
The falconer approached unperceived and seized them both.
Even thus those kinsmen who fall out with one another for the sake of wealth
fall into the hands of the enemy, like those birds I have cited.
Eating together, talking together—these are the duties of kinsmen.
Those kinsmen who with loving hearts wait on the old
become unconquerable, like a forest guarded by lions,
while those who, having won enormous riches, still behave like mean-minded men
always contribute to the prosperity of their foes.
Kinsmen, O Dhritarashtra, are like charred brands that blaze up when united
but only smoke when disunited. I will now tell you something else
that I saw on a mountain breast. Having listened to that also, do what is for your
best.
Once we repaired to the northern mountain, accompanied by some hunters
and a number of Brahmanas fond of discoursing on charms and medicinal
plants.
That northern mountain, Gandhamadana, looked like a grove.
As its breast was overgrown on all sides with trees and various medicinal herbs,
it was inhabited by siddhas and Gandharvas.
And there we all saw a quantity of honey of a bright yellow color,
and of the measure of a jar, placed on an inaccessible precipice of the mountain.
That honey, which was the favorite drink of Kuvera, king of the Yakshas,
was guarded by snakes of virulent poison. And it was such that a mortal, drinking
of it,
would win immortality, a sightless man would obtain sight, and an old man
would be a youth.
Those Brahmanas, conversant with sorcery, spoke about the honey.
The hunters desired to obtain it. And they all perished in that inaccessible
mountain cave
abounding with snakes. In the same way, your son desires to enjoy the whole
earth,
without a rival. He beholds the honey but from folly does not see the terrible
fall.
On a single car Arjuna conquered the whole earth.
At the head of their hosts, Bhishma and Drona and others were frightened by
Arjuna
and utterly routed at the city of Virata. Remember what took place on that
occasion.
O Dhritarashtra, take King Yudhishthira on your lap,
since both parties can, under no circumstances, have victory."

33

Sikhandini

Duryodhana consulted with Bhishma, whose wisdom was equaled only by his
    strength,

and he asked the grandsire what to expect in the coming battle.

"Many mighty warriors, kings, and other rulers, headed by the invincible Krishna,

have assembled for the sake of Pandu's son," said Bhishma.

"These are principally the maharathas, atirathas, and half-rathas of the Pandavas,

and these, O king, will lead in battle the terrible army of Yudhishthira,

which is protected, again, by the diadem-decked Arjuna, who is like the great
    Indra.

It is with them that I shall contend in battle, expecting victory or death.

I shall advance against these two foremost among car warriors, Krishna and
    Arjuna,

bearing, respectively, Gandiva and the discus, and resembling the sun and the
    moon

as seen together in the evening. I shall, on the field of battle,

encounter also those other car warriors of Yudhishthira at the head of their
    troops.

The maharathas and atirathas and half-rathas upon whom my eyes may fall

I will withstand. But I will not strike or slay Sikhandini, the prince of Panchalas,

even if I see him rushing against me in battle with weapons upraised.

The world knows how, from a desire of doing what was agreeable to my father,

I gave up the kingdom in the observance of the Brahmacharya vow.

Having made public my godlike vow among all the kings of the earth,

I shall never slay a woman or one who was formerly a woman.

It may be known to you, O king, that Sikhandini was formerly a woman.

Having been born as a daughter, she afterward metamorphosed

into the male sex. I shall not fight against him. I shall smite all other kings in
    battle.

I will not, however, O king, be able to slay the sons of Kunti!"

Duryodhana said: "Why will you not slay Sikhandini,

even if you see him approaching you as a foe with arms upraised?

You formerly told me: 'I will slay the Panchalas with the Somakas.'

O son of Ganga, tell me the reason for this reservation."

Bhishma said: "Listen to this history that will explain why I will not slay
    Sikhandini,

even if I behold him in battle. My father, Shantanu, celebrated over all the world,
paid his debt to nature in time. Observing my pledge, I then installed my
    brother,
Chitrangada, on the throne of the extensive kingdom of the Kurus.
After his demise, obedient to the counsels of Satyavati,
I installed, according to the ordinance, Vichitravirya as king.
Young in age, but having been installed by me, the virtuous Vichitravirya
looked to me in everything. Wanting him to marry, I set my heart on procuring
    daughters
from a suitable family. I heard that three maidens, all unrivaled for beauty—
Amva, Amvika, and Amvalika, daughters of the ruler of Kasi—
would select husbands for themselves, and that all the kings of the earth had
    been invited.
Among those maidens Amva was the eldest, Amvika the second,
while the princess Amvalika was the youngest.
Going on a single car to the city of the ruler of Kasi, I beheld the three maidens
adorned with ornaments, and all the kings of the earth who had been invited
    there.
Then, challenging to battle all those kings who were ready for the encounter,
I took up those maidens on my car and said to all the kings assembled there
    these words:
'Bhishma, the son of Shantanu, is carrying away these maidens by force.
You kings, strive to the best of your power to rescue them!
By force I take them away, making you spectators of my act!'
At these words of mine, those rulers of the earth sprang up with weapons
    unsheathed.
And they angrily urged the drivers of their cars, saying: 'Make ready the cars!
Make ready the cars!' On their cars resembling masses of clouds,
or fighting from elephants, or on their stout steeds, those kings surrounded me.
With a shower of arrows, I stopped their onrush and vanquished them,
like the chief of celestials vanquishing hordes of Danavas.
With ease I cut down their variegated standards with my blazing shafts.
In that combat I overthrew their steeds, elephants, and drivers, each with a
    single arrow.
Beholding that lightness of hand of mine, they desisted and broke.
And having vanquished all those rulers of the earth, I came back to Hastinapura
and made over those maidens to Satyavati, intending them for my brothers,
                and represented to her everything I had done."
Bhishma continued: "Then, approaching my mother and saluting her,
I said: 'Having vanquished all the kings, these daughters of the ruler of Kasi,
with beauty alone for their dowries, I have abducted for the sake of Vichitravirya!'
Then Satyavati, with eyes bathed in tears, smelled my head and joyously said:
'By good luck it is, O child, that you have triumphed!'
When, with Satyavati's acquiescence, the nuptials approached,
the eldest daughter of the ruler of Kasi said in great bashfulness:
'O Bhishma, you are conversant with morality and well versed in all our
    scriptures!

Hearing my words, it behooves you to do toward me what is consistent with
   morality.
Some time ago, I had mentally chosen the ruler of the Salwas as my lord.
By him also, without my father's knowledge, I was privately solicited.
How would you, O Bhishma, born as you are in Kuru's race,
transgress the laws of morality and cause one who longs for another
to live in your abode? Knowing this, and deliberating in your mind,
you must accomplish what is proper. It is clear that the ruler of the Salwas waits
   for me.
Therefore, permit me to depart. Be merciful to me, O hero devoted to truth.'"
Bhishma continued: "I then placed the matter before my mother, as also all our
   counselors,
and also before our special and ordinary priests, and then permitted the eldest
   maiden,
Amva, to depart. She then went to the city of the ruler of the Salwas.
She had for her escort a number of old Brahmanas and also her own nurse.
Having traveled the whole distance between Hastinapura and Salwa's city,
she approached King Salwa and said: 'I come to you, O high-souled one!'
But the lord of the Salwas said with a laugh: 'I no longer desire to make a wife
of you who were to be wedded to another. Therefore, go back to Bhishma's
   presence.
I no longer desire you who were forcibly ravished by Bhishma.
Indeed, when Bhishma, having vanquished the kings, took you away,
you went with him cheerfully. Having humiliated all the kings of the earth,
Bhishma took you away, and I no longer desire you as a wife.
How can a king like myself, acquainted with all branches of knowledge,
who lays down laws for others, admit into his abode a woman
who was to have been wedded to another?
                              Go wherever you wish, without waste of time.'
Amva then addressed Salwa, saying: 'Say not so, O lord of the earth, for it is not so!
I was not cheerful when Bhishma took me away!
He took me by force, having routed all the kings, and I wept all the while.
I am an innocent maiden and attached to you. Accept me, O lord of the Salwas!
Having solicited Ganga's son, who never retreats from battle,
and having at last obtained his permission, I come to you!
Indeed, the mighty-armed Bhishma, O king, did not desire me!
I heard that his action in this matter was for the sake of his brother.
My two sisters, Amvika and Amvalika, who were abducted with me at the same
   time,
have been bestowed by Ganga's son on his younger brother Vichitravirya.
O lord of the Salwas, I swear by touching my own head
that I have never thought of any husband but you!
I do not come to you as one who was to have been wedded to another!
Take me, a maiden come to you of her own accord,
one never betrothed to another, one desirous of your grace!'
Although she spoke in this strain, Salwa rejected that daughter of the ruler of
   Kasi,

like a snake casting off his old skin. Indeed, although that king was earnestly solicited
with diverse expressions such as these, the lord of the Salwas
still did not manifest any inclination for accepting the girl.
Then the eldest daughter of the ruler of Kasi, filled with anger
and with her eyes bathed in tears, said these words in a voice choked with grief:
'Cast off by you, wherever I may go, righteousness will protect me,
for truth is indestructible!'
It was thus that the lord of the Salwas rejected that maiden
who addressed him in language such as this and was sobbing with grief.
'Go, go,' were the words that Salwa said to her repeatedly.
'I am in terror of Bhishma and you are Bhishma's capture!'
Thus addressed by Salwa, that maiden left his city wailing like a she-osprey."
Bhishma continued: "Amva reflected in this strain: 'There is not in the whole world
a young woman as miserable as I! destitute of friends, I am rejected by Salwa also!
I cannot go back to the city named after an elephant,
for I was permitted by Bhishma to leave, expecting a welcome of Salwa!
Whom then shall I blame? Myself? Or the invincible Bhishma?
Or that foolish father of mine who made arrangements for my self-choice?
Perhaps it is my own fault! Why did I not leap down before from Bhishma's car
when that fierce battle took place, and flee to Salwa?
That I am so afflicted now, as if deprived of my senses, is the result of my omission!
Cursed be Bhishma! Cursed be my own wretched father of little understanding,
who had arranged prowess to be my dower, sending me out
as if I were a woman available for a consideration! Cursed be myself!
Cursed be King Salwa, and cursed be my creator, too!
Cursed be they through whose fault such great misery has been mine!
Human beings always suffer what is destined for them.
The cause, however, of my present affliction is Bhishma, the son of Shantanu.
I see that at present my vengeance should fall upon him,
either through ascetic austerities or by battle, for he is the cause of my woe.
But what king is there who would venture to vanquish Bhishma in battle?'
Having settled this, she repaired to an ashram of high-souled ascetics of virtuous deeds.
That night, she stayed there surrounded by those ascetics
and told them all that had happened to her, with the minutest details,
about her abduction and her rejection by Salwa.
There lived in that asylum an eminent Brahmana of rigid vows,
and his name was Saikhavatya. Endowed with ascetic merit of a high order,
he was a preceptor of the scriptures and the Aranyakas.
The sage Saikhavatya, of great ascetic merit, addressed that afflicted maiden,
that chaste girl sighing heavily in grief, and said: 'If it has been so, O blessed lady,
what can high-souled ascetics residing in their retreats and engaged in penances do?'

The maiden answered him: 'Let mercy be shown to me. I desire a life in the woods,
having renounced the world. I will practice the severest of ascetic austerities.
All that I now suffer is certainly the fruit of those sins that I committed
from ignorance in my former life. I do not venture to go back to my relatives,
rejected and cheerless as I am and humiliated by Salwa.
You who have washed away your sins, I desire that you should instruct me
in ascetic penance. Let mercy be shown to me!'
Thus addressed, that sage then comforted the maiden by examples from the scriptures.
And having consoled her, he and the other Brahmanas promised to do what she desired."
Bhishma continued: "Those virtuous ascetics then set themselves to their usual vocations,
thinking all the while about what they should do for that maiden.
Some among them said: 'Let her be taken to her father's abode.'
And some set their hearts upon reproaching me.
And some thought that the ruler of the Salwas should be solicited to accept the maiden.
But others said: 'No, that should not be done, for he has rejected her.'
And after some time had passed, those ascetics of rigid vows once more said to her:
'What can ascetics do for you? Do not devote yourself to a life in the woods,
renouncing the world! Listen to these words that are beneficial to you!
Depart, blessed be you, to your father's mansion!
The king, your father, will do what should be done.
O auspicious one, surrounded by every comfort, you may live there in happiness.
You are a woman! At present, therefore, you have no other protector but your father.
A woman has either her father for her protector or her husband.
Her husband is her protector when she is in comfortable circumstances,
but, plunged in misery, she has her father for her protector.
A life in the woods is exceedingly painful, especially to one who is delicate.
You are a princess by birth. Beyond this, you are very delicate, O beautiful maiden!
There are many discomforts and difficulties attached to a life in a retreat in the woods,
none of which you shall have to bear in your father's abode.'
Other ascetics, beholding that helpless girl, said to her:
'Seeing you alone in deep and solitary woods, kings may court you.
Therefore, set not your heart upon such a course.'
Hearing these words, Amva said: 'I am incapable of going back to my father's abode,
for without doubt I shall then be scorned by all my relatives.
I lived there with my father during my childhood. I cannot now go back there.
Protected by the ascetics, I desire to practice ascetic austerities
so that in a future life such sore afflictions may not be mine!'"
Bhishma continued: "When those Brahmanas were thinking thus about her,

there came into that forest that best of ascetics, the royal sage Hotravahana.
The ascetics reverenced that king with worship and words of welcome and
    courtesy,
a seat, and water. After he was seated and had rested for a while,
those forest denizens once more addressed that maiden in the hearing of the
    royal visitor.
Hearing the story of Amva and the king of Kasi, that sage of great energy
became very anxious at heart. Hearing her speak in that strain,
and beholding her distressed, the high-souled Hotravahana was filled with pity.
Then, O lord, that maternal grandsire of hers rose up with trembling frame,
caused that maiden to sit on his lap, and comforted her.
He then asked of her the details of that distress of hers from its beginning.
She told him minutely all that had happened, and he was filled with pity and
    grief.
He decided what she would do. 'Do not go back to your father's abode,' he said.
'I am the father of your mother. I will dispel your grief. Rely on me, O daughter!
Great indeed must your affliction when you are so emaciated!
At my advice, go to the ascetic Rama, the son of Jamadagni.
Rama will dispel this great affliction and grief of yours.
He will slay Bhishma in battle if the latter does not obey his command.
Go to that foremost one of Bhrigu's race who resembles the *yuga* fire in energy!
That great ascetic will place you once more on the right track!'
Hearing this, that maiden, shedding tears all the while,
saluted her maternal grandsire, Hotravahana, with a bend of her head
and addressed him, saying: 'I will go at your command!
But shall I succeed in obtaining a sight of that reverend sire celebrated over the
    world?
How will he dispel this poignant grief of mine?
And how shall I go to that descendant of Bhrigu?'
Hotravahana said: 'You will behold Jamadagni's son, Rama,
who is devoted to truth and endowed with great might
and engaged in austere penances in the great forest.
Rama always dwells in that foremost among mountains, called Mahendra.
Many rishis, learned in the Vedas, and many Gandharvas and Apsaras also dwell
    there.
Go and tell him these words of mine, having saluted that sage of rigid vows
and great ascetic merit with your bent head. Tell him also, O blessed girl,
all that you seek. If you name me, Rama will do everything for you,
for Rama, the heroic son of Jamadagni, that foremost among bearers of arms,
is a friend of mine highly pleased with me, and he always wishes me well.'
While King Hotravahana was saying all this to that maiden,
there appeared Akritavrana, a dear companion of Rama. And on his arrival,
those munis by the hundreds, and the Srinjaya king, Hotravahana, old in years,
all stood up. Those denizens of the forest, uniting with one another,
did him all the rites of hospitality. They all took their seats surrounding him.
And, filled with joy, they started various delightful and charming subjects of
    discourse.

After their discourse was over, that royal sage, the high-souled Hotravahana,
inquired of Akritavrana about Rama, that foremost among great sages, saying:
'O you of mighty arms, where, O Akritavrana, may that foremost among persons
    be seen?'
Akritavrana answered: 'O lord, Rama always speaks of you as his dear friend.
I believe he will be here tomorrow morning. As regards this maiden,
why, O royal sage, has she come to the woods? Whose is she, and what is she
    to you?'
Hotravahana. said: 'The favorite daughter of the ruler of Kasi, she is my
    daughter's child.
She is known by the name of Amva. Along with her two younger sisters,
she was in the midst of her Swayamvara ceremonies.
The names of her two younger sisters are Amvika and Amvalika.
All the Kshatriya kings of the earth were assembled together at the city of Kasi.
Great festivities were going on there on account of the self-choice of these
    maidens.
And in the midst of these, Shantanu's son, Bhishma of mighty valor,
    disregarding all the kings,
abducted the girls. Vanquishing all the monarchs, the pure-souled prince
    Bhishma
then reached Hastinapura and, representing everything to Satyavati,
ordered his brother Vichitravirya's marriage to take place with the girls he had
    brought.
But this maiden addressed Ganga's son in the presence of his ministers
and said that within her heart she had chosen the lord of the Salwas to be her
    husband.
Hearing these words of hers, Bhishma took counsel with his ministers
and at last, with Satyavati's consent, dismissed this maiden.
Permitted thus by Bhishma, she gladly repaired to Salwa, the lord of Saubha.
Salwa, however, rejected her, suspecting the purity of her conduct.
Since then she has come to these woods, to devote herself to ascetic penances.
I recognized her from the account that she gave of her parentage.
As regards her sorrow, she considers Bhishma to be its root.'
After Hotravahana had ceased, Amva herself said:
'O holy one, it is even as this lord of earth, this author of my mother's body,
Hotravahana of the Srinjaya race, has said. I cannot venture to go back to my
    own city,
                         for shame and fear of disgrace!'
Akritavrana said: 'Of these two afflictions of yours, for which do you seek a
    remedy?
Is it your wish that the lord of Saubha should be urged to wed you?
The high-souled Rama will certainly urge him from desire of doing you good.
Or, if you wish to behold Ganga's son, Bhishma, defeated in battle by Rama,
he will gratify even that wish. Hearing what Srinjaya has to say,
and what you also may have to say, let it be settled this day what should be done
    for you.'
Hearing these words, Amva said: 'O holy one, I was abducted by Bhishma

acting from ignorance, for he did not know that my heart had been given away
    to Salwa.
Thinking of this in your mind, you should decide which is consistent with justice,
and then let steps be taken to accomplish that goal. Do, O Brahmana,
what is proper to be done toward that tiger among the Kurus
or toward the ruler of the Salwas or toward both of them!
I have told you truly about the root of my grief.
O holy one, you must do what is consistent with reason.'
Akritavrana said: 'What you say is indeed worthy of you. Listen, however, to what
    I say!
If Ganga's son had never taken you to the city called after the elephant,
then, O timid girl, Salwa would, at Rama's behest, have taken you on his head!
It is because Bhishma bore you away that King Salwa's suspicions were awakened.
Bhishma is proud of his manliness and is crowned with success.
Therefore, you should cause your vengeance to fall upon him and no other!'
Amva answered: 'The desire I have cherished in my heart is that, if possible,
Bhishma should be slain by me in battle!
Be it Bhishma or be it King Salwa, punish that man whom you think to be guilty,
and through whose act I have been so miserable!' "
Bhishma continued: "In conversation such as this, that day passed and the night
    also,
which with its delicious breeze was neither cold nor hot. Then Rama appeared
    there,
beaming with energy. And that sage, wearing matted locks on his beard
and attired in deerskins, was surrounded by his disciples.
He had his bow in hand. And bearing also a sword and a battle-ax,
that sinless one approached the Srinjaya king, Hotravahana, in that forest.
And the ascetics dwelling there and that king also, beholding him, all stood up
and waited with joined hands. That helpless maiden did the same,
and they all cheerfully worshipped Bhargava, offering honey and curds.
Rama sat with Jamadagni's son and Hotravahana beside him, and they began to
    discourse.
Afterward, the sage Hotravahana said importunately to Rama of mighty strength:
'O Rama, this is my daughter's daughter and is the daughter of the king of Kasi.
                    She needs something to be done for her!'
Rama addressed that maiden, saying: 'Tell me what you have to say.'
At these words, Amva approached Rama, who resembled a blazing fire,
and worshipped both his feet with her bent head, touched them with her two
    hands,
and stood silently before him. Filled with grief, she wept aloud,
and she then sought the protection of that descendant of Bhrigu,
who was the refuge of all distressed persons. Rama said: 'Tell me
what grief is in your heart. I will act according to your words!'
Thus encouraged, Amva said: 'O holy one, today I seek your protection!
O lord, raise me from this unfathomable ocean of sorrow.' "
Bhishma continued: "Beholding her beauty, and her youthful body and its great
    delicacy,

Rama began to think: *What will she say?* And that perpetuator of Bhrigu's line
sat long in silence, filled with pity as she represented everything truly to him.
And Jamadagni's son, hearing these words of the princess,
and having first settled what he should do, addressed that damsel, saying:
'O beautiful lady, I will send word to Bhishma, that foremost one of Kuru's race.
Having heard what my behest is, that king will certainly obey it.
If, however, the son of Jahnavi does not act according to my words,
I will then consume him in battle, with all his counselors!
Or, O princess, if you desire, I may address the ruler of the Salwas to the matter
   in hand.'
Amva said: 'I was dismissed by Bhishma as soon as he heard that my heart
had previously been freely given to the ruler of the Salwas.
Approaching then the lord of Saubha, I addressed him in language that was
   unbecoming.
Doubtful of the purity of my conduct, he refused to accept me.
Reflecting on all this, with the aid of your own understanding,
you must do what should be done in view of these circumstances.
Bhishma, however, is the root of my calamity, for he brought me under his power,
taking me up on his car by violence. Slay him, for whose sake I suffer such misery!
Bhishma is covetous and mean and proud of his victory. Therefore, give him his
   deserts.
While I was being abducted by him, this was the desire I cherished in my heart:
that I should cause that hero of great vows to be slain.
Therefore, gratify this wish of mine! Slay Bhishma, even as Purandara slew
   Vritra.' "
Bhishma continued: "Rama replied to the weeping girl: 'O daughter of Kasi,
I do not take up arms now except for the sake of those conversant with the Vedas.
Tell me, therefore, what else I can do. Both Bhishma and Salwa are obedient
   to me.
Do not grieve. I will accomplish your object. I will not, however, take up arms
except at the command of Brahmanas. This has been my rule of conduct.'
Amva said: 'My misery should be dispelled by you by any means you choose.
That misery has been caused by Bhishma. Slay him, therefore, without much
   delay.'
Rama said: 'O daughter of Kasi, say but the word, and Bhishma,
however deserving of reverence from you, will take up your feet on his head!'
Amva said: 'O Rama, slay that Bhishma, who roars like an Asura,
if you wish to do what is agreeable to me. You must make your promise to me
   true.' "
Bhishma continued: "While Rama and Amva were talking thus with each other,
the rishi Akritavrana of highly virtuous soul said: 'You must not desert this girl
who seeks your protection! If, summoned to battle,
Bhishma comes to the encounter and says, "I am vanquished,"
or if he obeys your words, then that which this maiden seeks will be
   accomplished,
and the words spoken by you, O hero, will also be true!
This also was the vow then made by you, O Rama, before Brahmanas,

after you conquered all the Kshatriyas: that you would slay in battle the person,
be he a Brahmana, a Kshatriya, a Vaisya, or a Sudra,
who would be a foe to the Brahmanas. You further promised that as long as you
lived
you would not abandon those who came to you in fright and sought your
protection,
and that you would slay that proud warrior who would vanquish in battle
all the assembled Kshatriyas of the earth!
O Rama, Bhishma has achieved such success over all the Kshatriyas!
Approaching him, encounter him now in battle!'
Rama said: 'O best of rishis, I recollect that vow of mine.
I will, however in the present instance do that which conciliation may suggest.
That task the daughter of Kasi has in mind is a grave one!
Taking this maiden with me, I will repair myself to where Bhishma is.
If Bhishma, proud of his achievements in battle, does not obey my order,
I will then slay that arrogant man. This is my fixed resolve.
The arrows I shoot do not stick to the bodies of creatures but pass through them.
This is known to you from what you saw in my encounters with the Kshatriyas!'
Having said this, Rama then, along with all those seekers of Brahma,
resolved to depart from that ashram. The great ascetic rose from his seat.
Then all those ascetics who passed the night there
performed in the morning their Homa rites and recited their prayers.
Then they all set out, eager to take my life. And Rama and those devotees of
Brahma
then came to Kurukshetra, with that maiden in their company.
Those high-souled ascetics, with that foremost one of Bhrigu's race at their head,
having arrived on the banks of the stream of Saraswati, quartered themselves
there."
Bhishma continued: "After he had quartered there, on the third day
Jamadagni's son
sent a message to me, saying: 'I have come here. Do what is agreeable to me.'
Hearing that Rama of great might had come to the confines of our kingdom,
I speedily went with a joyous heart to that master, who was an ocean of energy.
I went to him with a cow placed in the van of my train,
and accompanied by many Brahmanas and ordinary priests of our family
and by others resembling the gods in splendor, employed by us on special
occasions.
Seeing me arrive in his presence, he accepted the worship I offered to him and
said:
'Divested of desire, with what mood of mind, O Bhishma, did you abduct,
on the occasion of her self-choice, this daughter of the king of Kasi and then
dismiss her?
By you this famous lady has been dissociated from virtue!
Contaminated by the touch of your hands, who can marry her now?
She has been rejected by Salwa because you abducted her.
Take her, therefore, to yourself, O Bharata, at my command.
Let this daughter of a king be charged with the duties of her sex!

It is not proper that this humiliation should be hers!'
Seeing him plunged into sorrow on her account, I said: 'O Brahmana,
I cannot bestow this girl on my brother. It was to me that she said: "I am Salwa's!"
And it was by me that she was permitted to go to Salwa's city.
As far as I am concerned, this was my firm vow, which I cannot abandon from
    fear,
                 or pity, or greed, or lust!'
Rama answered me with eyes rolling in anger, saying: 'If you do not act
according to my words, I will slay you this very day along with all your
    counselors!'
Indeed, Rama in great wrath told me these words repeatedly. I besought him
in sweet words, but he did not cool down. Bowing my head to that best of
    Brahmanas,
I then inquired of him the reason for which he sought battle with me.
I also said: 'While I was a child, it was you who instructed me in the four kinds of
    arms—
hurled, held, hurled or held, or shot. I am, therefore, your disciple!'
Rama answered: 'You know me, O Bhishma, to be your preceptor,
and yet you will not accept, to please me, this daughter of the ruler of Kasi!
I cannot be satisfied unless you act in this way! Take this maiden and preserve
    your race!
Having been abducted by you, she cannot obtain a husband.'
To Rama I replied: 'This cannot be, O rishi! All your labor is vain.
Remembering your old preceptorship, I am striving to gratify you!
As regards this maiden, she was refused by me
before I knew what are the faults, productive of great evil, of the female sex.
Who would admit into his abode a woman whose heart is another's
and who on that account is like a snake of virulent poison?
I would not, even from fear of Vasava, forsake my duty!
Be gracious to me, or do to me without delay what you think proper.
This couplet is heard in the Puranas, O lord, sung by the high-souled Marutta:
"The renunciation is sanctioned by the ordinance of a preceptor who is filled
    with vanity,
who is destitute of the knowledge of right and wrong, and who treads in a
    devious path."
You are my preceptor, and it is for this that I have from love reverenced you
    greatly.
But you do not know the duty of a preceptor, and for this reason I will fight
    with you.
I would not slay any preceptor in battle, especially a Brahmana,
and especially not one endowed with ascetic merit. For this reason I forgive you.
It is a well-known truth, gatherable from the scriptures,
that he is not guilty of slaying a Brahmana who kills in battle a person of that
    order
who takes up weapons like a Kshatriya and fights wrathfully without seeking to
    flee.
I am a Kshatriya accustomed to the practice of Kshatriya duties.

One does not incur sin or any harm by behaving toward a person exactly as he
deserves.

When a person acquainted with the proprieties of time and place,

and well versed in matters affecting both profit and virtue, feels doubtful about
anything,

he should without scruple of any kind devote himself to the acquisition of virtue,

which would confer the highest benefit on him.

And since you, O Rama, in a matter of doubtful propriety,

act unrighteously, I would certainly fight with you in a great battle.

Behold the strength of my arms, and my prowess that is superhuman!

In view of such circumstances, I shall certainly do what I can.

I shall fight with you on the field of Kurukshetra!

O Rama of great effulgence, equip yourself as you like for single combat!

Come and station yourself on the field, where, afflicted with my shafts in great
battle

and sanctified by my weapons, you may obtain those regions you have won

through your austerities. There I will approach for battle you who are so fond of
battle!

There, O Rama—where in the old days you propitiated your deceased fathers

with oblations of Kshatriya blood—slaying you there,

I will propitiate the Kshatriya you slew! Come there, O Rama, without delay!

There I will curb your old pride, about which the Brahmanas speak.

For many long years, O Rama, you have boasted, saying:

"I have, single-handed, vanquished all the Kshatriyas of the Earth!"

Listen now to what enabled you to indulge in that boast!

In those days Bhishma had not been born, or any Kshatriyas like Bhishma!

Kshatriyas really endowed with valor took their births later on!

As regards yourself, you have consumed only heaps of straw!

The person who would easily quell your pride of battle has since been born!

He is no other than myself, Bhishma, that subjugator of hostile cities!

Without doubt, O Rama, I shall quell your pride of battle!'"

Bhishma continued: "Rama addressed me, laughingly saying:

'By good luck it is, O Bhishma, that you desire to fight with me in battle!

Even now I go with you to Kurukshetra! I will do what you have said!

Let your mother, Ganga, behold you dead on that plain, pierced with my shafts,

to become the food of vultures, crows, and other carrion birds!

Let that goddess worshipped by siddhas and charanas,

that blessed daughter of Bhagiratha in the form of a river, who begat your
wicked self,

weep today, seeing you lying miserably on that plain,

however undeserving she may be of seeing such a sight!

Come, O Bhishma, and follow me and take your cars and all other equipment of
battle!'

Hearing these words of Rama, I worshipped him with a bend of my head

and answered him, saying: 'So be it!'

Rama then went to Kurukshetra, eager for combat,

while I returned to our city and represented everything to Satyavati.

Then, causing propitiatory ceremonies to be performed for my victory,
and being blessed also by my mother, and making the Brahmanas utter
    benedictions,
I mounted a handsome car made of silver to which were yoked steeds white in hue.
The car was well built and exceedingly commodious and covered with tigerskin.
And it was equipped with many great weapons and furnished with all
    necessaries.
And it was ridden by a charioteer who was wellborn and brave,
who was versed in horse lore, careful in battle, and well trained in his art,
and who had seen many encounters. I was accoutered in a coat of mail white
    in hue
and had in hand my bow, which was also white in hue.
Thus equipped, I set out, O best of Bharata's race! A white umbrella was held
over my head. And I was fanned with white fans and clad in white
with white headgear, and all my adornments were white.
Eulogized by Brahmanas wishing me victory. I ventured forth from the city
to Kurukshetra, which was to be the field of battle!
Those steeds, fleet as the mind or the wind, urged by my charioteer,
soon bore me to that great encounter. At the field, both Rama and I, eager for
    battle,
wanted to show each other our prowess. I took up my conch and blew a loud
    blast.
And many Brahmanas and many ascetics, having their abodes in the forest,
as also the gods with Indra at their head, were stationed there to witness the
    encounter.
Many celestial garlands and diverse kinds of celestial music
and many cloudy canopies could be seen there.
And all those ascetics who had come with Rama as spectators stood around the
    field.
At this juncture, O king, my divine mother, devoted to the good of all creatures,
appeared before me in her own form and said: 'What is this that you seek to do?
I will go to Jamadagni's son and solicit him, saying: "Do not fight Bhishma
who is your disciple!" O son, being a Kshatriya, do not set your heart on a battle
with Jamadagni's son, who is a Brahmana!' It was thus that she reproved me.
And she also said: 'Rama, equal in prowess to Mahadeva himself,
is the exterminator of the Kshatriya order!'
I saluted the goddess reverentially and replied to her with joined hands,
giving her an account of all that had happened in that self-choice of the
    daughter of Kasi.
I also told her everything about how I had urged Rama to desist from the
    combat.
I gave her a history of Amva's acts. Then my mother, the great river, going to
    Rama,
besought the rishi of Bhrigu's race: 'Do not fight Bhishma, who is your disciple!'
Rama, however, said 'Go, and make Bhishma desist! He does not execute my
    wish!

It is for this reason that I have challenged him!'

Thus addressed by Rama, Ganga returned to me.

But I, with my eyes rolling in anger, refused to do her bidding.

Just at this time, the mighty ascetic Rama appeared in my sight.

And I challenged him again to the encounter."

Bhishma continued: "I said to Rama: 'I am on my car, and I do not wish to fight with you

if you are on the ground! Mount on a car and encase your body in mail

if you wish to fight me in battle!' But he replied: 'The earth, O Bhishma, is my car,

and the Vedas, like good steeds, are the animals that carry me!

The wind is my car driver, and my coat of mail is constituted

by Gayatri, Savitri, and Saraswati, those mothers in the Vedas.

Well protected by these in battle, I will fight!'

Rama then covered me on all sides with a thick shower of arrows.

I then beheld him stationed on a car equipped with every kind of excellent weapon.

And the car he rode, of wonderful appearance, had been created by a fiat of his will.

Celestial steeds were yoked to it, and it was well protected by the necessary defenses

and decked all over with ornaments of gold. It was well covered with tough skins

and bore the devices of the sun and the moon. Rama was armed with a bow

and equipped with a quiver, and his fingers were encased in leather gloves.

Akritavrana, the dear friend of Bhargava, well versed in the Vedas,

did the duties of a car driver for that warrior. And Rama summoned me to battle, saying:

'Come, come. Gladden my heart!'

I had then obtained as my adversary Rama, that invincible exterminator of the Kshatriya race,

risen like the sun himself in splendor, and eager to fight in single combat!

After he had poured three showers of arrows on me, I curbed my steeds,

came down from my car, put my bow aside, and proceeded on foot

to that best of rishis. Arriving before him, I worshipped him with reverence.

And having saluted him duly, I told him: 'O Rama, whether you are equal

or superior to me, I will fight with you, my virtuous preceptor, in battle!

O lord, bless me, wishing me victory!' Rama replied: 'O foremost among Kuru's race,

he who desires prosperity should act even thus!

Those who fight with warriors more eminent than themselves have this duty to perform.

I would have cursed you if you had not approached me thus!

Go, fight carefully, summoning all your patience!

I cannot, however, wish you victory, for I myself stand here to vanquish you!

Go, fight fairly! I am pleased with your behavior!'

Bowing to him, I came back, mounted my car, and once more blew my conch.

Then the combat commenced between us.

It lasted for many days, each of us trying to vanquish the other.

In that battle, it was Rama who struck me first, with nine hundred and sixty arrows

furnished with vulturine wings. And with that shower of arrows,
my four steeds and my charioteer were completely covered!
Notwithstanding all this, I remained quiet in that encounter in my coat of mail.
Bowing to the gods, and especially to the Brahmanas, I then addressed Rama:
'Although you have shown little regard for me,
yet have I fully honored your preceptorship! Listen again, O Brahmana,
to some other auspicious duty that should be discharged if virtue is to be earned!
The Vedas that are in your body, and the high status of Brahmana that is also
    in you,
and the ascetic merit you have earned by the severest of austerities—
I do not strike at these. I strike, however, at that Kshatriya-hood which you have
    adopted.
When a Brahmana takes up weapons, he becomes a Kshatriya.
Behold now the power of my bow and the energy of my arms!
Speedily shall I cut off that bow of yours with a sharp shaft.'
Saying this, I shot a sharp broad-headed arrow and cut off one of the horns of
    his bow.
It dropped to the ground. I then shot at his car a hundred straight arrows
winged with vulturine feathers. Piercing through Rama's body,
and borne along by the wind, those arrows coursing through space seemed to
    vomit blood
and resembled snakes. Rama, with blood issuing from his body,
shone in battle like the Sumeru mountain with streams of liquid metal
rolling down its breast, or like the asoka tree at the advent of spring
when covered with red bunches of flowers, or like the kinsuka tree
when clad in its flowery attire. Taking up then another bow, Rama, filled with
    wrath,
showered upon me numerous arrows of excessive sharpness, furnished with
    golden wings
of tremendous impetus, resembling snakes, or fire, or poison, and coming from
    all sides.
They pierced my very vitals and caused me to tremble.
Summoning all my coolness, I steeled myself for the encounter and, filled with
    rage,
I pierced Rama with a hundred arrows. He seemed to lose his senses.
Filled with pity at the sight, I stopped of my own accord and said:
'Fie on battle! Fie on Kshatriya practices!' And, overwhelmed with grief, I said:
'Alas, great is the sin committed by me through observance of Kshatriya
    practices,
since I have afflicted with arrows my preceptor, who is a Brahmana with a
    virtuous soul!'
After that, O Bharata, I did not strike Rama anymore.
At this time, as the thousand-rayed luminary, having heated the earth with his rays,
proceeded at the close of day to his chambers in the west,
                     the battle between us ceased."
Bhishma continued: "After the battle had been suspended, my charioteer,
well skilled in such operations, drew out from his own body,

from the bodies of my steeds, and from my body as well the arrows that had
    struck there.
The next morning, when the sun rose, the battle commenced again,
my horses having been bathed and allowed to roll on the ground
and having had their thirst slaked and having been thereby reinvigorated.
Seeing me coming quickly to the encounter, attired in a coat of mail
and stationed on my car, the mighty Rama equipped his car with great care.
And I too, beholding Rama coming toward me to battle, placed aside my bow
and descended from my car. Saluting him, I reascended it and, ready to give
    battle,
stood fearlessly before him. I then overwhelmed him with a thick shower of
    arrows,
and he too covered me with a shower in return.
Filled with wrath, he once more shot at me a number of shafts of great force.
But I, shooting sharp shafts by the hundreds and thousands, repeatedly cut off
    his arrows
in midair before they could come at me. Then he began to hurl celestial
    weapons at me,
all of which I repelled with my weapons. Loud was the din that then arose in
    the sky
as I hurled at Rama the weapon named Vayavya, which he neutralized
by the weapon called Guhyaka. Then I applied, with proper mantras,
the weapon called Agneya, but Rama neutralized that weapon of mine
by one of his, called Varuna. And it was in this way that I neutralized
the celestial weapons of Rama and that he also neutralized mine.
Then, filled with wrath, suddenly wheeling to my right, he pierced me in the
    breast.
At this I swooned. And my charioteer, seeing me unconscious, bore me from the
    field.
All the followers of Rama, including Akritavrana and others
and the princess of Kasi, filled with joy, began to shout aloud!
Regaining consciousness then, I addressed my charioteer, saying:
'Go where Rama is! My pains have left me, and I am ready for battle!'
My charioteer soon took me to him with the aid of my exceedingly handsome
    steeds
that seemed to dance as they coursed over the plain with the speed of the wind.
Approaching Rama then, and filled with wrath, I overwhelmed him with arrows!
But Rama, shooting three for every single one of mine, cut into fragments
every one of my straight-going arrows in midair before any of them could
    reach him!
Seeing this, all the followers of Rama were filled with joy.
I then shot at Rama a good-looking arrow of blazing effulgence
with death's self sitting at its head. Struck forcibly, and succumbing to its impetus,
Rama fell into a swoon and dropped down to the ground.
And exclamations of 'Oh!' and 'Alas!' arose on all sides,
and the whole universe was filled with confusion and alarm,
such as would be witnessed if the sun were ever to fall from the firmament!

All those ascetics, together with the princess of the Kasi race,
hurried with great anxiety toward Rama and, embracing him,
began to comfort him with the touch of their hands, chilled by contact with
    water.
Rama rose up and, fixing an arrow to his bow, addressed me in an agitated voice:
'Stay, Bhishma! You are already slain!' And he fired that arrow and pierced my
    left side.
I trembled like a tree shaken by the tempest. Slaying my horses then in terrific
    combat,
Rama, fighting with great coolness, covered me with swarms of winged arrows
shot with remarkable lightness of hand. I also shot arrows with great lightness of
    hand
to obstruct Rama's arrows. His arrows and mine filled the sky and stayed there
without failing down. Enveloped by this cloud of arrows, the sun's rays
could not pass through them. The winds were unable to pass through them.
Then—because of the obstructed motion of the wind, the rays of the sun,
and the clash of the arrows against one another—a conflagration arose in the
    heavens.
And then those arrows blazed forth because of the fire they had generated
and fell to earth, reduced to ashes!
Rama, filled with rage, covered me with hundreds and thousands
and hundreds of thousands and hundreds of millions of arrows!
I too, O king, with my arrows resembling snakes of virulent poison,
cut into fragments all those arrows of Rama and caused them to fall to earth.
And it was thus that the combat took place. But when the shades of evening
    approached,
my preceptor withdrew from the fight."
Bhishma continued: "The next day, the combat was frightful again between
    Rama and me.
Rama began to use diverse celestial weapons. Regardless of life itself,
which is so difficult to sacrifice, I baffled all those weapons with such of mine
as are capable of doing that. And seeing all his weapons fended off,
he then hurled at me a fierce lance, blazing like a meteor
and resembling the dart hurled by death himself!
With my arrows, I cut that dart into three fragments
resembling in effulgence the sun that rises at end of the *yuga*!
At this, breezes charged with fragrant odors blew around me.
Rama hurled a dozen others at me, the forms of which, O Bharata,
I am incapable of describing because of their great effulgence and speed.
They were like the dozen suns that arise at the time of the destruction of the
    universe,
and I was filled with fear. We exchanged many deadly volleys
and overwhelmed each other with arrows and celestial weapons.
In our last exchange of the day, I was covered with arrows, as was my preceptor.
That mass of Brahmanic merit, mangled with that downpour, began to bleed
copiously and continuously. And, like him, I too was densely pierced with arrows.
When at last the sun set behind the western hills, our combat came to an end."

Bhishma continued: "The next morning, when the sun rose brightly, the combat
  recommenced.
Rama rained on me a thick downpour of arrows, and my beloved charioteer,
hit by some of them, swerved from his place on the car and lost consciousness.
He fell to earth in a swoon and soon gave up his life. Then fear entered my
  heart.
I was still lamenting for him when Rama began to shoot at me many death-
  dealing shafts.
Even while endangered by the death of my charioteer, I was grieving for him,
when he of Bhrigu's race drew his bow with strength and pierced me with an
  arrow!
That blood-drinking shaft struck my breast and pierced me through,
and it and I fell simultaneously upon the earth!
Thinking I was dead, Rama roared aloud like the clouds and rejoiced!
He sent forth stertorous shouts along with his followers, while all the Kauravas
who stood beside me and those who had come to see the combat were afflicted
  with woe.
While lying prostrate, I beheld eight Brahmanas endowed with the effulgence of
  the sun.
They stood surrounding me on that field of battle and supported me on their
  arms.
Borne up by those Brahmanas, I did not touch the ground.
Like friends, they supported me in midair while I breathed heavily.
And they sprinkled me with drops of water. Repeatedly they said to me: 'Do not
  fear!
                    Let prosperity be yours!'
Comforted then by those words of theirs, I rose up and beheld my mother, Ganga,
that foremost among rivers, stationed on my car. Indeed, it was that great river
  goddess
who had controlled my steeds in the combat after my charioteer's fall!
Worshipping then the feet of my mother and my ancestors, I ascended my car.
My mother then protected my car, steeds, and all the implements of battle.
With joined hands, I entreated her to go away.
I myself restrained those steeds and fought with Rama until the close of day!
Then I shot at Rama a powerful and heart-piercing arrow endowed with great
  speed.
Rama, his bow loosened from his grasp, fell down to his knees,
bereft of consciousness and pouring a copious shower of blood!
Meteors by the hundreds fell, and there were thunder rolls causing the earth to
  tremble!
Suddenly Rahu enveloped the blazing sun, and rough winds began to blow!
Vultures and crows and cranes alit in joy!
All the points of the horizon seemed to be ablaze, and jackals yelled fiercely!
Drums, unstruck by human hands, began to produce harsh sounds!
Indeed, when the high-souled Rama, bereft of consciousness, embraced the
  earth,
there were all these frightful and alarming omens of evil!

Then, suddenly rising up, Rama approached me once more to do battle,
forgetting everything and deprived of his senses by anger.
And that mighty-armed one took up his bow and a deadly arrow.
But I resisted him successfully. Then the great rishis who stood there
were moved with pity at the sight, while he of Bhrigu's race was filled with wrath.
I took up a shaft resembling the blazing fire that appears at the end of the *yuga*,
but Rama of immeasurable soul fended off that weapon of mine.
The splendor of the solar disc, covered by clouds of dust, was dimmed,
and the sun went to the western mount. Night came with its delicious, cool
    breezes,
and both of us desisted from the fight. In this way the fierce battle ceased.
The next day, with the reappearance of the sun, it recommenced,
                    and it lasted for three and twenty days together."
Bhishma continued: "I lay down on my bed, and in the solitude of my room
reflected: *For many days this fierce combat has gone on between Rama and me.*
I am unable to vanquish him on the field of battle. If I am competent to vanquish him,
then let the gods kindly show themselves to me this night!
Mangled with arrows, I lay asleep on my right side.
Toward morning, those Brahmanas who had raised me when I had fallen from
    my car
and had held me up and said, 'Do not fear'—these showed themselves to me in
    a dream!
They stood surrounding me and said: 'Rise, O Ganga's son, you need have no
    fear!
We will protect you, for you are our own body!
Rama will never be able to vanquish you in battle! You will be his conqueror!
This beloved weapon, O Bharata, called Praswapa,
appertaining to the lord of all creatures and forged by the divine artificer,
will come to your knowledge, for it was known to you in your former life!
Neither Rama nor any person on earth is acquainted with it.
Remember it, therefore, and apply it with all your strength! It will come to you
    of itself!
With it, you will be able to check all persons endowed with mighty energy!
Rama will not be slain outright by it, so you shall not incur any sin by using it!
Afflicted by the force of this weapon, he will fall asleep!
Vanquishing him thus, you will awaken him in battle
with that dear weapon called Samvodhana!
Do what we have told you in the morning, stationed on your car.
Asleep or dead, we reckon it as the same, but Rama will surely die!
Apply, therefore, this Praswapa weapon so happily thought of!'
Having said this, those Brahmanas, eight in number and resembling one
    another in form,
                    vanished from my sight!"
Bhishma continued: "After the night had passed away, I awoke, thought of my
    dream,
and was filled with great joy. Then between him and me the combat began
that was fierce and unrivaled. Rama poured on me a shower of arrows,

which I baffled with a shower of mine. Then, filled with wrath
at what he had seen the day before and what he saw that day,
Rama hurled at me a dart as hard as Indra's thunderbolt
and possessed of an effulgence resembling that of Yama's mace!
It came toward me like a blazing fire, drinking up, as it were, all the quarters of
    the field.
Then it fell upon my shoulder, like the lightning's flame that ranges the sky.
Wounded thus, I began to bleed copiously,
my blood flowing like streams of red earth from a mountain after a shower!
Filled with wrath, I then shot at Rama a deadly shaft, fatal as the poison of a snake,
which struck him in the forehead and appeared as beautiful as a crested hill!
Extremely angry, that hero then changed his position and drew his bowstring,
aiming at me a terrible shaft resembling all-destructive death himself!
That fierce arrow fell upon my breast, hissing through the air like a snake.
Covered with blood, I fell down to the earth. Regaining consciousness, I hurled
    at Rama
a frightful dart, which fell upon his bosom.
Deprived of his senses, he trembled all over. Then his friend Akritavrana, that
    great ascetic,
embraced him and soothed him with words of comfort.
Rama was then filled with vindictiveness, and he invoked the great Brahma
    weapon.
To fend it off, I used the same excellent weapon.
The two weapons, clashing against each other, blazed forth brightly
without being able to reach either myself or him.
Instead, they met each other in midair, and the bowl of the sky seemed to be
    ablaze,
and all creatures were terrified. The rishis, the Gandharvas, and the gods
were all greatly pained, and the earth, with her mountains and seas and trees,
    trembled.
The firmament was set ablaze, and the ten points of the horizon were filled with
    smoke.
This was the time I thought to shoot the Praswapa weapon, as those Brahmanas
who had appeared to me in my dream had commanded!
The mantras also for invoking this excellent weapon suddenly came to my mind!"
Bhishma continued: "When I had formed this resolution, a tumult of voices
    arose in the sky.
It said: 'O son of Kuru's race, do not use the Praswapa weapon!'
Notwithstanding this, I still aimed that weapon at Rama.
When I had aimed it, Narada addressed me, saying:
'Yonder, Bhishma, are the gods in the sky! They are forbidding you today to do
    this!
Do not aim the Praswapa weapon! Rama is an ascetic possessed of Brahmanic
    merit,
                    and he is your preceptor! Do not humiliate him.'
While Narada was telling me this, I beheld those eight Brahmanas stationed in
    the sky.

Smilingly, O king, they said to me slowly: 'Do what Narada says.
That will be highly beneficial to the world!'
I then withdrew that great weapon called Praswapa and invoked
according to the ordinance the weapon called Brahma in the combat.
Beholding the Praswapa weapon withdrawn, Rama was in a great huff,
and he exclaimed: 'Wretch that I am, I am vanquished, O Bhishma!'
Then he beheld before him his venerable father and his father's fathers.
They stood surrounding him and said these words of consolation:
'Never display such rashness again as engaging in battle with Bhishma,
or with any Kshatriya, O descendant of Bhrigu's race. To fight is the duty of a
    Kshatriya!
Study of the Vedas and practice of vows are the highest wealth of Brahmanas!
For some reason, before this, you had been ordered by us to take up weapons.
You then perpetrated that terrible and unbecoming feat.
Let this battle with Bhishma be your last, for you have had enough fighting
    already.
Leave the combat, throw your bow aside, and practice ascetic austerities!
Behold! Bhishma, the son of Shantanu, has been restrained by all the gods!
They are endeavoring to pacify him, repeatedly saying:
"Desist from this battle! Do not fight with Rama, who is your preceptor.
It is not proper for you to vanquish Rama in battle!
Show this Brahmana every honor on the field of battle!
We are your superiors, and we forbid you!"
Bhishma is one of the foremost among the Vasus! O son, it is fortunate that you
    are still alive!
A celebrated Vasu as he is, how can Bhishma be defeated by you? Desist,
    therefore!
That foremost among the Pandavas, Arjuna, the mighty son of Indra,
has been ordained by the Self-Created to be the slayer of Bhishma!' "
Bhishma continued: "Rama answered them, saying: 'I cannot give up the combat.
This is the solemn vow I have made. Before this, I never left the field, giving up
    in battle!
You, grandsires—if it please you, cause Ganga's son to desist from the fight!
As regards myself, I can by no means desist from this combat!'
Hearing these words of his, those ascetics with Richika at their head
came to me with Narada in their company and told me: 'Desist from the battle!
Honor that foremost among Brahmanas!' For the sake of Kshatriya morality, I
    replied:
'This is the vow I have taken in this world—that I would never desist from battle,
turning my back or suffering my back to be wounded with arrows!
I cannot—from temptation, or distress, or fear, or love of wealth—abandon my
    eternal duty!'
Then all those ascetics with Narada at their head, and my mother, Bhagirathi,
occupied the field of battle before me. I stayed where I was, waiting quietly
with arrows and bow as before, resolved to fight.
Once more they turned toward Rama and said: 'The hearts of Brahmanas
are made of butter. Be pacified, therefore, O Rama, and desist from this battle.

Bhishma is incapable of being slain by you, as indeed you are incapable
of being slain by him!' Saying these words while they stood obstructing the field,
the Pitris caused that descendant of Bhrigu's race to place aside his weapons.
Just at this time, I once more beheld those eight Brahmanas,
blazing with effulgence and resembling bright stars risen on the firmament.
With great affection they said to me, stationed for battle as I was: 'Go to Rama,
who is your preceptor! Do what is beneficial to all the worlds.'
Seeing then that Rama had desisted, owing to the words of his well-wishers,
I also, for the good of the worlds, accepted the words of my well-wishers.
Though mangled exceedingly, I still approached Rama and worshipped him.
Then the great ascetic Rama, smilingly and with great affection, said to me:
'There is no Kshatriya equal to you on the earth!
Go now, O Bhishma, for in this combat you have pleased me highly!'
Summoning then in my presence that maiden, the daughter of Kasi,
Rama sorrowfully said to her these words in the midst of all those high-souled
    persons:
'O damsel, in the very sight of all these persons, I have fought to the best of my
    power
and displayed all my prowess! By using even the very best of weapons,
I have not been able to obtain any advantage
over that foremost among wielders of weapons!
O beautiful lady, go wherever you wish! What other business of yours can I
    accomplish?
Seek the protection of Bhishma himself! You have no other refuge now,
for Bhishma has vanquished me!'
            Having said this, the high-souled Rama sighed and remained silent.
That maiden then addressed him, saying: 'O holy one, it is even as you have said!
This Bhishma of great intelligence is incapable of being vanquished in battle
by even the gods! You have done my business to the best of your power.
You have displayed in this battle energy incapable of being resisted.
You have yet been unable to obtain any advantage over Bhishma in combat.
As regards myself, I will not go a second time to Bhishma.
I will, however, go where I may obtain the means to slay Bhishma in battle
    myself!'
Having said this, that maiden went away,
her eyes agitated with wrath, and thinking to compass my death.
She firmly resolved to devote herself to asceticism.
Then that foremost one of Bhrigu's race, accompanied by those ascetics,
bade me farewell and departed for the mountains from which he had come.
I also, ascending my car and praised by the Brahmanas, entered our city
and represented to my mother, Satyavati, everything that had happened,
and she uttered benedictions on me.
I then appointed persons of intelligence to ascertain the doings of that maiden.
Devoted to my good, those spies of mine brought to me accounts
            of her words and actions from day to day."

✦

Bhishma continued: "When that maiden went to the woods, resolved on ascetic austerities,

I became melancholy. I lost heart. I told Narada and Vyasa what the maiden had done.

They both said: 'Do not give way to sorrow on her account.

Who would venture to defeat destiny by individual exertion?'

Meanwhile, that maiden entered a number of retreats and practiced austerities beyond human powers of endurance.

Without food, emaciated, dry, with matted locks and begrimed with filth,

for six months she lived on air only and stood unmoved, like a streetpost.

And forgoing all food, she passed a whole year standing in the waters of the Yamuna.

Angry as she was, she passed the next year standing on her big toes

and ate only one fallen tree leaf.

Thus for twelve years she made the heavens hot by her austerities.

And though dissuaded by her relatives, she could not be dissuaded

from that course of action. She went to Vatsabhumi, resorted to by the siddhas

and charanas, that retreat of high-souled ascetics of pious deeds.

Bathing frequently in the sacred waters of that retreat, the Kasi princess roamed at will,

proceeding next to the ashrams of Narada and of Uluka and of Chyavana;

and to the spot sacred to Brahmana; and to Prayaga, the sacrificial platform of the gods;

and to that forest sacred to the gods; and to Bhogawati;

and to the ashram of Kusika's son, Viswamitra; and to that of Mandavya,

and also to that of Dwilipa; and to Ramhrada; and to that of Garga.

She performed ablutions in the sacred waters of all these,

observing all the while the most difficult of vows.

One day, my mother from the waters said to her: 'O blessed lady,

why do you afflict yourself so? Tell me the truth!'

That damsel answered her with joined hands, saying:

'O you of handsome eyes, Rama has been vanquished in battle by Bhishma.

What other Kshatriya king would then venture to defeat him?

I am therefore practicing the severest penances for his destruction.

I wander the earth, O goddess, so that I may slay him!

In everything I do, O goddess, this is the great purpose of my vows!'

The oceangoing River Ganga replied to her: 'O lady, you are acting crookedly!

This wish of yours you shall not be able to achieve.

And if you observe these vows for the destruction of Bhishma,

and if you take leave of your body while observing them,

you shall in your next birth become a river, crooked in her course

and with water only during the rains! All the bathing places along your course

will be difficult to approach, and you shall be dry for eight months of the year!

Full of alligators and other frightful beasts, you shall inspire fear in all creatures!'

My mother, that highly blessed lady, in seeming smiles then dismissed the princess.

That highly fair damsel then continued to practice her vows,
forgoing all food, and even water, sometimes for eight months and sometimes
    for ten!
And she wandered hither and thither for her passionate desire of *tirthas*
and then came back to Vatsabhumi. And it is there, O Bharata,
that she is known to have become a river, filled only during the rainy seasons,
abounding with crocodiles, crooked in her course, and with no easy access to
    her water.
And, O king, in consequence of her ascetic merit, only half her body became
    such a river,
while with the other half she remained a maiden as before!"
Bhishma continued: "Then all those ascetics that dwell in Vatsabhumi,
seeing the princess of Kasi firmly resolved on ascetic austerities,
dissuaded her and asked of her: 'What is your business?'
She answered: 'I have been expelled by Bhishma
and prevented by him from the virtue that would have been mine by having a
    husband!
My observance of this vow is for his destruction and not for the sake of regions
    of bliss.
Peace will be mine when I will have accomplished the death of Bhishma. This is
    my resolve.
He for whom my grief has been continuous, he for whom I have been deprived
of what would have been mine if I could have obtained a husband,
he for whom I have become neither woman nor man—
that son of Ganga I will slaughter in battle.
What I have said is the purpose that is in my heart.
I have no longer any desire to be a woman. I am resolved to obtain manhood,
for in that way I will be avenged upon Bhishma. I will not be dissuaded, even
    by you.'
Soon the divine lord of Uma, bearing the trident, showed himself in his own
    form
to that female ascetic among those great rishis. Asked to solicit a boon,
she begged of the deity my defeat. 'You shall slay him,' the god said to that lady.
Thus assured, the maiden, however, once more said to Rudra:
'How can it happen, O god, that as a woman I shall be able to achieve victory in
    battle?
O lord of Uma, I am a woman, and my heart is quite stilled.
But you have promised me, O lord of creatures, the defeat of Bhishma.
O lord, having the bull for your mount, act in such a way
that your promise may become true and that I may slay Bhishma in battle.'
The god of gods, having the bull for his symbol, then said to that maiden:
'The words I have uttered cannot be false. You shall slay Bhishma
and even obtain manhood. You shall also remember all the incidents of your
    present life,
even when you obtain a new body. Born in the race of Drupada,
you shall become a Maharatha. Quick in the use of weapons, and a fierce
    warrior,

you shall be well skilled in battle. All that I have said will be true.'

                    Having said this, the god of gods disappeared.

Then, that faultless maiden of fairest complexion

procured wood and made a large funeral pyre on the banks of the Yamuna.

Having set fire to it, she entered that blazing fire with a heart burning with wrath,

and uttering the words 'I do this for Bhishma's destruction!' "

✦

Duryodhana said: "Tell me, O grandsire, how Sikhandini,

having been born a daughter, afterward became a man."

Bhishma said: "O great king, the eldest and beloved queen of King Drupada

was childless at first. During those years, King Drupada

paid his adoration to the god Sankara for the sake of offspring,

resolving in his mind to accomplish my destruction and practicing the austerest
    penances.

He begged Mahadeva, saying: 'Let a son, and not a daughter, be born to me.

I desire, O god, a son to revenge myself upon Bhishma.'

Thereupon that god of gods said to him: 'You shall have a child

who will be a female and a male. Desist, O king. It will not be otherwise.'

Returning then to his capital, he addressed his wife, saying: 'Great has been my
    exertion.

Undergoing ascetic austerities, I paid my adorations to Shiva,

and I was told by Sambhu that my child becoming a daughter first

would subsequently become a male person. And though I solicited him
    repeatedly,

yet Shiva said: "This is Destiny's decree. It will not be otherwise.

                 That which is destined must take place!" '

Then the queen of King Drupada, when her season came,

observing all the regulations about purity, approached Drupada.

And in due time his wife conceived, agreeably to destiny's decree.

And that lady of eyes like lotus petals held the embryo in her womb.

The mighty-armed King Drupada, from paternal affection,

attended to every comfort of his dear wife.

And the wife of that lord of earth, the royal Drupada, who had been childless,

had all her wishes gratified. In due time, the queen gave birth

to a daughter of great beauty. Thereupon the strong-minded wife of that king,

the childless Drupada, gave out that the child she had brought forth was a son.

Then King Drupada ordered all the rites prescribed for a male child to be
    performed

in respect of that misrepresented daughter, as if she were really a son.

And saying that the child was a son, Drupada's queen kept her counsels very
    carefully.

No other man in the city knew the sex of that child,

and, believing these words of that deity of unfading energy, the king, too,

concealed the real sex of his child, saying: 'She is a son.'

And he caused all the rites of infancy prescribed for a son to be performed for that child, and bestowed the name of Sikhandini on her.

I alone, through my spies and from Narada's words, knew the truth,

informed as I had been of the words of the god and of the ascetic austerities of Amva!"

Bhishma continued: "Drupada bestowed great attention on everything

in connection with that daughter of his, teaching her writing and painting and all the arts.

And in arrows and weapons that child became a disciple of Drona.

The child's mother then urged her husband to find a wife for her, as if she were a son.

Drupada, beholding that daughter of his to have attained the full development of youth,

and assured of her sex, consulted with his queen. Drupada said:

'This daughter of mine that so enhances my woe has attained her youth.

She had hitherto been concealed by me at the words of the trident-bearing deity!'

The queen replied: 'They can never be untrue!

Why indeed would the lord of the three worlds say what would not occur?

If it pleases you, O king, I will speak. Listen to my words, and having listened to me,

follow your own inclination! Let the wedding of this child

with a wife be performed carefully. The words of the god will be true. This is my belief!'

Then that royal couple, having settled their resolution of that affair,

chose the daughter of the king of the Dasarnakas as a wife to Sikhandini.

The king of the Dasarnakas was named Hiranyavarman,

and he gave away his daughter to Sikhandini. He was a powerful monarch,

incapable of being easily vanquished, and possessed of a large army.

Sometime after the wedding, the daughter of Hiranyavarman attained her youth

while the daughter of Drupada also had attained hers.

And Sikhandini, after the marriage, came back to Kampilya.

The former soon came to know that the latter was a woman like herself.

And the daughter of Hiranyavarman bashfully represented to her nurses and companions

everything about the so-called son of the king of the Panchalas.

Then those nurses of the Dasarnakas country, filled with great grief,

sent emissaries to their king who represented to him everything that had taken place.

The king was filled with wrath and sent a messenger to Drupada's abode.

And the messenger approached Drupada, took him aside, and said to him in private:

'The king of the Dasarnakas, O monarch, deceived by you and enraged at the insult,

has said these words to you: "You have humiliated me! It was not wise of you to do so!

You had, from folly, solicited my daughter for your daughter!

O wicked one, reap now the consequence of that act of deception!

I will now slay you, with all your relatives and advisers! Only wait a little!" ' "

Bhishma continued: "King Drupada, like a thief caught in the act, could not speak.

He exerted himself greatly by sending to them sweet-spoken emissaries
with his own instruction, saying, 'This is not so,' in order to pacify his brother.
King Hiranyavarman, however, ascertaining once again that the child
of the king of the Panchalas was really a daughter, issued forth immediately from
    his city.
He sent messages to all his powerful friends about that deception
of which he had heard from the nurses.
Then, having mustered a large army, he resolved to march against Drupada.
King Hiranyavarman held a consultation with his ministers
about the ruler of the Panchalas. And it was settled among those high-souled kings
that if Sikhandini was really a daughter, they should bind the ruler of the
    Panchalas
and drag him from his city, installing another king over the Panchalas,
and should slay both Drupada and Sikhandini.
King Hiranyavarman once more sent an envoy to the descendant of Prishata,
    saying
                         'I will slay you; be assured.'"
Bhishma continued: "King Drupada was not naturally courageous.
He therefore approached his wife and took counsel with her, saying:
'My powerful brother, King Hiranyavarman, having mustered a large force,
is coming toward me in anger. Fools that we both are, what are we now to do
about our daughter? Your son, Sikhandini, has been suspected to be a daughter.
O you of beautiful hips, tell us now what is true or false in this.
Hearing from you first, I will settle how to act.
I am very much endangered, and this child, Sikhandini, is equally so.
Indeed, O queen, you too are threatened with danger! For the relief of all,
tell me what the truth is! Although I have been deceived by you
as to the duties I owe toward a son, yet from kindness I will act toward you both
in a suitable manner. Tell me how may I act so that all may yet turn out well!'
Indeed, although the king knew everything, yet he addressed his wife
in the presence of others, in this way to proclaim his own innocence before
    these others.
His queen then answered him and represented to him the truth
about her daughter, Sikhandini. She said: 'Childless as I was, from fear of my
    co-wives
I told you when Sikhandini, my daughter, was born that she was a son!
For your love of me, you corroborated it and performed all the rites prescribed
    for a son
for this daughter of mine! You then married her, O king,
to the daughter of the king of the Dasarnakas. I did not prevent it,
remembering the words of Shiva: "Born a daughter, she will become a son!"'
Hearing all this, Drupada informed all his counselors of these facts.
And the king then took counsel with his ministers for the proper protection of
    his subjects.
Although he had himself deceived the king of the Dasarnakas,
yet he gave it out that the alliance he had made was proper.
He began to settle his plans with undivided attention.

King Drupada's city was naturally well protected.

Yet, at the advent of danger, they began to protect it all the more carefully

and fortify it with defensive works. But the king and the queen were greatly afflicted,

thinking of how to avoid a war with his brother.

Reflecting on this, the king began to pay his adorations to the gods.

His respected wife, beholding him relying on the gods and paying his adorations to them,

then addressed him and said: 'Homage to the gods is productive of benefits!

It is, therefore, approved by the righteous. What shall I say of those

who are sunk in an ocean of distress? Pay homage to those who are your superiors,

and let all the gods also be worshipped, making large presents to the Brahmanas!

Let oblations be poured on the fire to pacify the ruler of the Dasarnakas.

O lord, think of the means by which, without a war, you may pacify your brother!

Through the grace of the gods, all this will happen.

For the preservation of this city, you have taken counsel with your ministers.

Do all that those counsels suggest, for reliance on the gods,

when supported by human exertion, always leads to success.

If these two do not go hand in hand, success becomes unattainable.'

While husband and wife were thus conversing with each other, both filled with grief,

their helpless daughter, Sikhandini, was filled with shame.

She then reflected, saying within herself: *It is for me that these two are plunged into grief!*

Thinking so, she resolved upon putting an end to her life.

Having formed this determination, she left home, filled with heavy sorrow,

and went into a dense and solitary forest that was the haunt of a very formidable Yaksha

called Sthunakarna. From fear of that Yaksha, men never went into that forest.

And within it stood a mansion with high walls and a gateway

plastered over with powdered earth, and rich with smoke

bearing the fragrance of fried paddy. Entering that mansion, Sikhandini reduced herself

by forgoing all food for many days. Thereupon the Yaksha, also called Sthuna,

who was endowed with kindness, showed himself to her and said: 'For what object

is this endeavor of yours? I will accomplish it. Just tell me!

I am a follower of the lord of treasures. I can grant boons! I will grant you

even that which cannot be given!' Sikhandini represented everything that had happened.

And she said: 'My father, O Yaksha, will soon meet with destruction.

The ruler of the Dasarnakas marches against him in rage. Therefore, save me,

my mother, and my father! Indeed, you have already pledged yourself

to relieve my distress! Through your grace, O Yaksha, I would become a perfect man!'"

Bhishma continued: "The Yaksha, after reflecting in his mind, said:

'Indeed, it was ordained to be so, and it was ordained for my grief!'
The Yaksha continued: 'I will certainly do what you wish!
Listen, however, to my condition. For a certain period I will give you my
    manhood.
You must, however, come back to me in due time. Pledge yourself to do so!
Possessed of immense power, I am a ranger of the skies,
wandering at my pleasure, and capable of accomplishing whatever I intend.
Through my grace, you may save the city and your kinsmen!
I will bear your womanhood, O princess! Pledge your troth to me
and I will do what is agreeable to you!' Sikhandini said to him:
'O holy one of excellent vows, I will give you back your manhood!
O wanderer of the night, bear my womanhood for a short time!
After the ruler of the Dasarnakas, who is encased in golden mail, departs from
    my city,
I will once more become a maiden, and you will become a man!'"
Bhishma continued: "They made a covenant and imparted their sexes
to each other's bodies. The Yaksha Sthuna became a female,
while Sikhandini obtained the blazing form of the Yaksha.
Then Sikhandini entered his city in great joy and approached his father
and told him what had happened. Drupada was very glad.
And he forthwith sent a messenger to the ruler of the Dasarnakas, saying:
                    'My child is a male. Believe it!'
The king of the Dasarnakas, meanwhile, filled with sorrow and grief,
approached Drupada, and at Kampilya, after paying him proper honors,
dispatched an envoy who was one of the foremost among those conversant with
    the Vedas.
He addressed the envoy, saying: 'Say to that worst of kings of wicked
    understanding:
"Having selected my daughter as a wife for one who is your daughter,
you shall today harvest the fruit of that act of deception." '
The Brahmana set out for Drupada's city as Dasarnaka's envoy and went to
    Drupada.
Then the king of the Panchalas, with Sikhandini, offered the envoy a cow and
    honey.
The Brahmana, however, without accepting that worship, said to him
the words that had been communicated through him:
'O you of vile behaviors, I have been deceived by you through your daughter!
I will exterminate you, with your counselors and sons and kinsmen!'
Having been made by that priest to hear those words, fraught with censure
and uttered to him amid his counselors by the ruler of the Dasarnakas,
King Drupada then assumed a mild demeanor, from motives of friendship, and
    said:
'The reply to these words of my brother that you have delivered to me, O
    Brahmana,
will be carried to that monarch by my envoy!'
And King Drupada then sent as his envoy to the high-souled King Hiranyavarman
a Brahmana learned in the Vedas, to say the words

with which Drupada had entrusted him. He said: 'My child is really a male.
Let it be made clear by means of a witness. Somebody has spoken falsely to you.'
Then the king of the Dasarnakas, having heard the words of Drupada,
was filled with sorrow and dispatched a number of young ladies of great beauty
to ascertain whether Sikhandini was a male or a female.
Those ladies, having ascertained the truth, joyfully told the king of the Dasarnakas
that Sikhandini was a powerful person of the masculine sex.
The ruler of the Dasarnakas, filled with joy, went to his brother Drupada
and passed a few days with him in happiness. The king gave Sikhandini much
    wealth,
many elephants, steeds, and cattle; and, worshipped by Drupada, he then
    departed,
having severely rebuked his daughter. Sikhandini also rejoiced."

✦

Bhishma continued: "Meanwhile, sometime after the exchange of sexes had
    taken place,
Kuvera, who was always borne on the shoulders of human beings,
in the course of a journey came to the abode of Sthuna. Staying in the sky
above that mansion, the protector of all the treasures saw that the excellent
    abode
of the Yaksha Sthuna was well adorned with beautiful garlands of flowers
and perfumed with fragrant roots of grass and many sweet scents.
It was decked with canopies and with standards and banners.
It was filled with edibles and beverages of every kind.
And beholding that abode of the Yaksha decked out all over and filled with gems,
and well watered and well swept, the lord of the Yakshas
addressed the Yakshas who followed him, saying: 'This mansion of Sthuna
is well adorned! Why, however, does that man of wicked understanding not
    come to me?
And since that wicked one, knowing I am here, does not approach me,
some severe punishment should be inflicted on him! This is my intention!'
The Yakshas said: 'The royal Drupada had a daughter of the name of
    Sikhandini!
To her, for some reason, Sthuna has given his manhood,
                            and having taken her womanhood upon him, he
    stays within his abode!
Bearing as he does a feminine form, he does not approach you and is ashamed!
Hearing all this, do what may be proper!'
'Let the car be stopped here! Let Sthuna be brought to me,' the lord of the
    Yakshas said.
'I will punish him!' Summoned then by the lord of the Yakshas,
Sthuna, bearing a feminine form, came and stood before him in shame.
Then the giver of wealth cursed him in anger, saying: 'You Guhyakas,
let the femininity of the wretch remain as it is!' And the high-souled lord of the
    Yakshas

also said: 'Since humiliating all the Yakshas, you have given away your sex to Sikhandini

and taken her femininity from her. You have done what has never been done by anybody.

Therefore, from this day, you shall remain a woman, and she shall remain a man!'

At these words of his, all the Yakshas began to mollify Vaisravana

for the sake of Sthunakarna, repeatedly saying: 'Set a limit to your curse!'

The high-souled lord of the Yakshas then said to all those Yakshas who followed him:

'After Sikhandini's death, this one will regain his own form!

Therefore, let this high-souled Yaksha Sthuna be freed from his anxiety!'

Having said this, the illustrious and divine king of the Yakshas, receiving due worship,

departed with all his followers, who were capable of traversing a great distance

within the shortest time. And Sthuna, with that curse on him, continued to live there.

In a timely way, Sikhandini came to that wanderer of the night and said:

'I have come to you, O holy one!' Sthuna then answered him: 'I am pleased with you!'

Indeed, beholding that prince return to him without guile, Sthuna told Sikhandini

what had happened. The Yaksha said: 'For you, I have been cursed by Vaisravana.

Go now, and live happily among men as you choose. Your coming here, I think,

was ordained long ago. All this was incapable of being prevented!'"

Bhishma continued: "Sikhandini returned to his city filled with great joy.

He worshipped with diverse scents and garlands of flowers and costly presents

persons of the sanctified class, deities, big trees, and crossways.

And Drupada, the ruler of the Panchalas, along with his son Sikhandini,

whose wishes had been crowned with success, and with also his kinsmen,

became exceedingly glad. The king then gave his son, Sikhandini,

who had been a woman, as a pupil to Drona. And he obtained the whole science of arms,

with its four divisions. His brother Dhrishtadyumna of Prishata's race

also obtained the same. Indeed, all this was represented to me, O sire, by the spies,

disguised as idiots and as persons without the senses of vision and hearing,

whom I had set upon Drupada. It is thus that that best of Rathas, Sikhandini,

the son of Drupada, having first been born a female, subsequently became a male.

And it was the eldest daughter of the ruler of Kasi, celebrated by the name of Amva,

who was born in Drupada's line as Sikhandini. If he approaches me, bow in hand

and desirous of fighting, I will not look at him even for a moment nor smite him!

This is my vow, known all over the world: that I will not shoot weapons at a woman,

or one who was once a woman, or one bearing a feminine name,

or one whose form resembles a woman's. I will not, for this reason, slay Sikhandini.

If Bhishma slays a woman, the righteous will all speak ill of him."
Hearing these words of Bhishma, King Duryodhana of Kuru's race,
reflecting for a moment, thought that this behavior was proper for Bhishma.

✦

When morning came, Dhritirashtra's sons once more, in the midst of all the
    troops,
said to their grandsire: "O son of Ganga, this army of Pandu's son
that abounds with men, elephants, and steeds; that is crowded with maharathas;
that is protected by Bhima and Arjuna and others headed by Dhrishtadyumna;
that is invincible and incapable of being withstood; that resembles the
    unbounded sea;
this sea of warriors incapable of being agitated by the very gods in battle—
in how many days can you annihilate it? And that mighty bowman,
our preceptor Drona; and also the mighty Kripa;
and Karna, who takes pleasure in battle;
and the son of Drona, Aswatthaman—in what time can each annihilate it?
We desire to know this, for the curiosity we feel in our hearts is great!"
Bhishma said to Duryodhana: "You ask about the strength and weakness of the foe.
This indeed is worthy of you. Listen as I tell you the utmost limit of my power in
    battle,
or of the energy of my weapons, or of the might of my arms!
As regards ordinary combatants, one should fight with them artlessly.
As regards those who are possessed of powers of deception,
one should fight with them aided by the ways of deception.
This is what has been laid down as the duty of warriors.
I can annihilate the Pandava army, O blessed monarch,
taking every morning ten thousand ordinary warriors and one thousand car
    warriors
as my share from day to day. Encased in mail and exerting myself,
I can annihilate this large force according to this arrangement
as regards both number and time. If, however, stationed in battle,
I shoot my great weapons that slay hundreds and thousands at a time,
I can finish the slaughter in a month." King Duryodhana then asked Drona:
"O preceptor, in what time can you annihilate the troops of Pandu's son?"
Drona said smilingly: "I am old, O mighty-armed one! With the fire of my
    weapons
I, like Shantanu's son Bhishma, can consume the army of the Pandavas
I think in a month's time. This is the limit of my power and my strength."
Then Saradwat's son Kripa said that he could annihilate the foe in two months'
    time.
Drona's son, Aswatthaman, pledged himself to annihilate the Pandava army in
    ten nights.
Karna, however, acquainted as he was with weapons of high efficacy,
pledged himself to achieve that feat in five days. Hearing the words of the
    Suta's son,

the son of the oceangoing Ganga laughed aloud and said:
"As long, O son of Radha, as you do not encounter in battle
Arjuna with his arrows, conch, and bows, rushing to combat on his car
with Krishna in his company, so long may you think so!
You are capable of saying whatever you please!"

✦

Hearing these words of the leaders of the Kuru army,
Yudhishthira, summoning all his brothers, said to them in private:
"The spies I had placed in the army of Dhritarashtra's son brought me this.
Duryodhana asked Ganga's son in what time he could annihilate our troops.
He answered the wicked Duryodhana: 'In a month!' Drona also declared
that he could achieve the same feat in about the same time. Kripa indicated
    twice that period.
Drona's son said he could achieve it in ten nights. Karna said that he could
    achieve it in five days.
Therefore, O Arjuna, I desire to hear in what time you can exterminate the foe."
Thus addressed by the king, Arjuna, casting a look upon Krishna, said:
"All these, Bhishma and others, are high-souled and accomplished warriors.
Without doubt, O king, they can exterminate our forces even as they have said!
But let your heart's anguish be dispelled. I tell you that with Krishna as my ally,
I can, on a single car, exterminate the three worlds with even the immortals—
indeed, all mobile creatures that were, are, and will be—in the twinkling of
    an eye.
That terrible and mighty weapon—which Mahadeva, the lord of all creatures,
    gave me
on the occasion of my encounter with him in the guise of a hunter—I still have."

34

Engagement

When the night had passed away, the noise made by the shouting kings grew loud,
all exclaiming: "Array! Array!" With the blare of conchs and the sound of drums,
with the neigh of steeds, the clatter of car wheels, the blare of obstreperous
    elephants,
and the shouts, clapping of armpits, and cries of roaring combatants, the din was
    very great.
The large armies of the Kurus and the Pandavas rose at first light
and completed their arrangements. Then, when the sun rose, the fierce weapons
and the coats of mail of the Kauravas and the Pandavas became fully visible.
There were elephants and cars, adorned with gold, that looked as resplendent
as clouds mingled with lightning. The ranks of cars in profusion looked like cities.
The warriors, armed with bows and swords and scimitars and maces, javelins and
    lances
and bright weapons of diverse kinds, took up their positions in their respective
    ranks.
And there were resplendent standards set up by the thousands, belonging to
    each side,
made of gold and decked with gems and blazing like fire.
Those banners in the thousands endowed with great effulgence looked beautiful
as the heroic combatants, encased in mail, gazed at them, longing for battle.
The foremost men, with quivers and with their hands in leather gloves,
stood at the heads of their divisions with their bright weapons upraised.
Endowed with great bravery and possessing arms that looked like maces,
the performers of sacrifices with plentiful gifts to Brahmanas stood
each at the head of an *akshauhini* of troops. Many other kings and princes,
mighty car warriors conversant with policy and obedient to the commands of
    Duryodhana,
were stationed in their respective divisions. All of them, wearing black deerskins
and accomplished in battle, and cheerfully prepared, for Duryodhana's sake,
to ascend to the region of Brahma, stood there commanding ten efficient
    akshauhinis.
The eleventh great division of the Kauravas, consisting of the Dhartarashtra
    troops,
stood in advance of the whole army. There in the van of that division was
    Shantanu's son.

With his white headgear, white umbrella, and white mail, Bhishma of unfailing
   prowess
looked like the risen moon. His standard, bearing the device of a palmyra of
   gold,
was stationed on a car made of silver, and the Kurus and the Pandavas
beheld that hero looking like the moon encircled by white clouds.
The great bowmen among the Srinjayas, headed by Dhrishtadyumna
and beholding Bhishma, looked like little animals when they see a yawning lion.
Indeed, all the combatants headed by Dhrishtadyumna repeatedly trembled in
   fear.
                         These were the eleven splendid divisions of the Kurus' army.
So also the seven divisions of the Pandavas were protected by the foremost
   among men.
Indeed, the two armies facing each other looked like two oceans at the end of
   the *yuga,*
agitated by fierce sea creatures and abounding with huge crocodiles.
Never before had anyone seen or heard of two such armies encountering each
   other.
The seven large planets, as they appeared in the firmament, all blazed like fire.
The sun, when he rose, seemed to be divided in twain.
Jackals and crows, expecting dead bodies to feast upon, uttered fierce cries.
Bhishma, fully conversant with every duty, summoned all the kings, saying:
"This broad door is open to you for entering heaven. Go through it
to the region of Sakra and Brahman. The rishis of olden times
have shown you this path. Honor yourselves by engaging in battle with attentive
   minds.
Nabhaga and Yayati and Mandhatri and Nahusa and Nriga
were crowned with success and obtained the highest region of bliss by feats like
   these.
To die of disease at home is a sin for a Kshatriya. Death in battle is his eternal
   duty."
Thus addressed, the kings, looking beautiful in their excellent cars,
proceeded to the heads of their respective divisions.
Only Vikareana's son Karna and his friends and relatives laid aside their weapons
for the sake of Bhishma. Without Karna, then, all the Kuru kings proceeded,
making the ten points of the horizon resound with their leonine roars.
And their divisions shone brightly, with white umbrellas,
banners, standards, elephants, steeds, cars, and foot soldiers.
The earth was agitated with the sounds of drums, tabors, and cymbals
and the clatter of car wheels. The mighty car warriors,
decked with their bracelets and armlets of gold and with their bows,
looked resplendent, like hills of fire. With his large palmyra-bearing standard
decked with five stars, Bhishma, the generalissimo of the Kuru army,
looked like the dazzling sun himself.
Those mighty bowmen of royal birth who were on the Kuru side
all took up their positions, as Shantanu's son had ordered.
King Saivya of the country of the Govasanas, accompanied by all the monarchs,

went out on a princely elephant worthy of royal use and graced with a banner on
    its back.

And Aswatthaman, of the complexion of the lotus, went out ready for every
    emergency,

stationing himself at the head of all the divisions, with his standard

bearing the device of the lion's tail. Srutayudha and Chitrasena and Purumitra

and Vivinsati, and Salya and Bhurisravas, and that mighty car warrior Vikarna

followed Drona's son behind, but in advance of Bhishma.

The tall gold standards of these warriors, adorning their cars, were most
    resplendent.

The standard of Drona, that foremost among preceptors, bore the device of a
    golden altar

decked with a water pot and the figure of a bow. The standard of Duryodhana,

guiding many hundreds and thousands of divisions, bore the device of an
    elephant

worked in gems. Paurava and the ruler of the Kalingas and Salya took up their
    positions

in Duryodhana's van. On a costly car with his standard bearing the device of a
    bull,

and guiding the van of his division, the ruler of the Magadhas marched against
    the foe.

That large force of the Easterners, looking like the fleecy clouds of autumn,

was protected by the chief of the Angas, Karna's son Vrishaketu,

and by Kripa of great energy. Stationing himself in the van of his division,

with his beautiful standard of silver bearing the device of the boar,

the famous Jayadratha looked highly resplendent.

A hundred thousand cars, eight thousand elephants, and sixty thousand cavalry

were under his command. Directed by the royal chief of the Sindhus,

that large division, occupying the very van of the army

and abounding with untold cars, elephants, and steeds, looked magnificent.

With sixty thousand cars and ten thousand elephants,

the ruler of the Kalingas, accompanied by Ketumat, sallied forth,

his huge elephants resembling hills and adorned with the catapults called
    yantras

and with lances, quivers, and standards, looking exceedingly beautiful.

And the ruler of the Kalingas, with his tall standard as effulgent as fire

and his white umbrella and golden cuirass and the yak tails with which he was
    fanned,

shone brilliantly. And Ketumat also, riding on an elephant with beautiful tusks,

was stationed in battle like the sun in the midst of black clouds.

King Bhagadatta, blazing with energy and riding on that elephant of his,

went out like the wielder of the thunder. The two princes of Avanti,

named Vinda and Anuvinda, who were regarded as equal to Bhagadatta,

followed Ketumat, riding on the necks of their elephants.

And arrayed by Drona and the royal son of Shantanu and Drona's son

and Valhika and Kripa, the Vyuha formation, consisting of many divisions of
    cars,

was such that the elephants formed its body; the kings, its head; and the steeds,
  its wings.

With face toward all sides, the Vyuha formation seemed to smile, ready to spring
  upon the foe.

Soon after, there was a loud uproar, causing the heart to tremble.

Indeed, with the sounds of conchs and drums, the grunts of elephants,

and the clatter of car wheels, the earth seemed to rend in twain.

And soon the sky and the earth resounded with the neigh of chargers

and the shouts of combatants. The troops of the Kauravas and the Pandavas

trembled when they encountered each other.

There the elephants and the cars decked in gold looked like clouds adorned
  with lightning.

And standards of diverse forms belonging to the combatants,

ornamented with golden rings, glittered like fire.

Those standards resembled the banners of Indra in his celestial mansions.

The foremost warriors among the Kurus, with excellent bows

and weapons upraised for striking, with leather gloves on their hands,

and with eyes as large as those of bulls, all placed themselves at the heads of
  their divisions.

And these protected Bhishma from behind: Dussasana and Durvishaha and
  Durmukha

and Dussaha and Vivinsati and Chitrasena and that mighty car warrior Vikarna.

And among them were Satyavrata and Purumitra and Jaya and Bhurisravas and
  Sala.

And twenty thousand car warriors followed them. The Abhishahas, the
  Surasenas,

the Sivis, and the Vasatis, the Swalyas, the Matsyas, the Amvashtas, the Trigartas,

and the Kekayas, the Sauviras, the Kitavas,

and the dwellers of the eastern, western, and northern countries were all
  resolved

to fight, reckless of their lives. And these protected the grandsire with an array
  of cars.

And with a division that consisted of ten thousand elephants, the king of
  Magadha

followed that large car division. They who protected the wheels of the cars

and they who protected the elephants numbered a full six millions.

And the foot soldiers who marched in advance, armed with bows, swords, and
  shields,

numbered many hundreds of thousands. And the eleven Kuru *akshauhinis*
  looked like Ganga separated from Yamuna.

◆

Seeing Dhritarashtra's divisions arrayed in order of battle,
King Yudhishthira addressed Arjuna: "Men know from the words of that great rishi
Vrihaspati that one must make the few fight by condensing them,
while one may extend the many according to one's pleasure.

In encounters of the few with the many, the array to be formed should be
the needle-mouthed one. Our troops, compared with the enemy's, are few.
Keeping in view this precept of the great rishi, array our troops accordingly."
Arjuna answered: "That immovable array known by the name of Vajra,
designed by the wielder of the thunderbolt, is the one that I will make for you.
Bhima, that foremost among smiters, who is like the bursting tempest
and is incapable of being resisted in battle by the foe, will fight at our head.
Conversant with all the appliances of battle, he will be our leader, crushing the foe.
Beholding him, all the hostile warriors headed by Duryodhana will retreat in
    panic,
like smaller animals beholding the lion, and all of us, our fears dispelled,
will seek his shelter as if he were a wall, like the celestials seeking the shelter
    of Indra.
The man does not breathe who could bear to cast his eyes on that bull
    among men
when he is angry." Arjuna then did as he had said, disposing his troops in battle
    array.
And the mighty army of the Pandavas, beholding the Kuru army move,
looked like the full, immovable, and quickly rolling current of Ganga.
Bhimasena, and Dhrishtadyumna endowed with great energy,
and Nakula and Sahadeva and King Dhrishtaketu became the leaders of that
    force.
And King Virata, surrounded by an *akshauhini* of troops
and accompanied by his brothers and sons, marched in their rear, protecting
    them.
The two sons of Madri, both of great effulgence, were the protectors of Bhima's
    wheels,
while the five sons of Draupadi and the son of Subhadra protected Bhima from
    behind.
That mighty car warrior Dhrishtadyumna, the prince of Panchala,
with those bravest of combatants and those foremost among car warriors, the
    Prabhadrakas,
protected these princes from behind. And behind him was Sikhandin,
who in his turn was protected by Arjuna, behind whom was Yuyudhana
of mighty strength. And the two princes of Panchala, Yudhamanyu and
    Uttamaujas,
became the protectors of Arjuna's wheels along with the Kekaya brothers
and Dhrishtaketu and Chekitana of great valor. King Yudhishthira took up his
    position
in the center of his army, surrounded by huge elephants that looked like moving
    hills.
The high-souled Yajnasena, the king of the Panchalas, stationed himself behind
    Virata
with an *akshauhini* of troops for the sake of the Pandavas.
And on the cars of those kings were tall standards bearing diverse devices,
decked with excellent ornaments of gold, and as effulgent as the sun and the
    moon.

Causing those kings to make space for him, that mighty car warrior
     Dhrishtadyumna,
accompanied by his brothers and his sons, protected Yudhishthira from behind.
Transcending the huge standards on all the cars on both sides
was the standard with the gigantic ape on Arjuna's car. Foot soldiers
by the many hundreds of thousands, armed with swords, spears, and scimitars,
proceeded ahead to protect Bhimasena. And ten thousand elephants of great
     courage,
blazing with golden armor, followed behind the king, like moving mountains.
The invincible Bhimasena, whirling his fierce weapon, seemed to crush the Kuru
     army.
He was incapable of being looked at, like the scorching sun,
so that none of the combatants could bear to look at him from any near point.
And this array, called Vajra, fearless and having its face turned toward all sides,
having bows for its lightning sign, and extremely fierce, was protected
by the wielder of the Gandiva. Disposing their troops in this counterarray,
               the Pandavas waited for battle, invincible in the world of men.
As both armies stood at daybreak, waiting for sunrise, a wind began to blow,
with drops of water falling although there were no clouds,
and the roll of thunder was heard. Dry winds blew all around, showering
     pointed pebbles,
and thick dust arose, covering the world with darkness. Meteors began to fall
     eastward,
striking against the rising sun, and broke in fragments with loud noise.
When the troops stood arrayed, the sun rose, divested of splendor, and the earth
     trembled
and cracked in many places. The roll of thunder was heard on all sides.
The tall standards of the combatants—furnished with strings of bells,
decked with golden ornaments and garlands of flowers and rich drapery,
graced with banners, and resembling the sun in splendor—were shaken by the
     wind
and gave a loud jingling noise, like that of a forest of palmyra trees in a gale.
It was thus that those tigers among men, the sons of Pandu, stood,
having disposed their troops in counterarray against the army of the Kurus—
sucking, as it were, the strength of their warriors—as they eyed Bhimasena,
stationed at the Pandavas' head, mace in hand. Both armies were equally joyful.
Both armies looked beautiful, assuming the aspect of blossoming woods,
and both armies were full of elephants, cars and horses.
Both armies were vast and terrible in aspect, and neither could bear the sight of
     the other.
Both were arrayed for conquering the very heavens, and both of them
consisted of excellent persons. The Kauravas, belonging to the Dhritarashtra party,
stood facing the west, while the Pandavas stood facing the east, prepared to fight.
The troops of the Kauravas looked like the army of the chief of the Danavas,
while those of the Pandavas looked like the army of the celestials.
The wind blew from behind the Pandavas, against the face of the forces of
     Dhartarashtra,

and the beasts of prey began to yell against the Dhartarashtras.

The elephants belonging to the Kauravas could not bear the strong odor of the juice

emitted by the huge elephants of the Pandavas. And Duryodhana rode on an elephant

of the complexion of a lotus, graced with golden kaksha beads on its back

and encased in an armor of steel netting. And he was in the very center of the Kurus

and was adored by eulogists and bards. A white umbrella of lunar effulgence

was held over his head, graced with a golden chain. Sakuni, the ruler of the Gandharas,

followed Duryodhana with mountaineers of Gandhara all around. The venerable Bhishma,

at the head of all the troops—armed with bow and sword,

with a white umbrella held over his head, white headgear, and a white banner on his car

that had white steeds yoked to it—looked like a snow-covered mountain.

In Bhishma's division were all the sons of Dhritarashtra, and also Sala,

who was a countryman of the Valhikas, and also all those Kshatriyas called Amvastas,

and those called Sindhus, and those also that are called Sauviras,

and the heroic dwellers of the country of the five rivers.

And on a golden car to which were yoked red steeds, the high-souled Drona—

bow in hand and with never-failing heart, the preceptor of almost all the kings—

remained behind all the troops, protecting them like Indra.

And Saradwat's son—that fighter in the van, that high-souled and mighty bowman

called also Gautama, conversant with all modes of warfare,

accompanied by the Sakas, the Kiratas, the Yavanas, and the Pahlavas—

took up his position at the northern point of the army. That large force,

well protected by mighty car warriors of the Vrishni and Bhoja races

as also by the warriors of Surashtra, well-acquainted with the uses of weapons,

was led by Kritavarman and proceeded toward the south. Ten thousand cars

of the Samasaptakas—who were created for either the death or the fame of Arjuna

and who, accomplished in arms, intended to follow Arjuna at his heels—

all went out, as also the brave Trigartas. In the Kuru army were a thousand elephants

of the foremost fighting powers. To each elephant was assigned a century of cars;

to each car, a hundred horsemen; to each horseman, ten bowmen;

and to each bowman, ten combatants armed with sword and shield.

Thus were their divisions arrayed by Bhishma, the son of Shantanu.

As each day dawned, he sometimes disposed the troops of the human army,

sometimes those of the celestial, sometimes those of the Gandharva, and sometimes those of the Asura.

Thronged with a large number of Maharathas, and roaring like the very ocean,

Dhartarashtra's army stood facing the west. That illimitable army looked formidable, but the army of the Pandavas, although it was not so great in number,

yet seemed to be very large and invincible, since Krishna and Arjuna were its
  leaders.

✦

Beholding the vast Kuru army ready for battle, King Yudhishthira gave way to
  grief.

Seeing that impenetrable array formed by Bhishma, and regarding his position

as hopeless, the king became pale and addressed Arjuna, saying:

"How shall we fight in battle with those who have the grandsire as their chief?

Immovable and invincible is this array that has been designed

by Bhishma according to the rules laid down in the scriptures.

With our troops, success is doubtful in the face of this mighty force."

Arjuna answered Yudhishthira: "Hear, O king, how soldiers who are few in
  number

may vanquish the many who are possessed of every quality.

The rishi Narada knows it, as do both Bhishma and Drona.

Referring to this means, the grandsire himself in days of old, at the battle

between the gods and the Asuras, said to Indra and the other celestials:

'They who are desirous of victory do not conquer by might and energy

so much as by truth, compassion, and righteousness.

Discriminating, then, between righteousness and unrighteousness,

fight without arrogance, for victory is where righteousness is.'

Because of this, know that victory is certain for us in this battle.

Indeed, as Narada said: 'There is victory where Krishna is.'

Victory is inherent in Krishna. Indeed, it follows him.

And as victory is one of his attributes, so is humility another.

Govinda is possessed of infinite energy. Even in the midst of immeasurable foes,

he is without pain. He is the most eternal of male beings.

Indestructible, and of weapons incapable of being resisted,

appearing as Hari in olden days, he said in a loud voice to the gods and the
  Asuras:

'Who among you would be victorious?'

Even the conquered said: 'With Krishna in the front, we will conquer.'

It was through Hari's grace that the three worlds were won by the gods headed
  by Indra.

I do not, therefore, see the slightest cause of sorrow in you.

You have the sovereign of the universe and the lord of the celestials wishing you
  victory."

Then King Yudhishthira, disposing his own troops in counterarray

against Bhishma's divisions, urged them on: "The Pandavas have disposed their
  forces

according to the scriptures. Fight fairly, hoping to enter the highest heaven."

In the center of the Pandava army were Sikhandin and his troops, protected by
  Arjuna.

And Dhristadyumna moved in the van, protected by Bhima.

The southern division was protected by that mighty bowman, the handsome
    Yuyudhana,
foremost combatant of the Satwata race, resembling Indra himself.
Yudhishthira was stationed on a car, worthy of bearing the great Mahendra,
that was adorned with an excellent standard variegated with gold and gems
and furnished with golden traces for the steeds in the midst of his elephant
    divisions.
His pure white umbrella with ivory handle raised over his head was truly
    beautiful,
and many great rishis walked around the king, uttering laudatory words.
Many priests and holy rishis and siddhas, singing hymns in his praise,
wished him well as they walked around him with japa beads and mantras,
efficacious drugs, and diverse propitiatory ceremonies.
That high-souled chief of the Pandavas, giving the Brahmanas cattle and fruits
    and flowers
and golden coins, proceeded like Indra, the chief of the celestials.
The car of Arjuna, furnished with a hundred bells, decked with Jamvunada gold,
endowed with excellent wheels, possessed of the effulgence of fire,
and yoked to white steeds, looked as brilliant as a thousand suns.
On that ape-bannered car, the reins of which were held by Krishna,
Arjuna stood with the Gandiva, arrows in hand, a bowman peerless on earth.
For crushing the Kuru sons' troops, that strong-armed Bhimasena—
he who assumes the most awful form, and who, divested of weapons, with only
    his bare hands
pounds to dust men, horses, and elephants—became, accompanied by the twins,
the protector of the heroic car warriors of the Pandava army.
The warriors on the Kuru side beheld the invincible Bhima stationed in the van
    of the army,
like the proud leader of an elephantine herd, and they trembled, weakened by
    fear,
                  like elephants sunk in mire.
To that invincible prince in the midst of his troops
Krishna said: "He who, scorching us with his wrath, stays in the midst of his forces;
he who will attack our troops like a lion; he who performed
three hundred horse sacrifices—that banner of Kuru's race, that Bhishma, stays
    away!
There rank around him great warriors, like clouds shrouding the bright sun."
Having heard these words of Krishna, Arjuna alit from his car
and intoned the following hymn with joined hands: "I bow to you, O leader of
    yogins,
O you who are identical with Brahman, O you who dwell in the forest of Mandara,
O you who are freed from decrepitude and decay, O Kali, O wife of Kapala,
O you who are of a black and tawny hue. I bow to you, O bringer of benefits.
I bow to you, O Mahakali, wife of the universal destroyer.
I bow to you, O proud one, you who rescue us from dangers
and have every auspicious attribute, who are sprung from the Kata race,
who deserve the most regardful worship. O fierce one, O giver of victory,

O you who bear a banner of peacock plumes and are decked with every ornament,
O you who bear an awful spear, O you who hold a sword and a shield,
O you who are the younger sister of the chief of cowherds,
O eldest one, O you who were born in the race of the cowherd Nanda,
O you who are fond of buffalo's blood, O you who were born to the race of Kusika,
O you who are dressed in yellow robes, O you who devoured Asuras,
assuming the face of a wolf, I bow to you, who are fond of battle!
O Uma, Sakambhari, O you who are white in hue,
O you who are black in hue, O you who have slain the Asura Kaitabha,
O you who are yellow-eyed, O you of eyes that have the color of smoke, I bow
    to you.
O you who are the Vedas, the Srutis, and the highest virtue,
O you who are propitious to Brahmanas engaged in sacrifice,
O you who have knowledge of the past,
O you who are ever present in the sacred abodes erected to you in the cities of
    Jamvudwipa,
I bow to you. You are the science of Brahma among sciences
and are that sleep of creatures from which there is no waking.
O mother of Skanda, O you who possess the six highest attributes,
O Durga, O you who dwell in accessible regions,
who are described as Swaha and Swadha, as Kala, as Kashta
and as Saraswati, as Savitra the mother of the Vedas, and as the science of Vedanta,
with inner soul cleansed, I praise you. O great goddess,
let victory always attend me through your grace. In inaccessible regions
where there is fear, in places of difficulty, in the abodes of your worshippers,
and in the nether regions you always dwell. You always defeat the Danavas.
You are the unconsciousness, the sleep, the illusion, the modesty,
the beauty of all creatures. You are the twilight, you are the day, you are Savitri,
and you are the mother. You are contentment, you are growth, you are light.
It is you who support the sun and the moon and make them shine.
You are the prosperity of those who are prosperous.
                The siddhas and the charanas behold you in contemplation."
Understanding the measure of Arjuna's devotion,
Durga, who is always graciously inclined toward mankind,
appeared in the firmament and, in the presence of Govinda, said these words:
"O invincible one, you have Krishna to aid you. You cannot be defeated by foes,
not even by the wielder of the thunderbolt himself." Then the goddess
    disappeared.
Krishna and Arjuna, seated on the same car, blew their celestial conchs.
The man who recites this hymn at dawn has no fear at any time of Yakshas,
    Rakshasas,
and Pisachas. He can have no enemies. He has no fear of snakes,
nor of any other animal that has fangs and teeth, nor of kings.
He is sure to be victorious in all disputes and, if bound, is freed from his bonds.
He is sure to conquer all difficulties, is freed from thieves,
is ever victorious in battle, and wins the goddess of prosperity forever.
With health and strength, he lives for a hundred years.

Bhishma was surrounded on all sides by the Pandavas,
like the sun in the firmament surrounded by the clouds at the end of summer.
Duryodhana addressed Dussasana, saying: "This heroic and great bowman
    Bhishma,
this slayer of heroes, has been surrounded on all sides by the brave Pandavas.
With our protection, our grandsire Bhishma will slay all the Panchalas and
    Pandavas.
Therefore, surround the grandsire with all our troops, and protect him
who always achieves the most difficult feats in battle."
Dussasana, surrounding Bhishma with a large force on all sides, took up his
    position.
Then Suvala's son Sakuni—with hundreds and thousands of horsemen
having bright spears and swords and lances in hand
and forming a proud, well-dressed, strong body bearing standards
and mingling with excellent foot soldiers who were all well trained
and skilled in battle—confronted Nakula and Sahadeva and Yudhishthira,
surrounding them on all sides. King Duryodhana sent ten thousand more brave
    horsemen
to resist the Pandavas. When these rushed like so many Garudas toward the
    enemy,
the earth, struck with their horse hooves, trembled noisily.
And the loud clatter of their hooves resembled the noise of a large bamboo forest
in conflagration on a mountain. And as these dashed over the field,
there arose a cloud of dust, which, rising to the sky, shrouded the very sun.
Because of these impetuous steeds, the Pandava army was agitated,
like a large lake with a flight of swans suddenly alighting on its bosom.
King Yudhishthira and the two sons of Pandu by Madri
checked the charge of those horsemen in battle, like the continent
bearing the force at full tide of the surging sea.
Then those three car warriors with their shafts cut off the heads of those horse
    riders.
They fell to earth, like mighty elephants tumbling into mountain caves.
Coursing all over the field, those Pandava warriors cut off the heads
of those cavalry soldiers with sharp-bearded darts and straight shafts.
Those horsemen's heads dropped like fruits from tall trees.
All over the field, steeds and riders were falling or fallen. And the steeds, in
    panic, fled
like smaller animals trying to save their lives, having sighted a lion.
The Pandavas, after vanquishing their foes in that great battle, blew their conchs
and beat their drums. Then Duryodhana, filled with grief on seeing his troops
    defeated,
addressed the ruler of the Madras and said: "There, the eldest son of Pandu,
accompanied by the twins in battle, routs our troops in your sight.
O mighty-armed one, resist him, like the continent resisting the ocean.
You are well known as possessing might and prowess that are irresistible."

Hearing these words, the valiant Salya proceeded with a large body of cars
to the spot where Yudhishthira was. Thereupon the son of Pandu
battled that large host of Salyas rushing impetuously toward him
with the force of a mighty wave. And King Yudhishthira in that battle
pierced the ruler of the Madras in the center of the chest with ten shafts.
Nakula and Sahadeva struck him with seven straight shafts.
The ruler of the Madras then struck each of them with three arrows.
And once more he pierced Yudhishthira with sixty sharp-pointed arrows.
Excited with wrath, he struck each of the sons of Madri also with two shafts.
Then that vanquisher of foes, the mighty-armed Bhima,
beholding the king in that great battle, ventured within reach of Salya's car,
as if within the very jaws of death, and quickly came to Yudhishthira's side.
When the sun had passed the meridian and was sinking,
there commenced a fierce and terrible battle on that part of the field.
The Pandavas surrounded the grandsire on all sides,
but Bhishma, unvanquished by that large body of cars, blazed up like a fire in a
     forest
and consumed his foes. His car was his fire chamber;
his bow constituted the flames of that fire;
swords, darts, and maces constituted the fuel;
his shafts were the sparks; and Bhishma was himself the fire
that consumed those foremost among the Kshatriyas. With shafts furnished with
     golden wings
and vulturine feathers and endowed with great energy,
with barbed arrows, and darts, and long shafts, he covered the hostile host
and felled elephants and car warriors also. He made that large body of cars
resemble a forest of palmyras shorn of their leafy heads.
That mighty-armed warrior, that foremost among wielders of weapons,
deprived cars and elephants and steeds of their riders.
And hearing the twang of his bowstring and the noise of his palms,
as loud as the roar of the thunder, all the troops trembled.
The shafts shot from Bhishma's bow did not merely strike the coats of mail
but pierced them through. And there were many cars, destitute of their brave
     riders,
dragged over the field of battle by the fleet steeds yoked to them.
Fourteen thousand car warriors belonging to the Chedis, the Kasis, and the
     Karushas,
of great celebrity and noble parentage, prepared to lay down their lives.
They stood firm on the field of battle, opposing Bhishma, who resembled the
     destroyer himself,
and all, with wide-open mouths, went to the other world
with their cars, steeds, and elephants. There were cars by the hundreds and
     thousands,
some with their axles and bottoms broken, and some with broken wheels.
The earth was strewn with broken cars and with the prostrate forms of car
     warriors
in beautiful but broken coats of mail. The ground was strewn with maces

and short arrows and sharp shafts, with bottoms of cars, with quivers and broken
  wheels,

with innumerable bows and scimitars, with heads decked with earrings,

with leather gloves and overthrown standards, with bows broken in various parts,

with elephants destitute of riders, and with slain horsemen of the Pandava army.

The valiant Pandavas, notwithstanding all their efforts,

could not rally those car warriors afflicted by the shafts of Bhishma who were
  fleeing.

Indeed, that mighty host, while being slaughtered by Bhishma,

broke so completely that no two persons fled together.

With its cars, elephants, and steeds overthrown, and with its standards laid low,

the army of the sons of Pandu, deprived of its senses, uttered loud exclamations
  of woe.

At that time, sire slew son and son slew sire and friend smote dear friend.

And many combatants of the Pandavas' army, throwing off their armor,

were seen flying in all directions with disheveled hair.

Indeed, the Pandava troops looked like bulls no longer restrained by the yoke,
  running wild in fear.

Then Krishna, beholding the Pandava army breaking up,

reined the excellent car and said to Arjuna: "The hour is come that you had
  hoped for.

Strike now, or you will be deprived of your senses.

Formerly you said, in that conclave of kings in Virata's city, in the presence of
  Sanjaya:

'I will slay all the warriors of Dhritarashtra's son, all of them with their followers,

including Bhishma and Drona, that would fight with me in battle.'

O chastiser of foes, make those words of yours true.

Remembering the duty of a Kshatriya, fight without anxiety."

Arjuna hung down his head and looked askance at Krishna.

And Arjuna replied very unwillingly, saying: "To acquire sovereignty with hell in
  the end,

having slain those who should not be slain; or to endure the woes

of an exile in the woods—these are the alternatives. Which of these should I
  achieve?

Urge the steeds. I will do your bidding. I will overthrow the Kuru grandsire
  Bhishma,

that invincible warrior." Krishna then urged those steeds of silvery hue toward
  Bhishma,

and that large host of Yudhishthira rallied and came again to the fight,

seeing the mighty armed Arjuna proceeding for an encounter with Bhishma.

Bhishma repeatedly roared like a lion and covered Arjuna's car with a shower of
  arrows.

Within a trice, that car of his with its steeds and charioteer became entirely
  invisible

                                        because of that thick hail of arrows.

Krishna, however, without fear, mustering patience and endowed with great
  energy,

urged those steeds mangled with Bhishma's shafts. Arjuna, taking up his
celestial bow
with a twang as loud as the roar of the clouds, caused Bhishma's bow to drop
and cut it into fragments with sharp shafts. Then the Kuru hero,
whose bow had thus been cut off, strung another bow in the twinkling of an eye.
Arjuna, however, cut also that bow of his. The son of Shantanu applauded
the lightness of hand displayed by Arjuna, saying: "Well done, well done,
O mighty-armed one. Well done, O son of Kunti."
Having addressed Arjuna thus, Bhishma took up another beautiful bow
and shot many arrows at Arjuna's car.
And Krishna showed great skill in the management of steeds,
displaying the circling maneuver so that he baffled all of Bhishma's arrows.
Mangled with the arrows of Bhishma, those two tigers among men
looked beautiful, like two angry bulls marked with the scratches of horns.
Then Krishna, beholding that Arjuna was fighting mildly
and that Bhishma was incessantly scattering his arrows, could no longer bear it.
Abandoning Arjuna's steeds, and filled with wrath, that great lord of Yoga power
jumped down from the car. Repeatedly roaring like a lion,
the mighty Krishna of great energy, the lord of the universe, with eyes as red as
copper,
having his bare arms alone for his weapons, rushed toward Bhishma,
whip in hand, eager to slay him, and he seemed to split the universe itself with
his tread.
All the combatants, seeing Krishna about to fall on Bhishma, were stupefied.
"Bhishma is slain, Bhishma is slain," men exclaimed.
Krishna, robed in yellow silk and as dark as the lapis lazuli,
looked as beautiful as a mass of clouds charged with lightning as he pursued
Bhishma.
Like a lion rushing toward an elephant, that bull of Madhu's race rushed toward
Bhishma.
And Bhishma, beholding him of eyes like lotus petals thus approaching him,
drew his bow
and addressed Krishna, saying: "Come, come. O god of the gods, I bow to you.
Throw me down today in this great battle. O god, when I am slain by you in
battle,
great will be the good done to me, O Krishna.
Among all in the three worlds, great is the honor done to me today in battle.
Strike me as you please, for I am your slave, O sinless one."
Meanwhile, the mighty-armed Arjuna, quickly following behind Krishna,
seized him by encircling him with his two arms. Even seized by Arjuna,
Krishna still proceeded with great speed, bearing Arjuna with him.
The mighty Arjuna, however, forcibly catching hold of Krishna's legs,
stopped him with great difficulty at the tenth step.
Then Arjuna, Krishna's dear friend, filled with sorrow, affectionately addressed
Krishna,
who was then sighing like a snake, and whose eyes were troubled with wrath,
saying:

"Stop, O Krishna. It behooves you not to make those words false
that you had spoken before: 'I will not fight.' People will say that you are a liar.
This burden rests on me. I will slay the grandsire. I swear, O Krishna,
by my weapons, by truth, and by my good deeds, that I will do
whatever the destruction of my foes may require."
Krishna spoke not a word but in anger once more mounted the car.
And then on those two tigers among men stationed on their car
Bhishma again poured his shower of arrows, like the clouds pouring rain
on a mountain breast. He took the lives of the hostile warriors,
like the sun sucking with his rays the energies of all things during summer.
As the Pandavas had been breaking the ranks of the Kurus in battle,
so did Bhishma now break the Pandava ranks.
The routed soldiers, helpless and heartless, slaughtered in the hundreds and
thousands,
were unable even to look at him in that battle as he blazed in splendor.
Indeed, the Pandavas, afflicted with fear, watched Bhishma,
who was then achieving superhuman feats in that battle.
The Pandava troops, thus fleeing, failed to find a protector, like cattle in a shoal
of ants.
While he was thus grinding the Pandava army, the thousand-rayed maker of day
repaired to the setting hills, and there came the dreadful hour of twilight,
when the battle could no longer be seen.
King Yudhishthira—seeing that his troops, slaughtered by Bhishma,
had thrown aside their weapons and, stricken with fear, were fleeing the field;
and seeing Bhishma also, excited with wrath and afflicting everybody in the
fight;
and noticing that the mighty car warriors of the Somakas had been vanquished—
reflected a little and ordered the troops to withdraw.
And the Kuru forces also withdrew at the same time.
Afflicted by the shafts of Bhishma, and reflecting on that hero's feats in battle,
the Pandavas had no peace of mind. Bhishma also, having vanquished
the Pandavas and the Srinjayas in battle, was worshipped by the Kurus
and glorified by them. Then, in that first hour of night, the Pandavas, the Vrishnis,
and the invincible Srinjayas sat down for a consultation.
All those mighty persons coolly deliberated about what could be beneficial to
them
in view of their immediate circumstances. King Yudhishthira, having reflected
for a time,
said: "Behold, O Krishna, the high-souled Bhishma of fierce prowess.
He crushes my troops, like an elephant crushing a forest of reeds.
We dare not even look at him. Like a raging conflagration, he licks up my troops.
The valiant Bhishma, when excited with wrath in battle, and bow in hand,
becomes as fierce as the mighty Naga Takshaka of virulent poison.
Indeed, the angry Yama is capable of being vanquished,
or even the chief of the celestials, armed with the thunder,
or Varuna himself, noose in hand, or the lord of the Yakshas, armed with his mace.
But Bhishma, excited with wrath, is incapable of being vanquished in battle.

When this is the case, O Krishna, I am, through the weakness of my
    understanding,
plunged into an ocean of grief, having Bhishma as a foe. I will retire into the
    woods.
My exile would be for my benefit. I no longer desire battle. Bhishma slays us
    always.
As an insect, by rushing into a blazing fire, meets only with death,
                            even so do I rush against Bhishma.
In putting forth prowess for the sake of my kingdom, I am led to destruction.
My brothers have all been afflicted with arrows.
In consequence of the affection they bear me, their eldest brother,
they had to go into the woods, deprived of the kingdom. For myself alone
has Krishna been sunk into such distress. I regard life to be of high value.
But life now seems difficult to save. If I live, the remnant of my life I will pass
in the practice of virtue. If, with my brothers, O Krishna, I am worthy of your
    favor,
tell me what is for my benefit without contravening the duties of my order."
Hearing these words of his, Krishna, from compassion, said in reply:
"Do not indulge in sorrow, you who have these invincible heroes for your
    brothers.
Arjuna and Bhimasena are both endowed with the energy of wind and fire.
The twin sons of Madri also are both as valiant as the chief of the celestials.
From the good understanding that exists between us, you set me also to this task.
I will fight with Bhishma. Directed by you, O great king,
what is there that I may not do in battle? Challenging Bhishma, I will slay him in
    battle
in sight of the Kurus, if Arjuna does not wish to slay him.
If you see victory to be certain after the slaughter of the heroic Bhishma,
on a single car I will slay that aged grandsire.
I will overthrow from his car that warrior, who always shoots mighty weapons.
He who is an enemy of the sons of Pandu is my enemy also.
Those who are yours, are mine, as those who are mine, are yours.
Your brother Arjuna is my friend, relative, and disciple.
I will, O king, cut off my own flesh and give it away for the sake of Arjuna.
And this tiger among men also would lay down his life for my sake.
This is our understanding—that we will protect each other.
Therefore, command me, O king, in what way I am to fight.
Formerly, at Upaplavya, Arjuna had, in the presence of many persons, vowed:
                          'I will slay the son of Ganga.'
These words of the intelligent Arjuna should be observed in practice.
Indeed, if Arjuna requests it of me, without doubt I will fulfill that vow.
Or let it be the task of Arjuna himself in battle. It is not onerous for him.
He will slay Bhishma, that subjugator of hostile cities.
Excited in battle, Arjuna can achieve feats of which no others are capable.
Arjuna can slay in battle the very gods exerting themselves
along with the Daityas and the Danavas.
What need be said of Bhishma, therefore, O king?

Endowed with great energy, Bhishma is now of perverted judgment,
of decayed intelligence, and of little sense. He does not know what he should do."
Yudhishthira replied: "It is even as you say, Krishna.
All these together are not competent to bear your force.
I am sure of always having whatever I desire, when I have you on my side.
I would conquer the very gods, with Indra at their head, when I have you for my
 protector.
What need I say, therefore, of Bhishma, though he is a mighty car warrior?
But, O Krishna, I dare not, for my own glorification, falsify your words.
Therefore, render me aid, as you promised before, without fighting for me.
In this battle an agreement was made by me with Bhishma.
He said: 'I will give you counsel, but I shall never fight for you,
since I shall have to fight for Duryodhana's sake.'
Therefore, Bhishma may give me sovereignty by giving me good counsel.
Therefore, all of us, accompanied by you, will once more repair unto Devavrata
to ask him about the means of his own death.
All of us then, O best of persons, going to Bhishma without delay, will ask his
 advice.
He will give us beneficial counsel, and I will do in battle what he says.
Of austere vows, he will give us counsel and also victory. We were children and
 orphans.
By him were we reared. And him, our aged grandsire, I wish to slay—
him, the sire of our sire. O! shame on the profession of a Kshatriya."
Krishna answered Yudhishthira: "These words of yours, O king, are to my taste.
Bhishma is skilled in weapons. With only his glances he can consume the foe.
Go to that son of the oceangoing Ganga, and ask him about the means of his
 death.
He will certainly tell the truth."
Having thus deliberated, the heroic sons of Pandu and the valiant Krishna
all proceeded toward the abode of Bhishma, casting aside their coats of mail
and their weapons and then entering his tent. They all bowed to him and,
 worshipping him,
sought his protection. The Kuru grandsire then addressed them, saying:
"Welcome are you! Welcome are you, O Arjuna. Welcome to you, King
 Yudhishthira.
And to you, O Bhima. Welcome also to you twins. What am I to do to enhance
 your joy?
Even if it be exceedingly difficult, I will yet do it with all my soul."
To the son of Ganga, who thus spoke to them with such affection,
King Yudhishthira, with a cheerful heart said: "You are conversant with everything.
Tell us how we shall obtain victory and acquire sovereignty.
How may this destruction of creatures be stopped? Say all these things to me, O
 lord.
Tell us also the means of your own death. How can we fight against you in battle?
O grandsire, you do not give your foes even the most minute hole to pick in
 your defense.
You are seen in battle with your bow ever drawn to a circle.

When you take your shafts, when you aim them, and when you draw the bow,
none is able to mark. O slayer of hostile heroes, constantly smiting cars and steeds
and men and elephants, we behold you on your car, resembling a second sun.
What man is there who can vanquish you, scattering showers of arrows in battle
and causing great destruction?"
Shantanu's son said to the son of Pandu: "As long as I am alive, victory cannot be
    yours.
Truly do I say this to you. But after I am vanquished in the fight, you may have
    victory.
If, therefore, you desire victory in the battle, strike me down without delay.
I give you permission. Strike me as you please. I am thus known to you
in what I regard as a fortunate circumstance. After I am slain, all the rest will be
    slain.
                    Therefore, do as I bid."
Yudhishthira said: "Tell us the means by which we may vanquish you in battle,
you who are, when excited with wrath in the fight, like the destroyer himself
armed with his mace. The wielder of the thunderbolt may be vanquished,
or Varuna, or Yama. You, however, are incapable of being defeated in battle
by even the gods and Asuras united together, with Indra at their head."
Bhishma said: "What you say is true. When I have weapons and my large bow in
    hand
and I contend carefully in battle, I am incapable of being defeated by the very gods
and the Asuras, with Indra at their head. If, however, I lay aside my weapons,
even these car warriors can slay me. One who has thrown away his weapons,
one who has fallen down, one whose armor has slipped off, one whose standard
    is down,
one who is flying away, one who is frightened, one who says, 'I am yours,'
one who is female, one who bears the name of a female,
one who is no longer capable of taking care of himself, one who has only a
    single son,
or one who is a vulgar fellow—with these I do not like to battle.
Hear also of my resolve, formed long ago. Beholding any inauspicious omen,
I would never fight. That mighty car warrior, the son of Drupada,
whom you have in your army, who is known by the name of Sikhandin,
who is wrathful in battle, brave, and ever victorious,
was once female but later obtained manhood. How this took place, you all know.
Brave in battle and clad in mail, let Arjuna, keeping Sikhandin before him,
attack me with his sharp shafts. When that inauspicious omen will have appeared,
especially in the form of one who was once female, I will never seek,
though armed with bow and arrow, to strike him.
Obtaining that opportunity, let Arjuna pierce me on every side with his shafts.
Except for the highly blessed Krishna and Arjuna, I do not behold the person
in the three worlds who is able to slay me while I exert myself in battle.
Let Arjuna, therefore, armed with weapons, struggling carefully in battle,
with his excellent bow in hand, and placing Sikhandin or something else
    before him,
throw me down from my car. Then the victory will be certain.

Do, O great king, exactly what I have said to you.
You will then be able to slay all the Kauravas assembled together in battle."

✦

Saluting the Kuru grandsire, the Pandavas then went back to their tents.
Arjuna, burning with grief and his face suffused with shame, said:
"How, O Krishna, shall I fight in battle with the grandsire,
who is my senior in years, who is possessed of wisdom and intelligence,
and who is the oldest member of our race?
While sporting in days of childhood, I used to smear the body of this illustrious one
with dust by climbing on his lap with my own filthy body. He is the sire of my sire.
As a child, I once called him father, and he said, 'I am not your father
but your father's father!' How can I slay him? Let my army perish.
Whether it is victory or death that I obtain, I will never fight against him.
                         What do you think, O Krishna?"
Krishna said: "Having previously vowed the slaughter of Bhishma,
how can you now abstain from slaying him, as required by the duties of a
     Kshatriya?
Throw down from his car that Kshatriya who is invincible in battle.
Victory can never be yours without your slaying Ganga's son.
Even thus shall he go to the abode of Yama. This has been settled by the gods.
What has been destined must happen. It cannot be otherwise.
None except you, not even the wielder of the thunderbolt himself,
would be capable of fighting with Bhishma, who is like the destroyer
with wide-open mouth. Slay Bhishma without anxiety.
Listen also to these words of mine that are what Vrihaspati of great intelligence
said to Sakra in days of old: 'One should slay even an aged person
endowed with every merit and worthy of reverence if he comes as a foe.'
This is the eternal duty sanctioned for the Kshatriyas—that they should fight,
protect subjects, and perform sacrifices, all without malice."
Arjuna said: "Sikhandin will certainly be the cause of Bhishma's death,
for Bhishma, as soon as he beholds that prince of the Panchalas, will abstain
     from striking.
Therefore, keeping Sikhandin at our head, we will overthrow the son of Ganga.
I will hold in check the other great bowmen with my shafts.
Sikhandin will fight with Bhishma alone.
I have heard from that chief of the Kurus that he would not strike Sikhandin,
because he was born as a woman and only subsequently became a male person."

✦

Toward the hour of sunrise, with the beating of drums and cymbals and smaller
     drums,
and with the blare of conchs of milky whiteness, the Pandavas went out for battle.
They marched out in an array, destructive of all foes,
and Sikhandin was stationed in the very van of all the troops.

Bhimasena and Dhananjaya became the protectors of his car wheels.

And in his rear were the sons of Draupadi and the valiant Abhimanyu.

Those mighty car warriors Satyaki and Chekitana became the protectors of the
last.

Behind them was Dhrishtadyumna, protected by the Panchalas.

Next to Dhrishtadyumna marched the royal lord Yudhishthira,

accompanied by the twins and filling the air with leonine roars.

Next behind him was Virata, surrounded by his troops.

Next to him marched Drupada and the five Kaikeya brothers

and the valiant Dhrishtaketu, protecting the rear of the Pandava troops,

who rushed against the Kuru host and prepared to cast away their lives.

Similarly, the Kauravas, placing that mighty Bhishma at the head of their host,

proceeded against the Pandavas. Bhishma was protected by Dhritirashtra's
hundred sons.

Behind them was the great bowman Drona and his mighty son Aswatthaman.

Then came Bhagadatta, surrounded by his elephant division.

And behind him were Kripa and Kritavarman;

Sudakshina, the mighty ruler of the Kamvojas; Jayatsena, the king of the
Magadhas;

and Suvala's son and Vrihadvala. Similarly, many other kings, all great bowmen,

protected the rear of that host. As each day came, Bhishma formed arrays in
battle,

sometimes after the manner of the Asuras, sometimes after that of the Pisachas,

and sometimes after that of the Rakshasas. Then commenced the battle,

both parties smiting one another and increasing the population of Yama's
kingdom.

The Pandavas, with Arjuna at their head and with Sikhandin in the van,

proceeded against Bhishma, scattering diverse kinds of arrows.

And afflicted by Bhishma with his shafts, many Kuru warriors,

profusely bathed in blood, repaired to the other world.

Nakula and Sahadeva and the mighty car warrior Satyaki, approaching the
Kauravas,

afflicted their army with great vigor. Their warriors, unable to resist that vast host
of the Pandavas,

were slaughtered by them everywhere and fled in all directions.

With cheerful hearts, the brave sons of Pandu encountered Duryodhana's host,

slaughtering whomever they met. That carnage of human beings, elephants, and
steeds,

that destruction by the foe of the Kurus in battle, Bhishma could not endure.

Reckless of his very life, he poured on the Pandavas, the Panchalas, and the
Srinjayas

showers of long shafts and arrows with heads shaped like a calf's tooth or a
crescent.

And he checked with his shafts and with showers of other weapons,

both offensive and defensive, the five foremost car warriors of the Pandavas,

who had been struggling vigorously in battle. Excited with wrath,

he slaughtered in that battle countless elephants and steeds.

And throwing down many car warriors from their cars, and horsemen from their
  horses,
and crowds of foot soldiers, and elephant warriors from the backs of the beasts
  they rode,
Bhishma struck terror into the foe. The Pandava warriors all rushed together
  against him,
struggling in battle with great activity, like the Asuras rushing together
with the thunderbolt in hand. While Bhishma fought in that battle, his large bow,
resembling that of Sakra himself, seemed always to be drawn to a circle.
Beholding those feats, Dhritirashtra's sons, filled with wonder, worshipped the
  grandsire.
The Pandavas cast their eyes, with cheerless hearts, on the heroic Bhishma
struggling in battle like the celestials upon the Asura Viprachitti in days of old.
They could not resist that warrior, who then resembled the destroyer himself.
In that battle, on the tenth day, Bhishma, with his sharp shafts,
consumed the division of Sikhandin like a conflagration consuming a forest.
Sikhandin, resembling an angry snake of virulent poison, pierced him
with three shafts in the chest. Bhishma saw that it was Sikhandin who had done
  this.
Excited with wrath, but unwilling to fight with Sikhandin, Bhishma laughingly
  said:
"Whether you choose to strike me or not, I will never fight with you.
You are that Sikhandin which the creator had first made. You are still a woman."
Sikhandin, deprived of his senses by wrath, and licking the corners of his mouth,
addressed Bhishma, saying: "I know you to be the exterminator of the Kshatriya
  race.
I have heard also of your battle with Rama, Jamadagni's son.
I have heard much also of your superhuman prowess. But, doing what is agreeable
to the Pandavas and what is agreeable to myself, I will today fight with you in
  battle,
and I will of a certainty slay you. I swear this!
Hearing these words of mine, do what you should.
Whether you choose to strike me or not, you shall not escape with your life.
                    O Bhishma, look your last on this world."
Having said this, Sikhandin, having already wounded him with his verbal arrows,
                    pierced Bhishma with five straight shafts.
The mighty Arjuna, regarding Sikhandin as Bhishma's destroyer,
urged him on, saying: "I will fight behind you, routing the foe with my shafts.
Excited with fury, rush against Bhishma of terrible prowess.
The mighty Bhishma will not be able to afflict you in battle.
Therefore, O mighty-armed one, encounter Bhishma with vigor.
If you return without slaying Bhishma, you will be an object of ridicule to the
  world,
as will I. Seek to do that in battle by which we may not incur scorn. Slay the
  grandsire.
Drona, and Drona's son, and Kripa, and Suyodhana, and Chitrasena, and
  Vikarna,

and Jayadratha the ruler of the Sindhus, Vinda and Anuvinda of Avanti,
and Sudakshina the ruler of the Kamvojas, and the brave Bhagadatta,
and the mighty king of the Magadhas, and Somadatta's son,
and the brave Rakshasa who is Rishyasringa's son, and the ruler of the Trigartas
along with all the other great car warriors of the Kurus
I will check, like the continent resisting the surging sea.
Indeed, I will hold in check all the mighty warriors of the Kuru army assembled
  together.
                          You just slay the grandsire."
For ten days, while fighting in that battle, neither the bow nor the car of
  Bhishma
had suffered any injury. He had been slaying the foe with straight shafts.
Many thousands of mighty Kuru car warriors and elephants and steeds well
  harnessed
had proceeded to battle, with Bhishma in the van.
The Panchalas and the Pandavas had been unable to bear that great bowman's
  prowess
as he battled them and slew his foes with his shafts.
By the tenth day, the hostile army had been torn into pieces by Bhishma
with his shafts by the hundreds and thousands.
The sons of Pandu had been incapable of defeating the great Bhishma in battle.
Then the unvanquished Arjuna arrived, frightening all the car warriors.
Roaring like a lion, and repeatedly drawing his bowstring
and scattering showers of arrows, Arjuna careered on the battlefield like death
  himself.
The Kurus fled in terror. Duryodhana, himself terrified, said to Bhishma:
"That son of Pandu, with white steeds yoked to his car and with Krishna as his
  charioteer,
consumes all my troops, like a conflagration consuming a forest.
Behold all our troops, slaughtered in battle, who are fleeing.
As the herdsman belabors his cattle in the forest, even so is my army belabored.
Broken and driven away on all sides by Arjuna,
the invincible Bhima is also routing this already broken host of mine.
And Satyaki and Chekitana and the twin sons of Madri
and the valiant Abhimanyu are also routing my troops.
The brave Dhrishtadyumna and the Rakshasa Ghatotkacha also
are vigorously breaking and driving away my army.
I do not see any other refuge save you, O tiger among men,
              who are possessed of prowess equal to that of the celestials."
The son of Shantanu reflected for a moment and, settling what he should do,
  said:
"O Duryodhana, listen calmly to what I say. Formerly I vowed before you
that every day, slaying ten thousand Kshatriyas, I would come back from the battle.
I have fulfilled that vow! Today I will achieve an even greater feat.
Today I will either sleep, myself having been slain, or will slay the Pandavas.
I will today free myself from the debt I owe you, arising out of the food you
  gave me,

casting away my life at the head of your army." Having said these words,
that invincible warrior attacked the Pandava host.
And the Pandavas then resisted the son of Ganga, who was in the midst of his
forces
and excited with wrath like a snake of virulent poison.
On that tenth day of the battle, Bhishma, displaying his might,
slew hundreds of thousands and drained the energies of those royal car warriors
who were foremost among the Pandavas,
like the sun sucking up the moisture of the earth with his rays.
Having slain ten thousand elephants of great activity, and ten thousand steeds
also
along with their riders, and a full two hundred thousands of foot soldiers,
Bhishma shone resplendent in battle, like a fire without a curl of smoke.
No one among the Pandavas was capable even of looking at him,
who then resembled the burning sun at the northern solstice.
The Pandavas, however, though afflicted in battle by that great bowman,
still rushed ahead, accompanied by the mighty car warriors of the Srinjayas,
to try to slaughter him. Battling with myriads upon myriads around him,
Bhishma then looked like the cliff of Meru, covered on all sides with masses of
clouds.
The Kurus, however, stood fast, surrounding Bhishma on all sides
with a large force to protect him against the Pandavas.

35

Akampana

Having penetrated into the Kaurava array by means of his sharp shafts,
Abhimanyu, son of Arjuna, made all the kings turn away from the fight.
Then Drona and Kripa and Karna and Drona's son and Vrihadvala
and Kritavarman, the son of Hridika—these six car warriors encompassed him.
The other combatants of the Kuru army, seeing that Jayadratha, king of the Sindhus,
had taken upon himself the heavy duty of fending off the Pandavas,
supported him by rushing against Yudhishthira. Many among them, drawing their bows
full six cubits long, showered on the heroic Abhimanyu downpours of arrows.
That slayer of hostile heroes, however, paralyzed with his shafts all those great bowmen.
He pierced Drona with fifty arrows and Vrihadvala with twenty,
and Kritavarman with eighty shafts and Kripa with sixty.
And he pierced Drona's son Aswatthaman with ten arrows equipped with golden wings,
endowed with great speed, and shot from his bow drawn to its fullest stretch.
And the son of Arjuna pierced Karna—in the midst of his foes, on one of his cars—
with a bright, well-tempered, bearded arrow of great force.
Felling the steeds yoked to Kripa's car, as also both his Parshni charioteers,
Abhimanyu pierced Kripa himself in the center of the chest with ten arrows.
The mighty Abhimanyu then, in sight of Dhritarashtra's heroic sons,
slew the brave Vrindaraka, that enhancer of the fame of the Kurus.
While Abhimanyu was thus engaged in slaying one after another of those foremost warriors,
Drona's son Aswatthaman pierced him with five and twenty small arrows.
The son of Arjuna, however, in sight of all the Dhartarashtras,
quickly pierced Aswatthaman in return with many whetted shafts.
Drona's son, however, in return pierced Abhimanyu
with sixty fierce arrows of great impetuosity and keen sharpness
but failed to make him tremble, for the latter stood immovable, like the Mainaka mountain.
Endowed with great energy, the mighty Abhimanyu then pierced his antagonist
with three and seventy straight arrows equipped with wings of gold.

Drona, desirous of rescuing his son, then pierced Abhimanyu with a hundred
  arrows.

And Aswatthaman pierced him with sixty arrows, to rescue his father.

And Karna struck him with two and twenty broad-headed arrows,

and Kritavarman struck him with four and ten. And Vrihadvala pierced him with
  fifty

and Saradwata's son, Kripa, pierced Abhimanyu with ten. Abhimanyu, however,

pierced each of these in return with ten shafts. The ruler of the Kosalas struck
  Abhimanyu

in the chest with a barbed arrow. Abhimanyu, however, quickly felled

his antagonist's steeds and standard and bow and charioteer.

The ruler of the Kosalas, thus deprived of his car, took up a sword

and wished to sever Abhimanyu's head from his trunk.

Abhimanyu then pierced King Vrihadvala, the ruler of the Kosalas, in the chest

with a strong arrow. The latter, with riven heart, fell down.

Beholding this, ten thousand illustrious kings broke and fled.

Those kings, armed with swords and bows, ran away,

uttering words inimical to King Duryodhana.

Having thus slain Vrihadvala, the son of Subhadra careered in battle,

paralyzing the Kuru warriors with downpours of arrows as thick as rain.

Arjuna's son once again pierced Karna with a barbed arrow

and, to anger him still further, pierced him with fifty more shafts.

Karna pierced Abhimanyu in return with as many shafts.

Abhimanyu, covered all over with arrows, then looked exceedingly beautiful.

Filled with rage, he caused Karna also to be bathed in blood.

Mangled with arrows and covered with blood, the brave Karna also shone greatly.

Both those illustrious warriors resembled a pair of flowering kinsukas.

The son of Subhadra then slew six of Karna's brave counselors, conversant with
  all modes of warfare,

with their steeds and charioteers and cars. As regards other great bowmen,

fearless Abhimanyu pierced each of them in return with ten arrows.

That feat of his seemed highly wonderful.

Slaying next the son of the ruler of the Magadhas,

Abhimanyu, with six straight shafts, slew the youthful Aswaketu,

with his four steeds and charioteer. Then, dispatching with a sharp razor-headed
  arrow

the Bhoja prince of Martikavata, bearing the device of an elephant on his banner,

the son of Arjuna uttered a loud shout and began to scatter his shafts on all sides.

Then the son of Duhsasana pierced the four steeds of Abhimanyu with four shafts,

his charioteer with one, and Abhimanyu himself with ten.

The son of Arjuna, piercing Duhsasana's son with ten fleet shafts,

addressed him in a loud tone and, his eyes red with wrath, said:

"Your sire has fled like a coward. It is well that you know how to fight.

You shall not, however, escape today with your life."

Abhimanyu then sped a long arrow, well polished by a smith's hand, at his foe.

The son of Drona cut that arrow with three shafts of his own.

Arjuna's son, leaving Aswatthaman alone, struck Salya in return, fearlessly piercing him in the chest with nine shafts equipped with vulture's feathers.

The son of Arjuna then cut off Salya's bow and slew both his Parshni charioteers.

Abhimanyu then pierced Salya himself with six shafts made wholly of iron.

Thereupon the latter, leaving that steedless car, mounted another.

Abhimanyu then slew five warriors named Satrunjaya and Chandraketu and Mahamegba and Suvarchas and Suryabhasa.

He then pierced Suvala's son. The latter pierced Abhimanyu with three arrows and said to Duryodhana: "Let us all together grind this one, or else, fighting singly with us, he will slay us all. O king, think of the means of slaying this one, taking counsel with Drona and Kripa and others." Then Karna, the son of Vikartana, said to Drona: "Abhimanyu grinds us all. Tell us the means by which we may slay him."

Drona answered: "Observing him with vigilance, have any of you been able to find any defect in this youth? He careens in all directions.

Yet have any of you been able to detect today the least weakness in him?

Behold the lightness of hand and quickness of motion of this lion among men, this son of Arjuna. In the track of his car, only his bow drawn to a circle can be seen, so quickly does he aim his shafts and so quickly does he let them go.

Indeed, this slayer of hostile heroes gratifies me, although he afflicts my vital breath and stupefies me with shafts.

Even the mightiest car warriors, filled with wrath, are unable to detect any flaw in him.

I do not see that in battle there is any difference between the wielder of the Gandiva himself and this one, of great lightness of hand, filling all points of the horizon with his shafts."

Karna once more said to Drona: "Afflicted with the shafts of Abhimanyu, I am staying in battle only because it is my duty as a warrior.

Indeed, the arrows of this youth of great energy are exceedingly fierce.

Possessed of the energy of fire, they are weakening my heart."

Then the preceptor, slowly and with a smile, said to Karna:

"Abhimanyu is young. His prowess is great. His coat of mail is impenetrable.

This one's father had been taught by me the method of wearing defensive armor.

This subjugator of hostile towns assuredly knows the entire science of armor.

With shafts well shot, you can, however, cut off his bow, his bowstring, the reins of his steeds, the steeds themselves, and two Parshni charioteers.

Making him, by this means, turn back from the fight, strike him then.

With his bow in hand, he is incapable of being vanquished by the very gods and the Asuras together. If you wish, deprive him of his car and divest him of his bow." Hearing these words of the preceptor, Karna quickly cut off, by means of his shafts, the bow of Abhimanyu as the latter was shooting with great activity.

Kritavarman then slew Abhimanyu's steeds, and Kripa slew his two Parshni
    charioteers.
The others covered him with showers of arrows after he had been divested of
    his bow.
Those six great car warriors—with great speed, when speed was so necessary—
ruthlessly covered with showers of arrows that carless youth fighting single-
    handed with them.
Bowless and carless, but mindful of his duty,
handsome Abhimanyu, taking up a sword and a shield, jumped into the sky.
Displaying great strength and great activity, and describing the tracks
called Kausika and others, the son of Arjuna fiercely coursed through the sky,
                        like the prince of winged creatures, Garuda.
He may fall upon me sword in hand, each of those mighty bowmen thought,
and they were on the lookout for Abhimanyu and pierced him, gazing upward.
Then Drona, with a sharp arrow, quickly cut off the hilt, decked with gems,
of Abhimanyu's sword. Radha's son Karna, with sharp shafts, cut off his excellent
    shield.
Deprived of his sword and shield, Abhimanyu came back down, with sound
    limbs, to earth.
Then, taking up a car wheel, he rushed in wrath against Drona.
Bright with the dust of car wheels, and holding the car wheel in his upraised arms,
Abhimanyu looked exceedingly beautiful, and, imitating Krishna with his discus,
he became awfully fierce for a while in that battle.
His robes dyed with the blood flowing from his wounds, his brow formidable
with the wrinkles on it, and uttering loud leonine roars, Abhimanyu
of immeasurable might looked exceedingly resplendent on the field of battle.
With the ends of his locks waving in the air, and with that supreme weapon in his
    upraised arms,
his body became incapable of being looked at by the very gods.
The kings, beholding both his body and the wheel in his arms, were filled with
    anxiety
and cut the wheel into a hundred fragments. Then the son of Arjuna took up a
    mace.
Deprived by the kings of his bow and car and sword, and divested also of his
    wheel,
the mighty armed Abhimanyu, mace in hand, rushed against Aswatthaman.
Beholding that mace upraised, which looked like a blazing thunderbolt,
Aswatthaman, that tiger among men, rapidly alit from his car
and took three long leaps to avoid Abhimanyu.
Slaying Aswatthaman's steeds and two Parshni charioteers with that mace of his,
Subhadra's son, pierced all over with arrows, looked like a porcupine.
Then that hero pressed Suvala's son, Kalikeya, down into the earth
and slew seven and seventy of his Gandhara followers.
Next he slew ten car warriors of the Brahma-Vasatiya race, and then ten huge
    elephants.
Proceeding next toward the car of Duhsasana's son,
he crushed the latter's car and steeds, pressing them down into the earth.

Then the invincible son of Duhsasana, taking up his mace,
                    rushed at Abhimanyu, saying: "Wait! Wait!"
Then those cousins, those two heroes, with upraised maces began to strike each
    other,
each trying to achieve the other's death, like three-eyed Mahadeva
and the Asura Andhaka in days of old. Each of those chastisers of foes,
struck with the other's mace ends, fell to earth,
like two uprooted standards erected to the honor of Indra.
Then Duhsasana's son, that enhancer of the fame of the Kurus,
rising up first, struck Abhimanyu with the mace on the crown of his head,
just as the latter was on the point of rising. Stupefied by the violence of that
    stroke,
as also by the fatigue he had undergone, that slayer of hostile hosts fell to earth,
deprived of his senses. Thus was slain in battle one by many,
one who had ground the whole army, like an elephant grinding lotus stalks in a
    lake.
As he lay dead on the field, the heroic Abhimanyu looked like a wild elephant
slain by hunters. The fallen hero was then surrounded by Kuru troops.
And he looked like an extinguished fire in the summer season
after having consumed a whole forest, or like a tempest divested of its fury
after having crushed mountain crests, or like the sun arrived at the western hills
after having blasted the earth with his heat, or like Soma swallowed up by Rahu,
or like the ocean bereft of water. The mighty car warriors of the Kaurava army—
beholding Abhimanyu, whose face had the splendor of the full moon
and whose eyes were rendered beautiful by lashes as black as the feathers of the
    raven,
lying prostrate on the bare earth—were filled with great joy.
They uttered leonine shouts. Indeed, they were in transports of joy,
               while tears fell fast from the eyes of the Pandava heroes.
Beholding the heroic Abhimanyu lying on the field of battle,
like the moon dropped from the firmament,
various creatures said aloud: "Alas, this one lies on the field, slain while fighting
    singly
by six mighty car warriors of the Kuru army, headed by Drona and Karna.
               This act has been an unrighteous one."
Upon the slaughter of that hero, the earth looked resplendent,
like the star-bespangled firmament with the moon, strewn as it was with shafts
equipped with wings of gold, and covered with waves of blood.
And scattered everywhere were the beautiful heads of heroes
bedecked with earrings and variegated turbans of great value,
and banners, and yak tails, and beautiful blankets,
and weapons of great efficacy set with gems, and the bright ornaments of cars
    and steeds,
and men, and elephants, and sharp and well-tempered swords
looking like snakes freed from their old skins,
and bows, and broken shafts, and darts, and lances,
and diverse other kinds of weapons. It was a beautiful prospect.

And because of the steeds, dead or dying but all covered in blood,
with their riders lying about them, the earth in many places was impassable.
With iron hooks, and elephants equipped with shields, and weapons, and
    standards
lying about crushed with shafts, and with excellent cars
deprived of steeds, and charioteers, and car warriors lying scattered on the earth,
crushed by elephants and looking like agitated lakes,
and with large bodies of foot soldiers decked with diverse weapons lying dead on
    the ground,
                        the field of battle inspired all timid hearts with terror.
Beholding Abhimanyu lying on the ground, the Kuru troops were in transports
    of joy,
while the Pandavas were filled with grief. When the youthful Abhimanyu fell,
the Pandava divisions fled in sight of King Yudhishthira.
Seeing his army break up, Yudhishthira addressed his brave warriors, saying:
"The heroic Abhimanyu, who without retreating from battle has been slain,
has surely ascended to heaven. Stay, then, and fear not, for we shall vanquish our
    foes."
King Yudhishthira, saying such words to his grief-stricken soldiers,
endeavored to dispel their stupor. The king continued: "Having in the first
    instance
slain in battle hostile princes resembling snakes of virulent poison,
the son of Arjuna has given up his life. Having slain ten thousand warriors,
Abhimanyu, king of the Kosalas, who was even like Krishna or Arjuna himself,
has assuredly gone to the abode of Indra. Having destroyed cars and steeds
    and men
and elephants by the thousands, he was not yet content with what he had done.
We certainly should not grieve for him who has performed such meritorious feats.
He has gone to the bright regions of the righteous,
                        regions men acquire by meritorious deeds."

◆

After the slaughter of that hero, the Pandava warriors,
leaving their cars and putting off their armor and throwing aside their bows,
sat surrounding King Yudhishthira and brooded over their grief,
their hearts fixed on the deceased. Indeed, King Yudhishthira, overwhelmed
    with sadness
at the fall of Abhimanyu, that heroic nephew of his,
indulged in these lamentations: "Alas, Abhimanyu, from desire of achieving my
    good,
pierced the array formed by Drona and teeming with his soldiers.
Encountering him in battle, mighty bowmen endowed with great courage,
accomplished in weapons, and incapable of being easily defeated in battle
were routed and forced to retreat. Abhimanyu, meeting our implacable foe
    Duhsasana in battle,
caused that warrior to fly from the field, deprived of his senses.

Alas, the heroic son of Arjuna, having crossed the vast sea of Drona's army,
was ultimately obliged to become a guest of Yama's abode.
Now that Abhimanyu is slain, how shall I cast my eyes on Arjuna
and also on the blessed Subhadra, deprived of her favorite son?
What senseless, disjointed, and improper words shall we have to say today
to Hrishikesa and Dhananjaya? Desirous of achieving what is good,
and expecting victory, it is I who have done this great evil to Subhadra
and Krishna and Arjuna. He who is covetous never beholds his faults.
Covetousness springs from folly. Collectors of honey see not the fall that is
    before them.
I am even like them. He who was only a child, and who should have been provided
with good food, with vehicles, with beds, and with ornaments,
alas, even he was placed by us in the van of battle. How could good come
to a child of tender years, unskilled in battle, in such a situation of great danger?
Like a horse of proud mettle, he sacrificed himself instead of refusing
to do the bidding of his master. Alas, we also shall lay ourselves down on the bare
    earth,
blasted by the glances of grief cast by Arjuna filled with wrath.
Arjuna: liberal, intelligent, modest, forgiving, handsome, mighty,
possessed of well-developed and beautiful limbs, respectful to superiors,
heroic, beloved, and devoted to truth—the very gods applaud his feats.
That valiant hero slew the Nivatakavachas and the Kalakeyas,
those enemies of Indra having their abode in Hiranyapura.
In the twinkling of an eye he slew the Paulomas, with all their followers.
Endowed with great might, he grants quarter to implacable enemies asking for
    quarter!
Alas, we could not protect today the son of even such a person from danger.
A great fear has overtaken the Kauravas, endowed though they be with strength.
Enraged by the slaughter of his son, Arjuna will exterminate them.
It is evident also that the mean-minded Duryodhana,
that destroyer of his own race and partisans, having mean counselors,
will, beholding this extermination of the Kaurava army, give up his life in grief.
As I behold this son of Indra's son, of unrivaled energy and prowess on the field
    of battle,
neither victory nor sovereignty nor immortality nor abode with the celestials
                                    causes me the least delight!"
While Yudhishthira was indulging in such lamentations,
the great rishi Vyasa came to him. Yudhishthira, duly worshipping Vyasa and
    inviting him to be seated,
said: "Alas, while battling with many mighty bowmen,
the son of Subhadra, surrounded by several great car warriors
of unrighteous propensities, has been slain on the field.
The son of Subhadra was a child in years, and of childish understanding.
He fought in battle against desperate odds. I asked him to open a passage for us
    in battle.
He penetrated within the hostile army, but we could not follow him,
obstructed by the ruler of the Sindhus. Alas, those who devote themselves to battle

as a profession always fight with antagonists equally circumstanced.
This battle, however, that the enemy fought with Abhimanyu was an unequal one.
It is that which grieves me and prompts my tears.

           Thinking of this, I fail to regain peace of mind."

The illustrious Vyasa, addressing Yudhishthira thus unmanned by sorrow,
said: "O Yudhishthira, you who are master of all branches of knowledge,
persons like you never suffer themselves to be stupefied by calamity.
This brave youth, having slain numerous foes, has ascended to heaven.
Indeed, that best of persons, though a child, acted like one of mature years.
O Yudhishthira, this law is incapable of being transgressed:
death takes all—gods, Dhanavas, and Gandharvas—without exception."
Yudhishthira said: "Alas, these lords of earth who lie on the bare earth,
slain in the midst of their forces, bereft of consciousness, were possessed of great
    might.
Others of their class possessed strength equal to that of ten thousand elephants.
Others again were endowed with the impetuosity and might of the very wind.
They have all perished in battle, slain by men of their own class.
Endowed with great prowess, they were possessed of energy and might.
Alas, they who used to come to battle with the hope firmly implanted in their
    hearts
that they would conquer—even they, possessed of great wisdom, are lying on the
    field,
struck with weapons and deprived of life. The significance of the word *death*
has today been made intelligible, for these lords of earth, of terrible prowess, are
    all dead.
Those heroes, lying motionless and bereft of vanity, have succumbed to foes.
Many princes, filled with wrath, have been victimized by the fire of their
    enemies' wrath.
A great puzzlement seizes me. From where does death come? Whose offspring is
    death?
What is death? Why does death take away creatures?

           O Vyasa, O you who resemble a god, tell me this."

The illustrious rishi, comforting Yudhishthira, said:
"The answer, O king, is in this ancient story of what Narada had said long ago
to King Akampana. While in this world, the king was afflicted with unbearable
    grief
on account of the death of his son. I will now tell you his story
and the story of the origin of death. Having listened to it, you will be freed from
    sorrow
and the touch of affection's tie. This story extends the period of life,
kills grief, and is conducive to health. It is sacred, destructive of large bodies of
    foes,
and auspicious among all auspicious things. Indeed, this story is as the study of
    the Vedas.
It should be heard every morning by those foremost among kings
who are desirous of long-lived children and of their own good.
In days of old, O sire, there was a king named Akampana.

Once, on the field of battle, he was surrounded by his foes and nearly
overpowered.
He had a son called Hari, equal to Narayana himself in might,
who was exceedingly handsome, accomplished in weapons, gifted with great
intelligence,
and possessed of might, and who resembled Indra himself in battle.
Surrounded by countless foes on the field of battle, Hari sped thousands of shafts
at those warriors and at their elephants. Having achieved the most difficult feats
in battle,
that scorcher of foes was at last slain in the midst of the army.
Performing the obsequies of his son, King Akampana cleansed himself.
Grieving for his son day and night, the king failed to regain happiness of mind.
Informed of the king's grief on account of the death of his son, the celestial rishi
Narada
came into his presence. The blessed king, beholding the celestial rishi,
told the latter everything that had happened to him—his defeat at the hands of
his foes
and the slaughter of his son. And the king said: 'My son was endowed with great
energy
and equaled Indra or Vishnu himself in splendor. That mighty son of mine,
having displayed his prowess on the field against countless foes, was at last slain!
O illustrious one, who is this death? What is the measure of his energy,
strength, and prowess? I desire to hear all this truly.'
Hearing these words, Narada recited the following elaborate history,
destructive of grief on account of a son's death. Narada said:
'In the beginning, the grandsire Brahma created all creatures.
Endowed with mighty energy, he saw that the creation bore no signs of decay.
Therefore, the creator began to think about the destruction of the universe.
Reflecting on the matter, the creator failed to find any means of destruction.
He then became angry, and because of his anger a fire sprang from the sky.
That fire spread in all directions, consuming everything in the universe.
Heaven, sky, and earth—all became filled with fire.
And thus the creator began to consume the whole mobile and immobile
universe,
and all creatures, mobile and immobile, were destroyed.
Indeed, the mighty Brahma, frightening everything with the force of his wrath,
did all this.
Then Hara—otherwise called Sthanu or Shiva, with matted locks on his head,
that lord of all wanderers of the night—appealed to the divine Brahma,
the lord of the gods. When Shiva fell at Brahma's feet, wanting to do good to all
creatures,
the supreme deity said to that greatest of ascetics: "What wish of yours
shall we accomplish for you, who deserve to have all your wishes fulfilled?
You were born of our wish! We shall do all that may be agreeable to you!
Tell us your wish."
Shiva said: "O lord, you took great care in creating diverse creatures.
Indeed, creatures of diverse kinds were created and reared by you.

Those very creatures are now being consumed by your fire.
Seeing this, I am filled with compassion. O illustrious lord, be inclined to grace."
Brahma said: "I had no desire of destroying the universe.
I desired good for the earth, and it was for this that wrath possessed me.
The goddess Earth, afflicted with the heavy weight of creatures,
urged me to destroy the creatures on her. I could not, however, find any means
for the destruction of the infinite creation. At this, wrath possessed me."
Shiva said: "Be inclined to grace, O lord of the universe.
Do not cherish your wrath for the destruction of creatures.
Let no more creatures, immobile or mobile, be destroyed.
Through your grace, O illustrious one, maintain the threefold universe
of the future, the past, and the present. You, O Lord, blazed up with wrath.
From your wrath, a substance like fire sprang into existence.
That fire is even now blasting rocks and trees and rivers and all kinds of herbs
      and grasses.
Indeed, that fire is exterminating the immobile and the mobile universe
and reducing it to ashes. Be inclined to grace, O illustrious one!
Do not give way to wrath. This is the boon I solicit.
Let your wrath be annihilated in yourself.
Inspired with the desire of doing your creatures good, cast your eye on them.
Do that by which creatures endowed with life may not cease to be.
Let these creatures, with their productive powers weakened, not be exterminated.
O Creator of the worlds, you have appointed me their protector,
                    and for this reason I say these words to you." '
Narada continued: 'Hearing these words of Shiva, the divine Brahma,
from desire of benefiting creatures, held his wrath that had been roused within
      himself.
Extinguishing the fire, the divine benefactor of the world, the great master,
declared the duties of production and emancipation.
And while the supreme deity exterminated that fire born of his wrath,
there came out from the doors of his diverse senses a female
who was dark and red and tawny, whose tongue and face and eyes were red,
and who was decked with two brilliant earrings and diverse other brilliant
      ornaments.
Issuing from his body, she looked at those two lords of the universe
and then set out for the southern quarter. Then Brahma, that controller
of the creation and destruction of the worlds, called her by the name of Death.
And Brahma said to her: "Slay these creatures of mine!
You were born of that wrath of mine, which I cherished for the destruction of
      the universe.
At my command, kill all creatures, including idiots and seers.
                    By doing this, you will be benefited."
The lotus lady called Death reflected deeply and wept aloud in melodious accents.
The grandsire caught with his two hands the tears she shed,
for the benefit of all creatures, and he comforted her.'
Narada continued: 'The helpless lady, suppressing her sorrow within herself,
addressed, with joined hands, the lord of the creation,

bending with humility like a creeper. She said: "O foremost among speakers,
how shall I, created by you and being a female, commit such a cruel and evil act,
knowing it to be cruel and evil? I fear unrighteousness greatly.
O divine lord, be inclined to grace. Sons and friends and brothers and sires and
    husbands
are always dear. If I kill them, they who will suffer those losses will seek to
    injure me.
It is this that I fear. The tears that will fall from the eyes
of woe-stricken and weeping persons inspire me with fear, O lord!
I seek your protection. O divine being, I will not go to Yama's abode.
O boon-giving one, I implore you for your grace, bowing my head and joining
    my palms.
O grandsire of the worlds, I solicit the accomplishment of this wish at your hands!
I desire, with your permission, to undergo ascetic penances. O lord of created
    things,
grant me this boon, O divine being, O great master!
With your permission, I will go to the excellent ashram of Dhenuka!
Engaged in adoring yourself, I will undergo the severest austerities there,
but I will not be able, O lord of the gods, to take away the dear life's breath
of living creatures weeping in sorrow. Protect me from unrighteousness."
Brahma said: "O Death, you were intended for achieving the destruction of
    creatures.
Go, destroy all creatures. You need have no scruples. This must be;
it cannot be otherwise. Do as I command. Nobody in the world will find fault
    in you." '
Narada continued: 'Thus addressed, that lady became very much frightened.
Looking at Brahma's face, she stood with joined hands. Desiring to do good to
    creatures,
she could not set her heart on their destruction. The divine Brahma also,
that lord of the lord of all creatures, remained silent.
And soon the grandsire became pleased with himself.
Casting his eyes over all the creation, he smiled.
And thereupon creatures continued to live as before, unaffected by premature
    death.
And now that the invincible and illustrious lord had shaken off his wrath,
the damsel left his presence without having agreed to destroy creatures.
The damsel called Death speedily proceeded to the retreat called Dhenuka,
where she practiced excellent and highly austere vows. She stood there on one leg
for sixteen billions of years, and fifty billions also,
through pity for living creatures and from desire of doing them good,
all the time restraining her senses from their favorite objects.
And once again she stood there on one leg for one and twenty times ten billion
    years.
And then she wandered for ten times ten thousand billion years
with the creatures of the earth. Next, repairing to the sacred Nanda,
which was full of cool and pure water, she passed in those waters eight thousand
    years

and cleansed herself of all her sins. Then she proceeded first of all to the sacred
  Kausiki.

Living on air and water only, she practiced austerities there.

Repairing then to Panchaganga and next to Vetasa,

that cleansed damsel, by diverse kinds of special austerities, emaciated her own
  body.

Going next to the Ganga and thence to the great Meru,

she remained motionless as a stone, suspending her life's breath.

From there, going to the top of Himavat, where the gods had performed their
  sacrifices

in days of yore, that amiable and auspicious girl remained for a billion years,

standing on one toe only. Wending then to Pushkara and Gokarna

and Naimisha and Malaya, she emaciated her body, practicing austerities

agreeable to her heart. Without acknowledging any other god,

with steady devotion to the grandsire, she dedicated herself to the grandsire in
  every way.

Then the unchangeable creator of the worlds, gratified, said to her

with a softened heart: "O Death, why do you undergo austerities so severe?"

Death replied: "Creatures, O lord, are living in health. They do not injure one
  another

even by words. I shall not be able to slay them.

O lord, I desire this boon at your hands. I fear sin, and I am engaged in austerities.

O blessed one, undertake to remove forever my fears.

I am a woman in distress, and without fault. I beg you, be my protector."

The divine Brahman, acquainted with the past, the present, and the future, said:

"You shall commit no sin, O Death, by slaying these creatures.

My words can never be futile, O amiable one!

  Therefore, slay these creatures.

Eternal virtue shall always be yours. That regent of the world, Yama,

and the diverse diseases shall become your helpmates. I myself and all the gods

will grant you boons so that, freed from sin and perfectly cleansed,

you may acquire glory."

That lady, joining her hands, once more said:

"If, O Lord, this is not to be without me, then your command I place upon my
  head.

Listen, however, to what I say. Let covetousness, wrath, malice, jealousy, quarrel,
  folly,

shamelessness, and other stern passions tear the bodies of all embodied
  creatures."

Brahman said: "It will be, O Death, as you say. Meanwhile, slay creatures duly.

Sin shall not be yours, nor shall I seek to injure you, O auspicious one.

Those teardrops of yours that are in my hands will become diseases,

springing from living creatures themselves. They will kill men,

and if men are killed, sin shall not be yours. Therefore, do not fear.

Devoted to righteousness, and observant of your duty,

you shall hold sway over all creatures. Therefore, take the lives of these living
  creatures,

casting off both desire and wrath. Thus will eternal virtue be yours.

Sin will slay those who are of wicked behavior. By doing my bidding, cleanse
  yourself.

It will be yours to sink them in their sins who are wicked.

Therefore, cast off both desire and wrath, and kill these creatures endowed with
  life." '

Narada continued: 'That damsel, seeing that she was persistently called
by the name of Death, feared to act otherwise.

And in terror of Brahma's curse, she said yes to taking the lives of living creatures
when their time came. It is only living creatures that die.

Diseases spring from living creatures themselves.

Disease is the abnormal condition of creatures—they are pained by it.

Therefore, indulge not in fruitless grief for creatures after they are dead.

The senses, upon the death of creatures, go with them to the other world
and, achieving their respective functions, once more come back with them
when the creatures are reborn. Thus all creatures, the very gods included, going
  thither,
have to act like mortals.'

Then Narada said to King Akampana: 'The wind, which is awful, of terrible roars
  and great strength,
omnipresent and endowed with infinite energy, is the wind that will destroy
the bodies of living creatures. Even gods have the appellation of mortals
attached to them. Therefore, O lion among kings, do not grieve for your son!

Repairing to heaven, the son of your body is passing his days in perpetual
  happiness,
having obtained those delightful regions that are for heroes.

Casting off all sorrows, he has attained to the companionship of the righteous.

Death has been ordained by the creator himself for all creatures!

When their hour comes, creatures are destroyed. The death of creatures
arises from the creatures themselves. Creatures kill themselves.

Death does not kill anyone, armed with her bludgeon!

Therefore, they who are wise, knowing death to be inevitable and ordained by
  Brahma,
never grieve for the dead. Knowing this death to be ordained by the supreme god,
cast off, therefore, without delay, your grief for your dead son!' "

Vyasa continued: "Hearing these words of grave import spoken by Narada,

King Akampana, addressing his friend, said: 'O illustrious one, O foremost
  among rishis,
my grief is gone, and I am contented. Hearing this history from you,
I am grateful and I worship you.'

That foremost among superior rishis, that celestial ascetic of immeasurable soul,
thus addressed by the king, proceeded to the woods of Nandava.

The frequent recital of this history for the hearing of others
is regarded as cleansing, leading to fame and heaven and worthy of approbation.

Having listened to this instructive story, cast off your grief, O Yudhishthira,
reflecting on the duties of a Kshatriya and the state of blessedness attainable by
  heroes.

Abhimanyu, that mighty car warrior endowed with mighty energy,
having slain numerous foes before the gaze of all bowmen, has attained to
    heaven.
That great bowman, that mighty car warrior, struggling on the field,
has fallen in battle, struck with sword and mace and dart and bow.
Sprung from Soma, he has disappeared in the lunar essence, cleansed of
    impurities.
Therefore, mustering all your fortitude, you and your brothers,
without allowing your senses to be stupefied, set out, inflamed with rage, for
    battle."

36

The End of Bhishma

Arjuna covered with his straight shafts the mighty car warrior Salya,
who was struggling vigorously in battle. And he pierced Susarman and Kripa
with three arrows each. And in the battle with that car warrior,
Arjuna afflicted the Kuru host and struck the ruler of the Pragjyotishas,
and Jayadratha the king of the Sindhus, and Chitrasena, and Vikarna, and
    Kritavarman,
and Durmarshana, and the princes of Avanti, those two mighty warriors,
piercing each with three arrows winged with feathers of the kanka bird and the
    peacock.
Jayadratha, staying on the car of Chitrasena, pierced Arjuna in return
and then Bhima, too, without loss of time. Salya and Kripa both pierced Jishnu
with arrows capable of penetrating into the very vitals. Those sons of Kunti,
    however,
began in that battle to afflict the mighty host of the Trigartas.
Susarman in return pierced Arjuna with nine swift arrows and uttered a loud
    shout,
frightening the vast host of the Pandavas.
Other heroic car warriors pierced Bhimasena and Arjuna
with many straight-going arrows of keen points and golden wings.
Amid these car warriors, those two bulls of Bharata's race looked exceedingly
    beautiful.
They seemed to sport in the midst of the foe like two furious lions among a herd
    of cattle.
Cutting off in various ways the bows and arrows of many brave warriors,
they felled combatants by the hundreds upon hundreds.
Innumerable cars were broken, and steeds by the hundreds were slain,
and many elephants along with their riders were laid low on the field.
Car warriors and horsemen and elephant riders in large numbers,
deprived of life, were seen moving in convulsions all over the field.
The earth was covered with slain elephants, and foot soldiers in large bands,
and steeds deprived of life, and cars broken in diverse ways.
The prowess of Arjuna was amazing as, holding in check all those heroes,
he caused a great slaughter. Kripa and Kritavarman
and Jayadratha, the ruler of the Sindhus, and Vinda and Anuvinda of Avanti
did not forsake the battle. Then that great bowman Bhima

and that mighty car warrior Arjuna began in that battle to rout the fierce
Kaurava host.
The kings in that army quickly sped at Arjuna's car myriads upon myriads
and millions upon millions of arrows furnished with peacock feathers.
Arjuna, however, checking those arrows by means of his own volley of arrows,
sent those mighty car warriors to Yama's abode. The great car warrior Salya,
excited with wrath and as if sporting in that battle,
then struck Arjuna in the chest with some straight shafts of broad heads.
But Arjuna replied, cutting off with five shafts Salya's bow, and he pierced Salya
deeply
with many arrows of keen points. Taking up another bow that could bear a great
strain,
the ruler of the Madras then attacked Arjuna furiously with three arrows
and Krishna with five. And he struck Bhimasena in the arms and the chest
with nine arrows. Then Drona and the ruler of the Magadhas,
commanded by Duryodhana, both came to that spot where Arjuna and
Bhimasena
were slaughtering the mighty host of the Kuru king.
Jayatsena, the king of the Magadhas, pierced Bhima with eight sharp arrows,
and Bhima pierced him in return with ten and once more with five,
and with another broad-headed shaft he felled Jayatsena's charioteer from the car.
The steeds of his car, no longer restrained, ran wildly in all directions
and thus carried away the ruler of the Magadhas from battle, in sight of all the
troops.
Meanwhile, Drona, noticing an opening, pierced Bhimasena with eight keen
shafts
furnished with heads shaped after the frog's mouth. Bhima, however,
ever delighting in battle, pierced the preceptor with five broad-headed arrows
and then with sixty. Arjuna hit Susarman with a large number of arrows
made wholly of iron and destroyed his troops, like a tempest destroying masses
of clouds.
Then Bhishma and Duryodhana and Vrihadvala, the ruler of the Kosalas,
excited with rage, advanced upon Bhimasena and Arjuna.
At this, the warriors of the Pandava army and Dhrishtadyumna, the son of Prishata,
rushed in battle against Bhishma, who was advancing like death himself
with wide-open mouth. Sikhandini also, sighting the grandsire of the Bharatas,
was filled with joy and rushed at him, abandoning all fear of the mighty car
warrior.
Then all the Parthas with Yudhishthira at their head, placing Sikhandini in the van
and uniting with the Srinjayas, fought with Bhishma in battle.
Similarly, all the warriors of the Kaurava army, placing Bhishma in their van,
fought in battle with all the Parthas, headed by Sikhandini.
The fighting then between the Kauravas and the sons of Pandu,
for the sake of Bhishma's victory or victory over Bhishma, was exceedingly
terrible.
Indeed, in that game of battle, played for the sake of victory or the reverse,
Bhishma became the stake on which the victory of the Kuru army depended.

Then Dhrishtadyumna commanded all the troops: "Rush against the son of
   Ganga.
Do not fear!" And the warriors of the army of the Pandavas advanced quickly
   against Bhishma,
ready to lay down their lives in that dreadful battle. Bhishma received that large
   host,
like the continent receiving the surging sea. Day after day, many mighty car
   warriors
of the Kuru army, excited with wrath, were dispatched to the other world
by the diadem-decked Arjuna. The ever-victorious Kuru warrior Bhishma
also caused great carnage in the Partha army. Seeing Bhishma
at the head of the Kurus and Arjuna at the head of the Panchalas, one could not
   say truly
on which side the victory would declare itself. On the tenth day of battle,
when Bhishma and Arjuna encountered each other, the carnage was horrific.
Bhishma, with mighty weapons, repeatedly slew thousands upon thousands of
   warriors.
On that day Bhishma slew many whose names and families were not known
   but who
with great bravery were not retreating from battle but standing fast.
Scorching the Pandava army for ten days, Bhishma of virtuous soul
gave up all desire of protecting his life. Wishing his own slaughter, he thought:
No more shall I slay large numbers of these foremost among warriors.
Seeing Yudhishthira near him, he addressed him, saying:
"Yudhishthira, you are acquainted with every branch of learning.
Listen to these righteous words: I no longer desire to protect this body of mine.
I have passed much time in slaying large numbers of men in battle.
If you wish to do what is agreeable to me, strive to slay me,
placing Arjuna with the Panchalas and the Srinjayas in the van."
Ascertaining this, King Yudhishthira and Dhrishtadyumna urged their array on.
Yudhishthira said: "Advance! Fight! Vanquish Bhishma in battle.
You will all be protected by that conqueror of foes, Arjuna of perfect aim.
You Srinjayas, entertain no fear today of Bhishma in battle.
We will vanquish him today, with Sikhandini in our van."
Having on the tenth day of battle made such a vow, the Pandavas, resolved to
   conquer
or go to heaven, advanced, blinded by rage, with Sikhandini and Arjuna to the
   fore.
And they made the most vigorous efforts for the overthrow of Bhishma.
Then diverse kings of great might, urged by Duryodhana
and accompanied by Drona and his son and a large force
and by the mighty Dussasana at the head of all his brothers, proceeded toward
   Bhishma.
Those brave warriors, placing Bhishma of high vows in their van,
battled with the Parthas, headed by Sikhandini.
The ape-bannered Arjuna, supported by the Chedis and the Panchalas
and placing Sikhandini ahead, proceeded toward Bhishma, the son of Shantanu.

When the combatants of both armies rushed against each other with awful
    prowess,
the earth shook under their tread. The divisions of both armies mingled with
    one another,
and with a great din those warriors, burning with rage, rushed against each other
with the blare of conchs and the leonine shouts of the soldiers.
The splendor, equal to that of either the sun or the moon, of bracelets and
    diadems,
was dimmed. And the dust that rose looked like a cloud,
the flash of bright weapons constituting its lightning.
The twang of bows, the whiz of arrows, the blare of conchs, the loud beat of
    drums,
and the rattle of cars of both the armies constituted the fierce roar of those
    clouds.
And the welkin over the field of battle, because of the bearded darts,
the javelins, the swords, and the showers of arrows from both armies, was
    darkened.
Car warriors killed car warriors, and horsemen felled horsemen in that dreadful
    battle.
And elephants killed elephants, and foot soldiers slew foot soldiers.
The battle that took place there for Bhishma's sake between the Kurus and the
    Pandavas
was fierce in the extreme, like that between two hawks for a piece of flesh.
The son of Drona, excited with wrath in that battle, forcibly struck Satyaki in the
    chest
with fierce arrows. The grandson of Sini struck the preceptor's son in every vital
    limb
with nine shafts winged with the feathers of the iron-billed kanka bird.
Aswatthaman then struck Satyaki in return with nine shafts
and once more, quickly, with thirty in his arms and chest.
Then that great bowman of the Satwata race, possessed of great fame,
deeply pierced by Drona's son, pierced the latter in return with many arrows.
The mighty car warrior Paurava, covering Dhrishtaketu in that battle with his
    shafts,
mangled that great bowman, and the mighty car warrior Dhrishtaketu
quickly pierced the former with thirty arrows. Then the mighty car warrior
    Paurava
cut off Dhrishtaketu's bow and, uttering a loud shout, pierced him with whetted
    shafts.
Dhrishtaketu then took up another bow and pierced Paurava with three and
    seventy shafts
of great sharpness. Those two, both of gigantic stature, pierced each other
with showers of arrows. Each succeeded in cutting off the other's bow,
and each slew the other's steeds. And both of them, thus deprived of their cars,
encountered each other with swords. Each took up a beautiful shield made of
    bull's hide
and decked with a hundred moons and graced with a hundred stars.

Each of them also took up a polished sword of brilliant luster.
Thus equipped, they rushed at each other like two lions in the deep forest
both seeking the companionship of the same lioness in her season.
They wheeled in beautiful circles, advanced and retreated,
and, seeking to strike each other, displayed other movements.
Then Paurava, excited with wrath, addressed Dhrishtaketu, saying "Wait! Wait!"
And he struck Dhrishtaketu on the frontal bone with that large scimitar of his.
The king of the Chedis then struck Paurava on his shoulder with his scimitar of
    sharp edge.
Those two repressors of foes, thus encountering each other in battle
and thus striking each other, both fell down on the field.
Then Jayatsena, taking Paurava up on his car, removed him from the field of
    battle.
As regards Dhrishtaketu, the heroic Sahadeva, son of Madri, bore him from the
    field.
Chitrasena, having pierced, with many arrows made wholly of iron, Susarman—
not the king of the Trigartas but another warrior of that name—
once more pierced him with sixty arrows and then again with nine.
Susarman, however, excited with wrath, pierced Chitrasena with hundreds of
    arrows.
He then, full of rage, pierced his adversary with thirty straight shafts.
Susarman, however, pierced Chitrasena again in return.
In that battle for the destruction of Bhishma, Subhadra's son, enhancing his fame,
fought with Prince Vrihadvala, putting forth his prowess for aiding his sire,
    Partha,
and then proceeded toward Bhishma's front. The ruler of the Kosalas,
having pierced the son of Arjuna with five shafts made of iron, once more
    pierced him
with twenty straight shafts. Then the son of Subhadra pierced the ruler of the
    Kosalas
                        with eight shafts made wholly of iron.
He did not succeed, however, in making the ruler of the Kosalas tremble,
and he therefore again pierced him with many arrows.
And Arjuna's son then cut off Vrihadvala's bow and struck him once more with
    thirty arrows.
Vrihadvala then took up another bow and pierced the son of Arjuna with many
    arrows.
Truly, the battle that for Bhishma's sake took place between them,
each of them excited with rage and each conversant with every mode of fight,
was like the encounter of Vali and Vasava in days of old,
on the occasion of the battle between the gods and the Asuras.
Bhimasena, fighting against the elephant division, looked resplendent,
like Sakra armed with thunder after splitting large mountains.
Indeed, elephants as huge as hills, slaughtered by Bhimasena in battle,
fell down in numbers on the field, filling the earth with their shrieks.
Like massive heaps of antimony, and of huge proportions,
those elephants, with frontal globes split open, lying prostrate on the earth,

resembled mountains strewn over the earth's surface.

The mighty bowman Yudhishthira, protected by a large force,
afflicted the ruler of the Madras, encountering him in that dreadful battle.
The ruler of the Madras in return, displaying his prowess for the sake of Bhishma,
afflicted in battle the son of Dharma, that mighty car warrior.
The king of Sindhus, having pierced Virata with nine straight arrows of keen
    points,
once more struck him with thirty. Virata, however, struck Jayadratha
in the center of his chest with thirty shafts of keen points.
The ruler of the Matsyas and the ruler of the Sindhus—
both armed with beautiful bows and beautiful scimitars,
both decked with handsome coats of mail and weapons and standards,
and both of beautiful forms—looked resplendent in that battle.
Drona, encountering in dreadful battle Dhrishtadyumna, prince of the
    Panchalas,
fought fiercely. Then Drona, having cut off the large bow of Prishata's son,
pierced him deeply with fifty arrows.
That slayer of hostile heroes, the son of Prishata, taking up another bow, sped
    arrows
at Drona, who was contending with him. Drona, however, cut off all those
    arrows,
striking them with his own. And then Drona sped at Drupada's son five fierce
    shafts.
The son of Prishata, excited with rage, hurled at Drona a mace like that of death
    himself.
Drona, however, checked by means of fifty arrows that mace decked with gold
as it coursed toward him. Thereupon the mace, cut into fragments, fell to earth.
The son of Prishata, seeing his mace warded off, hurled at Drona an excellent
    dart
made wholly of iron. Drona, however, cut that dart with nine shafts
and then afflicted the son of Prishata. Thus took place the awful battle between
    Drona
                            and the son of Prishata for the sake of Bhishma.
Arjuna, rushing at Bhishma, afflicted him with many arrows of keen points.
King Bhagadatta, however, of great prowess, then rushed at Arjuna
and checked his course in battle with showers of arrows.
Arjuna then hit Bhagadatta's elephant, coming toward him
with many polished arrows of iron that were all as bright as silver
and furnished with keen points. The son of Kunti, meanwhile, urged Sikhandini,
    saying:
"Proceed, proceed toward Bhishma, and slay him!"
Then the ruler of Pragjyotishas, abandoning that son of Pandu, proceeded
against the car of Drupada. Arjuna thereupon hurried toward Bhishma,
placing Sikhandini ahead. And then there took place a fierce battle,
for all the brave combatants of the Kuru army rushed with great vigor against
    Arjuna,
shouting loudly. It was wonderful, like the wind dispersing in the summer

masses of clouds in the sky, as Arjuna dispersed divisions of the Kurus.

Sikhandini, however, without anxiety, coming up to the grandsire of the
   Bharatas,

pierced him with a great many arrows. Bhishma's car was then his fire chamber.

His bow was the flame of that fire. And swords and darts and maces were the fuel.

The showers of arrows he shot were the blazing sparks of that fire,

with which he was then consuming Kshatriyas in battle.

As a raging conflagration with a constant supply of fuel

wanders in the midst of masses of dry grass when aided by the wind,

so did Bhishma blaze up with his flames and scatter his celestial weapons.

The Kuru hero slew the Somakas, who followed Partha in that battle.

Indeed, that mighty car warrior checked also the other forces of Arjuna

by means of his straight and whetted shafts furnished with wings of gold.

Filling in that dreadful battle all the points of the compass with his leonine
   shouts,

Bhishma felled many car warriors from their cars and many steeds with their
   riders.

He caused large bodies of cars to look like forests of palmyras shorn of their
   leafy heads.

That foremost among wielders of weapons in that battle deprived cars and steeds

and elephants of their riders. Hearing the twang of his bow and the slap of his
   palms,

both resembling the roll of the thunder, the troops trembled all over the field.

His shafts were never ineffectual as they fell.

Indeed, shot from Bhishma's bow, they never fell, only touching the bodies of
   the foe

and piercing them through in every case. Crowds of cars deprived of their riders,

but to which fleet steeds were still yoked, were dragged on all sides with the
   speed of the wind.

A full fourteen thousand great car warriors of noble parentage—

prepared to lay down their lives, and standing fast with gold-decked standards

belonging to the Chedis, the Kasis, and the Karushas—approached Bhishma

and were dispatched with their steeds, cars, and elephants to the other world.

There was not a single great car warrior among the Somakas

who, having approached Bhishma in that battle, returned alive from that
   engagement.

Beholding Bhishma's prowess, people regarded all those warriors who
   approached him

as already dispatched to the abode of the king of the dead.

Indeed, no car warriors ventured to approach Bhishma in battle except the
   heroic Arjuna,

with those white steeds yoked to his car and with Krishna for his charioteer,

and Sikhandini, the prince of Panchala, of immeasurable energy.

Sikhandini, approaching Bhishma in battle, struck him in the center of his chest

with ten broad-headed arrows. The son of Ganga, however,

only looked at Sikhandini with wrath, as if consuming the Panchala prince with
   that look.

Bhishma, remembering Sikhandini's former femininity, declined in sight of
  everyone to strike.
Sikhandini, however, did not understand this.
Then Arjuna addressed Sikhandini, saying: "Rush quickly, and slay the old man.
Slay Bhishma. I do not see any other warrior in Yudhishthira's army
who is competent to fight with Bhishma in battle save you, O tiger among men."
Sikhandini quickly covered the grandsire with diverse kinds of weapons.
The Pandavas began to overwhelm Bhishma, like the clouds covering the maker
  of day.
Surrounded on all sides, Bhishma consumed many brave warriors in that battle,
like a raging conflagration in the forest consuming numberless trees.
The prowess that was then beheld there of Dussasana was wonderful
inasmuch as he battled with Arjuna and protected Bhishma at the same time.
With that feat of Dussasana, all the people there were highly gratified.
Alone he battled with all the Pandavas, having Arjuna among them,
and he fought with such vigor that the Pandavas were unable to resist him.
Many car warriors were in that battle deprived of their cars by Dussasana.
And many mighty bowmen on horseback and many mighty warriors on
  elephants,
pierced with Dussasana's keen shafts, fell to earth.
And many elephants, afflicted with his shafts, ran away in all directions.
As a fire fiercely blazes forth with bright flames when fed with fuel,
so did Dussasana blaze forth, consuming the Pandava host.
No car warrior of the Pandava host ventured to proceed against that warrior
of gigantic proportions except Arjuna, having Krishna for his charioteer.
Then Arjuna vanquished Dussasana in battle, in sight of all the troops,
and proceeded against Bhishma. Dussasana, although vanquished,
repeatedly comforted his own side, relying on the might of Bhishma's arms,
and battled the Pandavas with great fierceness.
Then Sikhandini in that battle pierced Bhishma with many arrows
as fatal as the poison of the snake. These arrows, however,
caused Bhishma little pain, for the son of Ganga received them laughingly.
Indeed, as a person afflicted with heat cheerfully receives torrents of rain,
even so did the son of Ganga receive those arrows of Sikhandini.
The Kshatriyas there beheld Bhishma in that great battle
as a being of fierce visage who was consuming the troops of the high-souled
  Pandavas.
Duryodhana, addressing all his warriors, said: "Rush against Arjuna from all sides.
Bhishma will protect you." The Kaurava troops, casting off all fear,
fought with the Pandavas. And once more Duryodhana said to them:
"With his tall standard bearing the device of the golden palmyra,
Bhishma will stay, protecting the honor and the armor of all the Dhartarashtra
  warriors.
The very gods, striving vigorously, cannot vanquish the illustrious and mighty
  Bhishma.
What need be said of the Parthas, who are mortals? Therefore, do not flee from
  the field.

I myself, striving vigorously, will today fight with the Pandavas,
uniting with all of you as you exert yourselves strenuously."
Hearing these words, many mighty combatants, excited with rage,
belonging to the Videhas, the Kalingas, and the tribes of the Daserkas, fell upon
   Arjuna.
And many combatants also, belonging to the Nishadas, the Sauviras, the
   Valhikas,
the Daradas, the Westerners, the Northerners, the Malavas, the Abhighatas,
the Surasenas, the Sivis, the Vasatis, the Salwas, the Sakas, the Trigartas,
the Amvashthas, and the Kekayas, similarly fell upon him, like flights of insects
   around a fire.
The mighty Arjuna, calling to mind diverse celestial weapons
and aiming them at those great car warriors at the heads of their respective
   divisions,
then quickly consumed them all with those weapons of great force.
And while that firm bowman was creating with his celestial weapons
thousands upon thousands of arrows, his Gandiva was resplendent under heaven.
Those Kshatriyas, afflicted with those arrows, with their standards torn and
   overthrown,
could not even together approach the ape-bannered Arjuna.
Car warriors fell down with their standards, and horsemen with their horses,
and elephant riders with their elephants, attacked by Arjuna with his shafts.
The earth was soon covered on all sides with the retreating troops of those kings,
routed by the shafts shot from his weapons. Arjuna then, having routed the
   Kauravas,
sped many arrows at Dussasana. Those arrows with iron heads, piercing him
   through,
all entered the earth like snakes through anthills.
Arjuna then slew Dussasana's steeds and then felled his charioteer.
And with twenty shafts he deprived Vivingsati of his car.
And, piercing Kripa and Vikarna and Salya with many arrows made wholly of
   iron,
he deprived all of them of their cars. Thus vanquished in battle, Kripa and Salya
and Dussasana and Vikarna and Vivingsati all fled.
Having vanquished them in the forenoon, Arjuna then blazed up like a
   smokeless fire.
Scattering shafts all around, like the sun shedding rays of light,
he felled many other kings and, making mighty car warriors turn their backs on
   the field
with his showers of arrows, he caused a large river of blood to flow in that battle
between the hosts of the Kurus and the Pandavas.
Large numbers of elephants and steeds and car warriors were slain by car warriors.
And many were the car warriors slain by elephants,
and many also were the steeds slain by foot soldiers.
And the bodies of many elephant riders and horsemen and car warriors,
cut off in the middle as also were their heads cut off,
fell down on every part of the field, which was strewn with slain princes,

falling or fallen, decked with earrings and bracelets.
It was also strewn with the bodies of many warriors severed by car wheels
or trodden by elephants. Foot soldiers ran away, and horsemen also.
And many elephants and car warriors fell down on all sides.
And many cars, with wheels and yokes and broken standards, lay scattered on
the field.
The field, dyed with the gore of large numbers of elephants, horses, and car
warriors,
looked beautiful, like a red cloud in an autumn sky.
Dogs and crows and vultures and wolves and jackals and many other frightful
beasts
and birds set up loud howls at the sight of the food that lay before them.
Diverse kinds of winds blew in all directions,
and Rakshasas and evil spirits were there, uttering loud roars.
Cloth embroidered with gold in costly banners waved in the winds.
Thousands of umbrellas and great cars with standards attached were strewn over
the field.
Then Bhishma, invoking a celestial weapon, rushed at Arjuna in sight of the
bowmen.
Thereupon Sikhandini, clad in mail, rushed at Bhishma, who was dashing
toward Arjuna.
When the combatants of both armies were thus disposed in battle array,
all those steadfast heroes set their hearts on the region of Brahma.
In the course of the general engagement that followed,
same classes of combatants did not fight with same classes of combatants.
Car warriors did not fight with car warriors, nor foot soldiers with foot soldiers,
nor horsemen with horsemen, nor elephant warriors with elephant warriors.
Rather, the combatants fought with one another like madmen.
Great and dreadful was the calamity that overtook both armies.
In that fierce slaughter, when elephants and men spread themselves on the field,
all distinctions between them ceased, and they fought indiscriminately.
Then Salya and Kripa and Chitrasena and Dussasana and Vikarna
remounted their bright cars, causing the Pandava host to tremble.
Slaughtered in battle by those high-souled warriors,
the Pandava army began to reel, like a boat on waters tossed by the wind.
As a wintry blast cuts cattle to the quick, so did Bhishma cut the sons of Pandu.
As regards the Kaurava army also, many elephants, looking like newly risen clouds,
were felled by the illustrious Arjuna. Many warriors were crushed by that hero.
And, struck with arrows and long shafts in the thousands, many huge elephants
fell down,
uttering frightful shrieks of pain. The field of battle looked beautiful,
with the bodies still decked with the ornaments of high-souled warriors deprived
of life
and the heads still wearing earrings. In that battle, destructive of great heroes,
when Bhishma and Arjuna put forth their prowess, the Kurus,
beholding the grandsire exert himself, approached him with their troops placed
ahead.

Desirous of laying down their lives in battle and making heaven their goal,
they approached the Pandavas. The brave Pandavas also—
bearing in mind the many injuries of diverse kinds inflicted on them,
casting off all fear, and eager to win the highest heavens—cheerfully fought the
    Kauravas.
Then the generalissimo of the Pandava army, the mighty car warrior
    Dhrishtadyumna,
addressing his soldiers, said: "You Somakas, accompanied by the Srinjayas,
                    rush at Ganga's son."
The Somakas and the Srinjayas, though afflicted with showers of arrows,
rushed at the son of Ganga. And Bhishma, full of wrath, began to fight with the
    Srinjayas.
In days of old, the intelligent Rama had imparted to Bhishma
instruction in weaponry that was greatly destructive of hostile ranks.
Relying on such instruction, and causing great havoc among the troops of the foe,
the old Kuru grandsire slew ten thousand warriors of the Ratha, day after day.
On the tenth day, however, Bhishma, single-handed, slew ten thousand
    elephants
and then seven great car warriors among the Matsyas and the Panchalas.
In addition to all these, in that dreadful battle he slew five thousand foot soldiers
and one thousand tuskers and ten thousand steeds through skill acquired by
    education.
Having thinned the ranks of all the kings, he slew Satanika, the dear brother of
    Virata.
And he then felled fully a thousand Kshatriyas with his broad-headed shafts.
Besides these, all the Kshatriyas of the Pandava army who followed Arjuna,
as soon as they approached Bhishma, had to go to Yama's abode.
Covering the Pandava host from every side with showers of arrows,
Bhishma stayed in battle at the head of the Kaurava army.
On the tenth day, Bhishma achieved the most glorious feats as he stood between
    the two armies,
bow in hand. None of the kings could even look at him,
for he resembled the hot midday sun in the summer sky.
As Sakra scorched the Daitya host in battle, so did Bhishma scorch the Pandava
    host.
Seeing him thus put forth his prowess, Krishna cheerfully addressed Arjuna
and said: "There stands Bhishma, son of Shantanu, between the two armies.
Slaying him by putting forth your might, you may win victory.
There, at that spot from which he breaks our ranks, check him with all your
    strength.
No one other than you ventures to bear the arrows of Bhishma."
The ape-bannered Arjuna, with his arrows, made Bhishma, his car, his steeds,
    and his standard
invisible. That foremost among Kurus, with his own showers of arrows,
pierced Arjuna's shafts. Then the king of the Panchalas, and the valiant
    Dhrishtaketu,
and Bhimasena the son of Pandu, and Dhrishtadyumna of Prishata's race,

and the twins Nakula and Sahadeva, and Chekitana, and the five Kaikaya
    brothers,
and the mighty-armed Satyaki, and Subhadra's son, and Ghatotkacha,
and the five sons of Draupadi, and Sikhandini, and the valiant Kuntibhoja,
and Susarman, and Virata, and many other powerful warriors of the Pandava
    army—
all, afflicted by the shafts of Bhishma, seemed to sink in an ocean of grief.
Arjuna, however, rescued them all.
Then Sikhandini, taking up a mighty weapon, and protected by Arjuna,
rushed alone, impetuously, toward Bhishma. The unvanquished Arjuna,
knowing what should be done after that, then slew all those who had followed
    Bhishma
and had then rushed at him. And Satyaki and Chekitana and Dhristadyumna
    and Virata
and Drupada and the twin sons of Madri by Pandu, all protected by Arjuna,
rushed against Bhishma. Abhimanyu and the five sons of Draupadi also,
with mighty weapons upraised, rushed against him and hit him
                    in diverse parts of his body with well-aimed shafts.
Disregarding all those shafts of the Pandava host, Bhishma penetrated
into the Pandava ranks, deflecting all their arrows, as if it were sport.
Frequently looking at Sikhandini, prince of the Panchalas,
Bhishma aimed not a single arrow at him, on account of his femininity.
On the other hand, he slew seven great car warriors belonging to Drupada's
    division.
Confused cries of woe soon arose among the Matsyas, the Panchalas, and the
    Chedis,
who were together rushing at that single hero.
With large numbers of foot soldiers and steeds and cars and with showers of
    arrows
they overwhelmed Bhishma, like the clouds overwhelming the maker of day.
Then, in that battle between him and them,
the diadem-decked Arjuna, placing Sikhandini before him, pierced Bhishma
    repeatedly.

✦

Thus all the Pandavas, with Sikhandini before them,
pierced Bhishma repeatedly from all sides.
All the Srinjayas, uniting together, struck him with dreadful weapons:
spiked maces, and battle-axes, and mallets, and short thick clubs, and bearded
    darts,
and arrows furnished with golden wings, and lances, and long shafts,
and arrows with heads shaped like a calf's tooth, and rockets.
Thus afflicted by many, his coat of mail was pierced everywhere.
But Bhishma, though pierced in every vital part, felt no pain.
On the other hand, he then seemed to his enemies to resemble in appearance
the all-destructive fire that rises at the end of the *yuga*.

His bow and arrows constituted the blazing flames of that fire.
The flight of his weapons constituted its breeze.
The rattle of his car wheels constituted its heat,
and his mighty weapons constituted its splendor.
His beautiful bow formed its fierce tongue;
and the bodies of heroic warriors, its profuse fuel.
Bhishma seemed to roll through the midst of the crowds of cars belonging to
    those kings,
or to emerge at times and then course once more through their midst.
Disregarding the king of the Panchalas and Dhrishtaketu,
he penetrated into the midst of the Pandava army. He pierced the six Pandava
    warriors—
Satyaki and Bhima and Dhananjaya the son of Pandu, and Drupada
and Virata and Dhrishtadyumna of Prishata's race—
with many excellent arrows of great sharpness and dreadful whiz and impetuosity,
capable of piercing every kind of armor.
Those mighty car warriors, however, checking those keen shafts,
afflicted Bhishma with great force, each of them striking him with ten shafts.
And those mighty shafts which the great car warrior Sikhandini shot,
whetted on stone and furnished with golden wings, penetrated deep into
    Bhishma's body.
The diadem-decked Arjuna, alive with wrath and placing Sikhandini ahead,
rushed at Bhishma and cut off his bow.
Thereupon Drona and Kritavarman, and Jayadratha the ruler of the Sindhus,
and Bhurisravas and Sala and Salya and Bhagadatta,
inflamed with rage by that act of Arjuna, rushed at him.
Those mighty car warriors, invoking celestial weapons,
fell with great wrath upon that son of Pandu and covered him with their arrows.
As they rushed toward Arjuna's car, the noise they made
resembled that made by the ocean itself when it swells in rage at the end of the
    yuga.
"Kill! Bring up our forces! Take! Pierce! Cut off!"
These words and phrases combined to make a furious uproar around Arjuna's car.
Hearing it, the car warriors of the Pandava army rushed forward to protect
    Arjuna.
They were Satyaki and Bhimasena and Dhrishtadyumna of Prishata's race
and both Virata and Drupada and the Rakshasa Ghatotkacha and Abhimanyu.
These seven, enraged and armed with excellent bows, rushed with great speed.
And the battle that took place between these and the Kaurava warriors was
    fierce,
making the hair stand on end and resembling the battle of the gods with the
    Danavas.
Sikhandini, that foremost among car warriors, protected in the battle by Arjuna,
pierced Bhishma with ten shafts after the latter's bow had been cut off.
And he struck Bhishma's charioteer with other shafts and cut off his standard
    with one.
The son of Ganga took up another bow that was tougher.

That, too, was cut off by Arjuna with three sharp shafts.
Indeed, he who was capable of drawing the bow with even his left hand
cut off all the bows that Bhishma took up, one after another.
Then Bhishma, licking the corners of his mouth, took up a dart that could rive
a hill.
In rage, he hurled it at Arjuna's car. Seeing it course toward him like a bolt from
heaven,
Arjuna fixed five sharp broad-headed arrows on his bowstring
and with those five arrows cut into five fragments the dart that Bhishma had
hurled.
That dart then fell down, like a flash of lightning separated from a mass of clouds.
Bhishma was filled with rage and began to reflect.
He said to himself: *With a single bow I could have slain all the Pandavas,*
if the mighty Vishnu himself had not been their protector.
For two reasons, however, I will not fight with the Pandavas—
their invincibility, and the femininity of Sikhandini.
When my sire wedded Kali, he was pleased with me and gave me two boons—
that I should be incapable of being slain in battle, and that my death should depend
on my own choice. I now wish my death, this being the proper hour.
Ascertaining this to be the resolve of Bhishma,
the rishis and the Vasus stationed in the firmament said:
"That which you have resolved is approved by us also, O son!
Act according to your resolution. Withdraw your heart from the battle."
At the conclusion of those words, fragrant and auspicious breezes
charged with particles of water began to blow in a natural direction.
And celestial cymbals began to beat. A flowery shower fell upon Bhishma.
The words spoken by the rishis and the Vasus were heard by none save Bhishma
himself.
Great was the grief that filled the hearts of the celestials
at the thought of Bhishma, that favorite of all the worlds, falling down from his car.
Having listened to these words of the celestials, Bhishma rushed out at Arjuna,
even though he was being pierced with sharp arrows capable of penetrating any
armor.
Then Sikhandini, excited with rage, struck the grandsire of the Bharatas in the
chest
with nine sharp arrows. Bhishma did not tremble
but remained unmoved, like a mountain during an earthquake.
Then Arjuna, drawing his bow called the Gandiva, with a laugh pierced the son
of Ganga
with five and twenty arrows. And once more, with great speed and excited with
wrath,
he struck him in every vital part with hundreds of arrows.
Thus pierced by others with thousands of arrows, the mighty car warrior
Bhishma
pierced those others in return. And as regards the arrows shot by those warriors,
Bhishma checked them all with his own straight arrows.
Those arrows, however, which Sikhandini shot in that battle,

though endowed with wings of gold and whetted on stone, scarcely caused
 Bhishma any pain.
Then Arjuna approached nearer to Bhishma once again and cut off his bow,
pierced him with ten arrows, and cut off his standard with one.
He struck Bhishma's chariot with ten arrows and caused him to tremble.
The son of Ganga took up another bow that was stronger,
but in the twinkling of an eye Arjuna cut that bow also into three fragments
with three broad-headed shafts. Thus the son of Pandu cut off all the bows of
 Bhishma,
and after that Bhishma no longer desired to battle with Arjuna.
The latter, however, then pierced him with five and twenty arrows.
That great bowman, thus greatly pierced, addressed Dussasana and said:
"Behold, Arjuna pierces me with many thousands of arrows.
He is incapable of being vanquished in battle by the wielder of the thunderbolt
 himself.
As regards myself also, the very gods, Danavas, and Rakshasas united together
cannot vanquish me. What shall I say, then, of mighty car warriors among men?"
While Bhishma was thus speaking to Dussasana, Arjuna with sharp shafts,
and with Sikhandini to the fore, pierced Bhishma with many more keen-pointed
 arrows.
Once more Bhishma addressed Dussasana with a smile and said:
"These arrows coursing toward me in one continuous line,
whose touch resembles that of heaven's bolt, have been shot by Arjuna.
These are not Sikhandini's. Cutting me to the quick, piercing through my coat
 of mail,
and striking me with the force of clubs, these arrows are not Sikhandini's.
Of touch as hard as that of the Brahmana's rod of chastisement,
these arrows are afflicting my vital forces.
Of the touch of maces and spiked bludgeons, those arrows are like messengers
 of death,
commissioned by the grim king himself. They are not Sikhandini's.
Like angry snakes of virulent poison flicking their tongues out,
they are penetrating into my vitals. They not Sikhandini's.
These cut me to the quick, like the cold of winter cutting cattle to the quick.
Except for the wielder of the Gandiva, all other kings united together cannot
 cause me pain."
Saying these words, Bhishma, the valiant son of Shantanu,
as if to consume the Pandavas, hurled a dart at Arjuna.
Arjuna, however, cutting it into three fragments with three shafts,
caused that dart to drop down in sight of all the Kuru army.
Wanting either death or victory, the son of Ganga then took up a sword
and a shield decked with gold. But before he could come down from his car,
Arjuna cut that shield into a hundred fragments with his arrows.
And that feat of his seemed exceedingly wonderful.
King Yudhishthira urged his own troops, saying: "Rush at Ganga's son.
                              Do not entertain the slightest fear."
Then, armed with bearded darts and lances and clubs and axes

and excellent scimitars and long shafts of great sharpness
and broad-headed and calf's-tooth-shaped arrows, from all sides they rushed at
that single warrior.
Then arose from among the Pandava host a loud shout.
The Kauravas, desirous of Bhishma's victory, surrounded him with leonine roars.
Fierce was the battle between the two sides on that, the tenth day,
when Bhishma and Arjuna met together.
Like the vortex that occurs at the spot where the Ganga meets the ocean,
for a short while a vortex occurred there where the troops of both armies met
and struck one another down. And the earth, wet with gore, assumed a fierce
form
in which the even and the uneven spots on its surface could no longer be
distinguished.
Although Bhishma was pierced in all his vital parts,
yet he stayed calmly in the battle, having slain ten thousand warriors.
The great bowman Arjuna, at the head of his troops, broke the center of the
Kuru army.
The Kauravas then, afraid of Kunti's son Arjuna with his white steeds attached to
his car,
and afflicted by him with polished weapons, fled the battle.
The Sauviras, the Kitavas, the Easterners, the Westerners, the Northerners, the
Malavas,
the Abhishahas, the Surasenas, the Sivis, the Vasatis, the Salwas, the Sayas, the
Trigartas,
the Amvashthas, the Kaikeyas, and other illustrious warriors, afflicted with
arrows
and pained by their wounds, abandoned Bhishma while he was fighting
with the diadem-decked Arjuna.
With his foes in that battle slain by the hundreds and thousands,
there was not on all of Bhishma's body a space of even two fingers' breadth
not pierced with arrows. Thus was he mangled with arrows of keen points
by Arjuna in that battle. He fell from his car with his head to the east
a little before sunset, and there resounded in the welkin loud cries of "Alas!"
and "Oh!"
uttered both by the celestials and by the kings of the earth.
Beholding the high-souled grandsire falling down from his car,
the hearts of all the Kurus fell with him. That foremost among bowmen,
that mighty-armed hero, fell like an uprooted standard of Indra, making the
earth tremble.
Pierced all over with arrows, however, his body did not touch the ground.
At that moment, a divine nature took possession of him,
lying as he was on a bed of arrows. The clouds poured a cool shower over him,
and the earth shook. While falling, he had marked the sun in the southern
solstice.
That hero, therefore, would not permit his senses to depart,
thinking that it was an inauspicious season for death. All around in the heavens
he heard celestial voices crying: "Oh! Why should Ganga's son,

that foremost among warriors of weapons, yield up his life during the southern
  solstice?"
The son of Ganga replied: "I am alive!" Although fallen upon the earth,
Bhishma, preferring the northern solstice, did not suffer his life to depart.
Ascertaining that this was his resolve, Ganga, the daughter of Himavat,
sent to him the great rishis in swanlike form. Those rishis, inhabiting Lake
  Manasa,
quickly rose up and came together to obtain a sight of the Kuru grandsire
  Bhishma
where that foremost among men was lying on his bed of arrows.
Those rishis in swanlike form alit, looked at Bhishma on his bed of arrows,
walked around him, and, with the sun then in the southern solstice,
addressed one another in these words: "Being a high-souled person,
why should Bhishma pass out of the world during the southern solstice?"
Bhishma reflected and said to them: "I will not pass out of the world while the sun
is in the southern solstice. I will proceed to my own ancient abode
when the sun reaches the northern solstice. You swans, I tell you this truly.
Until the northern solstice, I will hold on to my life. I will postpone my death
  until then.
The boon granted me by my sire was that my death would depend upon my own
  wish.
Let that boon become true. Since I have control in the matter, I will hold on to
  life."
Then the swans flew away, proceeding toward the south.
And having said these words to the swans, Bhishma continued to lie there on his
  bed of arrows.

✦

When Bhishma fell, the Pandavas and the Srinjayas roared like lions.
Duryodhana had no idea what to do. All the Kurus, deprived of their senses,
sighed and wept and remained perfectly still, without any heart for battle.
As if seized by the thighs, they stood motionless, unable to proceed against the
  Pandavas.
Bhishma had been regarded as unslayable, but now he was slain,
and all the Kurus thought that the destruction of their king was now at hand.
Vanquished by Arjuna, with their foremost heroes slain
and mangled with sharp arrows, they did not know what to do.
The Pandavas, having obtained the victory and a blessed state in the other world,
blew their great conchs. And the Somakas and the Panchalas all rejoiced.
Then, when thousands of trumpets were blown, the mighty Bhimasena
slapped his armpits and shouted loudly. When the all-powerful son of Ganga was
  slain,
the heroic warriors of both armies lay down their weapons and began to reflect.
Some shrieked and some fled, and some were stunned and unable to move.
Some censured the practices of the Kshatriya order, and some applauded
  Bhishma.

The rishis and the Pitris all applauded Bhishma of high vows.
And the deceased ancestors of the Bharatas also praised Bhishma.
Meanwhile, Bhishma, son of Shantanu, having recourse to that Yoga
which is taught in the great Upanishads, and engaged in mental prayers,
remained quiet, expectant of his hour.

✦

Slain in the evening, Bhishma saddened the Dhartarashtras and delighted the
Panchalas.
Falling down, he lay on his bed of arrows without touching the earth with his body.
When Bhishma had been thrown down from his car and had fallen upon the
earth,
cries of "Oh!" and "Alas!" were heard among all creatures.
When Bhishma, that boundary tree of the Kurus, fell down, fear entered the
hearts
of the Kshatriyas of both armies. Seeing Bhishma with his standard overthrown
and his armor cut open, the Kurus and the Pandavas also were filled with gloom.
And the bowl of the sky, too, was enveloped with gloom. The sun himself
became dim.
The earth seemed to groan when the son of Shantanu was slain.
When Bhishma, grandsire of the Bharatas, was slain, the Kaurava princes
wore an expression of grief, and the splendor of their countenances abandoned
them.
All of them stood in shame, hanging down their heads. The Pandavas, on the
other hand,
having won the victory, stood at the heads of their ranks and blew their large
conchs.
When, in consequence of their joy, thousands of trumpets were sounded there,
the mighty Bhimasena, son of Kunti, sported in great glee,
having slain many hostile warriors endowed with enormous strength.
A great swoon overtook all the Kurus. And Karna and Duryodhana drew long
breaths.
Seeing that Bhishma had fallen, Dussasana entered the division commanded by
Drona.
Clad in mail, and at the head of his own troops, he had been placed by his elder
brother
for the protection of Bhishma. But now he came, with the troops he had
commanded
plunged into grief. The Kauravas surrounded him, eager to hear what he had
to say.
Dussasana informed Drona of Bhishma's slaughter.
And Drona, hearing those tidings, fell from his car.
Then he recovered his senses and forbade the Kuru army to continue the fight.
Seeing the Kurus desist from battle, the Pandavas also,
through messengers on fleet horses, countermanded their orders and ceased to
fight.

The kings of both armies, putting off their armor, all repaired to Bhishma.
Desisting from the fight, thousands of other warriors then proceeded
toward the high-souled Bhishma, like the celestials toward the lord of all creatures.
Approaching him who was then lying on his bed of arrows,
the Pandavas and the Kurus stood there, having offered him their salutations.
Then Bhishma addressed the Pandavas and the Kurus, who had reverenced him
and now stood before him. He said: "Welcome to you, you highly blessed ones!
Welcome to you, you mighty car warriors! Gratified am I to see you,
who are the equals of the very gods." He continued: "My head is hanging down
    greatly.
Let a pillow be given to me!" The kings then fetched excellent pillows that were
    very soft
and made of the most delicate fabrics. The grandsire, however, refused them.
That tiger among men then said with a laugh: "These do not become a hero's
    bed."
To Arjuna he then said: "O Dhananjaya, my head hangs down.
Give me a pillow such as you regard to be fit!"
Stringing then his large bow and reverentially saluting the grandsire, Arjuna,
with eyes filled with tears, said: "O foremost one among the Kurus,
you who are first among all wielders of weapons, command me, for I am your
    slave!
                        What shall I do, O grandsire?"
"Give me a pillow that would become my bed," Bhishma said,
"for you are conversant with the duties of Kshatriyas and are endowed
                        with intelligence and goodness!"
Arjuna said: "So be it!" And he took up the Gandiva and a number of straight
    shafts.
Inspiring them with mantras, and obtaining permission of that illustrious car
    warrior,
he then with three keen shafts supported Bhishma's head.
Seeing that Arjuna had divined his thought and had achieved that feat,
Bhishma became highly pleased. After that pillow had thus been given to him,
he applauded Arjuna and thanked him. And he said: "You have given me a
    pillow
that becomes my bed! If you had acted otherwise, I would have cursed you!
Even thus should a Kshatriya, observant of his duties, sleep on the field of battle,
                        on his bed of arrows!"
He then said to all those kings and princes who were present:
"Behold the pillow that the son of Pandu has given me!
I will sleep on this bed until the sun turns to the northern solstice.
Those kings who will then come to me will behold my death.
When the sun on his car of great speed to which are yoked seven steeds
proceeds toward the direction occupied by Vaisravana,
then will I yield up my life, like a dear friend dismissing a dear friend.
Let a ditch be dug here around my quarters, you kings!
Thus pierced, with hundreds of arrows, will I pay my adorations to the sun.
As regards yourselves, abandon enmity and cease from the fight."

Then there came to him some surgeons well trained in their science
and skilled in plucking out arrows with all appropriate appliances of their
    profession.
But the son of Ganga said: "Let these physicians, after proper respect being paid
    them,
be dismissed with presents. Brought to such a plight, what need have I of
    physicians?
I have won the most laudable and highest state ordained in Kshatriya observances!
You kings, lying as I do on a bed of arrows, it is not proper for me to submit now
to the treatment of physicians. With these arrows in my body, you rulers of men,
               I must be burned!"
Duryodhana then dismissed those physicians, having honored them as they
    deserved.
Then those kings of many realms, seeing Bhishma's constancy, were filled with
    wonder.
Having given him a pillow, the Pandavas and the Kauravas, united together,
once more approached the high-souled Bhishma lying on that excellent bed
    of his.
Reverentially saluting that high-souled one and circumambulating him thrice
and stationing guards all around for his protection,
those heroes, with bodies drenched in blood, repaired for rest toward their own
    tents,
their hearts plunged into grief, and thinking of what they had seen.
Then, at the proper time, the mighty Krishna, approaching the Pandavas
cheerfully seated together and filled with joy at the fall of Bhishma,
said to Yudhishthira: "By good luck has victory been yours!
By good luck has Bhishma been overthrown, he who is unslayable by men!
Or perhaps, as destiny would have it, that warrior who was master of every
    weapon,
having obtained you for a foe, you who can slay with your eyes alone,
              has been consumed by your wrathful eye!"
King Yudhishthira said: "Through your grace is victory, through your wrath is
    defeat.
You are the dispeller of the fears of those who are devoted to you. You are our
    refuge.
It is not wonderful that they should have victory whom you always protect in
    battle,
and in whose welfare you are always engaged. Having you for our refuge,
              I do not regard anything as wonderful."
Krishna answered with a smile: "O best of kings, these words can come from you
    alone!"
After the night had passed away, all the kings, the Pandavas and the
    Dhartarashtras,
repaired to Bhishma. Those Kshatriyas then saluted that bull of their order,
that hero lying on a hero's bed, and stood in his presence.

Maidens by the thousands, having repaired to that place, gently showered over him
powdered sandalwood and fried paddy and garlands of flowers.
Women and old men and children and ordinary spectators
all approached Shantanu's son, like creatures of the world desirous of beholding
     the sun.
Trumpets by the hundreds and thousands, and actors, and mimes,
and skilled mechanics also came to the aged Kuru grandsire.
And—ceasing to fight, putting aside their coats of mail, and laying aside their
     weapons—
the Kurus and the Pandavas, united together, came to the invincible Bhishma,
that chastiser of foes. Assembled together as in days of old,
they cheerfully addressed one another according to their respective ages.
That conclave of Bharata kings by the hundreds, with Bhishma among them,
blazed like a conclave of gods in heaven engaged in adoring their grandsire,
     Brahman.
Bhishma, suppressing his agonies with fortitude, though burning with the arrows
still sticking to his body, sighed like a snake.
Nearly deprived of his senses, in consequence of his wounds,
Bhishma cast his eyes on those kings and asked for water.
Those Kshatriyas brought excellent viands and several vessels of cold water.
Looking at that water brought for him, he said: "I cannot now use any article
of human enjoyment! I am removed from the pale of humanity. I lie on a bed of
     arrows.
I am waiting here, expecting only the return of the moon and the sun!"
Having spoken these words, and thereby having rebuked those kings,
                              he said: "I wish to see Arjuna!"
Arjuna came and, with joined hands, said: "What shall I do?"
Bhishma said: "Covered all over with your shafts, my body is burning greatly!
All the vital parts of my body are in agony. My mouth is dry. Give me water, O
     Arjuna!
You are a great bowman! You are capable of giving me water!"
The valiant Arjuna said: "So be it." He mounted his car and began to stretch his
     Gandiva.
Hearing the twang of his bow and the slap of his palms, which resembled the
     thunder,
the troops and the kings were all inspired with fear.
Then that warrior on his car circumambulated the prostrate chief of the
     Bharatas,
that foremost among wielders of weapons.
Aiming then a blazing arrow, after having inspired it with mantras,
and identifying it with the Parjanya weapon,
Arjuna pierced the earth south of where Bhishma lay, and there arose a jet of
     water
which was pure and auspicious and cool and which, resembling nectar,
was of celestial scent and taste. With that cool jet of water
Arjuna assuaged the thirst of Bhishma.
And at that feat, all those rulers of earth were filled with great wonder.

Beholding that feat of superhuman prowess, the Kurus trembled like cattle
afflicted with cold.

And all the kings there, from wonder, waved their garments in the air.

Loud was the blare of conchs and the beat of drums then heard all over the
field.

Bhishma, his thirst quenched, then addressed Arjuna and said:

"This is not wonderful in you, O Arjuna. Narada spoke of you as an ancient rishi.

Indeed, with Krishna as your ally, you will achieve many mighty feats,

which the chief of the celestials himself with all the gods will not venture to
achieve.

They who have knowledge of such things know you to be

the destroyer of the whole Kshatriya race.

You are the one bowman among the bowmen of the world!

You are foremost among men. As Garuda is foremost among winged creatures,

as the ocean is foremost among receptacles of water,

as the cow is foremost among quadrupeds, as the sun is foremost

among luminous bodies, as Himavat is foremost among mountains,

and as the Brahmana is foremost among castes, so are you foremost among
bowmen.

Duryodhana did not listen to the words repeatedly spoken by me and Vidura

and Drona and Rama and Janardana and also by Sanjaya.

Reft of his senses, like an idiot, Duryodhana placed no reliance on our
utterances.

Past all instruction, he will certainly have to lie down forever,
                                  overwhelmed by the might of Bhima!"

Hearing these words, King Duryodhana became of cheerless heart.

Shantanu's son, eyeing Duryodhana, said: "Listen, O king! Abandon your wrath!

You have seen how the intelligent Arjuna created that jet of cool, nectar-scented
water.

There is no one else in this world capable of achieving such a feat.

The weapons appertaining to Agni, Varuna, Soma, Vayu, and Vishnu,

as also those appertaining to Indra, Pasupati, and Paramesthi,

and those of Prajapati, Dhatri, Tashtri, Savitri, and Vivaswat,

are all known to Arjuna alone in this world of men.

Krishna, the son of Devaki, also knows them. But there is no one else here who
does.

This son of Pandu is incapable of being defeated in battle

even by the gods and the Asuras together. The feats of this high-souled one

are superhuman. With that truthful hero, that ornament of battle,

that warrior accomplished in fight, let peace, O king, soon be made!

As long as the mighty-armed Krishna is not possessed by wrath,

O chief of the Kurus, it is fitting that peace should be made with the heroic
Pandavas.

As long as this remnant of your brothers is not slain, let peace be made.

As long as Yudhishthira, his eyes burning with wrath,

does not consume your troops in battle, let peace be made.

As long as Nakula and Sahadeva and Bhimasena, the sons of Pandu,

do not exterminate your army, it seems to me that friendly relations should be
    restored
between you and the Pandavas. Let this battle end with my death, sire!
Make peace with the Pandavas. Let these words of mine be acceptable to you.
This is what I regard to be beneficial both for yourself and for the Kuru race.
Abandoning your wrath, let peace be made with Parthas.
What Arjuna has already done is sufficient. Let friendly relations be restored
upon the death of Bhishma. Let this remnant of warriors live! Relent, O king!
Let half the kingdom be given to the Pandavas. Let King Yudhishthira go to
    Indraprastha.
O chief of the Kurus, do not achieve a sinful notoriety among the kings of the
    earth
by incurring the reproach of meanness and by fomenting internecine
    dissension.
Let peace come to all with my death! Let sire get back the son,
let sister's son get back the maternal uncle. If from want of understanding,
and possessed by folly, you do not hearken to those timely words of mine,
you will have greatly to repent! What I say is true. Therefore, desist, even now!"
Having said, from affection, these words to Duryodhana in the midst of the
    kings,
the son of the oceangoing Ganga fell silent.
Though his vitals were burning with the arrow wounds, still he applied himself
    to yoga,
prevailing over his agonies. But Duryodhana, for his part, like a dying man
    refusing medicine,
rejected Bhishma's wise words.

✦

After Bhishma had become silent, all those rulers of earth
returned to their respective quarters. Hearing of Bhishma's condition, Radha's
    son Karna,
partially inspired with fear, came there and beheld that hero on his bed of
    arrows.
With his voice choked by tears, Karna approached that hero who lay with eyes
    closed.
He fell at his feet and said: "O chief of the Kurus, I am Radha's son,
upon whom you have looked with hate!"
Hearing these words, the son of Ganga, whose eyes were covered with film,
slowly raised his eyelids and caused the guards to be removed.
Seeing the place deserted by all, he embraced Karna with one arm,
like a sire embracing his son, and said: "Come, come!
You are an opponent of mine who always challenges comparison with me.
If you had not come to me, it would not have been well with you.
You are Kunti's son, not Radha's. Nor is Adhiratha your father.
I heard all this about you from Narada as also from Vyasa. Without doubt, all this
    is true.

I tell you that I bear you no malice. It was only to abate your energy
that I used to say such harsh words to you. With no reason, you speak ill of the
 Pandavas.
Sinfully did you come into the world. It is for this that your heart has been as it is.
Through pride, and owing also to your companionship with the low,
your heart hates even persons of merit. It is for this that I spoke such harsh
 words
about you in the Kuru camp. I know your prowess in battle,
which can with difficulty be borne on earth by foes.
I know also your regard for Brahmanas, your courage,
and your attachment to almsgiving. You resemble a very god—
among men there is none like you.
For fear of internecine dissension, I always spoke harsh words about you.
In bowmanship, in aiming weapons, in lightness of hand, and in strength of
 weapons,
you are equal to Arjuna himself, or to the high-souled Krishna.
O Karna, proceeding to the city of Kasi alone with your bow,
you crushed the kings in battle to procure a bride for the Kuru king.
The mighty and invincible King Jarasandha, ever boastful of his prowess in
 battle,
could not match you in fighting. You are devoted to Brahmanas. You always fight
 fairly.
In energy and strength, you are equal to a child of the celestials
and certainly much superior to men. The wrath I harbored against you is gone.
Destiny is incapable of being avoided by exertion. The sons of Pandu are your
 brothers!
If you wish to do what is agreeable to me, unite with them.
O son of Surya, let these hostilities end with me!
               Let all the kings of earth be today freed from danger!"
Karna said: "I know this! All this is as you say.
As you tell me, O Bhishma, I am Kunti's son, and not the son of a Suta.
I was, however, abandoned by Kunti, and I have been reared by a Suta.
Having so long enjoyed the wealth of Duryodhana, I dare not falsify myself now.
Like Krishna's son, who is firmly resolved for the sake of the Pandavas,
I also am prepared to cast away my possessions, my body itself,
my children, and my wife, for Duryodhana's sake.
Death from disease does not become a Kshatriya.
Relying upon Duryodhana, I have always offended the Pandavas.
This affair is destined to take its course. It is incapable of being prevented.
Who is there who would venture to overcome destiny by exertion?
You noticed various omens indicating the destruction of the earth, O grandsire,
and you declared this in the assembly. It is well known to me that Arjuna and
 Krishna
are incapable of being conquered by other men. But even with them we venture
 to fight.
I will vanquish Arjuna in battle! This is my firm resolve.

I am not capable of casting off this fierce animosity that I cherish against the
   Pandavas.
With a cheerful heart, and keeping the duties of my order before my eyes,
I will contend against Arjuna. Firmly resolved as I am on battle,
I ask you to grant me your permission. I will fight. This is my wish.
You must also forgive me for any harsh words that I may ever have uttered
   against you,
and for any action that I may ever have taken against you from anger or
   inconsideration."
Bhishma said: "If indeed you are unable to cast off this fierce animosity,
I permit you, Karna, to fight, moved by the desire of heaven.
Without anger and without vindictiveness, serve the king according to your
   power
and according to your courage, and observant of the conduct of the righteous.
You have then my permission, O Karna. Obtain that which you seek.
Through Arjuna you will obtain all those regions hereafter that can be had
by fulfilling the duties of a Kshatriya. Freed from pride and relying on your
   might,
fight, since a Kshatriya cannot have greater happiness than in righteous battle.
For a long while I made great efforts to bring about peace.
               But I could not succeed in this task. Truly do I say this to you."
After the son of Ganga had said this, Karna saluted him
and, having obtained his forgiveness, hastened toward Duryodhana's
   headquarters.

37

The Funeral

Until the winter solstice, Bhishma lay on his bed of arrows,
a bed always coveted by heroes, and when the Pandavas were sitting around him,
Yudhishthira of much wisdom asked the grandsire many questions about
    morality
and had all his doubts resolved. He heard also what the ordinances are
that apply to the subjects of gifts, of righteousness, and of wealth.
When Bhishma at last fell silent, the entire circle of kings seated around him
became silent also and motionless, like figures painted on canvas.
Then Vyasa, the son of Satyavati, having reflected for a moment,
addressed the royal son of Ganga, saying: "O king, the Kuru chief Yudhishthira
has been restored to his place along with all his brothers and followers.
With Krishna of great intelligence by his side, he bends his head in reverence
    to you.
            You must give him leave to return to the city."
Bhishma then dismissed Yudhishthira and his counselors,
saying to his grandson in a sweet voice: "Return to the city, O king!
Let the pain of your heart be dispelled. Adore the deities in diverse sacrifices
distinguished by large gifts of food and wealth.
Devoted to the practices of the Kshatriya order, gratify the Pitris and the deities.
You shall then earn great benefits. Gladden all your subjects.
Assure them and establish peace among them all.
Also honor all your well-wishers with such rewards as they deserve.
Let your friends and well-wishers live, depending on you for their means,
even as birds live, depending on a tall tree that stands full of fruit on a sacred
    spot.
When the hour comes for my departure from this world, come here, O king.
The time when I shall take leave of my body is that period when the sun,
stopping in his southward course, begins to return northward."
The son of Kunti answered: "So be it." And he saluted his grandsire with
    reverence.
He then set out with all his relatives and followers for the city called after the
    elephant.
Placing old King Dhritarashtra at the head and also Gandhari,
who was exceedingly devoted to her lord, and accompanied by the rishis and
    Krishna,

as also by the citizens and the inhabitants of the country and by his counselors,
that foremost one of Kuru's race entered Hastinapura.
He assured all his subjects by diverse acts of goodwill and set upon earning
the blessing of the Brahmanas, of the foremost military officers, and of the
    leading citizens.
Then, having passed fifty nights in the capital, he recollected that the time
indicated by his grandsire as the hour of his departure from this world had come.
Accompanied by a number of priests, he then set out, taking with him clarified
    butter
and floral garlands and scents and silken cloths and excellent sandalwood
and agarwood and dark aloe wood for cremating the body of Bhishma.
Various kinds of costly gems also were among those stores.
Yudhishthira of great intelligence, accompanied by Krishna and Vidura of great
    wisdom
as also by Yuyutsu and Yuyudhana and by his other relatives and followers,
    formed a large train
with Dhritarashtra placed ahead along with Queen Gandhari, celebrated for her
    virtues,
and his own mother, Kunti, and all his brothers also,
and proceeded while eulogists and bards hymned Bhishma's praises.
The sacrificial fires of Bhishma were also borne in the procession.
Thus the king set out from his city like a second chief of the deities.
Soon he came to the spot where the son of Shantanu was still lying on his bed of
    arrows.
He beheld his grandsire waited upon with reverence by Parasara's son Vyasa,
by Narada, by Devala, and by Asita as also by the remnant of unslain kings
                        assembled from various parts of the country.
Indeed, the king saw that his high-souled grandsire, as he lay on his heroic bed,
was guarded on all sides by the warriors appointed for that duty.
Alighting from his car, King Yudhishthira with his brothers saluted his grandsire.
They also saluted the rishis with the island-born Vyasa at their head.
They were saluted in return. Accompanied by his priests as also by his brothers,
Yudhishthira then approached that spot where Bhishma lay on his bed of arrows
                        surrounded by those reverend rishis. King
    Yudhishthira then addressed
                        that foremost one of Kuru's race, the son of the
    River Ganga, saying:
                        "I am Yudhishthira, O king! Salutations to you!
If you hear me still, tell me what I am to do for you!
Bearing with me your sacrificial fires, I have come here, O king, and wait upon you
at the hour indicated! Preceptors of all branches of learning, Brahmanas, all my
    brothers,
and King Dhritarashtra of great energy are all here with my counselors
                        and also Arjuna of great prowess.
The remaining unslain warriors and all the denizens of Kurujangala
                        are also here.
Opening your eyes, O chief of Kuru's race, behold them!

Whatever should be done on this occasion has all been arranged and provided
for by me.
Indeed, for this hour, which you indicated, all things have been kept ready!"
The son of Ganga opened his eyes and saw all the Bharatas assembled there.
Bhishma, taking the strong hand of Yudhishthira, addressed him:
"By good luck, you have come here with all your counselors, O Yudhishthira!
The thousand-rayed maker of day, the holy Surya, has begun his northward
course.
I have been lying here on my bed for eight and fifty nights.
Stretched on these sharp-pointed arrows, I have felt this period to be as long
as if it were a century. The lunar month of Magha has come.
This is, again, the lighted fortnight, and a fourth part of it ought to be over."
Having said this, Bhishma then saluted Dhritarashtra and spoke to him as
follows:
"O king, you are conversant with duties. All your doubts relating to the science
of wealth
have been well solved. You have waited upon many Brahmanas of great learning.
The subtle sciences connected with the Vedas, all the duties of religion,
and the whole of the four Vedas are well known to you.
You should not grieve, therefore, O son of Kuru. What was preordained has
happened.
It could not be otherwise. You have heard the mysteries relating to the deities
from the lips of the island-born rishi himself. Yudhishthira and his brothers
are morally as much your sons as they are the sons of Pandu.
Observant of the duties of religion, cherish and protect them.
In their turn, they are always devoted to the service of their seniors.
King Yudhishthira is pure-souled. He will always prove obedient to you.
I know that he is devoted to the virtues of compassion and abstention from
injury.
He is devoted to his seniors and preceptors. Your sons were all wicked-souled.
They were wedded to wrath and cupidity. Overwhelmed by envy,
they were all of wicked behavior. You must not grieve for them."
Having said this much to Dhritarashtra, the Kuru hero then addressed Arjuna:
"O holy one, O god of all gods, O you who are worshipped by all the deities and
Asuras,
O you who covered the three worlds with three steps of yours, salutations to you.
O wielder of the conch, the discus, and the mace,
you are Krishna, you are of golden body, you are the creator of the universe,
you are of vast proportions. You are Jiva. You are subtle.
You are the supreme and eternal soul. O lotus-eyed one, rescue me!
Give me permission, O Krishna, to depart from this world,
O you who are the supreme felicity and foremost among beings.
The sons of Pandu should ever be protected by you. You are indeed their sole
refuge.
Formerly I said to the foolish Duryodhana of wicked understanding
that where righteousness is, there Krishna is,
and that there is victory where righteousness is.

I counseled him that with Krishna as his refuge, he should make peace with the
    Pandavas.
Indeed, I repeatedly told him: 'This is the fittest time for you to make peace!'
The foolish Duryodhana of wicked understanding, however, did not do my
    bidding.
Having caused great havoc on earth, at last he laid down his life.
You, O illustrious one, I know to be that ancient and best of rishis
who dwelled for many years in the company of Nara, in the retreat of Vadari.
The celestial rishi Narada told me this, as also Vyasa of austere penances.
You and Arjuna are the old rishis Narayana and Nara, born among men.
O Krishna, grant me leave, and I shall cast off my body.
Permitted by you, I shall attain to the highest end."
Krishna said: "I give you leave, O Bhishma! O king, attain to the status of the
    Vasus.
O you of great splendor, you have not been guilty of a single transgression in this
    world.
O royal sage, you are devoted to your sire. For that reason, death waits upon
    your pleasure,
                even as your slave is attentive to anticipating your pleasure."
Having heard these words, the son of Ganga once more addressed the Pandavas,
headed by Dhritarashtra, and other friends and well-wishers of his:
"I desire to cast off my life's breath. You must give me leave.
You should strive for attaining to truth. Truth constitutes the highest power.
You should always live with Brahmanas who are of righteous conduct, devoted to
    penances,
and ever abstaining from cruel behavior, and who have their souls under
    control."
Bhishma then addressed Yudhishthira once more, saying:
"O king, let all Brahmanas—especially those who are endowed with wisdom—
let them who are preceptors, let them who are priests capable of assisting at
    sacrifices,
                be reverenced in your estimation."

✦

Bhishma remained silent for some time. He then held forth his life's breath
    successively
in those parts of his body which are indicated in Yoga.
The life's breath of that high-souled one, restrained duly, then rose up.
Those parts of the body of Shantanu's son, because of his adoption of Yoga,
became painless one after another. In the midst of those high-souled persons,
including those great rishis with Vyasa at their head, the sight seemed a strange
    one.
Within a short time, the entire body of Bhishma became arrowless and painless.
The life's breath, restrained and unable to escape through any of the outlets,
at last pierced through the crown of the head and proceeded upward to heaven.
The celestial kettledrums began to play, and floral showers rained down.

The siddhas and holy rishis, filled with delight, exclaimed: "Excellent!
Excellent!"
The life's breath of Bhishma, piercing through the crown of his head,
shot up through the heavens like a large meteor and soon became invisible.
Even thus did Shantanu's son, that pillar of Bharata's race, unite himself with
eternity.
Then the high-souled Pandavas and Vidura, taking a large quantity of wood
and diverse kinds of fragrant scents, made a funeral pyre.
Yuyutsu and others stood as spectators of the preparations.
Then Yudhishthira and the high-souled Vidura wrapped Bhishma's body
with a silken cloth and floral garlands. Yuyutsu held an excellent umbrella,
and over it both Bhimasena and Arjuna held a pair of yak tails of pure white.
The two sons of Madri held two headgears in their hands.
Yudhishthira and Dhritarashtra stood at the feet of the lord of the Kurus
and, taking up palmyra fans, stood around the body and began to fan it softly.
The Pitri sacrifice of the high-souled Bhishma was then duly performed.
Many libations were poured on the fire. The singers of Samans,
those hymns of the Sama Veda, sang many Samans.
Then, covering the body of Ganga's son with sandalwood and black aloe
and bark wood and other fragrant fuel, and setting fire to it,
the Kurus with Dhritarashtra and others stood on the right sight of the funeral
pyre.
Those foremost among Kuru's race, having thus cremated the body of the son of
Ganga,
proceeded to the sacred Bhagirathi River, accompanied by the rishis.
They were followed by Vyasa, by Narada, by Asita, by Krishna,
by the ladies of the Bharata race, and also by such of the citizens of Hastinapura
as had come to the place. All of them at that sacred river offered oblations of
water
to the high-souled son of Ganga.
The goddess Bhagirathi, after those oblations of water had been offered to
her son,
rose up from the stream, weeping and distracted by sorrow.
In the midst of her lamentations, she addressed the Kurus:
"You sinless ones, listen to me as I tell to you all that occurred with respect to
my son.
Possessed of royal conduct and disposition, and endowed with wisdom and high
birth,
my son was the benefactor of all the seniors of his race. He was devoted to his
sire
and was of high vows. He could not be vanquished by even Rama of Jamadagni's
race.
Alas, he has been slain by Sikhandini. Without doubt, my heart is made of
adamant,
for it does not break even at the disappearance of that son from my sight!
At the self-choice at Kasi, he vanquished on a single car the assembled Kshatriyas
and abducted the three princesses for his stepbrother Vichitravirya!

There was no one on earth who equaled him in might.
Alas, my heart does not break upon hearing of the slaughter of that son of mine!"
The puissant Krishna, hearing the goddess of the great river lamenting,
consoled her with these words: "O amiable one, be comforted. Do not yield to
    grief,
O you of beautiful features! Your son has gone to the highest region of felicity!
He was one of the Vasus of great energy.
Through a curse, he had to take birth among men. You must not grieve for him.
Agreeably to Kshatriya duties, he was slain by Arjuna on the field of battle.
He was not slain, O goddess, by Sikhandini. The very chief of the celestials
    himself
could not slay Bhishma in battle when he stood with stretched bow in hand.
Your son has, in felicity, gone to heaven. Do not grieve for that son of Kuru's race.
                Let the fever of your heart therefore be dispelled."
That foremost among rivers, thus addressed by Krishna and Vyasa, cast off her
    grief
and became restored to equanimity. And all the kings there present, headed by
    Krishna,
having honored that goddess duly, received her permission to depart from her
    banks.